FIELDING'S
BORNEO

Fielding Titles

Fielding's Alaska Cruises/Inside Passage
Fielding's Amazon
Fielding's Australia
Fielding's Bahamas
Fielding's Belgium
Fielding's Bermuda
Fielding's Borneo
Fielding's Brazil
Fielding's Britain
Fielding's Budget Europe
Fielding's Caribbean
Fielding's Caribbean Cruises
Fielding's Caribbean East
Fielding's Caribbean West
Fielding's Europe
Fielding's European Cruises
Fielding's Far East
Fielding's France
Fielding's Freewheelin' USA
Fielding's Guide to the World's Most Dangerous Places
Fielding's Guide to Kenya's Best Hotels, Lodges & Homestays
Fielding's Guide to the World's Great Voyages
Fielding's Hawaii
Fielding's Holland
Fielding's Italy
Fielding's Las Vegas Agenda
Fielding's London Agenda
Fielding's Los Angeles Agenda
Fielding's Malaysia and Singapore
Fielding's Mexico
Fielding's New York Agenda
Fielding's New Zealand
Fielding's Paris Agenda
Fielding's Portugal
Fielding's Rome Agenda
Fielding's San Diego Agenda
Fielding's Scandinavia
Fielding's Southeast Asia
Fielding's Southern Vietnam on Two Wheels
Fielding's Spain
Fielding's Thailand Including Cambodia, Laos, Myanmar
Fielding's Vacation Places Rated
Fielding's Vietnam
Fielding's Worldwide Cruises
The Indiana Jones Survival Guide

FIELDING'S BORNEO

The adventurous guide to the island of Borneo

covering Brunei, Kalimantan, Sabah and Sarawak

by
Robert Young Pelton

Fielding Worldwide, Inc.
308 South Catalina Avenue
Redondo Beach, California 90277 U.S.A.

Fielding's Borneo
Published by Fielding Worldwide, Inc.
Text Copyright ©1995 Robert Young Pelton.
Icons & Illustrations Copyright ©1995 FWI
Photo Copyrights ©1995 Robert Young Pelton other photos copyright as marked.

FIELDING WORLDWIDE INC.

PUBLISHER AND CEO **Robert Young Pelton**
DIRECTOR OF PUBLISHING **Paul T. Snapp**
ELECTRONIC PUBLISHING DIRECTOR **Larry E. Hart**
PUBLIC RELATIONS DIRECTOR **Beverly Riess**
ACCOUNT SERVICES MANAGER **Christy Harp**

EDITORS

Linda Charlton   **Kathy Knoles**

PRODUCTION

Gini Sardo-Martin   **Chris Snyder**
Craig South   **Diane Vogel**
Janice Whitby

COVER DESIGNED BY **Digital Artists, Inc.**
COVER PHOTOGRAPHERS - Front Covers **Robert Young Pelton**
INSIDE PHOTOS **Robert Young Pelton**
with additional photos by **Coskun Aral, C.L. Chan, Tony Lamb, A. Phillips, Jon Rees**

Inquiries should be addressed to: Fielding Worldwide, Inc., 308 South Catalina Ave., Redondo Beach, California 90277 U.S.A., ☎ *(310) 372-4474*, Facsimile *(310) 376-8064*, 8:30 a.m.–5:30 p.m. Pacific Standard Time.

ISBN 1-56952-026-7

Library of Congress Number

94-068337

Printed in the United States of America

Letter from the Publisher

In 1946, Temple Fielding began the first of what would be a remarkable new series of well-written, highly personalized guidebooks for independent travelers. Temple's opinionated, witty, and oft-imitated books have now guided travelers for almost a half-century. More important to some was Fielding's humorous and direct method of steering travelers away from the dull and the insipid. Today, Fielding Travel Guides are still written by experienced travelers for experienced travelers. Our authors carry on Fielding's reputation for creating travel experiences that deliver insight with a sense of discovery and style.

You are reading the latest in our series of guides written on remote regions for adventurers by adventurers. Other titles include *Vietnam* and *Southern Vietnam on Two Wheels*, the *Amazon* and *Kenya*. The concept of adventurous travel has never been bigger. Our policy of *brutal honesty* and a highly personal point of view has never changed; it just seems the travel world has caught up with us.

RYP

Robert Young Pelton
Publisher and CEO
Fielding Worldwide, Inc.

Dedication

This book is dedicated to my wife Linda and our daughters, Lisa and Claire. They have taught me that true adventure can not only be found in fear and danger, it can also be found in love.

Acknowledgements

When I first committed to the creation of this book I had little idea of just how much of my life it would consume. I am grateful for the many people who made it happen. It takes much more than an idea to bring these adventures to life. The expeditions in this book took months of planning, a lot of money, the support of staff, expeditors, rivermen, pilots, doctors, support personnel and the unpaid time of hundreds of people, who helped push my crazy concept one step closer to reality. Most importantly, it takes the blessing and patience of my family, clients and staff who help me maintain my sanity in my other endeavors. They are quite used to explaining that I am "somewhere in Southeast Asia" when people ask my whereabouts.

For this particular book I must thank two people who accompanied me on the bulk of the expeditions:

Jon Rees: Outward Bound instructor, river guide and fellow explorer. His knowledge of Sabah and willingness to head into the unknown with a crazy Canadian and a Turk made our expeditions easier and more educational.

Coskun Aral: A combat photographer for SIPA and television journalist in Istanbul. Coskun's idea of getting dressed for work is putting on a flak jacket, and documenting the horrors of war. I thank him for his humor and fellowship during the many days in the jungle and on the river.

I would like to thank the following people for their assistance in making my dream and this book possible:

Paul Sumner	**Chuck Bailey**
Annuar Ghani	**Yamin Vong**
Jerry Butler	**George Hayward**
Ron Lennard	**Beverly Reiss**
Christy Harp	**Lilian Tse**
Jasmin Favell	**Ray Laskowitz**
Linda Charlton	**Clive Marsh**
Richard Lucik	**Mike Armijo**
Tony Lamb	**The Tenom Research Center**
Jesus Cedes	**Pelita Air Services**
Pempbung Anya	**Venetia Simonds**
Francis Herbert	**The Royal Geographical Society**
Tommy Chang	**Malaysian Tourism**
Ric Williams	**Dr. Dev Sidhu**
Doc Teoh	**Bob Teoh**
Joe Seliski	**Mike Olsen**

THE JOURNEY OF DEATH

When a Kenyah of noble birth dies, his soul goes on a difficult journey to heaven. The soul comes to a land that is dark, where all things are opposite. Light is dark, black is white, yes is no. It is then that his dark intricate tattoos begin to radiate light so that he may continue his journey to find peace with his ancestors.

Like the last of the Kenyah, Borneo is traveling from life to death. The quiet forest is being ripped apart by the sounds of bulldozers leaving a land of opposites. Wet becomes dry, cool becomes hot and the world's most exotic ecosystem hangs in a delicate balance. It is a time of darkness. The Kenyah no longer create their tattoos to guide them beyond death and the souls of their ancestors will be lost forever in the darkness.

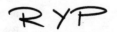

About the Author

Robert Young Pelton

Robert Young Pelton, 40, began his adventurous career at 10 when he became the youngest boy to attend St. John's Cathedral school. Called "the toughest boys' school in North America" by the *Globe & Mail*, the curriculum included intensive education combined with feats of endurance—25 and 50 mile snowshoe marathon races in the dead of winter and 1000 mile canoe trips tracing voyageur routes in the spring.

Since then, Pelton has combined his love of knowledge and adventure by traveling through 50 countries including living with the Dogon people in West Africa, being a professional adventurer in Colombia and Central America, bicycling through Canada and Europe and off-roading in Africa, Mexico and California. He accompanied the American team in the 1991 Camel Trophy in retracing the routes of the great explorers overland from Dar es Salaam to Bujumbura.

To create this guidebook, Pelton has flown, driven, hiked, climbed, caved, trekked, canoed, partied, crawled and crashed throughout most of Borneo over the last six years.

He is the author of *The World's Most Dangerous Places*, and *Fielding's LA Agenda*. He contributes to *Fielding's Far East, Fielding's Southeast Asia* and *Fielding's Malaysia and Singapore*.

Pelton lives in Southern California, with his wife and twin daughters. When he isn't *ulu*, he raises avocados and black swans. He is a fellow of the Royal Geographical Society and is a trustee of the Laguna Art Museum.

Fielding Rating Icons

The Fielding Rating Icons are highly personal and awarded to help the besieged traveler choose from among the dizzying array of activities, attractions, hotels, restaurants and sights. The awarding of an icon denotes unusual or exceptional qualities in the relevant category.

RATINGS

Fielding Award | Author Selection | Money Saver | Expensive | Quality | Warning | Danger | Inexpensive

Spacious | Cramped | Mild Disapproval

CULTURAL

Museum/Art | Interesting Architecture | History | Book Reference | Artistically Important | Musically Interesting | Cultural Archeology | Crafts

Theater | Festivals

SIGHTS

Picturesque | Great Scenery | Market | Beaches/Resorts | Cultural | Fortress | Church

WHERE TO STAY

Simple | Luxurious | Cottage | Bed & Breakfast | Scenic | Business

TRAVEL TIPS

Arrival/Departure | By Air | By Water | By Train | By Car | Bus/Local Transit | Barge

Calendar | Itinerary | Compass | Kids

ACTIVITIES	Water Sports	Sailing	Scuba Diving	Snorkeling/ Diving	Deep-sea Fishing	Freshwater Fishing	Cycling	Workout
	Swimming	Hiking	Walking	Relaxing	Golf	Tennis	Horseback Riding	General Sports
SPECIAL INTEREST	Nightlife	Singles	Romantic	Spectacular Cuisine	Shopping	Cafe Stops	Mystery	

Currency Exchange Rates			
Country	**Currency**	**Foreign to US$1**	**US$1 to Foreign**
Malaysia	**Ringgit**	0.441197	2.26
Indonesia	**Rupiah**	0.000539	1855.00
Brunei	**Dollar**	0.7790	1.28
Singapore	**Dollar**	0.7709	1.29

Source: Thomas Cook Foreign Exchange, July 18, 1995

TABLE OF CONTENTS

LIST OF MAPS

Pulau Banggi

Kudat

SULU SEA

Tuaran
Kinabalu
National Park
Sepilok
Sanctuary
KOTA KINABALU
Poring Hot
Springs
Ranau
Turtle Islands National Park
Tanjung Aru
Beaufort
Sandakan
Gomantong
Caves
Pulau Labuan
Danum
Valley
Lahad Datu
BANDAR SERI
BEGAWAN
Batu
Punggul
Maliau
Basin
Tungku
Kuala Belait
Semporna
Miri
Kalabakan
Tawau
Lambir Hills
National Park
Gunung Mulu
National Park
Rumah
Lagan
Long Lama
Bario
Pa Dali
Tawau Hill
State Park
Tarakan
Lio Matoh
SULAWESI SEA
Tanjung Selor

Gunung Berau Reserve

Tanjung Redeb

Muara Blemlelakidau

Muarabu
Kombeng
Caves
Lasan
Sangkulirang
Pulai
Batu Kelau
Muara Wahau
Sengata
Muara Kaman
Reserve
Betapau
Kutai
National
Park
Genting Tanah
SAMARINDA
Muara Badak
Tajung Balai
Kersik Luwai
Orchid Forest
Reserve
Tenggarong
Selpinang
Samboja
Muara Merunga
Balikpapan
Muara
Koman
PALANGKARAYA
Tanjung
MAKASSAR STRAIT
Amuntai
Tabudarat
Rantau
Kandangan
BANJARMASIN
Kotabaru
Martapura
Kutn
Floating
Market
Pelaihari
Martapura Reserve
Pelaihari

Preface

The reason for this book is simple and urgent. After years of travel and adventures in exotic regions I realized upon each return to Borneo that much of the awe and spectacle I took for granted was disappearing. I was finally motivated to put these travels on paper. These experiences have not just changed me but I have tried to create change wherever I have traveled. Subtly at first, but there is a greater sense of urgency as the world's wild places and peoples slip into memory. In 1989, I journeyed across the length of Borneo by foot, airplane, canoe and Land Rover. When I returned just one year later I was shocked to find many of the great forests turned into wastelands of scarred earth. These undiscovered realms are being assaulted by boats of eco-tourists and indigenous tribesmen sporting Ninja Turtle T-shirts. Change is coming much too fast and without the understanding of the effects of this change. The goal of this and future Fielding guidebooks on remote regions is to help adventurers, travelers and the simply curious how to understand and experience these vanishing worlds. Informed tourists and the dollars they leave behind may be the best way for many of these areas to be preserved.

The other reason this book must be written is that it is only through books that the overwhelming drama and beauty of these last wild places can be captured before they are lost forever.

A Pilgrimage to the Golden Age of Adventure

Gunung Mulu in Sarawak

Somewhere in Borneo - I am squatting in a small clearing at night in the Borneo jungle. The rain continually pours down, making me wonder how the sky can hold so much water for so long. Sounds of tree frogs, insects, birds and other nocturnal animals are almost deafening. The rain makes plopping and hissing sounds on the large leaves. Here, nighttime belongs to the leopards. Silent death for most small mammals. The apes have the luxury of sleeping high in the trees where the leopards cannot climb. I am on the ground where huge insects walk somnambulantly. Should I be in a tree, or in a cave? It doesn't feel right on the ground. I have the one thing that separates me from these apes and other animals: fire.

The small fire sputters and hisses under the deluge. Occasionally a six inch moth will fly out of the darkness and land on my face illuminated by the flames. They are soft, inquiring and ultimately doomed to escape my curious grasp and leap into the fire. My umbrella for the evening is a large palmetto leaf. I am happy here; soaked to the bone, a steaming rank animal in the middle of primitive jungle. As the sun comes up high above and paints the sky a tired blue, I am content.

I am determined to come back to this verdant, mysterious place, but I cannot set my direction or purpose from within this green maze to get to where I must go. I must start at the beginning.

London, England - The morning dawns cold, and blustery grey clouds scud across the Victorian rooftops. As I walk through Hyde Park, cavalry officers exercise their horses in the damp cold. I pass the pale yellow daffodils and brilliant green lawns. The scene of blanketed cavalry officers along Rotten Row could almost be a hundred years earlier. I have chosen to start my trip to Borneo here in this grey place at the heart of adventure. Just as young people are thrilled by the launch of the space shuttle, 100 years ago this was a place that stirred souls and sent adventurers into the unknown.

It is difficult for Americans to understand why Borneo has had such a strong attaction for the British. Here, Borneo is the soul of adventure and I am heading for the most famous launching pad in history—The Royal Geographical Society.

Ahead, across the park, is my destination, tucked between the red brick elegance of Albert Hall and the embassy recently damaged by the S.A.S. counterattack on terrorists. The grim reminder that England's once far-off battles of occupation are now being fought by enemies in the heart of London disturbs my Victorian reverie. Things have changed.

As I make my way across the street, I can't help noticing the stern, polar-clad statue of Shackleton tucked in an alcove of the building above. A statue of the great African explorer Dr. Livingstone peers inquisitively around the corner from his niche in the wall. A simple sign on the red brick building tells me that I have arrived at the starting point for many of the world's great explorations for over 150 years.

The Society was founded in May of 1830 by a group of well-travelled London gentlemen who determined they would form a society, "whose sole object shall be the promotion of that most important and entertaining branch of knowledge—geography."

Today the RGS has not only the best collection of maps, diaries and artifacts from explorers, but also runs an Expedition Advisory Center that stocks books on how to mount just about any kind of expedition you can dream up. I am here to find maps and information about the island of Borneo and to absorb some of the mystique of this hallowed place.

The Map Room is a musty room, walled on three sides by worn leather-bound tomes. Faded black and white blowups of the Himalayas teeter on top of the bookcase. After a discussion of my needs with the director of the map room, I am led through the corridors under the gaze of past RGS presidents and British kings and queens to a reading room. Sunlight streams through the paned glass window, illuminating a scale model of Everest. On the walls are stern, yellowed portraits of Henry Morton Stanley, Speke, Livingstone, Ross, Everest and other notables. Inside this august institution that sent Franklin to find the Northwest Passage and Livingstone to find the source of the Nile, geographic endeavors are not taken lightly.

Every map tells a story and has a purpose. I browse through the steel-engraved maps of early explorers to the computer generated maps of today: ancient Chinese trading maps, Dutch and British colonial maps, OSS military maps of WWII showing navigable waterways and indigenous peoples. There are oil and mineral company exploration maps and the most recent aviation maps showing every *sungai* (river), *kampung* (village) and *gunung* (mountain. More than just geographical indicators, the shifting borders, the names of discovered regions, and the increasing level of detail tell a romantic history of discovery. Each map shines a bit more light on this dark region.

As I progress through the ages I am heartened by the blank areas that remain like obstinate blind spots. Even in this age of daily satellite imagery and helicopters, there is too much cloud-cover over Borneo to create an accurate map. I look up at my august companions in oil and am thankful that, yes, there are still wild places to explore and adventures to be had. I am neither a soldier, an explorer, a scientist, nor even a journalist like the great explorers of the Victorian age, I am just curious and it remains to be seen what adventures await me. There are no wars to win, pirates to quell, or even any lost missionaries to find. I will descend into the dark nameless depths of Borneo, drawn like a moth to the bright white spots on the map.

The men who would be kings

To understand the soul of the adventurer you cannot just browse through their journals, notes and maps. You have to look them straight in the face to find out why they have made the hard choice between reading about adventure or living it. Trapped on this small island, and smothered by rules, class and blandness, it is not surprising that England has sent their best into the most far-flung regions of the world. My next stop is the National Portrait Gallery; a gallery dedicated to paintings, photographs and sculptures of great Englishmen. Wandering through the hushed halls, I am greeted by row after row of austere pasty countenances of mid-19th century England. Stern expressions, ill-fitting clothing and dark suits are set against grim, grey backgrounds.

I climb the marble stairs to the third floor and there I find the reason for my visit. In a small room, out of the way and easy to miss, are portraits of the great English explorers of the Victorian era. An elderly, balding museum attendant sleeps peacefully under the fierce portrait of Captain Sir Richard Francis Burton. The errant linguist, much maligned explorer, celebrated translator of *1001 Tales of the Arabian Nights* and other "questionable" books is one of my heroes. Whether it was boldly walking into the city of Harrar, where all white men were instantly killed, making a pilgrimage to Mecca, visiting the bloodthirsty kings of West Africa or visiting battlefields in South America, Burton had an inextinguishable curiosity that was only matched by his contempt for Victorian society. The man produced an endless stream of tomes on everything from dueling, exotic sexual practices, to gold mining, and even translated Portuguese poetry.

The small painting of Burton is more than a portrait, it is a statement. Upon closer inspection, I see that Burton's blazing countenance is not a mistake but a deliberate attempt by the artist to communicate the burning intensity of the man. Pea-sized globs of white paint have been added to his dark eyes to make them glare across the room. This is obviously a man who does not sit willfully for a portrait. The physical size of the portrait is small, as befits Burton's legend and modesty. Burton is famous for his love of the desert and mastery of languages of the Middle and Far East. The many stories told under the desert stars gave flavor and spice to his masterful translation of the *Arabian Nights.* There are no monuments to Burton, no place names, not even a tiny river named after this adventurer.

Across the doorway from Burton is a representation at the other end of the spectrum. An oversized, rather foppish, windblown portrait of a young Sir James Brooke, the rajah of Sarawak. In an effort to capture his fame and accomplishments, the painter portrays Brooke like a caricature from *Boy's Own* magazine. His boyish good looks and the breezy setting contrast sharply with Burton's dark, hard intensity. Brooke was to spend his inheritance on a well armed ship and seek fame and fortune in the turbulent Far East. He was to find both. Through bravery, ambition and a dash of trickery he became the ruler of Sarawak, master of a nation, and the first in a line of three White Rajahs who ruled uncontested until the realities of World War II ended their dynasty.

Two other portraits sum up the mood of the era. Further to the right is Lord Kitchener standing fiercely in the deserts of Egypt, his bristling whiskers and intense stare betrayed by his soft schoolboy eyes. Next to him is Sir Baden Powell founder of the Boy Scout movement, stiff and uncomfortable.

One last portrait graces the faded red flocked wallpaper. It, too, is of modest size and displays a soft-featured, balding man against a background of books, staring wistfully out a window. This is Rudyard Kipling, the man who would write books about adventure and lionize the peculiar British trait of seeking adventure for its own sake. *The Man Who Would be King, The Jungle Book, Gunga Din* and *Kim* colorfully captured the feeling of exotic adventures in faraway countries.

This odd assortment of characters comprises the complete adventurer: Burton, the pariah of polite society; Brooke, the empire builder; Kitchener, the soldier, Powell, the creator of millions of little adventurers; and finally, Kipling, the dreamer who turned hard realities and hard people into fascinating tales of adventure.

The Last Adventure

There is one last stop. On the outskirts of London, in an overgrown, nondescript, Roman Catholic churchyard stands an incongruous monument. Tucked hard against a cement wall that hides the aging cemetery from the working-class suburb is a curious monument. It is a stone carving of an English campaign tent. It is slightly Arabic in flavor and stained by the moss and lichen that cover its surface.

These are the graves of Captain Sir Richard Burton and his devoted wife, Isabel. Burton's grave was not of his choosing but rather a fanciful remembrance by his wife. They did not bury Burton in Westminster Abbey for good reason. His fame was more for his bawdy, but faithful, translation of *1001 Tales of the Arabian Nights* rather than for his incredible travels on almost every continent. He was fascinated by people, their culture and their most private acts. He spent the greater portion of his life as an underpaid diplomatic servant who abused his fame as a great explorer in Africa to its fullest. Whether visiting cannibals in West Africa or Mormons in Salt Lake City, he was the paragon of the Victorian adventurer and a tolerated curiosity of Victorian society. He was smitten with a terminal wanderlust and curiosity. It is in his spirit that this book was created. The pursuit of adventure for knowledge, camaraderie and self-enlightenment. It is a sobering thought to realize that most of his works sit idle in musty antiquarian bookshops and that only he understood the meaning of his thousands of adventures, loves, pains, sorrows and joys.

My pilgrimage to London has made me feel comfortable in what I am about to do. There is no prospect of wealth or fame ahead of me, only the satisfaction that I have to live a piece of my life to the fullest before complacency and age catch up with me. This book is my simple recording of my pleasures and solid advice to the next person—a worn and battered remembrance before my thoughts and memory dim and I, too, lie still and cold in a forgotten overgrown graveyard.

My silence is disturbed by the 747s on final approach to Heathrow. I look up. It is time to start my journey.

Who Is This Guide For?

French expedition member Jean Loup Roy makes a jungle fashion statement. True adventure requires innovation, creativity and a healthy disrespect of guidebooks.

At first glance the casual reader might decry the lack of hotel ratings, restaurant choices or even descriptions of tours. If you are looking for comfort and frills, head for Europe. If you are seeking a glimpse into one of the world's last wild places and want stories to tell your children, then Borneo may be for you. Fielding's *Borneo* is a return to the tradition of adventure guidebooks. Travel guides used to be a cross between scientific textbook and ethnographic tome. In between the lines were romance, adventure, fear and death. This book is written for people who need to understand how the world works—people who balance a sense of the romantic with the pragmatic. There are many adventures awaiting you in Borneo. The last place you want to be is in an air-conditioned bus.

Our faithful guide promised us there would be a road here. Technically he was right, he just forgot to accurately describe the size of the pothole.

A Word About Guidebooks

Guidebooks, even this one, aren't the end-all for managing your Borneo adventure. It took me six years to write this book. I am painfully aware that the lush rainforests may have turned into sun-scorched dust by now. You, gentle reader, will have to push further upriver, haggle longer and spend more time to capture the innocence and beauty I have found. Sadly, I get wistful when I thumb through archival photos of Borneo's past and see sights I was too late to see. So remember, things change, towns spring up almost overnight, forests disappear, and hopefully you will find new areas to discover by using this guide as a springboard.

On a happier side, I have taken pains to make sure the listing material on hotels, customs and travel restrictions was updated just before we went to press. My thanks to Sam Mitani who went to Sarawak to double check some of the hotel information. In any case, Malaysia, Brunei and Indonesia are rapidly developing into wealthy countries and change is a fact of life. Don't be afraid to pick up the phone and call the hotel or tour group you want to talk to. Send or ask for faxed information. The tourism folks stateside are as helpful as they can be considering their slim budgets and overworked staff.

10,000 miles, 16 inches and 20 hours

There is a price you will pay for your adventurous tastes. For Europeans or North Americans, Borneo is on the other side of the world. There is no avoiding one of the world's longest and most uncomfortable airplane rides. Twenty-odd hours aboard a plane or two or three and you're there. Almost. you will probably end up in Singapore, Jakarta or Kuala Lumpur first. I have flown the 20 plus hours and there are only two solutions—stop overs or business class. Most government-owned carriers fly full. They make money by cramming in as many smiling countrymen as possible.

If you fly on some national carriers prepare to experience "the bus that flies." On one Garuda flight the passengers were packed in so tight I had to measure the seat width. They were exactly 16 inches wide, inside arm to inside arm. Plenty of room for most Malaysians and Indonesians but a curious form of torture for most Americans. I am 6' 4" and I have counted every minute on some flights. The first six hours are the worst. If you choose Singapore Airlines or a business carrier, life is a little easier. They don't fly any faster but time seems to go by faster. None of the carriers can be faulted for the quality of the flight attendants. All are exemplary and friendly.

What's It Like?

In case you didn't know, it rains quite a bit in Borneo and it is known to get rather muddy.

The purpose of this book is to answer that question in detail, but from a first timer's view, be prepared for some unsettling differences.

It's hot: From the second they open the aircraft door to when you board the plane again it will be tropical. A hot heavy, sweaty feeling that you either like or hate. Remember to pack light, wear loose cotton and keep out of the midday sun.

It smells: It is hard to describe the kaleidoscope of olfactory delights and horrors that await you. Fragrant flowers and rotting carcasses, lemongrass and raw sewage, durians and diesel. All at the same time. When I return from Borneo I always find it curious what little work our noses have in North American cities.

Things work differently: Once you are outside of Borneo's main cities, you will wonder how to fix things, buy food, sleep, even how to go to the bathroom. Don't be afraid to ask and don't be afraid to laugh with your hosts if you do something really dumb. You will learn to eat with your fingers, use a *mandi*, a ladle type of bath, how to sleep with cockroaches, spiders and domestic animals sharing your bed.

This book offers a lot of tips, but once again, watch, ask and mimic. Remember you are the weird one there.

People think and act differently: You will be exposed to Muslims, animists, Chinese businessmen and a multitude of strangers who will have preconceptions about who you are and why you are there. Despite some well meaning philosophies about the family of man, people are different. Malays are devout Muslims who do not use profanity or drink alcohol but do engage in many western activities. You will be judged on your morality, your positive attitude and dedication to family, God and country. Chinese businessmen will check out what type of watch you wear, what type of booze you order and how loud you laugh at their jokes. Dayaks will be curious to see how well you can deliver a speech, how accurately you can throw a spear, how hard you can paddle a canoe, if you can drink all night and still be dancing when the sun comes up. All these people are part of Borneo just as you will be.

It is colorful: Tropical fish, rare orchids, fruits, birds, sunsets all conspire to make you expand your color vocabulary. Borneo is the richest island in the world for exotic flora and fauna.

Everything is alive: With the exception of some of the dull industrial towns rebuilt after WWII and logged areas, Borneo can be an exciting panorama of people, color, costume, scenery and activity.

They speak different languages: Most English speaking visitors will have no problem conversing in the main cities. As you get more than five miles out of town, Bahasa Indonesian or Malay is the lingua franca of Borneo. It is a simple language much like Swahili, another Arab trading language. The trouble is that by the time you learn it, you will be packing your bags to go home.

BORNEO AT A GLANCE				
COUNTRY	AREA (SQ. MI.)	POPULATION	LANGUAGES	RELIGIONS
Brunei	2227	300,000	Malay, English, Chinese, Iban	Islam
Indonesia	736,000	199 million	Indonesian (dialects)	Muslim, Protestant, Catholic
Malaysia	128,328	19.5 million	Malay, Chinese, English, Tamil	Muslim, Hindi, Buddhism, Taoism, Christianity

Is it Safe?

There is little to fear from warfare terrorism or violence since the turbulent 60s. There is still **piracy** in the Sulu seas (northeast Borneo) and there are cases of petty theft in the large cities. But overall, Borneo still has a small town atmosphere. There is danger in the general **bush travel** usage of small canoes, rough roads and travel through remote mountainous terrain as there is any country. Just be careful, wear life preservers in canoes, wear your seatbelt and do not be surprised if there are none of either in sight.

What about the headhunters you say? Well, headhunting was last revived in the '40s when the British paid a bounty to the locals for Japanese heads. There were some beheadings by scouts working with the SAS during the *Konfrontasi* but no activity since then. Even then very few tourists were ever at risk of losing their craniums.

If you smuggle **drugs** you will find Brunei, Singapore and Malaysia very dangerous. Travelers get plenty of notice when they go through customs about the severe penalties for drug smuggling in Malaysia (and Singapore). Unfortunately, by then it is probably too late. Remember that U.S. citizens are subject to the laws and legal practices of the country in which they are traveling and the embassy can't do much except arrange to have your body shipped back home after you are hung. Malaysia strictly enforces its drug laws. Malaysian legislation provides for a mandatory death penalty for convicted drug traffickers. Individuals arrested in possession of fifteen grams (1/2 ounce) of heroin or two hundred grams (7 ounces) of marijuana are presumed by law to be trafficking in drugs.

Malaria, particularly quinine resistant malaria (*falciparum malaria*), is endemic in Borneo. It is a serious danger to the unprotected traveler. Malarial infection can be at its most virulent around the logging camps. Consult your doctor before you go and consult a doctor once in country for his recommendations. Local doctors see and treat a lot more cases of malaria than a doctor in Iowa. They will probably prescribe chloroquine and Fansidar only to be taken if you contract malaria. Fansidar is not usually prescribed in the U.S. but most doctors will recommend you carry it with you in case you come down with a resistant strain. Contrary to popular belief, taking medicine to prevent malaria does not guarantee you won't come down with it. Many countries have strains of malaria that are resistant to traditional prophylaxis. Contact the **Center for Disease Control**; ☎ *(404) 332-4559*, and your local doctor for more information. The mosquitoes that carry malaria bite at dusk and during the evening so taking precautions when you eat and sleep is important.

A few simple rules to prevent problems with malaria:

- Plan on taking your medicine before you leave and remember to continue to take it after you return. Malaria can strike long after you return from your trip.

- Pick a time of day for taking your medicine that is easy to remember.

- Use a small portable mosquito tent available from camping stores like REI.

- Do not scratch your bites, they can become infected. Dab them with anti-itch sticks or vinegar.

- Apply insect repellant with a high percentage of diethyltoluamide or DEET. Remember that most mosquito repellants are flammable. Use in shoes or under clothing can cause rashes. DEET can cause rashes, iritation, nervous system disorders and other problems. So consult your doctor if you have sensitive skin.

- Use mosquito coils containing Pyrethrum available in most local stores in Borneo. Place them at four corners of your bed or so that the prevailing breeze draws the smoke over you. Use a nonflammable holder or container. Keep well away from mosquito netting.

If you follow the above you should not get malaria and you should eliminate a few million mosquitoes while you are there.

The author inspects a walking stick up close and vice versa.

Insects

Though technically not a danger, many people recoil in horror when they see the giant cockroaches, centipedes, moths or rhinoceros beetles that are commonly found in the jungles. If you are not a fan of insects you may not be pleased to learn that some of the world's largest insects are found in Borneo (like the 20-inch walking stick).

Microbes

The lifeforms that pose a real danger are much smaller—the tiny bacteria that multiply in the dank tropic heat. Use common sense when eating in Borneo. Watch food being cooked, boil it or peel it. Luckily Asian food is usually cooked fresh. Not so with some of the street vendors found in larger towns. Stay away from anything that attracts flies, such as uncooked meats, unbottled juices, the usual breeding grounds for hepatitis A. A shot of gamma globulin before you leave can be a deterrent but is not guaranteed to protect you. I have never been sick in Borneo but I have had food poisoning in the States three times. Asian and Muslim food is usually prepared fresh and with a level of cleanliness that can exceed Western standards. Water can be safe in the major cities but it doesn't hurt to drink and brush your teeth with bottled water. Some people eat vegetarian and some like the fact that your chicken dinner was twitching just 20 minutes ago. There are even Chinese restaurants that double as zoos up in the hills behind Kota Kinabalu.

Here are some common sense tips:

- Eat freshly prepared hot foods such as soups, fish, or noodles.
- Avoid meats or prepared meals that sit out more than 20 minutes.
- Drink bottled water and brush your teeth with it as well.

- Wash your hands often and keep your fingers out of your mouth and eyes.

- Keep clean and pay attention to your toilet hygiene.

- Peel fruit, don't eat raw foods, stick to canned foods, drink bottled beverages.

- If flies are on your food think twice.

- Treat any cut, scratch or rash with antibiotic and keep it clean and dry.

The best way to avoid diseases is to get all your shots before you go, eat smart, keep clean and take care of any cut or irritation with medication.

If you come down with the trots, you don't necessarily have a major problem. Hepatitus A or jaundice is identified by the yellowness of the eyes and skin. Common diarrhea can be caused by heat, lack of water, minor bugs in food and water. If you have the runs, start by drinking a lot of bottled water mixed with an electrolyte designed to combat dehydration. I use a banana flavored powder that goes by the appealing name of Stop Trot. A minor amount of table salt mixed with your water also can do the trick.

AIDS

Although Borneo will never compete with Bangkok, sex is very available in every hotel, small town and bar. Where there are working men there are working girls. The larger hotels have health clubs where rotating groups of Filipino and Chinese girls put in two to four week stints. These girls demand the use of condoms and are generally considered safe. The smaller towns have clubs where Dayak girls do not use or can't get condoms. The locals consider these clubs "safe." The reality is that any sexual contact carries the threat of AIDS. It is a sick joke but a deadly reality that Thai girls are now working large health clubs in Kuala Lumpur due to the pressure on sex tourism in Thailand. Asian businessmen now come to Malaysia because they believe that Americans have infected the prostitutes in Bankkok with AIDS and that Malaysian girls are still "safe." T'ain't so.

The AIDS virus can also be transmitted by blood transfusions and using needles that have been previously used to inject infected patients. Incidentally, although the spotlight is on AIDS, you can still get the good old fashioned STDs like herpes, syphilis (both normal and penicillin resistant strains) gonorrhea, crabs, chlamydia, genital warts, lice, and Hepatitis B. The only compensation is that Borneo is still a backwater place, and maybe, just maybe your chances of having good healthy, clean sex are still excellent.

Scorpions are not a food group. This one has been dispatched and its tail removed. Don't try this at home kids.

Snakes, scorpions, crocodiles and other nasties

There are plenty of poisonous snakes, venomous scorpions (just lift the bark off any old log to find 3–5" long scorpions) both above and under water. Rather than scare you with true stories of ten foot cobras chasing and attacking people without provocation, I will just tell you to be careful, wear boots, long pants and long sleeve shirts, watch where you put your hands or your butt, sleep off the ground in a cot and carry a first aid kit that includes antihistamines, a first aid manual and, of course, good old common sense.

- If you are bitten by a snake, do not make a cut and suck out the poison. You can cause a very nasty infection and a lot of pain. Try to bring in the snake or at least the head of the snake that bit you to the medical personnel who will treat your bite. Apply a tourniquet between the bite and your heart to prevent the venom from spreading.

- Watch out for coral reefs, wear running shoes to protect you from coral cuts, spiny urchins and stone or scorpion fish.

The crocodiles of Sarawak are legendary for their size and terrify the locals. Aggressive cobras are still killed in homes and shops. It is a measure of how civilized Borneo has become that sightings of either are becoming rare. Still ask about any nasties before you jump into that muddy river.

The author makes an inelegant exit from a vehicle that he has just rolled.

Accidents

I cannot predict whether you will be the victim of a car crash or even a coral rash but Malaysia has excellent medical facilities in the main cities and little to no services in the boonies. Singapore, Kuala Lumpur, Brunei or Balikpapan would be your best bet for serious medical care.

For up-to-the-minute recorded information on these and any hot spots call the U.S. State Department's travel advisory line, ☎ *(202) 647-5225.*

Useful information on guarding valuables and protecting personal security while traveling abroad is provided in the Department of State pamphlet, "A Safe Trip Abroad." It is available from the Superintendent of Documents, U.S. Government Printing Office, Washington, D.C. 20402.

Entirely Unfair Capsules
of the Borneo Regions
Brunei

Brunei is diffident towards tourists. It's a small, boring, expensive and easy to miss country. The best places to see are the remote jungles and inside the royal palace. Of course those are exactly what you can't see. Strictly for country counters and expats.

Highlights

The **palace**, the **museums**, and of course the scary feeling of being in a utopian society.

Indonesia

The world's largest Muslim nation is a seething powerhouse of diversity. To describe it as a country is a mistake. If anyone could visit all 17,508 islands there would still be plenty to see underwater. Indonesia is best known for the Aussie and German tourist mecca of **Bali**. It's an acquired addiction of seasoned travelers. Kalimantan is cheap, exotic and ultimately depressing because of its military regime. The people are magical and getting to know them is why you should experience this backwater wonderland. Kalimantan is not Indonesia at its best but there are many adventures awaiting the bold.

Highlights

Tanjung Puting, the **floating market** at Banjarmasin, trekking the **Apo Kayan**, a slow lazy trip down the **Mahakam** and the food.

Malaysia

For the genteel or the adventurous. Malaysia's split personality makes it the Southeast Asia with training wheels. Lots of English spoken, clean, great food, happy people, great infrastructure. No Kalishnakovs, no cheap Soviet-made uniforms—just the well-oiled machinery of a country hitting the big time. Even the flag looks like ours. Sarawak for first timers and Sabah for the brave.

Highlights

Visit the Iban in Sarawak or the Muruts in Sabah. Historic Kuching, The Sarawak Museum, the caves of **Mulu**, climbing **Mt. Kinabalu**, diving **Sipadan**, orang utans in **Sepilok**, and the forests of **Danum**. The upper reaches of the Belaga, Rejang and Batang Ai will provide a memorable **longhouse** experience. If you don't like trees, heat, Chinese hotels or dusty roads try Sarawak. If you want to experience colonial exotica just hang around Kuching.

Before You Go

Some folks like to be prepared for anything.

Travel Documents

Before you even schedule your trip, you'll need to get a passport. Check to find the closest passport agency in your area. Passport agencies are located in most large cities and selected post offices across the country. Passports cost $65 ($55 to renew). You'll need two passport photos (most photo shops can shoot them for you) and an original birth certificate. No copies. Allow about 30 days for processing. You'll need visas to visit some countries for purposes other than tourism, although many nations will stamp U.S. and Canadian passports with stays from two weeks up to 90 days free of charge. Visas, where they're necessary, can be had by contacting the consulates of the countries you'll be visiting. Obtain your visa before entering the country. But relax, they all don't need to be had in the U.S. You can also get them on the road.

Visas for Borneo

BRUNEI

Passport required. Visa not required for tourist or business stay up to 90 days. Yellow fever vaccination needed if arriving from infected area. For more information, contact **Embassy of the State of Brunei Darussalam**, *Suite 300, 2600 Virginia Ave., N.W., Washington, D.C. 20037* ☎ *(202) 342-0159* or Brunei Permanent Mission to the U.N., *866 United Nations Plaza, Rm. 248, New York, NY 10017* ☎ *(212) 838-1600.*

INDONESIA

Valid passport and onward or return ticket required. Visa not required for tourist stay up to two months (non-extendable.) For longer stays and additional information consult **Embassy of the Republic of Indonesia**, *2020 Mass. Ave., N.W., Washington, D.C. 20036* ☎ *(202) 775-5200* or nearest Consulate: CA ☎ *(213) 383-5126* or *(415) 474-9571*, IL ☎ *(312) 938-0101*, NY ☎ *(212) 879-0600* or TX ☎ *(713) 626-3291.*

MALAYSIA
(and the Borneo States, Sarawak and Sabah)

Passport required. Visa not required for stay up to three months. Yellow fever and cholera immunizations necessary if arriving from infected areas. AIDS test required for work permits. U.S. Test sometimes accepted. For entry of pets or other types of visits, consult **Embassy of Malaysia**, *2401 Mass. Ave., N.W., Washington, D.C. 20008* ☎ *(202) 328-2700* or nearest Consulate: Los Angeles ☎ *(213) 621-2991* or New York ☎ *(212) 490-2722.*

FOR U.S. CITIZENS: GETTING VISAS		
COUNTRY	WHERE TO OBTAIN	GOOD FOR
Brunei	On arrival	*1 week*
Hong Kong	On arrival	*1 month*
Indonesia	On arrival	*2 months*
Malaysia	On arrival	*3 months*
Philippines	On arrival	*21 days*
Singapore	On arrival	*1 week*
Thailand	On arrival	*15 days*

Health Certificates

Some countries will require that you have, under International Health Regulations adopted by the World Health Organization, an International Certificate of Vaccination against yellow fever. Travelers arriving from infected areas will be required to show proof of vaccination against yellow fever. The certificate will also be stamped with the other inoculations that you have received. Any medical center will be able to provide this service or advice.

International Drivers License

These can be obtained at your state's department of motor vehicles offices or through AAA and other automobile associations. The fee is approximately $7. If you're planning on driving in Asia, get one.

International Student Identity Card

The ISIC card can help with discounts on airline tickets and lodging. There's been a surge in bogus cards, which have been readily available in mainland Malaysia.They won't do you much good in Borneo except in museums and city attractions. To get a real one, contact the Council on International Educational Exchange (CIEE) at *205 E. 42nd Street, New York, NY 10017-5706;* ☎ *(212) 661-1414.*

Cheap Airfares

If you are flying over to Asia you will want to pay the least amount of money for the best flight. For smart travelers that means a lot less than the best advertised fare. Well you are in luck. Unlike Eastern Europe or the CIS countries, Malaysia, Brunei and Indonesia have invested heavily in American jumbo jets and new airports. There are frequent flights to every major city with plenty of connections to smaller towns on a daily basis. Also there are significant discounts available to the dedicated shopper. Here is a partial list of who can get you to Asia as cheaply as possible:

DISCOUNT TICKET BROKERS	
American Travel Ventures	☎ *(310) 274-7061*
Angels International Travel	☎ *(800) 400-4150*
BiCoastal Travel	☎ *(800) 9-COASTAL*
Discover Wholesale Travel	☎ *(800) 576-7770*
Eros Travel	☎ *(213) 955-9695*
Falcon Wings Travel	☎ *(310) 417-3590*
Moon Travel & Tours	☎ *(800) 352-2899*
Sky Service Travel	☎ *(800) 700-1222*
Silver Wings Travel	☎ *(800) 488-9002*

DISCOUNT TICKET BROKERS

Supertrip Travel	☎ *(800) 338-1898*
Travel Mate	☎ *(818) 507-6283*

The last bit of good news is that Singapore Airlines, Cathay Pacific, Garuda, and Malaysian Air Services all price their flights aggressively. Now the bad news. Asian airlines, particularly MAS and Garuda like to fly full. Not American Airlines full where they fill up the aisle and window seat and leave a hole in the middle, I mean full where every single seat has a warm body in it.

The second bit of bad news is that Asians tend to be smaller than Americans if you hadn't noticed. This means seats can have an unbelievable width of 16 inches (like Garuda) and leg room that is a good two inches less than the length of your thigh bone.

The final bit of bad news is that the Concord only flies to Europe. That means you are looking at a flight of around 20 hours no matter which airline you fly.

Now combine full airplanes, with ridiculously small seat space and long flights and you have enough reason to spend your vacation on the jungle ride in Disneyland.

This applies whether you are paying full fare or next to nothing to get to Asia, so be forewarned. The flight attendants on MAS and Garuda can make the flight worthwhile but my advice is to meet them in the hotels in KK and fly to Asia on a Western carrier.

There are plenty of European and American carriers that go to Asia. Keep in mind that most Western carriers fly through Singapore.

Air Carriers

British Airways	☎ *(800) 247-9297*
Cathay Pacific	☎ *(800) 233-2742*
China Airlines	☎ *(800) 334-6787*
Garuda Air	☎ *(800) 342-7832*
Japan Air Lines	☎ *(800) 525-3663*
Malaysia Air Services	☎ *(800) 421-8641*
Northwest Airlines	☎ *(800) 225-2525*
Philippine Airlines	☎ *(800) 435-9725*
Singapore Airlines	☎ *(800) 742-3333*
Thai International	☎ *(800) 426-5204*
United Airlines	☎ *(800) 538-2929*

If you are flying Garuda or MAS ask about special fares inside the country that can significantly reduce the cost of flying internally. These special fares can only be purchased with your trans-Pacific fare and cost about $200. You must prebook your trips at least 21 days in advance and you can take up to five free flights within regions. Also think about breaking up your trip with stopovers in Hawaii, Japan, Taiwan, Hong Kong, Singapore, Jakarta or other places your airline stops along the way to Borneo. Keep in mind that New Yorkers will end up flying east through Europe and Asia to get to Singapore then Borneo. This increases your choice of airlines to include KLM, Lufthansa, Air India, and even Aeroflot. Tickets to Asia are always cheaper in the bucket shops in London, Amsterdam or Athens.

High season for airfares to Asia is early June to late August (school holidays) and mid December to early January (Christmas and school holidays). During these high seasons tickets go up 20 percent and there is significantly less choice of departure dates. Also if you miss or change your flight once over there, it can be next to impossible to get a flight home without waiting for a cancellation.

Average prices hover around $1000 roundtrip LA - KL and $1200 from New York. If you leave from a less direct airport like Atlanta, Miami, Montreal or Houston expect to pay an additional $200–$400 more.

The cheapest place to fly to in Asia is Bangkok. From there you can travel down the peninsula and fly out of KL or Singapore. Next cheapest is Singapore, followed by KL and then Jakarta. MAS has the cheapest flights to KK and Kuching while Garuda has the cheapest flights to Balikpapan and other points in Kalimantan. Brunei is the most expensive (about $1200 - $1500 return from LA) place to fly into. An excellent alternative for the serious traveler is a RTW or around the world fare that can be as cheap as $900. These fares usually include Singapore so all you have is the flight from Singapore to KK to worry about.

Insider Tip

One minor tip on baggage, MAS has an extra baggage allowance for dive bags. That doesn't mean you have to have dive equipment inside, you just have to point to the scales and the dive bag and you will avoid some of the rather hefty excess baggage charges.

Tours

Taking a tour isn't the cop-out you might think it is. Tours can actually be a better alternative to independent travel if you have only a week or two. You won't experience the delays, language problems or other time-consuming idiosyncracies inherent in the culture you're visiting. Of course you won't be truly experiencing the culture with a few of the tours. Others, though, give you a surprising amount of freedom.

Although most tours to Borneo will not save you money they can increase your enjoyment and prevent you from wasting money on useless attractions, waiting for connections and getting permits.

Tour Operators	
Abercrombie and Kent	☎ *(800) 323-7308*
Bolder Adventures	☎ *(800) 642-2742*
Cos & Kings	☎ *(800) 227-8747*
Creative Adventure Club	☎ *(800) 544-5088*
Maluku Adventures	☎ *(800) 566-2585*
Mountain Travel-Sobek	☎ *(800) 227-2384*
Natrabu Indo-America Travel	☎ *(800) 628-7228*
Nature Expeditions	☎ *(504) 484-6529*

Maps and Travel Guides

There has yet to be a decent map of Borneo. Maps made by Nelles are the prettiest but the road information on any map to this region can be unreliable. Logging roads go up faster than daffodils in the springtime and disappear just as fast. The maps in the Periplus guides are excellent and look like they are created by the same folks who put together the Nelles maps. There are various maps available in Sabah and Sarawak and none available in Kalimantan. Guidebook maps in Lonely Planet, Rough Guide, Trade and Travel and this book are your best bet. See the section in the back for a complete rundown on books available on Borneo. All books are cheaper in the States than overseas. Also take along a Bahasa Indonesia or Malay phrasebook and a couple of good books on Borneo. I would recommend *The Best of Borneo* from Oxford in Asia Paperbacks or any other of their commendable reprints of older travel journals.

Those who find nonfiction tedious should buy *Shooting the Boh* by Tracy Johnston, *Into the Heart of Borneo* by Redmond O'Hanlon and anything on Asia by Joseph Conrad or Somerset Maugham. Put your books in plastic sandwich bags to protect them from the constant moisture. Give them away as gifts after you've read them. See page 615 for more info on travel guides and fiction on Borneo.

Don't Take Drugs

If you are traveling from liberal countries like Thailand or America do not import or carry any drug into Borneo. As the locals like to say "Dada is death." Malaysia has the death sentence for people caught trafficking in drugs. Singapore and Brunei have equally harsh laws for any type of drug. Heroin is the big no. Having sat with a local Sabahan who drove 20 miles out of town to watch him smoke one joint in the middle of the jungle, I can attest to the paranoia caused by this harsh treatment and the effectiveness of the enforcement. If you do find yourself in a situation where locals are using drugs, do not prolong the social intercourse and remember that in Asia drugs are neither cool nor healthy.

Insurance

If you are the nervous type contact your insurance agent about insurance for your body and your personal possessions. Look into medical insurance that provides repatriation or medivac flights from Borneo to your country of choice.

When to Go

As you can see by the following chart the only choice you have is how hot and how wet you would like your weather. You can expect more variation in temperature as you change altitude. The mornings are cool and moist. The solar energy builds up until noon where you can almost feel your skin crackle except for the streams of sweat pouring off you. Then the heat breaks with a downpour usually between 2:00 to 3:00 p.m. The evenings are damp and cool and the rain usually begins again during the night leaving the next day fresh and cool.

In the monsoon season expect absolutely torrential downpours, strong gusts of wind and flooding. Even birds do not fly in the heavy rains. These rains come in sudden bursts and then the sun appears again. During the dry season there may be as much as two weeks without rain (very unusual) and the heat builds up to an intolerable level making you wish it would rain.

After a few weeks in country you will learn to love the close sensual heat and wonder why Europeans would ever leave this region for northern climes.

If you are planning to travel quite a bit keep this in mind:

- Travel between March and July when the rains are at their weakest. Many roads are flooded and bridges are washed out when the heavy December and January monsoons hit. This will put a wrinkle in your travel plans if you are using ground transportation.

- Avoid Ramadan when Muslims must fast during the day and are trying to preserve their energy. Things take longer and tempers can flare.

- Try to take in at least one major festival such as Sabah's Kadazan harvest festival in late May—worth scheduling a trip around. Sarawak has a similar whoop up in June. Kalimantan has the Erau festival in Tenggarong from the 23–28th of September. Due to the crowds, when visiting major attractions or flying, you should avoid the school holidays or weekends.

- Use air transportation as much as possible. This will ensure that you will arrive sooner and you will not waste as much time on rivers or on creaky local buses.

- Try to use a local guide or the help of a tour company to get the most from your trip and money. Independent travelers may find their mode of travel more expensive when visiting remote regions.

THE WEATHER IN BORNEO												
CITY	Jan.	Feb.	Mar.	Apr.	May	Jun.	Jul.	Aug.	Sep.	Oct.	Nov.	Dec.
AVERAGE TEMPERATURES IN SOUTHEAST ASIA												
Bangkok	81	83	85	88	85	83	82	82	81	80	79	79
Singapore	78	79	80	81	81	80	80	79	79	79	79	79
Jakarta	78	78	79	80	80	79	79	79	80	80	79	79
Kota Kinabalu	81	82	83	83	82	82	82	81	81	81	81	81
Manila	78	80	83	85	85	83	80	79	79	80	79	78
COMPARATIVE RAIN & HUMIDITY												
Balikpapan	85	85	86	85	85	84	83	84	84	85	85	85
Inches of Rain	7.9	6.9	9.1	8.2	9.1	7.6	7.1	6.4	5.5	5.2	6.6	8.1
% Average Humidity	74	72	72	74	76	75	75	75	72	70	71	73
Labuan	85	86	87	89	89	88	88	88	87	87	87	86
Inches of Rain	4.4	4.6	5.9	11.7	13.6	13.8	12.5	11.7	16.4	18.3	16.5	11.2
% Average Humidity	81	81	80	78	79	78	78	76	77	78	78	79
Kuching	85	86	88	90	90	91	90	91	89	89	88	87
Inches of Rain	24	20.1	12.9	11	10.3	7.1	7.7	9.2	8.6	10.5	14.1	18.2
% Average Humidity	75	74	73	71	70	66	66	68	79	71	74	75

The tourism industry in Borneo is a tight knit group and having a guide along can smooth many ruffles. The bigger the tour group you hire, the faster hotels become available, boats are safer and locals open up more. You won't find the European big glass bus, blaring megaphone, shove' em in a greasy restaurant type of guided tours here (unless you arrive on a cruise ship). The tourism business is built on personal service and unless you understand the *adat* or customs of each ethnic group, you could wonder what the heck you are looking at.

All the Nasties

Crime

The state department considers Malaysia a "low threat" environment for both resident and visiting Americans. The 1989 accord between the government of Malaysia and the Communist party of Malaya was the last time the only known indigenous terrorist-like threat was in the news. Malaysia has large ethnic Chinese and Indian populations, and remains over 50 percent Muslim. During the Gulf War the U.S. Embassy received a number of threats, bomb hoaxes, and crank phone calls. Anti-coalition demonstrations were held near the embassy and one embassy guard was a victim of a shooting. After the war ended, these activities fell off drastically. The U.S. Embassy in Kuala Lumpur expects anti-American sentiments to remain at their current very low level (actually none) unless tensions between Muslims and the U.S. occur again.

Scams

Although you may be surprised at how readily your credit cards can be used in Malaysia and Indonesia you should be on your guard in Malaysia regarding your carbons, or having people look over your shoulder when making purchases. Think twice before using your card at hole-in-the-wall stores. Credit card fraud is a growing threat and the counterfeiting of U.S. currency is quite prevalent so visitors should conduct their financial dealings in banks or reputable hotels.

Health

Rather than give you a long dry treatise on the various diseases and afflictions the tropical world has in store for you I thought I would throw in a little sex in the middle to liven it up. The chances of coming down with a bug are pretty good once you leave the antiseptic Western world. I used to think that the locals had built up resistance to the various bugs that strike down Westerners. Once in-country you realize just what a toll disease takes on the Third World. Not only are many people riddled with malaria, river blindness, intestinal infections, hepatitis, sexual diseases and more; but they are also faced with malnutrition, poor dental care, toxic chemicals and hard environmental conditions.

There are a lot of good doctors in Sabah and Sarawak—not so many in Kalimantan. Obviously the large cities are your best bet for medical care. Out in the boonies there are no doctors. There are quite a few small air strips as well as enough oil companies to support a fairly large fleet of helicopters and small planes. If you are injured in a remote area the chances are good that you can be evacuated if your guide makes it to an airstrip or radio operator.

A lot of the drugs you need a prescription for in North America can be obtained over the counter in Asia. Be careful because you will be sold whatever you want. I would strongly advise spending a few minutes with a local doctor asking him what should go in your medicine kit for wasp stings, painkillers, and most important malaria prophylaxis. Doctors can also help with anti-diarrheal drugs such as codeine, Imodium or Lomotil. Also include antiseptic and a laxative. The cost of medical treatment and drugs are quite reasonable in Malaysia and Brunei, and doctors are very open to walk in visits.

A minor note. Do not hand out medicine when in remote *kampungs*. In the past, I have tended to slashed feet, swollen eyes and other problems but I never leave strong medicine behind. If there is a missionary or trained medical specialist ask them if they are in need of your surplus medicines.

Shots

You should receive inoculations against **yellow fever**, **hepatitis B**, **tetanus**, **typhoid**, **cholera** and **tuberculosis**. An **influenza** shot couldn't hurt either. Keep in mind that these shots do not prevent you from getting sick but strengthen your resistance. There have been outbreaks of dengue fever in areas of Borneo and AIDS and STDs are potential dangers.

Ask your doctor about malaria pills. Lariam is the pill of choice but remember that there are many resistant strains of malaria and local doctors can prescribe additional types for these strains. Fansidar (which is banned for malarial prevention) is one pill that you should carry with you but never take unless you come down with malaria.

Unwanted Souvenirs

My least favorite bugs are the helminthic infections, or diseases caused by intestinal worms. Unlike the more dramatic and deadly diseases, these parasites are easily caught through ingestion of bad water and food and cause long term damage. Just to let you know who's out there you can choose from angiostrongyliasis, herring worm, roundworm, schistsomiasis, capillariasis, pin worm, oriental liver fluke, fish tapeworm, guinea worm, cat liver fluke, tapeworm, trichinosis and the ominous sounding giant intestinal fluke (who's eating who here?) All these little buggers create havoc with your internal organs and some will make the rest of your life miserable. Your digestive system will be shot, your organs under constant attack and the treatment or removal of these buggers is downright depressing. These can be prevented by maintaining absolutely rigid standards in what you eat, breathe or stick inside your body. Not easy since most travelers find wearing a biohazard suit a major impediment to picking up chicks or doing the limbo.

Think of yourself as a sponge, your lungs as an air filter and all the moist cavities of your body ideal breeding grounds for tropical diseases. It is better to think like Howard Hughes than Pig Pen when it comes to personal hygiene. Traveling down the rivers of Indonesia might give you pause when you feel refreshed by the spray coming off the bow of the boat. Consider yourself being spritzed with effluent from about 30-100 villages. Not a pretty thought.

The Fevers

The classic tropical diseases that incapacitated Stanley, Livingstone, Burton and Speke are the hemorrhagic fevers. Many of these diseases kill but most make your life a living hell and then disappear. Some come back on a regular basis. It is surprising that most of the African explorers lived to a ripe old age. The hemorrhagic fevers in Borneo are carried by mosquitoes, ticks, rats feces or even airborne dust that gets into your bloodstream and lets you die a slow, demented death as your blood turns so thin it trickles out your nose, gums, skin and eyes. Coma and death can occur in the second week. There are so many versions they just name them after the places where they are found. These are not featured in any glossy brochures for the various regions. Various blood thinning killers found around the world are called Chikungunya, Crimean, Congo, Omsk, Kyasanur Forest, Korean, Manchurian, Songo, Ebola, Argentinian, Hantaan, Lassa and Yellow Fever. In the jungles of Borneo just drinking out of crystal clear streams that a rat has urinated in can cause your downfall from leptospirosis.

The Most Dangerous Creature in the Jungle

Tiny mosquitoes, not fanged carnivores, are the traveler's worst enemy. Malaria was once thought to be caused by the bad air (mal area) given off by swamps. Now we know better. It is estimated that there are over 300 million people with malaria worldwide.Over a million people in Africa are killed by malaria every year. The female *anopheles* mosquito is small, pervasive and hungry for your blood. As they seek out blood to nurture their own offspring they leave *plasmodium* parasites in your blood system. The symptoms can start with a flulike attack followed by fever, chills, then lead to failure of multiple organs and then death. In many cases the symptoms of malaria do not start until the traveler has returned home and is in a nonmalarial zone. Remember that current chemoprophlylaxis does not prevent malaria. Lariam, Fansidar, and chloroquinine can lower the chances of getting malaria but do not provide any guarantee of being malaria proof. Two of my fellow travelers (one in Africa and one in Borneo) did not realize they had malaria because they believed that Lariam would prevent or protect them from the disease. Both did not have symptoms until a week after they arrived home. Luckily they sought treatment in time.

Malaria is a very real and common danger in most tropical countries. Most malaria in Asian and African areas is now quinine resistant and requires multiple or more creative dosages to avoid the horrors of the disease. The *anopheles* mosquito likes to bite in the cool hours before and after sunset. The most vicious strains of malaria *(Plasmodium falciparum)* attack your liver and red blood cells creating massive fevers, coma, acute kidney failure, and eventually death. There are four types of malaria in the world: *Plasmodium falciparum* is the most dangerous, *Plasmodium malariae, Plasmodium vivax* and *Plasmodium ovale* (found only in West Africa).

The *anopheles* mosquito is the most dangerous insect in the world and there are few contenders for its crown. Other biting insects that can cause you grief include the *Aedes aegypti* mosquito which carries yellow fever. His kissing cousins, the *Culex, Haemogogus, Sabethes* and *Mansonia*, can give you filariasis, viral encephalitis, dengue and other great hemorrhagic fevers.

Next on the list are tsetse flies, fleas, ticks, sandflies, mites and lice. We won't even bother to discuss wasps, horseflies, deerflies, or other clean biters.

These insects are an everyday part of life in tropical, endemic or Third World countries. They infect major percentages of the local population and if you don't take precautions, it is only a matter of time and luck before you become a victim.

Prevention is rather simple but ineffective. Protect yourself from insects by wearing long sleeved shirts and long pants. Use insect repellant, sleep under a mosquito net, avoid swampy areas, use mosquito coils, don't sleep directly on the ground, check yourself for tick and insect bites daily, and last but not least, understand the symptoms and treatment of these diseases so you can seek immediate and effective treatment no matter what part of the world you are in.

Sex: The Good, the Bad and the Ugly

It is only because of my Puritan ethic that I put sex in with the nasty stuff. Being happily married I must resort to less accurate reportorial methods to provide guidance to the curious. The quest for sexual adventure used to be a major part of the joy of travel, and in some places like Bangkok, manages to fill jumbo jets full of Koreans and Japanese on a daily basis. On Borneo, the Muslim governments frown on drugs. They will hang you for trafficking in drugs but they seem to turn a blind eye to sex and gambling. AIDS is an overblown but still a very real danger to the traveler. I say overblown because of all the diseases that can strike you dead in the tropics, AIDS is a very minor contender compared to malaria or even leptospirosis. Whorehouses around the world have not gone out of business, junkies still share needles and dentists in many Third World countries still grind and yank away with improperly sterilized instruments. Westerners blame HIV, Hepatitis B and other sexually transmitted diseases on the Third World, and the Third World blames them on the West. In Borneo you will find the availability of prostitution on a level that matches hairdressing. In fact many whorehouses advertise themselves as hairstylists (always found on the second floor). If you do need a haircut and are used to Ed the barber shearing you like a dog while reciting baseball statistics, you might enjoy a clipping here. The hairstylist will provide you with a cup of tea and provide a wonderful neck and head massage. You will be so relaxed and tingling you might even forget the godawful haircut you got.

The curious traveler will more than likely come in contact with the infamous hotel "health club." The health club is usually staffed with a group of 5–20 girls who are shipped around Malaysia as prostitutes. There are also ladies who do nothing but give massages. You can ask for a massage girl or a sex girl without risk of embarrassing the attendant. You can also call down for room service, the attendant will then send up a lady for a hotel massage or plain old sex or whatever accommodation you can discuss.

If you go downstairs the rates will be cheaper. At the desk you can ask for a sex girl or a massage girl. Usually the girls will be Chinese or Filipino. It is very rare that you will find a Malay girl in a health club. You are given a towel and slippers to wear and shown to a simple room. You will be expected to disrobe completely and lie on the massage table. The lady will come in and ask you if you would like a bath first. If you take a bath you will be washed like a small child and then toweled off. The massage can be quite thorough and in some cases painful. If you request a sex girl for a massage it is similar to being beaten up by a dwarf—short and painful, also a little embarrassing.

Each girl has her own inimitable style and these skills can be discussed with the desk. At or towards the end of the massage you will be asked if you wish to be masturbated. This is considered quite normal in the health clubs and in a very Chinese way is considered healthy.

If you wish to have sex there will be a discussion of the additional fee. In the big hotels in Kuching and KK, nonlocals will be nicked $70–$100 US dollars. In the smaller towns $20–$50 is about the norm. Since I cannot vouch for each person's idea of a good time it is best left to the imagination if this is an erotic event or similar to milking time at the dairy farm. The girls in the health clubs do not perform fellatio, do not generally like Western men (too big, carry AIDS, smell bad, etc.) and would send most men running back to their girlfriends or wives for real affection. The women do not provide emotional satisfaction; they do however provide those itty bitty cheap Asian condoms and a good massage. The sexual experience can be summed up by one of my fellow travelers (an ex-marine with much time in the bars of Saigon) who once explained the experience by drawling "I would've said no but I was too tired to jack myself off." Ahh such is love.

This is pretty much the routine in the Chinese business hotels and resorts in Malaysia. In Kalimantan there are certain hotels with bars where men go to have a good time. There is no pretense of massage or even health in the smoke filled rooms. It is a sociable atmosphere and the women are available for between $10 and as little as $2 US. In these places of ill repute you can usually find the police chief, military officers and probably your guide.

There are also men's dance clubs where lonely businessmen can choose a numbered lady from behind a glass window. They then spend the evening drinking expensive drinks, dancing to lame Asian grinders and doing absolutely nothing carnal. They do laugh at your jokes and drink expensive champagne.

In the larger cities you will find the women very welcoming and decidedly friendly. In many cases western men will be coyly approached by young girls and few single women will turn down an offer of dinner and showing you around. As for the opposite sex, Western women describe Indonesian and Malaysian men as very shy, sophomoric in their intent and absolutely without pretense. Do not be surprised if any social encounter includes meeting and traveling with numbers of the immediate family. Those of my friends who have had romantic encounters with Malaysian and Indonesian women all go on for hours about the special romantic feeling that Asian women have inspired.

The more skeptical might be thinking "Yeah that's all fine, but what about getting AIDS?" Keep in mind that although most prostitutes in major cities use condoms with Western clients (they assume that AIDS is spread by Westerners having sex with Asian women and men) there is a growing contingent of Thai girls being passed off to tourists as Malaysian. As for the general population, incidence of AIDS is much lower than North America but growing rapidly.

Your chances of catching AIDS through unprotected sex depends on frequency and type of contact. So before you slap on the Old Spice and dust off those Engelbert Humperdinck records remember the wild cards: people infected by blood transfusions, prostitutes, frequent drug users, hemophiliacs, homosexuals, and the millions of people who will get HIV this year from heterosexual sex will continue to make HIV a danger, if not an overwhelmingly ominous one.

The Invisibles

Some might think it unfair that I should burden the eager traveler with the following list of bugs that exist in Southeast Asia. I have been sick as a dog in

Mexico and lived out my own version of the "Sheltering Sky" in North Africa. Now saying this, I traveled to Borneo with a fellow American who proceeded to catch malaria on a kayak trip in remote Sabah, and I've heard enough stories about malarial insect bites on airplanes to make me sleep with one eye open.

After reading this list, don't just run off to be the next bubble boy and spend the rest of your life in a hermetically sealed dome. For travelers these diseases are relatively rare and mostly avoidable. To put the whole thing in perspective the most frequent complaints tend to be diarrhea followed by a cold (usually the result of lowered resistance caused by fatigue, dehydration, foreign microbes and stress). The important thing is to know when you are sick versus very sick. Tales of turn of the century explorers struck down by a tiny mosquito bite are not legend. Malaria is still a very real and common threat. Just for fun bring back a sample of local river water from your next trip and have the medical lab analyze it. You may never drink water of any kind again.

Here are some very unscientific pointers on healthy habits in the tropics

People cause most bugs. The refuse and waste from populated areas are a major source for disease. Avoid these and head for the forests.

Understand the dangers, practice the cure

Know when mosquitoes bite, what bugs lie in stagnant water, and then acquaint yourselves with the proper first aid procedures, cures, and methods of healing. I am always surprised how few Americans understand how malaria is caused or even take precautions.

Wash your hands

You would be surprised how many times you transfer germs from your hands to your face and then into your body.

Inspect the nasties

Try to wash yourself as much as you can and do a daily inspection of every sweaty nook and rude cranny for bites, ticks, scratches etc. Don't be shy about asking your fellow travelers to oblige.

Don't drink out of anything that isn't fresh and cooked well.

Forget about the old wives tale about washing fruit. If half the village just defecated in the river upstream you were better off eating that fruit peel and all. Cook all meat well and avoid pork like the plague.

Don't do stupid things

Go ahead and seduce every bar wench in Asia, drink out of dirty rivers, use rusty razors to remove thorns and eat anything that's put in front of you. The chances are good that absolutely nothing will happen to you. Then again you could get run over by a car on the way home from the airport. The lesson here is the more care you take and the more aware you are of problems, the greater the chance you will live long enough to die at home in bed.

Diseases

Diseases listed below are important and you should be conversant with both symptoms and cures.

WARNING:

THIS INFORMATION IS NOT INTENDED AS MEDICAL ADVICE. IT IS A SIMPLE LIST DESIGNED TO GIVE YOU AN OVERVIEW OF THE VARIOUS NASTIES THAT AWAIT YOU. IF YOU NEED MEDICAL ADVICE, SEE A DOCTOR OR AN EXPERT ON TROPICAL DISEASES.

Tropical countries are the most likely to cause you bacterial grief. Keep in mind that most of these diseases are a direct result of poor hygiene, travel in infected areas and contact with infected people. In other words stay away from people if you want to stay healthy. Secondly follow the common sense practice of having all food cooked freshly and properly. Many books tell you to wash fruit then forget that the water is probably more bug filled than the fruit. Peel all fruits and vegetables and approach anything you stick in your body with a healthy level of skepticism and distrust. If you are completely anal you can exist on freeze dried foods, Maggi Mee (noodles) fresh fruit (peeled remember) and tinned food.

Remember that the symptoms of many tropical diseases may not take effect until you are home and back into your regular schedule. It is highly advisable that you contact a tropical disease specialist and have full testing done (stool, urine, blood, physical) just to be sure. Very few American doctors are conversant with the many tropical diseases by virtue of their rarity. This is not their fault since many tourists do not even realize that they have taken trips or cruises into endemic zones. People can catch malaria on a plane between London and New York from a stowaway mosquito that just came in from Bombay. Many people come in close contact with foreigners in buses, subways and on the street in Los Angeles and New York. Don't assume you have to be up to your neck in pig wallows to be a risk.

Many labs do not do tests for some of the more exotic bugs. Symptoms can also be misleading. It is possible that you may be misdiagnosed or mistreated if you do not fully discuss the possible reasons for your medical condition. Now that we have scared the hell out of you, your first contact should be with the Center for Disease Control in Atlanta ☎ *(404) 332-4559.*

Remember that many childhood diseases like measles, mumps, polio, and whooping cough are prevalent in remote villages. If you have not had these unpleasant but not life threatening diseases or have not been inoculated, you could be in for a surprise.

AIDS (Acquired Immune Deficiency Syndrome)

Cause: Advanced stage of HIV (Human Immunodeficiency Syndrome) which causes destruction of the natural resistance of human to infection and other diseases. Death by AIDS is usually a result of unrelated diseases which rapidly attack the victim. These range of diseases are called ARC (AIDS-related complex.)

Carrier: Sexual intercourse with infected person, transfusion of infected blood or even from infected mother through breast milk. There is no way to determine if someone has HIV except by blood test. Male homosexuals, drug users, prostitutes are high risk groups in major urban centers in the West. AIDS is less selective in developing countries with Central and Eastern Africa being the areas of highest incidence. Southeast Asia is rapidly catching up to Africa and the West.

Symptoms: Fever, weight loss, fatigue, night sweats, lymph node problems. Infection by other opportunistic diseases such as Karposi's sarcoma and pneumonia are highly probable and will lead to death.

Treatment: There is no known cure. Use of condoms, refrain from sexual contact, do not receive injections or transfusions in questionable areas. Avoid live vaccines such as gama globulin and Hepatitis B in developing countries.

Amebiasis

Cause: A protozoan parasite carried in human fecal matter. Usually found in areas with poor sanitation.

Carrier: Entamoeba histolytic is passed by poor hygiene. Ingested orally in water, air or food that has been in contact with the parasite.

Symptoms: The infection will spread from the intestines and cause abscesses in other organs such as liver, lungs and brain.

Treatment: Metronidazole, iodoquinol, diloxanide furoate, paromomycin, tetracycline plus chloroquinine base.

How to Avoid: Avoid uncooked foods. Boil water. Drink bottled liquids. Be sure that food is cooked properly. Peel fruits and vegetables.

Brucellosis (undulant fever)

Cause: Ingestion of infected dairy products

Carrier: Untreated dairy products infected with the brucellosis bacteria

Symptoms: Intermittent fever, sweating, jaundice, rash, depression, enlarged spleen and lymph nodes. The symptoms may disappear and go into permanent remission after 3 to 6 months.

Treatment: Tetracyclines, sulfonamides, and streptomycin.

How to Avoid: Drink pasteurized milk, avoid infected livestock.

Cholera

Cause: Intestinal infection caused by the toxin Vibrio cholerae O group bacteria

Carrier: Infected food and water contaminated by human and animal waste

Symptoms: Watery diarrhea, abdominal cramps, nausea, vomiting and severe dehydration as a result of diarrhea. Can lead to death if fluids are not replaced.

Treatment: Tetracycline can hasten recovery. Replace fluids using an electrolyte solution.

How to Avoid: Vaccinations before trip can diminish symptoms up to 50 percent for a period of 3 to 6 months. A threat in refugee camps or areas of poor sanitation. Use standard precautions with food and drink for developing countries.

Chikungunya Disease

Cause: Alphavirus transmitted by mosquito bites

Carrier: Mosquitoes who transmit the disease from the host (Monkeys)

Symptoms: Joint pain with potential for hemorrhagic symptoms.

Treatment: None but symptoms will disappear. In hemorrhagic cases avoid aspirin.

How to Avoid: Standard precautions to avoid mosquito bites. Insect repellent, mosquito nets, cover exposed skin areas.

Ciguatera Poisoning

Cause: Ingestion of fish containing the toxin produced by the dinoflagellate *Gambierdiscus toxoids*.

Carrier: 425 species of tropical reef fish

Symptoms: Up to 6 hours after eating, victims may experience nausea, watery diarrhea, abdominal cramps, vomiting, abnormal sensation in limbs and teeth, hot cold flashes, joint pain, weakness, skin rashes and itching. In very severe cases victims may experience blind spells, low blood pressure and heart rate, paralysis and loss of coordination. Symptoms may appear years later.

Treatment: There is no specific medical treatment other than first aid. Induce vomiting.

How to Avoid: Do not eat reef fish (including sea bass, barracuda, red snapper or grouper).

Dengue Fever (Breakbone fever)

Cause: An arbovirus transmitted by mosquitoes

Carrier: Mosquitoes in tropical areas, usually bite during the daytime.

Symptoms: Two distinct periods. First period consists of severe muscle, joint and headaches combined with high fever (the origin of the term "break bone fever." The second phase is sensitivity to light, diarrhea, vomiting, nausea, mental depression and enlarged lymph nodes.

Treatment: Designed to relieve symptoms. Aspirin should be avoided due to hemorrhagic complications.

How to Avoid: Typical protection against daytime mosquito bites: Insect repellent with high DEET levels, light colored long sleeve pants and shirts.

Diarrhea

Cause: There are many reasons for travelers to have the symptoms of diarrhea. It is important to remember that alien bacteria in the digestive tract is the main culprit. Many travelers to Third World countries may find themselves doubled up in pain, running for the nearest stinking toilet wondering why the hell they ever left their comfortable home.

Carrier: Bacteria from food, the air, water or other people can be the cause. Dehydration from long airplane flights, strange diets, stress and high altitude can also cause diarrhea. It is doubtful you will ever get to know your intestinal bacteria on a first name basis but *Aeromonas hydrophila, Campylobacter, Jejuni pleisiomonas, salmonellae, shigellae, shielloides, Vibrio cholerae* (non-01), *Vibrio parahaemolyticus, Yersinia enterocoliticia* are the most likely culprits, along with *Escherichia coli.* All these bugs would love to spend a week or two in your gut.

Symptoms: Loose stools, stomach pains, bloating, fever and malaise.

Treatment: First step is to stop eating and ingest plenty of fluids and salty foods, secondly try Kaopectate or Pepto Bismol. If diarrhea persists after 3–4 days, seek medical advice.

How to Avoid: Keep your fluid intake high when traveling. Follow common sense procedures when eating, drinking and ingesting any food or fluids. Remember to wash your hands carefully and frequently since you can transmit a shocking number of germs from your hands to your mouth, eyes and nose.

Encephalitis

Cause: A common viral infection carried by insects in Southeast Asia.

Carrier: The disease can be carried by the tick or mosquito. The risk is high.

Symptoms: Fever, headache, muscle pain, malaise, runny nose and sore throat followed by lethargy, confusion, hallucination and seizures. About one fifth of infections have led to death.

Treatment: A vaccine is available for those traveling to endemic areas.

How to Avoid: Avoid areas known to be endemic. Avoid tick infested areas such as forests, rice growing areas in Asia (mosquitoes), or areas that have a large number of domestic pigs (tick carriers). Use insect repellant. Do not drink unpasteurized milk.

Filariasis (lymphatic, river blindness)

Cause: A group of diseases caused by roundworms and carried by mosquitoes.

Carrier: Mosquitoes and biting flies in tropical areas.

Symptoms: Lymphatic filariasis, onchocerciasis (river blindness), loiasis, mansonellasis all have similar and very unpleasant symptoms. Fevers, headaches, nausea, vomiting, sensitivity to light, inflammation in the legs including the abdomen and testicles. Swelling of the abdomen, joints and scrotum, enlarged lymph nodes, abscesses, eye lesions that lead to blindness, rashes, itches and arthritis.

Treatment: Diethylcarbamazine (DEC, Hetrazan, Notezine) is the usual treatment.

How to Avoid: Avoid bites by insects with usual protective measures and insect repellent.

Flukes, Oriental

Cause: the liver fluke *(Clonorchis sinensis)* and the lung fluke *(Paragonimus westermani)* which lead to paragonimasis.

Carrier: Carried in fish that has not been properly cooked.

Symptoms: Obstruction of the bile system, along with fever, pain, jaundice, gallstones, inflammation of the pancreas. There is further risk of cancer of the bile tract after infection. Paragonimasis affects the lungs and causes chest pains.

Treatment: Treatment for paragonimasis is with Prazanquantel. Obstruction of the bile system can require surgery.

How to Avoid: To avoid liver flukes do not eat uncooked or improperly cooked fish—something most sushi fans will decry. Paragonimasis is found in uncooked shellfish, like freshwater crabs, crayfish and shrimp.

Giardiasis

Cause: A protozoa Giardi lamblia that causes diarrhea.

Carrier: Ingestion of food or water that is contaminated with fecal matter.

Symptoms: Very sudden diarrhea, severe flatulence, cramps, nausea, anorexia, weight loss and fever.

Treatment: Giardiasis can disappear without treatment but Furazolidone, metronidizole, or quinacrine HCI is the usual method of treatment.

How to Avoid: Cleanliness, drink bottled water, and strict personal hygiene in eating and personal contact.

HEMORRHAGIC FEVERS

Some of the more well known hemorrhagic fevers are yellow fever, dengue, lassa fever and the horror movie calibre Ebola fever from Africa (not found in Asia) . Outbreaks tend to be localized and subject to large populations of insects, or rats. Don't let the exotic sounding names lull you into a sense of false security since there was a major outbreak in the American Southwest caused by rodents spreading the disease.

Cause: Intestinal worms carried by insects and rodents.

Carrier: Depending on the disease it can be transmitted by mosquitoes, ticks, rodents (in urine and feces)

Symptoms: Headache, backache, muscle pain and conjunctivitis. Later on the thinning of the blood will cause low blood pressure, bleeding from the gums and nose, vomiting and coughing up blood, blood in your stool, bleeding from the skin, and hemorrhaging in the internal organs. Coma and death may occur in the second week.

Treatment: Consult a doctor or medical facility familiar with the local disease.

How to Avoid: Avoid mosquitoes, ticks, and areas with high concentrations of mice and rats.

Hepatitis, A, B, Non-A, Non-B

Cause: A virus that attacks the liver. Hepatitis A, Non B and Non A can be brought on by poor hygiene. Hepatitis B is transmitted sexually or through infected blood.

Carrier: Hepatitis A is transmitted by oral-fecal route, person to person contact, or through contaminated food or water. Hepatitis B is transmitted by sexual activity or the transfer of bodily fluids. Hepatitis Non A and Non B is spread by contaminated water or from other people.

Symptoms: Muscle and joint pain, nausea, fatigue, sensitivity to light, sore throat, runny nose. Look for dark urine and clay colored stools, jaundice along with liver pain and enlargement.

Treatment: Rest and a high calorie diet. Immune Globulin is advised as a minor protection against Hepatitis A. You can be vaccinated against hepatitis B.

How to Avoid: Non A and B require avoiding infected foods. Hepatitis B requires no unprotected sexual contact, avoiding unsterile needles, dental work and infusions. Hepatitis A requires proper hygiene and avoiding infected water and foods.

Hydatid Disease (echinococcosis)

Cause: A tapeworm found in areas with high populations of pigs, cattle and sheep.

Carrier: Eggs of the echinococcosis

Symptoms: Cysts form in the liver, lungs, bone or brain.

Treatment: Surgery for removal of the infected cysts. Mebendazole and albendazole are used as well.

How to Avoid: Boil water, cook foods properly, avoid infected areas.

Leishmaniasis

Cause: Protozoans of the genus Leishmania

Carrier: Sandflies in tropical and subtropical regions

Symptoms: Skin lesions, cutaneous ulcers, mucocutaneous ulcers in the mouth, nose and anus. Intermittent fever, anemia and enlarged spleen

Treatment: Sodium stibogluconate, rifampin, and sodium antimony gluconate. Surgery is also used to remove cutaneous and mucocutaneous cysts.

How to Avoid: Use insect repellant, a ground cover when sleeping, bednets and cover arms and legs.

Malaria

Malaria is by far the most dangerous and likely disease for travelers to Third World countries. Protection against this disease should be your first priority. As a rule be leery of all riverine, swampy or tropical places. Areas such as logging camps, shanty towns, oases, campsites near slow moving water, resorts near mangrove swamps are very likely to be major areas of malarial infection. Consult with a local doctor to understand the various resistances and the prescribed treatment. Many foreign doctors are more knowledgable about the cure and treatment of malaria than domestic doctors.

Cause: The plasmodium parasite injected into the victim while the mosquito draws blood.

Carrier: The female anopheles mosquito

Symptoms: Fever, chills, enlarged spleen in low level versions, *plasmodium falciparum* or cerebral malaria can also cause convulsions, kidney failure, hypoglycemia.

Treatment: Chloroquinine, quinine, pyrimethamine, sulfadoxine, and mefloquine. Note: Some people may have adverse reactions to all and any of these drugs.

How to Avoid: Begin taking a malarial prophylaxis before your trip, during and after. (Consult your doctor for a prescription) Avoid infected areas, protect yourself from mosquito bites, (netting, insect repellant, mosquito coils, long sleeves and shirts) especially during dusk and evening times.

Salmonellosis

Cause: A common bacterial infection; *Salmonella gastroenteritis* that is commonly described as food poisoning.

Carrier: Found in fecally contaminated food, unpasteurized milk, raw foods, water

Symptoms: Abdominal pain, diarrhea, vomiting, chills and fever usually within 8–48 hours of ingesting infected food. *Salmonella* only kills about one percent of its victims usually small children or the aged.

Treatment: Purge infected food, replace fluids. Complete recovery is within 2–5 days.

How to Avoid: Consume only properly prepared foods.

Sandfly Fever (3 day fever)

Cause: Phleboviruses injected by sandfly bites

Carrier: Transmitted by sandflies, usually during the dry season.

Symptoms: Fever, headache, eye pain, chest muscle pains, vomiting, sensitivity to light, stiff neck, taste abnormality, rash and joint pain.

Treatment: There is no specific treatment. The symptoms can reoccur in about 15 percent of cases, but typically disappear

How to Avoid: Do not sleep directly on the ground, sandflies usually bite at night.

Schistosomiasis (bilharzia)

Bilharzia is one of the meanest bugs to pick up in your foreign travels. The nasty little creatures actually burrow through unbroken skin and lodge themselves in your gut. If not treated it can make your life a living hell with afternoon sweats, painful urination, weakness and other good stuff. There is little you can do to prevent infection since the Schistosoma larva and flukes are found where people have fouled fresh water rivers and lakes. Get treatment immediately since the affliction worsens as the eggs multiply and continue to infect more tissues. About 250 million people around the world are believed to be infected.

Cause: A group of parasitic Schistosoma flatworms (*Schistosoma mansoni, Schistosomajaponicum* and *Schistosoma haematobium*) are found in slow moving, tropical fresh water.

Carrier: The larvae of Schistosoma are found in slow moving waterways in tropical areas around the world. They enter the body through the skin and then enter the lymph vessels and then migrate to the liver.

Symptoms: Look for a rash and itching at the entry site followed by weakness, loss of appetite, night sweats, hivelike rashes, and afternoon fevers in about 4–6 weeks. Bloody, painful and frequent urination, diarrhea and later victims become weaker and may be susceptible to further infections and diseases.

Treatment: Elimination of *S. Mansoni* requires oxamniquine and praziquantel. *S. japonicum* responds to praziquantel alone and *S. haematobium* is treated with praziquantel and metrifonate.

How to Avoid: Stay out of slow moving fresh water in all tropical and semitropical areas. This also means wading or standing in water.

Tainiasis (tapeworms)

Cause: A tapeworm, usually discovered after being passed by the victim.

Carrier: Ingestion of poorly cooked meat infected with tapeworms.

Symptoms: In advanced cases there will be diarrhea, and stomach cramps. Sections of tapeworms can be seen in stools.

Treatment: Mebendazole, niclocsamide, paromomysi, and praziqunatel are effective in killing the parasite.

How to Avoid: Tapeworm comes from eating meats infected with tapeworm or coming into contact with infected fecal matter through poor hygiene or ingestion.

Tetanus (lockjaw)

Cause: A bacteria caused by the bacteria *Clostridiium tetani.*

Carrier: Found in soil and enters body through cuts or punctures

Symptoms: Restlessness, irritability, headaches, jaw pain, back pain and stiffness and difficulty in swallowing. Then within 2–56 days stiffness increases with lockjaw and spasms. Death occurs in about half the cases, usually affecting children.

Treatment: Human tetanus immune globulin is administered with nerve blockers for muscle relaxation.

How to Avoid: Immunization is the best prevention with a booster recommended before travel.

Trachoma

Cause: A chlamydial infection of the eye, that is responsible for about 200 million cases of blindness.

Carrier: Flies, contact, wiping face or eye area with infected towels,

Symptoms: Constant inflammation under the eyelid that causes scarring of the eyelid, in turned eyelash and eventual scarring of the cornea and then blindness.

Treatment: Tetracyclines, erythromycin, sulfonomide, surgery to correct turned in lashes.

How to Avoid: Common in Africa, the Middle East and Asia it is spread primarily by flies. Proper hygiene and avoidance of fly infested areas are recommended.

Trichinosis

Cause: Infection of the *Trichinella spiralis* worm.

Carrier: Pork that contains cysts. The worm then infects the new host's tissue and intestines.

Symptoms: Diarrhea, abdominal pain, nausea, prostration, and fever. As the worm infects tissue it causes fever, swelling around the eyes, conjunctivitis, eye hemorrhages, muscle pain, weakness, rash and splinter hemorrhages under the nails. Less than 10 percent of the cases result in death.

Treatment: Thiabendazole is effective in killing the parasite.

How to Avoid: Proper preparation, storage and cooking of meat.

Tuberculosis

Cause: A disease of the lungs caused by the *Mycobacterium tuberculosis* bacteria or *Mycobacterium bovis*.

Carrier: By close contact with infected persons, (sneezing, coughing) or in the case of *Mycobacterium bovis* contaminated or unpasteurized milk.

Symptoms: Weight loss, night sweats and a chronic cough usually with traces of blood. If left untreated death results in about 60 percent of the cases after a period of 2 and a half years.

Treatment: Isoniazid, Rifampin, Pyrazinamide, Streptomycin and Ethambutal are used to control the disease.

How to Avoid: Vaccination and isoniazid prophylaxis.

Typhoid Fever

Cause: The bacterium *Salmonella typhi*.

Carrier: Transmitted by contaminated food and water in areas of poor hygiene.

Symptoms: Fever, headaches, abdominal tenderness, malaise, rash, enlarged spleen. Later symptoms include delirium, intestinal hemorrhage and perforation of the intestine.

Treatment: Chloramphenicol.

How to Avoid: Vaccination is the primary protection although the effectiveness is not high.

Typhus Fever

Cause: Rickettsia

Carrier: Transmitted by fleas, lice, mites and ticks found in mountainous areas around the world.

Symptoms: Fever, headache, rash, and muscle pain. If untreated death may occur in the second week due to kidney failure, coma, and blockage of the arteries.

Treatment: Tetracyclines or chloramphenicol.

How to Avoid: Check for ticks, avoid insect bites, hygiene to prevent lice and avoiding mountainous regions.

Yellow Fever

Cause: A virus transmitted by mosquito bites.

Carrier: The tiny banded legged *aedes aegpyti* is the source for urban yellow fever and the Haemogogus and Sabethes mosquito carry the jungle version.

Symptoms: In the beginning, fever, headaches, backaches, muscle pain, nausea, conjunctivitis, albumin in the urine and slow heart rate. Followed by black vomit, no urination, and delirium. Death affects only 5–10 percent of cases and occurs in the fourth to sixth day.

Treatment: Replace fluids and electrolytes.

How to Avoid: Vaccination is mandatory when entering or leaving from infected areas.

Language and Culture

Aren't you glad that you don't look like a tourist?

Asians are probably more concerned about respecting your Western sensi-
bilities than you are about theirs. This is natural since our polyglot culture
erases many of the rigid social courtesies. The further you go into the back-
woods the more important cultural signals become. At the same time don't
be afraid to let your hosts in on some of our curious habits. Just try to explain baseball cards or chewing gum to an Iban headhunter to see how far
our two worlds are apart.

- **Be calm and attentive.** If Americans can do one thing to dispel the
  ugly American label it would be to listen and talk softly. Yanks
  have an annoying habit of talking louder as language fails them.
  This shouting is usually matched with exaggerated hand movements in case the puzzled local is deaf as well as blind. Speak slowly
  and clearly with enough room for the other to take in what you
  have said.

- **Control your emotions:** Outbursts of anger or affection are considered crass and rude. Never show anger, regardless of the situation.
  Asians abhor conflict. Equally as offensive are public displays of
  sexual affection. Kissing and holding hands are discouraged in
  most Muslim communities. However Indonesian men and women
  will hold hands with the same sex while strolling.

- **Dress simply and cleanly:** This means rather dull attire. Black T-shirts with skulls, military type pants, short skirts, all have very real and negative messages to Asians and Muslims.

- **Remove your shoes:** When entering an individual's home, remove your shoes. This is always the case at people's homes, although rarely so at hotels and public structures other than religious temples.

- **Don't pat people on the head**, including children. The head contains the person's soul. It's a sign of disrespect. Conversely, the Chinese like to rub the heads of blond children to bring them good luck.

- **The left hand is unclean.** What you do with your hands, do with both hands or your right hand only. You don't have to use your left hand for the purpose your hosts assume you do but it might help explain why the sinister is less popular than your dexter. Most rural Asians and Muslims do not use toilet paper and wash themselves with their left hand and water. Does that help you remember why you should use the right hand when, greeting, eating and passing objects to other people? Lefties may take an instant dislike to Asia but would you want your Charmin-free hosts to use their left hand to pass you your food?

- **Feet** are considered unclean as well. When seated, don't point your soles in anyone's direction.

- **Eating** with chopsticks or with your fingers is acceptable depending on your host's lead. Place chopsticks horizontally across your bowl when finished. Eat all the food you take or else your host will think you didn't like the meal. You can use both hands to eat with if using your fingers, and yes, you can slurp your soup.

- **Behaving in temples:** Despite the exotic and sometimes fierce look of Muslim, Hindu or Chinese temples, visitors are usually welcome. But be very careful not to talk loudly, take pictures without permission or act disrespectfully. Always remove your shoes before entering an Asian temple of worship. And if seated before a Buddha, sit on your knees, thigh and hip, with your feet extending behind you. Do not sit in the lotus position (cross-legged). No shorts in temples, although some guides will tell you that it's okay. (They just don't want to offend you.) Cameras may or may not be permitted. Usually they're not, but inquire first.

Just as you wouldn't necessarily shoot a guest for picking their nose at breakfast, your hosts are not about to stone you for being culturally insensitive. Think Asian, ask first and keep a sense of humor.

Borneo

A Green And Deadly Place

Headhunting exists only in history books and in the blackened skulls in longhouses. This is a 100-year-old photo of Penan heads collected by the Iban.

Borneo: ancient, primitive, exotic, wild. When you spin the globe certain names evoke romantic images. The island of Borneo is one of them. Pirates, headhunters, white rajahs, rare animals and deep mysterious jungles are all part of the appeal of this equatorial paradise. But there is more than just mystery and romance to recommend Borneo for adventure. There is the wicked omnipresent feeling of death and wildly exploding life.

Sit with me in the jungle. Be silent. Look around you. The jungle is a deadly place. I don't mean deadly to humans, but there is no other place I can think of that brings death so quickly to mind. The jungle lives on death. Decay is life. A mere fingernail-scratch beneath the thin ground cover, the rotting leaves, is the barren red sandy clay. Tree roots sit on top of the dirt sending out wavy curtainlike roots to delicately balance their great height. Once exposed to wind and erosion and left naked by logging, they topple over in the slightest breeze or deluge. Plants survive as sponges clinging to their hosts to soak up rain and nutrients. Here in the jungle the food chain has no mercy, no pecking order. Plants kill animals, animals feed ants, termites dismember towering trees, strangling figs choke trees, snakes swallow pigs and deer, bacteria can fell humans. Here there is rot, putrefaction, dampness and mold. Living organisms seem to dismantle and decay before your very eyes. Animals and birds have the shy desperate look of one that knows it does not have long to procreate before losing the battle to age, disease or another species. It is easy to picture how long our bodies would last in this primeval charnel house. I once asked why Dayaks looked so healthy in the jungle. I was simply told "If you get sick, you die." Darwin would have loved Borneo.

We are in the incubator of life. Evolution is sped up here. Like a giant agar jar, the rapidity and diversity that occurs here breeds bizarre symbiotic relationships: flowers that smell like rotting carcasses to attract pollinating flies, fruit that can be smelled from over a kilometer away, animals that fly, birds that walk, snakes that fly, squirrels that fly, insects that look like leaves, sticks, African masks...centipedes that look like nuts, orchids that slam unsuspecting bees against their private parts to pollinate themselves... Giant everything: earthworms, crocodiles, squirrels, bats... But I am getting ahead of myself. Walk with me into the light.

As we leave the dim wetness of the forest we come out onto a logged clearing. The mud is five feet deep, smashed wood is everywhere, there are rainbow puddles of diesel and grease, old oil cans, crude wooden buildings. The heat is stifling, the brightness blinds you. Here is the silence of real death. The death that comes of annihilation. Here the vines, weeds and brush will take over within five years, in ten years trees will tower above us, birds, insects, some mammals will return but it will not be the same. The rainforest that has existed in a delicate balance between life and death will have died.

A Peculiar and Romantic History

Today Borneo is a place of growth, wealth, poverty, waste, energy and devastation. Like many romantic places, some of the stories are true, some are fables. For an island that has been known since the second century after Christ (Ptolemy mentioned the land mass in his book *Geographia*) the island is still very wild and remote. There are many stories about Borneo. Some are still true today. Pirates still terrorize, Sultans still rule, giant crocodiles exist, elephants and rhinoceros still roam the dark jungles. Thousands of species of exotic birds, plants and animals continue to inspire wonder. But headhunters do not take heads anymore, the wildman of Borneo was a Barnum & Bailey circus fake and what many visitors mistake for virgin rainforest is actually secondary growth from ancient logging.

Borneo may not be ideal for the first time visitor to Asia. Unlike the elegant temples of Bali or the cultural complexity of Singapore, the island of Borneo is an Asian frontier; much like Alaska or Australia were frontiers. There is good money to be made here, room to live and there is the promise of uncontrolled growth and exploitation. Things have changed since A.D. 700 when the Chinese first started trading with the natives. Today Borneo has its modern shopping malls, cellular phones and expensive cars (the one manufacturer that builds cars in Sarawak is BMW) but just a few miles from the major towns hard reality sets in. Logging trucks, ramshackle *kampungs* and dusty, tumbledown logging towns are the norm.

Burial pole from Belaga now outside the Sarawak Museum

One person might come away with the distinct impression that Borneo is a hopeless wasteland of endless miles of denuded countryside stripped by avaricious politicians, with labor supplied by exploited indigenous people who will be cast aside once they have destroyed their own home. Another person might marvel at the untouched wonder of a virgin rainforest, experience the laughter and camaraderie of a native guide and come away amazed at the future potential for this garden of Eden and the intensity of its people and government in wanting to preserve a better future. I have come away with both images and this book will explore the shades of grey in between. Like most large geographic and geopolitical areas, Borneo cannot be painted with a broad brush. There is hope and there is fear. There is good and there is bad.

I have been traveling to Borneo on and off since 1989. I am in love with the people, the promise of adventure, the immense rainforests. I cannot predict the future. You gentle reader must form your own opinion.

Mt. Kinabalu in Sabah

Geography

Borneo is 746,309 sq. kms. (288,150 sq. mi): the third largest island after Greenland and New Guinea. The population is 17 million. Indonesia, Malaysia and Brunei share domain of this equatorial island.

It is one of the oldest islands in the Indonesian archipelago. Part of the Sunda shelf, Borneo was once linked to the mainland and shares many species with Southeast Asia. The island is not volcanic like many Indonesian islands but is formed by a fold in the earth's crust. This means that there has been very little upheaval or change in its ecosystem. It also means that there are large mineral deposits with significant amounts of coal, oil and gas reserves.

The backbone of Borneo is formed by the Crocker Range and the Muller Range that separates Malaysian Borneo from Kalimantan. The highest point on the island is Mount Kinabalu at 4101 meters (13,445 ft.). These mountainous highlands feed the huge river systems that flow down into the lowlands of Kalimantan, Sabah and Sarawak. Most of Borneo is comprised of the lowlands of Kalimantan which spread over the southern area creating vast, inhospitable mangrove swamps. In fact, half of Borneo's land is under 150 meters; the majority being in Kalimantan. The soils of Borneo are not rich but can sustain crops like oil palm, cocoa and swidden; slash and burn agriculture.

Borneo has a monsoon climate. The weather at the coast receives an average of (3m) ten feet of rain a year and up to (4m) 13 feet inland. There are dry winds from the southeast from May through September and moisture-laden winds from the northwest from October through March. The heaviest rains occur from November through January. Borneo is at its driest from July through September. For some, this is the best time to visit although it is hot and dry and may not be to some people's liking. Those who wish to experience the full impact of a monsoon, flash flooding and the power of the heavens may wish to visit during the monsoon season. I actually prefer the monsoon season for its drama and coolness. The average temperature on the coast reaches up to 97 F (37 C). Inland temperatures average 75–79 F (24–26 C).

The Giant Rafflesia is a parasitic plant—its odor of rotting flesh attracts the flies that pollinate it.

Plants

No one has successfully taken an inventory of all the plant and animal life that remains hidden within Borneo's forests and swamps. Latest research estimates there are: 9000 species of flowering plants; 1000 species of butterflies; 570 species of birds; 250 species of freshwater fish; 200 species of mammals and 100 species of snakes. There are enough plant species in one, 25 acre section to equal all of the species found in North America.

There are so many species of trees that they are typically lumped into three classes of hardwood: heavy hardwoods, medium hardwoods and soft hardwoods.

Forest is divided by elevation and by soil type: lowland rain forest (mixed dipterocarp) which is found up to 600 meters; montane forest which occurs above 600 meters and mossy forest which is above 1200 meters. We will visit all three of these types of forest during our safari. We will also travel through other species of forest found on the island of Borneo: the mangrove forests of the lowlands; heath forests (called *kerangas* which means "land on which rice cannot grow"); casuarina forests, which feature stands of 25 meter conifers and nasty nipah palm, and the bakau mangrove forests along the ocean.

The orang utan or "man of the forest"

Wildlife

The wildlife of Borneo is exotic, varied, and in many cases unique. Borneo requires a little more sophistication, patience and a lower level of expectations when searching for game. The large mammals of Borneo tend to be secretive, widely spaced and remote.

Borneo's most famous resident is the orang utan or "man of the forest." The orang utan is an ape and like his relatives, the gorilla and chimpanzee, is highly intelligent and socially evolved. The orang utan is different in it lives a solitary existence and requires a large area of virgin jungle to sustain itself on its diet of wild fruit and nuts. We will also come to know more about the proboscis monkey, the hornbill, the rhino, the elephant and the rare Sumatran rhino as we travel through Borneo.

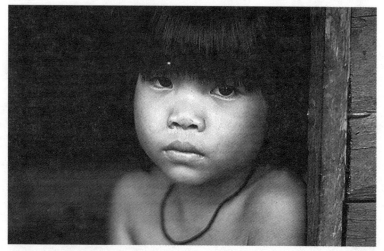

A young Penan girl from Sarawak

Indigenous People

In the late '50s, a 35–40,000 year-old Australoid skull was discovered by Tom Harrisson. The skull, called Niah Man, is one of the oldest Homo sapien remains ever found. The first people of Borneo were the Australoids, who were replaced by the Austronesians. Linguistic evidence traces their origin to Mongols who first arrived from Taiwan, via outrigger canoes, around the year of 5000 B.C. Their descendants are the aboriginal people of Borneo who are called Dayaks by outsiders. There are over 200 tribes, each with their own dialect, customs and lifestyle. The word "Dayak" is never used by these tribes to describe themselves and is considered to be a pejorative term by some. Bit by bit the Dayaks take on the modern world, slowly abandoning their centuries-old traditions for the conveniences of technology.

Traditional Dayaks live in multi-family longhouses, or *lamin*, that can be as long as 600 feet (180m). Built on stilts, they are ideal for the climate. Dayaks have a remarkable sense of design and motif. The terrible and frightening decorations found on their houses are actually positive symbols. The "asu dragon" is a symbol of prosperity and is a common motif on Kenyah homes, clothing and shields. The tendrils, huge fangs and exotic designs are common through many tribal art forms.

The most famous trait of the Dayaks is headhunting. Blackened skulls still hang in remote longhouses. These skulls are the remains of enemies killed long ago. Their skulls were smoked over a fire and preserved to protect the longhouse and tribe from harm. Dayaks believed that the longer the skull hung in the house, the weaker its magic power became. The addition of new skulls solved this problem. Headhunting was forced out of existence by the 1920s and reappeared in the '40s when British soldiers encouraged Japanese head taking in the Kelabit Highlands.

Rattan is a vine found only in primary forest and used for furniture, baskets, rope and other household items.

Early Traders

There were many indigenous peoples on the island of Borneo, but the influence of trade from the outside and outside opportunists had more to do with the shaping of modern day Borneo than anything else. Although there is evidence of Indian influence as far back as the 4th century, documented trade with the outside world began with the Chinese in A.D. 600. Items that brought great amusement to the locals were in demand by the Chinese. They traded the world's finest and most advanced goods of the day: silks, delicate porcelains, brass teapots, intricately carved gongs and other wonders, for the bladder stones from monkeys, the cave nests of swiftlets, the heads of hornbills and even the horns of rhinoceros.

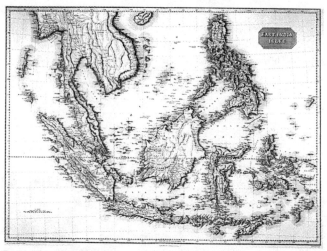

Borneo has been known by traders since A.D. 700.

In Brunei, Chinese coins have been found that date to A.D. 618 along with numerous artifacts like brass gongs and pottery. The Hindus and Arabs also traded with the north and south. By the early 1800s over 300 trading posts had been established in Borneo. Ever since Magellan's fleet, Western traders have been returning from Borneo exciting the West with tales of riches, exotic wonders and danger.

Brunei

The Chinese called the island *Puni*. Puni was influenced by the Sumatran Srijaya empire. China first mentions this faraway island in the 9th century as Po-ni. In 1408 the ruler of Po-ni is said to have visited the court of the Emperor Yung Lo of China. After Yung Lo's death in 1424 the Chinese stopped trading directly with Borneo and the sultans of Brunei began to trade with the Malaccans on the Malaysian peninsula. The sultanate of Brunei prospered trading their unusual commodities of sharkfins, medicinal plants, rhinoceros horn, elephant ivory, pearls, resin, aromatic woods and rattan gathered from the dark jungles.

Brunei claims to be one of the longest continuous sultanates in the world. The current sultan can trace his ancestry back to 1476. The Sultans of Brunei who reigned over the northern coast between the 14th and 19th centuries were wealthy and controlled much of the trade with China and the outside world. In the mid-1400s, Islam came to Borneo by way of trade with Arab traders.

Sultan Bolkiah ruled the area from the Southern Philippines to the far West of Borneo. All the river tribes were under his control and traded through him. The first Westerners arrived in Borneo toward the tail end of this golden era and were suitably impressed. On July 8, 1521, Magellan's chronicler, Antonio Pigafetta's description of his voyage around the world and of a wealthy court living in a lavish palace surrounded by a city built on stilts, would be identical to a modern traveller's description of Brunei today. He chronicles everything from the brightly decorated elephants to the fine porcelain on the Sultan's table. To find this wealth in the center of primitive jungle would be an amazing experience then—just as it is today—except the elephants have been replaced with Bentley Turbos and polo ponies.

Five years later, the Portuguese established a trading partnership with Brunei and it wasn't until Portugal came under Spanish rule in 1580 that Brunei was successfully overcome by Europeans. The Spanish favored the Sultan of Sooloo (Sulu) in the southern Philippines and the Sultan's influence was spread over most of northeastern Borneo.

Sarawak

In 1841, the Sultan of Brunei, Omar Ali Saiffuddin, ceded Sarawak and its dependencies to James Brooke for helping him put down a rebellion by a *pangiran* (lesser nobleman) named Makota. Brooke dispatched the tyrant with the help of his modern gunboats.

Shooting the Limbang River

The British Navy, under the command of Sir Thomas Cochrane, took advantage of a palace coup in 1846 to chase out the Sultan of Brunei into the jungle and he ceded the island of Labuan to the British Crown. In 1847, the Sultan promised not to give up any more territory without the Queen's consent.

Brooke continued to fight the Balanini and Illanun pirates that preyed on shipping and towns knowing that this would strengthen his claim to his ill-defined territory. In 1849, Brooke killed 1500 pirates, sank 87 of their ships and his faithful Iban chased the survivors deep into the jungle, beheaded them and burned down their villages. Despite Brooke's success with the pirates and the romantic popularity his exploits were gaining with British press, England refused to make his territory a protectorate in 1874. In 1853 Brooke was finally given absolute control over Sarawak.

Sabah

In 1845, the Americans signed a trade treaty with the Sultan of Brunei. It wasn't long until the American Ambassador, Claude Lee Moses, convinced the Sultan to give him land in Sabah. Moses quickly "flipped" the deal to two Yanks living in Hong Kong who fancied themselves cut in the mold of Brooke. These Yanks formed the American Trading Company which was abandoned in 1866 when the laborers began to starve and one of the entrepreneurs died of malaria. An Austrian, Baron Gustav von Overbeck, then bought the Americans' rights from the Sultan. He received financing for the deal from Alfred Dent, an English businessman who also extended the area covered to include most of what is now modern day Sabah. The problem arose within a few days of signing the deal in 1877 when he found out that the Sultan of Sulu had been given the same area 173 years earlier. Baron von Overbeck's solution was to pay the Sultan of Sulu 5000 Straights dollars and the Sultan of Brunei 15,000 Straights dollars. When Dent received a royal charter from Queen Victoria, who conveniently insisted that it be a completely British undertaking, Von Overbeck was forced out. The first managing director was appropriately, a former gunrunner and adventurer, William C. Cowie.

To counter Brooke's success that covered his reputed holdings of territory to the east, a chartered company known as British North Borneo was established to exploit the natural resources found in the area. Today, this area is known as Sabah. The problem was that the Sultan of Sulu claimed that he only agreed to "rent out" Sabah to the British for their exploitation. As recently as 1989 the current Sultan of Sulu, the antithesis of the current Sultan of Brunei, was trying to get his "rental property" back through the Philippine government. He was unsuccessful and continued to expand his domain under the 50 year rule of his nephew Charles Johnson (who changed his name to Brooke).

The area once claimed by Brunei continued to be carved up by the British and Brooke until insult was added to injury in 1890 when Brooke annexed the Limbang strip that today splits Brunei in half.

But, the Sultan has had his revenge. The tiny piece of land left by the British turned out to be all he needed to become the wealthiest man in the world. The discovery of oil in 1929 put what little was left of Brunei back on the map. Today, Brunei is the wealthiest country in the world on a per capita basis.

Kalimantan

The history of Kalimantan is separate from the birth and growth of the northern areas. In the 12th century, the son of a merchant from India founded Kalimantan; the first kingdom in what is now Banjarmasin in the southeast corner of the island. Called Negara-dipa, it later came under the influence of Java's Hindu kingdom of Majapahit. The first ruler to convert to Islam was the Hindu ruler, Pangeran Samudera (the Prince from the Sea). This began a long line of rulers (22) who controlled all of what is now Kalimantan.

The enterprising Dutch decided to capture what they could of the lucrative spice trade in Asia and they soon controlled the clove trade in the Mollucas. Following Portugal's abortive attempt to control Banjarmasin and its lucrative pepper trade, they were unsuccessful even though they destroyed the entire city in the process. The Dutch even expelled a British attempt to trade in Banjarmasin. The problem was that the Chinese had been dealing with the locals for about a thousand years longer and offered better prices and finer goods in barter. The Chinese also bought more profitable raw materials such as camphor, sharkfins and birds nests.

Finally, in 1785, an army of Celebes Warriors attacked the Banjarmasin Sultanate. The Dutch, seeking an opportunity, lent their assistance. The price was a puppet Sultan who quickly ceded most of what the previous sultan had controlled, but it was the majority of the east coast of Borneo which he had never even seen.

In 1817 the Sultan of Banjarmasin gave the Dutch what they thought were the rights to most of Kalimantan. This established Holland as a premier trader in spices and diamonds; even today Amsterdam is still the diamond cutting center of Europe. In 1860 the Dutch took the questionable step of abolishing the Sultanate which sparked off a four year war led by Pangeran Antasari, who is now a state hero.

An early Dutch expedition into the interior

Unlike Sarawak where the benevolent dictatorship of Brooke had a laissez-faire attitude towards the culture of the Dayaks, the Dutch quickly began to stamp out the culture of the Dayak. Missionaries were allowed to proselytize the interior, heads and pagan symbols were burned and the concept of long-house living was frowned upon in favor of individual homes. During the mid-1800s, The Netherlands opened the interior to missionaries and despite several setbacks, the colonial government, in conjunction with the missionaries, soon brought western order and protestant "decency" to even the most remote villages. In fact, the more remote the villages, the better the chances of it being almost European; faded T-shirts, radios, wide footpaths, western style wooden houses, bridges over the rivers, a clapboard church on the hill might remind some visitors of the deep South instead of remote Borneo.

The Postwar Era

World War II was the first great modern shaper of today's Borneo. Kuching fell on Christmas day of 1941 and the oilfields of Tarakan, Balikpapan and

Brunei fell to the Japanese in late 1942 and early 1943. The petty ambitions of businessmen, adventurers and colonialists were dwarfed by the savagery and completeness of the Japanese occupation. All Europeans were interned. In British North Borneo, 2 740 Europeans were forced to build an airfield at Sandakan and then forced to march 240 km to Ranau. Only six men survived. A brief rebellion in October of 1943 that liberated Jesselton (Kota Kinabalu), Tuaran and Kota Belud resulted in retaliatory bombing of these cities by the Japanese and the capture and mass beheading of 175 rebels. In Dutch Borneo the Japanese pursued fleeing Europeans into the very center of Borneo and then, after forcing them to dig their own graves, beheaded everyone including women and children.

Tom Harrisson, an erudite British scholar and adventurer from Oxford, parachuted in and helped to organize a resistance movement. His idea of "ten bob a nob," brought back headhunting with a vengeance. His efforts in Sarawak can be seen where the Japanese heads are displayed in remote up-river longhouses.

Aerial bombardment during the Allied liberation destroyed the cities of Sandakan and Jesselton. Today, unlike Kuching, there is little of the past in Sandakan and Kota Kinabalu.

The aftermath of WW II was demonstrated when Sabah was sold to the British Crown for 1.4 million pounds in 1946. The elderly Vyner Brooke asked that his Sarawakian subjects accept the King of England as their new ruler. Transfer of power was not without protest or reaction from his anachronistic relatives, Anthony and Bertram Brooke, who felt they had been betrayed. The new governor was assassinated in Sibu in 1949. The assassin and his cohorts were sentenced to death. Anthony Brooke bitterly gave up his resistance in 1951.

In Kalimantan the locals were not pleased at all with the handing back of their homeland to the Dutch. They quickly declared independence and set up a government in Jakarta. The issue was complicated by the Japanese insistence on surrendering to the Indonesians in 1945. After fierce fighting against the Dutch and British, the Indonesians under Sukarno, won their freedom from the Netherlands in 1949.

Brunei remained a Sultanate, something its growing oil wealth allowed. Although the Sultan promised to allow the people to elect a free government, a communist insurgency created an emergency excuse to enact a state of emergency which remains in effect today. The Sultan maintains close ties with Britain and even rents an army of Gurkhas and can expect any further help if he has need of military assistance again. Indeed, Brunei was invaluable not only as a jungle training area, but for the British Special Air Services (S.A.S) in the Konfrontasi launched by Sukarno of Indonesia in 1963.

The Modern Era

In 1963, it became obvious Indonesia took a dim view of the alliance of Malaya, Singapore, Sarawak and Sabah. Brunei wanted no part of the alliance since it was better off without poorer neighbors to support. Singapore opted out for the same reason. Peace was over in the area. Malaysian backed insurgents attacked Brunei and the Indonesian army launched raids along the border of Sabah. Sarawakian communists, along with Indonesian communists, staged raids deep into Sarawak. Three hundred saboteurs were landed in Singapore and began a bombing campaign. The Philippines gave support to rebels in Sabah. Sabah provided a haven for Moro insurgents who attacked the Philippines. In the 1960s, the first inklings of Indonesia's plan to open Kalimantan began with Soviet aid. There is a straight road that goes 35 miles from Palangarkaraya directly into the jungle. At the end of this road, there is nothing but jungle. This was supposed to be the site of a new city; Brasilia-style in the heart of Borneo.

Sukarno's fall from power in 1966 quickly ended the Konfrontasi in Sabah but not before dozens of British, Malayan, Ghurka and Indonesians lost their lives in the rugged jungle between Sabah and Kalimantan. The communist insurgents in Sarawak fled to the hills and were active until the '70s. The last rebels came out of hiding in 1990; Sarawak is still sensitive to this today. Brunei has existed under a state of emergency since 1963 and has not suffered any further attacks.

The Future

Malaysia may be one country but you still need a passport and border checks to travel between its sister states. The mountainous border between Sabah and Kalimantan is now open to land travel; its previously closed status the last relic of the ill-will between these two states. Sarawak has loosened its paranoid censorship policy towards journalists and travel to remote regions. Brunei is in splendid affluent isolation; a virtual "Disneyland" in the rain forest. Mainland Malaysia still feuds with Sabah over oil rights and sharing the wealth. Kalimantan is trying to ease the population explosion in Java by resettling these people in Kalimantan.

The end of World War II signaled the end of the colonial exploration of Kalimantan and the beginning of the Indonesian army's exploitation of the natural resources. The wholesale exploitation of the regions began. Logging, oil exploration and mining brought quick money into the fledgling countries. Eager foreign investors, pork barrel governments, poorly formed or inadequate resource management policies started the juggernaut in motion. Malaysia and Indonesia, angry that rich western nations should tell them how to dispose of their resources, gladly sold their forest as fast as they could cut it down. Short term timber leases, and rampant entrepreneurialism, created overnight millionaires in small towns, military circles and government posts. The volume and rate of deforestation is staggering. The world's largest forest fires occurred in Kalimantan in 1982-83, in 1991 and again in 1994. The fires in 1991 were spread by a combination of an unequalled dry spell caused by El Nino, low lying coal deposits and large open areas, setting a section of 29,000 kilometers ablaze causing air traffic in Singapore to be diverted. The rain forests burned at temperatures of up to 600 degrees celsius.

Before Westerners are too quick to criticize, it must be remembered that no one loves or needs the jungle, the wildlife and its vital support system more than the Malaysians and Indonesians. We need only to look around in our own backyard to see how quick profits and the lure of a better life have seduced us into biocide.

Malaysia

The Shah Alam Mosque in Kuala Lumpur is the new symbol of this Asian and Islamic powerhouse.

It was in 1957 when the Union Jack was lowered for the last time in the Malay Peninsula. Hoisted in its place was a new flag, one with 11 stripes with a star and crescent symbolizing the birth of a new nation under the faith of Islam. The nation was to be called Malaysia.

The government has recently decided to promote tourism more aggressively, and major improvements to roads and public transportation have taken a priority in their budget. A recent survey by Visa International revealed that the capital, Kuala Lumpur, has the lowest rates in terms of postage, five-star hotels, food and taxi fares in Asia.

Once there, you'll find that Malaysia is a land of many faces. Some parts, such as the large cities are buzzing with activity, while in the countryside, life is slow and simple. So what's there to do for the vacationer lusting for some adventure? The list is endless.

Walking along almost any street, you'll witness Islamic, Chinese and Indian festivities practiced today as they have been for hundreds of years. The Malaysian calendar is filled with holidays and events from all over the world. You can

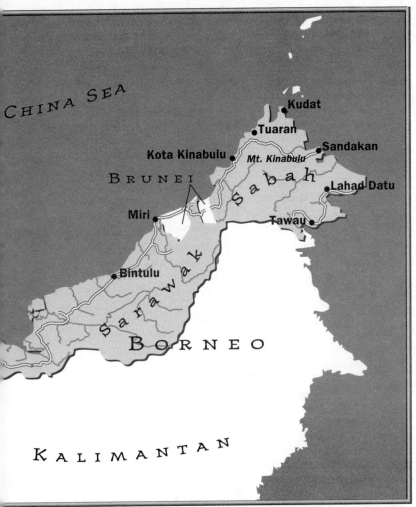

join the Pesta Munai festival in Sabah to welcome the rice spirit Bambaazon. Or spend a snowless Christmas Eve listening to carolers sing your favorite Christmas song.

One of my favorite memories of Malaysia is the country's warm and friendly people. Malaysia's 19.5 million inhabitants are made up of three main races, Malays (54 percent)—or bumiputra (which translates to "sons of the soil"), the Chinese (35 percent), and the Indians (10 percent). The remaining percentage consists of Arabs, Pakistanis, Indonesians, Japanese, Koreans and western folk.

Because the country was founded as a multiethnic country, racial tension has for the most part been absent, yet there were years of struggle between the Malays and the Chinese. However, the government was quick to suppress racially-motivated violence after the outbreak of a major riot in 1969.

Islam is the country's official faith, with virtually all Malays following the writings of the Koran. However, Malaysia's constitution grants freedom of religion, therefore, there are many Buddhists, Hindus and Christians.

Malaysia is geographically a small country (332,370 square kilometers) situated between Thailand and Indonesia, almost directly above the equator. It consists of two regions 644 km apart: Peninsular Malaysia, located on the southern part of the Malay Peninsula, and Sarawak and Sabah, located on the northern part of the island of Borneo. The country consists of 13 states—11 on Peninsular Malaysia and two in Borneo.

About 70 percent of the country is covered by a dense rainforest—the oldest rainforest in the world. At 130 million years, it's far older than those found in Africa or South America. Most of the uncleared areas of Malaysia are commonly referred to as the jungle, but this isn't an entirely accurate description. The mangrove and nipa palm areas are really "swamp forests" that are virtually impenetrable by land. The major portion of the rainforest is made up of trees that are about 100 feet high, and whose canopy is so dense that everything underneath is hidden almost entirely from the sun.

The lush plant life is mainly due to the climate of Malaysia, which is hot and wet year round. Malaysia is known as a country with only one season. The basic feature of this season is heavy rainfall, high humidity, and a uniform temperature of 21 C. to 32 C. (69°F–88°F).

October through February is the monsoon season, where rainfall can be much heavier than usual. This extra rain usually means flooding, particularly on the East Coast of Peninsular Malaysia. The precipitation falls at an average of 2540 mm per year, with about 180 days out of the year with rain.

Brief Facts

Capital: Kuala Lumpur

Official Language: Malay (official), Chinese, Tamil, English Form of Government: Constitutional monarchy

States: Johor, Kedah, Kelantan, Malacca, Negri Sembilan, Pahang, Penang, Perlis, Perak, Sabah, Sarawak, Selangor, Terengganu

Paramount Ruler: Tuanku Ja'afar, Sultan of Negri Sembilan
Current Prime Minister: D.S. Mahathir Bin Mohamad

Area: 127,320 sq. miles
Population: 19,060,000
National religion: Islam
Currency: Ringgit

History

Once a colony of Britain, Malaysia retains much of its British heritage.

Malaysia is quite young—only 32-years old—but the land has been inhabited by man since prehistoric times. Human skeletons, found during archaeological excavations in the Niah Caves on Borneo, date back as far as 35,000 B.C.

Malaysia today is primarily known as a land of immigrants—a nation of multiracial cultures. And no wonder, people have been immigrating into Malaysia long before the birth of Christ. The first known immigrants to arrive to the Malay Peninsula were from southern China, around 2000 B.C. The Proto-Malays, as they are now called, took up residency along the coastline of the peninsula and stayed there for roughly 1700 years. Around 300 B.C., Duetero-Malays—an interracial mix that branched out from the Proto-Malays—overpowered the Proto-Malays and forced them inland. The Duetero-Malays are believed to be the direct ancestors of Malays today.

The Prosperity of Malacca

In the years after Christ, Peninsular Malaysia was a popular stopover for traders who went back and forth between China and India. Indian traders brought not only their goods to the Malay Peninsula, but also their customs and cultures—most notably their religion, Buddhism and Hinduism.

In the early 1400s, a Sumatran prince named Parameswara founded the city of Malacca. Before long, Malacca became a thriving metropolis, as Parameswara took advantage of its location. Malacca was ideally located in the middle of many trading routes. Malacca soon gained international popularity, and in 1405, Admiral Cheng Ho of China visited the city and gave Malacca the blessing of the Ming Court.

The Arrival of Islam

Malacca was first exposed to the faith of Islam toward the end of the 13th century when Muslim traders from India arrived and spread the religion among the masses. Parameswara, himself converted to the faith when he took control of Malacca and soon the entire region followed suit. By the 15th century, virtually all of the Malacca kingdom, which included Pahang, the west coast and the east coast of Sumatra, were practicing Islam.

The Europeans

A hot spot such as Malacca doesn't remain a secret forever, especially from the Europeans. In 1511, the Portuguese took control of Malacca, adding this port city to their already extensive empire. However, their reign was short lived. In 1641, the Dutch invaded and conquered the main Portuguese fort, A Famosa, and Malacca soon fell under Dutch jurisdiction.

Then the British came. In 1786, Captain Francis Light claimed the island of Penang for the British Empire, and not much later, Singapore and Malacca soon joined it. This new formation came to be known as the Straits Settlement, or "British Malaya." Britain would control the destiny of the Malay Peninsula for the next 155 years.

It didn't take long for the Brits to discover that their new land was rich in natural resources. In 1864, British prospectors began traveling south in search of tin. And they found it...lots of it. In 1864, Kuala Lumpur, whose Malay name is translated as the "muddy estuary," was founded at the confluence of the Klang and Gombak rivers. Although the town was an unimpressive outback at first, Kuala Lumpur soon become a tin-mining boomtown. At the turn of the century, as the Brits began filling the swamp land with houses and official buildings, they declared Kuala Lumpur the capital of Malaya.

Here, the Brits began planting on a grand scale. As an experiment, they planted Brazilian rubber trees sent from the Kew Gardens. The result was an unexpected bonanza. Malaya became and continues to be the world's largest single supplier of Brazilian rubber. Timber also became a lucrative export. Life was pleasant for all concerned, and continued peacefully into the next century...then came World War II.

The Japanese

On December 8, 1941, British battleships patrolling the South China Sea, were attacked and sunk by Japanese invaders. Hours later, the Japanese army had set foot onto Peninsular Malaysia. From the shores of Kota Bharu, located in the northeastern state of Kelantan, the Japanese army proceeded south in everything from tanks to bicycles. Within two months, they had captured Singapore.

While the British were preoccupied with protecting their own country from the nearby Germans, the Japanese Imperial Army met with little resistance and they did as they pleased in Malaya. Nothing and no one could stop them. Then, on that fateful day in 1945, the sound of the first atom bomb was heard around the world. Japan soon surrendered to the Allied forces. Japanese occupancy in Malaya ended in the same year.

The Communists

After the conclusion of WWII, communism was gaining momentum all over the world. Malaysia did not escape its extensive reach. During British reoccupation of Malaya after the conclusion of WWII, communist radicals in Malaysia, organized years before during Japanese oppression, began to revolt. The time had come for them to emerge from the shadows of the rain forest.

The Communist invasion was led by a man named Chin Peng, and his group terrorized the land using violence in order to disrupt the country's economy. They came from nowhere—they would strike and then disappear. The Brits had a difficult time tracking them down because they lived and operated out of the rain forest. The Brits found themselves with their backs against the wall. This situation became known as "The Emergency."

Instead of fighting the radicals head-on, the Brits decided to relocate Malays most vulnerable to the Communist influence. They took them from remote areas where their villages were located to safer places with better government protection. The Communists, however, answered by simply attacking the new settlements. A bad move. The government forces proved too strong and gradually the Communists were overpowered. In a matter of months, The Emergency was over.

The Birth of Malaysia

In 1956, as Britain was slowly disbanding its incredible empire that consisted of territories all over the world, the British government agreed to grant Malaya independence. On August 31, 1957, Malaya became a full-fledged nation. Its 11 states were symbolized by a new flag with an 11-pointed star.

On September 2, the new king and ruler of the Federation of Malaya took office. His official title was the Yang di Pertuan Agong, and he would govern for a period of five years, after which another one of the 10 sultans would succeed him.

In September of 1963, Sabah, Sarawak and Singapore joined Malaya to become the Federation of Malaysia. However, this union was short-lived; political differences between Malaysia and Singapore led to the seceding of Singapore from the Federation. Singapore became an independent nation.

On May 13, 1969, disaster struck the country in the form of racially motivated riots. The riots, started by Malays who were unhappy that Chinese were reaping the rewards of successful businesses, left several hundred Chinese dead. A state of emergency was declared, and a new national ideology emphasizing the unity of all peoples was proclaimed.

The New Economic Policy (NEP), as it was called, was highly successful. It eradicated poverty and restructured society so that racism and associated economical stereotypes was eliminated.

The current prime minister of Malaysia is Dato' Seri Dr. Mahathir Mohamad, who took the office in 1981. His rise in Malaysian politics began a little more than a decade after his ouster from UMNO, the country's major political party, following an outspoken attack on its leaders in the wake of the 1969 riots. Because of the unprecedented scale of UMNO-led victory in the following year's elections, Mahathir was quick to consolidate with the party. His right-hand man is Anwar Ibrahim, former leader of the Islam-based Muslim Youth Movement of Malaysia, and very possibly the heir to the office.

Malaysia Today

Malaysia is currently a strong member of the Association of South East Asian Nations (ASEAN) which was formed to promote greater economic, social, and cultural association between its members.

But the nation is now in the midst of a tremendous shift. Following years of rapid industrialization, Malaysia is now experiencing a period of consolidation. It faces the challenge of dealing with worldwide financial success while also dealing with a labor shortage, infrastructure obstacles and the threat of inflation. The government is attempting to somewhat slow growth to a sustainable rate while diversifying the economy.

Malaysia is the world's largest exporter of computer chips and the third-largest chip producer, after the United States and Japan. The country has also become a major producer of VCRs and air-conditioning units.

Malaysia is the largest producer of palm oil, accounting for roughly half of the world's production in recent years. Traditional exports such as tin and rubber have declined because of falling prices. Oil has taken their places as the country's largest export earner. Most of the exported oil goes to Singapore, Japan, South Korea and Thailand.

In a joint venture with Mitsubishi, Malaysia has been assembling its own national cars, the Proton Saga and the Wira. Sales in Malaysia have been astronomical because heavy taxes are levied on imported automobiles, which gives the Proton an "unfair" advantage. Nevertheless, the quality of the car is world class; thus Malaysia has introduced the Proton in the international market, exporting it to such faraway places as the United Kingdom.

It's simple to see that Malaysia's current transition stage is directed toward economic growth. It has set a goal of becoming a fully developed nation by the year 2020 in a plan the Prime Minister calls Vision 2020. At the rate it's going now, Malaysia may become a formidable economic powerhouse well before that time.

The Malaysians

Malaysians are a diverse people with strong cultural ties to their origins.

Why are Malaysians so friendly? Because Malaysians pride themselves in being a peaceful, highly-civilized race. To many of them, being Malaysian means being courteous, responsible and respectful. They seldom risk offending others, and in turn, do not expect to be offended. For example, they rarely lose their temper in public and they dress quite conservatively.

When interacting with a Malaysian, remember to be on your best behavior; always be considerate, refrain from using vulgar phrases, or emotional outbursts. Remember the small courtesies like taking off your shoes before entering a home. Once you get to know a Malaysian, chances are he or she will loosen up, and the risk of offending becomes increasingly less. If a Malaysian finds you amicable, you've made a friend for life.

The country's natives are the Malays who comprise roughly 48 percent of the population. But immigrants, especially the Chinese, who make up 34 percent, have a tremendous presence in the country—in some ways more so than the Malays. The next largest group are the Indians who comprise about 9 percent. The rest are made up of small numbers of Arabs, Indonesians, Filipinos and Pakistanis.

Some of the country's races are created within its own borders. Fifteenth-century Chinese arrivals intermixed with native Malays to create a new group called **peranakans**—Straits-born people with a mixture of Chinese/Malay in food, customs and language.

When the Portuguese arrived in the 16th century, their offspring from marriage to the locals produced a small population of Eurasians.

All the races now live harmoniously together while being "peacefully" segregated. By this I mean that although the different races come in close contact professionally and socially, their communities continue to be residentially segregated. Private lives rarely mix—family gatherings, weddings and banquets are usually restricted to one race. This "apartness" is a primary reason why cultures are so well preserved in Malaysia.

Since the new economic policy was implemented, racial incidents are all but absent. The people have all found a way to maintain their ancestral identity, yet still have a national Malaysian identity. Sabah is most resistant to this change because of the large Christian and Kadazan population while Sarawak with its large Chinese population and very different history seems to ignore Malaysia all together.

The Malays

As the natives of the country, the Malays occupy a stronghold in Malaysian politics. Together with the Orang Asli and the indigenous peoples of Sabah and Sarawak, Malays are known in their own tongue as **bumiputra** (translated as "sons of the soil"). This designation entitles them to have a "special" status in the country as representatives of Malaysia's national identity. The bumiputra are afforded more social privileges than recent immigrants. These include getting loans from Islamic banks, being given good positions in companies (all Malaysian companies are supposed to have at least 51 percent Malay shareholders and must employ a Malay at a senior level). This creates friction with many of the Chinese-held companies in Borneo.

Many of the Malays who live in the countryside are usually found in **kampong** villages—made up of crude houses, often sitting atop stilts. The people here lead simple lives as fishermen and farmers, reveling in the peace and simplicity of their life-styles. The central mosque and religion play a large part in their lives and ambitions. You're sure to see more than a few kampong villages during a trip out of town.

In the large cities such as Kota Kinabalu, Malays aren't much different than you or me. Adults commute daily to their jobs. Teenage children, when they're not in school, spend their free time dancing to the latest rhythms at a popular nightclub or hanging out at the local shopping mall. (Malaysia even has its share of mall rats.)

Muslim Malays aren't as "radical" as the Muslims of the Middle East but the tenants of Islam are inseparable from the laws of the country. This creates friction with the differing beliefs of Chinese and Dayaks. Before traveling into Malaysia, it's a good idea to familiarize yourself with the laws of Islam and how they pertain to Malays in particular.

Aside from not consuming alcohol, pork is strictly forbidden from the Muslim diet. You probably won't find a side of bacon or a ham sandwich in a Malay restaurant. It would be rude to even ask for one. The consumption of beef and chicken is allowed, but only if the animals are slaughtered and prepared in a special way called **halal**.

Don't make the mistake of offering to take a devout Muslim to a Chinese restaurant or to a bar.

Muslim Malays pray several times a day. In most seaside cities and towns, the call to prayer is broadcast through loudspeakers or on the radio. Most mosques blare out their call to prayer before dawn, so make sure you find accommodations away from the mosques.

Like their Middle Eastern counterparts, Muslim Malays follow the writings of the Koran and are identified by Arabic names.

Sultans are regarded as the rulers of the land. In all the states of Peninsular Malaysia except Penang and Malacca, there is a sultan, usually with a large extended family. Members of the royal family are treated with great devotion, and they occupy a totally different social world than that of the commoner. Every five years, a new supreme sultan, or Paramount Ruler, is chosen from the Conference of Rulers—the other 10 Sultanates. These rulers actually rotate their terms of being in power.

Muslim Malays almost never marry outside of their faith; they only let outsiders in if the outsider is willing to convert to the faith of Islam. Of course, many of these laws are interpreted differently by different individuals, and some do make slight exceptions, but don't forget that all Malays take their faith very seriously, and an unkind word toward their religion is an extreme insult.

The Chinese

The Chinese comprise 34 percent of Malaysia's population. See page 262 for in-depth coverage of their origins and contributions.

The Indians

The Indians represent the third largest mainstream group in Malaysia, comprising 10 percent of the country's total population.

Although they were among the first traders to set foot on Peninsular Malaysia, it wasn't until the 1800s that they began arriving in large numbers. Most of the immigrants are from southern India—the majority being Tamils and Hindus—but other groups such as the Sikhs (or the Punjabis, those who wear turbans), Malayees, Telungus and Parsis are also present. The Indian community itself is separated by religious beliefs, with a significant number of Indian Muslims (who consider themselves to be originally from Pakistan), Buddhists, and even a small number of Indian Christians, among the Indian population.

Unlike Malays and Chinese, the Indians are clustered in only a handful of areas, notably Penang, Perak and Selangor. However, don't let that fool you into thinking they're an insignificant minority; the influence of Indian culture in Malaysia is a formidable one indeed. Indian temples, such as the Sri Maha Mariamman in Kuala Lumpur, are found all over. Many Indian festivities, such as Thaipusam, where up to 200,000 Indian Malaysians pay homage to the statue of Subramanya in the Batu Caves, grace the Malaysian calendar. Banana-leaf curry is now considered a Malaysian dish, but it really came from India.

Indians found in urban neighborhoods are active in business life. They comprise a good portion of Malaysia's middle-class professionals.

The Orang Asli

Although there are no Orang Asli (translated into English as "original people") in Borneo it is important to know that there is an aboriginal race on the mainland. The Orang Asli aren't just one group of people or race, they're many different races, as many as 50,000, who belong to various tribes. The true origins of the Orang Asli have always been a mystery, but they live life as they have for hundreds of years—modestly, in simple houses in the middle of the jungle or near beaches where fish are plentiful.

Perhaps the most notable of the Orang Asli are the **Negritos**. As the name suggests they are dark-skinned people who bear a close resemblance to Africans. Although they are the smallest Orang Asli group, they are believed to be the oldest. They may well be the first people of Malaysia.

The largest Orang Asli group are the **Senoi**, who also possess dark skins, thus resembling the Negritos. Another major Orang Asli group are the **Orang Melayu Asli**, Proto-Malays made up of several different tribes.

The People of Borneo

Sabah and Sarawak (also referred to as East Malaysia), are so different in character and demographic make-up that many consider them separate countries altogether. The areas of Sabah and Sarawak are more diverse racially than Peninsular Malaysia. Away from developed areas such as Kota Kinabalu, most Borneo-Malaysians live in tribes much like their Peninsular Malaysian counterparts, the Orang Asli. Their villages are also located in the jungle or near the coast.

The list of different ethnic communities in Sabah and Sarawak seems almost infinite, with each having its own customs and languages.

In Sabah, **Primbumi** is the general classification, yet there are almost 30 separate categories under Primbumi. The largest of these are the **Kadazan** who inhabit the lowlands and the mountainous interior. They live in small villages and are primarily occupied in rubber cultivation. Farther inland are the **Murut**. In recent years, the number of Muslims has increased significantly in Sabah as a result of continued immigration and the conversion of the local peoples.

In Sarawak, the largest indigenous group are the **Iban** (or **Sea Dayak**). These people live in **longhouses**, large houses built on stilts that accommodate an entire community, usually found next to a river or stream. One longhouse can house up to 50 families, with each having a headman, or leader. Longhouses usually consist of several rooms, the largest one being the "sitting room." Here, the men often sit together and relax or work on their craft. The sitting room is also used to entertain visitors and to hold ceremonies.

Longhouses have traditionally been used as stopover places for river travel.

Malaysian Festivals & Holidays

FESTIVALS AND HOLIDAYS

It almost seems that Malaysians celebrate every festival known to man since their calendar includes holidays belonging to Christians, Hindus, Buddhists and Muslims—as well as many local and national events. It is quite a calendar and visitors are certainly encouraged to participate in any celebration underway!

*January 1	New Year's Day	
January	Thaipongal	*The first day of the Tamil month of Thai. Harvest Festival and pongal, or new grain, is cooked.*
January	Birthday of Prophet Muhammad	*Born April 20, A.D. 571. Processions and chanting of holy verses held throughout the country.*
January/ February	Chinese New Year	
February	Birthday of Tien Kung	*Chinese God of Heaven.*
February	Chap Goh Meh	*15th day of the Chinese New Year.*
February	Tua Pek Kong	*Festival of burning paper money, houses and cars for deceased relatives. Main celebration at San Ten Temple, Kuching, Sarawak.*
*March	Hari Raya Puasa	*End of month of fasting for Muslims. Great festivities with prayers, delicacies and offerings to the poor (date changes yearly, as it falls on the first day of Syawal, the 10th month of the Muslim calendar).*
March	Maha Siva Rathiri	*Pujas (ceremonies) performed in Hindu temples through the night. Devotees sing hymns in honor of Lord Siva.*
March	Pangguni Uttiram	*Day of prayers for Hindus that commemorates the marriage of Rama and Sita, hero and heroine of the Ramayana epic.*
March	Kuan Yin	*Day of worship for Chinese Goddess of Mercy, guardian of children.*
March 25	Police Day	*Recognition of service to the country by the police force.*
April	Good Friday	*Celebrated only in Sabah and Sarawak.*
April	Easter Sunday	
April	Cheng Beng	*All Soul's Day. Chinese pay homage to ancestors.*

FESTIVALS AND HOLIDAYS

April	Sri Rama Navami	*Marks descent of Lord Rama, seventh Avatar of Vishu Rama and hero of the Ramayana epic. Pujas performed by Hindus.*
April	Songkran	*New Year of the Thais. Water Festival.*
April/May	Chitra Pauranami	*Hindus offer pujas, carry kavadis and pay homage to Lord Subramaniam in temples throughout the country.*
May	Sipitaxg Tamu Besar	*Blowpipe competitions and ladies' football matches held in Sipitang, a coastal town in Sabah.*
May	Kota Belud Tamu Besar	*A tamu (open market) in Kota Belud, Sabah, with cock fighting, native dances, buffaloes for sale and handicrafts.*
May	Migratory Giant Turtles	*Giant leathery turtles from South China Sea make annual visits from May to early September to east coast beaches.*
May 1	Labor Day	
***May 7**	Hari Hol	*Public holiday in Pahang only that marks the anniversary of death of Sultan Abu Bakar.*
May	National Youth Week.	
May	Kadazan Harvest Festival	*Traditional thanksgiving by Kadazan farmers only in Sabah.*
May	Hari Pesta Menuai	*Festival for Kadazan farmers to appease rice spirit for good harvest.*
May	Ascension Day	
May	Teacher's Day	
May	Vesakhi	*Sikhs celebrate New Year.*
May	Wesak Day	*Commemorates birth, enlightenment and passing away.*
***May**	Isra' and Mi'raj	*Isra' is the journey by night of Prophet Muhammad from Al Haram Mosque in Baitul Muqaddis. Mi'raj is the ascent of Prophet Muhammad from Al Aqsa to Heaven to meet Allah. It was on this occasion Prophet Muhammad received orders from Allah to introduce the practice of praying five times daily to Mecca.*
June 1-2	Gawai Dayak	*Festival celebrates successful padi (rice) harvest. Dayaks offer traditional tuak, or rice wine and a bard recites poetry.*

FESTIVALS AND HOLIDAYS

June 2	Birthday of Dymn Seri Paduka Baingda Yang Dipertuan Agong	*Thanksgiving prayers offered in mosques, churches and temples throughout Malaysia.*
June 4	Martyrdom of Guru Arjan Dev	*Religious ceremonies in all Sikh temples.*
June	Dragon Boat Festival (Tuan Wu Chieh)	*Marks death of a Chinese minister, scholar and poet, who drowned himself rather than live corruptly like his colleagues.*
June	Nisfu Syaaban	*Muslims perform their religious duties at this time.*
July 1	International Cooperative Day	
July	Awal Ramadhan	*Beginning of month of fasting for Muslims.*
*July	Nuzul al Quran	*Holy verses of the Koran were revealed to Prophet Muhammad in Mecca; Muslims celebrate this day by religious gatherings.*
July	Heroes Day	*In remembrance of all Malaysians who fought and died for their country.*
August	Farmer's Day	
August	Festival of Seven Sisters	*A Chinese festival for single girls to pray for a happy marital future.*
August	Hungry Ghosts Festival	*A festival to celebrate the Chinese custom of offering food, joss sticks and paper money to ghosts who apparently come down to earth for a month and mingle with real people.*
August	Sri Krishna Jayanti	*Marks the descent of Sri Krishan as the eighth Avatar of Vishnu and hero of the Mahabharata epic of the Hindus.*
August 31	National Day	*Parade, cultural performance and musicals abound.*
September	Moon Cake Festival	*A time of great significance for Buddhists.*
September	Fire Walking Ceremony	*Devotees walk across a pit of glowing embers to fulfill their vows.*

FESTIVALS AND HOLIDAYS

*September	Hari Raya Haji	*Muslim celebration for those who have become haji (those who visited the holy city of Mecca).*
September	Vinayaka Chaturti	*A special day for Hindus, when they worship Ganapathy, the elephant-headed god who blesses devotees.*
September	Armed Forces Day	
October	Deepavali	*The Hindu festival of lights marks the victory of light over darkness, good over evil and wisdom over ignorance.*
*October	Awal Muharram	*First month in the Hijrah (Islamic) calendar. Marks the journey of Prophet Muhammad from Mecca to Medina.*
October	Universal Children's Day	
October	Festival of Loy Krathong	*Buddhist festival of lights. Candles are floated on artificial lotus flowers in memory of Lord Buddha's footprint.*
November 1	All Saints' Day	
November	All Souls' Day	
November 30	Birthday of Guru Nanak	*Founder of Sikhism. Day of prayers, hymns and religious lectures.*
December	Tung Chih Festival	*Chinese pay homage to ancestors. Marble-sized rice balls (tung yuan) are served to symbolize family reunion.*
December 25	Christmas Day	
December	Prophet Mondi's Birthday	

*Muslim holidays follow the lunar calendar.

The Food of Malaysia

Malaysian cuisine consists of a unique blend of British, Indian, Chinese, Thai, Arabic and Malay cooking.

The mainstream dishes are primarily Malay, Chinese and Indian foods, with rice and noodles as a main part of virtually every dish. However, these foods have gone through a certain assimilation—each cuisine adopting various characteristics from the others—creating a style unique to Malaysia.

The complexity of Malaysian foods means they can be hot, spicy, cool, sweet and sour all at the same time.

Food is offered in a number of various forms of establishments, from elaborate restaurants to simple street-side stalls, or hawkers, that are located all over Malaysia. Although the eating environment of some of these stalls may not be quite up to your standards—the tables could be a bit dirty, the silverware modest—it's a favorite of locals, especially late at night when everything else is closed. And it's unbelievably cheap!

Malay Dishes

The staples of Malay food are noodles and rice. And they find a number of ways of preparing them. Typically, Malay cuisine is spicy. Seafood is a big part of the Malaysian diet, followed by chicken and beef. However, you won't find pork in Malay establishments because its consumption is prohibited by their religion. Even chicken and beef must conform to a rule called **halal**—a special way of slaughtering and preparing the animals. It's common to find signs on the windows of fast-food establishments indicating that they serve halal food.

Satays are probably Malaysia's most popular and tastiest dish. It's also the most palatable for foreigners because its preparation is similar to our style of barbecue. Marinated pieces of beef or chicken are barbecued over an open charcoal flame, and then served with a sweet and spicy peanut sauce. Satays come in the form of what we call shishkebabs—a long thin stick holding the meat together—and are usually served with rice cakes, cucumber slices and onions. It is normal for restaurants to have a satay vendor outside the restaurant. So don't be surprised if you see your waiter paying cash for your satay on the street.

Another popular Malay dish is **nasi lemak**. Usually eaten at breakfast, nasi lemak is rice with seasoning cooked in coconut milk and served with dried anchovies, hard boiled egg, peanuts and cucumber slices. **Rendang**, a spicy meat dish is usually included. **Nasi padang**, usually eaten for lunch, consists of rice served with a number of different dishes, including rendang and curry. Other popular dishes include **laksa johor**, spaghetti-like noodles in a fish curry gravy and vegetables; and **mee jawa**, noodles in a thick gravy served with prawn fritters, potatoes and tofu.

Popular Malaysian soups include **sago melaka**, sago with brown sugar syrup; **sup ekor**, a spicy ox-tail soup; and **soto ayam**, a spicy chicken soup with rice cubes and vegetables.

Chinese Dishes

Chinese food is everywhere in Malaysia. Much like its Malay counterpart, rice and noodles are a main part of the cuisine. Pork is a big part of the Chinese diet, and beef and chicken are not required to be halal. The common reply if you ask what a favorite Chinese dish is would be, "If the sun shines on its back, the Chinese will eat it." Meaning that humans are the only animals that walk upright.

Don't expect the Chinese food in Malaysia to taste exactly like what you find in restaurants in America. For the most part, the food is much more basic in nature, especially in the modest places, and much of the rich sauces are absent. Many of the dishes have been influenced by Malay food, so you'll no doubt find entrees unique to this country. Regardless, you probably won't recognize a lot of the food on the menu. The Chinese are also fond of exotic food like dog, bat and other "medicinal" animals.

The country's most elaborate restaurants are usually Chinese. In these opulent places, you'll find the food comparable to Chinese food found in America.

A popular Chinese dish found in Malaysia is **Hainanese chicken rice**, rice cooked in chicken stock and served with either steamed or roasted chicken. Some places offer sweet or barbecued pork in the place of the chicken. **Ngah poh fan** is also a favorite Chinese dish. It consists of rice cooked in a clay pot with chicken, sausages and vegetables. When your appetite is modest, **fried rice**, rice fried with meat and vegetables, and **wantan mee**, noodles served in a soup with prawn and pork, will no doubt do the job.

A dish not to be missed, which is somewhat a mixture of Chinese and Malay, is **assam laksa**. This is a specialty of Penang, but can be found almost everywhere in Malaysia. *Assam laksa* is rice noodles served in fish gravy with shredded cucumbers and pineapples, with prawn paste added to the side. One of my favorites is **curry laksa**, noodles served in a curry with boiled chicken, cockles, tofu and bean sprouts.

An interesting variation to Chinese cooking is **Nonya** cuisine. Nonya is the local term for a Straits-born Chinese woman (Baba is the male equivalent). Although Nonyas are notorious for jealously guarding their family recipes from generation to generation, there are some modest restaurants around that serve authentic Nonya dishes. Most of the dishes begin with a generous helping of **rempah**, a mixture of ground spices. Some of the more recognized dishes are **curry kapitan**, an unusual chicken curry; **otak otak**, a fish pate flavored with spice and coconut cream, wrapped in leaves and grilled; **inche kabin**, a spicy deep-fried chicken; and **poh poh**, a savory stuffed pancake.

Indian Dishes

Indian food has been part of the Malaysian diet since traders brought curry and other various spices with them to the region. The cooking styles range from subtle North Indian dishes to the extremely spicy South Indian ones. You'll find that some Indian dishes incorporate lamb rather than beef because of religious beliefs.

Indian dishes found in Malaysia have assimilated somewhat with the Malay style of cooking, nevertheless, rice and curry are the staples of Indian food.

Popular Indian dishes include **nasi briyani**, rice cooked in ghee with spices and vegetables, and served with either beef or chicken; **roti canai**, griddle-fried layered pancake served with curry or **dhall**—lentil-based gravy. When roti canai is stuffed with a mixture of minced beef, egg and onion served with curry, the result is **murtabak**. **Mee goreng** is another popular dish; it consists of noodles fried with chile paste, tomatoes, prawns and eggs. A favorite Indian salad is **rojak**, made from flour cake, beansprouts, shredded cucumber, turnip, hard-boiled egg, squids and prawns, topped with a spicy peanut sauce.

Wash all this food down with **teh tarik**, a vanilla flavored tea with milk. It's worth trying just to see how it is made. A man mixes the tea with the milk using two separate cups where he pours one into the other using the full extension of his arms. Satisfy your sweet tooth with **cendol**, shaved ice with coconut milk, green noodles and palm sugar.

INSIDER TIP

I have found that the best places to eat in Malaysia are the food stalls. Although at first they may seem too simple and not very orderly, once you've tried the food, you'll find there's no going back. There are many areas in cities of almost all sizes where a number of food stalls serve different types of food: Malay, Chinese and Indian. You can find some extravagant seafood as well, such as giant fried prawns, lobster and all kinds of fish. The food is delicious and has a genuinely local flavor. And best of all it's cheap. Expect a party of four to eat well and pay no more than M$20.

When you visit a market in Malaysia it is worth sampling unique fruits like these starfruits.

The Fruits of Borneo

With all the plant life in Malaysia, it's understandable that there's an endless variety of tropical fruits. Many of them will sound familiar to you, but there are those that will sound as foreign as some of the dishes listed in the previous section. I encourage you to try as many of these as possible because all are delicious and very easy to find. You'll find many being sold along the roads of the countryside. Just stop the car, pick out what you want and head back on your way. It's the perfect snack for a long day's drive.

Odd exotic taste treats await the adventurous traveler.

Banana *(Musacae)*

Bananas (*pisang*) are a staple diet in Malaysia and fall into two main categories—those eaten raw and those that must be cooked. The ready-to-eat raw bananas are sweet when eaten ripe and are called *pisang mas*, or golden banana. Cooked bananas are made into what is called *goreng pisang*, where the banana is coated with batter and deep fried.

Durian *(Durio putih)*

Malaysia's most famous (or infamous) fruit is the durian. It's green, spiky and shaped like a football. The durian is seasonal, available in the summer and winter months and known for the thick, mushy consistency of its flesh, and its incredibly vile aroma. The stench of durians is so intense that many hotels don't allow you to bring them into your room. A popular saying in Malaysia about the durian is, "Smells like hell, but tastes like heaven." The durian is not that bad going down but your first burp will tell you that you've made a dreadful mistake. The taste is similar to a septic tank mixed with diesel oil and lasts a long, long time. The durian's odor helps attract orang utans and other animals to its location in the jungles of Borneo. Botanists are currently at work breeding less offensive strains of the custardlike fruit. The durians are at their peak in July and August and November to January.

Jackfruit *(Artocarpus heterophyllus)*

The Jackfruit or *nangka* is a larger cousin of the durian and the breadfruit but with less odor and aftertaste. The skin is green, with knobs instead of spikes. The seeds can be eaten once roasted.

Mango *(Mango indica)*

Mangos are abundant in Malaysia—from small green tart-sized ones to large yellow ones. Mango varieties include the Apple Mango, the Indian Papaya Mango, the Philippines Mango, the Taiwan Mini Apple Mango, and the Indian Coconut Mango. When ripe, mangos are a popular delicacy for dessert. They are also processed into juice, jams, jellies and ice cream.

Mangosteen *(Garcina mangostena)*

The mangosteen is a native fruit of Malaysia found in the same seasons as the durian. Mangosteens are the size of a baseball, with a thick brown skin and white puffy flesh and primarily sweet in flavor.

Papaya *(Carica papaya)*

Papayas have been growing in Malaysia for a few hundred years now. The Malaysian papaya is known for its delicate flavor and its color that ranges from yellow to red. Unripe Papayas are usually used for tenderizing meat, but when ripe they are best served chilled and freshly cut. The papaya has an enzyme that also aids in digestion so have a ripe papaya with a squeeze of lime to start you off in the morning.

Pomelo *(Citrus)*

The pomelo is the biggest citrus fruit in the world. Available all throughout the year, the *limau bali* is roughly the size of a basketball. They are very popular during the Chinese festive seasons and often exchanged as gifts. The fruit can be highly acidic and taste like a bland grapefruit.

Rambutan *(Nephelium lappaceum)*

These furry little red buggers will turn most first time shoppers off until they taste the sweet white flesh within.The rambutan is a relative of the lichee nut and can also be bought tinned. Batches can vary but the ripe ones are sweet, juicy and thirst quenching when eaten raw. *Rambut* means hairy in Malay.

Salak *(Salacca edulis)*

Popular along the coasts and lazy rivers of Kalimantan. The salak is picked from a nasty spiked relative of the rattan. They seem to keep forever and are great for quenching thirst, with a crunch apple sweet taste and chestnut texture.If you don't mind the lizardlike outer skin the salak is a great pack stuffer.

Starfruit *(Belimbing)*

The starfruit is another popular fruit because of its unusual shape. When sliced, each piece of the *carambola* resembles a multi-pointed star. Its flavor varies from sour to sweet, similar to a tart apple and is available year round. Usually eaten fresh or chilled, the starfruit, with its high content of Vitamin C and Vitamin A, is a healthy, refreshing way of fighting the heat. Get your starfruits juiced to really appreciate the taste.

Shopping

All of Borneo's crafts are still painstakingly handcrafted.

Batik

Batik is everyone's favorite purchase, as the lovely materials can be used for many things and for all occasions. Clothing is the most popular usage and Malaysians themselves dress both formally and casually in their batik. You can also find such items as tissue box covers, hats and bags, cushion covers, bedspreads, curtains and table mats or napkin sets. The batik industry is concentrated on the East Coast and visitors may have the opportunity to visit factories to observe the production first-hand and make their purchases on the spot.

Batik painting

Batik painting has become, in recent years, another of Malaysia's contributions to the world of art. The batik artist needs the same skill, craftsmanship and patience necessary in the making of batik. The only difference between the maker and the artist is that the artist's patterns may be bolder because the cloth is sized and framed and not worn on the body or used as household accessories. Batik paintings make excellent souvenirs because they can be framed later and take up little room in a suitcase.

Songket

Another indigenous fabric and the pride of Malaysia. It is a fabric much entwined with the country's history and culture; it has long been worn by royalty and used by the courts for ceremonial occasions. It has also been successfully adapted for Western evening wear. Songket is woven with the finest silk available and the gold-threaded patterns are reproduced from ancient designs (which are often a secret passed from generation to generation). The art of weaving songket dates from as early as the 15th century and it is said that no two pieces of the cloth have ever been alike. Even the design of the loom has not changed with time and many weavers now employ valuable antiques in their making of the cloth. Naturally, a piece of songket (1.8m in length) is expensive in comparison to other Malaysian traditional crafts, but anyone able to purchase one will never fail to enjoy its exquisite beauty.

Vases

The colorful **vases** of Sarawak come from the capital, Kuching, where Chinese from Kwantung province brought their skill. The vases are quite unusual, however, because the hand-applied designs feature local folklore. You can appreciate figures of Iban hunters, Murut men in traditional dress, or the stylized dragons from the Bidayuh, Kayan and Kenyah tribes.

Pandan weaving

Pandan weaving is another cottage industry in the East Coast state of Terengganu. The short pandan, or screw-pine leaves are used to make narrow sleeping mats, fans, baskets, tobacco pouches, slippers, purses and colorful table mats. The longer mengkuang leaves are used for floor mats. Visitors who wish to see this interesting weaving process can visit several village houses, open daily, from Kuantan to Kuala Terengganu. Primarily a woman's vocation, the process includes a great sense of camaraderie as the women chat and laugh together while they work. Though the craft looks simple, even a small purse may take an entire day to complete. Considered an East Coast tradition, the weaving is also popular among the women of Malacca, Selangor and Negri Sembilan.

Rattan

Rattan, or *rotan* in Malay, is abundant in this country because it is a jungle vine that thrives in dense, tropical rainforests. The furniture made from this vine is inexpensive, attractive and extremely durable. Basketware is also popular. Although a bit difficult to transport in a suitcase, rattan can be viewed at handicraft centers throughout Malaysia.

Birds nest

Finally, the "caviar of the East" is said to be the **birds' nests** found in the Niah caves and Baram in Sarawak and the Gomantong caves and Madai in Sabah. The Chinese insist that the birds' nests not only are tasty and nourishing, but also have aphrodisiacal powers. Uh, huh. So does bat stew. If you don't have the time or interest to collect your own, good quality nests are available from medicine shops (expensive) or packed in plastic bags at supermarkets. You don't eat the nest, rather the saliva that's used to keep them together. Before you tell all your friends with a wok what to expect, check with the U.S. Department of Agriculture. Birds' nests may be classified as plants and not allowed to be imported individually.

Malaysian handicrafts are readily available at the government-sponsored handicraft centers in major cities. However, the best and most enjoyable way to purchase your souvenirs is at the local markets.

Nuts & Bolts

Malaysia is the fastest growing of the ASEAN tigers with the highest growth rate (8% a year) and most aggressive investment policy. Its economy is in warp drive and it will soon join the world as a major manufacturer of electronic parts and other light industry goods. For now Malaysia is using its raw resources to fund that growth. Almost half of the world's timber products come from its jungles and Sarawak is estimated to be cutting down its trees at four times the sustainable rate. When the timber runs out Malaysia still has almost 4 billion barrels of sweet crude still to be sucked up and significant supplies of minerals and agricultural products. Malaysia is the largest exporter of palm oil and is even trying to develop an engine that runs solely on the product of this West African palm tree. Rubber and cocoa are still important exports with continual experimentation with new crops. Malaysia's goal is to have full self sufficiency by industrial means by 2020 under the guidance of Dr. Mahathir Mohammad, the prime minister since 1981.

The politics of Malaysia are a blend of old world sultanates (there are seven rotating sultans) and the democratic election of UNMO, the party that has been in power since independence from Britain in 1947. This is not expected to change anytime soon. Mahathir uses this comfortable power base to lash out at the U.S. and other developed nations. He roundly criticizes the pressure put on Malaysia to conserve its forest while the U.S has virtually no first growth forests left. Luckily Malaysia is not a bellicose country and despite its increasing Islamification it coexists peacefully with all its neighbors. Its biggest potential enemy is China who is laying claim to the Spratleys and other poorly defined territories.

The composition of Malaysia is 48% Malay, 34% Chinese, 9% Indian and 9% indigenous peoples. The religion of the country is Islam but Buddhism, Christianity, Hinduism, and other faiths are common and tolerated.

Malaysians tend to be rural people with each state having one major city. The Chinese control most businesses in the mainland and Borneo, leading the government to favor Malays over other ethnic groups when awarding contracts or promotions. In fact, in 1970 the New Economic Policy spelled out the special benefits that will be accorded Malays as a reaction to race riots that same year. The result is that Chinese and Indians (who make up a large number of the professional class) are siphoning their money into Singapore and other safe havens.

Luckily (or unluckily depending on how you look at it) soft adventure tourism has been chosen as a major area of development. Of the 7.5 million people who visit Malaysia every year the bulk of them arrive through Singapore for short one or two day visits. Tourism is expected to double every two years as more facilities are built. 1998 is expected to be a banner year for Malaysia as the Commonwealth games arrive and the country hosts its third "Visit Malaysia Year." The first event (that rotates between ASEAN countries) in 1990 established tourism as Malaysia's third largest foreign exchange source. Seventy new beach resorts are scheduled to be built before the year 2000.

The Climate

Malaysia virtually sits atop the equator, therefore the climate is hot and humid the year round. The best time to go is away from the monsoon season, October through February. Nevertheless, always expect rain. Flooded roads are commonplace in cities from November to January when the heaviest rains hit. So if you go during the monsoon season, don't forget to bring an umbrella and proper footwear.

More Information

Because of the great potential in revenue from tourism, Malaysia's semi-government organization, Tourism Malaysia, also known as The Malaysia Tourism Promotion Board, is working hard to welcome more and more visitors each year. In the Fourth Malaysia Plan, the country's blueprint for increasing development, tourism-related projects have taken the forefront, and incorporates various items intended to make travel within the country easier, such as highway extensions and railroad improvements. Also, more first-class hotels are being built in places like Penang and Kuala Lumpur.

If you require specialized information on Malaysia that no book can provide, contact Tourism Malaysia; they will be more than happy to answer any questions you may have.

Headquarters for **Tourism Malaysia** is *25th Floor, Menara Dato'Onn, Putra World Trade Centre, 45, Jalan Tun Ismail, 50480 Kuala Lumpur, Malaysia*. They have regional offices all over the world.

Malaysian Tourism Promotion Board,

818 W. 7th St.,
Los Angeles, CA 90017
☎ *(213) 689-9702; FAX (213) 689-1530.*

In Canada:

Malaysian Tourism Promotion Board,

830 Burrard St.,
Vancouver, B.C. V6Z2K4, CANADA
☎ *(604) 689-8899; FAX: (604) 680-8804 .*

Visas

Visas are not required for citizens of the Commonwealth (except India), British Protected Territories and those from the Republic of Ireland, Switzerland, the Netherlands, San Marino and Liechtenstein.

U.S. citizens, with valid U.S. passports, are not required to obtain a visa if the intended stay is 14 days or less. An extension can be granted up to three months if you show proof of solvency, respectable dress and airline tickets. Longer stays must be approved with the Malaysian Embassy.

Please note that entering Sabah and Sarawak is not the same as entering the other states in Peninsular Malaysia. Sabah and Sarawak are treated like different countries, so you'll need to go through customs all over again in each of those states if you're coming from Peninsular Malaysia or even if you're simply coming and going between the two states.

Malaysia is a federal parliamentary democracy with a constitutional monarch.

Getting In

A passport is required. Visas are not required for stays of up to three months. Yellow fever and cholera immunizations are necessary if arriving from infected areas. For further information the traveler can call the **Embassy of Malaysia**, *2401 Massachusetts Avenue, N.W., Washington, D.C. 20008;* ☎ *(202) 328-2700.*

Major crimes against tourists are uncommon but be aware that Malaysia has one of the highest rates of credit card fraud in the world. Petty crimes such as pickpocketing and purse-snatching are common in tourist areas.

The **U.S. Embassy** is located at *376 Jalan Tun Razak 50400 Kuala Lumpur,* mail: *P.O.Box No. 10035, 50700 Kuala Lumpur;* ☎ *(60-3) 248-9011.* FAX *(60-3) 242-2207,* the FAX number for the Consular Section is *(60-3) 248-5801.*

Inoculations

Unless you're coming from an endemic area, inoculations are not required, but tropical diseases such as malaria are still a threat in the jungles of Peninsular Malaysia and Borneo, so before venturing into unknown regions, please check with your doctor or the **Center for Disease Control** in Atlanta: ☎ *(404) 639-3311.*

INSIDER TIP

The malaria strains spread by mosquitoes are rapidly becoming resistant to quinine-based medication. Remember that Lariam is not 100 percent successful in preventing malaria. Since Fansidar is banned in the U.S. but commonly prescribed in Asia and Africa, make sure you know the pros and cons of malaria prophylaxis before venturing into remote, bug-infested regions. Also, if you're not on any medication, you may want to buy more malaria pills in Malaysia. It cost me about US$80 to get a prescription for them in the States, but you can buy them over the counter in Malaysia for about M$3, or just over a U.S. dollar.

Customs

Duty free in Malaysia are the usual items: cameras, watches, pens, lighters, cosmetics, perfume and portable radios. Those who bring in dutiable items such as video equipment may have to pay a deposit for temporary importation, refundable on their return. Usually this fee is up to 50 percent of the item's value.

Beware that pornography—such as X-rated video tapes and magazines—is strictly forbidden in Malaysia. Also, trafficking illegal drugs into Malaysia carries the death penalty. And it is enforced!

The Currency

The unit of currency of Malaysia is the ringgit (M), or the Malaysian dollar. One hundred sens equals one ringgit. Currency notes are divided in denominations similar to those in the U.S.: M$1, M$5, M$10, M$20, M$50, M$100, M$500, M$1000. Coins are issued in 1 sen, 5 sen, 10 sen, 20 sen, 50 sen and M$1.

Although the exchange rate for any two international currencies is never constant, there are **M$2.26 to US$1**. Please note that the Malaysian dollar no longer has the same worth as the Singapore and Brunei dollar and is no longer interchangeable. Both finished goods and raw materials are cheap in Malaysia. A laborer makes about 14 ringgits a day while a white collar worker might make 1000 a month.

Traveler's Checks and Credit Cards

There are more than 40 different commercial banks in Malaysia. Most banks in the larger cities exchange traveler's checks, as do money agencies including one in Kuala Lumpur's International Airport. But be warned, not all hotels exchange traveler's checks. And always remember to have your passport ready.

Most shops and restaurants in cities, such as Kuala Lumpur, take major credit cards (I have found more to take American Express than Visa or MasterCard), but smaller shops farther away from civilization probably won't pay any attention to plastic.

In Malaysia, the best way to travel outside of the main cities is with cash in hand. Make sure you have plenty, because if you run out, you may find yourself in a hopeless situation.

Setting Your Clock

Local time in Malaysia is Greenwich Mean Time plus eight hours. Peninsular Malaysia and the states of Sabah and Sarawak on Borneo were finally on the same time New Year's Day 1982 as a symbol of unity. When setting your watch, keep in mind that Malaysia does not utilize daylight savings. Malaysia is 16 hours ahead of PST time.

Electricity

Local current in Malaysia is 220 volts, 50 cycles, but don't expect appliances to work too well outside the leading hotels. Some luxury hotels will have 110 outlets but the safest bet is to bring an adaptor or disposable razors.

Water

The tap water throughout Malaysia is potable; however, there is an abundance of bottled water and soft drinks available for the timid. The farther you get out of town, the less you should drink from the tap. If you find yourself away from the city without bottled water, boil the tap water, just in case. I usually stock up on bottled water wherever I stay in the country.

Health Services

Even in small towns, private clinics are easy to find. In major cities, your best bet is to visit medical centers, where private doctors render their services inexpensively. Also they dispense medicine on the spot. Approximate fee for a private medical visit to a clinic is M$20 including medicine. There is one doctor for every 2708 persons with clinics in many small towns.

Keep in mind that the various government hospitals scattered throughout the country are geared to serve the local population, not foreign tourists—with the exceptions of emergencies of course.

What to Wear

Lightweight clothing is the rule in Malaysia. When packing, load up on your coolest, lightest, most conservative, and most important of all, most comfortable clothes. Cotton is preferable because it breathes better than polyester or other similar fabrics.

Unless the occasion is formal, people in Malaysia tend to dress casually. Formal occasions usually require a suit and tie for men and dresses for women. Alternatively, batik, a local fabric, is worn. Women may be requested to don a head cover when visiting a mosque or other holy places.

Always be prepared for rain. An umbrella is ideal for Malaysia's torrential rainstorms that come from nowhere and leave after several drenching minutes. Ponchos or plastic wraps may keep you dry from the rain, but they keep heat in, so you end up drenched in your own perspiration. Keep in mind that many hotels and restaurants are air-conditioned, so a shawl or sweater may be necessary when dining out. Sandals are worn by everyone and aren't a bad idea considering the rain and the fact that shoes are not allowed in Muslim monuments. Inexpensive straw hats and the strongest available sun screen are also helpful to those not accustomed to the tropical sun.

If you forget to pack something, don't sweat it (forgive the pun). There are heaps of stores with brand names and great prices for just about any kind of clothing you need.

INSIDER TIP

Save space. Pick up a cheap umbrella, a straw hat or any cotton clothing you may need in the main cities. But if you're tall or large, don't expect much of a selection. Give 'em away before you leave.

A Polaroid photo is an ideal icebreaker.

Photography Tips

Kuching and the Iban longhouses are the most photogenic places for photographers. The wild places of Sabah are also challenging. The jungles are the least inspiring for color. Having considerable experience in these regions, I can pass on some advice:

Your camera equipment will be trashed.

The moisture, dust, humidity, bumpy roads, airplane trips, high heat and intense sunlight are exactly what you are supposed to avoid. Your best bet is a manual camera carried in a Pelican case. The next best solution is to put your lenses in heavy duty freezer bags. Remember that what keeps moisture out works equally effectively at keeping it in. Video cameras are the most sensitive to tropical journeys because of their delicate working parts, refusal to work when damp and susceptibility of electronics to dampness and dust. When you get back home you will need to have your cameras taken apart and all the rusty springs and mildew removed.

Remember that cameras hate going from air-conditioned hotels and buses into the steaming humidity. They will fog up as soon as you take the lens cap off. Every once in a while let your cameras and lenses heat up at noon (the lowest humidity level of the day). Lenses off, backs open. Take the film out first. Some folks like silica gel but I think it is fairly useless in high humidity.

Consider taking along all weather cameras but be prepared for them to be trashed when the expansion of the camera casing actually sucks moisture into the body and it won't come out.

Your film will be fried.

Heat affects film dramatically—more so after your pictures are exposed than before. Buy fresh film from a professional camera dealer. Ask for same batch, latest date emulsion. Shoot a roll to test your camera, meter, emulsion and lens diaphragms. Try different exposures to zero in on the best ASA to use. Don't be bullied by the manufacturer into shooting Kodachrome 200 at ASA 200. For example Fuji Velvia is rated at 50 but should be shot at ASA 32. Develop the roll and judge the results. Freeze the film until you are ready to travel. Take all the film out of the paper packaging and store it by emulsion type in large clear freezer bags. Have your film hand-inspected. If you like, bring along those freezer packs to help regulate temperature.

Shoot lots of pictures being careful to bracket your tricky exposures. Keep the film cool by storing it in the middle of your luggage or in a separate bag with a wet towel on top. If you go back to a hotel, keep it in the fridge. When you get home make sure it is hand-inspected (X-ray damage is cumulative and destroys the D-max or dark areas of your pictures.)

You will miss a lot of great shots.

The jungle is very dark and even ASA 200 film will yield dull blobs and shapes. Overexpose by one stop because your meter will be reading the bright spots. Always shoot small, focus on details and don't expect a rhinoceros to come stumbling into your viewfinder. Look for orchids, insects, fungi, ants and the occasional stick insect or butterfly.

Carry a hand tripod, fast telephoto lenses and a mini softbox for your strobe. Those great nature shots of Asian wildlife took years of being in the same place and dumb luck.

What's bad about photography in Borneo

Birds sit too high up in the trees. Animals come out at night or in heavy rainfalls. The sun barely comes out some days. Danum Valley and other remote places require a lot of patience and specialized equipment to capture mammals or interesting insects. Caves are just about impossible to capture and the lush forests are too big and too dark to communicate on film. River rides just soak your camera. Trekking quadruples the weight of your equipment and provides absolutely no viewpoints or vistas. Climbing a mountain just reveals a carpet of green and if you have seen one tree you have seen them all.

Good things about photography in Borneo

The people are very photogenic and proud to be photographed. The Malays and Bajau will not let you leave until every member of their family has been photographed. Much of the tribal artwork, dress and crafts are very photogenic and the people are happy to let you click away. There is little paranoia about photography.

Festivals are the best time to be shutter happy and the people expect you to capture them on film. Wildlife or nature photographers should head straight for the Agricultural Center in Tenom, and The Orang Utan Rehabilitation center at Sepilok is ideal for clicking away. Orchid lovers will also get great shots at Poring Hot Springs and the Orchid Center in Tenom. The Sarawak Cultural Centre is the best place for housing and crafts. Mount Kinabalu could easily occupy a lifetime of nature photography with its pitcher plants, moss forests and wildlife. Tamus and marketplaces provide excellent subject material and the people are not shy about posing. Underwater photographers could spend the rest of their lives and money photographing Sipadan and Layang Layang. Lovers of insects, ferns, flowers,reptiles, butterflies, or even ants could spent two lifetimes just documenting the hundreds of known and unknown species of the island.

Never leave your film in a warm area...

And now a true story to show you just how useless guidebook advice is. I bought the freshest, "all same" professional emulsion in L.A. I random tested on recently calibrated Leicas and Linhofs. I kept it cool in jungle streams, hotel meatlockers, holes dug in the ground and taped to air conditioning vents. Soon I had about 200 rolls ready for shipment back to the States. The photos were of my plane crash, two new species of plants, a remote area that we had explored and most of the documentation for this book. I carefully labelled and wrapped each roll in plastic. I arranged for a local person to meet us as we came out of the bush. I gave the person explicit instructions on how to ship it. When we came out of the bush two weeks later, we found the film sitting in the truck, all our windows rolled up tightly with a note saying "Too heavy." Aghast at my film sitting in a 150 degree truck for two weeks, I had another local drive to KK where they were instructed which customs broker was to receive the film and how it was to be sent.

Never leave your film in a warm area...

Coming out of the bush again I called my office. No film had arrived. I called the the customs broker. Good news and bad news. The bad news was that his warehouse caught on fire and everything was either burnt, melted or water damaged. The cartons that were left were all opened so that the insurance company could ascertain the damage. So my film was either burnt, destroyed or exposed to light. What was the good news? The insurance company would reimburse me for each roll of film (about $3–$5 per roll.)

There are moments when you want to give up and scream but something about the tone of his voice made me ask more questions. Like a mother who wants to ID her dead son, I asked "What happened to the boxes and where are they now?" They had been moved to "the other warehouse." A warehouse that apparently had no name, address or telephone number. Aha there was hope.

To make a long story short, the Chinese owner had spirited away to his home anything of value that could be resold. After days of getting the runaround and demanding to talk to the insurance inspector, I told him I was going to the other "warehouse" or to his home until I saw proof. Finally the truth emerged. He had brought home a pile of boxes that he thought contained books and auto parts. Tucked underneath those boxes were my two boxes of film. The boxes were scorched, stained from water and half burnt, but every one of my rolls of film was intact. Oh, and the film turned out perfectly. So forget all that guidebook advice. Just don't ever let your film out of your sight.

Tipping

For the most part, tipping is considered unnecessary in Malaysia. A service charge of 10 percent is added to most hotel and restaurant bills, plus a five percent government tax. However, you should always reward service with a smile. Malaysians are sincere, honest people and the gratuitous dispersal of money can be taken the wrong way.

Telephones and Faxes

Telephones rates are cheap in Malaysia. Public telephone booths are found in most towns in Malaysia, especially at supermarkets and post offices. Local calls are 10 sen. If you need to make a long distance call, you should do so at your hotel using an operator or direct dial. But if you absolutely need to make a direct call from a public phone, look for one with International Subscriber Dialing (ISD). For a significant fee, you can hook up to the U.S., Australia, Japan, Britain, Germany, Hong Kong, Bangkok, Switzerland, Italy and Tahiti. International calling rates are reduced during the hours of 6 p.m. to 7 a.m.

Keep in mind that Jahatan Telekom Malaysia is changing the telephone numbers throughout Malaysia, usually from six to eight digits. If you need assistance or information regarding a new number, contact the Assistance Center by dialing 1060 and give them the old number.

Fax service is widely available at hotels and public offices. Or you can send them from various telegram offices.

Cellular phones are quite common and provide service in the most remote regions.

MALAYSIA

TO CALL ANY NUMBER IN THIS BOOK FROM THE USA:

DIAL 011 then 60 then the area code (no 0) and the number

To reach a local directory assistance operator dial T103

The area code for KK is 088, Kuching 082, Labuan 087, Miri 085 and
Sandakan 089.

To reach an operator for general assistance dial 102

For help with international calls dial 108

There are two kinds of cardphones; Kadfon and Unicard. Telephone
cards can be purchased at airports, gas stations and convenience
stores. Insert your card, dial the number and remember to push the
button once the other person answers. Cellular phone service is
excellent but requires line of sight to an cell antennae to operate
properly. To place a long distance call in a small town go to the Telekom office.

Borneo is 16 hours ahead of Los Angeles time so that when it is 8 a.m. in Malaysia, it
is 4 p.m. the previous day in Los Angeles.

Getting There and Getting Around

By Air

Malaysia Airlines, formerly known as Malaysia Airline System (MAS), offers services to
and from the United States, Europe, the Middle East, India, Australia, Korea, Japan and
Mexico City.

If you visit Borneo via Malaysia you will need to stop in Singapore or KL first. Royal
Brunei, Singapore Airlines and MAS all offer similar prices but very different levels of service. Singapore is number one with the others trailing a long way behind. The new Kuala
Lumpur International Airport is currently under construction in nearby Sepang, Selang-
or, and is scheduled to become operational in stages in 1997.

Malaysia Airlines also offers an extensive network of domestic routes within the country and special deals for flights between states if you buy tickets at the same time you book
your international flight.

By Sea

Although it's a stop for various cruise liners, most of Malaysia's ports are intended for
cargo ships. Cruise ships do stop at Sandakan where ground transportation is available for
tours to the orang utans at Sepilok, and the famous caves.

By Rail

Other than the tiny rail line that runs along the Padas Gorge in Sabah there is no rail
transport in Borneo.

By Bus Or Taxi

Rental cars are usually available on an unlimited mileage basis, but overall, they don't represent as much of a bargain as taxi travel. The daily rates range from M$240 for economy cars to M$350 for the luxury models. Weekly rates are also available. Many of the nicer hotels in Kuala Lumpur have rental-car agencies.

The most popular method of travel in Borneo (besides boat) is bus. They are cheap, slow, crowded and ubiquitous. Buses usually leave from the square next to the markets.

By Car

Although the traffic rules are basically the same, cars in Malaysia are *right-hand drive* like in England and Japan. Also, traffic flow is reversed—you drive on the right side of the road not left. When first driving there, drive with caution; driving on the opposite side of the car on the opposite side of the road is more awkward than you might expect. You'll have a strong natural tendency to look the wrong way and drive into the wrong lane when turning. Also, you may find yourself veering onto the right side of the road when avoiding oncoming traffic. This also applies when walking on the street. So do as your mother told you and look both ways before crossing the street.

The road signs in Malaysia are still mostly written in Bahasa Malay, so study the table below before setting out on the road. And keep your speed down, speeding is strictly enforced and carries a heavy fine.

An *International Driving Permit* is required for foreign drivers but you can usually rent a car with an American photo ID driver's license. If you have a valid state or national driver's license, you can pick one up for a small fee. Expect to pay about $US50 a day for a flimsy Proton Saga and four times that for a 4 wheel drive vehicle. You will also be hit up for a collision waiver of about $US20 a day for the Proton and correspondingly more for the truck.

Insider tip

Blammo—you just splattered a chicken that never will cross the road. Well believe it or not you are in big trouble. God help you if you kill or maim one of those miserable dogs that seem to lie on the road taunting you to flatten them. If you kill an animal while driving you will be expected to pay for it. A chicken will only cost about 20 ringgit and a scabby dog (elevated in death to the finest hunting dog in Sabah) could cost you around 400 ringgit. One of our drivers on an expedition struck a mangey cur and wounded it. The owner wanted full compensation; we argued that the dog still had value for breeding, warmth, etc. and was only worth half that. The owner, hoping that his dog would learn how to play dead, had to admit that we had not removed the full value of his flea bitten mut and accepted our offer.

Rental cars can be booked from a variety of agencies in Sabah and Sarawak. You must be 23 or older and have had a clean driving license for one year (how they can check this is beyond me). Malaysian drivers tend to be casually deadly and the bad roads tend to slow them down, keeping them alive for a longer than normal period. Signage and direction are good in some areas and missing completely in others. The main roads are smooth, efficient and reliable. The smaller roads should be driven with care since children, dogs, bicycles and other objects occupy the road equally. Dogs are a particular menace in the small kampungs since they will not move a single muscle even when logging trucks bear down on them at 60 miles per hour.

If you have the misfortune of driving on *logging roads* please remember this: Directional signs must be obeyed regardless of how stupid they sound. If you are told to "Ikut Kanan" and you know you are supposed to be on the left it is because the logging trucks swing wide. You better be huddled to the right or in the case of "Ikut Kiri" to the left.

Speeding tickets are not common in the boonies in Borneo but are very common coming into the major cities. The fee is a whopping $US200 and many police will offer to work it out on the spot. Do as your conscience or wallet dictates.

When heading for a tight bridge whoever flashes their lights first has the right of way. Fuel is cheap, diesel is the most common outside the cities. If you are in a pinch, logging camps will sell you diesel from their supply at usurious rates. In town driving is best left to the Chinese cab drivers or trishaw drivers.

By Trishaw

The best way to commute short distances are trishaws. Trishaws are bicycles with a small carriage attached to the rear. They serve as a relaxing and slow way to travel short distances, but not all towns and cities have them. They cost about M$1 per kilometer, but always agree on the price beforehand or it may cost you more than a limousine.

IMPORTANT ROAD SIGNS	
AWAS	CAUTION
BERHENTI	STOP
IKUT KIRI	KEEP LEFT
IKUT KANAN	KEEP RIGHT
KURANGKAN LAJU	SLOW DOWN
JALAN SEHALA	ONE WAY
UTARA	NORTH
SELATAN	SOUTH
TIMUR	EAST
BARAT	WEST

Business in Malaysia

Because Malaysia is a country of rich cultural diversity, be careful when conducting business. Normal business practices in the States may not be necessarily so in Malaysia.

Business Hours

Government offices in Malaysia usually operate from 8:15 a.m. to 12:45 p.m. and from 2 to 4:15 p.m. Monday through Friday (with a little extra time off on Friday afternoon for communal Jumaah prayers at the mosques).

Banking hours are 10 a.m. to 3 p.m. Monday through Friday; 9:30 to 11:30 a.m. on Saturday. In Kedah, Perlis, Kelantan, and Terengganu, banks are open from 9:30 to 11:30 a.m. on Thursday and are closed on Friday. Offices and shops usually begin their day at 9 a.m. and close anywhere from 5 to 10 p.m. Saturdays are half-days and Sunday is a holiday.

However, the five states in the eastern part of the peninsula still maintain the Muslim half-day on Thursday, full holiday on Friday (the holy day), and full working days on Saturday and Sunday. The best rule is to always confirm appointments and check hours of business.

Tips on Doing Business in Malaysia

Malaysians usually like to take time studying any business proposal. They are very cautious and like to shop around so be sure to give them plenty of time to make up their minds.

The Malaysian date documents like the Europeans. Day/Month/Year. Make sure you date documents accordingly or February 5, 1995 will read like May 2, 1995.

Malaysia is an Islamic nation so make sure you schedule meetings and such around their prayer times.

If the need arises to hire a lawyer, you may want to hire a local attorney or one familiar with the British system for that is what Malaysian law is based upon.

Try not to say "no" directly or harshly. Listen to the entire proposal, and then politely refuse. Malaysians will act the same way, so expect subtle negative remarks.

Always expect Malaysians to be late for an appointment. This is not to say that they are tardy people, but in my experience, being on time didn't seem like a priority.

Lodging in Malaysia

Finding a place to stay is reliable and cheap in Sabah and Sarawak. The forms of lodging follow a fairly predictable pattern. They can be divided into resorts, business hotels, resthouses and other. Other would include campsites, longhouses, and anywhere other than a hotel.

Resorts

There are only a handful of resorts in Sabah and Sarawak. The Batang Ai, Holiday Inn at Damai Beach and Royal Mulu are examples of this fairly new breed of high roller tourist fare. None can compare to the more exotic versions on Bali, Tahiti or Hawaii but they do offer high standards and an invigorating ambience.

Business Hotels

Unlike the more rugged parts of the world, every small town in Sabah and Sarawak has a collection of Chinese run hotels that offer a thin mattress, clean sheets (sometimes) and a roof over your head. These are the "Motel Sixes" of Borneo and they have overstated names like "Cosy," the "Premier" and the "Mandarin." Many go by a Chinese name. On the low end you will have to wait while they drag a mattress into your room and find a lightbulb for the swinging socket. Most are family run and lower room rates than published in this book can be negotiated. Air conditioning is something you have to ask for and will be provided via a wheezing mildewed wall mount unit. The hotels tend to be as cheap as they are noisy as the family or friends will play dominoes or watch TV late into the night. There is a certain fairness in what you will be charged so expect to get what you pay for. Bare bones joints that can't even afford cockroaches go for about $US10 and don't take credit cards. These hotels are called *rumah persinggahan*

On the upper end there is usually one good business hotel in every city in Borneo. Almost all are musty, worn at the corners and still offer good value. These hotels will have internal or wall mount AC, color TVs with in-room movies, clean bathrooms with 110 sockets, direct dial phones and comfy mattresses with clean sheets. Most will have a restaurant, a coffee shop, a health club (see the Sex section) and diffident service. Expect to pay between $US20–100 a night for the spiffier joints and you can usually use your Visa or Mastercard. The large hotels also have a wide latitude in what they can charge. All except the resorts are open to negotiation. Ask for the corporate rate (even if you are a student) or call a local travel agency to shop around.

Other

Many travelers will want to spend at least one night in a **longhouse**. Although the idea of partying every night and being tortured by gong music does not appeal to all folks it still is the only way to find lodging in the remote regions. You can ask the headman if you can stay, offer a gift or small amount of cash, and other than sharing the evening meal and breakfast, be left to your own devices. A longhouse is a large elevated apartment with a common veranda and private apartments towards the back for each family. There is plenty of paraphernalia around for pounding rice, cooking dinner, as well as a Bruegel-like assortment of dogs, children and old women. Longhouses are usually built near a "lazy" or tributary or a main river, and of course they are long houses.

A *rumah rehat* is a **resthouse** usually built by the government to provide very low cost lodging to government employees, students or locals traveling. These places are always full, have clean accommodations and can be quite interesting if you like to meet the locals since there is usually a common cooking and dining area.

Camping in Sabah and Sarawak is for fools like myself. If you have a choice between a resthouse, longhouse, tin shed or even making a bamboo platform, go for it. Carrying a soggy tent, sleeping in the mud and trying to prevent yourself from drowning or being eaten alive by insects is a futile and frustrating experience. Tents are oppressively hot, are not waterproof in heavy downpours and a general nuisance to pack around. Having spent many, many nights in the bush and having tried all sorts of high tech, all mesh, lightweight tents, I have settled on a simple collapsible mosquito tent, a thin sleeping bag (with cotton lining) and a plastic sheet or tarp. In remote regions I simply create a raised platform covered with palm leaves and/or a tarp. Since there are no campsites in Brunei, none in Kalimantan and a pathetic few in Sabah and Sarawak, I would recommend doing as the locals do and planning on spending your nights above ground level with a roof over your head. If you want to rough it then learn how to fashion lean-tos like the Penan.

The funny thing is I always ended up selling every tent I took to Borneo to some local person who usually was fascinated with the potential for high tech camping.

2:00 a.m. in the mountains of Sabah—The second night in the jungle was a memorable one. Sleepless, tired and fatigued, we were fighting the land-slides, mud and hills as best we could. This country was not made to be driven through but we were going to try. The screaming of over-revved engines and the shouting of men straining against obstinate vehicles echoed through the cool, misty mountains. Overloaded trucks slithered and fishtailed as they fought for every inch of steep muddy track. High-powered fog lights blasted eerie shadows of mud-splattered men through the fog and against the solid dark wall of rainforest. During all of this, monkeys hooted and cicadas tinkled like a thousand tiny bells, all underscored by the steady jungle downpour. The whole enterprise smacked of futility and I was in heaven.

A boat is considered the ideal method of transportation through Borneo. In this case a Land Rover does just fine.

The warm rain and the thick tropical smells wrapped me like a woollen blanket as the deep, heavy mud pulled hard at my boots. The smell of hot sweat on a cool jungle night felt warm and enveloping—the tension and camaraderie of men desperately trying to beat nature to avoid being cut off by the swollen rivers ahead. Misery and fatigue threatened to overtake us as I pushed and cajoled my topless green Land Rover along the slick trails. We had chosen this place in this season to fight the elements and to test ourselves against the stubborn hand of nature. I was in the middle of Borneo, driving a battered army-green Series II Land Rover 88, my gear lashed under the dirty canvas cover and covered in mud from head to toe. This was adventure!

There are hundreds of trails and abandoned logging roads in Borneo. Most require permission to pass from the owners of the timber concessions.

Adventure in a Box

A group of Malaysians who had previously participated in the Camel Trophy expedition in Kalimantan and Madagascar had decided to attempt a crossing of Borneo by off-road vehicle, canoe and foot. An east to west crossing of Borneo had never been done before, and this fact captured the imagination of various sponsors including the government and airlines. It also attracted the attention of the world's press, film and television journalists. I was invited to join as both an advisor and the U.S. team representative.

Borneo is an island where most explorations have been made by river or by foot. Its primary attraction for me was its massive and relatively unexplored jungle, a forest accessible only by small canoe or logging roads, which was exactly where the Trans Borneo was to take us. The idea of linking together a series of new logging roads, rivers and paths made the prospect even more appealing because I could see firsthand what was happening to this fertile island.

The only positive aspect of the miles of logging roads that creep further and further into the virgin forest every year is they allow exploration into untouched territory. These extensive roads are unmapped and carefully guarded. Journalists are absolutely not allowed in these areas, and in Sarawak many journalists had actually been asked to sign a form that they would not be critical of the government or logging policy.

There are also practical reasons for keeping tourists and journalists off these roads. Active logging roads are ruled by 50-ton logging trucks that hurtle up and down at breakneck speeds. These trucks make full use of every inch of road and do not stop for tourists.

Off-Roading the Asian Way

In America, off-roading is viewed as the domain of beer swilling, gun toting, tobacco chewing, blue collar workers. The reality is that more off-road vehicles are driven by suburban housewives picking up their children from school. In Asia the difference is even more pronounced, sport utility vehicles are for the strictly wealthy. They impart a macho, worldly image and cost an extraordinary amount of money to buy, insure, equip and run. There are many utilitarian Land Cruisers in more utilitarian hands but few can afford to take them on expeditions. Winches, spare gas tanks, driving lights, safety equipment and hi lift jacks are very expensive here. To then take what is in effect a luxury vehicle and run it into the ground takes another load of money. In Sabah, many people start a business just to be able to afford to insure and register their off-road vehicles.

Into the Orient

Our journey began in Kota Kinabalu (KK) in Sabah, a rugged, mountainous region to the northwest. We followed a circuitous route from KK around the most easterly point in Sabah and then back across Borneo, ending up in Kuching, the capital of Sarawak.

The flight to Kuala Lumpur, the jumping off point for Borneo, was uneventful and a constant reminder of the difference between Asian and American frames. MAS flies direct to Kota Kinabalu and a connecting flight to KK leaves at least twice a day.

Kuala Lumpur is a sight to behold. Not as frantic as Hong Kong, not as commercial as Singapore, and not as exotic as Bangkok, it is still very much the restrained ex-colonial capital. Buses run on time and the streets are clean. The evidence of Malaysia's entrance into the mainstream of world economy is demonstrated by the frenetic shopping by locals and the construction of skyscrapers by outside investors.

Some things struck me as slightly peculiar: cabs charge 20 percent more for air conditioning; they sentenced a kidnapper to life in jail *and* six strokes of the roatan (a kind of whip); and the latest gimmick advertised on TV was a $6000 wireless remote control water closet from Japan. I had come here for adventure, yet I was feeling I had arrived 10 years in the future.

Since the expedition was organized with the assistance of the government and the participation of adventurers around the world, it was a good time to get to know the journalists and participants. There were people from Japan, Italy, Turkey, France, Australia, the United States, Sweden and Malaysia; a true United Nations of adventurers. As we drank and swapped stories in the ultramodern air-conditioned bar at the Holiday Inn until the early morning, I kept thinking that I could have been in Kansas City for a Shriner's convention. Surely this couldn't be the adventure I had come thousands of miles for.

As I slipped into bed on the upper floors, a huge flash of light outside my hotel room awoke me. Despite my fatigue, I had to see this display. Climbing out on the roof, I watched the giant thunderheads soaring thousands of feet into the night sky pulsing with an internal light. Not really caring that I was an attractive lightning rod, I watched the sound and light show as Shah Alam mosque glittered far below in the dawn. The awesome power and force of the lightning storm and the mystical hold of the world's largest domed mosque told me I had not come to Malaysia in vain. Behind the veneer of the modern city, there were powerful natural and spiritual forces to reckon with.

The next day my flight from Kuala Lumpur to Kota Kinabalu on the island of Borneo was through sheets of solid rain. Thunder cracked and shook the Boeing 737 as the engines screamed to break contact with the flooded runway. The plane creaked and shuddered as it fought the storm. The engines would suddenly speed up or slow down depending on the air pressure, and the few peeks of blue sky were negated by the awesome size and darkness of the thunderheads we were trying to avoid. To say it rains in Malaysia is an understatement.

Kota Kinabalu

On our arrival in Kota Kinabalu we were met by our local expedition members in their clattering 4 wheel drive vehicles. Kota Kinabalu (or KK) is not the ugliest city I have seen but it would be up there in the finalists. The major difference between Sabah and the rest of Malaysia is its utilitarian ambience. It also didn't help that the Japanese and the Americans bombed the major ports of Jesselton (now KK) and Sandakan (then British North Borneo) into rubble during World War II.

The buildings have a definite Eastern European work camp influence. There is quite a bit of money made here in timber and oil but it is definitely not spent on architecture. Fueled by the exotic images of Sarawak or Kalimantan, I was not quite prepared for the dullness of it all. Our hotel was a musty version of what would have been an American luxury hotel in 1962.

There is not much to see in and around Kota Kinabalu unless you like to shop or do business. There are numerous shopping malls that stretch in endless mazes of identical corridors. The Centrepoint complex was the shiniest, and the largest of the shopping centers, complete with the obligatory health club/whorehouse on the top floor and a Yoahan's with the bowing, scraping sales clerks on the ground floor. There is little that cannot be bought here: cameras, auto parts, clothing. Restaurants and stores repeat themselves in a mind numbing procession. Clean, antiseptic and air-conditioned, the malls, office buildings and supermarkets let you know that Sabahans are an industrious race in love with the trappings of the Western world—and they can afford it.

Kota Kinabalu was not the jungle outpost I pictured, in fact, some of the foreign crews had brought their own toilet paper and water purification tablets, expecting to barter for water and food when they arrived. I just went to the camping and food department and bought everthing I needed and charged it to my credit card.

The Journey Begins

This expedition was as modern and as industrious as the rest of the region. Designed to promote adventure tourism, eco-travelers and investment, we found ourselves paraded about in our khaki gear like foreign poster children for an entire regime of ever-smiling politicians.

At the ceremonial dinner we were seated adventurer, politician, adventurer, politician and so on. After being regaled with mind-numbing cultural displays, hearty speeches and polite mush mouthing questions such as,"What do you think of our fine state," or "what do you think of the cultural differences between our two societies?" we ground our way through the endless procession of dead animals killed and prepared on our behalf. We kept going by knowing that there must be a point at which the politicians have to leave with their cute office administrators, and we would be left to the serious work of having a good time. I have a lot more respect for the drudge work that royalty does after this. My face hurt the next morning from so much smiling, and my voice was hoarse from shouting polite answers across eight foot tables.

Our briefing the next morning was simple and to the point. A large scale map of Borneo was presented with varicose veins drawn all over it. We were told that this road was closed due to rain, that this path may be open, etc., etc., and to generally ignore the carefully drawn route map. We also learned that we would not be going through Brunei because quite simply, Brunei didn't want us. Instead we were instructed to go around Brunei using canoes and on foot. Our vehicles would be ferried from Lawas to Miri. There was much spirited discussion as to the painfully obvious fact that the route drawn on the map meandered through completely unmarked territory that had no roads or towns and that the varicose veins were rivers which continually crossed our paths.

Rivers must be crossed using winches or tow straps.

Flag-Off

At the flag-off point in Kota Kinabalu, we met all the local participants for the first time after having spent sufficient time in the hotel bar meeting the international competitors and journalists. Twenty vehicles were to take part in the expedition, ranging from new factory prepared Nissans to old, taped-together Land Rovers. The starting lineup looked more like a used 4 x 4 lot and most vehicles looked as if the major use of the sponsor's stickers was to hold their body panels together.

The bulk of local participants were from Kuching, Kuala Lumpur and Kota Kinabalu. The Japanese had traveled here at great expense complete with spotless Mitsubishi-made Jeeps. They were outfitted in the latest American expedition gear, bristling with every photographic and video innovation known to man, complete with every spare part, freeze-dried meal and camping requirement available. We got underway after an evening and morning of waiting and speech making. Our overloaded trucks climbed through the mountain scenery as we ground into the rugged interior of Sabah.

Our first taste of action came soon along an abandoned logging trail. Here the rapid growth quickly reclaims any man-made clearings. Most of our time was taken up with clearing fallen trees and undergrowth. I learned quickly that roatan and vines can carry very sharp and painful spines after grabbing a branch and finding my hand impaled shut with two inch thorns. In addition to my personal damage and a few nasty cuts, the vehicles began to take on a well worn look: the fancy driving lights took the worst of the beating as branches and creepers smacked and twisted off the expensive accessories.

Our crisp fatigues and cool demeanor soon wilted as the sun rose in the sky. The lack of breeze, 80 to 100 degree heat and 100 percent humidity sucked the water out of our bodies like a sponge. The oozing sweat stings your eyes and soaks your clothes. Once exposed to the equatorial sun, Westerners not only burn quickly, but run the risk of heatstroke. The only relief from the heat inside my cramped, hot Land Rover was an overworked metal fan that swung back and forth in a drunken arc.

As we fought our way towards the higher elevations that would bring cooler temperatures, we received our first rain shower. You soon learn to differentiate between the various types of rain in Borneo: fine mist, light drizzle, heavy downpour, blowing gusts and so on. Whatever the weather, you can count on Borneo to be hot and wet. Luckily, our first rain was a soft cooling drizzle, which combined with the day's dirt and sweat to create a greasy, malodorous mixture. We had chosen the monsoon season to attempt this crossing because it would make it "more interesting."

On the second day, the rain began in earnest. The rainy seasons in Borneo are divided into two monsoons: the Northeast, which brings rain from November until April and the Southwest, which covers the rest of the year from May to October.

Some of the calmer sections made us forget the mountains and the rains that awaited us.

On our way up to the higher elevations, we stopped at a riverside campsite for lunch. Rain began to fall, slowly at first, then into the heavy torrents more typical of a monsoon. While sitting in the pouring rain, we watched a small brown stream turn into a boiling torrent of brown mud, threatening to wash away the Bailey bridge we were soon to cross. Quickly we packed and jumped into our vehicles as the water rose within inches of the bridge.

Now that the monsoons had started, the rains would be a regular feature of our days and nights. Since we were to cross several makeshift bridges over the next few days, it was important to move as quickly as possible. Most of the logging bridges ahead of us were made of enormous hardwood logs stacked on top of each other and packed with mud. Every year the monsoon washes them away, every year they are rebuilt. The risky part of driving on abandoned roads at this time is the good chance of falling though the gaping craters between the massive logs.

This day we are on a recently abandoned road slithering through eight to 10 inches of solid mud. The more it rains, the deeper the mud gets. Driving is a delicate balance between wheel spin and forward motion. Too little gas, you get bogged down, too much, you slither off an 80 foot drop-off. My little green Rover is packed to the gunnels, making the rear continually try to slide around to meet the front end. My biggest problem is staying between the loose muck on the steep side of the road and the ever narrowing drop-off on the other side. Between all this maneuvering, I tried to glimpse the ever changing scenery that unfolded at every turn.

Most rivers required us to build bridges or to ford the narrow sections.

Mud is omnipresent and unavoidable. By late afternoon, the entire outside and inside of our vehicle was again covered in mud. Cleated tires were balls of reddish brown dough, windows were streaked triangles where the wipers valiantly ground back and forth; reddish brown was the color of everything: thick, goopy chunks of mud that would weigh down your boots and stick to everything you touched. Mud that stuck to mud, making walking, driving, sleeping and eating a constant battle to find a clean area. After a while you gave up. You slept in the mud, picked it out of your food, picked it out of your ears, and even began to like the feel of it squishing between your toes.

Occasionally, we stopped to stretch our legs and take pictures of the magnificent, mist-shrouded mountains we were passing through. Despite the hardships, at least we weren't walking. This was off-road adventure at its finest. To see, feel and smell the jungle in its primeval state is an experience everyone should have at least once.

As the day wore on, we kept up the pace to make a remote bridge before it was washed out. The unseen sun, set high above the rain clouds, bathed the jungle with a glowing orange light that slowly faded into a deep red. It was getting dark, the rain kept falling and the evening's fun was soon to begin.

At the bottom of a steep hill, the convoy stopped to consider the next move. It seems we had met our match. One by one, like knights charging a dragon or the glass mountain, we set off to challenge the hill. With wheels spinning, elbows flying and engines whining, we all ended up ignobly sliding back down again, forced to bow to the enemies of off-roading: gravity and traction. The first and only team to make it up were the Japanese. Being first to try, they avoided the ever-deepening ruts and were poised at the top of the hill, waiting for our next move.

Putting our heads together, we struck upon a labor intensive, but workable plan. We would stage the three Japanese Willys that had made it up the hill, a hundred feet apart, so that they would be anchored together like one massive ski lift. The downside was the twenty vehicles that had to be winched a foot at a time up the precipitous slope. A quick calculation told us that it would take about 40 minutes per vehicle, and this was just the first hill of three ahead.

The drenching rain had turned the hill into a mass of gelatinous slime. It was almost impossible to walk, let alone drive. I was trying to carry a heavy steel cable up the hill. I'd get halfway up and then slither down again to the bottom. On hands and knees, I dragged the cable up to the Japanese team's truck. Finally, I could slide down the hill without swearing, and actually enjoying the rich dark mud.

Slowly, with motors revving, mud flying and everyone yelling directions in different languages, we pushed and shoved the vehicles from winch to winch. Then we ran the mud-caked cable to the next vehicle waiting at the bottom of the hill. After the vehicles came over the hill, we joined, muddy and tired, at the bottom of the next hill to repeat the process. Although we were from different countries, we worked as a team, sliding and cursing good naturedly as we pulled up vehicle after vehicle. Far away from the winching bridges, we could hear the sounds of the jungle.

As the night wore on, people began to fall asleep in their vehicles. We were still confined to the narrow roadway that hugged the mountains. At about 3:00 a.m., with most people asleep, we decided to press on since the continuous rain might wash out a bridge we had yet to cross. It is tricky enough to negotiate windy mountain roads in daylight, but in the dark, in the pouring rain, half asleep, well, that is something to experience.

All I could see through my fogged-up windshield were raindrops and flying mud glistening in the dim light of the flickering headlights. Then the two miserable headlights began blinking on and off, turning every blind corner into a game of Russian roulette. All that kept us from driving over the cliff edge was our trancelike adherence to the deep ruts of the vehicles in front.

In one sense, what you don't know won't hurt you. Our maps were rudimentary and our faith completely in the hands of our organizers ahead of us, who had traversed the course months earlier going in the opposite direction. We could only hope they would not drive off the road, since we would be sure to follow.

What could stop us now? Well, because the route had been plotted the opposite way in daylight, junctions that had made perfect sense were now invisible. Simply put, we were lost. The convoy bunched up on the precarious cliff-side road. We figured if we were lost, it would be better not to continue driving blindly into the night.

Building bridges was a peculiar joy of the Japanese teams.

We decided to camp where we stood, literally. "Stood" is an appropriate word, since there was barely enough room for the vehicles in single file. Most people slept upright in their seats. I spent the rest of the night trying to get a couple of hours sleep in our cramped Land Rover cab. Just before dawn, the chatter of birds roused me. I pried myself out of the cab to watch the sun come up. Limping stiffly between the vehicles, I made my way to the edge of the cliff. It had stopped raining and I was treated to a spectacular view of Mount Kinabalu shrouded in mist. We were up high above an ocean of low-lying fog. As the sun turned the 12,000 foot mountain glorious shades of red, pink and yellow, the camp slowly came to life. One by one, the men stretched and groaned as they added their contribution to the evening rainfall. The disheveled appearance of our expedition gave new meaning to the words: cold, tired and dirty.

On the side of the road, I noticed what looked like a discarded rag start to move. It turned out to be the deflated tent of the photographer from Italy. When asked how he slept, he paused, carefully searching for the correct words to describe both his appearance and demeanor. His reply, "I think that I am a dog."

When we recced to determine our location, we discovered that, by some stroke of luck, we had stopped at the exact junction we were looking for. Impossible to see in the dark, it was down a steep embankment and across a low bridge that had survived the evening's deluge.

We were off again—this time, sore, stiff and with a little less faith in our leaders. The sun shone brilliantly on the third day. The mounting heat quickly dried three days of rain-soaked mud into a hard-packed trail. Today was hot, very hot. Soon the hard-packed mud became a fine dust that drifted into the air, clinging to sweat, covering cameras, dusting hair and eyebrows and filling noses. Surgical masks were handed out to prevent the formation of large blocks of concrete in our lungs, but they were useless against the fine, choking dust.

We were back in active logging areas. Large dust clouds heralded the arrival of the mammoth logging trucks that sent us scurrying into ditches. We were to see our fill of these behemoths over the next few days—battered, overloaded Nissans, Toyotas and Mercedes, easily identified by the twin trails of water used to continuously cool their brakes, and driven at high speeds by ever- smiling, miniscule drivers.

Most logging roads are temporary and are washed out every year.

Poring Hot Springs

Our next destination was Poring Hot Springs. This hot mineral springs is situated in a lush tropical forest also famous for being home of the rafflesia, the world's largest flower. As we arrived in this welcome outpost of civilization, we jockeyed for the few available beds. Hot showers were first on the list, a cold drink was second. Tomorrow we would explore the park and carry out any maintenance and repairs on our vehicles.

Later that evening, we discovered that the trouble-prone Volvo military transport and the overloaded Land Rover 109 carrying some journalists has not come in yet. The Japanese sacrificed a soft bed and a good night's sleep to head back into the jungle to retrieve the lost vehicles. It seemed the Volvo did break down but was repaired and waiting with the Land Rover. The 109 was not so fortunate. In a freak series of mishaps, it had been stranded by a broken half-shaft, burned out its wiring and tipped on its side, emptying out all the fuel. The only consolation was while they were in their second night of splendid, but weary, isolation one of the journalists claimed to have sighted a *Tapirus indicus*, the rare Malay tapir, supposedly only found on the mainland. I also knew that the Swede, who was with them all night is known to maintain a well stocked bar at all times, even under the most grueling conditions. We assumed what they actually saw was a wild pig.

The next morning the tired, tattered and grimy journalists pulled up in their refueled Land Rover. While they caught up on their sleep, the rest of us explored an impressive new addition to the park; a series of aluminum walkways suspended high above the jungle floor built with funds from the Smithsonian Institute. An excellent concept on paper that might give most tourists pause as they find themselves dangling hundreds of feet above the ground suspended only by thin wires on flimsy aluminum walkways! To show us how well the walkway was constructed, one of the guides climbed over the side and hung by a cable until we told him we had enough pictures.

The jungle floor tends to be dark and very bleak. Most of the activity and color are found in the canopies of the 100–300 foot hardwood trees. Although the canopy is truly the zoo of the jungle, the forest floor also has some interesting denizens: well-adapted creatures like the dreaded leeches of Borneo. We saw our first leeches close up while we were casually sitting on a fallen log. Leeches actually stand on their hind sections "sniffing" out their next meal. They then inch along as fast as their slimy little bodies will take them and attach themselves to the first exposed fleshy spot they can find. They will drill through your socks, climb all the way up your pants, and even hitch a ride in your shoes to get you.

After a refreshing day viewing the orchid gardens and hot springs, we were back on the road. Back to the grind of off-roading the remaining distance to Kuching and back to our Keystone Cops mode; driving like madmen trying to make our rendezvous points or sitting for hours waiting for the last vehicle to catch up. We were also shuffling journalists since no provision had been made to transport them and their luggage. Directions and convoy rules were fuzzy, bordering on useless.

A leisurely drive through the final stages in Sarawak.

By now we were becoming used to the long days of driving. Spectacular scenery was becoming commonplace, cliff-hanging roads, endless vistas of mist-shrouded jungle, constant flailing through mud and rivers was becoming just another bumpy commute. We were longing for the peace and silence of the jungle without mechanized transport.

The end of the expedition was feted with much celebration and speeches. Having the unusual perspective of seeing the entire country in a two week period made me hunger for more—to go deeper into forests and higher into the mountains and to hopefully spend more time just sitting and watching this magical place.

We had crossed Borneo too fast, too easily and I was determined to do it right.

Sabah

Mt Kinabalu

Welcome to the wild east of Borneo. One can imagine America in the 1890s having much of the appeal of Sabah in the 1990s. Tattooed ex-head-hunters stroll down hastily constructed towns next to young Chinese businessmen on their cellular phones. Air-conditioned shopping malls are minutes away from the virgin rainforest. Towering mountains, dark swamps, massive caves and animals are all within a half-day's drive of the main city, Kota Kinabalu. Not as exotic as Sarawak, more rugged than the mainland and more compact than Kalimantan, Sabah is home to an industrious and forward thinking people. Everyone seems to have business here; hotels and transportation are expensive, designed more for business travelers than tourists. The road system is evolving from logging roads to paved highways and tourism is a relatively new but rapidly growing industry.

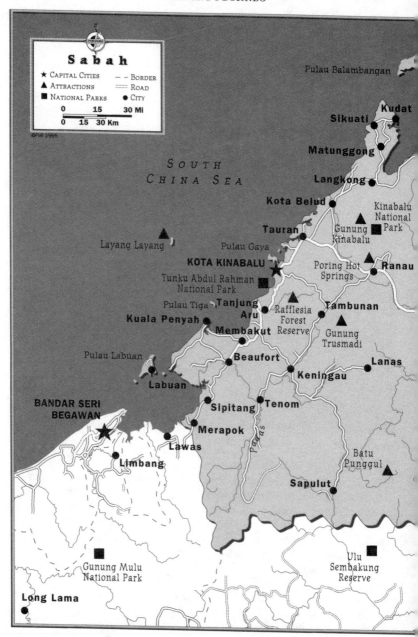

There are many fortunes to be made here in the next decade and it seems exporting raw resources will probably be one of the most popular—if not so by the environmentalists. So you better be fast if you want to discover the mythical, verdant island of Borneo. They are cutting the great canopy forests down as fast as they can. The only hope is that the impact of tourism will provide an alternative source of income to slow the rapid loss of one of the world's great ecosystems.

I don't recommend driving around Sabah unless you have a sturdy 4WD vehicle, a good guide and don't mind eating dust and dodging logging trucks. Traveling by air is recommended and Malaysian Air Service usually has a special fare for travel between airports in Sabah and Sarawak. Once you arrive, taxis can be hired for an entire day. Taxi drivers will take care of your luggage, recommend bad restaurants and laugh at your jokes. Local tour operators are also a good deal since they usually are just like you (and your companions) and prefer to avoid nasty surprises (like getting lost on new logging roads).

Sabah is actively seeking adventure travelers, and the region has hosted a number of international events such as the Trans Borneo, Raid Gauloises and the Camel Trophy.

Sabah, whose coastline stretches 1440 kilometers, washed by the Sulu and Celebes Seas on the west and the South China Sea in the east, is often referred to as the "Land Below the Wind" because of its location beneath the typhoon belt. Sabah's general terrain is mountainous with lush tropical rainforests known to be the oldest in the world.

History of Sabah

Sabah was and is still very much a frontier. The major port cities were the entry to the dark interior. Like Sarawak and Brunei, Sabah was an ill-defined area that provided raw materials to Chinese traders. Charles Lee Moses, the American consul to Brunei, took advantage of this and obtained the rights to exploit the area from the Sultan of Brunei. This lease was flipped between Asian, Austrian, English and Italian interests until the English trader Alfred Dent ended up with absolute ownership of British North Borneo between 1881 to 1946. The sultan of Sulu (or Sooloo) in the Philippines didn't see eye to eye with this since he also claimed domain over the uncharted area much as the Sultan of Brunei laid claim to vague areas east and west of his capital.

To show their displeasure, the Sulu sultan's relative, Mat Sallah, and the Bajau and Murut people loyal to him, began a fairly successful uprising between 1896 until Sallah was killed in 1900. Despite this bloody but eventually unsuccessful revolt at the turn of the century, British North Borneo was very British and very colonial. Browsing through old issues of the British *North Borneo Herald* there is little news about the uprising or the state of the world in general. Instead there are stories of dog stealing, rogue elephants, bird nest smuggling, rewards posted for the capture of a man-eating crocodile and even a story about a king cobra that was killed in the dining room. Turn of the century British North Borneo was very much a frontier outpost. The abolition of headhunting, sea monsters dragged out of the ocean, murdered missionaries, the revolution in the nearby Philippines and piracy were major concerns. Topics of the day included the correctness of branding coolies, how to care for pianos in the tropical heat and how to prevent beri beri, malaria and other tropical diseases. Timber was the major export, with Sandakan the main port for its export. Back then, much of the primary forest was used to build the Chinese rail system, chiefly for railroad ties. The logged areas were planted with rubber and tobacco plantations. Today oil palms from West Africa sprout up on clear cut land.

Sabah's wealth came from exporting oil, gutta percha, coconuts, hemp, tea, oil, rubber, tobacco and timber.

After the quelling of the revolt in 1900 there was another uprising of the Muruts in 1915 that was put down quickly and brutally. For the most part Sabah's major enemies then became pirates, fires and boredom. Kudat was the first capital but repeated attacks by pirates forced a move to Sandakan in 1884 and then to Kota Kinabalu (formerly Jesselton) after WWII when there was literally nothing left of Sandakan due to the skilled bombing raids against the Japanese occupier.

It is a credit to Sabahans' industriousness that the history of North Borneo was relatively uneventful until the arrival of the Japanese on Pulau Labuan on New Year's Day in 1942.

The Japanese were extremely brutal in their treatment of captured soldiers and locals, particularly the Chinese who were punished severely for their uprising against the Japanese in Jesselton and Labuan. The most infamous event in Borneo was the Death March where only six out of 2400 Australians survived the forced march from Sandakan to Ranau. Borneo was thrust into the global spotlight on September 9, 1945 when the Japanese surrendered on Pulau Labuan.

After the war both Sarawak and British North Borneo became crown colonies of Britain. This arrangement prevented Indonesia from destabilizing and eventually gobbling up the tiny areas into its vast archipelago. Indonesia had always wanted the entire island of Borneo for extending its reach into what it felt was its domain. *Konfrontasi* was the Indonesian word for its displeasure with Singapore's and Malaysia's meddling. Over 60,000 British

Ghurka, and Australian troops were stationed along the border with Kalimantan and fought bloody skirmishes with the Indonesian Army between 1963 and 1966. The war was not widely publicized but accounts for the large military presence found along the border between Sabah and Kalimantan. Fellow expedition organizers and myself have tried for years to set up a Sabah-Kalimantan crossing but animosity still prevents this. It has only been in the last two years that border crossing restrictions have been relaxed.

After Sabah and Sarawak joined the Malaysian federation in August of 1963, there was a backlash against Peninsular Malays now controlling what was essentially a Chinese dominated region. Low level guerilla war supported by the Chinese was waged primarily in Sarawak but created tension between ethnic Chinese and Malays throughout Malaysian Borneo, Brunei and Singapore. Business leaders in Singapore saw the advantage of a Chinese run area as vast as Borneo. The steady push by the Malays in Kuala Lumpur has not been accepted by the mostly Christian Sabahans either. Outside influences increased the pressure until race riots broke out in 1964 and in August 9, 1965 Singapore was ousted from the Malaysian Federation and became an independent country.

There is still quite a distance between KK and Kuala Lumpur. Only five percent of oil revenues from Sabah trickle back into the state and it was only recently that the KL based government broke the Kadazan and Christian political resistance against long term goals for Malaysia. Today the man in charge in Sabah is really Dr. Mahathir Mohammed, leader of the ruling UNMO party. He is a tough voice against the Western world's demand for conservation of resources. He has made Malaysia one of the fastest growing countries in the world and continues to look to Singapore and other local sources for funding in his ambitious plans. His policy of creating opportunities for Malays over the interests of Indian, Chinese and native interests have been widely criticized and do not make him popular in Sabah. In fact, in Sabah conversion to Islam is rewarded with a cash payment. Today Sabahans quite rightly believe that Mahathir is building success for Malaysia on the back of Borneo's petroleum, palm oil, timber and minerals. They would like a larger share of Malaysia's new success. Today, most of the industrial development to replace natural resources is still concentrated on the mainland.

Sabah's traditional defiance of the Malay government ended when Jeffery Kitingan was arrested as a seccessionist conspirator and was accused of bleeding $1.5 billion from the Sabah Foundation. His brother, Joseph, the chief minister, was also charged with corruption. The entire PartiBersatu Sabah, the only Christian political party to hold power, evaporated in the 1994 elections. The chief minister is now a Muslim, Tan Sri Sakaran Dandai, and it remains to be seen what benefits this will bring Sabah.

The People of Sabah

The people of Sabah differ greatly from the people of Kalimantan or Sarawak. They all speak languages from a common root: Dusunic. They are primarily slash and burn cultivators and grow rice. Kadazan is the term used to describe these peoples. There are also large groups of Filipino immigrants and Timorese who are for the most part illegal immigrants. The Chinese are well represented, but they comprise a much smaller presence than in Sarawak.

Getting In

The best time to visit Sabah is the dry season between May to September. Although you probably will travel from Malaysia or Singapore, Sabah wants to plant its own stamps in your passport. The major airport is Kota Kinabalu. Cruise passengers will disembark at Sandakan and travelers from Sarawak will pass through Pulau Labuan or Sandakan.

From	Flights	Cost	Via
VIA AIR TO KOTA KINABALU			
BRUNEI			
Brunei	3 weekly	**M$117**	**Royal Brunei**
HONG KONG			
Hong Kong	3 weekly	**M$650**	**Dragon Air**
Hong Kong	2 weekly	**M$650**	**MAS**
INDONESIA			
Tarakan	3 weekly	**M$185**	**Bouraq**
Tarakan	2 weekly	**M$210**	**MAS**
MALAYSIA			
Johor Bahru	4 daily flights	**M$347**	**MAS**
Kuala Lumpur	7 daily flights	**M$437**	**MAS**
Kuching	6 daily flights	**M$228**	**MAS**
Labuan	5 daily	**M$52**	**MAS**
Lahad Data	3 daily	**M$106**	**MAS**
Lawas	1 weekly	**M$47**	**MAS**
Limbang	2 weekly	**M$60**	**MAS**
Kudat	2 weekly	**M$50**	**MAS**
Miri	5 daily	**M$104**	**MAS**

From	Flights	Cost	Via
Sandakan	5 daily	M$83	MAS
Tawau	5 daily	M$96	MAS
PHILIPPINES			
Manila	3 weekly	M$472	Philippine Airlines
Manila	daily	M$500	MAS
SINGAPORE			
Singapore	daily	M$419	MAS
VIA BOAT			
BRUNEI			
Leave from Customs & Immigration Station			
Labuan	3 daily	M$25	
Lawas	daily 11:30am	M$25	
Limbang	frequent daily	M$10	
INDONESIA			
Tarakan- Tawau	2 -3 weekly		Ferry
PHILIPPINES			
Zambaongo	Private Charter		Note: This is illegal
VIA LAND			

There are no legal land connections between Indonesia and Sabah.

Getting Around

The best way to see Sabah is with a tour or a guide. The labyrinth of logging roads are off limits to most travelers but a local can get permission to travel on most. Be forewarned that there are few road signs and even the most experienced still can get lost.

Air

The best way to get around Sabah is by MAS. Inquire about specials MAS offers when you book your return ticket to Malaysia. You can usually get a special ticket that lets you travel internally much cheaper than if you decide to do it later. The Malaysian Airlines are modern (usually *Boeing 737s, Twin Otters* or *Fokker F-27s*) but with one maddening frustration. You must reconfirm your flight 72 hours before departure or you will be automatically bumped. This can wreak havoc if you are disappearing into the jungle for long periods of time and emerging hours before your flight leaves. The best solution is to stop in at any local MAS office, chat up the friendly agents and explain your situation. Most are happy to show that you have reconfirmed. Worst case, ask about cancellations or first class seats when you show up at the airport. Like most of Southeast Asia the airlines fly at full capacity and reservations are a necessity. You can book your tickets through travel agents for no extra costs.

Airline offices in KK

MAS, *Kompleks Karamunsing* ☎ *(088) 213555*
There is also a MAS office at the airport. Open 5 am to 7pm daily

Philippines Airlines, *Kompleks Karamunsing* ☎ *(088) 239600*

Cathay Pacific, *Kompleks Kuwasa* ☎ *(088) 54733*

Royal Brunei Airlines *Kompleks Kuwasa* ☎ *(088) 242193*

Singapore Airlines, *Kompleks Kuwasa* ☎ *(088) 55444*

Thai Airlines, *Kompleks Kuwasa* ☎ *(088) 232896*

Train

Borneo's only train is an ancient affair (circa 1902) that travels between Beaufort and Tenom. Ideal for a tourist outing, the train leaves Beaufort at 8:25 a.m. and 3:50 p.m. and makes its way along the Padas River until it reaches its other terminus only two hours and fifteen minutes later. The trip costs $8.35 and is well worth it. The return journey from Tenom to Beaufort is at 6:40 a.m. and 4 p.m. Other departures via cargo and diesel trains are not worth taking. Grab a seat up front and don't be surprised to see the engineer carrying a chainsaw to take care of any downed trees that often block the tracks. Buy your tickets at the station.

Rafting

There are rafting trips down the Padas River. Book the trip out of KK and expect a thrilling ride regardless of the water level (less water is better). The Padas River through Tenom Gorge is rated Class IV, the Kinabatangan River is Class II and III and the Papar is Class I and II. Api Tours in KK can set you up with a rafting trip. **Api Tours** *Lot 49, Bandaran Berjaya* ☎ *(088) 221230, FAX 212078.*

Helicopter

Expensive but unmatched in spectacle. Sabah Air rents out JetRangers starting at $250 an hour.

Four Wheel Drive

The chances of renting a four-wheel-drive and actually being able to find your way around Sabah by yourself are slim to none. Experienced guides can take you around the island and deal with the realities of winching, changing tires and repairs. Travel on logging roads requires prior permission, none of the roads are signed and there are no service facilities to speak of outside the towns. Although you can rent a heavy duty four-wheel-drive vehicle like the Land Cruiser (M$350 per day) from most car rental agencies in the large hotels and Wisma Sabah shopping center, be forewarned that the roads are very dangerous. Even if you are not fazed by ice-like mountain roads, washed out bridges, canyon sized potholes, deep river crossings or even the bewildering maze of logging roads, it pays to have a driver with a properly equipped vehicle. See list of car rental agencies below.

Cars

The roads in Sabah range from silky smooth, to rough dirt, to bone jarring asphalt nightmares. The Trans Sabah highway from Sandakan to Tawau is essentially islands of asphalt ringed with deep potholes. (Allegedly the contractor saved a few dollars by not putting in the proper road bed.) Driving on the better roads like the KK to Sandakan is smooth and efficient. The heavy downpours can make the going dicey and wipe out visibility as can the clouds that regularly obscure the higher roads. Although cars can be rented in KK, I would suggest sticking to taxis, local buses or aircraft. The fares are cheap and the scenery can be a little repetitious. You can rent Proton Sagas (M$150) a day from:

Ais

Lot 1 Block A Ground Floor, Sinsuran Kompleks, ☎ *(088) 238953*

Adaras Rent a Car

Lot G07, Ground Floor, Wisma Sabah, ☎ *(088) 222137*

Kinabalu Rent a Car

Hyatt Kinabalu International, ☎ *(088) 221234 or at the Tanjung Aru Beach resort* ☎ *(088) 58711*

Getting Out

"I am sorry, sir, your reservation has been cancelled."

I stared incredulously at the clerk; this cannot be. I just booked it two days ago. I needed to get from Sandakan to KK to catch my outbound flight to L.A. If I missed this leg I would be stuck in the damnation of cancellation hell, sitting at the airport waiting for cancellations all the way from KK to KL to Tokyo to Hawaii. The clerk solemnly spoke as if pronouncing sentence.

"I am sorry; you must reconfirm at least 72 hours in advance of your flight."

"How can I confirm a ticket three days in advance when I only booked it two days ago" I asked.

"I do not know sir, but this is our policy."

The long lines waiting to get on the plane stared at me patiently but with the air of watching the condemned being hanged. My discussion of logic, the modern calendar, common sense and pure pity could not move the adamant MAS clerk. I didn't confirm my ticket therefore I didn't have a reservation. After 20 minutes of trying to convince him of the relative inaneness of his stance, a simple thought struck me.

"Could you check to see if there are any seats available?" After a lengthy cross check tabulation he confirmed that, yes, there were plenty of seats. Would I like one?

This little story might save you mountains of grief. Airline employees tend to mindlessly follow the specific rules and regulations of the airlines. In the example above the first class section was also wide open with a surcharge of 20 dollars.

I bring this to your attention because if you miss a connecting flight and you are bumped, the chances of you getting a cancellation or a seat during the holidays will be slim.

On another note, you may come across ivory antiques, mounted butterflies, turtle shells and other exotic souvenirs. Keep in mind that these items will be confiscated if discovered upon your arrival back in the states. You will most likely go through customs in Hawaii where they have a good deal of experience in sniffing these out. Also if you are stopping over in Japan, remember that they too have stringent rules about the importation of certain protected animal parts.

Typical road conditions in the dry season

Batu Punggul

The Cave, The Rock,
And The Hunter

Flying over Borneo you can be lulled into the monotony of green below. Once in a while the green carpet will be slashed through by brilliant white limestone spires. The Salikularang Peninsula in Eastern Kalimantan, Mulu and Batu Punggul provides tantalizing glimpses into what awaits the intrepid explorer. Inspection from the air reveals twisted formations and ghoulish orifices in the cliffs. From the forest floor the explorer could wander for years without ever seeing these impressive structures. It is almost impossible to see these cliffs in the dense jungle, even when standing directly under them.

One unique formation that slices through the dense forest is Batu Punggul. Situated in a remote area of southeast Sabah, it is a spectacular combination of natural splendor, giant caves and cultural wonder, since there is now a Murut longhouse at the base of the rock. The Muruts are the hunters of Borneo—stolid, practical people who have taken up farming as their ancestral forest is destroyed.

To get there you drive on paved road through Tawau and then through unpaved logging areas to the town of Sapulut which marks the end of any passable road. Here we would meet our guide, Lantier, and take a boat to a Murut longhouse across the river from the rock.

There is not much to recommend the coastal or inland towns of Sabah. The usual exotic colors and elegant architecture of Asia are missing. Sabah is still a frontier. Life and architecture are utilitarian and transitory. What little heritage there was, got bombed into mud by the Japanese and then later by the Allies. There are towns like Keningau, logging towns where everything is covered with dust and great trucks rumble and clatter to the smoking sawmills that surround the gray town. Smaller habitations like Tawau are ancient seaports, sharp with the stench of sewage and rotted fish. Other towns like Tenom are just a confused jumble of dirty white boxes, tiny shops below tiny apartments above. Mud spattered, clattering four-wheel-drive vehicles abound. These boom towns are crawling with young people, Chinese, Indians, Malays, Muruts, Kadazans, even the occasional negroid-featured Timorese. The distinct smells of curry, ginger, cooking oil, diesel, sewage and sweat blend into the uniquely Asian smell. Here money is being made and the past being discarded in rapid bounds.

Once out of the main towns the forest seems to go on forever.

As we drove through the small towns and tiny *kampungs*, or villages, of Sabah we took in this squalid atmosphere of hanging laundry, scurrying roosters, multicolored pickup trucks and naked children interrupted by endless rows of plantations. Along the way we crossed narrow bailey bridges, dodged mangy dogs and waved at the shy, giggling girls with telltale, duck-like kampung feet. Less excited were the ever-burdened, gentle-faced old ladies and cheerful, chain smoking men with haircuts like Moe of the Three Stooges. The people are very placid considering that they are being forced fast-forward into a future that we have had 200 years to come to grips with.

Despite its rural and seemingly impoverished atmosphere, Sabah is doing just fine. These Muruts have come for the timber jobs. Many of these men have traveled for weeks to work. They will do their time in the timber camps, save their money and travel back to their families in Kalimantan and the remote regions of Sabah. They proudly lug home oversized radios, fans, TVs and other gifts just as they once arrived with severed sticky heads. Oil, timber and oil palm millionaires are here in abundance. There is little ostentatious wealth here and when the Chinese do display their wealth, it can be bizarre. One of my local acquaintances bought a perfectly good Range Rover, ripped the body off and plunked the top half of a Toyota Land Cruiser cab on top and then stuck in a massive truck diesel engine. Voila! The world's first Range Cruiser (or is it a Land Rover?) Inside was a hurricane sized air conditioning unit, refrigerator and every electronic gizmo the parts store could find. (If you look closely you will see young Chinese men carrying cellular phones and wearing gold Piaget watches and Polo golf shirts.) The owner of a simple shop may return to a palatial home and secretly count his gold at night. Thousands of dollars are spent in restaurants and on gambling and air-conditioned Japanese four-wheel-drives. Here there is enterprise in everything from rhino horns to birds' nests to timber. In Sabah money does grow on trees.

As you pass through the bustling commerce of the towns and the endless oil palm plantations you begin to understand the dynamics of Borneo. Here is a natural world ripe for the picking. Descending like locusts, opportunists strip the country of timber, leaving a jumble of patchwork plantations, substandard towns and leaving behind a nation of poor people wearing faded Batman T-shirts.

We wound our way from Tawau on the coast of the Sulu Sea past the plantations and into the freshly cut timber concessions. We turned off the main road to wind our way through the unmapped maze of logging roads that cut further every day into the forest.

Although I had been here a year ago, I could not recognize the landscape. Virgin forest was now shattered and all that was left was muddy ground; clear cut and naked. Before, you knew you were getting remote because the trucks only came at you down the mountain. Now overloaded logging trucks were hauling raw logs and passing fully loaded trucks, from both directions, which bore freshly processed two by fours. This meant there were no more frontiers in this part of Borneo.

We were lost in the web of new timber roads. When we stopped the drivers of the many beat-up, green pickup trucks, we got one set of directions. When we asked the timber workers, we got conflicting directions. Everyone we met had a different way to get out of the maze. Each person was right, since they drove in on their own road between the timber camp and the cut. They really didn't know where the other roads led. This too was an ominous sign that there were timber cutters encroaching from all sides.

Typical road conditions during the wet seasons.

I had visited this area three years ago when a new cut road had allowed us to visit a virgin stand of timber inhabited by elephants. We passed a road that I dimly remembered spending an entire night winching up on my Trans Borneo trip. Now it was a smoothly graded road, worn flat by bulldozers and polished by an endless procession of logging trucks.

The afternoon rain began to fall and the road was soon impassible to the great logging trucks. When it rains in Borneo the logging trucks stop dead while the drivers sleep. Traction is lost on the slippery mud and the over-taxed vehicles just slide right off the road. The drivers do not have doors on these trucks because they want to be able to jump clear. We made our way to Sapulut through a wasteland. Before, this had been jungle. Now, it was eroded dirt with a ragtag cover of weeds.

The end of the road was just past the village of Sapulut. The road begins bold and wide through the lowlands and then nervously winds along the edge of a mountain range, dips into a couple of streams and finally gives up when it meets the river. From this point on the river rules, as it has done forever in Borneo.

We started our trip to Batu Punggul at the village of Sapulut, staying at the KPD Agricultural rest house. We would be going upstream past the village of Tataluan to stay at the KPD (Korpeasi Perbangunan Desa which means "rural development corporation") resthouse in Batu Punggul. This was a poor area and the goal was to provide employment to the locals. The local people were expecting us and had promised to put on a do when we arrived.

Batu Punggul, one of the more dramatic limestone spires in Borneo, is a 600 plus foot limestone pillar which rises vertically from the riverside. Once an ancient reef bed, it was pushed up thousands of years ago and has been weathered into a tall delicate pinnacle that houses an impressive cave system that the rain has hollowed out inside.

Getting there is a three to six hour boat ride, depending on water levels. If the water is low there is a lot of pushing to get up the rapids. If it has been raining nonstop, the water level is extremely high and the river fast.

We boarded our large longboat and after a few adjustments to the seating positions, we were on our way. It was a pleasant trip as we passed longhouses along the river. Some were very well built with shingle roofs of *bilian* or ironwood, others looked like scrap heaps complete with rusted tin roofs. Along the way, there was a very large oxbow lake, where the passengers walk to the other bank of the river while the boatman blasts around the oxbow, then picks them up on the other side. It took us about five minutes on foot, but it took the boat about twenty minutes.

Batu Punggul

While we were waiting in a house in the village above the river we chatted with the owners. In the corner a young girl was bouncing a young baby like a yo-yo on a small hammock suspended by a bungie. Looking around the house we noticed a dead dove, a sleeping dog and three young fruit bats in wire cages. One bat was near death, breathing slowly and lying listlessly on its back. The others were twitching nervously as they hung upside down. We asked two young children if they liked bats. They rubbed their stomachs as if to say, "Yummy." We learned that these bats would be for dinner.

We inspected the baby bats. Unlike most bats, these fruit bats, or flying foxes were quite attractive. They looked very much like miniature dogs or foxes. They had a dull stare as if they were wearing dark goggles. (It is only when they sink their hooks into your arm in a desperate attempt to get themselves upside down again that you realize that they are indeed bats. When put on the ground, they drag themselves to the nearest suspension point with their sharp hooked front claws. Once suspended, they are happy. They wrap their heads in their membrane-like wings and flutter spastically until they are comfortable.) The people explained that the bats would be boiled whole, head, wings, lice, feet and all, in a broth with a garlic and ginger seasoning. Muruts consider this a delicacy but in my opinion it sounds as if it would taste like boiled thongs with a dash of gritty river water. We passed on the lunch special.

Back in the boat our trip resumed. The river narrowed and the jungle closed in. It was noticeably cooler. The rapids became more frequent. As we turned a corner, an impressive, giant white pillar of twisted, tortured limestone loomed over the river. This was Batu Punggul.

The Hunters: Another Long Night in a Longhouse

Before we climb to the summit we will spend an evening of celebration with our Murut hosts. Below Batu Punggul and across the river is a Murut longhouse reconstructed by the government in the traditional style. Constructed on stilts, there are two woven floors of bamboo slats. In the center is a *lansaran*, or a primitive trampoline, sort of a combination jungle gym/entertainment center. Here the Muruts chant monotonous songs, bang on gongs and compete to see who can jump the highest.

Tonight I ask the people if they can play some gong music before the festivities, which always includes extensive drinking. If there is a tune, I figure I can have a better chance of finding it while the musicians are sober. It turns out the music sounds a lot better when you're drunk. They begin to play a rhythmic tune with an interesting syncopation. After ten minutes I ask them to play another tune. At first, I think it is the same as the first. After five minutes of this version, they play a third. This time, I am pretty sure that the

Murut "top of the pops" consists of one song with three different names, sung three different ways.

The entrance to a longhouse is a notched pole that is taken up at night.

That evening people gather for the party. It begins with the guests taking deep drinks from the large brown *tapai* jars. There is a moment of foreboding because the rows of oddly matched ceramic jars look suspiciously like the Chinese burial jars the Murut use to bury and ferment their dead. My suspicions are confirmed when I inquire about the similarity. I remind myself to watch for lumps. Closer inspection yields some interesting details. First of all, there are ominous bubbles gurgling up from the depths of the brown jars. There is definitely something alive or dead in there. There is a round wooden disc which is mercifully shielding the view of what lays inside. A hole has been punched for a grass reed straw, and a notched indicator much like the old gas pumps you find in Midwestern towns tells the imbiber when it's time to pass out or pee.

Tapai is a traditional fermented rice wine made of cooked rice with yeast and a little beetroot. I perceive that the basic difference between *tuak* of Sarawak and *tapai* of Sabah (other than *tuak* can be made of fermented coconut) is the manner of consumption. Whereas *tuak* is served out of old, dirty bottles for single shots, *tapai* is consumed from huge earthen jars by straws in all night drinking contests. A *tapai* drinking bout is not for the faint hearted since there is a devious method to measure your consumption and the rice wine can be replenished indefinitely just by pouring in more brown river water.

Like all native hooch, *tapai* is easy to make. Rice and yeast are put into earthen jars, sealed and left to ferment ideally for a year but more typically for three to four weeks. Water from the river is added just before drinking and as the jar is drained, more and more water is added. The first sip is the killer since the jars have been percolating awaiting their first victim. As a guest in the longhouse, you are expected not only to have the first drink, but to show your prowess by seeing how many notches down the bamboo measuring stick you can drink without taking a breather. Three notches is respectable, two for tourists and one is an insult. Four notches will ensure heroic fame and liver failure, as well as fierce competition from your hosts. For this evening, people have come from all around to see the three crazy white men drink *tapai*. Their enthusiasm also stems from the fact *orang puti* have a reputation for being notorious pantywaists when it comes to consuming the odious fermentation. Their glee is also heightened by our having paid for this party with no hope of us leaving with a ceramic doggy bag.

The home chug-a-lug team gets ready to embarrass the visiting team.

After much ceremony and pompous blathering, the three of us (Coskun, Jon and myself) are commanded to sit facing the jars, bent over until our mouths reach the straws. Like a patient executioner, the headman measures to make sure that we are sitting just so and that everyone's jar is filled to the brim and that no one is cheating by pulling his stick up to expose the notches. The fact that he is giggling while doing this makes me nervous.

At the sound of the gong, a chant begins and the drinking commences. My first pull is a short exploratory one. My brain tells me I have just swallowed a mouthful of ice cold vomit and my stomach burns. Ignoring these signals I take a heavy duty pull. My tastebuds confirm the previous message and my brain pauses for further directions. The Muruts see the expressions on our faces and are laughing and patting each other on the back. I wonder whether they have substituted buffalo urine just to see the expressions on our faces. Jon, who is a veteran tapai drinker sits up, belches and compliments the headman on his *tapai*. I do my best to keep pace with the rest of the crew lined up at the jars. I keep my head down and pull the icy liquid into my protesting gut.

It is hard work. Not only trying to keep from throwing up, but to continuously pull at a straw without breathing. Every once in a while, a piece of rice jams the straw and must be backflushed. Not very sanitary, but effective. More doom for the next drinker. Not wanting to lift our heads, we take a cockeyed stare at each other's indicator to see who is ahead. Nobody's indicator has budged. After much tut tutting and insults, I manage to push the vile brine down only a notch and half. Jon is good for two while Coskun, a Muslim, finds new reason to strengthen his faith in the tenants of Islam and begs off.

The home team lines up and sucks at the jars, their friends clustered around shouting and cheering. They all manage two notches and I am beginning to think there's a trick to all this. The headman fills up the jars again by priming a funky garden hose that runs all the way to the river. Not sanitary but effective. Back for a second round, my head is beginning to spin so I go for distance rather than volume. The closer to the bottom you get, the more rancid and repulsive the brew tastes. At the end of round one, Jon Rees comes out a clear winner in the consumption race. His wife is Murut and he is definitely in his element now. I beg off at second place and the Muruts, thankful that we have consumed the foul first pressing, now descend on the tapai jars like mosquitoes in a hemophiliac's ward.

The dancing begins. The women enter dancing with delicate hand motions. I would describe it as similar to hand models selling Lee Press-on nails. Their hands flutter and wave in a very prim and proper dance, eyes downward. The men follow behind dancing as gracefully as the women. Then the headman dances with his head sword, and cap decorated with Argus pheasant and hornbill feathers. It is a gentle dance of death. Like a kung fu movie played in slow motion, he is telling a story of taking heads and hunting. The constant monotony of the gongs and the tai chi-like movements of the headman serve to remind us that he is a great hunter and has taken many heads.

Then the dancing begins on the *lansaran*. A *lansaran* is a uniquely Murut device. The uses of the *lansaran* are part entertainment, part religious and part betting pool. Down below the longhouse long, flexible trees are roped together to create what we would call a trampoline. It is surprisingly supple and flexible.

Men and women form a circle and rotate on the *lansaran* chanting back and forth as they invoke the spirits. Moving in a circular motion, they slowly pick up the pace and rhythm. They begin to jump in unison to keep rhythm. Later the men of the longhouse will try their skill at jumping. There is a decorated stick hanging high above the *lansaran*. Guests tie money to it to see if anyone can jump high enough to claim it. Four men, one at each corner, crouch down and catapult a man in the center as high as they can. You can jump as high as six feet doing this. The money is lowered as each person fails until finally one man claims it. I managed to reach the money in a previous *lansaran* bout but politely left the money for a local to win. The fact that I am 6 foot 4 inches tall, gives me a decided edge on the diminutive Muruts. The trick is to pump the *lansaran,* and then when you stop, the motion throws the central "missile" man in the air. It is all a matter of timing and being about two feet taller than our guests.

The dancing begins.

The guests must now dance as is the custom in all longhouses. Being somewhat of a veteran, I do my best imitation of the headman's dance. I dream I am a rooster. Then I give them my best tourist headhunter dance. The headman provides his sword, with a gentle warning that only he can unsheathe the aged blade. I do my best, "sneaking-up-on-and-decapitating-thousands-of-victims," dance. Despite my serious attempt the audience laughs and claps at the antics of a fool. During the dance I am aware of another difference between longhouses. Unlike the more robust Kenyah or Iban floors made of rock hard bilian wood, the Murut longhouse floor is constructed of delicately woven bamboo in two layers. I find myself crunching through the top layer and am trying to avoid falling completely through the floor every time I stomp. I have already crashed one leg through a section to find that it is twenty feet straight down. Thankfully, the sharp ends of the bamboo grasped my leg like a Chinese finger trap and all I got were a few slices.

We are all dragged up one after another. Jon does a good job but since he weighs about 220 lbs. and has had a significantly greater amount to drink, the sound of the crunching floor is most alarming. Coskun does a cross between a belly dance and a hula. I wonder who is going to rethatch the floor in the morning.

Sometime during the night Jon urges me to taste *gerok*. Described as a "local delicacy" I should have known better. The alcohol must have subdued the screaming sound my brain was making. By now I have learned that any "local delicacy" is guaranteed to be inedible and sure to provide hours of merriment for the hosts when the traveller actually eats the offered atrocity. Tonight seems to be my night for unique taste experiences. Lovers of *gerok*, know that it is merely rancid beef that has been packed into a bamboo tube along with some vile concoction, buried in the ground and left to fester until the owner is drunk enough or hungry enough to dig it up. Muruts love it and I am sure that along with oysters, beer and durians all real adventurers will learn to love it too. My first taste actually reinforced my preliminary mental image that it would be similar to eating a decayed corpse that had drowned in a vat of brine. To this day I shudder when I think of eating *gerok*.

Unlike the tender, almost mystical night with the Iban, this night is a "plain ole" house party. Lots of shouting, banging on things and excessive consumption of alcohol were the centerpiece. I have a suspicion the strident gong music is to prevent the participants from lapsing into a coma from drinking too much. The brief silences while the musicians took their turn drinking from the jars, seem like symphonies.

The gongs continue throughout the night. I have a theory that the lack of wildlife in Borneo might be due to the high suicide rates amongst animals here. If I were a rhino I would prefer extinction to listening to Muruts partying all night. Finally, at some predawn senseless moment, we steal away and half stagger/half fall down the slippery notched pole that is supposed to keep marauding headhunters out. As we leave our hosts, people sleep in haphazard fashion in their rooms and in the main party area the stalwart few keep topping off the jars and sucking them dry.

The lansaran is a combination home entertainment center and jungle gym for the Muruts.

The next morning we can smell the sour stench of *tapai* and urine outside the longhouse. The party continues until 3 p.m. the next day when the *tapai* and fellowship finally cannot be stretched any further. The gong music mercifully ceases and the peace returns to the surrounding jungle. We spend the day recovering from the evening/late morning revelry and rebuild our liver cells by sleeping.

After showering in the simple resthouse that night, I find that I have roommates: two very shy, but very large (four- and five-inch) spiders, night wasps and bees are crawling on the floor. If you step on a night wasp you will know it. The experience is described as being similar to having a three-inch red-hot nail driven through your foot. There are various species of ants, some sedentary watching curiously, some busily commuting across beams and walls. The two other residents are a mother cat and a day-old kitten sitting on top of the crude dresser. They call out to each other during the night oblivious to my need for sleep and recovery. There is much calling back and forth until thankfully they are reunited.

The Rock

The next day our goal is to climb to the summit of the great white rock, Batu Punggul. The rock is a constant fixture of this area. Peeking over the jungle canopy in the morning, it reveals itself like a coquette as the mists gently wrap and unwrap it from sight. In the middle of the day it stares down hard, it's white light illuminating the dark jungle like a fill light on a movie set. At dusk it is a spooky blue silhouette lurking over the river.

Batu Punggul is actually a large ridge of karst limestone punctured by caves.

We set off across the river into the wet darkness of the jungle below the rock. It is muddy here and there are great limestone boulders that have tumbled down from the cliffs above us. Creepers and vines snake around the rocks, seemingly the only thing holding them together since there is little soil under the leaf litter. The cracks, splits and crevices support trees and moss with the rainfall they catch. We need an early start because climbing the rock too late in the day will fry us like an egg if we are caught between the equatorial sun and the dazzling white limestone.

As is typical of karst topography, any time there are limestone outcrops, there are sure to be caves. It is difficult to find them in the jungle since the openings may be tiny slits or buried under rubble. As we skirt the base of the cliffs below Batu Punggul, we can smell the caves before we see them. The sharp smell of bat droppings carried on the damp breeze that comes from the cool interior of the rock, leads us to the opening.

Caves have the unmistakable odor of fear and darkness. We climb higher slipping on the slick roots and wet mud. The cave is large and leads down into a shallow grotto. There is little evidence of animals. We push back further into the dark cave and hear the swoosh of swallows narrowly missing our heads. Trusting that they can navigate better than we can, we do not bother to duck. After I get a sharp flick in the ear, I realize that I am confusing their visual navigational ability with the more precise sonar of bats. I decide to duck next time. Using the beam of our powerful Mag-Lite flashlight, I inspect the swallows in their teacup-sized nests high above.

Above us there are dark crescents with a constant stir and chatter from disturbed birds. These are low quality nests compared to the highly prized crystalline type. The black nests, which have a higher concentration of saliva are only worth about one tenth what the white nests fetch The white nests are usually built high on the roof of the cave and are composed of almost pure saliva. These are also the inedible mossy nests, not the highly prized nests of the swiftlets used for bird's nest soup. These have a small amount of crystalline saliva used to adhere the sticks, branches, feathers and moss of the nest to the cave wall. At eye level the birds calmly watch us as we inspect their tiny homes. Next to our head sits a six-inch spider, also calmly watching us.

The cave leads us back, lower and lower. Some rooms are small antechambers with no exits, but one leads into a large cool chamber. The flashlight reveals that the roof is about a hundred feet high with a small crack of light. It takes on the atmosphere of the Sistine Chapel with a bold, single shaft of light illuminating the wall. Here bats circle noisily, uncomfortable with our presence. We discover a single, thin stone standing on edge. When we ask our guide what it is, we are told it is an ancient grave marker, but no one knows who put it there. We are also told that the Muruts believe that these caves were once longhouses and were turned to stone. Their belief is based on the existence of a large wooden beam in the roof of one of the big caves.

We press on to the big cave, Batu Tinahas. Circling higher along the cliff wall, we pass tiny portholes with strong blasts of ammonia gases. We descend into a gaping hole in the side of the rock. This entrance is protected by a single spikelike stalactite at the entrance. Beyond this Damoclean guard is a curtain-like wall suspended from five to a hundred feet up. Colored in greens, rust and ocher, it almost appears that someone has painted the walls in an attempt to decorate the entrance.

We pause in the entrance to let our eyes adjust to the light. Compared to the last cave, this one is massive. The delayed echoes of dripping water make the cave seem endless. We begin the hike into the cave. I jump forward onto what appears to be a dark dirt floor and sink two feet into a wet black muck. I have sunk into pure bat shit. My eyes slowly make out moving forms around my knees. There are thousands of cockroaches and centipedes crawling in and out of the black guano. The combination of water seeping through the roof and the soft bat droppings, makes the world's best fertilizer. Properly "bat-ptized," my shoes and pants black and rank, I press on into the dank interior. Any one with a phobia for crawly insects may think twice about exploring the caves of Borneo.

As we push into the cave, we can understand just how vast this one cavern is. It is at least 400 feet wide by 600 feet long. Towards the back I enter through what looks like arches from a dungeon. It is another chamber. This one looks like a set from the movie *Alien*, or the royal chamber of a medieval castle. A hole high above sends a shaft of light down to illuminate what could be a throne. Around the lower edges are small keyholes, as in an old castle, that let in air and light. The bat guano is deeper here, and we are surrounded by agitated bats and swallows. Up above, where the flashlight beam begins to dim, are the remains of the highly prized crystalline swallows nests.

Through the second chamber lies a third chamber. This one steps down and comes out on the other side of the rock. The cave outlet here forms a small walled garden. Here I come across two unusual plants that look like mottled green snakes with a palm tree at the top. These are *phallus Lambii*, named for Tony Lamb, who we spent some time with in the Maliau. We make our way back through the caves and come into the fresh air and sunlight.

We decide that even though it is late now, we will still attempt to climb the rock. Not only will we have seen it from afar, we will have seen it from within and then from above.

Up the Rock

Climbing the mammoth rock is not that daunting. Many people have climbed Batu Punggul without incident. Most of them were probably hung over. The important thing our guide Lantier tells us, is to take your time, observe the flower species and do not attempt the climb in the middle of the day. Naturally, by the time we leave the caves, we are in a hurry and it is the middle of the day.

The base is scaled with the help of thick ropes, but once past the first hundred feet there is no shortage of handholds. The limestone face is weathered and honed to a lacerating edge. The best description of our climb that day would be to imagine climbing a hill of razor blades under a magnifying glass in the Sahara. The serrated ridges cut through hands, shoe bottoms and clothes. Thankfully the heat of the rock can be used to cauterize many of the cuts. We press the deeper cuts against the hot limestone and voilà, instant suture and congealed cuts. This cooktop environment is a strange place in which to find flowering plants, mosses and lichens. The daily rains run down the barren rock and collect in pockets. Here tiny plants cling for life in this little insulated crotch of moss and coolness. These islands of green also make us slip, sliding along until our arms or legs are stopped dead by a crisp scalpel of thin limestone. Climbing the rock, we get used to constantly wiping the stinging sweat from our eyes with our blood-soaked and torn shirt.

Hornbill skull

As we gingerly pull ourselves over a ridge, we realize we are finally on the top. The peak is a few yards away. The top of the rock is a group of pinnacles sharpened like Indian arrowheads, forcing us to jump from point to point.

Our guide cautions me to be careful as I nonchalantly leap over a four foot gap.

The reconstructed longhouse at Batu Punggul

Wondering what made that leap any different than the others, I go back for a peek. Through the crack I can see almost 200 feet straight down to the tops of trees below. The rock is like a great cracked arch with a huge cavity in the middle. The two pieces of the great rock meet in a sparkplug-thin gap at the top that has claimed at least two lives. We are told that a Murut girl had attempted the leap and fell to her death on the sharp rocks below. When her boyfriend tried to help her, he too fell to his death. They are still there if you care to look for them (if the story is true.)

As I look down on the canopy 600 feet below, I am learning that one part of Sabah can look pretty much like any other. A dark green ocean extends in every direction. Down below, the brown river snakes through the green. We cannot see the longhouse or any sign of habitation, yet we are dangling almost directly over it. A breeze cools the sweat of our soaked clothes. A small native canoe appears on the river briefly then disappears into the soft covering. This a scene from a hundred years ago.

I gingerly make the descent, hoping not to tear open my many freshly sealed wounds. My once new canvas high-tops are black from bat crap and shredded like a bag lady's second pair of gloves.

Lantier, Jon and I make it down to the bottom where Coskun has opted to catch forty winks, still recovering from our previous good times.

That night we have *opikayu*, or tapioca leaves and *pakus*, or ferns—a staple meal of the Muruts and quite tasty. A squeezed lime and red chiles add a nice balance to the tedium of boiled jungle plants and rice. We ask Lantier, our guide, about the legend of Batu Punggul. He tells us a long and convoluted story about a Murut boy, his girlfriend across the river, a leech, a dog, a chicken and a giant block of ice dropped on them for making fun of the leech. He apologizes at the end of the lengthy story explaining that even he doesn't know what the legend means. We figure we'll have to let this tale stretch and age a bit before it can entertain the out-of-towners.

Lantier decides to celebrate by hooking up a TV and VCR brought in for the occasion. A truck battery charged by a tiny portable generator is pressed into service as the Muruts sit enthralled by an Indonesian kung fu movie. Even after running the movie for the fourth time, they still scream with laughter at the same jokes and yell in surprise at the same points as hundreds of bad guys (who wear black) are beaten into submission by the false-mustachioed-sound-effects-assisted hero (who wears white). As the evening rains pour down, the generator begins to waiver and then expires. As the movie plays for the fifth time, the battery valiantly does its best to power these modern inventions. But, the hero disappears mid-kick and we are plunged into darkness and the eternal sound of the jungle.

Batu Punggul

2–4 hrs by boat from Sapulut

Batu Punggul is an impressive sight as it looms out of the mist. The 200m-high white rock is a massive ridge of karst that is punctured by **spectacular caves** and fissures. There are also a variety of jungle walks. You can climb the rock (leave early!) or explore the impressive caves. If you're squeamish about wading in about 1–2 feet of bat droppings, cockroaches, spiders or bats, you may want to pass. The caves are large, open to the light and very interesting. Recently opened to visitors is a KPD (Korperasi Pembangunan Desa or local development agency) rest house. There is also a very nice replica of a Murut longhouse.

Batu Punggul   ★ ★ ★

(Across the river via suspension bridge.)
A sheer limestone outcrop that looks like a pinnacle but is actually part of a long ridge. Surrounded by virgin forest, it is a dramatic experience. If the forest and the peak weren't enough, the ridge is full of large dramatic caves.

Batu Tinaha   ★ ★ ★

(About 20 minutes from Batu Punggul)
The most impressive cave in Sabah. There are a series of chambers that look like they were part of a sci-fi movie set or medieval throne room. Up above swiftlets build nests and bats come up at dusk. The caves have not been fully explored and it is known that there are at least three levels of caves here.

Getting in

Arrange a tour at KPD, Inanam at the corner of Jalan Tuaran and Jalan Kelombong; ☎ *(088) 428910*, ext. *240*. If you can get to Sapulut there may be a chance to arrange a boat up the river. It's actually cheaper to book a tour. They typically like to book the tour for groups so they can drag the nearby villagers up to put on a cultural show for you. The villagers and their *tapai* or rice wine party fuel will cost you M$15 per head. After you have done your obligatory *taipai* chugging contest and made a fool out of yourself on the *lansaran* (an ingenious native trampoline), they will leave you in relative peace as the villagers polish off the rest of the rice wine. Boats from Sapulut to Batu Punggul are M$250 per boat (maximum 6). If you visit between January to March remember it's dry season so you may be pushing the boat for quite a bit of the ride. Don't bring too much luggage and wear sturdy shoes. You will need a guide for jungle trekking, M$20 to see the caves and M$30 to climb the rock.

Where to Stay in Batu Punggul

You must take a 2–4 hour boat ride in, and there are a variety of government workers, students and tourists coming through Batu Punggul so you must make your bookings in advance. There is a canteen at the site so you can buy simple meals as well as beer and refreshments.

KPD, Inanam (corner Jalan Tuaran & Jalan Kelombong) ☎ *(088) 428910 ext 240*

Batu Punggul Resort   M$30– 60

The word resort is ambitious here. Very simple accommodations complete with stray cats and very large spiders. Don't be surprised if you are mobbed by one of the local tour groups, government workers and/or kept up all night by the party animals 100 meters away in the longhouse. There are cooking facilities as well as meals provided by the simple canteen.

Murut Longhouse   M$6

If you really want to get rustic this is the place. You enter along a notched log and sleep on woven platforms. All this and bedding for about M$6. If you signed on for the "typical Murut welcome" don't bother trying to get any sleep. If you want to set up your own tribal wingding, entertainers hire out at M$15 per entertainer. You might as well hire 'em by the dozen to guarantee a rip-roaring good time. The fee includes enough jars of the traditional *tapai* to irrigate three or four acres of surrounding jungle. Don't worry about how much to order. Every jar of rice wine will be consumed *in toto* by your paid guests and they will take home the empties.

Campsites   M$2

If you want to save four ringgit you can camp out. In fact you can even rent a tent if you really want to get wet and muddy.

Beaufort

100m from KK

Beaufort's main street

Beaufort is a curious backwater town known more for being the terminus of the ancient railway built at the turn of the century. The tiny railroad only carries about 10–12 passengers and hobbles between Beaufort and Tenom. What makes the two-hour trip worthwhile is the view of the Padas river and its gorge. (The front seats have the best views.) After you have seen how angry the river is, you may want to think twice about arranging a **white water rafting** tour out of KK. If you wondered why the old wooden buildings near the river are so high off the ground it is because of the flooding during the heavy monsoons. There is a market on Saturdays.

There are a handful of simple Chinese-run hotels—the Beaufort and the Padas across from the fishmarket. We recommend the Beaufort Hotel for obvious reasons.

Where to Stay in Beaufort

Hotel Beaufort   **M\$30–36**

P.O. Box 147. ☎ *(087) 211911*
Air-conditioned rooms with television. Modest but acceptable.

Beaufort Inn   **M\$35**

Lot 19 -20 Lochung Park ☎ *(087) 211911*
Essentially overflow for the Beaufort Hotel.

Mandarin Inn   **M\$30–35**

Jalan Beaufort Jaya. ☎ *(087) 212800.*
A cleaner hotel than the competition worth the five minute walk from the center of town, on the other side of the river.

New Padas Hotel   **M\$35**

P.O. Box 147. ☎ *(087) 211411.*

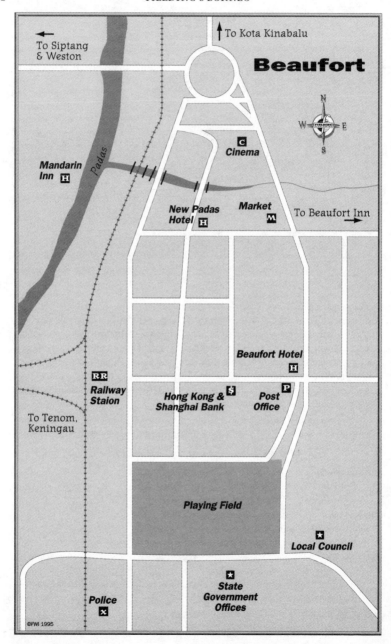

22 rooms.

Do you really want to stay opposite the fish market?

Crocker Range Park

At this time this mountainous area has no visitor facilities despite the fact that the 1399 sq km park is the second largest in Sabah. The park can be reached by taking any one of the two roads that pass through it. The park is just a few minutes from KK.

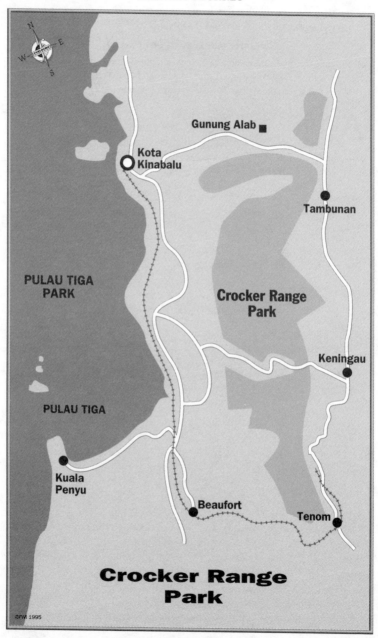

Crocker Range Park

Danum Valley
Land Of The Leviathans

M

y eyes sting from the constant dripping of perspiration. It is dark, no, more like Stygian here. Dead leaves, stinging centipedes, tangled roots and loose vines constantly trip us. My muddy Converses have turned a dull, dark brown from blood from leech bites. They bite, get rubbed off inside my sock and bite again.I have blood not dripping, but streaming from dozens of neat round holes. I hesitate to check my crotch and thighs but the blood soaking through my jungle pants tells me the more industrious of leeches have crawled to juicier quarters. The heat is within and without. Down here on the dark forest floor, 150 feet below the canopy, it is steaming. Sweat drenches your clothing, rain and moisture mix with the sweat and the blood to create a feeling of primeval ooze. This is the ancient forest of the Danum Valley.

This is not the storybook rainforest of Burrough's *Tarzan* or Kipling's *Jungle Book*. This is the real thing. The constant drone of cicadas and unseen birds add to the droning heat. To the first time visitor, each corner of the rainforest looks pretty much like the next. The trick is to stop and observe. Like the desert each square yard is a world unto itself. Also, the description "rainforest" is much like calling any body of water a sea. Specifically, we are in one of the world's finest stands of lowland dipterocarp forest; lowland because of the elevation—dipterocarp (or two-winged seeds) because of the profusion of fruiting hard and softwood trees that have winged seeds to spread their range.

There is little color here. No lush banana leaves, no parrots, no tigers, no brightly colored fruits. Nothing to tell the visitor that this is the most diverse plant and insect system in the world. The lowly footbound traveler stumbles through the green twilight wondering what all the fuss is about.

Danum Valley is a mere 438 sq km of a million square kilometers granted by the government to the Sabah Foundation (which is owned by the public of Sabah.) The goal of the Sabah Foundation is to study and use the natural resources of the land. The resulting income provides social services for the people. The Sabah Foundation has designated Maliau and Danum Valley as conservation areas. These areas are unique but for different reasons.

Danum Valley is home to 12–15 scientists working on everything from soil nutrients to tracking tiny deer. Danum has become one of the world's largest rainforest labs. The facility is also designed to accommodate about 35 students in a hostel and there are a few rooms for visitors.

The area is comprised of lowland forest with some peaks that reach over 6000 feet where lower montane forest can be explored. It has the largest concentration of large mammals anywhere in Borneo. Animals such as elephants, Sumatran rhino, sun bear, barking deer, and just about any inland

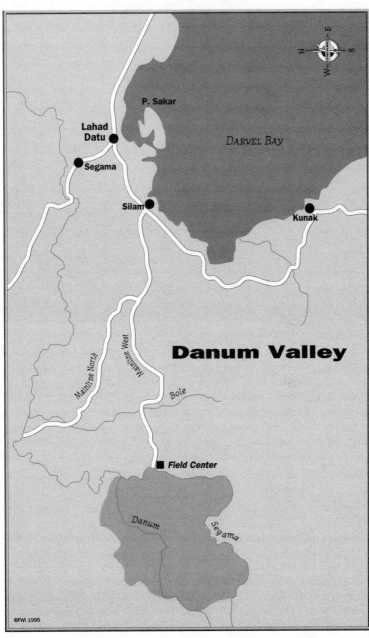

©FWI 1995

animal to be found in Sabah, can be found here. There are 30 kms of marked
trails from a 7 km to an 18 km trek to Kuala Subran.

The annual rainfall is about 80 inches with the driest months being May to
October and the wettest months being November to February. Danum is
not immune from severe flooding. In January of 1968 the Segama River rose
60 feet above its banks.

Danum Valley Research Center

For those with more time to explore, there are the Segama Highlands, an
area of sharp peaks, narrow ridges and steep slopes where gorges, river rapids
and waterfalls are common There is a salt lick north of Sungai Hantu in the
Tingkayu region that is ideal for stalking rhino. The Borneo Rainforest
Lodge has 12 kms of trails and 35 kms of road to explore. There are a variety
of minor entertainments around the lodge like night spotting, bird watching
from towers or just watching the flying squirrels sailing 60 feet across the
river as they return to the forest at dusk.

Despite Danum Valley being billed as uninhabited, there is evidence of
human habitation here.

Whether the dead were brought here to be buried or lived here and were
buried is open to discussion. We found buffalo coffins near the site of the
new lodge high up on a cliff face. There are also significant amounts of charcoal from about two to three hundred years ago. Scientists carbon dated it
and found out that Danum may have suffered a major forest fire meaning
that Danum actually could be a very mature secondary forest. There have
been great forest fires caused by drought as a result of El Nino conditions.
Like the great forest fires in Kalimantan in the early '80s, they may be caused
by manmade or natural conditions. The average life span of the trees in the

rainforest is about 100 years with trees growing about a centimeter a year. Parts of Danum Valley are logged however. Danum is an attempt to see if various forms of controlled logging can regenerate the precious hardwoods that sustain Sabah's timber industry.

When the North Borneo Company took control of what is now Sabah, there were expeditions to look for gold in the Danum Valley. You can still find gold flakes in the river but no major deposits of gold were ever found. Mount Tribulation and Dismal Gorge were named by early explorers who had a very tough portage around the rapids.

There had been no further activity in the Danum area until Dr. Clive Marsh, of the Sabah Foundation, set up the beginnings of what is today the Danum Research Center. His philosophy (and so far it has proved correct) is that simply creating legislation does not guarantee that a park can survive. There have been cases of a park being removed by the stroke of a minister's pen. His approach is longer lasting: Create enough activity and publicity around an area to guarantee that no politician would dare log or exploit the area. The reason we have chosen Danum for an expedition is that it is actually owned by Sabah's largest timber company: The Sabah Foundation. The Sabah Foundation or Yasahan Sabah is a positive exercise in responsible conservation of Sabah's largest visible resource: timber. Over one million hectares of prime forest land have been deeded to the foundation on the premise that they be maintained in perpetuity for the good of the people. This means logging to generate income and, hopefully, long term management to ensure a continual supply of timber. At this moment there is no replanting of the original dipterocarp forest and there is growing concern that bit-by-bit the fragile ecosystems of Borneo are being destroyed. The rainforest is a verdant, but complex environment. Danum is an excellent way to learn just what a tropical rainforest is and isn't.

Many people are surprised to find that Danum Valley is owned by the state logging company.

We hiked to the site of the Borneo Rainforest Lodge. We took a steep trail that went up a ridge to a lookout that overlooks the entire valley. Below the granite outcrop is a burial site with the undisturbed remains of people from the Idahan tribe; the first known peoples of Sabah's history.

Going down from the lookout we came to our first waterfall called Dribblers Fall. It is about 200 feet in height and is host to frogs and ferns. From there we crossed over to another unnamed river that cascaded down into a wonderful swimming pool. As we followed the waterfall down to the Jungle Lodge each waterfall pool or cataract became even more idyllic until we came upon the "piece de resistance," an elegantly carved series of waterfalls and waterways that cascade into a pool at the bottom.

If you stop and look carefully you will see life all around you in Danum Valley.

The area is truly a Garden of Eden. From the Jungle Lodge, nature trails go out to explore the surrounding jungle. One trail climbs a steep hill to an ancient gravesite with the undisturbed remains of people from the Idahan tribe; the first known recorders of Borneo's history and then to a scenic vista of the valley. Following the same trail down takes the traveler along a series of waterfalls and rock formations that can only be described as the romantic's perception of what the rainforest must be like.

We drove from the Kinabatangan River to the bustling port of Lahad Datu. Taking the logging road is somewhat unsettling since most visitors are surprised to see the perimeter of a conservation area so heavily logged. The World Wildlife Fund and Sabah Forestry Foundation estimate that 1000 or more elephants are found here. The elephants actually prefer logged areas and can be seen moving in heavy rain along many points along the road. It has been dry here for a while so the rain is welcome. After the rain, mists rise from the jungle. We passed through canyons of fresh timber stacked by the roadside in neat, numbered piles. Danum Valley is in a timber concession and is actually a research center that does not encourage tourism but is available for local students, bird watchers, nature lovers and other visitors interested more in the forest rather than the accommodations.

Up early, five-thirty, for a walk along South Ridge Trail. There are two observation towers and one, 120 foot platform built in 1991. The two other platforms provide an excellent view of the surrounding jungle and come complete with blinds for wildlife photography. It is very dark in the jungle so bring plenty of fast film and lenses. If you are after wildlife you will probably be disappointed, but it's a good idea to walk in the rain to mask noises. The other way is to be very patient: walk slowly and deliberately, taking time to stop and listen.

Since Danum is a research center, there are many marked trees, plots and boundaries along the paths. Some of these areas are off-limits. A very organized system of marked trails will take you through a good variety of jungle.

The leviathans of the forest; dipterocarp trees.

EVERYTHING YOU WANTED TO KNOW ABOUT RAINFORESTS

Rainforest is a generic term used to describe forest that is influenced by 80 inches of rain annually. Just as we call the indigenous tribes of Borneo "Dayaks", there is much more diversity than one word can describe. There are vast differences in rainforests, not only between the cold mist-shrouded coasts of British Columbia and the tropics of Borneo, but also within the rainforest. Just an elevation of 500 feet or a slight difference in soil can create a completely different environment.

EVERYTHING YOU WANTED TO KNOW ABOUT RAINFORESTS

Rainforests were created 140 million years ago during the Cretaceous period. Rainforest origi-nally covered over six million square miles, twice the three million square miles it covers today. In 1990, the United Nations estimated the rainforest is disappearing at the rate of 55,000 square miles a year, resulting in the extinction of at least one species of bird, mammal or plant every day. For an estimated ten million species, the rainforest is the last refuge. There are many esti-mates of how fast the rainforest is disappearing but like the cedars of Lebanon, the oak forests of England or even the towering stands of Sequoias in California, it will not be long before stands of virgin rainforest become curiosities visited by tourists who wonder what it must have been like when these giant forests covered the entire equatorial belt.

A fantastic array of species has been able to adapt to the micro climates of the tropical forests because of constant temperatures that make the tropical forest a giant incubator. For example, the entire native tree flora of Canada and the United States can only muster 700 species. The tropics boast about 50,000 species of trees and two thirds of the world's plants. Today Sabah is missing about 60% (or 44,000 sq kms) of its primary forests–a better statistic than Sarawak who some say has lost 80% (and counting) but sobering.

This spectacular bio-diversity is found mostly in the canopy. To most Northerners, the world of the rainforest is topsy-turvy. Over half the plants and animals live in the canopy, rarely descending to the jungle floor. Tem-perate forests are just the opposite: the diversity is on the ground.

Down below in the dark, tannin-stained leaf litter supports little. The red clay or sand dirt is rarely more than an inch below the surface. Here the world is populated with the undertakers of the rainforest: termites, milli-pedes and fungi go about grimly breaking down the dead leaves, animals, branches, and other unfortunate plants that have lost their purchase in the bright light of the canopy.

Rainforests are in close cahoots with the insect world, without one another they cannot survive. Many plants in Borneo's rainforest exist because of the reciprocal needs of just one insect species. For example, The giant Rafflesia is pollinated only by the bluebottle fly. Some species of orchids have spring loaded petals that are sprung by the weight of an insect. The built-in spring slams the unsuspecting insect against the orchid's reproductive parts ensur-ing furthering of the species. To remove one species can destroy another here in the interlocked world.

A casual inspection of a fallen tree limb will reveal a world unto itself. Highways of ants wind their way through orchid roots, moss and other epi-phytic plants. Epiphytes are a diverse group of 29,000 species of moss, li-chens, orchids, ferns, bromeliads, gesnerads, figs, arums and members of the pepper family. They draw their nutrition from rainfall and organic material that collects on branches. They grow in huge confused masses on the trunks and branches, using the trees as support.

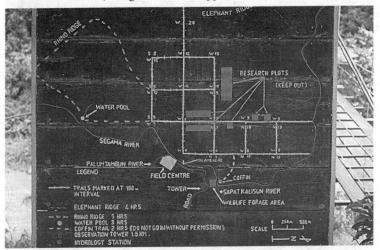

There are a variety of trails as well as study plots across the Segama River from the Research Center.

The Scientists

We fall into the ritual of the research center: up before dawn for our jungle walks, back by 3:30 when the heavens open up and rain pours down in earnest.

The colonial atmosphere of Sabah is still much in evidence since at four we go to tea. The scientists who live in the compounds down the road and work in the adjoining labs wander up to the dining room and balcony. They have the look of people who have been together too long and do not have much to talk to each other about. Thin, anemic, with close-cropped hair and faded T-shirts, they are here for a variety of reasons: tracking barking deer, studying ants, measuring soil nutrients and reforestation and cataloging trees. They don't drink, laugh or chatter. They politely eat their dinner and retire to do their "computer work." The new arrivals have the most cheerful dispositions. Some who have been here six months may act like "lifers." Some scientists will be here for up to five years.

The forest canopy

Back in my room I discover that I am covered with hundreds of microscopic ticks that are busy burrowing under my skin making red welts. Apparently I had stood in a pig's nest and now must spend the rest of the afternoon cutting them out with my knife.

Next morning I go out for another stroll. Sweat forms little pools in creases of my stomach as I sit in the jungle looking at frogs, lizards and hospital termites with endless armies of burden carrying slaves. We are getting used to the pace and rhythm of the rainforest and sit for long periods of time taking in the complex beauty. Hiking along the Segama River we go for a swim in the fast flowing water and discover that yellow river leeches are more vicious than their landborne cousins. Along the shores yellow, orange and neon green butterflies taste the sweat on our grimy clothes.

Sitting on the rocks drying out I watch an old branch actually get up and walk slowly into the forest. Upon closer inspection I find a large example of the walking stick insect. Much like a praying mantis, the walking stick is ideally suited for the forest. It is obviously quite uncomfortable away from the trees. When it is put back in the branches it immediately strikes a silent pose and blends perfectly into the branches.

We head back for lunch at two. Like clockwork the rain comes just as we cross the suspension bridge. Soaked by sweat, thirsty and tired from our trek, I stand under the edge of the building and enjoy a thunderous downpour of cool rainwater from the eaves. Drying off inside I listen to the geckos clucking in the eaves above me.

That night brings out the nocturnal dwellers and we watch an owl sitting patiently above a spot on the badminton court, waiting for the large beetles to seek out the brilliant light. This owl apparently likes the white leeches. He turns up his nose at the giant black rhinoceros beetles we offer him.

In our room, we are greeted by dozens of stinging night wasps, the carcasses of a giant moth, a three-inch cicada and a bee twice the size of a bumblebee.

A Night in the Canopy

We spend the night in the platform. Built by Phil Hurrel in exchange for food, lodging and beer (and also to apparently avoid taking around a well known National Geographic photographer), it is a marvelous contraption and the best way to truly experience the rainforest.

Constructed of wood supported by cables, there is no damage to the tree as a support member. An aluminum ladder with a metal safety grate climbs straight up into the heavens with an excellent view of the surrounding canopy. The tree platform is built about halfway up its host tree. It extends out around the tree about three feet, allowing a spectacular view of the branches above. We are determined to be the first to spend an evening high above the leeches, mud and leaf litter below.

We start off clean, cool and refreshed. After a 300 meter hike to the base of the platform, our pants are soaked from sweat. In the light of the head flashlights, bats flicker like fighter planes as they speed down the trail corridor. Animals and birds fall silent as they see two beams of light sweep through the night. We pull our equipment up on a rope, 120 feet times three. The air is still. The canopy overhead is silhouetted by the silver clouds.

After we have settled in, we lie back and look at the magnificent panorama of silhouetted branches, broken by exotic outlines of tree ferns and hanging moss. After about ten minutes of watching the thin clouds drift by and listening to classical music on the digital recorder, I am immersed in the jungle. The beads of sweat on my chest sparkle like diamonds in the moonlight as they form little rivers and run down onto the mat.

At ten minutes to eleven, it begins to rain. The cool drops are a wonderful sensation. Common sense prevails as I remember that these gentle drops may be the calling card of the huge deluges that are the real rain here. A dark cloud is sailing in from the north. I had almost forgotten we were in Borneo. Quickly we threw up our makeshift protection from the rain. Drinking cold coffee and orange juice that was too sweet, we told orang utan jokes and recorded the sounds of the night.

The forest floor is a damp, dead place except for scavengers like this millipede.

In the early morning around four is when the jungle noises are at their loudest. There is no hint of the coming dawn, but the birds and monkeys have replaced the insects as the noisemakers. The beam from the flashlight shows that we are in a deep fog that blankets everything with a wet, glistening sheen. The giant ants that travel up and down the trunks of trees seem tireless in their tasks. When I shine my torch on them they become confused, stop and do a silly jig. As soon as I turn the light off, they continue their endless journey.

A large group of hornbills descends on the tree next to us. Noisy in flight, they are even noisier at rest. It is unusual to be this close to hornbills. They cackle and honk as if they have just come back from a night out on the town. At the first sign of light, they lift off, as if by some secret signal and continue their noisy trip through the jungle. Throughout the night our favorite sound is a bird call that can best be described as the sound of a drunk whistling a tuneless version of a Frank Sinatra melody while searching for his keys.

Now the fog bathes the canopy in an eerie light. About 5:15 a.m., a blue glow begins the new day. Gibbons make their appearance in the jungle orchestra. Each jungle sound has a unique personality and it would not be too hard to anthropomorphize the sound of the gibbon as a shy person tentatively seeking his mother. Other calls are raucous. Many sound like bad imitations of bird calls. Some are just downright strange. Gleeps, kronks and braats all form a tropical symphony. As the blue gets more intense, the canopy gets quieter as if the animals are embarrassed to be seen making their strange calls. The only sound is the perfect matchup between the intense humid heat and the droning sound of cicadas.

Every tiny part of Danum is a critical link to survival.

The sun finally slices through the damp mist at around six-thirty. The jungle falls silent. The ferns and moss are backlit in the bright light of morning. As the heat rises in damp fetid waves, it is time to go back down. As we descend from the bright light and airiness of the canopy into the endless twilight of the dark jungle floor, we are one night richer for our experience in Borneo's jungle.

Danum Valley★★★

About 85 kms west of Lahad Datu.

How can a logging company also be a social agency *and* the owner of a large forested park? Easy, when that company is the Sabah Foundation. Despite my incessant criticism of logging practices in Borneo, I have to praise Clive Marsh and the Sabah Foundation. Clive worked to create this area to find new and better ways of forest management. To do this, he has invited scientists from around the world to help him. By doing so, he has also made it very difficult for anyone to cut down his 438-sq.-km outdoor laboratory. You can stay in the simple visitors' quarters, which may be full of visiting schoolchildren or crane-necked birdwatchers. Meals are served and you will bump into the scientists (who work across the way and live up the road) at coffee breaks or teatime. They study everything from ants to orang utan nests and are a storehouse of knowledge, as well as pleasant company. There are 220 species of birds here alone. They have yet to identify all the tree species.

Danum's uniqueness lies in its lack of habitation and natural disasters. (Clive admits that there may have been a major burn centuries ago and a few nomadic hunters.) Here you will find all the major land mammals—birds, insects and more plant species than the entire continent of Europe and America combined. If you came to Borneo to see elephant, kijang, argus pheasant—or just to jungle walk—this is the place.It costs $25 to get in and guides run about $20 for half a day.

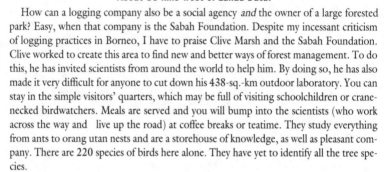

INSIDER TIP

Don't be too impressed by the number of species rattled off in nature guides. Asian forests may have a high diversity of species but a low biomass. This means you will be amazed at the species you see, but unlike East Africa don't expect to see a whole lot of animals, birds or insects in one place at one time. The animals are not only shy but need large habitats to survive in these meager conditions. Best spot for elephants is mile 20 marker on the way into the park during heavy downpours.

Where to Stay in Danum Valley

Borneo Rainforest Lodge   **M$40–150**   ★★★

☎ *(088) 243245.*

The Borneo Rainforest Lodge is modeled after Tigertops in India or the Ark in Kenya. There are 24 twin rooms with meals included. The goal is to keep the traffic down and the quality of the experience up. I spent some time here with the scientists looking for orang utans to see if they would habituate the area but it appears that the slightest appearance of man drives them further and further into the bush. Here you will be able to spend a night surrounded by pure wilderness with the chance to set out on foot the next day. The trails are spectacular. Having been given a sneak preview, I can say it is well worth the price of admission. The trails will take you to an ancient Dusun burial ground, past waterfalls, racing gorges and through some of the best pristine lowland dipterocarp forest in Asia.

Danum Valley Field Centre   M$36

Technically not a tourist attraction, but you can apply at the Sabah Foundation in KK ☎ *354496* (the big shiny skyscraper that looks like a tree stump) or the Forestry Division in Lahad Datu ☎ *81092*. The rooms are inexpensive and the meals simple. It is a beautiful lodge situated with a sweeping view of the jungle. The company of the resident scientists can also make it a very educational experience. The simple rooms at the Field Center run about $36 per person.

INSIDER TIP

Elephants and other animals are best seen along the road leading into the park boundaries. Elephants like to move in heavy rain and in aging logging cuts...Start out at dusk and be patient.

There are no set itineraries or programs for visitors, but your guide or the staff can set up an itinerary for you. Ask if there has been any activity recently. The 30 km of trails include the survey plots laid out across the river. There are also elevated blinds that offer excellent viewing and an unusual tree platform that will work up a sweat. I recommend spending the night in a blind or on the tree platform. You won't see much but it is a great experience.

You can buy maps, a guide map and rent binoculars in the sparse store. Spend about a week here if you can; you will truly learn to love the lowland dipterocarp forest. The best way to visit the park is through a tour booked from Kota Kinabalu.

Camping

You can pitch a tent for $15 a day.

Labuan

10kms west of the Klias Peninsula

Once a coaling station for British ships in the 1800s, Labuan is now a booming free trade zone, duty free port and offshore banking center for Southeast Asia.

During World War II the island was the staging point for Japanese forces into Borneo and was the site of the Japanese surrender in September 9, 1945.

Labuan Lalang (also known as Teluk Terima) with its deep-water harbor and coal reserves made this an excellent spot for Rajah James Brooke to fight pirates from. The former penal colony and then colonial administration center for the British North Borneo was manned by drunken civil servants who were the source for many of the despondent, besotted characters created by Conrad and Maugham.

Today Pulau Labuan is tax-free Federal Territory that has generated much notoriety as a center of smuggling and piracy. It's a bustling center of commerce and barter for raw goods and finished luxuries between the Philippines and Malaysia. Filipinos trade raw goods and leave bulging most boats with expensive manufactured goods. For all you cautious travelers, we should warn you that you must check your weapons when you enter the port just as the heavily armed sailors must. The marine police will return them to you when you leave. Labuan is also a military base, a major oil drilling center and a **WWII battle site**.

Labuan Lalang is an excellent spot for a **wreck dive**. Borneo Divers, KK, offers an intriguing six day dive trip (16 hours by boat.) Also contact Coral Island Cruises in KK. You can get to the island via ferry from Kota Kinabalu, Brunei, Limbang Lawas and Menumbok.

Lahad Datu

272km from KK by air

Most folks pass through this grubby backwater town on their way to Danum Valley. Lahad Datu is famous for pirate raids, illegal Timorese and the Filipino immigrants and vast oil palm plantations. If you get hungry or get tired hanging out to absorb the seediness, try the fish and chips at the Evergreen Snack Bar and Pub. As with most small Sabahan towns there is a motley collection of no name cheap Chinese hotels that will run you about M$30 a night. There is a Government Resthouse out towards the airport that goes for a trifling M$12.

The World's Greatest Forest Fire Part 2

In a case of depressing deja vu in August of 1994 once again smoke from forest fires in south Sumatra and South Kalimantan choked the skies from Singapore to Jakarta. The dry conditions triggered an exact replay of the great fires of the early 1980s.

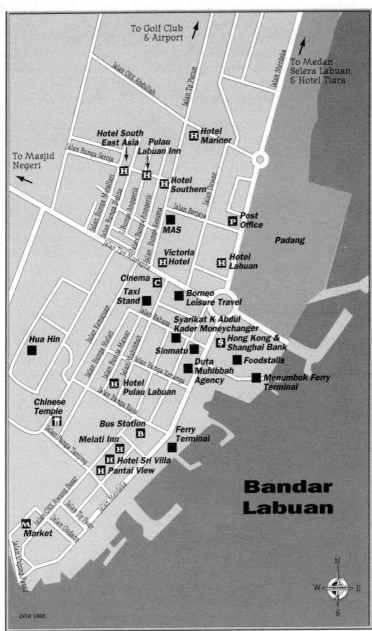

To Golf Club & Airport

Jalan OKK Abdullah

Jalan Tg Purun

Jalan Merdeka

To Medan Selera Labuan & Hotel Tiara

Hotel South East Asia

Pulau Labuan Inn

H Hotel Mariner

Jalan Bunga Seroja

To Masjid Negeri

Jalan Bunga Dahlia

Jalan Bunga Anggerik

J. Bunga Anggerik

Jalan Bunga Anggerik

Jalan Bunga Kesuma

Jalan Tun Mustapha

H

H

H **Hotel Southern**

Jalan Dewan

Jalan Berjaya

MAS

P **Post Office**

Padang

Victoria H Hotel

H Hotel Labuan

Cinema C

Taxi Stand

Borneo Leisure Travel

Jalan Bahasa

Syarikat K Abdul Kader Moneychanger

Hua Hin

Jalan Kemajuan

Jalan Bunga Melati

Jalan Bunga Mawar

Jalan Muhibbah

Jalan Bunga Kehanga

Sinmatu

$ **Hong Kong & Shanghai Bank**

■ **Foodstalls**

Duta Muhibbah Agency

■ **Menumbok Ferry Terminal**

H Hotel Pulau Labuan

Jalan Bunga Raya

Chinese Temple

Jalan Bunga Tanjong

Bus Station B

Melati Inn

Ferry Terminal

H

H Hotel Sri Villa

H Pantai View

Bandar Labuan

Jalan OKK Awang Besar

Jalan Tg Pasir

Jalan Merdeka

Jalan Gudang

M **Market**

Jalan Hujang Pasar

N
W E
S

FIELDING

©AWI 1995

Layang Layang ★★★★

Layang Layang is the world's hottest new dive spot in more ways than one. Just as Sipadan was contested by the Indonesian and Malaysian governments, it seems that this tiny 7 km long, 5 km wide island may also be hotly contested. For now Layang Layang offers the most pristine, unexplored diving on this planet. Wall dives that are 1500 meters straight down, visibility up to 60 meters, dolphins, barracuda, tuna, sea turtles, grey reef sharks, eagle rays, and hammerheads abound in the silent undisturbed depths. A rainbow of coral, sponges and anemones color the dramatic dive spots. Golden Wall has one of the richest collections of plant and animal life available to the scuba enthusiast. And it has never been touched. The island is part of the North Borneo Banks and is one of the 60 islands that make up the Spratleys. The Spratleys are being contested by Malaysia, Brunei, the Philippines, China, Taiwan and Vietnam. They are not squabbling about who gets to own the diving rights, they want the black gold that lies beneath, oil. The dive resort was opened in 1993 and has already become the insider's dive spot. The dive boats also travel to three other atolls: Dallas Reef, Ardaiser Reef and Mariveles Reef. Deep sea fishermen also head out to the Spratleys for some very impressive catches. Four to nine day packages including airfare from Singapore run about $1500 per person.

Getting There

Layang Layang is the southernmost island in the Spratleys and can be reached via MAS from KK. Two operators, Tropical Dive Adventures and Coral Island Cruises operate 22 passenger boats to the island. Once on Layang Layang you stay aboard a permanently stationed dive boat.

Asia Aquatic

> *#07-37 Cuppage Centre, 55 Cuppage Road, Singapore*
> ☎ *738-8158, FAX 738-8153*
> Runs dive trips on the *Spirit of Borneo*.

Coral Islands Cruises Tours & Travel

> *G19, Ground Floor Wisma Sabah*
> *Jalan Haji Saman, 88851 Kota Kinabalu, Sabah*
> ☎ *(088) 223490, FAX 223404*
> Offers diving and deep sea fishing tours to Layang Layang.

Madai Caves

An unremarkable but see-it-while-you're-here spot. The Idahan nest gatherers will show you around the caves if you really need to see another guano lined swiftlet hatchery. Inside are some coffins. The chambers are quite large and quite dark.

Maliau

The Lost World

Seeking out the last wild places for this book was not as easy as simply picking a green spot on the map. I spent a long time looking for areas in Borneo that could be future ecological and cultural highlights. Our goal was to publicize threatened and significant areas in Borneo that are important not only to the region, but to the world. One area needed no discussion: a perfectly balanced environment, untouched by man, home to a diverse array of species and biosystems... and in danger of becoming a coal mine.

"Ever heard of the Maliau?" Jon Rees asked. "No." "The Lost World, the last wild place in Borneo." "Really? Tell me more." The phone line between Malaysia and Los Angeles gave its characteristic echo as our voices sped up to satellites and down again, bridging the thousands of miles between us.

"There have only been four expeditions into the Maliau, three scientific and one I did just for the hell of it. Now a surveyor is there mapping coal seams. I think it's the right time for the world to find out about the Maliau Basin."

We talked at length about what was needed to get in and out of the basin. On my topographical aviation map, the Maliau looks like a giant volcanic basin. It is not. The Maliau Basin is a sedimentary formation of eroded sandstone and mudstone. The steep cliffs surrounding the basin, one of the features that has earned it the name, "Lost World," make it almost inaccessible. The only way in, at the lower end, is guarded by a series of impressive waterfalls and gorges.

The Maliau Basin is unique in that it is an area that has lain unvisited and untouched since the dawn of time. Now the area is getting serious attention from logging companies, coal mining and oil drilling interests.

Maliau means "murky" in the Murut language which is a good description of its past and possibly of its future.

Expeditions Into the Maliau

In 1947, a pilot flying from the west coast of British North Borneo to Tawau experienced a rude shock when he narrowly avoided colliding with a wall of steep cliffs emerging from the misty jungle. This minor incident is the first recorded mention of the Maliau Basin. The "Lost World" was recorded in the *Borneo Bulletin*—and then quietly slipped back into obscurity.

The nearest Dusun villagers lived only four days away, but their belief that a fierce dragon inhabited Lake Limunsut at the base of the cliffs didn't encourage exploration. Muruts along Sungai Sapulut were known to have reached the lower basin, calling it the "Mountain of Stairs" in reference to the many waterfalls and limestone ledges.

The first Western attempt to enter the "Lost World" was in 1976 during a forest service expedition to Lake Limunsut. They tried in vain to scale the escarpment but were forced to turn back just forty feet from the upper edge.

Maliau is a raised plateau washed by an ocean of fog.

Four years later, the Sabah Museum mounted an expedition to penetrate this remote area. The expedition ran out of supplies, was felled by malaria, and had to give up before they could conquer the escarpment.

In 1982, they managed a brief reconnaissance by helicopter, landing on a gravel bar near the falls. This preliminary mission was designed to lay the groundwork for a more intensive expedition a year later. They were greeted by animals that had never seen man before: a docile 22 foot, 400 pound python, mildly curious bearded pigs and a *kijang*, deer. In all, this brief foray into the wilderness posed more questions than it answered.

Finally, in April-May of 1988, a 43 man expedition spent three weeks in the Maliau unlocking its secrets. What they found was impressive. The 390 square kilometer basin covers an area of 25 kilometers across and is protected by an encircling escarpment that climbs up to 1500 meters. The highest point is Gunung Lotung, estimated to be 1900 meters high, but it has yet to be properly surveyed.

This expedition identified 47 species of mammals, including rhino, proboscis monkey and clouded leopard; 175 species of birds, including the Bulwer's Pheasant (once thought extinct in Sabah); and 450 species of plants, many of them rare species. Their scientific finds and increased understanding of this absolutely untouched region led them to declare it a conservation area. But, along with the numerous rare plants and unusual ecosystems, the expedition also discovered significant coal seams.

There had also been a more adventurous and less scientific foray into the Maliau. Jon Rees walked in from Sapulut with three other Americans, a New Zealander and a Brit. They had heard there was a place no one had ever been, so they hiked through solid jungle from Sapulut for three days, plunged down into the Maliau River, walked along the ridge trail for five days, spent time in the central area and then devised a curious way to exit the basin. They had carried in canisters of two chemicals, used in boat building to create a buoyant foam. They also carried in two presewn plastic socks sewn in the shape of a Hobie cat.

The group tried to create hulls by hanging the socks in a tree, mixing the chemicals and pouring the chemical mixture into the socks. However, instead of a light, crisp vessel, they got two soggy bananas. The foam did not expand to its full volume, due either to altitude, heat, humidity or to all three. Nonetheless, they made a platform with roughly hewn crossbars and an old tennis net, tied sticks to the sawed-off blades of paddles, and proceeded to float down the Kuamut for 10 days to get out.

Their total time in the country was 27 days longer than any other outsider before them. During their foray they came across all the major mammals of Borneo except the rhino, and discovered "Jalan Babi," the curious highway used by pigs to enter the Maliau. The profusion of coniferous and oak trees attracts the pigs in impressive numbers every year.

Because of the area's inaccessibility, various expeditions had passed the Maliau Basin by, or skirted its perimeter. The Maliau has a curious history of being discovered and then undiscovered. The purpose of our trip was to bring this area to the attention of the world and by so doing provide incentive for the government of Sabah and Malaysia to preserve the touristic and environmental importance of this region.

Into the Maliau

Mention the Maliau in Sabah, and the name Tony Lamb always seems to come up. Tony is a dedicated scientist, whose fascination and experience with the Maliau Basin made him the perfect choice for our expedition. Tony was in charge of the Tenom Research Center, now retired, and his special interest is in the identification, propagation, and domestication of tropical fruits. He also has a vast knowledge of local insects, birds and mammals. His knowledge of the orchids and plants is encyclopedic. Only accurate identification of the multitude of trees prompts him to defer to a tree expert.

Tony was born in Ceylon, (now Sri Lanka) and grew up on a tea plantation during the British colonial period. Being educated in England and spending many years in Malaysia, another former British colony, may explain his genteel and pleasant nature.

The impenetrable canopy hides the spectacular beauty that lies below

The helicopter descended: white, clean and gleaming. We waited; brown, mud-dirty and disheveled, from our previous adventure in Batu Punggul. Once on board and aloft, the complexities of the jungle intermingled into a rich, green blanket. The heavy heat became an icy coolness as the Bell 206 gained altitude.

From above the miles and miles of jungle carpet, the ground was unbroken, except by a few large rivers that had cut the dirt right down to the sandstone. Here, there was diversity, but also a monotony of endless green: a carpet of color every few miles from a flowering tree, subtle shades of green, blending from dark brownish green to light green and even yellowish green. If the helicopter went down in this canopy, we would never be found.

Off in the distance we saw the crisp shape of a continent rising above an ocean of mist. The sharp outline of the steep cliffs cut an exact shoreline in this cloud as if it were an island.

We asked the pilot to take us higher to get a better idea of the shape of this vast island within an island. It looked like an elephant track in hard dirt that has been washed by rain. The basin also could be described as a crown shape that rises in the north to a tiara-like configuration and slopes down on each side to where rivers have cut a series of jagged canyons through which they spill like wax from a candle. The Maliau is an important drainage basin that creates the Sungai Maliau, which tumbles down to create the Maliau Falls, then drains into the Kuamut, which links up with the Kinabatangan.

The area is so vast that we flew long and hard before we found the chain of rapids and waterfalls spilling out of the basin seen by so few people. The drainage of the entire 25 kilometer-wide basin made a most impressive showing. As the pilot dived and maneuvered between the steep cliffs, the ground turned from a smooth carpet to individual giants. What had looked like strewn pebbles were house-sized boulders. What had looked like rapids, were 20-30 foot waterfalls that cascaded into basin after basin. An extraordinary sight.

We were thankful that we did not have to walk in. The only ground access in is a full day hike from the nearest timber camp on the Tawau Keningau timber road. The downside to this method is a very steep and dangerous cliff ascent late in the day or early the next morning. For those pressed for time, a helicopter can be chartered from KK or Sandakan. It will not be cheap.

We decided to drop our gear at a helipad first, then have the pilot drop us off at the highest helipad. We would then walk down to the base camp from where we would explore the basin. The first day would be an ambitious, but easy, walk of about 8 kilometers through dense jungle. That was our plan. Things did not quite turn out that way. We were in the "Lost World," subject to its whims and desires.

The pilot tapped his gauge, alerting us to his low fuel. We broke out of our aerial reverie and began to search for the helipad. Crude helipads had been hacked out of the dense jungle to let the research and survey teams in. Our goal was to pick the most remote site and then walk along the ridge to the confluence of the two good sized rivers.

The helicopter touched down. We leaped out and immediately sank up to our chests in moss. Shocked by the lack of solid footing, we realized that the firm peat forest floor was an illusion. The stumps of the trees poked through three to four feet of moss and leaf litter before rooting in the thin hard bedrock.

A series of waterfalls on the sungai Maliau act as another natural barrier.

We labored like horses in deep snow to get the gear away from the rotor wash. As the chopper lifted back into the bright sunlight, we had a chance to record our first impressions of the Maliau Basin.

It was cool near the rim. The altitude and humidity created an agreeable atmosphere. There was moss everywhere. The curious lack of soil and depth of the moss was typical of a peat forest. The trees were not the typical lowland dipterocarps. Here, there were conifers. Big conifers.

It was a discomforting feeling to descend from the clear, piercing blue sky into the dark grasps of the jungle. The trees towered above us. The contours of the basin, which had seemed gentle and caressing, were now wickedly steep and forbidding. Instead of seeing clearly in 360 degrees, we were now confined to staring at patches of sky through 60-100 foot trees.

Our weight restrictions and the distance we needed to fly to get to the Maliau dictated that we make two trips. Our solution was to send Jon back with the pilot to help find the helipad.

We flew into helipad four and set up camp at the base of the hill, lugging our gear and crashing through the dense brush like drunk elephants.

We were just five minutes down the trail and suddenly Tony asked us to stop. It appeared he had already made a discovery. He pointed to a thimble-sized plant that closely resembled a cross between an alien spaceship and a Victorian light standard. He collected the second finding ever of a small saprophytic plant; *Thysmia aescananthus*. The tiny plant is nestled under the roots of a tree and would have been easily crushed. Tony mentioned in a casual manner that the first time this plant was found was in exactly this same spot on an earlier expedition. The uniqueness and fragility of this area began to sink in.

The steep cliffs and tough terrain have isolated the Maliau until recently.

Tony explained that we were in unique coniferous forest dominated by huge Agathus (related to the New Zealand cowrie pines), dacridiums and podocarpus trees, mixed with oaks and casserinas as it mixes with the lower hill dipterocarp forest.

This was truly pristine forest. There was no evidence of fire. There have been no natural calamities. There are no people to disturb the forest and there is no wind. Nothing to disturb the test tube-like conditions for creating new species. The only major trauma is the life cycle of the giant trees as they grow, die, and then crash into the forest, unheard and unseen, creating a gaping hole in the canopy for their offspring to fill.

A wet fantasy world of rivers, landscapes and silence exists under the canopy.

Night on the Edge of the World

We began our trek to the rim and then down along the edge to our rendezvous at a preagreed base camp. For navigation we had a compass and a crude map.

The size of the Maliau is overwhelming. Like most wilderness areas, there is a mixture of monotony and surprise: smooth skinned gum trees, disrobed and red in the normally green jungle; streams that run with tea-colored water; pitcher plants that festoon trees like Christmas decorations. As we increased in altitude the trees became stunted, the moss became thicker and the forest wetter.

We could tell when we were close to the rim because we hit a green wall of moss. There is a distinct rim forest that lives in the constant wash of the mist and fog that pours over the rim. The trees are twisted and gnarled with their roots raised as if to keep their feet dry. The moss is constantly wet. Walking through the almost impenetrable maze of roots and branches drenches you as they squish their burden of water. It is chilly. It is also silent. There does not appear to be any life along the rim.

Another surprise was that the spectacular view we thought would greet us, did not exist. The dense growth at the rim blocked any chance to get a clear view of the surrounding jungle. We were floating in a "sea of mist" that stretched as far as the eye could see. "Sea" is an appropriate description because the mist bobs and ebbs like an ocean. It hits the cliffs, curls up and then floats above the trees, spraying a fine cool mist over the trees and moss.

I pushed out to get a view over the ledge and had a gut wrenching revelation. When the mist cleared for a few seconds, I saw below me over a thousand feet of sheer cliff. More correctly, "behind" me was over a thousand feet of sheer cliff. I had learned another intriguing fact about the rim forest. The roots of the trees grew far out over the cliffs. Covered with moss and detritus and being continually moist, the roots support more plants and trees, encouraging the process to repeat itself. I should have learned my lesson when we leaped off the helicopter into a mossy trap. Wiser, I gently returned to the safety of the cliff five feet behind me.

Tony and I, realizing that the day was getting late and that we had a long hike ahead of us, made haste along the rim. From the air, the rim looks like a smooth, clean edge sloping softly to a basin. Toiling antlike on the ground, it is a wonderland of ravines, cliffs, gullies and inaccessible smaller cliffs. In some places, water too impatient to flow into the central basin, has sliced through the edge of the precipice, creating a magical series of waterfalls and ledges ending in one last leap of escarpment. The water never hits the ground, dissipating into mist and drops of moisture.

We made our way through alleys of 20 feet high, five feet wide and 60 feet long slabs of sandstone. We clambered up the root-bound cliffs and slid down the other side. We passed the remains of a camp. This was the first evidence of man after the helipad—further evidence of the search for coal. In the coming days we would come upon holes dug to measure the depth of soft black coal. They had picked a most impressive spot: water had carved a notch in the cliff face providing a picture window view of the top of the mist sea.

Soon the path flattened out. Instead of the steep climbing and tumbling, we were dodging, ducking and twisting around the chaotic moss forest. I couldn't help but think of British Columbia or the Olympic National Park in Washington. It was cool, green and refreshing when we were moving at a clip. We took a short breather. As soon as we stopped, the chill attacked.

We pressed on. Tony vaguely remembered there is a quicker route further down the rim. I chose to travel along the rim in my quest for a photograph that would capture the congested wet moss forest and the ocean of fog that gave us tantalizing peeks, but never the full picture.

A typical scene in the Lost World

The game path was now marked with survey sticks and occasionally flagging tape. We had been walking for a full day without food or water. Luckily, we were travelling light and the cool wet rim had made water abundantly unnecessary.

Tony's muttering, normally an ongoing description of plant life and other information, turned to concern. He didn't remember that ridge. We should be higher up. It was getting rather late.

Our crude maps showed we were still quite a long way from the helipad and eventual base camp where our gear was stored. Looking back, I could see the profile of the cliff that matched the map. The problem was, I was looking up at the ridge and it was behind me.

We continued. We were losing altitude at an alarming rate. It was getting darker. Now Tony and I were sure something was wrong. The map showed a smaller plateau below the cliff edge. We had been mindlessly following a game trail that we assumed would follow the ridge. Instead, we had found a way out of the basin and down the cliff.

We discussed our situation. We could turn back, but we didn't know exactly where we went off the ridge and down onto this lower plateau. Since the path winds and curves tree by tree there would be no sure way of knowing where the path diverged, if it diverged at all. Plus, it was getting dark. Being lost in unexplored jungle at night with sheer cliffs was not a welcome feeling.

We decided to go forward because it would take us closer to our rendez-vous. We would then cut in towards the cliff face as we got to the end of this minor plateau. There might be a way up, similar to the way we were fooled into coming down.

We continued losing height until we were in the depths of a black swamp. Trees blocked the light as our feet were sucked into the dark ooze. We were tired. It was late and the swamp was a depressing place to spend the night. Noxious gases were released as we struggled to pull our feet free. A blue oily film floated on the surface of the mosquito infested slime.

We decided that the swamp was the last place we wanted to spend our first evening in the Maliau. We could see the cliffs looming above us. We made a bold decision. We would push up the cliffs since the path we were taking went deeper and deeper into the lowland jungle.

Tony was tired. He had been helicoptered in from his comfortable desk job and he was now sitting in a dark swamp, about to cliff climb with a stranger, at night, in one of the most remote jungles in the world.

I was concerned about him. He had twenty years on me, but he was the one who suggested that we haul ourselves up the cliff. All he asked was that we have a good rest before we attempted the ascent. I gave him what little water I had, knowing it would be the last of our water for some time.

A wet wonderful world that has yet to be fully explored.

The sun had set, but there was still a dull light that illuminated our climb. The first section up was through tight brush and razor-sharp roatan. It was demanding, but doable.

We hit the first ledge. Using cracks in the rock, we pulled ourselves up. We hit our second ledge. Once again there were enough crevices to gain a purchase. Then we hit the wall—sheer cliff that ended in a green cornice of tangled, moss-covered roots. Momentarily set back, we explored the base of the cliff for a way up. We were drenched by the constant fall of water from the moss forest high above us. We had followed a narrow game trail along the base. We could spend the night here in the overhang below the face, but the sight of our quest, after working so hard, drove us on.

We had no ropes, no climbing gear, so it would be tough going. Office building-size chunks of cliff had fallen off and blocked our way on the side. Occasionally there was a collapsed section but they ended up in sheer overhangs. Finally, we found what we were looking for: a section of the cliff that had fallen away leaving a crack that enabled us to get tantalizingly close to the green overhang—more importantly, a large tree root that gave us something that would allow us to hike up the clean, cliff face.

I climbed up to see if it was possible. I pointed out to Tony that once we were over, we could not come back down. We could find another cliff face just as high, if not higher, beyond this climb. Tony told me to go first. We could barely see in the dusk. We were soaked with sweat, hungry and thirsty after our climb. We didn't know if we had the energy to make this climb.

I began to climb. I fell back, a handful of moss and dirt clutched in each hand. I burrowed my hands to find something solid. I began to climb slowly and nervously. A slight tug or pressure could bring down tons of rock and trees on top of me.

As I gained in height, the chance of going back down seemed dimmer and dimmer, making each upward move that much more desperate. My muscles were shaking with exertion as I reached the cornice. What looked like a green ledge was now a four foot overhang covered in slippery moss and elastic roots. For awhile I was baffled. I could not get a grip on anything to move myself back and then over. I could not go down, sideways or up. My muscles were turning weak and my mouth was dry. I locked my legs around the dangling roots and jammed my hand into the deep moss. Still nothing to hold onto. If there was nothing to hold onto, maybe I could use that to my advantage. Desperately, I began to burrow through the roots and moss with my bare hands. I almost laughed with the sight I must have presented as I broke through the dirt and moss to finally find a tangle of solid roots above. My strength was drained as I wedged my arm in like a stick and threw my leg up to avoid falling back to the rocks below.

The nepenthes or pitcher plant is actually a leaf tip.

Catching my breath, I found myself in the cloud forest of the rim. I crawled the remaining fifty feet under roots and over moss to discover that we were back on the rim.

Covered in dirt and my clothes dripping, I weakly made my way to the ridge. I yelled to Tony we had made it. I searched for a creeper or vine to help Tony up.

I tore off a creeper and dangled it down for Tony to tie his pack to. Tony said, "Don't worry. I'll come up with my pack." He began to climb using the vine for support. When he reached the green wall that I had to burrow through, he used the vine to crawl over. As he tried to lift his leg up for the final push, he paused, looked at me and then fell back down. It all happened in slow motion. I almost laughed as Tony calmly looked at me as he slowly shrank in size and fell to the rocks below. When he hit, back first, I don't think he even blinked. No screams, yells, or grunts. He just lay there calmly, eyes wide open. I assumed he was dead.

Now I was faced with a decision. Go down and apply first aid (or last rites) or climb up and go for help to carry him to the helipad. Thankfully, before I had time to decide which action to take, Tony quietly said, "I think I hurt myself." Surprised he was alive, I asked if he needed assistance.

"No, just let me lie here awhile."

He had fallen a sickening distance. Later we discovered what had saved his life. He had fallen in the crevice of two large moss covered rocks. In the crevice, the moss was almost three feet thick. Twelve inches either way, he would have had only two inches of moss to cushion the impact.

He rested for quite a while. This time, I hauled his pack up and then used the vine to take him all the way up. It was dark now. We shivered with cold as the temperature dropped and the sweat from our exertion chilled us. It looked like rain.

I found a hollow tree large enough to hold two people in moderate comfort. Lining it with fern fronds, it made a passable bivouac for the night. Tony's pack held a cornucopia of treasures: a tin of sardines, one can of orange juice, newspaper, plastic bags—and eureka!—a pack of matches.

After planting Tony in his fern bower, I set about building a fire to dry our clothes and to provide some heat. It was not easy to create fire with wood that has been continuously wet.

After a few false starts and with the last of the dry newspaper, the fire reluctantly smoked to life. It is almost perverse to say we spent quite an enjoyable evening with a roaring fire on the edge of the cliff inside a fern-lined hollow tree. It is hard to describe the pleasures of relative existence. I say "relative" because we might have had to spend the night in the swamp. We might have had no matches, no food, and Tony could be dead.

The rain came down in polite periods, allowing us to dry out in front of the fire. Each onset was heralded by gentle showers before the deluge.

Tony became consumed by thirst, so I set off to find water, using the large plastic bags Tony brought to collect plant samples. At night the confused tangle of trees turned into a nightmare of dead ends, pits, and the ever present cliff face.

I tried walking down to where the water eventually gathers in small streams before joining the rivers that flow everywhere in the Maliau Basin. In the blackness I realized that by going down and then coming back up, it would be impossible to know if I should go left or right to return to our camp, despite the light from the roaring fire, which disappeared within 20 feet. I yelled to see if sound travels. The thick moss absorbed all sound. I wisely decided to follow the edge.

I walked for about a mile in the dark along the rim in search of water and almost fell into an open pit. Open is not a good description because it was full of brown water. I kneeled down and drank my fill from the gritty stagnant water. I kindly did not tell Tony where I found the water.

The morning dawned cold and wet. The fire was still smoldering. The sun skittered across the top of the mist, creating a strange sunrise. I climbed out on an overhanging limb to take a picture. The trees grew out and over still blocking a clear view of the golden ocean below. I still couldn't capture the sense of being on the edge of a lost world. I was barred in by the jungle.

The Maliau can be a trackless nightmare for the uninitiated.

As we warmed up in the sunlight, Tony took stock of his damage. His leg had been twisted in the fall. His back had been bruised by landing on his pack. He could walk, but in great pain. We made our way slowly to the base camp. At every steep descent or ascent, Tony's condition worsened. But he still stopped to point out rare plants and unusual species. We also passed signs of people—traps set by the logging camp workers for deer, pigs and rhino. A single rhino horn can be worth a year's wages. Poachers dig large pits near the wallows and come back once a month to check on their luck.

We met up later that day with Coskun and Jon. They had spent a cold and wet night listening to civets fighting with rats. They looked tired and haggard.

In my pack, I had the foresight to bring a bottle of cognac. After our first meal and a celebratory toast, we set up camp for the next week. We spent the following days exploring the basin and the highways of water that led down to the great waterfalls below. Walking in the cool water on the flat sandstone bottom was pleasant.

The rivers run reddish brown from the tannin that leaches from the podsol, or heath forest. Podsol (a Russian word) forests have poor acidic soils and leaves full of tannin. The constant percolation of the water creates the tea-colored stain in it.

The sandstone bed rivers of the Maliau are stained brown by the tannin from the podsol forests.

The foam in the water is caused by saponins in the leaf matter. This creates the impression that the water is dirty and full of detergents. The truth is, this is pure water collected from rain, which drains into the Kuamut river. If coal mining is allowed to affect the natural water retention and drainage, not only would there be flash floods, but sulphur from the coal would pollute the water downriver.

The Future of the Maliau

There is a considerable amount of coal in the Maliau Basin. Borneo is cursed with low sulphur coal and oil; the finest available. It runs in shallow seams about four to seven feet thick, close to the surface. Initial estimates of income to be derived from this coal are significant. The unknown factor is that coal sells very cheaply in the Third World and the discovery in Kalimantan of the world's purest coal casts a shadow over the feasibility of the Maliau being an efficient source of coal.

Thankfully, the Maliau is identified by the Sabah Foundation, the state owned timber concession, as an area for preservation. Scientists like Tony Lamb and others have identified many rare species in the unique eco and biosystem of the Maliau. Also, the world famous international expedition, the Camel Trophy, will attempt to walk into the Maliau Basin, focusing much needed attention on the area.

One morning the Iban workers and the surveyor from the coal company stopped by our base camp. We were aware of their presence but had never run into them before. They were surveying the area's coal seams, and the orange flagging tape was sprouting like wild flowers. We carried the scars on our shins from hitting the punji-like stakes they leave when they clear the survey trails, or *rentuses*.

We chatted with Tony Voon, the head surveyor. He is a pleasant Chinese man who is an old hand in the Maliau. He has worked on and off surveying coal for the Kuching-based Broken Hill Coal Company for the last six years. He has surveyed the 40 kilometer rim path and most of the basin. Like the few people who have made it into the "Lost World," he has come to love the Maliau, despite the long term implications of his work. The poignancy of this dilemma was highlighted when he came by one morning with a bright magenta orchid; a rare Dendrobium Aegle. His find was the second known plant of its type on earth. The delicate plant he held in his hand had been found only once before and that was in Borneo. The man who had discovered the first of its species was Tony Lamb, who found it first in Gunung Alab in 1991.

I found it hard to understand how two people with such dissimilar goals could share in such a similar joy of discovery. If the Maliau is not protected soon, it will surely become the "Lost World."

Maliau Basin★

90 km from Danum Valley

You will probably hear stories of the Maliau Basin or the "Lost World" of Borneo. It is a truly remote and beautiful place. An uninhabited 390sq km basin shaped like a tiara with Gunung Lotung being the highest peak at 5468m. It is protected by sheer cliffs and surrounded in mist. Once in the lost world, you are surrounded by *podsol* (heath) forest that ranges from lowland dipterocarp to mossy forest. The tea-colored water drains out of the Basin through a network of tablelike rivers that ends in a series of dramatic waterfalls. There is an area put aside for research and conservation. In the future, it may become a popular adventure destination. If you want to explore the Maliau, contact Jon Rees at **White Water Adventures,** *P.O. Box 13076, KK, (088) 223924* in KK. All supplies will have to be hiked or helicoptered in. The cost will depend on whether you want to be dropped in by chopper or hike in from the steadily encroaching logging roads.The Maliau is part of the Danum Valley Conservation Area and can be reached by hiking in from a nearby logging road or by helicopter.

Keningau

128kms from KK by road

If you want to see the rate at which Sabah is bleeding timber, spend a few hours in downtown Keningau sipping ice cold beer and counting the timber trucks. Keningau is an outpost before you head into the maze of logging roads that vein Sabah. I always seem to end up in Keningau to get fuel or supplies or dropped off by helicopter in the sports stadium, but I would not recommend it to anyone who wants anything but cold beer or needs their truck repaired. For the masochist tourist there is a Chinese temple next to the bus terminal and a large tamu on Thursdays. The best hotel is the Hotel Perkasa Keningau.

Where to Stay in Keningau

Hotel Perkassa-Keningau   **M$92–200**

Jalan Kampung Keningau, ☎ *(087) 331045, FAX 334800*

A hotel populated by the timber crowd 1 km from the center of town towards Tambunan. There is a disco, small restaurant and the usual amenities the Chinese business crowd seeks. The hotel is old and tired (the last rehab was in 1983) probably due to the fact that there is no competition here.

Government Resthouse   **M$40**

Across the street from Hotel Perkassa, Book a room in the resthouse at the District Office
☎ *(087) 331535*

Penny pinchers can choose the Government resthouse across the way which will cost them M$40.

The Cloud Forest

Down Mt. Kinabalu

Mount Kinabalu is actually a large plateau located at the northern end of the Crocker range. The massive mountain rises to 13,455 feet (4101 m) to become the highest peak in the Malay Archipelago. There are two very plausible sources for the name Kinabalu. The first and most likely source for the name is the Dusun, or Kadazan term, *Aki Nabalu* or "Revered Place of the Dead." The other is a more fanciful Chinese derivative; A Chinese Prince arrived in search of a large pearl on top of the mountain. The pearl was guarded by a dragon which he quickly slew and soon after he married a beautiful Kadazan girl. He soon grew homesick for China and promised his wife he would return. She climbed the mountain every day to search for his returning ship but it never came. She lay down and died and was turned to stone. The mountain was given the name *kina balu*, or Chinese widow. Take your pick, but the mountain was not climbed until just over 100 years ago. The local Kadazan refused to climb it and even made regular sacrifices to the gods that lived on the mountain.

Today the mountain is laughably simple to traverse as you are passed by groups of local school children wearing tennis shoes. You have to wonder why it took three attempts over the 37 years, between 1851 when Sir Hugh Low made the first unsuccessful attempt, and its final scaling by a zoologist named John Whitehead in 1888. The fact that almost 200,000 visitors walk up and down the mountain with little more than a day pack and a water bottle does remove some of the adventure. There are places on the mountain that have not been climbed but, then again, nobody has climbed the Sabah Foundation building either. In 1994 a group of soldiers got lost trying to climb Low's Gully, so there is always the potential for danger. The unique beauty of Kinabalu is its commanding position as the most diverse mountain ecosystem on earth. As for the walk to get there, I think Sir Low's words sum it up best: "The most tiresome walk I have ever experienced."

Most people reach Mount Kinabalu driving from Kota Kinabalu in the early morning. They then check in at park headquarters at 6000 feet, hire guides and ascend along a path used since the 1950s. The path is cleared and has handrails, steps and bridges. There are more difficult routes ranging from three to ten days. Normal ascent time is four to seven hours to Laban Ratah. Many people suffer from the combination of the high altitude and the tough hike. On the way down, the many muddy patches and gnarled roots can cause a nasty sprain.

We decide to take the helicopter up to Laban Ratah (Laban Ratah is a rest house for climbers who stay overnight) or the Paka Cave helipad and walk down. This would allow us to walk up to the summit in three hours, down to Laban in two hours, and then down to headquarters in three to four hours. It's expensive, but worth every penny.

Laban Ratah guesthouse below the summit of Mt. Kinabalu

When you begin the hike you are in lower montane forest: oak trees, nepenthes, tree ferns and rhododendrons. As you climb, you enter montane forest. The plants become smaller due to the lower temperature, and mosses and liverworts begin to appear. The next step is mossy forest, or cloud forest, typified by continual mist. The richest altitude for orchids, rhododendrons and pitcher plants is between 8–10,000 feet. The richest altitude for birds (drongos, minivets, tree pies and tailorbirds) is from 6000 to 9000 feet.

Everyone who goes up the mountain needs a guide. They can be hired from the main office for 50 ringgits a day. Along the way are many little paths leading off the main trail. Be careful when going off the path since there are many park and university studies going on.

The night before the helicopter ride, the night is alive with an electrical storm. Our one hour flight in a Sabah Air *Jet Ranger 206* helicopter at 6:30 a.m. gives us a front row seat to a cinematic sunrise. We can understand the true majesty of this mountain as it emerges out of the cool blue of night and is crowned by the golden rays of the sun ringed by a white satin cloud. We land at Laban Ratah, a flat place. Majid, our pilot, flies us over the mist-covered jungle towards the mountain and we take photographs as it grows in size. We land at 10,300 feet, just below the summit. At this altitude and early hour, there is nothing tropical about this place. The air is cool and blustery. It looks like the Scottish moors. Moss stunted trees and lichens abound. Water is everywhere. Curious people from the resthouse come out to see us and walk up to take our picture. The equatorial sun at 13,000 feet can pack quite a punch.

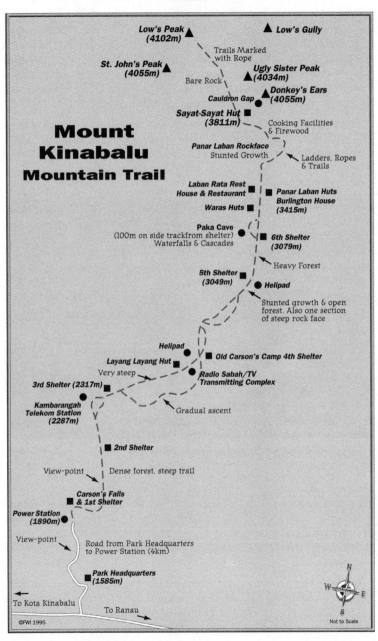

Low's Peak
(4102m)

Low's Gully

Trails Marked
with Rope

St. John's Peak
(4055m)

Ugly Sister Peak
(4034m)

Bare Rock

Donkey's Ears
(4055m)

Cauldron Gap

Sayat-Sayat Hut
(3811m)

Cooking Facilities
& Firewood

Mount
Kinabalu
Mountain Trail

Panar Laban Rockface
Stunted Growth

Ladders, Ropes
& Trails

Laban Rata Rest
House & Restaurant

Panar Laban Huts
Burlington House
(3415m)

Waras Huts

Paka Cave
(100m on side trackfrom shelter)
Waterfalls & Cascades

6th Shelter
(3079m)

Heavy Forest

5th Shelter
(3049m)

Helipad

Stunted growth & open
forest. Also one section
of steep rock face

Helipad

Layang Layang Hut

Old Carson's Camp 4th Shelter

Very steep

Radio Sabah/TV
Transmitting Complex

3rd Shelter (2317m)

Kambarangah
Telekom Station
(2287m)

Gradual ascent

2nd Shelter

View-point

Dense forest, steep trail

Carson's Falls
& 1st Shelter

Power Station
(1890m)

View-point

Road from Park Headquarters
to Power Station (4km)

Park Headquarters
(1585m)

To Kota Kinabalu

To Ranau

©FWI 1995

N
W   E
S

Not to Scale

Rumpled hikers who have been roused at 3:00 a.m. to climb to the summit eye us enviously as we arrive showered, well fed and relaxed after our high level view of the sun's arrival. For those who want to have a cold chilly night but less of a walk in the morning there is a mountaineer's hut on the other side of the mountain that is available to experienced climbers with prior permission from the park authorities. It is called the West Gurkha Hut because the Gurkha regiment in Brunei assisted in carrying it up.

We walk down rickety stairs; handmade steps of well-polished logs, and we stop at the second helicopter pad. We pause to admire the view. The mist is being sucked up and shaped into eerie vortices, dancing, fading and then rushing up again. You can see why the Murut thought this was home to the spirits of their dead.

The mists swirl and twist creating dragonlike shapes.

We sit in the crisp morning air and watch the brilliant white shapes of mist get stretched and torn by the updrafts. The long fantastic shapes look just like dragons with evil curls and serpentine tails. Each wisp of mist is torn upwards in an exotic symphony. Behind me the blue-green jungle canopy stretches as far as the eye can see. Either giddy from the high altitude or the mesmerizing effect, I understand the mystical attraction the mountain has over people.

We visit Paka cave. Before the colonials made it to the top, it was the highest point visited by the Muruts. Don't just peek in and keep walking. Behind and past the cave is a beautiful stream and waterfall with pools—a green, cool and mossy place ideal for a breather before pushing on.

The curious pitcher plant is found in great abundance here.

The major attraction of Southeast Asia's highest mountain is the montane forest—1200 species of orchids, 26 species of rhododendrons, 450 species of ferns, the trisania tree. The patient can try to spot the 518 species of birds and the energetic will come across rafflesia, pitcher plants and orchids.

Along the way we see giant mosses, pitcher plants, wild raspberries, rhododendrons, bird's nest ferns, orchids and other natural curiosities. If you are truly patient you may sight some of the more curious denizens of this lofty ecosystem—giant earthworms, giant squirrels. We spend the day photographing the various *nepenthes* plants at various altitudes in the quiet solitude. Soon the mist blows in and cools the temperature. The sounds of the first hikers making their way up the mountain disturb the reverie and we make our way down the mountain.

Kinabalu National Park

Even though Mt. Kinabalu is more of a steep hike than a climb, it can get awfully tiring if you aren't in shape or have just finished a 20-hour plane ride. You might want to save the climb towards the middle or end of your trip to Sabah. Carry water, sunglasses and an extra layer of clothing for the crisp weather at the summit and protection against the sun and rain.

Say it with pebbles

In March of 1994 five British soldiers were lost for 34 days during an attempt to climb Mt. Kinabalu via Low's Gully. Four hundred soldiers and volunteers searched for the missing men without success until a helicopter saw the letters SOS spelled out in white stones. The men were on a training expedition and had survived on 10 days of rations.

The objective is Low's Peak, the top of Mount Kinabalu. The best time to begin your ascent from the Power Station is at 7 a.m. An hour and a half climb will take you to your first stop, Kambarangoh, 2286 meters above sea level. Then it's on to Pakka Cave, Panar Laban and Sayat-Sayat, all about an hour and a half apart. The target for the end of the first day is the cabin at Panar Laban, 3350 meters. Here you'll eat a meal cooked from the fire started by your guide and sleep like the dead. Get some sleep, you'll need it because the next day is going to be tough and long.

You'll start early—about 3 a.m. not a pleasant experience after the previous day's climb and in cold weather—but if the weather is right, you'll be rewarded by one of the most piercingly beautiful sunrises you'll ever see. You'll proceed on to Sayat-Sayat, and then to Low's Peak (at this point you'll be wondering if you'll ever get to the top). After an hour of heavy climbing, you've made it! And the scenery is breathtaking; you can see almost all of Sabah before the morning clouds roll in.

The descent from the peak to the Power Station is much easier, so you should make it back by nightfall. And you'll never forget this two-day experience. Don't get cocky on the way down because it is very easy to slip or trip and spend the rest of your trip hobbling around.

INSIDER TIP

Watch for pitcher plants (nepenthes), rhododendrons and orchids. Despite what the other guidebooks tell you, pitcher plants are not "carnivorous" and the water found in the base of the plant is quite refreshing. Use your teeth to strain out the bugs.

Getting There

Kinabalu Park is about 138 km from Kota Kinabalu, Sabah's capital. By car, the journey takes roughly two hours. Taxis can be chartered from Kota Kinabalu, but negotiate the price first. Expect roughly M$80 for four passengers per taxi. Taking a minibus is the most affordable way to get there. The buses depart daily from Kota Kinabalu to Ranau, stopping at Kinabalu Park along the way. The fare is about M$8 per person one-way. Getting back to Kota Kinabalu from the park requires you to stand alongside the main road, from noon to 1 p.m., and flagging down taxis or buses. Groups can charter buses with the price of one 24-seat bus costing roughly M$225 for non-air-conditioned and

M$300 for air-conditioned. Groups of up to 12 people can also charter 4-wheel-drive vehicles from Kota Kinabalu.

Tips on Climbing Mt. Kinabalu

For starters, you need to make necessary arrangements for transportation, accommodation and climbing reservations before arrival. You need to be accompanied by a registered mountain guide, which must be arranged at least a day in advance at Kinabalu Park. Because these guides aren't actual park employees, they charge about M$60 for their services. You also need to obtain a climber's permit at Kinabalu Park or in advance from **Sabah Parks Office**, *Sinsuran Complex, P.O. Box 10626, Kota Kinabalu Sabah, Malaysia* before the climb. These are relatively cheap, costing about M$10.

INSIDER TIP

Pick up the guidebook to the park at the park office. As you ascend, try to let the groups pass you and take a few detours off the path to rest and take in the constantly changing plant species and birds. Remember that as you change altitude, the species of plants will change.

The beginning of the ascent is at the Power Station, located at 1890 meters above sea level and about an hour's walk from the main office of Kinabalu Park. To save time, you can take the mini bus shuttle that shortens your vertical trek to the Power Station for about M$10 to M$20. The most important experience is seeing how the environment changes as you slowly gain altitude. Spend as much time absorbing the scenery as you can on the way up since you may not have the same sense of wonder as you stumble, dog tired, on your way down. The lack of trees at the summit is caused by lack of soil scraped off 3000 years ago by glaciers, not cold. In fact you will be frozen, then broiled as the sun comes up. You are supposed to hire a guide for your ascent of the mountain, so by all means, bring all the camera gear and nature guidebooks you need, up to 11kg. The guide will help find any specific plants or birds you seek, so let him know what you are looking for.

Location	Elev./Dist./Time	What to look for
Timpohon Gate	1830m/0km/0min	*Nepenthes fusca*, thick oak forests.
Pondok Kandis	1981m/0.9km/20min	Tree ferns, Kinabalu balsam.
Pondok Ubah	2095m/1.7km/15min	*Nepenthes tentaculata* off the trail.
Pondok Lowii	2286m/2.3km/30min	*Nepenthes lowii*, moss forest, orchids.
Pondok Mempening	2518m/3.1km/45min	Bamboo forest, birds, look for nests.
Carson's Camp	2621m/3.9km/30min	*Rhododendron lowii, Nepenthes villosa* (unique to Kinabalu), mist.
Pondok Villosa	2942m/4.9km/45min	Scrubby vegetation, thin air.
Pondok Paka	3052m/5.3km/30min	Paka cave, vegetation thins.
Panar Laban	3300m/5.8km/1hr.	Overnight rest house, edge of "tree line."
Summit	4101m/8.5km/3hrs	Go slow due to thin air, leave by 10:30 a.m. due to heavy mist.

Where to Stay at Kinabalu Park

Reservations at Kinabalu Park should be made well in advance, especially during public holidays. They get booked quite early. Weekend and holiday rates are quoted here and are 20 percent cheaper during the week. You should book in advance by contacting **Sabah Parks (Reservations)** *P.O. Box 626, Kota Kinabalu, Sabah* or call the reservation clerk at ☎ *(088) 211585*

On the mountain

Laban Rata Resthouse   **M$25**

at 3300 meters
A 54 bed resthouse that has one of the best views in Southeast Asia. Accommodation is in four bed rooms. There is a restaurant and it gets cold at night.

Waras, Panar Laban, Guntin Lagadan   **M$5**

at 3415 meters

These huts are used by students and do not have any heat or services. You can walk to the restaurant at Laban Rata for food or hot water. Waras & Panar have 12 beds each and Guntin Lagadan has 44 beds.

Sayat Sayat   M$10

at 3811 meters

A very crude 8 bed tin shack that has cooking facilities and firewood.

Park Headquarters

Raja Lodge   M$1000

5 bedrooms. This is the most expensive of the accommodation facilities. Prices can be as much as M$1000 per night.

Kinabalu Lodge   M$360

4 bedroom sleeps 8 people.

Chalets   M$50–250

There is a wide range of chalets in the park. You can choose from twin bed (sleeps two) cabins for M$50, annexes that sleep 4 for M$100, two bedroom chalets that sleep 6 for M$200. Deluxe chalets can sleep 5 and 7 people and go for M$200 and M$250.

Old/New Hostel   M$10

The old hostel has 46 beds, the new hostel has 52 beds. The hostels are kept up and have cooking areas and a fireplace.

Outside the Park

Hotel Perkassa Mt. Kinabalu   M$125–290

WDT 11, Ranau outside Kundasang ☎ *(088) 214142*

A posh 74 room resort hotel overlooking the Kundasang valley and mountain.The 1981 hotel is on 20 acres at an elevation of 4900 feet above sea level. You can choose one of the 18 luxury suites with refrigerator.

Kinabalu Rose Cabin   M$100–230

Before entrance to park, near Ranau, ☎ *(088) 889233*

Fairly new choice with well furnished rooms and suites.

Traveller's Cottage   M$200

Before entrance to park, ☎ *(088) 750313*

Two bedroom cottages that sleep six. With kitchen and sitting area.

Kinabalu Resort Hotel   M$70–90

Near the entrance to park, ☎ *(088) 810781*

Rooms with attached baths, TV and restaurant.

Searching for the proboscis monkey on a tributary of the Kinabatangan River.

Kinabatangan River★

115km, 3.5 hrs from Sandakan

The longest (560 km) river in Sabah meanders through a very important basin. Here you can find the Jimmy Durante-nosed, beer-bellied, proboscis monkey with great regularity. Orang utan nests and rhino tracks are common; traces of Asian elephants are also very common. This area is sparsely inhabited due to flooding and the continual threat from pirates. Whether you actually see animals is a matter of luck and stealth. This is one of the best areas in Sabah for accessible wildlife spotting. Best bet for spotting proboscis monkeys is before and shortly after dawn on a tributary of the Sungai Menanggol, where you can see the curious-looking monkey (*nasalis larvatus*) in the trees above. Thankfully, the female of the species is more attractive, with a pert upturned nose. Since the area is mostly mangrove swamp, the monkeys spend each evening and morning socializing, eating and mating in the trees.

Getting In

Book a tour in KK or contact the caretaker in the village of Sukau to stay at the rustic lodge 6 km down river. You will need a guide and a boat. The 1.5 hour boat ride from the market in Sandakan to Suad Lamba costs M$3 and leaves at 11:00 am. or you can take the 3.5 hour minibus ride (M$100, 115km) to Sukau.

Where to Stay on the Kinabatangan

Most folks stay at Uncle Tan's about a 45 minute longboat ride from Sukau. There is also the Sukau Resthouse in Sukau where you can arrange boat trips for about M$30 an hour.

Proboscis monkeys can be seen at dawn or dusk as they feed by the rivers.

Kota Belud

77km north of KK

This small Bajau town is worth visiting to experience the Sunday morning *tamu* or market. It is also an ideal place to buy local handicrafts of the Bajaus and Kadazans. Try to catch the Kadazan harvest festival, a very colorful and vibrant *gawai*.

There is a new luxury resort called Shangri-La RasaRia Resort under construction on the beach about 10 kms south of Kota Belud. The resort will be a lowrise ultra luxury affair with 333 rooms. Scheduled for opening in early 1996.

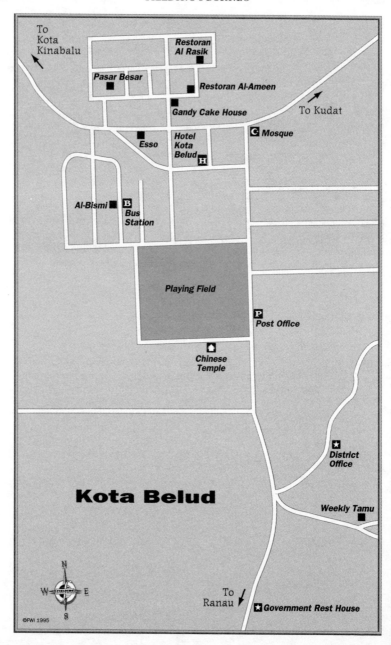

To
Kota
Kinabalu

Restoran
Al Rasik

Pasar Besar

Restoran Al-Ameen

Gandy Cake House

To Kudat

Esso

Hotel
Kota
Belud

G Mosque

H

Al-Bismi

B
Bus
Station

Playing Field

P Post Office

Chinese
Temple

Kota Belud

District
Office

Weekly Tamu

N

W   E

S

©FWi 1995

To
Ranau

Government Rest House

Kota Kinabalu or "KK" is just minutes from the pristine Crocker range.

Kota Kinabalu

1470kms from Singapore, 811kms from Kuching

This is Sabah's rather bland capital with a population of about 200,000; locals call it KK. The history is far more interesting that the current reality. KK was nicknamed Api Api (or fire, fire) because it was attacked and burned by pirates so many times and was flattened by the Allies in WWII. It's now an unappealing mix of dull modern structures and dull older structures. The only buildings that have survived are the Sabah Tourism Building (the old Post Office) and the Atkinson Clock Tower. KK is also busy reclaiming land from the sea so the quaint (but foul smelling) stilt villages will slowly be replaced by more nondescript apartment buildings.

The best advice is do your shopping, get your onward ticket reconfirmed and head out into the boonies. Before you go make sure you check out the:

State Mosque

(Best time to visit is during prayers)
Visit the gold-domed State Mosque (designed by an Italian architect in 1977) with its contemporary Islamic architecture.

Sabah Museum ★

(Open every day except Friday, 10a.m. -6p.m.)
This dramatic and large museum is a younger brother to the Sarawak Museum in Kuching. You should swing through here to see their collection and display of tribal artifacts. Don't miss the ornately carved Sea Bajau boat (called a *lipa lipa*) and the stuffed rhino upstairs. (Probably the only rhino you are going to see in Borneo.) Outside the museum is a re-creation of local village buildings.

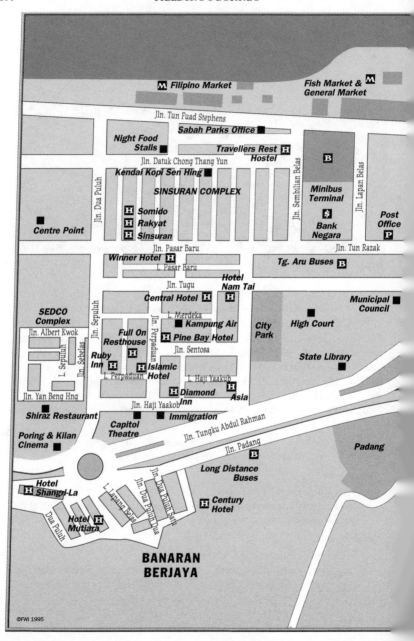

Filipino Market

Fish Market & General Market

Jln. Tun Fuad Stephens

Sabah Parks Office

Night Food Stalls

Travellers Rest Hostel

Jln. Datuk Chong Thang Yun

Kendai Kopi Sen Hing

SINSURAN COMPLEX

Minibus Terminal

Centre Point

Jln. Dua Puluh

Jln. Sembilan Belas

Jln. Lapan Belas

Somido
Rakyat
Sinsuran

Bank Negara

Post Office

Jln. Pasar Baru

Winner Hotel

L. Pasar Baru

Jln. Tun Razak

Tg. Aru Buses

Hotel Nam Tai

Jln. Tugu

Central Hotel

L. Merdeka

Municipal Council

SEDCO Complex

Jln. Albert Kwok

Jln. Sepuluh

Jln. Perpaduan

Kampung Air

City Park

High Court

Full On Resthouse

Pine Bay Hotel

Jln. Sentosa

State Library

Ruby Inn

L. Sepuluh

Jln. Sebelas

Islamic Hotel

L. Perpaduan

L. Haji Yaakub

Jln. Yan Beng Hng

Diamond Inn

Asia

Jln. Haji Yaakob

Shiraz Restaurant

Capitol Theatre

Immigration

Poring & Kilan Cinema

Jln. Tungku Abdul Rahman

Jln. Padang

Padang

Long Distance Buses

Hotel Shangri-La

L. Lapang Belas

Jln. Dua Puluh Satu

Dua Puluh

Century Hotel

Hotel Mutiara

Jln. Dua Puluh Dua

BANARAN BERJAYA

©FWI 1995

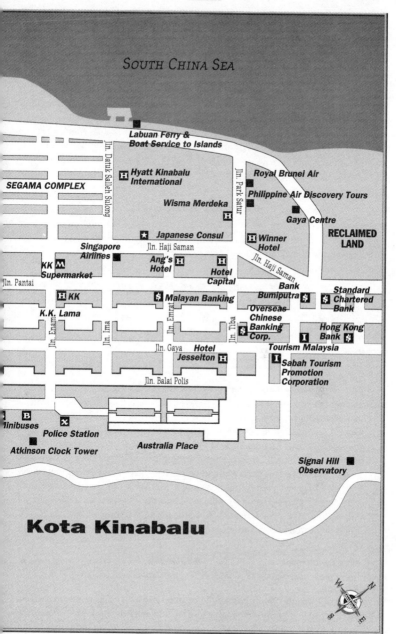

SOUTH CHINA SEA

Labuan Ferry &
Boat Service to Islands

Hyatt Kinabalu
International

SEGAMA COMPLEX

Wisma Merdeka

Royal Brunei Air

Philippine Air Discovery Tours

Gaya Centre

RECLAIMED
LAND

Japanese Consul

Jln. Haji Saman

Winner
Hotel

Singapore
Airlines

KK
Supermarket

Ang's
Hotel

Hotel
Capital

Jln. Haji Saman

Jln. Pantai

KK

K.K. Lama

Malayan Banking

Bank
Bumiputra

Standard
Chartered
Bank

Overseas
Chinese
Banking
Corp.

Hong Kong
Bank

Tourism Malaysia

Jln. Gaya   Hotel
Jesselton

Sabah Tourism
Promotion
Corporation

Jln. Balai Polis

Minibuses

Police Station

Atkinson Clock Tower

Australia Place

Signal Hill
Observatory

Kota Kinabalu

Kampung Ayer   ★

(Worth about an hour or so in the early morning or late afternoon.)

It's a quick boat trip across the bay to Kampung Ayer or Water Village to see houses and sidewalks on stilts. If you time your return for about 3:30 you can watch the fishing boats return and explore the colorful (but pungent) marketplace.

Getting In

The international airport is a quick 6 kms (15 minutes) from the center of town. You can take the bus for 65 sen or a cab for M$25. Any journey through Sabah starts and ends in dull but friendly KK, a boom town. It is the best place to arrange your adventures from. Mt. Kinabalu trips should be booked here first. Sabah Parks office is at ☎ *(088)211585 (Block K of Sinsuran Kompleks on Jalan Tun Fuad Stephens)*; the TDC office can be reached by calling ☎ *(088)211732*; it is in the Wing Onn Life Building on *Jalan Segunting*.

Getting Around

Taxis are by far your best bet. Although I have a low opinion on cabs on this side of the pond the cab drivers in Malaysia tend to be jolly trustworthy people who think nothing of carrying around your luggage all day and meeting you later in the afternoon to take you the few miles to your hotel.

Where to Stay in KK

Other than the Tanjung Aru Resort (which is a ways out of town) accommodation in KK is fairly bland. The aging Hyatt is your best bet if you want to be near the market and harbor.

Shangri-la' Tanjung Aru Resort   M$380–650   ★★★★

Jalan Aru, Tanjung Aru Beach. ☎ *(088) 225800, FAX: 217155.*
500 rooms.

The only choice in resort accommodations in KK. About 10kms from the airport and out in a residential suburb. This top class 500 room resort hotel was revamped and expanded in 1993. Rooms and suites with balconies and panoramic ocean views. There are four restaurants so you can take your pick of Continental, Italian (mediocre at best) Chinese, seafood and other Asian specialties. Lounge, poolside bar, disco-pub. Fitness center, two swimming pools, beach, outdoor Jacuzzi, four tennis courts, nine-hole pitch-and-putt golf course and color TV (CNN junkies will rejoice). There are nonsmoking rooms and wheelchair access. Staying here is truly feels like you are on vacation with the usual resort treatment. A great oasis and the only place to stay if you want to have a little fun and recreation while in KK. The health club harbors what is probably the most expensive whorehouse/health club in Borneo.

Hyatt Kinabalu International   M$310–550   ★★

Jalan Datuk Salleh Sulong ☎ *(088)221234, FAX: 225972.*
345 rooms.

A well worn, slighty musty business hotel with 315 rooms caters mostly to business travelers and tour groups who can't afford the Tanjung Aru resort. Most rooms face on to a central atrium which makes the rooms noisy when the band plays in the lounge downstairs. During heavy monsoons the rain beats like a drum on the Filon corrugated roof. Chinese and Malaysian restaurants. Hugo's grillroom. 24-hour cafe. 2 bars. Cocktail lounge. Entertainment. Swimming pool. Health center. Regency Club.

Capital Hotel **M$125–220**

23 Jalan Haji Seman. ☎ *(088) 23199, FAX 23722.*
One of the oldest hotels in KK built in 1920. Don't assume that this old 102 room hotel is also charming since it acquired its grim look when it was freshened up in 1967 and 1983. Dining room serving Western/Chinese cuisine. Cocktail lounge. Nightclub. Watersports and boating. 20 feet from ocean and in the harbor area.

Hotel Shangri-la **M$150–320**

75 Bandaran Berjaya ☎ *(088) 212800, FAX 212078*
Don't confuse this ten story downtown hotel with the resort. This 1974, 126 room hotel is unrelated in either location, ownership or quality. It was fixed up in 93 and is a budget alternative to the more expensive Capital and Hyatt. Rooms are all AC with CNN, phone, bath, hair dryer and minibar. Nonsmoking rooms available.

Jesselton **M$100–120**

69 Gaya ☎ *(088) 55633*

Moderate

Winner **M$65–85**

9 Haji Saman, ☎ *(088) 52688*

Asia Hotel **M$40–70**

68 Jalan Bandaran Berjaya (off Jalan Tunku Abdul Rahman) ☎ *(088) 53533*
A cheap and cheerful alternative amongst the budget bunks.

Rakyat **M$30–45**

Block 1, Sinsuran, ☎ *(088) 211100*

Ang's Hotel **M$28–32**

28 Jalan Bakau ☎ *(088) 234999, FAX 217867*
Probably one of the better deals for budget travelers AC, color TV phone and bath.

Cheap

If you don't want to stay in KK head out to Kampung Likas for lower prices and stress levels. Take a minibus or taxi.

Islamic Hotel **M$25–35** ★

27 Jalan Perpanderuan ☎ *(088) 54325*
Most backpackers seem to start here (probably because most guidebooks list it) and then wander up and down the street to cut their best deal. Don't be afraid to negotiate if there is no one else in the hotel or you can get a better rate down the street at any one of the other budget hotels.

Traveller's Rest **M$25–38**

3rd Floor Block L, Sinsuran Complex, ☎ *(088) 231892*

Likas Guest House **M$15–30**

371 Likas, Kampong Likas, ☎ *(088) 31706*

"KK" is a bustling, unattractive town.

Cecilia Bed & Breakfast   **M$12–30**

413 Saga, Kampong Likas ☎ *(088) 35733*
Many travelers stay here because they are going onward with owner Danny Chew
who offers tours around Sabah.

Kudat

240 kms (4 hours) from KK

Kudat is the home of the Rungus people and located a half day's drive from Kota Kinabalu. Inhabitants live in longhouses. The women wear black ankle-length *sarungs* (sa-
rongs). They weave baskets and hats, make beaded adornments and metal jewelry.
Because of Kudat's relative islolation in the north of Borneo it is a good spot to see the
locals living in longhouses and going on in a relatively undisturbed manner. If you continue north 11 kms to Bak Bak you can be truly alone on the wild and rugged beaches.
On Sunday there is a *tamu* in nearby Sikuati about 23 kms away. Kudat has a government
Resthouse (M$15) and a good selection of cheap hotels for the usual M$30.

Penampang Village

13 km from KK,

Penampang is popular with tourists who can get a quick view of the Kadazan tribe at
work, their traditional structures, activities and handicrafts.

Pulau Tiga Park

50 kms south of KK

Pulau Tiga or Three Island park is in fact three islands that can be reached from Kuala
Penyu. From there it's a 45 minute boat ride to the coral reefs and pristine environment.
If you want to take a boat directly from KK you can expect to pay $150 per person (max-
imum of four or M$200 if there are just two of you. There is a research facility on the is-
land and there is little to do if you do not snorkel.

The Canopy Walk at Poring Hot Springs

Poring Hot Springs

43kms from Mt. Kinabalu Park Headquarters, 19 km north of Ranau

Most people don't realize there is another side to Mt. Kinabalu National Park, but a trip to Poring Hot Springs is the ideal reward to a long day or two of climbing. These hot springs, first developed by the Japanese as a recreation center for officers during World War II, are now a hiker's delight. The Japanese built a series of baths using wooden tubs. There are also many other hot springs that are undeveloped. There is a butterfly orchid garden, small menagerie of local animals and rafflesia is found in this area.

The natural open-air baths contain sulphur that is deemed healthy to the skin. Don't expect anything exotic; the tubs are dram cement cubes that require you to fill them using the scalding hot water and moderating cold water to get the right temperature. It is ideal for a post hike soak. The next day you may want to explore the area around the baths that leads to rich-lowland forest, mountain rivers, waterfalls and bat caves. The last bus from the Park HQ leaves at 2:30p.m. *There is a M$2 entry fee, a M$5 for cameras and a small fee for video cameras. Admission to the park is free for overnight guests. The baths are open 7 a.m. to 6 p.m. daily.*

Jungle Canopy Walkway

(Up the hill from the Park HQ across the suspension bridge)
There is also the 150 foot high canopy walk sponsored by the Smithsonian that will take you up into the canopy of a Southeast Asian rainforest. You won't see much as you cross the three 200 foot spans to the four platforms except large insects, praying mantis and butterflies but at least you can tell people you have been there. The canopy walk is a stiff hike up a hill and then along a series of swaying aluminum platforms supported by cables. Try to experience the canopy early in the morning and

at dusk. Ask the ranger if there are any rafflesia in bloom and see what animals are in captivity at the zoo. The hours for the canopy don't allow you to truly experience the dusk, dawn and evening periods when the canopy is really alive but it beats carrying climbing gear. I had the opportunity to experience the canopy while it was under construction and during a variety of time periods and recommend it highly. Watch for flying squirrels, giant squirrels and birds. They are hard platforms, but you will have to tiptoe across the aluminum planks. *Hours for the canopy walk are 10am - 4pm. You can reserve ahead to experience the walkway at night for an additional cost of M$45 for 3 people plus another M$12 per extra person. Plan on a 30 minute hike to get to the walkway.*

Where to Stay at Poring Hot Springs

Rates are more expensive on weekends and holidays. There are student discounts of up to 50 percent. Ask for the cabins by the river. The lodging at Poring Hot Springs is being expanded so check for any new additions.

Poring Hostel   **M$10**

The 24 bed dormitory can be crowded with students. Blankets and pillows are provided. One room sleeps eight people. Kitchen with cooking facilities.

New Cabin   **M$60–80**

Cabins are preferable to the hostel. Two twin bedrooms sleep four.

Old Cabin   **M$75–100**

Three rooms.

Camp Ground   **M$2**

Camping is the least preferred lodging since it rains quite a bit and it gets chilly. Tents, blankets and pillows can be rented at the office.

Ranau
156 kms from KK, 18kms from Poring Hot Springs

Ranau is an agricultural area known more for its **war memorial** in Kundasang than for its scenery. After the Japanese forced Australian and British prisoners of war to build the airport at Sandakan, they force-marched 2400 of them (mostly Australian) to Ranau. Only six prisoners survived the 11-month, 240 km march. This act killed more Australians than any other single event in WWII. There is a particularly disturbing monument with a plaque that describes the beating, torture and death of one Australian.

Where to Stay in Ranau

Although there are a number of budget hotels like Hotel Ranau (M$30–65) your best bet is to spend your time at one of the hotels in the park or just outside.

Sandakan
388 kms from KK

Sandakan is the former capital of North Borneo and like the current capital has little to offer visitors other than a departure point for **Sepilok Orang Utan reserve**, the **Turtle sanctuary** and the **Gomontong caves**. This is a tourist rut for the infrequent cruise ships that stop here so tours that let you take in all these attractions are plentiful and cheap. Sandakan is a modern city at the edge of the sea, known for the **Sandakan Orchid House** with its exhibits and collections of rare orchids. See the **Forestry Exhibition** for displays of local handicrafts and tribal hunting weapons.

Turtle Sanctuary

3 hours by boat from Sandakan

Just north of Sandakan are three islands where green and hawksbill turtles come ashore to lay their eggs. August and September are the peak seasons. There is a Government resthouse on Pulau Selingan (4 person chalets are M$120, cabins are M$30). You must reserve your stay at the Parks office in Sandakan. Most people take a tour here since the cost of hiring a boat, guide and lodging can be too expensive.

Gomantong Caves

32kms south of Sandakan

Part of the Sandakan/cruise ship tourist rut that also includes Sepilok, Turtle Islands and the Crocodile Farms. The caves are still worth a visit for first time visitors. The main cave is Black Cave (30m wide by 20m high that leads to a chamber 90m high) and the smaller but more intriguing White Cave (which branches off to several smaller caves and has long passageways). See it at sunset for the memorable sight of two million bats going out for dinner. Famous for its collection of edible birds' nests created by delicate and nervous *burong layang layang* or swiftlet. The nests are knocked off the cave walls two to three times a year by the Orang Sungeti who have traded these nests with the Chinese since the 7th century AD. The caves are a long boat ride across the bay from Sandakan and then a bumpy 16km ride to the caves. Almost all visitors book a tour in Sandakan and have them take care of the necessary forestry permit.

Crocodile Farms

Mile 8, Labuk Road

What started as a hobby has turned into a thriving business. When the Sabah government banned the hunting of wild crocodiles, the farm became a profitable enterprise exporting skins and meat. There are about 2000 crocs at any one time but none the size of the monster Sarawak saurians that have been measured at over 10 meters.

Sandakan Prisoner of War Memorial

Taman Rimba, Mile 7 Labuk Road

A simple monument commemorates the spot where 2000 Australian and 750 British servicemen were held during WWII. By September 1944 only 1800 Australians and 600 British troops were alive. These men were then marched to Ranau where a year later only six survived. This single event killed more Australian soldiers than any other event in WWII.

Agnes Keith House

Keith, an American, is known for her three books on life in Sabah; *Land Below the Wind, Three Came Home* and *White Man Returns.* Her books cover her life in Sabah including internment in a prison camp on Berhala island. The house, like all of Sandakan was destroyed during the war but has been rebuilt.

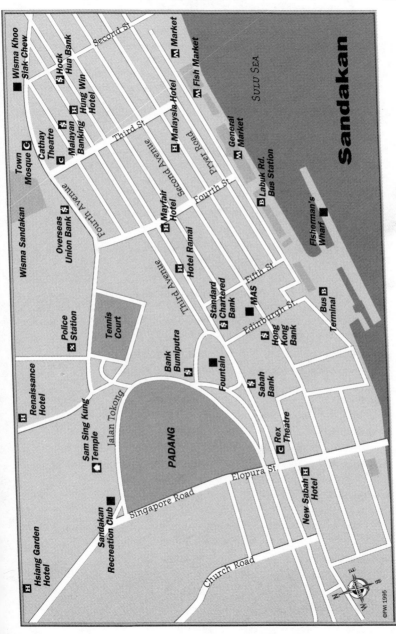

Sandakan

Wisma Khoo Siak Chew
Hock Hua Bank
Second St.
Market
Fish Market
SULU SEA
Hung Win Hotel
Town Mosque
Cathay Theatre
Malayan Banking
Third St.
Malaysia Hotel
Pryer Road
General Market
Wisma Sandakan
Overseas Union Bank
Fourth Avenue
Fourth St.
Second Avenue
Labuk Rd. Bus Station
Mayfair Hotel
Hotel Ramai
Fisherman's Wharf
Third Avenue
Standard Chartered Bank
Fifth St.
MAS
Police Station
Tennis Court
Edinburgh St.
Hong Kong Bank
Bus Terminal
Renaissance Hotel
Bank Bumiputra
Fountain
Sam Sing Kung Temple
Jalan Tokong
Sabah Bank
Rex Theatre
PADANG
Elopura St.
Hsiang Garden Hotel
Sandakan Recreation Club
Singapore Road
New Sabah Hotel
Church Road

©PWI 1995

Japanese Cemetery

Top level of the Japanese cemetery above Sandakan

A curious attraction where Japanese soldiers who died in Borneo during WWII and Japanese women brought to Sandakan as prostitutes are buried. The Japanese girls were tricked into coming to Sandakan at the turn of the century when they were seven to nine years of age. They were put to work until the age of twenty and then worked as prostitutes in the town's four brothels.

Palau Berhala

Outside entrance to Sandakan Bay

A dramatic ocean island with 200m cliffs on the southern side. There are a number of caves in the pink cliffs. The island is a popular picnicking spot but was once a leper colony and Japanese prisoner of war camp. Take a boat from the fishmarket in Sandakan for about M$10.

Where to Stay in Sandakan

Most cheap sleeps are on Jalan Tiga.

Sandakan Renaissance   M$295–475   ★★★★

Mile 1 Jalan Utara, ☎ *(089) 213299, FAX271271*

The top resort type hotel in Sandakan. Their 120 rooms are for the package tour and business crowd and offer marble bath (with bathroom phone!) hair dryer, mini-bar, movies in room, ironing board, direct dial phone and 24 hour room service and concierge. Built in 1991 the hotel is on the grounds of the 1911 Governors House and is a pleasant location.

Hsiang Garden   M$76–110

Jalan Leila Hsiang Garden Estate, ☎ *(089) 273122, FAX 273127*

Hotel Ramai   M$97–145

Km 2, Jalan Leila, ☎ *(089) 273222, FAX 271884*

Hung Win Hotel   M$25–30

Jalan Tiga, ☎ *(089) 218855,*

Hotel Malaysia   M$83–118

32 2nd Ave. ☎ *(089) 218322*

Hotel Mayfair   M$32–40

24 Jalan Pryer,

If you are really hurting and want to sleep in a dorm. Make your way to Batu 7out by the airport and try a lumpy bed at Uncle Tans.

Hotel New Sabah   M$44–55

Jalan Singapura, ☎ *(089) 218711*

Uncle Tan's   M$15–20

Mile 17.5, Labuk Road, ☎ *(089) 216227, FAX 271215*

A dorm set in a plantation, close to Sepilok. Price includes breakfast.

Logging trucks use a continuous stream of water to cool their red hot brakes.

Sapulut

116km from Keningau by road

The four hour trip to this backwater terminus is not much. The town of Sapulut is even less overwhelming. Sapulut is a company town where KPD operates a tapioca mill and oddly has developed a very dramatic region called Batu Punggul. Other than this pristine area there will be little to justify visiting this remote region since logging is quickly removing any scenery worth visiting. Most visitors come to Sapulut to continue on to Batu Punggul, the site of an interesting karst rock, dramatic cave system and replica Murut longhouse. As for finding the real thing, this area is home to a number of authentic longhouses about an hour down the Sapulut River. There is a large longhouse in Kampung Silungai. (See "Into Indonesia the Hard Way"). Penisangan area is also worth visiting.

Getting In

There is a daily bus to Sapulut from Keningau. Don't try to drive here yourself since the logging companies are putting in new roads daily and if you ask directions from the truck drivers you realize that they only drive the same road everyday and have no idea where all the other roads go. If you want to visit Batu Punggul you can set up a trip with most tour companies in KK or contact the KPD (Korperasi Pembangunan Desa or Rural Development Corporation) in KK at *9km, Tuaran Road* ☎ *(088) 428910*

Getting Around

The man who has a lock on visitors to Batu Punggul and longboat rentals is Lantier Bakayas and his Sapulot Adventurism Tourism Travel Company. He can set up boat trips, cultural dancing at the Murut longhouse in Batu Punggul and anything you need to experience this area. The return boat trip will run you M$250 and depending on luggage will take four to six people.

Semporna's Darvel Bay is actually the caldera of an ancient volcano.

Semporna★

106kms north of Tawau

You will probably end up here on your way to Sipadan but nondivers will enjoy the **Dragon Inn** ☎ *(089) 781088*, a rustic resort built out over the water with a restaurant that asks that you choose your dinner from the holding tanks. Charter a boat and visit the Sea Bajau, their stilt villages and the volcanic islands in the surrounding bay. They once had pearl farms here. Semporna is the least known but probably the most diverse Marine Park in Asia. There are 73,000 acres with 70 genera of coral and over 200 species of fish. Make sure you sample at least three or four of the species at the restaurant before you go diving. If the Dragon Inn is full (which is rare) try the **Hotel Semporna** ☎ *(089) 781378* which is dull and nowhere near as interesting.

Semporna Marine Park

This 73,000 acre marine park is centered around the crater of a long extinct volcano. The islands that ring the sunken caldera are home to stilt villages and sea bajau with their ornate *lipa lipa*. If you head out past the tidal flats you can make it all the way to the Philippines and the dangerous area ruled by pirates. There are more families of coral and fish than anywhere else on earth. There was once a cultured pearl industry here but piracy forced them out.

Getting Around

It is worthwhile visiting the many tiny islands that surround the area. Boats can be hired for between M$100-150 for the return trip. Best diving is on Sipadan but you could spend years exploring the tiny islands and rich coral atolls. Pack a picnic lunch and water.

The orang utan or man of the forest can be seen here every day at feeding time.

Sepilok Sanctuary★★★

25 km outside Sandakan

Don't be fooled into thinking you will be spotting the great red ape in his natural habitat. The chances of seeing an orang utan (literally man of the forest in Malay) calmly peeling a banana while you blow through ten rolls of Velvia is slim to none. Orangs are solitary animals that stay up in the high canopies. They even make nightly nests to bed down. Other than zoos, there are few opportunities to understand and feel what it would be like to come across this gentle creature in the wild. What Sepilok has done for 30 years is offer a close up view of young and orphaned orangs being fed on a daily basis. The young apes come crashing out of the forest to have their daily meal of milk and bananas. Although the rangers do not like humans to have contact with apes (they are susceptible to our diseases) the chances are good that an inquisitive ape will sneak up behind you and give you the fright of your life. The young apes are good natured but inquisitive.

I advise you to spend your time at platform A. If you are taking pictures, a couple of words of advice: first, use a tripod, a long lens and fast film. The apes usually spend most of their time on and around the platform. Do not leave your possessions unattended, because as you're concentrating on one ape, another will calmly swing down and steal your camera bag, hat, sunglasses or even your entire video outfit. It's all in good fun, but you may not get it back in one piece. Keepers try to discourage human contact, but once you hold the soft hand of a young orang utan and look him directly in the eyes, you will know there is someone in there. Scary.

There is also a pair of Sumatran rhinos being cloistered in the hopes that they'll breed. Visitors are no longer allowed to ogle without special permission. Sepilok is the most popular of Borneo's three Orang Utan Rehabilitation centers (40,000 visitors a year).

The others are Tanjung Puting in Southern Kalimantan—run by Canadian scientist Dr. Birute Galdikus—and Semonggoh in Sarawak, 32 km from Kuching. Sepilok is a 4530 hectare forest reserve used to protect orphaned or recaptured orang utans and to help them grow to maturity—to eventually be released in the wild. There are an estimated 5000 animals left in the wild, so each one is important. The park hopes that the apes will learn to fend for themselves and go off into the wild; their orangs need too large a space and enjoy human company too much. After all most of these wards are traumatized orphans.

Take a taxi to the preserve, go to Platform A just before 10:00 a.m. (There is another less well attended feeding at 2:30 p.m.). The youngest apes will come from out of nowhere to feed on bananas and milk. You can then take a rigorous hike out to Platform B for the 11:00 a.m. feeding but don't be surprised if no one shows up. If you get hungry there is a great little Chinese fantasyland/restaurant just outside the park. *Admission fee. Open 9:00 a.m. to 4:00 p.m. Monday through Sunday.*

Tambunan

80kms from KK by road

This is the usual base of operations for trips to **Crocker National Park**. Tambunan was also the stomping grounds of Mat Salleh, the charismatic rebel leader and military fort builder of the late 1800s. Mat Salleh initiated a series of "terrorist acts" against the British North Borneo Company that was stealing tribal land. He outwitted the various military forays against him and built a great fort of stone and wood on a plain outside Tambunan that withstood 10 days of shelling, until he was killed by a stray bullet in January of 1900. Today, he is considered a national hero by Sabahans. There is a memorial north of the town in Kampung Tibabar. There is also a 15m high waterfall, a two hour hike after you get to nearby Kampung Patau.

Tambunan is a dull little burg not worthy of a special trip but if you get stuck here, there is a government resthouse ☎ *(089) 774339* up on the hill or the rustic Tambunan Village Resort Centre ☎ *(087) 774076* (about a click out of town) that was built by student volunteers. Sample some of the local rice wine or *lihing* while you're there.

Tanjung Aru

5kms south of KK airport

Capital's seaside resort features beautiful beaches. **Prince Philip Park and Recreation Center** is located just 5 km south of Kota Kinabalu International Airport. It's a lovely spot to enjoy the sunset.

Tawau

272kms from KK by or 150 kms from Lahad Datu by road

Tawau is a grubby shipping port known for its nearby hot springs and illegal immigrants from Timor and the nearby Philippines. The southeastern part of Sabah is just a jumping-off point for Tarakan in Kalimantan, Indonesia for most travelers. Take a plane or a ferry to Tarakan but get your visa first. There is a 280 sq km park, **Tawau Hills Park**, a rough ride 24 kms NW, 30 minutes out of town. There are campsites, waterfalls, day facilities and little else to recommend the hilly jungle covered park. You can reach the hot springs in three hours by taking the trail from the park HQ.

Getting Around

If you are going to Indonesia via the ferry to Tarakan or by plane make sure you have a one month entry visa (M$15) from the **Indonesian consulate** on *1 1/2 Jalan Apas* ☎ *(089) 765930* a ways out of town on the main road. Typically visas are no problem but there can be delays. If you decide to cheap out and charter a boat to the island of Nunakan, the first Indonesian village across the border, and then to travel further into Tarakan you can count on being hassled when you try to leave Indonesia. Indonesia likes foreigners to enter through major ports via air or established sea ports. Since Tawau is the tail end of Sabah, there are good flight connections via MAS: twice weekly to Tarakan (M$180), 6 daily to KK (M$96) twice weekly to Semporna (M$40), daily to Lahud Datu (M$40), and twice daily to Sandakan (M$74). The **MAS office** is in *Wisma Sasco* and opens at 8 a.m. The office closes weekdays at 4:30 p.m., 3 p.m. on Saturday and noon on Sunday. If you want to get to Tarakan via Bouraq on their bizarre little Islander **Merdaka Travel**, *41 Jalan Dunlop* ☎ *(089) 771927* will sell you a ticket. I prefer the MAS Twin Otter flight for this usually violently bumpy 35 minute ride over mangrove swamps. The airport is 2kms (M$3) from the town center.

By Road

You can take the dusty roads back to Keningau via the Toyota Landcruisers (M$80) that leave when full or take mini buses back to Semporna (M$4, 90 minutes) and Lahad Datu (M$15, 2.5 hour) Buses leave from the town center. There is little to see except endless vistas of oil palm plantations and recently deforested landscapes.

By Boat

There is an 8:30 a.m. (sailings can be unreliable) ferry that goes to Tarakan in Indonesia via Nunakan. Buy your tickets by the Customs wharf (you can also change money here but the money changers back in town will give you a better deal). Make sure you have your visa first. The ferry travels to Tarakan but clears customs in Nunakan. The cost is M$65 to Tarakan and the trip takes about four to five hours.

Where to Stay in Tawau

Head to Jalan Stephan Tan by the market for a reasonable selection of drab budget accommodations. Upscale travelers will check in at the incongruously luxurious Marco Polo that holds a western (and I mean American Western) BBQ in the lot across the street and has Filipino bands in the lobby that sing all the American top 40 songs perfectly. Because of the transients and low lifes most budget hotels tend to be dirty and grubby so I would recommend springing for decent digs here.

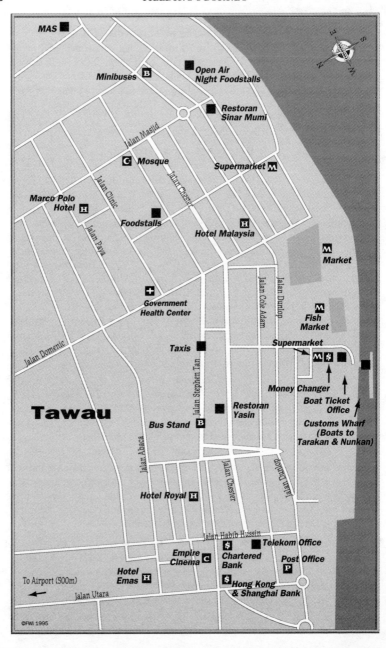

MAS

Minibuses

Open Air
Night Foodstalls

Restoran
Sinar Mumi

Jalan Masjid

Mosque

Supermarket

Jalan Clinic

Jalan Chester

Marco Polo
Hotel

Jalan Paya

Foodstalls

Hotel Malaysia

Market

Jalan Cole Adam

Jalan Dunlop

Fish
Market

Government
Health Center

Supermarket

Taxis

Jalan Domenic

Money Changer

Jalan Stephen Tan

Restoran
Yasin

Boat Ticket
Office

Tawau

Bus Stand

Customs Wharf
(Boats to
Tarakan & Nunkan)

Jalan Abaca

Jalan Dunlop

Hotel Royal

Jalan Chester

Jalan Habib Hussin

Telekom Office

Empire
Cinema

Chartered
Bank

Post Office

To Airport (500m)

Hotel
Emas

Jalan Utara

Hong Kong
& Shanghai Bank

©FWI 1995

Marco Polo   **M$115–370**   ★★

Jalan Abaca & Jalan Clinic ☎ *(089) 777988 FAX 761743*

The best and only business hotel in Tawau, built in 1985 centrally located (which isn't too hard in tiny Tawau) with AC, health club and a good Chinese restaurant. The 150 balconied rooms provide AC, cable TV, in-room movies, radio as well as views of the town and the ocean beyond. If you have been dying to try bird's nest soup, they will whip it up for you for M$120 if you give them a day's notice. Don't get your expectations or hunger too high.

Hotel Emas   **M$75–200**

Jalan Utara, ☎ *(089) 762000, FAX 763569*

If the Marco Polo is beyond your budget this is your best bet. All AC, there is a good restaurant.

Hotel Royal   **M$55– 65**

177 Jalan Bilian, ☎ *(089) 773100, FAX 772856*

Tenom

42kms from Keningau by road

Home of the Muruts, Tenom is reachable by Sabah's only railway.Trains to Beaufort leave at 7:30 a.m., 1:40 p.m. and 3:00 p.m. Tenom is a popular tourist area about a 30-minute drive from Kota Kinabalu. There are some interesting visits to the agricultural station of Tamu on market day. **Mengkabong Bajau** village is built over water. **Tamparuli** is for handicrafts and local specialties. Stroll across Sabah's longest suspension bridge. And make sure you visit the **Agricultural Research Center** (also called the Cocoa Research Station) about 10 km from Tenom. Although most people can't imagine why they would want to visit a cocoa research center, you will be pleasantly surprised.

Orchid Centre   ★★★

My friend and renowned botanist, Tony Lamb (now retired) has created one of the most unique botanical attractions in Asia with his collection of over 450 Bornean **orchids**. The best time to visit is between October to February when many of the orchids are in full bloom. A stroll around the center is impressive as you see the life work of the world's most dedicated collector of orchids. Serious students might want to set up a meeting with one of the staff's experts ☎ *(087) 735661* who can tell you volumes about the origin of each plant. There is also a definitive guidebook about orchids for sale at the center. *Hours are 8 a.m. to 1 p.m. Monday to Friday.*

Lagud Sebren Cacao Research Centre   ★★

Although the Orchid Centre is the center's jewel, what the scientists are supposed to be doing is collecting and breeding strains of indigenous and foreign plants, then convincing the locals to plant these new crops. Sabah has managed to select foreign and domestic plants and turn them into extremely profitable crops. Sabah has created cacao, rubber, palm oil strains that outproduce their home varieties and is the worlds largest supplier of cacao. The center's collection of thousands of **wild fruits and plants** is second to none and Lamb has managed to create a collection of every possible type of wild and domesticated tropical plant that could be useful to man. They are currently busy trying to tame the noxious traits of the wild durian. (Good

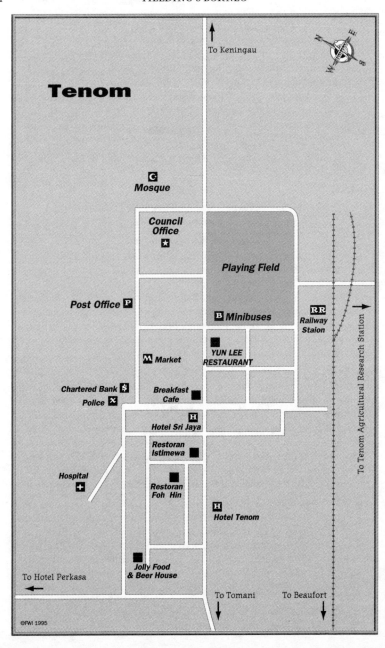

To Keningau

Tenom

C
Mosque

Council Office
★

Playing Field

Post Office P

B *Minibuses*

R·R
Railway Staion

M *Market*

■
YUN LEE RESTAURANT

Chartered Bank $
Police ✗

Breakfast Cafe ■

H
Hotel Sri Jaya

Restoran Istimewa ■

Hospital
✚

■
Restoran Foh Hin

H
Hotel Tenom

■
Jolly Food & Beer House

To Hotel Perkasa ←

To Tomani

To Beaufort

To Tenom Agricultural Research Station

©FWI 1995

luck!) The goal is to discover new agricultural products and resilient strains for export. Although the concept of wandering through acres of every type of passion-fruit, banana, vanilla nut and even many nameless trees may sound mundane, I can't think of where else you can get such a quick education in tropical fruits. The acres of hundreds of different fruits, nuts, fibres and medicinal plants are an education in themselves. *Open Monday to Thursday 7 a.m.–3 p.m., Friday till noon and Saturday til 12:30.*

Rock Carvings

(40kms south of Tenom, near Kampung Tomani at Kuala Tomani) Those looking for mystery might want to take a side trip to inspect the large boulder found near the Sungai Lumuyu in 1971. There is no explanation as to who made the carvings.

You can't see the forest for the trees.

If anyone was looking for a reason to save the forests of Borneo this may be it. The Agricultural Center contains many unusual plants that have yet to be fully tested on humans: medicinal plants, artificial sweeteners and potentially even a cure for AIDS. It's all here. The orchid center is an excellent introduction to the beauty of the world's most primitive, numerous and beautiful species.

The other major benefit of the center is to convince locals that they can actually plant fruit trees, shade trees, and balance crops beyond the nutrient-greedy rice, tapioca and maize they have traditionally grown. The new strains of seeds are bred, collected, typed and distributed free of charge.

Where to Stay in Tenom

Hotel Perkasa   M$75–86   ★

P.O. Box 225 ☎ *(087) 735811*
A massive luxury hotel that was intended to be a casino but is now a usually empty palace overlooking the town. If you book a room they will run down and pick you up from the town.

Tenom Hotel   M$30

Jalan Tun Datu Mustapha ☎ *(087) 735567*
One of the three leading budget choices with AC and TV.

Hotel Sri Jaya   M$30–35

Main Street ☎ *(087) 735669*

Research Station Resthouse   M$15

5km from the Research Centre, ☎ *(087) 735661*
I recommend this scenic rest house if you are visiting the research station with its sweeping views of the valley and pleasant breezes (they never did explain the chopped-up monitor lizard in the freezer!). You will need transportation since it is a 5 km drive from the Research Center or a M$1.5 minibus ride from town.

Green Turtle

Turtle Islands National Park

40kms (3 hours) from Sandakan by boat

These three islands are known for the regularity with which green and hawksbill turtles can be seen laying their eggs. The 17km sq park can be reached by chartering a boat from Sandakan for a very expensive M$500. You must have a permit from the park office in Sandakan and bring your own food and water. Tours are the recommended way to visit the islands. The turtles come up from the depths at night and spend hours franticly digging holes, laying their eggs and making their way back into the water. The turtles can be seen on just about every night, but August to October are peak periods. There are resthouses on the Selingaan island where green turtles are the most prevalent. Hawksbill turtles are more prevalent on Pulau Gulisaan. On Palau Bakkungan Kecil there is a curious mud volcano.

If you are in Sabah between July and October don't miss seeing the dozens of green and hawksbill turtles coming out of the water to lay their eggs. There is activity year-round if you can't make peak season. The females will come up after 8:00 p.m., while the male waits offshore. Be patient; it takes about 90–120 minutes for the laborious process. The number of spectators is limited to 20 and permits are required from the Sabah Parks Office in Sandakan. There are only three chalets, so taking a tour is best.

Getting There

Take a flight to Sandakan from KK. Visitors then must charter a boat. Currently, Wildlife Expeditions is providing the speedboats to the islands. The fares range from M$70 a passenger to M$100. For further information contact Sabah Park offices, ☎ *088-211652.*

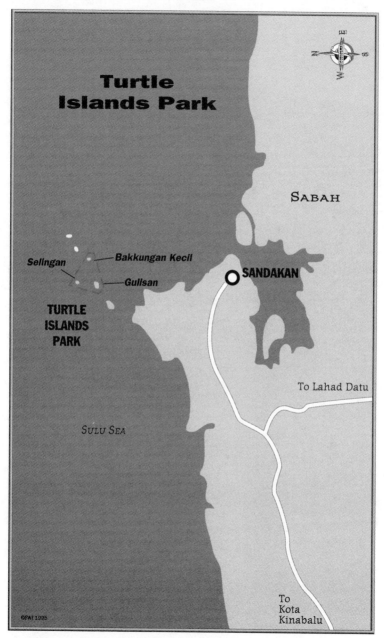

Logging trucks make their way carefully down the highest road in Sabah.

Mt. Trusmadi

70km south east of KK by road

Gunung Trusmadi is the poor brother to Gunung Kinabalu. Most people see Mt. Trusmadi from Gunung Kinabalu but never go there. It is the second highest mountain in Malaysia (2642m) and offers a truly challenging set of two climbs and a large and very rare pitcher plant to seek out. (*Nepenthes trusmadiensis*). There is a northern route that takes four days up and three days down. The two-day southern route is more difficult but takes less time. Stop in at the district office in Tambunan to hire guides and porters. March is the best time to visit the area. Those crazy enough to drive through here will have the distinction of traveling on the highest road in Borneo.

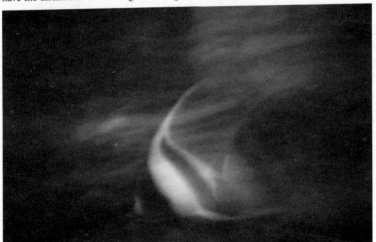

Borneo holds an equal number of attractions below sea level.

Sipadan★★★★

25 kms south of Semporna by boat

The east coast of Sabah is home to many secrets: the vanishing rhino, shy elephants, the lost world of Maliau, pirates, smugglers, caves and hundreds of undiscovered natural wonders. One such wonder is the island of Sipadan, a tiny, tear-shaped island that is one of the finest diving sites in the world. Discovered and developed by two expatriate divers, Sipadan is now available for exploration by the average diver. First discovered in the '30s and dived in the '70s, this tiny island is on the verge of being discovered, explored, exploited and ruined in just a decade.

Sipadan is assumed to be a version of the word *sempadan* or "border." It is one of the many islands whose ownership is disputed by Indonesia and Malaysia. Not surprising since it sits smack on the border between the two countries. The fact that it is visited weekly by a Malaysian gunboat might have something to do with its alignment with that country. Also, a small diving service created by Borneo Divers generates income that the Indonesian government eyes jealously.

We hastily booked a few days on the island from KK and soon found ourselves taking the forty-five minute trip to Sipadan starting along the shallow waters of Semporna and the stilt villages and then heading out to the open ocean past the Continental Shelf.

Sipadan looks like any other tropical island from above, but below the sea, Sipadan is unique. Formed as an undersea volcano, millions of years ago, it is the only deep water oceanic island in Malaysia. It rises 2000 feet (600 m) from the bottom of the sea. The other Malaysian islands sit in the shallows of the Continental Shelf, generally at depths of less than 400 feet.

The top 164 feet of Sipadan is a living coral reef where tidal currents, limestone and millions of tiny bluish, orange cup, and black corals form a reef wall that is known to a select few as the best wall dive in the world. The reef provides a habitat for barracuda, hammerhead sharks and shoals of brilliantly colored fish, some of which can be found only in Sipadan. Jacques Cousteau has called Sipadan, "an untouched piece of art."

Along the way, we flag down a fisherman and buy a "string" of crabs neatly tied together in a ladder of squirming blue crabs. As we leave the land behind, we see Sipadan is a dark speck on the horizon and we wonder just how far this small island is. The boat cuts through the shallow turquoise waters into the dark green deeper waters. Small silver fish flick nervously out of the clear waters. After you leave the scenic Darvel Bay behind, you wonder where the island could be. Then after a long stretch, it appears much smaller than you expected and magnificently isolated.

As the boat pulls up on the white beach, you get some sense of the uniqueness of Sipadan. The captain of the boat reminds us that if we're going to drop anything, drop it off the front of the boat since the water there is only three feet deep. Off the back of the boat, it is 2000 feet deep. You see why the water turns from crystal clear to dark green in a well-defined edge.

We are sitting on the top of an ancient volcano, turned atoll, turned coral reef. Sipadan is more than just another volcanic pimple in the sea. Below us are caves, overhanging gardens of coral, spawning sea turtles and probably the most diverse collection of underwater life in the tropics.

There must have been a period when Sipadan was high enough out of the water to let the natural seepage of the water form stalactites and stalagmites in its now underwater caves.

The structure of Sipadan is ideal for diving because of the wide variety of underwater topography in such a small area. Shaped like an arrowhead, the island offers steep cliffs, most with dramatic overhangs. When I say, "island," the actual area above the water is quite small compared to the total underwater area of the island. The land mass is towards the north end and is right on top of the drop-off.

Borneo Divers, run by expat Aussies, has christened various dive sites with romantic Western-sounding names: Hanging Gardens, Lobster Lairs, White Tip Avenue and Turtle Cavern. You will not find many Malaysians here since Sipadan is being developed as a dive spot that caters to Europeans, Singaporeans and Americans. The size of the island dictates that whatever development is made here must be small: Sipadan is only four hectares in size. It has one inhabitant called the "Turtle Man" who collects turtle eggs by virtue of his right to the island granted by the Sultan of Sulu. There is also a wildlife station to protect the sea turtles. The Hawksbill and Green Turtle are abundant here.

There is a full moon, so we go out to see if we can find the turtles. Finding them doesn't take long. The telltale signs are the tractorlike tracks as the heavy animals laboriously drag themselves over the coral shallows, across the sand and into the protection of the wooded areas. We hear labored sounds of things digging clumsily in the sand behind the trees. Following the tracks that show every detour she made, we find a large green turtle digging a hole. Why this spot? Why not the desert island? Each turtle has a homing instinct that tells it this is the special place.

Sipadan is a major nesting area for green and leatherback turtles.

It is one thing to see it on TV, yet another to experience the amount of energy and effort that the simple process of laying eggs requires. The turtle's breath is labored and comes in quick blasts. Her flippers dig out blindly, showering sand for ten feet behind. Over and over. Nothing happens fast. The turtle senses our presence and turns towards us. Her tears glisten in the full moon. Her tears, more a protective function, and deep hollow breaths make this seem like a painful experience. The process of digging continues for another hour. Then satisfied her nest is deep enough, the eggs begin to drop. By the time we give up counting, there are almost a hundred eggs. Although that seems like a lot, there are many predators and trials ahead of these turtles.

Into the Deep

One of the diving instructors gives us a preliminary checkout; then we head for the wall. We flop into the water and glide over the shallow reef towards the edge. When we sail over the edge I feel the dark abyss pulling me down. I have leaped off a skyscraper and there is no bottom. It is cinematic. Once you dive the walls of Sipadan you are spoiled for anything else. On the way down I notice the many caverns in the wall. Sitting, as if arranged carefully, are dozing sea turtles, one to a cave.

Since the beach is the leading edge of the island, I will make my way around the reef down to a depth of 120 feet. Most of the coral, rising and falling as the reef dictates, is in the top 150 meters. Wall dives are the best way to experience the enormity of sea life here. As if laid out for your inspection, every type of sponge, fish, coral and anemone is carefully placed on the ledges and nooks of this vast wall. In Sipadan, there is a complexity to the wall: caverns, overhangs, shelves, outcrops, hidden corners and nooks, all are magically adorned.

I drop to a depth of about 60 feet. I feel as if I am sitting too close to the screen at the movies. I cannot take it all in. I back up further. Then, further still. Now I am an astronaut floating alongside an enormous spacecraft. The current pulls me along in what seems like a gentle orbit. I recognize a few coral from my dive book: Dendronephthya coral and Melithaied sea fans are the most impressive. Fish—to truly describe the fish would take an entire book. Silver clouds of fish swirl around me: rays, barracuda, shark, parrotfish, puffers, groupers, batfish. I can't begin to identify the myriad species. They seem to neither resent nor notice our intrusion here.

Since the vast wall fades into blue darkness on either end, I am treated to an endless moving cyclorama of reef life forms. Behind me, beside me and above me are turtles, like fat birds, flapping gently through an azure sky. Deep below in the blackness appear flashes of silver: large predatory fish appear briefly, then retreat back to the depths. I have to be careful to monitor my air and time. This is truly mesmerizing. I move closer to the wall and realize I am moving at quite a clip. It takes all my strength to swim against the current to stay in one position. I decide to go with the ride. There is too much to see. Every square foot is a masterpiece of color, form and balance. I am picking up speed again. My air indicator needle in the red, I begin to rise. As I swim towards the edge of the underwater cliff, I feel a slight sadness. Before I was adrift in inner space, now I am simply a land-bound mammal breathing through a tank. I break the surface and the magic is lost.

After spending many days diving on Sipadan I cannot say I was bored for one minute. It is fair to say that you cannot get enough of the spectacular, ever-changing beauty. It is also fair to say that there is nothing else to do above land. We are clean, suntanned and healthy. Other than ripped neck muscles, coral cuts and sunburn, I leave refreshed and ready for my next adventure. About 30 acres in size, the island is actually the very tip of a mushroom-shaped pinnacle. Sipadan's claim to fame is twofold. First, it is one of the islands disputed by Indonesia (it is technically in Kalimantan, Indonesia) but the two governments are working it out and it offers dramatic diving afforded by its 2000-foot (600 m) underwater drop-off.

I first dove the Sipadan in 1989 and it was a very offbeat destination. Excellent PR and significant coverage in the world diving press have put it on every diver's Top Ten list since then. Today three dive companies have set up A frames on the island, putting about 30–120 divers on the island at any one time.

Visibility can range between 30–100 feet—the major factor being whether it has rained the night before. Keep in mind that the rainy season is smack during Christmas dive trip season, between mid December and mid February. Monsoon winds and waves can stir up the water as well. Regardless of the visibility, there are plenty of unique and interesting dive sites and even snorkeling areas. Drift dives along the sheer wall are amongst the most popular but require careful attention to depth air and location.

It can get rather boring if you don't dive—a walk around the island takes 35 minutes. You can eat and drink and snorkel if you don't do a lot of diving.

Turtle egg-laying season occurs during the summer (July–October). About an hour after sunset you can watch the lumbering giants drag themselves up from the water, across the beach and into the edge of the forest. They then laboriously dig a hole using their rear flippers, lay up to 100 eggs and then crawl slowly back into the water before sunrise. The turtles then hatch and scamper to the sea hopefully before being picked off by the terns.

If you want to explore the interior or watch the turtles lay eggs, you must look up the Sabah Parks Department ranger on the island who lives in a small hut near the Borneo Dive Resort. He'll be happy to take you around the interior and point out the limited but interesting natural inhabitants.

The crystal clear waters are home to 1200 species of fish.

Conservation measures by the dive operators include removal of all garbage from the island by boat several times a week.

Getting There

Once you get to Kuala Lumpur you can expect a two hour connecting flight and then a 45 minute flight from Kota Kinabalu and then an hour long van ride through the oil palm plantations that dominate the area around Tawau and then a 45 minute boat ride to the island. Once there you can be in the water within a hour.

Then you have an hour long motorboat out to the island. Expect to overnight in KL, or Kota Kinabalu and/or the rustic but exotic Dragon Inn in Semporna. All in all you can expect to arrive in the middle of the day in time for a brief lunch and a couple of dives.

You can get to Tawau via Malaysia Airlines (MAS) and other major airlines from Kuala Lumpur, Singapore, Hong Kong and Tokyo. Malaysia Airlines offers daily flights from Kota Kinabalu to Tawau, and from Tawau to Sandakan. (About $100 for the entire route, including the return to Kota Kinabalu.) Ask if there is a special deal for multiple travel between states.

When to Go

Dive packages start at $525 for two days and one night and can go up to $705 for five days, four nights. All prices include meals, but do not include equipment rental. Rental of a buoyancy compensator and regulator with gauges costs about $10 a day. Equipment is well used and they may not have all sizes so book ahead. Dive operators offer discounts for nondivers who wish to snorkel or just read.

INSIDER TIP

Try to visit between mid-February and mid-December, when visibility is a staggering 50-60 meters. If your interest is the turtles laying eggs, then August and September are the best times. There is no one best spot but ask what's happening when you arrive. Try to get in shape before you go—you'll be doing a lot of diving!

Novice divers can easily spend 3–4 days. Experienced divers may want to block out a 10 day trip during the dry season or sea turtle egg laying season. Professional dive photographers could easily spend a year here. Obviously Christmas and summer are the busiest times. Guests tend to be American and European. Spouses or significant others who don't dive might want to charter a speedboat to visit the surrounding islands or visit the tourist attractions around Sandakan.

Borneo Sea Adventures

Post Office Box 10134, Kota Kinabalu
☎ *(088) 55390 or 215475 or 218126, FAX 221106.*

Borneo Endeavour

Second Floor, Lot 10, Block A, Damai Plaza, Larong Pokok Kayu Manis, Luyang, Kota Kinabalu
☎ *(088) 249950, FAX 249946.*

Borneo Divers

Fourth Floor, Wisma Sabah, Kota Kinabalu
☎ *(088) 222226, FAX 221550*
The original and most experienced dive operators on Sipidan. They also offer the best A frames on the beach since they are the choice of most divers to Sipidan.

Pulau Sipadan Resort

Post Office Box 290 91007, Tawau
☎ *(089) 7652000*
Next to Borneo Divers, second choice.

Sipadan Dive Center

A1026, 10th Floor, Wisma Merdeka, Jalan Tun Razak, Kota Kinabalu
☎ *(088) 240584 or 21870, FAX 240415*
The most recent (It opened in 1992) but least favorably situated.

For those who prefer to make arrangements for a tour through an operator based in the United States, companies with experience in planning trips to Sipidan include:

Tropical Adventures

111 Second North, Seattle, Washington 98109
☎ *(800) 247-3483, (206) 441-3483, FAX 441-5431.*

Creative Adventure Club

3007 Royce Lane, Costa Mesa, California 92626
☎ *(714) 545-5888, (800) 553-9233 in California,*
(800) 544-5088 in the rest of the United States,
FAX (714) 545-5898.

Sea Safaris

3770 Highland Avenue, Suite 102 , Manhattan Beach, California 90266
☎ *(800) 821-6670, FAX (310) 545-1672.*

Accommodations on the island are rustic at best.

Where to Stay

You have a choice of three dive centers on Sipadan. There is little to differentiate in terms of costs, accommodations or food. There is a big difference in their situation. Borneo Divers were the pioneers on Sipadan and grabbed the best spots for their cabins. They also have the most convenient entry into the water, about 30 yards from equipment shed to drop off. Also there is no hard and fast rule that you can't socialize from site to site. They all charge extra for beer and sodas. Showers are not communal but require waiting for the shower stalls (and the toilets.)

You can choose from 10 rustic cottages that either face out towards the ocean or in-land.

Accommodations are simple, thatched roofed, A-frames about three by four meters with two beds per cabin. They can be a little leaky during heavy rains and the sound of the generator will put you to sleep before the rats scuttling in the eaves will wake you up again.

Late at night is when the rats come out. They will chew on any snacks you leave in your A-Frame and will even eat soap. There are also sand flies on the beach that come out at dusk plus mosquitoes at night. If you forgot to bring mosquito coils ask the management for some. They can also provide soap, pillows and a bottom sheet.

In the morning you can choose from one of the four 28 foot, 12 man fiberglass dive boats that go out to the various dive spots.

Tunku Abdul Rahman National Park★

About 10 minutes by boat from KK

A marine park with five islands is a short trip from Kota Kinabalu. The park is Sabah's most accessible sanctuary for beautiful coral and many varieties of fish. Despite the park's popularity with locals and visitors the beaches are uncrowded and offer superb snorkeling. Also popular for weekend picnics. Boat trips can be arranged with local fishermen. Pulau Gaya, the site of the first British settlers, is the largest and offers 20 kms of trails to explore the mangrove swamps. Pulau Sapi is the most popular island for its diving and white beaches. Pulau Sapi is the least developed.

Getting There

Take the longboat that embarks from the Marina jetty at the beach hotel in Tanjung. Aru. The boat leaves every hour and costs about M$20 per person. The fares from KK to Manukan Island and Mamutik Island are M$10 per person. You can charter boats at the jetty by the Hyatt in KK.

Where To Stay

There are 10 air-conditioned chalets at Manukan Island with two bedrooms each. Fortunately, there is a refrigerator, so be sure to bring plenty of food because there are no restaurants on the island. On Mamutik Island, a two-bedroom resthouse, accommodating eight to twelve people is available for M$60. For more information, call Sabah Parks, ☎ *51591*.Camping is allowed on all islands. There are facilities for cooking and washing but no stores or supplies.

The Sea Gypsies

On The Sulu Seas

One Monday morning in September of 1988, fifteen long-haired, dark-skinned men walked through the streets of Lahad Datu. There was something unsettling about these men. It wasn't their dark skin. Coffee-colored skin would have identified them as sailors, sunburnt from their honest work on the seas. Their long hair was unusual for this strict Muslim seaport but what really made the police nervous were the men's green army fatigues and the fact that they were carrying M16 rifles and mortars. The pirates of the Sulu Seas were back in business.

For the next two hours, all hell broke loose. The pirates robbed two banks, mortared the police station, sank a marine police boat, and killed ten people before they sped away in unmarked speedboats.

There are many more stories of piracy in the Sulu Seas. Pirates machine-gunned 33 of 51 passengers, making sure that all 23 males aboard were dead. They kidnapped three teenage girls, and left the wounded and dying to drift ashore to Tawau.

A year later, pirates used hand grenades to rob a jeweler in Semporna. Three pirates were killed and several people injured. Two months earlier, five pirates were killed in a shoot-out with police at sea. Entire islands are robbed, pearl farm managers are shot and killed, large passenger boats disappear. The stories continue.

Piracy is not new in this area. The Strait of Malacca, the Indonesian Archipelago and the Philippine Islands create thousands of narrow waterways and remote islands where piracy can flourish. The Indonesians blame the Malaysians, the Malaysians blame the Filipinos, the government blames immigrants, the military blames the people and the people blame the military. The combination of the military unrest in the Philippines and the large number of refugees who eke out a living on the northeast coast of Sabah make this region an excellent breeding ground for piracy. What makes these pirates different from ordinary landlocked thugs is they will kill a fisherman for only his outboard motor and they will strike anywhere, at any time, using high-speed power boats without fear of law enforcement.

I wanted to go straight to the nexus of this activity, the Sulu Sea off Semporna. Here we will not only search for pirates, but visit with their nomadic cousins the Sea Bajau. Pirates and gypsies are a magnet for adventurers.

Adventurers have a kinship with the nomad. Both are out of synch with the modern world—going where wind, necessity, and whim direct them. Most nomads are found in the great open areas of the world; the Gypsies of the Russian Steppes, the Tuareg of the Sahara, the Eskimo of the Arctic, the Bushman of the Kalahari, and the Sea Bajau of the Sulu Sea.

Borneo is also home to the last seaborne nomads of Asia, the Sea Bajau; the Gypsies of the Sulu Sea. Sulu, or sooloo, was once a Philippine-based kingdom of islands and ocean. Like earthbound kingdoms bound by roads, the sultanate of Sulu is a collection of trading routes connecting what are now the Philippines, Malaysia, Indonesia and China. The Sultan of Sulu controlled the trade between the East and West. Keeping the trading lanes open, guaranteeing safe passage and fair trading was his only claim to power.

Semporna and Sandakan, much like Timbuktu and Zanzibar, were fabled trading centers where exotic raw materials were traded for the elegant riches of civilization. Mountains of strange, crude bundles were pulled from the dark interior by natives and traded by the Chinese: Rattan, gutta percha gum, diamonds, elephant ivory, rhinoceros horns, stones from monkey bladders, and camphor wood. Bird's nests were exchanged at a fraction of their value for ceramic jars, brass gongs, steel, silk and beads. Explorers, traders and kings were fascinated by the diversity of riches that came from this green, steaming hell.

The forbidding shoreline of Sabah is home to pirates, smugglers and trespassers.

In October, pirate winds would carry the Moslem Moros in their hundred-man triremes from Sulu to terrorize the area as far west as Malacca and Singapore. The same Moslem Moros forced the U.S. Marines to adopt the 45-calibre slug because the army's old .38 caliber handgun could not stop a blood-crazed Moro in full charge.

The Sea Bajau came from the southern Philippines in the eighteenth and nineteenth centuries. Some now fish, others farm. Legend says they are descended from the escort of a Johor princess. To visit the Gypsies and to look for pirates we must have a boat. Semporna is a good place to begin our journey.

The camel shaped island of Palau Gaya

Semporna is not much of a town; rows of grim two-story cement buildings with goods spilling into the streets from the stores below. The Moros live here. It is a center for fishing and sea produce: pearls, seaweed farms. It is also a smuggling center to and from the southern Philippines a few miles away. Guns and cigarettes are smuggled from here to avoid taxes. Semporna is also a diving center, with Sipadan as the main attraction.

Since we are starting to look as if we belong in the jungle, we decide to treat ourselves to a hotel. We choose the Dragon Inn. Not much by Western standards, but a palace to us. The Dragon Inn is unique in that it is built over the water.

At Semporna we run the gauntlet of "black pearl hawkers," Ray-Banned, greasy-haired, most with a permanent smirk. They hover like flies at the entrance to the hotel. They look as if their source of income and employment is neither legal nor worth investigating.

We are also looking forward to a good meal. The Dragon Inn is famous for its fresh seafood. I am learning that the Chinese love to look at animals before they eat them. Having been to a mountaintop restaurant that doubles as a zoo, I am not surprised that the sharks, tuna, crabs, lobster and fish on display in the ocean "aquarium" in the Dragon Inn, are also on the menu. The seafood for the restaurant is kept in holding tanks for the customer to select. There is also a display of sharks and tuna that can be fed with small fish. It is quite acceptable to have your picture taken with your meal while it is still alive.

We have a dinner of both deep and shallow water lobster, grouper, fried rice and hot and sour soup. Sitting over the water, we watch the sun go down in a tropical sunset that fades through blues, purples, golds, yellows and then blood red, before revealing a canopy of brilliant stars against a deep blue sky.

Large families of Chinese and Malays sit at huge tables that seat twelve. The Chinese take great pleasure in the large multi-course meals. They slurp their tea noisily, chatter loudly, and end the meal with a loud pop by smacking their lanolin-soaked paper towels. Toothpicks protrude from every mouth. Once satiated, they push their round bellies back from the table, and like smiling Buddhas, they are happy.

After dinner we decide to go to a karaoke bar. It is not a difficult decision, since it seems that all bars in Semporna are karaoke bars. You are given a drink menu and a song menu, and your song request is shoved through a little slot in the disc jockey's booth. You sing along with the creeping, yellow lyrics running off a laser disc. The audience laughs at our attempt to sing Malaysian and Chinese love songs. Behind us, the sappy romance videos contrast with our unshaven, fatigued delivery.

Later we wander around the town. The pool halls are bustling, and we hear the quiet chatter of people eating dinner. Semporna takes on a different feeling at night. I go to sleep to the sound of lapping waves, interrupted by the sound of rats scurrying and scraping along the roof and inside the walls.

Our wake up call is the sound of outboard motors, and the cool green light of the water coming between the gaps in the hardwood floors. Quite rustic and touristy, this hotel is used mostly by divers as a stopping off point to Sipadan and by Chinese for a night out. The rooms are built of roughly hewn hardwood and split nibong palm, a thorny and fountain-like palm used for a rustic type of paneling. There are shutters and no windows.

You bathe out back using water scooped out of a large ceramic jar, or you can use the shower, which drains straight back into the ocean below. The toilet seems to go into a pipe, but since I have yet to see a functioning sewer system, it probably dumps straight into the crystal clear water. The multipurpose function of the ocean as provider and receptor is dubious when you consider that the dinner we had last night came out of the same ocean about 50 feet away.

The lipa lipa of the Sea Bajau

The Market

The next morning we decide to walk into town. My favorite time of the day is dawn. In Africa, morning breaks like the sharp click of a shell being ejected from a carbine. In Borneo, morning rises softly out of the sea. Clouds billow overhead and the sounds change slowly. We have a "hallal" (a Moslem restaurant usually run by Pakistanis) breakfast in an Indian restaurant.

We order "chapitas" (a light gooey Indian bread) with eggs and cheese. We are entertained by the ever-smiling cook's dervish-like spinning of the dough into a paper-thin pancake. The dough then lightly settles down onto the grill, capturing a large bubble of air. We walk to the market to get two papayas while Coskun shows the cook how to add cheese to the "chapitas." We force the cook to sample our concoction, and he thinks it will be a hit. We leave the rest of our cheese with him.

It is a glorious day. The call to prayer is played over and over as if to wake those who overslept. It is Saturday and after the morning monsoon showers clean the streets of last night's garbage and freshen the air, the sun comes up, bathing us in a honeyed light reflected from the gold painted domes of the mosque and beckoning us to the market.

The bustling marketplace of Semporna is built over the water and is a good introduction to the smells, sounds, and colors of this part of Sabah. Indonesians, Filipinos, Bajau, Malays, Chinese, Indians and Arabs mingle in this Asian kaleidoscope. We wander among clouds of fried grease and the smells of enticing spices, animals and exotic vegetables. Long silver fish grin back at me as they sit stacked in neat rows. We see barracuda, salted and split into ornate shapes; sharks, whose fins have been removed and sold to restaurants; siri leaves, a type of pepper used with betelnut; *tarap*, a yellow breadfruit with spiky flesh, found only in Borneo. There are giant jackfruits (*nangka*), starfruit, coffee grinders, ice shavers, and *sago* (brightly colored starch made into drinks). The rats slither like harried commuters between the crates and refuse while pus-ridden cats stare groggily at passersby.

Stares follow us as we push our way through narrow alleys. Conversations stop when we push into the darker, more remote areas. Men sip their coffee and wait until we pass. Back in the main alleys, there is gaiety and laughter again.

Old ladies perch on counters with the classic market pose—one leg under, one leg up, supporting a hand on the forehead. Their eyes flicker, waiting for the ever so slight hesitation that means someone may be interested. Sensing a customer, they click into their animated spiel: "We have the finest produce, there is no better price." Once they see you are just browsing, they revert to the pose. Prices are so low it is not even worth haggling, but it must be done. The next *orang puti*, or white man, will always pay what the most gullible has paid before. The Sea Bajau bring their dried fish and cucumbers here to exchange. The pirates meet here to exchange information and arrange smuggling contracts. Who is a gypsy and who is a pirate? Here, there is no line.

The slimy tidal muck is visible through the worn rounded planks. Great care has to be taken if you step towards the ends of these rotted boards, since great economy is taken with the use of nails. The marketplace is a microcosm of life. Everything must disappear to be renewed again. The process is as old as time. After the close, fetid smell of the market, the brilliant pure light of the ocean with its exotic silhouettes beckons.

Typical Sea Bajau village

On the Sulu Sea

That afternoon we arrange for a speedboat to take us out to meet the Sea Bajau, the Gypsies of the Sea. They can be found as far south as Papar, particularly in the area of the Tempasuk Plain, and on the west coast of Sabah, concentrated around Semporna.

The Bajaus are Filipino by descent. Today, they are fishermen, farmers, trappers of crabs, collectors of sea cucumbers and shellfish. Some also cut firewood in mangrove swamps. Their nomadic life dictates that their profession be waterborne. On the west coast of Sabah, Sea Bajaus are traditionally farmers; some grow rice, others rear cattle, bison, or ponies. The Spanish introduced horses to the Philippines, and the Bajau brought the horses with them. Because of their skill with horses, the Bajau (Bajow) horsemen are known as the "Cowboys of Asia."

The Sea Bajau that choose to live in villages build their homes over the tidal flats of Semporna. At first, it is disconcerting to see a rustic thatched village standing completely on its own and out of sight of any terra firma. There are two reasons why these villages make sense. First, the water is an amazing three to six feet deep for miles around, and second, being on the edge of the flats lets the fishermen build their homes on stilts directly over their fishing and crabbing grounds.

The nomads of the Sulu Sea

The Sea Bajau who live on boats have a simpler, more elegant existence. Their *lipo-lipo* are beautifully carved, some with intricately carved bows and lattice work windows. They have all the comforts of home: stove, sleeping areas, cages for animals. Many even drag their in-laws behind them in a separate boat. Typically there is a main boat that tows small canoes behind it, sometimes as many as three.

Our first destination is Pulau Gaya, the exotic-looking humpbacked island that is an ever-present sight in Semporna. It is actually just one in a series of islands that form the rim of an ancient volcanic caldera. As we get closer, the island looms above us. It is easy to see why the people have chosen to build their homes here in the protective nook of this massive cliff.

We cruise slowly into the waterborne village of Gaya, probably the most idyllically situated of the Sea Bajau villages. People peek at us through holes in the thatched walls of their rustic stilt houses. We see silhouettes of people inside the boats. As we near the first house, the sound of children giggling and jabbering at us begins. Another group of children runs to the balcony and waves. They see we are taking pictures. Parents drag their babies out and hold them up for us to take their pictures. Not quite the reaction to strangers we expected after our encounter with the dark recesses of the marketplace. As we cruise between the boats and houses, we create a wake of laughing behind us, jabbering, and shouting. We are probably the only entertainment they have had in months.

We move on to the village of Labuan Haji (the port of someone who has made the pilgrimage to Mecca). The reaction is the same: loud chattering, laughing, whistling, hissing. Even an argument between two women, screaming at the top of their lungs, chasing each other in comically tiny dugout canoes, is drowned out by the noise of the village. Small children, laughing and shouting, jump into the water and swim behind us.

We wave and take photos. The women are as shy as the children are gregarious. The women hide their faces. As they peek back and realize we have taken their picture, they smile.

Out to sea, I see a line of boats like elephants on parade. Their long graceful bows tell me these are the Gypsies of the Sulu Sea going to market. We rev the engine to catch up. Like Arab traders, this flotilla is a self-sufficient community. Their hand-carved wooden boats are faded to a light grey. Fish hang from sticks that protrude from the boats. Small fish are laid out to dry on thatched roofs. On one roof is a barracuda, slit and splayed in a delicate zigzag pattern. Chicken are kept in woven or wooden lattice cages. Laundry, tools, and supplies hang in careful arrangements. Towed behind, a small girl is cleaning giant clams in an equally tiny canoe. The look is very much Depression Era Okie, except these elegantly carved boats replace clattering pickup trucks. Their poverty is extreme, even by Asian standards, but it is apparent that these are happy people. It could be argued that because they depend on the sea and want for nothing, they, like most nomads, are rich.

An old couple sits on the lead boat watching us with some amusement. They laugh good naturedly when we try to talk to them. We ask what they have for sale. They show us the pearls and dried fish that are strung all over the boats. We ask one family where they are going and they point towards Semporna. We ask them where they have come from and they point in the opposite direction. I am sure they evoke peals of laughter as they tell stories for months to come of the stupidity of their Western visitors.

We give them gifts and Polaroid pictures of themselves and are thankful that unlike their brothers, the Penan, whose way of life is being destroyed by the loss of their beloved forest, the Sea Gypsies will have their ocean forever. At dusk, we head back to the Dragon Inn for another multi-course seafood dinner. On the way back, the outboard motors conk out. Ahmed, our boatman, busies himself sucking gas, cleaning plugs, and swapping engines every ten minutes until we slide into the dock. We clean up the debris in the boat and carefully pack it into a plastic bag we had brought. As we climb the ten feet up to the dock, Ahmed takes our carefully packed trash and empty film canisters and tosses them into the ocean.

The fishing villages are built in 3–4 feet of water on stilts.

The Pirates

Heading out at dawn on the ocean is actually late in the day for most fishermen around Semporna. Today we will wing it and see what we can see. After the friendly reception of the Sea Bajau, we decide to put a little edge on the trip and head out into the shipping lanes and small islands to search for pirates. As we leave the sight of land, the feeling that there is danger here increases. These are pirate waters. Not just the armed paramilitary that rob freighters, but vicious Indonesians and Filipino pirates that prey on gentle fishermen. Just one week ago, a gang of five pirates used M-16s to rob a local fisherman of his motor and a battery. There are weekly reports of fishing boats being stolen and people being killed, robbed and raped for their meager possessions. Banks are robbed in coastal towns, entire cargo ships are relieved of their safes, and sailors of their valuables. Our load of expensive cameras and other gear would definitely interest them. The fact that our outboards are cantankerous, to say the least, and that we are without food, water, or emergency equipment would probably qualify us as stupid, rather than as adventurous.

The pirates are not only a historic presence here. The recent resurgence is due to the massive influx of Filipino refugees escaping the separatist war between the Moros and the Philippine government. Some estimates say that there are half a million illegal immigrants in Sabah. In the early '70s Sabah was used as a training ground for the Moro National Liberation Front (MNLF) and as a shipment route for arms. Today there is still widespread smuggling as boats make the twelve hour crossing between Lahad Datu and Zamboanga. Smugglers may bring in items like San Miguel beer and Coca Cola. They arrive in the dead of night to exchange their goods for cigarettes and other mundane, but less taxed items and return to start all over again. Pirates prey on these and other smugglers as they crisscross the narrow channel.

Since we had some trepidation about the reliability of our outboard, we had asked our boatman, Ahmed, to bring snorkels, ice, and lunches, and of course, after swearing up and down that it would be no problem, he brought nothing. We silently decide which one of us will be eaten first, should we be set adrift. We all agree we will eat Ahmed.

As we head for open ocean, we pass a group of fishermen leaving their small island. The small border post flies the Malaysian flag, so we know we are getting close to Indonesia. The fishermen set out in a collection of dugout canoes, motorboats, pirogues and outriggers to perform a questionable act: fishing by bomb. Using fertilizer as a base, they concoct a mixture that creates a massive explosion that ruptures the internal flotation organs of the reef fish. Then they dive in the water to pick up the stunned and dead fish. You can tell if your fish has been caught by bombing because its insides are destroyed. No one has calculated how much damage has been done to the coral reefs by this crude method of fishing. But, it continues every day.

The reefs below us are also smashed and worn from the thousands of boat propellers and anchors that ploy these waters. Looking through the trash on the broken reefs, you can see starfish, sea snakes, and colorful fish. It is hard to understand how the ocean still manages to survive.

Palau Gaya

We see our destination: a tight collection of light gray houses built over the water. These are crabbing villages. They drop their baskets from their front doors and the waste from the village feeds the crabs. A simple, but questionable, exchange of resources. Once again we visit, take pictures, talk with the people. No pirates here.

Among the hundreds of tiny islands, we find a tiny spot of sand that is the best example of the mythical Desert Island I have ever seen, Pulau Umusan. One lonely coconut palm, a handful of grass shacks, a rusting hulk of a wrecked boat and 20 people who make their living collecting and drying sea cucumbers. The majority of them are Obian Filipino and Sulu. We stop for lunch. The women fastidiously arrange the sea cucumbers they gather to dry, turning them religiously. The children play in the water as if on vacation. We stop and share our lunch and marvel at the adaptability of people.

Granted, there are many Westerners who dream of moving to such a place. But here, there is not a drop of water, no way to communicate. One large wave would wipe the island clean.

We are unsuccessful in our quest for pirates. Coskun promises us if we go with him (he is a good friend of the leader of the Moro resistance) to the southern tip of the Philippines, only a few hours away by boat, we can meet all the pirates we want. The fact that they kidnap Westerners and Christians for ammo money, persuades me to decline.

The rain hisses on the water as we make our way back. We pass the stilt villages we visited earlier: Gagangun, Pulau Tiga, Pulau Putih. Off in the distance is the silhouette of the ever-present police boat.

The sun comes out. Mosque domes glow silver against the dark green coco palms. The twisted, rickety stilt villages are now shimmering silhouettes dwarfed by pure white tropical thunderheads in the dark blue sky. They could be mirages. Our thoughts of pirates gone, we head peacefully into the dock at Semporna. As we clean up our belongings, this time making sure that we will take our film boxes and refuse with us, one of the long-haired men looks down into the boat and notices our empty SX-70 Polaroid film battery packs. He yells to our boatman in a regional dialect that sounds like Tagalog. The boatman asks us in a curiously serious and polite tone, "Do you have need of these?" as he holds the flat batteries up.

I reply, not quite understanding Ahmed's sudden eco-correctness, "No, but they should be disposed of properly because they are caustic."

"My friend would like them," Ahmed replied, with his best shit-eating grin.

I look up to his Ray-Banned friend, complete with a dangling Marlboro and back down at Ahmed. He gives me his best "hello-to-my-tourist-friend" smile back.

"Why does he want them?" I inquire.

Guessing he should come clean and involve us in his need to avoid loss of our precious trash he tries telling the truth.

"They are worth a lot of money."

While I am racking my brain for what possible use a long-haired boatman and his dubious, deeply tanned associate would have for our used batteries, Ahmed finally comes clean.

"We need them for our bomb timers."

Suddenly it all clicks why we have been so unsuccessful in our pirate search over the last few days. I see identical expressions, and our dockside friend's Marlboro goes from slack to erect as they uniformly smile the smile of evil.

We have found our pirates.

Sarawak

The Sarawak Cultural Center has full size re-creations of ancient longhouses.

There is a distinct difference between Sabah and Sarawak. Sabahans are industrious, no nonsense, simplistic, spartan folks. The local handicrafts feature machinelike patterns and are hard-edged and practical. The cities are square and utilitarian, lacking ornament built for function not contemplation. On the other hand, Sarawak has an air of mystery, of sensual mysticism. The Sarawakians are languorous, sophisticated, they take longer to decipher, but are quicker to laugh. The cities are tumble-down, winding, ancient and reeking of spices and other less pleasant odors. My impression of Sabahans is that they are the beneficiaries of a fairly recent economic boon and the victims of relentless destruction during WWII and unbridled modern development.

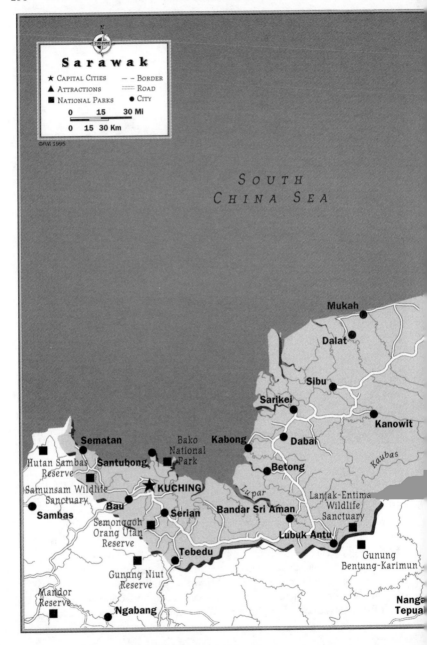

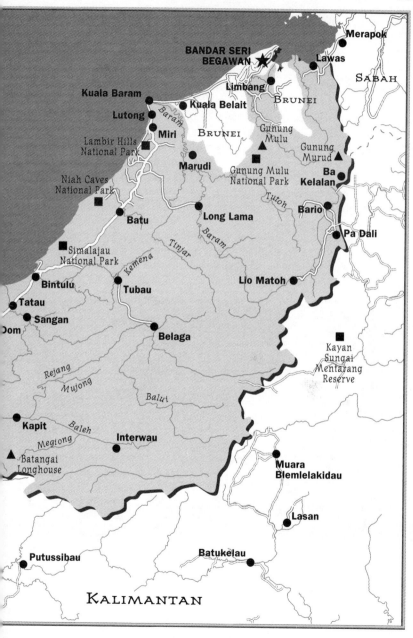

Merapok

BANDAR SERI
BEGAWAN

Lawas

SABAH

Kuala Baram

Limbang

BRUNEI

Lutong

Kuala Belait

Miri

BRUNEI

Gunung
Mulu

Gunung
Murud

Lambir Hills
National Park

Marudi

Gunung Mulu
National Park

Ba
Kelalan

Niah Caves
National Park

Baram

Tutoh

Bario

Batu

Long Lama

Pa Dali

Baram

Simalajau
National Park

Tinjar

Kemena

Lio Matoh

Bintulu

Tubau

Tatau

Sangan

Belaga

Kayan
Sungai
Mentarang
Reserve

Dom

Rejang

Mujong

Balui

Kapit

Baleh

Megiong

Interwau

Batangai
Longhouse

Muara
Blemlelakidau

Lasan

Putussibau

Batukelau

KALIMANTAN

Breathing Space

The governments of Indonesia and Malaysia announced they will create one of the world's largest wildlife sanctuaries in 1995. The park will straddle Kalimantan and Sarawak and will be managed by both countries as well as the Japanese based International Tropical Timber Organization.

The other difference can be directly traced to their method of government. The Sarawakians under Brooke enjoyed the rule of a family who respected the financial aspects of both Chinese traders and the cultural traditions of the Iban. Both cultures were left intact for hundreds of years. In Sabah the singular and pecuniary goal of the British North Borneo Corporation was to exploit the area and people for gain. Today, Sabahans, second after the Bruneians, strive to add a measure of responsibility to every economic endeavor. Unfortunately, the absolute and secretive rule of the Brookes also encouraged financial development but relied on the ruler to provide moderation or benefit to all. The system imposed by the Brookes is not far off the current system of benevolent dictatorship being imposed by the current Sultan of Brunei upon his subjects.

The rivers are the highways of Sarawak.

When the last Rajah of Sarawak took his leave in May 1946 and Sarawak was left to its own devices, the region embarked on a development plan of the country's timber that would make the Visigoths of Europe take pause and reconsider the plundering of Sarawak's forests.

Sarawak is about the size of New York State with 1.3 million people sparsely spread over 49,000 square miles. As of 1991, Sarawak was the largest source of unprocessed tropical timber in the world. Their imports of 19.6 million cubic yards of hardwood logs dwarf the next at 1.3 million cubic yards. When the government invited the International Tropical Timber Organization (ITTO) to defend its policy of logging, the ITTO reported that Sarawak was cutting down its forests at eight to ten times the sustainable rate and would be depleted within a decade. They recommended a cap at 2.6 million cubic yards per year.

Oops There Goes A Million Kilowatt Dam

About 5000 Dayaks are going to be floating if they stay on their ancestral lands and the Bakun dam project goes through. Malaysia is going to put in a $5.8 billion hydroelectric dam on the upper reaches of the Rejang River that will flood about 200,000 acres, roughly the size of Singapore.

The dam will not be completed for 10 years but it is creating tension amongst the locals who just started to feel good about Sarawak slowing down its rapacious need for denuding the forests. The Bakun will generate about 3000 megawatts of electricity and most of that power will go to mainland Malaysia via a 400 mile underground cable. The dam is estimated to provide 25% of Malaysia's energy needs. Naturally in keeping with SE Asian politics, the main contractor for the dam is a close personal friend of Prime Minister Mahathir Mohamad. The owner of Ekran, Ting Pek Khiing, 49, is a Sarawak-based entrepreneur who is involved in tourist resort development. The revenue from clearing the 80,000 hectares of timber is estimated to generate a profit between $1 - 2.4 billion dollars, half of the entire cost of the project. Ting flew in Mahatir on his private jet to announce that Ekran had won the contract. No bidding for his portion of the massive job was ever held.

Sarawak is the exotic Borneo that most people imagine. It is a place of headhunters, longhouses, unexplored jungles and semimythical creatures. Sarawak, like Sabah, has a colorful history thanks to adventurer James Brooke, who with the help of 19 men and one ship, managed to obtain a kingdom from the Sultan of Brunei for keeping the infestation of pirates down. Today, Sarawak is an excellent destination for those who seek the exotic and the wild. Not as rugged as Sabah, not as industrious as mainland Malaysia, Sarawak is a country unto itself. The high points are both cultural and natural: the Iban people, the town of Kuching, the Sarawak Museum and Gunung Mulu National Park and the miles of riverine adventure that await.

Sarawak, formerly known as the Land of the Headhunters, and now land of the hornbills is Malaysia's largest state. It occupies most of the northern part of Borneo, located west of Sabah. It was originally under the Sultanate of Brunei until it was placed under administration of British adventurer James Brooke, who arrived in his well armed ship, the *Royalist*, seeking adventure and fortune. He offered to help quell the Bidayuh and Malay uprising against the Sultan of Brunei. He was given control over the ill-defined region called Sarawak in September of 1842. His nephew Charles Brooke continued expanding their holdings by subduing tribes and annexing areas until 1917. The Japanese effectively ended any control the third and last White Rajah, Vyner Brooke, had over Sarawak in 1941. After the war Sarawak become a protectorate of the British until 1963, when the country became part of the Malaysian federation. The *Konfrontasi* between the communist insurgents based in Kalimantan and supported by some Chinese in Sarawak created tensions along the border until 1965 when the conflict ended. It has taken 30 years for both countries to begin relaxing travel restrictions between the two countries. The most recent tension caused by global criticism of Sarawak's logging practices has been replaced with a sense of fatalism as Sarawak cleans up the last remaining virgin forest stands left. Although large areas have been protected by recent parks, areas of triple canopy dipterocarps are more the exception than the rule now.

Sarawak's utilization of its timber and oil resources has allowed the region to grow both demographically and financially. The coming years will no doubt see more development. Sarawak is filled with jungles, mountains, rain forests, swamplands and rivers, and tourism is still a major provider of hard currency. The latest proposal to build one of the world's largest hydroelectric projects just to feed electrical power to mainland Malaysia seems to echo the same inside deals that denuded most of Sarawak's forest for the benefit of a few wealthy timber barons.

For now Sarawak offers the visitor an unusual cultural experience. It is fair to say there is no country quite like it. Kuching has preserved much of its romantic and historic past, while major parks like Gunung Mulu allow the short time visitor to experience one of the world's most majestic biospheres.

The Peoples of Sarawak

Part of what makes Borneo unique are the gregarious and artistic Iban. The Penan are one of the last truly nomadic tribes left on earth and the complex mix of other indigenous tribes from the Bukitan/Ukit to Kayan weave a rich tapestry of cultures. In the cities, the Chinese and Malays dominate business while pockets of Dutch expats or American missionaries give the areas a frontier feel. Outside of the main cities Sarawak is a simple world of subsistence farmers. Most of the Dayak subsist on rice farming or working in surrounding logging camps to feed their families. As young men come back from the cities they bring back generators, television sets and ghetto blasters. In 10–20 years the older generation with their tattoos, stretched earlobes and native dress will have completely disappeared from this land.

The Iban

The Iban are equal in number to the ethnic Chinese, about 30 percent of Sarawak's population. Although the Iban are the peoples most associated with headhunting in Borneo, the custom was practiced by most tribes. The Iban, along with the Kayan, managed to elevate the practice into a sport. Even today Iban are fiercely competitive whether its in a pool hall or at the local cock fights. The Iban were once called Sea Dayaks to differentiate them from the Land Dayaks or Bidayuh. The Sea Dayaks were assumed to be fierce pirates while the Bidayuh were peaceful agrarian peoples.

The Ibans are also agrarian people who live off the rice that comes from their *ladangs*, or rice growing areas, and the results of their daily hunting. They live in a tight knit family unit within a larger longhouse social unit and take care of their elderly. The Iban have a well defined culture that embraces an afterlife, the powers of man, of earth, animals, plants and the interaction between each other.

The Ibans are skilled at many things—the arts, ironwork, dance, hunting, warfare and weaving or *ikat*. Their habit of *bejalai* or going on a long extended trip to seek their fortune has been turned into an exodus from their longhouses into the logging camps.

The Ibans like most Dayaks of Borneo had no written language. It wasn't until almost a hundred years ago when Westerners promoted the concept of education that a written form of communication was developed.

The Iban pass down their history and culture through oral recitation of events. Like many indigenous tribes, they use a singsong rhythm to help them remember the lengthy tales. According to this oral history, the Ibans came either from the Indonesian island of Java to the south or from the north, in the area of what is now Cambodia. They originally settled in Sabah in the area of Merudu Bay.

Intense raids by the Sulu islanders from the Philippines forced them to the area around Bintulu. The Sultan of Brunei forced them to move south to Sambas in what is now Kalimantan.

The Ibans were industrious and gathered wealth and were working with the Majapahit government. When the kingdom fell the Iban fled. Afraid that they would be under the control of another tribe, they decided to move to new ground. They had not learned how to build dugout canoes and their rafts broke apart in the fast water. In frustration they moved overland. Later migrations took them to the head of the Kapuas river. Further migrations took them up the Skrang river and the River Padih.

Superstition has been, and still is, a major influence among Ibans. If the omen bird, (*rufous piculet*) flies from one longhouse to another, the inhabitants will abandon it until the evil omens are exorcised, usually by holding a *gawai*. Fighting cocks that carry *ubat kebal*, or protective amulets, are considered to be protected from razor cuts of its opponents. Wild boar tusks and deer horns contain magic that can protect men from bullets and others can make a man invisible. There are charms called *punti* that, if buried under a jungle path, will cause lameness or pain when the intended victim walks over them. The quiet chant or *puchau* is used in emergencies or desperate situations. The *puchau* is used in emergency or to defeat severe illness, similar in use to the Roman Catholic Hail Mary.

The Penan

The Penan (sometimes spelled as Punan or Penang) are the last nomads of the Borneo forest. Estimates put their population at 6000 in all of Borneo, of which 100–500 still live a truly nomadic life. They live in groups of 25–40 people, stay in one area for two to three weeks and live in temporary lean-tos called *sulaps*. They hunt for game and fruit using their hardwood blowpipes or *sumpit* with a spear at one end. The Penan can knock a monkey out of a tree 150 feet up with their poisoned darts. They track down wild boar and deer with the help of their trusty, but scabby, hunting dogs. When the food thins out they move on. They also are the traditional collectors of garu wood, gutta percha, damar resin, honey and rattan. They exchange this bounty of the forest for iron to fashion the spears that tip their blowpipes, beads and simple utensils.

Need a light?

When the bark of a jelitong *or other dipterocarps tree is damaged it bleeds a protective resin called damar. This resin hardens to crystalline chunks and is flammable. The Penan and other tribes also tap the meranti trees to create a constant source of resin. Damar is used to light torches and lamps in longhouses. Damar was also sold to caulk boats, to bind bark in a seamless cover for roofs, and was used as the basic ingredient in varnishes before being replaced by synthetics. Stingless bees also use the damar to build the entrance tubes to their nests. Trekkers should carry a small piece to provide an emergency source of light in heavy downpours when wood is wet.*

The Penan are also famous for being the finest fabricators of the blowpipe. Drilled from a single piece of Belian or ironwood, a Penan blowpipe is the "ne plus ultra" of jungle weapons. It is fashioned from a five to six foot rod using a chisel that is repeatedly hammered and twisted until the blowpipe is bored through. The tricky part is to bend the wood so that when held there is compensation for the sag. Using bamboo darts with a kapok base and a poisoned end there is little that a blowpipe cannot bring down. In fact, the blowpipe proved to be a marvelous "stealth" weapon during the Japanese occupation in WWII.

Many Penan have been resettled into longhouses, a concept as alien to the Penan as an igloo to an Arab. In 1990 some Penan were moved from the inside of Gunung Mulu park boundaries to longhouses close to the mouth of Clearwater Cave. Some 134 Penans were taught to make baskets, traditionally a woman's job and give up their nomadic hunting. It is not clear whether the government intends for this settlement to be a low budget audio-animatronic equivalent of the attacking native on the jungle cruise in Disneyland or whether the Penan have had a choice in selecting this spot. The fact that Miri based tour guides will offer trips to "primitive" Penan villages tips me off that this is not for the Penan's own good. For now the Penan in Mulu live inside a large zoo and all that is missing is the sign that gives us this *Homo sapiens* background and description of their natural habitat.

The Chinese

The Chinese today make up about 30 percent of Sarawak's 1.3 million inhabitants. As a percentage of population there are twice as many Chinese in Sarawak than Sabah and three times as many as in Brunei. Although the Chinese first came here as traders, their current presence is due to the large numbers of laborers that were brought from China to work the plantations, mines and land in the late 1800s. Many traders and shopkeepers from Hokkien, Hakka and Canton came to set up shop and export goods back to China. Later many set up their own plantations and began trading in pepper and rice. The first settlers came to Sarawak to work in the goldmines at Bau and then again to work the oil fields in the '30s. Today it is not an overstatement to say that the Chinese have gone from being the shopkeepers of Sarawak to being the captains of industry. Throughout their long history in Sarawak the Chinese have kept their language, culture and social structure intact. The Chinese virtually control the timber trade and are also dominant in local politics. The Chinese are predominately urban with a strong sense of community.

The Bidayuh

The Bidayuh are shy people known for their weaving and peaceful life-style. Today there are 30,000 Bidayuh in five subgroups: the Biatah, Bukar-Sadong, Jagoi, Lara and Selakau. Most live in towns but a few still cling to their traditional life-style or swidden agriculture and hunting. The Bidayuh were attacked relentlessly by the Iban during the time of James and Charles Brooke. Both men protected the peaceful tribes and prevented them from being enslaved by the Malays. Because they live away from rivers they have made wide use of primitive aqueduct systems using split bamboo. They also make a mean *tapai*. When the festivities begin the Bidayuh are quite musical and make a three stringed *tinton* or harp as well as a curious violin called a *rabup*. You could call the Bidayuh the hillbillies of Sarawak and not be far off in describing their quiet rural life-style and devotion to entertaining guests.

If you would like to visit the more traditional longhouses you can venture beyond Serian to Benuk, Anna Rais or Kampung Abang.

Getting There

Malaysia Airlines services flights to Sarawak daily from Kuala Lumpur to Kuching. As of now, you are still required to go through customs and pay a deportation tax of M$5. However, plans are well underway to treat Sarawak (and Sabah) no different than the states on Peninsular Malaysia. Remember that Miri is the major air hub for Sarawak.

From	Flights	Cost	Via
VIA AIR TO KUCHING			
MALAYSIA			
Johor Bahru	**daily**	**M$150**	**MAS**
Kuala Lumpur	**daily**	**M$240**	**MAS**
SINGAPORE			
Singapore	**daily**	**M$180**	**MAS**

From	Flights	Cost	Via
	INDONESIA		
Pontianak	weekly	M$	Merpati

Check for discounts for travel inside Malaysia and advance purchases

Getting Around

River

Sarawak was built on river transport. This is the major reason for the presence of only one east-west cross country road. The riverine transportation system is quite extensive and cheap. To find out where and when the various boat services leave, pick up a copy of the *Borneo Post*.

Express boats

You have to experience one of these overpowered bullet boats. Seemingly built out of an old aircraft, diesel locomotive and a canoe, these boats are the jumbo jets of the rivers. The boats can run at speeds of 60km per hour and have heavy steel hulls to survive the occasional floating log. Inside, the boats feel more like a submarine with aircraft seats, air-conditioning, tinted windows and non stop WWF wrestling matches or kung fu movies shown on a small, way-out-of-whack color TV set. To book a ticket look at the display that lists times and schedules displayed on the front of the boat. You can leave an object on the seat to reserve a spot and then show up ten minutes before the departure time. You can ride on the roof with the cargo if you like but be careful of the effects of the sun. Also breathing the spray from the polluted rivers can be just as bad as drinking from it.

Remember that long journeys via express (or *ekspres*) will stop at food stops or markets but you should be fairly self sufficient on these long trips with water and snacks. If you are going upriver from the coast, use the term *ulu*. If you are traveling with a group you may want to charter a boat once you get to the classic jump off points like Kapit. The easier way is to set up your itinerary with a Kuching or Miri based tour company. These boats ply the rivers and bay of Brunei.

From	To	Time	Cost
EXPRESS BOAT SERVICE			
Sibu	Kapit	3 hours	M$15
Kuala Baram	Marudi	2 hours	M$12
Kapit	Belaga	6 hours	M$20
Marudi	Kuala Apoh	2 hours	M$10
Kuala Apoh	Long Terawan	2 hours	M$8
Kuching	Sibu	4 hours	M$29

Note: low water levels during the dry season will cancel trips.

Longboats

The next level down from the express boat is the longboat. These large canoes are used when the water level is too low for an express boat to operate or when there isn't enough traffic. Many people use them for shorter trips as well. If you are going past scheduled boat service the method of determining the cost is quite democratic. The boatman will estimate the amount of gas required (usually in number of tanks) and then divide the cost between the number of passengers. A five gallon tank of outboard fuel takes about M$50 worth of gasoline. For example if you are going upriver from Belaga to Ukit it will take about eight tanks depending on the cargo weight, water level and speed of the river. If *orang putis* (white men) and luggage are the sole passengers, fuel consumption can rise dramatically. Then you can expect to pay a per diem for the boatman (M$30) his bowsman (M$20) his longboat (M$20) the engine (M$20–50 depending on power), gas (at least M$50 a day) and any food and lodging. If they have to go to unusually remote places or gas is hard to get, the prices go up from there. If you are stuck like I have been at times, they can charge any damn price they want. Throw these prices out the window if you are trying to apply this to travel in Indonesia where the boatmen are a lot more entrepreneurial, to put it kindly. Also agree on the total cost by writing it down on a piece of paper and waving it around and then shake on it.

If locals are coming along for the ride you can usually be assured of a fair shake. If you are taking a guide don't expect him to pay his share. The Dayaks of Sarawak tend to be very honest compared to the more predatory boatmen over in Indonesia so have some level of faith when negotiating in Sarawak. In any case, agree on a price before setting off and be steeled for the actual price of fuel in remote regions. In our example, the trip from Belaga to Ukit will cost one person M$400 one way or over $150 US.

Air

MAS offers the most convenient way to get to Sibu, Bintulu and Miri. Most flights are heavily booked. Local air schedules can be found in the *Borneo Post*, the newspaper of record in Sarawak. MAS runs large jets like Boeing 737s and Fokker Friendships between major cities and Twin Otters into the smaller strips. Even though most small towns boast daily air service, the Twin Otters only carry 21 people, very little baggage and mucho cargo, so passengers may be bumped.

Land

For short trips between major towns there are plenty of buses that leave in the morning. They do take a while and there is little to see other than endless clearings, pepper plantations and the occasional kampung. When the monsoons hit, travel by road is a risky affair. You may or may not make it due to bridge washouts, floodings and other natural obstacles across the road. If you have your heart set on hemorrhoids, cramped legs and a sore back you can get a bus schedule from the Kuching Tourist Office. The central terminus is Kuching with buses radiating outwards towards Sri Aman and Sarikei.In town the best mode of transportation is by foot, taxi or rickshaw. However, if you're planning on going into the forest to visit longhouses and such, you'll need to contact a local tour agency because most longhouses are accessible only by river.

Borneo
a journey

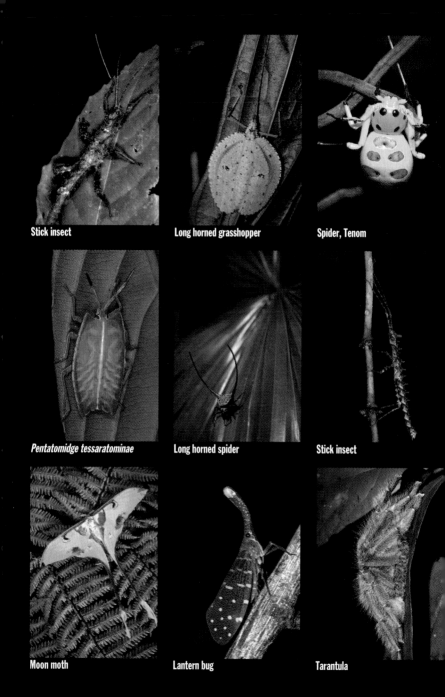

Stick insect

Long horned grasshopper

Spider, Tenom

Pentatomidge tessaratominae

Long horned spider

Stick insect

Moon moth

Lantern bug

Tarantula

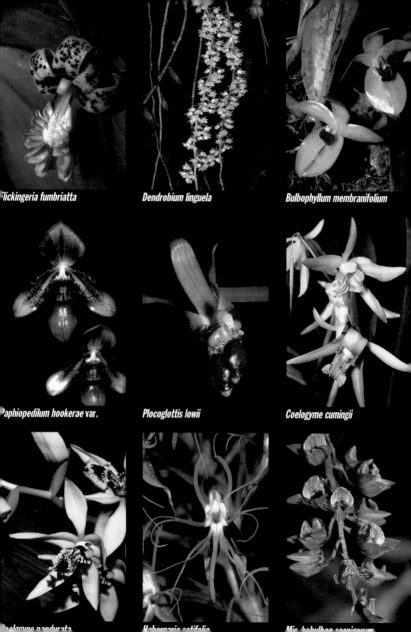

Flickingeria fumbriatta

Dendrobium linguela

Bulbophyllum membranifolium

Paphiopedilum hookerae var.

Plocoglottis lowii

Coelogyme cumingii

Coelogyne pandurata

Habernaria setifolia

Mic. bulbulbon ecaniverum

The Pinnacles, Mulu

Mt. Kinabalu

Orang utans at play in canopy, Sepilok

Mt. Kinabalu

Orchids

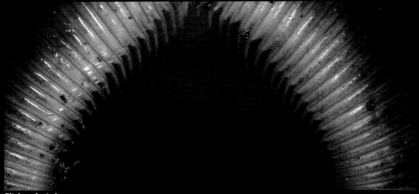

Pitcher plant close up

Gunung Mulu at dawn

ban chief

Rare *thysmia* plant

Maliau falls

Cave in Batu Punggul

Aerial of Sabah

Dipterocarp trees

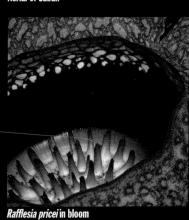
Rafflesia pricei in bloom

Maliau basin

The Lost World of Borneo

Maliau basin

Canopy at dawn, Danum Valley

The road past Sapulut

Sepilok Orang utan Rehabilitation Center

Murut Dancer

Batu Punggul

Murut hat

Belawing ceremony pole, Long Ampung

Kenyah baby carrier

Long Nawang before a thunderstorm

Long Nawang Baru

Star fungus

Dipterocarp tree

Coral reef

Burial decorations

Orchids

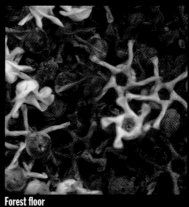
Forest floor

Fishing village near Semporna

Shoreline of Sabah

Indonesian fishing village

Indonesian puppets, Kalimantan

Movie poster, Kota Kinabalu

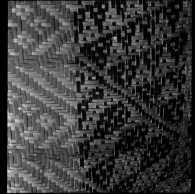

Dugout canoe

Longhouse wall

Murut basket design

Longhouse roof decorations

Unidentified spider

Buffy owl

Asian leaf frog

Rhinoceros hornbill

Orang utan

Kenyah sun hat

Tarakan, Kalimantan

Pet monkey, Kalimant...

Pontianak

Marudi

Mt. Kinabalu

Sandakan

Apo Kayan

Batu Punggul

Filipino children

Chinese fish hawker

Bajau mother

Penan nomad

Kenyah child

Bruneian fisherman

Logging road

Typical bridge, Sabah

Night river crossing

River running

Mt. Kinabalu

Abandoned logging road

Adult male orang utan

Nuts & Bolts

Sarawak is expensive for travel, but not as expensive as Sabah. The predominance of oil workers, timber camp workers and traders jack hotel rates up on the high end but there are plenty of Chinese fleabags for the impecunious traveler. Restaurants are cheap and plentiful. As elsewhere in this book I do not cover where to eat because food tends to be of a high quality, consistent with its ethnic origins and an adventure in itself. Can anyone compare *satay* in a logging town to a stir fry in a trading outpost? I think not. If you find an establishment that merits being singled out let me know. As for general costs, expect to pay twice what you paid in mainland Malaysia for gas, hotels, food and supplies. If you are heading upriver and are somewhat ambitious, be very careful that you don't run out of money or at least ringgits since costs can be extraordinary and banks are only in main centers. If you just want to hit the highlights, plan on three-four days. If you want to get to know one or two of the remote areas, plan on two weeks. If you want to really understand the country spend a minimum of five weeks. If you seek true adventure then just throw away your watch and max out your charge cards in Kuching. You will need at least a three day period to acclimatize to the heat, the food and the time zone, so for the sake of your sanity spend the first week doing the easy stuff, with plenty of sleep. If you want to hate this place, start your trip with the obligatory all night drunk at a longhouse right off the plane combined with a flesh searing trip on a river boat to end up in a hospital. All things in moderation, or at least one at a time.

Getting around to the main attractions is fairly simple. People are helpful, the infrastructure is reliable (until the monsoons hit between November to February) and the prices are reasonable for air, bus and boat fares on established routes.

For air transport or to reconfirm your tickets check in at the **MAS** office on *Jalan Song Thian* ☎ *244144*

Merpati (for flights to Pontianak in Indonesia) is at **Sin Hwa Travel**, *8 Jalan Temple, near the Kuching Hilton,* ☎ *246688*. If you want to make the overland to Pontianak in Indonesia the Indonesian consulate is on Pisang Road.

If you have problems or need visa extensions contact the State Government Complex on Jalan Simpang Tiga about three kms south of downtown Kuching on the way to the airport. **Immigration** hours are Monday to Friday 9:00 a.m. til 4:30 p.m. and Saturdays 9:00 a.m. to noon.

Permits are required for most trips upriver or to parks so check with local tour operators. Niah Cave permits can be picked up from the Sarawak Museum or at the park office in Miri or at the park itself. **Tours** can be booked from **Borneo Transverse**, *10B Wayang Street,* ☎ *257784* and **Interworld Travel Services** on *Green Road,* ☎ *(082) 252344*. Major hotels and the Tourism Promotion Board can also direct you to tour agencies. **Malaysian Tourist Promotion Board** is in the AIA building on Song Thian Cheok Road and is very helpful in providing information and literature. ☎ *246775*. The **Sarawak Tourist Association** is at the Main Bazaar ☎ *(082) 242218*.

Information or bookings for Sarawak's **National Parks** can be had at the **National Parks Office** on Jalan Satok on the 7th floor, about a click west of the town center, ☎ *(082) 248088*. There is also an office in Miri if you are going to Mulu or Niah.

Bako is close to Kuching and offers a wide variety of ecosystems for the traveler on a short schedule.

Bako National Park★

40 kms (2 1/2 hours) from Kuching

Sarawak's first national park is 2728 hectares of mangrove, heath forest and dipterocarp forest about two hours by speedboat upriver from Kuching. The major attractions are the dramatic cliffs and beautiful beaches. The popular getaway is a two hour bus trip to Bako village and then a 30 minute boat trip to the park. Don't forget to book your return trip if you charter a local boat (about M$3–$4). If you are really in a hurry you can take a taxi from Kuching for around M$40 which will reduce the land portion to one hour, but remember there is a ferry crossing that could add an hour on weekends or holidays. The less adventurous will simply book a packaged tour from Kuching and let them take care of everything.

Once inside the park there are fascinating plants and animals, including the pitcher plant, dwarf palm, proboscis monkey, flying lemur, civet cat and over 150 species of birds. The park has a good choice of easy hiking paths and government rest houses. **Tanjung Sapi** is the most dramatic of the many sculptured coves and headlands. There's good swimming in secluded bays located about 1.5 hours from Park headquarters. Teluk Pandan Kecil is probably the best bet.

Most visitors don't bother exploring the tiny 27sq. km. (10 sq. miles) park for a one day visit or hiking all 16 well marked paths. The circuitous Lintan trail is the best single choice. Ambitious hikers can walk to the eastern side of the island and camp overnight.

The Park HQ has a small store, toilets and other good stuff. July and August are crowded with locals on day trips to the park.

Where to Stay in
Bako National Park

Resthouses run about M$30 per house and about half for a room (There are two rooms to a bungalow and the entire house sleeps 10). There is also a hostel for half of the

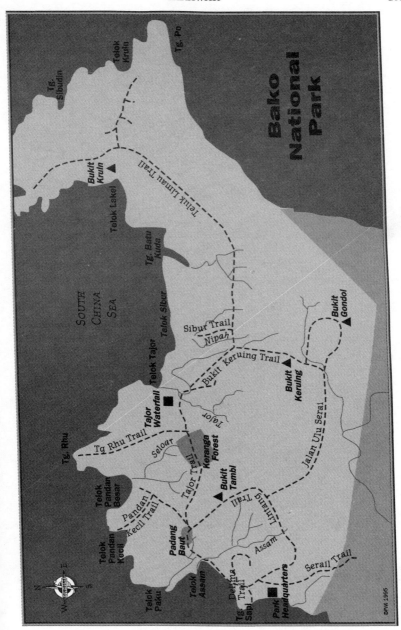

room cost. Single cost for a bed in the hostel is a mere M$1. If that is too pricey for you then you can pay the equivalent of 25 cents and camp at the headquarters site.

AUTHOR'S TIP

There are a lot of mosquitoes in Bako. After all, you are in a swamp. So bring lots of insect repellent and use netting when you sleep. The best place to see wildlife and escape picnickers is the trail towards the eastern end of the park.

TRAILS IN BAKO NATIONAL PARK

TRAIL	DISTANCE	TIME FROM PARK HQ	DESCRIPTION
Lintan Trail	5.35km	4 hours	*The most popular trail that will take you through the mangrove swamp, kerangas forest, 3 different types of nepenthes plants and lowland dipterocarp forest.*
Telok Limau	10.5km	7 hrs	*The longest trail to the Northeast point. There is a beachside campsite at the end of the trail. From there excursions can be made to P. Lakei for excellent snorkeling There is also another beach and freshwater pond at T.Kruin.*
Telok Delima	.25km	.75 hr	*The best trail to see the proboscis monkeys, off the Lintan trail.*
Ulu Serait	2.25km	3 hrs	*Summit trail (a mere 260m) but good chances of viewing pitcher plants.*
Telok Paku	2.75km	2 hrs	*Raised walkway path that ends up on a nice beach with interesting sandstone patterns. Ideal for exploring the mangrove swamp. Mudskippers, pitcher plants, crabs*

Bandar Sri Aman

135kms from Kuching by road

The Sungai Lupar is famous for two things: It is a river with a mean tidal bore that almost drowned Somerset Maugham in 1929. The episode inspired "Yellow Streak" in his book *Borneo Tales*. Also this is where James Brooke did most of his pirate and headhunter bashing. In 1849, 800 Ibans raiders who came storming downriver from the Lupar and Skrang rivers were killed at the battle of Batang Maru. Brooke was given this area by the Sultan of Brunei four years later and this became the second major chunk of land ceded to the English adventurer. It is now appropriately called the second division.

The only thing remaining of those bloodthirsty times are the Iban longhouses upriver and **Fort Alice** constructed in 1864 as a base for Brooke's pirate-quashing forays against the Ibans. Formerly called Simmanggang, Sri Aman is the administrative capital of Sarawak's second division.

Fort Alice

This very colonial looking fort with its turrets and drawbridge was the base for many punitive expeditions against the Ibans upriver and a fortification against pirates venturing from the sea. Charles Brooke lived in this area for 10 years. The fort was strategically built to control the Skrang, Lemanak and Ai rivers that flow into the Lupar.

The tidal bore ★

(Consult tidal charts or locals for best time to visit.) The Lupar River or sungai Lupar tightens up dramatically from its wide mouth creating a phenomenon called a tidal bore. There is also a tiny island that blocks the entry of the tide just downriver from the town. When the tide comes in it builds in intensity and then washes inland in great force. After that (and Fort Alice) you have seen all there is to see in this town.

Where to Stay in Bandar Sri Aman

There are four average Chinese run hotels in town. All offer AC, clean rooms and not much else. The Hoover is your best bet for a price that includes television, attached bathroom and air conditioning.

The Hoover   M$28–45

139 Jalan Club, ☎ (085) 321985.

The Alishan   M$20–34

120 Jalan Council, ☎ (085) 322578.

Champion Hotel   M$20–28

1248 Main Bazaar, ☎ (085) 320140.

The Sun Sun   M$20–25

62 Jalan Club, across from the market ☎ (085) 322191.

Around Bandar Sri Aman

Longhouses along the tributaries of the Lupar

When you book an "authentic" longhouse tour in Kuching chances are you will be taken to the longhouses along the Engkari, the Lemanak, the Skrang or the ulu Ai. The joke is, of course, that the more authentic looking longhouses are actually just south of Kuching where the tour agencies and longhouse owners have worked to prevent reality creep. Kampung Annah Rais is an example of a well visited but authentically maintained longhouse of over 100 doors.

If you do venture up the Skrang, try to get past the ones close to Pias or Lamanak which are main embarkation points for longhouse tours. The Banteng Ai region is about 40kms southwest of Bandar Sri Aman and has many traditional longhouses. If you are going solo you will need to take a bus to Lubok Antu, 50kms southeast of Bandar Sri Aman and then take a bus to the jetty on the Batang Ai reservoir. Here you can charter a boat to take you upriver. This area was flooded in the '60s but the remaining Iban live a fairly simple life.

Batang Ai is a convenient area to visit Iban longhouses.

Batang Ai National Park

275km, 4 hours from Kuching

Sarawak's newest national park is 24 hectares dedicated to preserving 90 plant species, 61 species of birds, 44 species of mammals and a unique water and land based series of trails.

Where to Stay in Batang Ai

Batang Ai Longhouse Resort   M$189–315   ★★★★★

Batang Ai Lake, P.O. Box 2396 Kuching, 93748 ☎ (82) 240281, FAX 425400

It would seem the real reason to visit Batang Ai is for the new M$28 million dollar resort built to attract eco-tourists and the well-heeled locals from Kuching. Built in the style of traditional Iban architecture, the hotel is part of a new breed of resorts that appeal to the ecologically sensitive by recreating "rustic experiences without the realities. Imagine air-conditioned longhouse suites, dirt roads that lead to the hotel to make you think you are entering the great unknown, and an 18 minute longboat trip that will take you into this longhouse experience. The park itself is a two hour longboat ride away. If the resort is too slick you can arrange a trip to a "real" Iban longhouse just up the river.

The hotel is managed by the Kuching Hilton folks, so one can imagine that everything is first class. There are 100 rooms all with AC, minibar, phone, etc. Nonsmoking rooms are available.

Belaga

150 kms upriver from Kapit

If Kapit is too civilized, Belaga is for folks who really like to get backcountry. This place was originally set up by Chinese traders in the early 1900s to deal in truly raw materials like beeswax, bezoar stones (monkey gallbladder stones), gutta-percha and rhinoceros horn. You will need a permit to get here (from the SAO office in the State Government Complex *(Pejabat Daerah)* in Belaga or in Kapit or from the District officer). If you don't mind taking a hell-bent-for-leather ride in a 12-cylinder *ekspres* speed boat, and shooting the 2.5 km long Pelagus Rapids, (all inside an hour into your trip to Belaga) you will enjoy the trip.

Longhouse tours along the Baleh

Sungai Baleh begins 10kms east of Kapit.

Visiting the local longhouses is popular; ask around to make sure you get the name of the type you like and then see if you can wangle an invite. You will get a kick out of the rustic funkiness of the town. There are slim pickings when it comes to hotels all grouped together for easy comparison. The longhouse in Tubau on the Kemana river is a popular overnight stop. If you want a more authentic longhouse experience try the Iban longhouses in the Baleh area on the Gaat and Merirai sidestreams. If you would like to find a ride to one of these longhouses, just hang around the jetty where the Baleh meets the Gaat and Meriri. There is an old logging camp at Putai. Past this point the river is fast and requires a smaller longboat with a good engine. There is a Kenyah longhouse about two hours past Putai on the upper Baleh. Now you can truly tell your friends that you have seen an authentic longhouse and spend some time with the aristocrats of Borneo. Although none of the longhouses have the grand architecture and massive support beams of old, the people and setting are close to what Borneo used to be like before White Rajahs, chainsaws and resort hotels. If you have been following Redmond O'Hanlon's book this far you will be able to see Batu Tiban. Not technically the geographic "Heart of Borneo" but close enough to the soul to make the trip worthwhile. If you are traveling alone and would like to visit this area you might be better served to set your trip up in advance through a Kuching based tour organizer.

Drowning the Dark Heart

Higher than Aswan at 111 meters, cranking out 3000 megawatts a year and backing up 44,000,000,000 cubic feet of water in a reservoir area 695 sq kms wide. This is the area of proposed Bakun dam project to be built above Belaga on the Rejang River in an area that is primarily virgin rainforest. Some reports say a series of dams are to be built in the area. There have been 17 technical studies carried out on Bakun over the last decade and a half. They remain classified under Malaysia's official secrets. The dam will be over 500km from the mouth of the Rejang and will require extensive roads and support services to be brought in. Long Murum and 14 other tribal longhouses will disappear under water and a way of life will come to an end.

The M$ 15 billion ($5.8 billion) project is expected to displace only 5000-8500 locals but will inundate over 80,000 hectares (197,000 acres) when it floods an area the size of Singapore in 10 years. Most of the 3000 megawatts of electricity will be siphoned off via a 650km (404 mile) cable to mainland Malaysia.

It is not known whether the forest is being cleared by Ekran, the local company owned by a close friend of the Mahatir in preparation for the dam being given the go ahead. It is estimated that the revenue generated from timber will pay half of the cost of the dam. The dam is expected to provide a quarter of Malaysia's electrical needs. During the last year prices of many tropical hardwoods have more than doubled in price. Needless to say the time to visit the Rejang is now.

Beyond Belaga ★

You would be foolish to come this far then jump on the twice weekly MAS flight and go home. You can choose from land or water in your quest for adventure.

There are a variety of land routes that connect with river sections. You can travel with a guide or just go for it if you get good instructions. The journey can take three-five days over the mountains into Bintulu via a well marked path. You can also set this up in Kuching or Bintulu before you go. You can take a truncated version where much of the walking is replaced by four-wheel-drive vehicle and a boat ride. If you want to go upriver longboats can be shared to Wong Jawa (2 hours, M$10) and Ukit (full day, M$35), price is dependent on how many people are on board. If the river is low then you will have to use a canoe and the length of the journey will be dramatically lengthened.

If you want to explore the longhouses upriver from Belaga don't be surprised to find that most have land connections through the maze of logging roads that terminate in Kapit. There are no maps but the local with trucks could advise you on which road goes where. You will need special permission from the logging concession owners to use roads and these are best handled by a local tour operator.

Pasang Rapids ★★

(2kms upriver from Belaga by longboat) The most powerful set of rapids in Sarawak can be seen (not run) about 2km up the Batang Belaga from town. If you charter a boat for about M$50 they will run you up to a cleared area above the rapids.

Beyond Belaga

From	to	Notes
BELAGA - BINTULU		
Belaga	Long Metik	*Take the express boat (M$60) to Long Metik.*
Long Metik	Tubau	*The Balui-Tubau Transport Co. will take you to Tubau for M$50 per person. Stay at the Angelina Inn (M$10) or at the longhouse nearby. There are some very nice longhouses on the sungai Kemena. (Iban) or sungai Tubau (Kenyah, Kayan) and Penan settlements on the sungai Jalalong. Guides from Tubau run about M$200 per trip to the longhouses.*
Tubau	Bintulu	*Take the express boat (M$14) to Bintulu.*
BINTULA - BELAGA		
Bintulu	Tubau	*Take Express boat(M$14) to Tubau.*
Tubau	Centre Camp	*Take longboat (M$3) to CentreCamp.*
Centre Camp	Long Metik	*At Centre Camp ask for a ride to Long Metik, a logging camp 20km upstream from Belaga on the Balui river Expect to pay M$30 per person.*
Long Metik	Belaga	*Take the express boat to Belaga(M$60).*

Where to Stay in Belaga

The most popular hotel in Belaga seems to be the Belaga Hotel mostly for its ever smiling owner and the good food in its cafe downstairs. Second choice goes to the Bee Lian.

Hotel Belaga   **M$15–30**
 14 Belaga Bazaar (086) 461244

Bee Lian Inn   **M$25**
 11 Belaga Bazaar ☎ (086) 461416

Hotel Sing Soon Huat   **M$20**
 27 New Bazaar ☎ (086) 461257 FAX 461346

Bintulu

120kms, (3 hours from Miri)

Bintulu is the site of a monstrous, ever-growing refinery complex and not much else. The **Niah caves** are nearby and the **Similajau National Park** is 20 kms away, as well as about two dozen longhouses (authentic but not unvisited) on the Kemana River. There are modern and inexpensive hotels in town (compared to Kuching). Similajau Adventure tours, Jalan Sommerville (in the PDA building) can set up trips to Niah, Belaga and Similajau. Last resort if the Kemana is full.

My Iban host checks out a bizarre offering, American baseball cards.

Where to Stay in Bintulu

If you ever have the misfortune to be stuck in Bintulu there are a collection of flea bags down by the waterfront that will ding you M$20 unless you bargain hard.

Plaza Hotel   **$160–280**   ★★★

    116 Jalan Abang Galau ☎ *(086) 335111, FAX 332742*
    A luxury business hotel for oil patch folks on expensive accounts.

Kemana Lodging House and Annex   **M$15–30**

    78 Keppel Road, ☎ *(086) 31533*
    Out near the airport and cheaper than the Plaza Hotel.

Capitol Hotel   **M$15–40**

    Keppel Road, ☎ *(086) 34667*

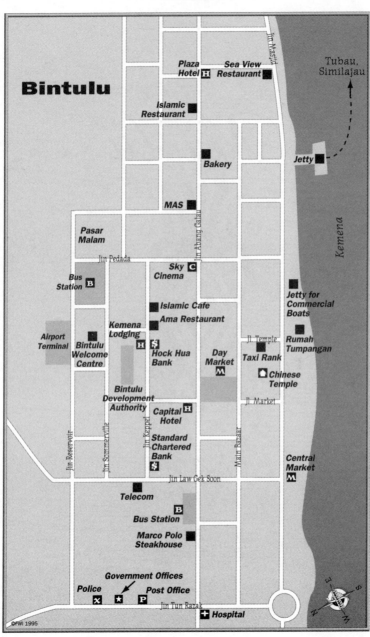

Bintulu

Tubau, Similajau

Plaza Hotel H Sea View Restaurant

Islamic Restaurant

Bakery

MAS

Pasar Malam

Jln Pedada

Sky Cinema C

Bus Station B

Islamic Cafe
Ama Restaurant

Kemena Lodging H S

Hock Hua Bank

Airport Terminal

Bintulu Welcome Centre

Bintulu Development Authority

Capital Hotel H

Standard Chartered Bank S

Jln Reservoir

Jln Sommerville

Jln Keppel

Jln Law Gek Soon

Telecom

Bus Station B

Marco Polo Steakhouse

Government Offices

Police ✕ ★ Post Office P

Jln Tun Razak

Hospital ✚

Jetty

Kemena

Jetty for Commercial Boats

Jl. Temple

Day Market M

Taxi Rank

Rumah Tumpangan

Chinese Temple

Jl. Market

Main Bazaar

Central Market M

©FWI 1995

T here are many parts of our world that will never be discovered—the everchanging wasteland of the poles, the harsh monotony of the desert and the faceless ocean that hides the majority of our accessible environment. One of the areas that keeps surprising us is right under our feet. Over the past few years there have been significant discoveries of cave systems in China, Mexico and Borneo. I had read about the results of a 1978 expedition to explore the Mulu caves. More than 115 scientists spent a year and three months exploring this remote and truly unexplored region. To date, 27 different cave systems and 137 kms of passages have been explored with many more awaiting discovery. The existence of Gunung Mulu at 2376 meters is overshadowed by these stygian finds. Mulu is still yielding new species and discoveries.

We should begin with the, by now, obligatory rattling off of Mulu's biodiversity. Mulu is home to 20,000 animal species, 8000 types of fungi, 3500 plant species, 1500 types of flowering plants, including: 170 types of orchids, 109 types of palm, 10 types of pitcher plants, 67 species of mammals, 262 species of birds; 8 of them hornbills, 74 species of frogs, 50 species of reptiles, 47 species of fish (9 of which are found in the caves), 12 species of bats, 281 species of butterflies, and even 458 species of ants. The 544 sq km area (210 sq. miles) defined as Gunung Mulu National Park is home to an unusual collection of unique species both above and below ground including cave flying fish and albino crabs.

Although there is now an airstrip carved out of the jungle to allow greater access to tourists and tour groups, I went in 1989 as part of an international expedition. I also wanted to explore the little visited area of Limbang, the curious thin little strip that divides Brunei in two. The area ceded to Brooke in 1890 must still vex the Sultan of Brunei every time he looks across the Gulf of Brunei or at a map of his tiny domain.

Leaving our vehicles to be ferried to Miri, we begin our journey from the port of Lawas, a rough and tumble place visited by few tourists. During the cool dawn we watch mother nature unfurl a spectacular multi-hued sunset as we sit atop the high speed express boat on our trip across the Gulf of Brunei to Limbang. Then we pile in a sweltering bus that takes us up to Kuala Medamit and finally pack ourselves into primitive longboats for the trip up the fast flowing Sungai Melinau.

When we arrive at the start of our river trip it doesn't take long to see that our ancient longboats were designed to carry much less than they are carrying now. Once loaded with our gear and crew it seems it is only surface tension that keeps the three glued-together planks that pass for a boat on top of the water. Our canoe rides barely one and a half inches from the water. I know this because when I hold the sides, my fingertips are under water.

At first we are quite amused at the agility of our bowman and steersman as they jump in and out of the boat pushing us through the many rapids. It isn't until we are rudely awakened to the fact that we are intended to be participants, not spectators, in this entertainment that the cruel joke sinks in. The outboard engines on the backs of the boats are for decoration, since we will be doing most of the propulsion on this long wet trip!

Further upstream, where the river becomes narrower and shallower, the passengers are pressed into service more often, jumping out when the boat hits the first rocks, then pushing and shoving the waterlogged boat over the rapids. Only after we are waist deep in the rapidly flowing water can we jump back in, filling the already sinking boat with more muddy water.

When I ask our bowman whether they have ever thought of using lighter boats, he confides that they have never done this before, with this many people, in this short a time. He winks and tells me the reason he jumps in and out so fast is due to the prevalence of large man-eating reptiles in the rivers.

Suddenly I developed a sprightly approach to entering and reentering our leaky craft. Bailing our leaking craft takes on a new urgency. In case you did not know, the largest crocodiles in the world are from Sarawak.

As we glide deeper and deeper into the jungle, the river banks grow closer together. The round smooth stones evolve into razor-sharp limestone formations, the vines and creepers hang down into the brackish water creating soft green curtains. We push the clumsy boats, cursing and slipping on the eerily sculpted rocks. Soon fatigue sets in. We have been smashing our shins and straining against the current for over six hours now. The light is failing and our steersman begins to peer nervously into the gloom, searching for hidden rocks or submerged logs. They do not like to travel on the water when it's dark. Since our campsite is miles up river and we are trapped on the river by the impenetrable walls of green on each side, there is no choice but to press on into the night. The rounded rocks that twisted our ankles are replaced by sharp painful rocks that bloody our shins and tear the soles off our heavy jungle boots.

Finally, the meager light that penetrates the canopy fails, leaving us to negotiate between walls of limestone and run rapids by flashlight. It is quite an experience. Hours later we are still splashing in and out of the canoe and pushing the damned thing up river, our only thought now being a warm, dry place to spend the night.

Into Mulu via the back door: the infamous Headhunters Trail.

At last we come to a halt on a rocky curve in the river. Soaked to the skin and shivering from exhaustion, we are glad to see the crude wooden compound that is seemingly modeled on a camp from a Japanese prisoner of war-movie. The raw light of the single kerosene lantern sways back and forth, projecting animated shadows of the giant bugs against the wall. We slop around in the mud and silently eat a simple meal of plain rice and noodles. We sleep the sleep of the dead, oblivious to the rain drumming on the tin roof and the rising river.

Four hours later we awaken to a predawn wake-up call consisting of a screeching siren and broken English blasted over an overamped bullhorn. I am now absolutely positive we are extras in a low budget remake of *The Bridge on the River Kwai.*

Our local guide bellows, "Good morning. Good morning, happy people. We must now hurry to be upriver before the river rises from the rain last night."

Hurry to where? Doesn't water start upriver and rush downriver? What he meant is that we have many more hours of pushing boats before we can begin our "death march" across the height of land.We should have chartered much lighter boats and we are now paying the price. The torrential rains have brought trees crashing down during the night, we have had to constantly move the boats to higher and higher ground and we are getting sick of "mee" or noodles for breakfast, lunch and dinner. On this cold shivering morning, adventure sucks.

On learning that yesterday's punishment was just a warm up, the television crew documenting our expedition has had enough. They commandeer three canoes to take them back down the river. That means more people in less canoe and of course more pushing. This morning the river is hard and cold from the recent rains and we shiver even more as we push the waterlogged boats into the current.

We fight even harder for every inch of progress in the narrow river since it is now blocked by fallen trees and choked with undergrowth. The river bed, carved out of solid limestone, becomes increasingly more convoluted and wicked. It now delivers razor sharp blows to already smashed shins, feet and arms.

We are almost too tired to notice the strange beauty that now surrounds us. The river is a green tunnel, every rock a soft cushion of thick moss. Brightly colored butterflies flit by, odd looking insects inspect us from every branch. Wild orchids of every color and variety spill down from the trees. Although pretty at first glance, each animal and plant must fight for survival in the thin soil and light of the jungle floor. This is the world as I imagine it would have been in prehistoric days—a beautiful but dangerous world where life is decided by its position on the food chain.

At long last we come upon the clearing that is the start of our overland journey. We are to hike five and a half hours across the height of land connecting us with Sungai Tujob, from where we will then take canoes down-stream into the headquarters and giant caves of Mulu National Park. I have a sneaking suspicion our boatman will just throw what is left of the canoes away and float down on the wreckage. Amazingly, they figure the leaking and smashed canoes have one more expedition left in them and they wave gleefully as they leave us in the jungle.

Our guide gives the uninitiated amongst us a brief lecture on leeches. Having suckled, nurtured and then killed more leeches than I can remember I have developed a grudging respect for them. After I lose my tan, scrapes and cuts, it seems the little white scars from leech bites are the last souvenir of Borneo to disappear.

Leeches can actually smell blood. I have seen them stand on their hind-quarters like bears and sniff for victims. Once they zero in on you, they hustle their little brown slimy butts as fast as they can. Although tiny, when they latch on they soon become engorged and black. Once removed, the antico-agulant will make the bite bleed long after your guest has been smashed to a pulp. If they are caught in your clothes while hiking they will latch on, bite, get knocked off, latch on again and bite ad nauseum until you look like you were attacked by an octopus with a chain saw. I still cannot get the blood stains out of my jungle clothes.

Our guide's description of blood-swollen leeches clinging from every tender orifice and appendage makes everyone check every zipper and tighten each lace just a little more. Over our guide's now hated and still over-amped bullhorn came the final plaintive warning, "Don't be afraid of our leeches.... Please,... don't be afraid." By this time I was pretty sure that even a leech would probably take pity and donate blood to our soaked and shrivelled group.

As we stagger in the gloom beneath 200 foot tall trees, we see the jungle from the inside. I say inside because from the jungle a river is a smooth green wall from the river bank to the canopy. As the jungle engulfs the river it becomes a tunnel still smooth, dark brown and ordered.

Once you break through the green wall, the jungle is a strange and intriguing place. It is wet, dark and muddy. It is also sharp, painful and deadening. There is little visible wildlife other than biting insects, and after your first "ass-over-a-tea kettle" introduction to the root system of the strangling fig plant, you pretty much spend most of your time looking at a small patch of muddy leaves directly ahead of you. Inside the forest there are some scenic respites from the boredom—huge bamboo groves, emerald snakes, giant insects and a host of delicate plants and flowers. But all in all, jungle trekking is just hot, dark and wet. After five hours of squish, squish, squish, you long for a peek of blue sky and a dry patch of land. Suddenly the land tilts down and "blam" we come out into a clearing. Our hands automatically go up to shield our eyes from the brilliant sun. After our eyes adjust we discover with some excitement that we have come upon a crystal clear mountain stream. We are so used to the tepid muddy rivers that this ice-cold stream is quite a novelty.

The source of our temporary blindness is not the sun but the reflection of the sun on the sheer granite cliffs of Melanau Gorge. The scene would rival the majesty of Half Dome in Yosemite or Bryce Canyon.

This brief and bright interlude is not to last. Ten feet from the ice cold river, we are plunged back into the steamy, midday gloom of the primeval forest. Although our expedition members would rather spend the rest of the day cooling off in the alpine waters, we must press on if we are to rendezvous with the boats that await us.

The boats that are to take us downriver to the lodge are much larger and look more suited to multi-passenger transportation than the tiny canoes we left behind. It is not long before we have fonder memories of the tiny canoes as we soon discover that pushing bigger boats down river requires much greater effort. New pleasures await us like the pain of continually smashing your shins as you leap into the boat across the two foot high gunnels or the rather strenuous activity of running on slippery boulders in waist-deep water to avoid being left behind. As you can guess, the novelty of boat pushing was wearing off. We pass under grotesque shaped limestone cliffs. Some look like skulls, others have ominous shapes.

Before we are to rest that day, we visit Deer Cave and Clearwater Cave. Deer Cave is probably the most thoroughly explored and known. The cave features the world's biggest cave mouth at 30 stories high and the biggest cave passage which, at 2.2 km long and 220 meters high, is impressive. The roof is never less than 100 meters in height. Deer Cave is well known as a place to hunt deer and for the most spectacular bat show in Sarawak. The deer lick the salted pools that drain off the guano and provide a regular source of quarry for the Penan that live in the area. Deer Cave is short by Mulu standards being only about 2 kilometers in length and open at both ends. Its easy access and great space make it ideal for bats of which over a million live high in the caverns.

The spectacle of the bats has been described endlessly but it is one of the more memorable visions of Mulu. Be sure to arrange your trip to Deer Cave around dusk. It is a spectacle that is both demonic and awe-inspiring. The sound of the "6:30 bug" or *ngingit* cicada is the cue for the over one million fret tailed bats to emanate from the cave. A continuous stream of bats explodes forth from the cave mouth over the next thirty minutes on their way to the coast where they will eat 10 tons of insects. The long black line of bats that curves and stretches off into the distance continues until dark. They return by nightfall and feed the cockroaches below with their droppings. This daily migration of bats is not unique to Deer Cave, but the number of bats in such a small area is.

The opening of Deer Cave

Clearwater Cave had just been discovered the year before our visit. Deep inside the cave is an underground river that can be navigated for 5 kilometers. Since the entire cave is estimated to be 60 kilometers long (38 miles), it is not a casual decision to go exploring. Mulu Visitors who are keen on seeing the world's largest cave chamber might be wise to be satisfied with the westernized descriptions of the Sarawak chamber being as big as sixteen football fields or eight 747s nose to tail and with room for 32 more at the sides. What the guidebooks fail to mention is that there is no lighting in the immense chamber. In other words, unless you brought in massive amounts of lighting equipment with special permission from the government, you will never see the true scale of this cave.

Entrance to various caves is regulated by the park. All parts of the cave systems are not open and you must have a park guide with you at all times. There are 25 major caves in Mulu discovered so far. There are also dozens of minor caves. It is estimated that only ten percent of the caves have been discovered. The park is opening more caves to the public and preserving others for scientific exploration only. Gunung Benarat at 1585 meters is still unclimbed. About 3000–5000 people visit the park each year and it is gaining rapidly in popularity. Most of these visitors are on overnight trips from Miri and do not venture into the remote areas of the park.

The Last People of the Forest

We stop to chat with the people in a Penan village. I talk with a man whose face is bisected by a scar that runs diagonally from his chin to his forehead. He shows me how to use a blow gun. I gather from his patient and slightly distant attitude that this is something they do quite regularly. They smile and endure us politely as we take their pictures. As we use our international sign language to converse with these "simple, primitive" people, I can't help noticing a young man using a gas powered weedwhacker to clear grass away from his "primitive" hut. The children run naked around the crudely built huts as the women modestly bathe in the river. A group of older children plays with a monkey chained to a veranda. The monkey lashes out, pulling the young Penan's hair.

In the background, government workers are busy putting up a longhouse that these people will move into. There will be proper displays of native skills and sales of handicrafts I am told. I look at the monkey, now sitting patiently, ignoring its tormentors and then at the quiet, sedate Penan. I can't help but see the similarity of their predicament. Glad to be back on the river I realize our incursion into these people's homeland has its price.

Known as the *orang ulu*, or people upriver, the Penan are one of the world's last wild people. Because they leave no mark upon the forest as shifting cultivators do, the government feels they do not have a claim to the land. When criticized for the forced resettlement of the Penan by the prime minister of Malaysia, the response was, "We don't intend to turn the Penans into human zoological specimens to be gawked at by tourists. There is nothing romantic about these helpless, half-starved and disease-ridden people." In 1989, 40 percent of Sarawak's forests had already been destroyed. The Sarawak government's response was to at first deny, then ignore and then ban journalists who would be "anti-logging" from entering the country. The fight for the forest was not just a PR scheme dreamed up by long haired people who also save whales on weekends. The military had put a price on the head of Bruno Manser, then a 33-year-old artist from Switzerland, who was causing great embarrassment to the government by helping to organize the Penan. When I came across a recently exploded bridge and left behind plastic explosives I was begged by the local people not to write about the incident because it would be bad for tourism. The local people had destroyed a bridge that allowed loggers to flagrantly log inside a National Park. The locals and the Penan were both "mad as hell" but the Penan had no formal way to make their displeasure known. Despite their lack of government representation, money, education, or even clothes, they were not going to take it anymore.

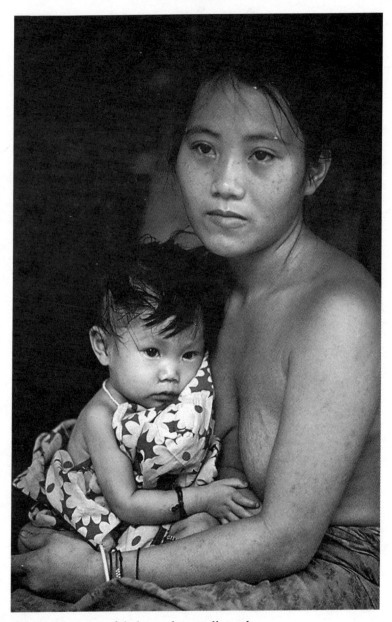

The Penan are some of the last truly nomadic peoples.

Gunung Mulu is a biosphere where people, plants and animals are protected.

Manser lived with the Penan and even adopted the bowl cut hairstyle and customs of the people. He showed them how to create blockades and worked to gain international attention. When I was there a serious manhunt for him was underway with much nervousness all around whenever a Westerner like myself was found wandering deep in the Sarawak forests.

The Penan are not a political race. Although a large percentage of modern Penan now work in logging camps in small towns doing menial labor, they view the forest as their home. The nonstop encroachment of logging slowly drove them to action. A very unusual step for this gentle and non warring people. The Penan have never taken heads, have no rigid social structure or even a method of organizing their people by race. But in March of 1987 they did.

Supported by outside organizers and world opinion, groups of Penan finally struck back and set up their first blockade in March of 1987 but were immediately arrested for blockading logging roads from 1987 to late 1989. Their roadblocks prevented millions of dollars worth of timber from getting to market. Armed with their traditional blow guns and spears they demanded that the loggers leave their homeland alone. The protestors were arrested and then these indigenous people, who have no use for currency, were asked to post two thousand ringgits as bail money. The government of Sarawak quickly passed a law that forbids blocking a logging road. The Penan's simple complaint is that the logging is scaring away wildlife, polluting rivers and killing fish. They want government to either compensate them for the loss of their land or stop the logging. Neither has occurred.

The tradition of Sarawakians being accountable only to themselves is evident in septuagenarian James Wong's attitude towards the unholy alliance of timber, money and politics. Like most Chinese timber millionaires in Borneo, he does not see any problem with his co-ownership of some of the largest logging concessions in Sarawak. His position as Minister of Tourism and the Environment for Sarawak didn't bother him in the least. He is also famous for his reply when asked if he was concerned about the lack of rainfall some blame on deforestation. He remarked that the rain was cutting into his golf games.

Licenses in Sarawak are usually granted to Malays who then grant timber licenses to ethnic Chinese who also own the trucking and barge companies required for removal of the timber. In 1962 in Sabah, a Japanese cartel established the Nanyozai trade agreement which has controlled the state-owned timber industry for the last decade.

Ninety percent of Japan's annual 18.2 million cubic yards of tropical wood comes from Malaysia, most of it from Sarawak. In 1990, Sarawak earned about $3 billion from timber sales. The wood is used for paper, furniture and construction. One curious attribute of Malaysian hardwoods is the ability to be processed into sheets, imprinted with a grain and printed to look like oak, maple or walnut. America bought about $7 million worth of Malaysian tropical timber. The Japanese moved to Malaysian timber in the '70s after the Indonesia government restricted and then banned raw log exports.

Sarawak is one of the most heavily logged regions in the world.

The Japanese had to switch to Indonesian timber after decimating the forests of the Philippines. In 1967 the military government of Suharto opened up Kalimantan to outside investment. The structure used foreign companies (such as Tacoma's Weyerhauser) or local Chinese capital with senior military people brought in as partners. As expected, companies like Mitsubishi, Marubeni and Nichimen, Japan's top importers of timber from Sarawak, insist that their trade is beneficial and has no effect on deforestation.

Finally, in March of 1992 the government of Sarawak set aside 12,000 hectares of forest in the Ulumelanar area on the border of the Limbang and Miri divisions, near, but not in, the Mulu area for the Penan to live in. The only condition set by the Chief Minister was that, "the Penans will be allowed to settle in the area on the understanding that they do not cut trees unnecessarily." Gunung Mulu has been the ancestral homeland of the Penan for 40,000 years. It is estimated that all primary growth timber will have been harvested in the next 20 years.

That night we arrive at the Alo Doda Inn near the park headquarters. After the prerequisite speech making, we settle in to having a good time. The hospitality and warmth of our hosts makes the long, hard journey here less painful. I even feel it was worth it as I survey the beautiful mountainous scenery from the comfortable chairs on the veranda of this rustic lodge.

Our hosts have brought a portable radio, gifts and enough beer to supply a small army. As the evening begins, a small stack of empty Heineken cans starts to grow on the Japanese team's table. It could have started because they were homesick for Mt. Fuji or just inspired by the mountainous scenery, but soon there is a majestic green and white mountain of beer cans towering above the revellers. Not satisfied with their rate of construction, the Japanese begin calling out for other members of our group to consume faster to help them complete their mountain sculpture. Still not content with the rate of consumption, a Japanese singsong is composed with the final verse requiring the victim to chug-a-lug his beer and add it to the pile.

Hour by hour the aluminum mountain grows and spreads from table to table. I can only wonder how our hosts knew to stock that much beer. That night we are treated to local dancers, a giant bonfire and a down-home barbecue that lasts early into the next morning.

The next morning I watch the mists curl and wrap around the granite peaks through somewhat blurry eyes. Beyond the caves of Mulu there is much more—The Pinnacles, a forest of six story limestone pinnacles about two thirds of the way up Gunung Api. There is also Gunung Mulu which is more of a hike than a climb. There are shelters along the way.

Mulu National Park is one place I could spend a year just exploring the many hills, caves and rivers. I would highly recommend it.

For us it is time to leave. Up before dawn and into the boats. As we squeeze into the huge canoes, we know we are leaving the jungle at its most innocent and hopefully at its most secure. The trip down river is anticlimactic. Although we travel by the dreaded boat today, mercifully, no pushing is required. Along the way we sight the fabled hornbill gracefully flying high overhead—a fitting good luck omen.

We catch a diesel-powered river boat. As the river slowly widens and the shores become further apart the signs of civilization return.

We stop briefly at Marudi to drop off passengers. While we are waiting, an elderly Iban walks straight up to us and stops within comfortable camera range. From the neck up he is dressed like an Iban chieftain complete with clouded leopard hat and leopard tooth fang earrings. From the neck down he is dressed like a tourist from Florida with bright red polyester shirt, cheap flip flops and bermuda shorts. We stare with amusement. He gruffly points to our cameras and then to his face as if to say, "Hey, can't you recognize a real Iban chief when you see one, stupid." We click off a few pictures to avoid being rude. Then he rubs his thumb and finger in the international symbol for "now pay me." We are definitely nearing civilization. As we twist and turn down the final miles to Miri to rejoin our vehicles, the forest becomes thinner and thinner and the devastation caused by logging reappears. Huge five story stacks of hardwood logs are piled along the shoreline as far as the eye can see. In one section, I measure an unbroken row of giant hardwood logs for four miles on both sides of the river before I give up counting. The jungle is bleeding.

Gunung Mulu National Park

Penan nomads, Gunung Mulu National Park

Gunung Mulu can be the adventure of a lifetime, for I can think of nowhere else to find such vast primeval beauty, accessible and mysterious, waiting to be truly explored. To see the park you will need a guide. I recommend letting a Miri-based outfitter take care of everything. Plan at least a week to really see it all. Here is a chart of just some of the things that await you.

Exploring Gunung Mulu National Park

Although the park was gazetted in 1974, there is much still to be discovered. Only a third of the estimated cave system has been explored. The sheer size (52,866 ha) and remoteness of the park invites discovery. Hard-core cavers and climbers can organize trips at HQ or through tour companies. Here are the highlights:

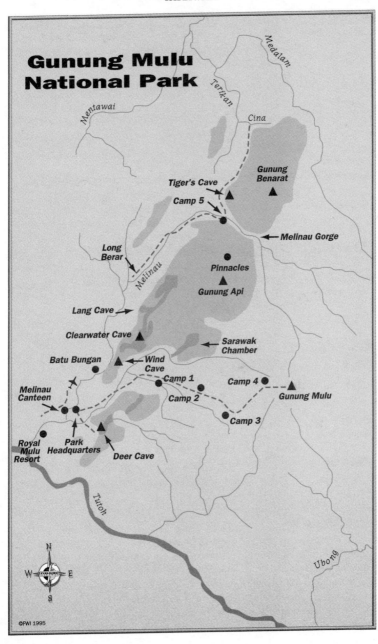

Gunung Mulu National Park

Mentawai

Medalam

Terikan

Cina

Gunung Benarat

Tiger's Cave

Camp 5

Melinau Gorge

Long Berar

Melinau

Pinnacles

Gunung Api

Lang Cave

Clearwater Cave

Sarawak Chamber

Batu Bungan

Wind Cave

Camp 1

Camp 4

Gunung Mulu

Melinau Canteen

Camp 2

Camp 3

Royal Mulu Resort

Park Headquarters

Deer Cave

Tutoh

Ubong

N
W   E
S

©FWI 1995

Exploring Gunung Mulu National Park

Clearwater Cave	*40-mile long underground river. At 62 km (38 miles), the longest underground passageway in SE Asia. It takes a half day and M$80 to charter a 8 passenger boat to reach the cave. You will pass by Clearwater cave on the way here.*
Deer Cave	*World's largest entrance, highest passage (22m). 1.2 km long and full of hoof prints from deer found near the entrance. Look for nightly exit of over one million bats. Visit Garden of Eden. Plan on 2 hours to make it here from the Park HQ. Bring a flashlight to find your way back after you watch the bats.*
Lang's Cave	*Lit cave, impressive stalagmites and stalactites.*
Cave of the Winds	*Visit King's room, constant breeze and interesting formations. Linked to Clearwater.*
Sarawak Chamber	*World's largest cave chamber (600m long, 450m wide, 100m high). Open with advance notice, four-hour walk from river. Big! Can hold 16 football fields. Bring powerful light sources.*
Melinau Gorge	*2-3 hr arduous climb to see the dramatic 1580m limestone cliffs visible intermittently through the thick canopy. Crystal clear, ice cold river and swimming hole (brrrr) await the hardy.*
The Pinnacles	*45m razor sharp needles at 1200m, 2-hour boat ride, then 5 km trek to Camp 5. Short morning ascent is 3 km (4-6 hours up, 4-5 down) of hell. Tough but worth it. Razor-sharp limestone and the hot sun will make you think you are climbing a red hot meat slicer.*
Gunung Api	*A 3-day round trip trek/climb to the 1710m summit. The experienced climb. First climbed in 1978. Hot, dangerous and a true accomplishment if you can climb it. (Same goes for the unclimbed Gunung Benarat across the river.) The highest limestone mountain between Thailand and New Guinea. The climb is over razor sharp limestone. Tangled roots above hide very deep sinkholes on top.*
Gunung Mulu	*4-day climb over ridge trail to 2326m summit. Shelters eliminate need for tents. Fixed ropes near summit. Medium tough.*
River Trips	*You can content yourself with the rip upriver or to the cave mouths.*
Jungle Treks	*There is plenty to keep you occupied if you just hike between camps or to the caves.*

We strongly recommend spending time setting up your trip with a Miri-based guide company to get the most from your stay.

Getting in

The most efficient way is to simply book a tour out of Miri. Expect to pay M$500 per person for a 6 day/5 night tour. Shorter stay 4 day 3 night trips are M$300 per person. The adventurous will take the long boat ride from Kuala Baram (make sure you have booked your accommodation and guides in the park before you set off) about a half hour $M16 taxi trip from Miri. The express boat to Marudi is a 3 hour, $M12 trip. Try to get the first boat at 7 a.m. to make it to the Park by nightfall. If you catch the last boat at

2 p.m. you can spend the night in Marudi. Marudi is a well known frontier town and the site of Fort Hose built in 1901. You can also take one of the 15 minute, $M29 flights to Marudi from Miri. From Marudi take the noon express boat to Long Panai/Kuala Apoh. There is one boat a day and the cost is $M10 and the trip takes 2.5 hours depending on the water level. From Long Panai take a 1 hour, $M10 canoe trip to the longhouse at Long Terawan. Here you can connect with the Park boat. If it has been a long day you can spend the evening here since the Park headquarters is still 3.5 hours away. The boat trip to the Park from Long Terawan is $M50 per person if it is full and possibly M$160 if you have to charter the entire boat. This part of the trip is very scenic but it will be getting dark by the time you reach the park. Once in the park you will need a guide. They will charge $M20 per day plus their accommodation at an additional $M10 per night. Hopefully you can see why booking an all inclusive tour is really the most economical and practical way to explore the park. Don't be afraid to set up your own itinerary. The less adventurous will simply fly directly to the airstrip and stay at the Royal Mulu.

Where to Stay in Mulu

Royal Mulu Resort   M$165–250   ★ ★ ★ ★
Sungair Melanau Baram, CDT 62, ☎ *(085) 421122, FAX 421088*
You knew it had to happen; the world's most remote place now has an airport and a luxury resort hotel complete with mini longhouse accommodations. Yes you can now rough it in Mulu while you watch color TV, rummage through the mini bar and wonder if the natives are restless tonight. There are 176 rooms in this 1993 resort.

Dormitory   M$63
There is a dormitory in the park HQ that sleeps 48 people in 8 rooms. Expect to pay $M63. (There are two private "luxury" suites with air conditioning if you don't feel communal).

Chalets   M$5
At Long Pala about 15 minutes by boat from the HQ there are two chalets that sleep 10 people each. For $M5.

Tour company resthouses   M$10
If there is room at one of the tour company resthouses on the other bank of the Melinau you can stay for $M10 a night. There are also resthouses for hikers and campers along the trails that lead in and through the park.

National Park HQ Hostels   M$5
Facilities for cooking, water and blankets are provided. There is a small store for tea, salt etc. but you should come well prepared.

Kelabit Highlands★★

12kms from Kalimantan Border

This is truly the remote heart of Borneo (along with its Indonesian border twin, the Apo Kayan in Kalimantan). Like most truly remote places it seems to attract more trekkers than the more accessible regions in Sarawak. Shrouded in mist and hidden even from modern satellite mapping, the Kelabit Highlands (sometimes called the Bareo Highlands) is the Holy Grail of hard-core trekkers. The gentle Kelabit inhabit a 1000m-high plateau of fertile fields and mountainous scenery. The fertile rice growing area is surrounded by a circle of mountains that has left this area remote and relatively unaffected by outsiders. I say relatively because the highlands have been heavily proselytized by Christian missionaries and was the center of very successful Allied guerilla activities against the Japanese during WWII. Led by Tom Harrisson, it is a modern day Lawrence of Arabia story that vaguely resembles the John Milius' movie *Farewell to the King*. It is worth reading Harrisson's own account of his wartime adventures organizing the Kelabit against the Japanese in his book *World Within*. Harrisson went on to be the director of the Sarawak museum and the discoverer of Niah man. The area today provides truly rugged mountaineering, hiking and trekking.The dramatic twin-peaked **Bukit Batu Lawi** (6703ft./2043m) and **Gunung Marudi** (7950ft./2423m) are a major attraction. Lawi seems to draw the most climbers and its nearby twin is Sarawak's highest peak. Both summits require climbing equipment and skill although you can climb the lower peak without too much gear. To explore the Kelabit Highlands, you must be self sufficient since there are no facilities other than one rest house and a few shops in Bario.

The silent sentinels of Bario

There is a continual discovery going on of stone monuments in the Kelabit highlands. Although they were known about for years more stone works are coming to light every year. There are currently 20 stone artifacts that have been recorded by the Kelabits but many more have yet to be cataloged or discovered. The stone monuments are in the form of either megaliths, monoliths, menhir and dolmens depending on their purpose. There are stone engravings (Batu Narit) large stone jars (Batu Nawe) sharpening stones for headswords (Batu Tukad Rini named for a Kelabit aristocrat) mausoleums (Batu Ritong) funerary stones (Batu Sinuped) and a massive 6 meter high rock near Pa Rumudu where the bones of Kelabit aristocrats were placed on top and the houses of commoners were placed in a hole below (Benato Batu Kitong) that opens to an underground river.

There have been some attempts by the mainly Christian Kelabits to create new carvings and monuments but they pale against the Bronze Age achievements of their ancestors.

Bario

Once you land in Bario you will feel like you arrived in an adventurer's Shangri-La. Bario is a one street town. You will feel that only the bold dare visit here and the guestbooks are full of tall tales, suggestions, curt directions and tips. The locals make their money by sending palefaced guests into jungles, up mountains and down

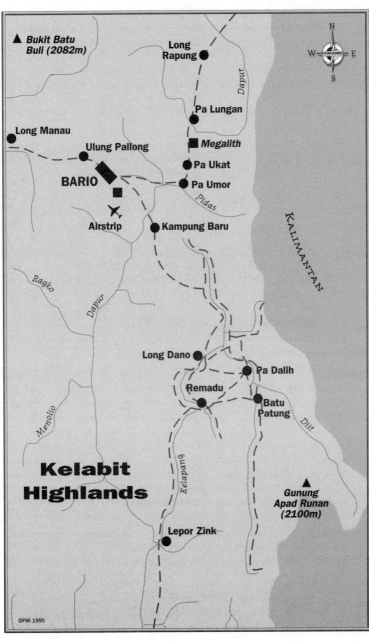

river so don't be afraid to change your plans if something exciting is offered to you. The Kelabit are also expert in lightening your load by charging rather steep prices for porters, guides and supplies so bargain hard but keep your sense of humor. The *penghulu* is the man you want to talk to when you arrive, and unlike many of the more touristed spots in Borneo you will find yourself being invited into just about every longhouse you come across, even if you don't want to spend the night! On the main street is a guest house called Tarawes that offers four rooms that sleep three people each. They serve meals and there are a couple of restaurants near the airline office.

Hospitality to strangers is part of Dayak life.

Trekking   ★★

Hiking here is not the alpine variety unless you come to climb Gunung Murud. There are well marked paths that the locals use to get between villages. The trails can be steep and muddy but for the most part they are quite easy to follow. They do however seem to go on forever towards the end of the day. The distances between villages are deceptively long and you better like sleeping on mats and eating rice, pig or jungle chicken. Staying and partying in the longhouses is a treat but can get old if you just want to crash after a 8 hour day of trekking. Plan on spending a couple of days in a village. The Kelabit are very industrious rice farmers, Christians and warm hearted people. There are some Penan villages that can show you a way of life that will soon be gone. Most Kelabit speak Malay but the Penan don't use it much.

It helps to have a guide and possibly a porter if you are carrying a lot of gear on the longer treks. Wildlife is scarce to nonexistent here other than an abundance of leeches (who always seem glad to accompany trekkers). The best you will see might be a glimpse of a hornbill, butterflies, a few insects and maybe a wild pig.

Getting In

There is daily air service to the middle, north and south of the Kelabit Highlands via Bario, Ba Kelalan and Long Lellang. Service is via MAS Twin Otter, a rugged 21 passenger Canadian made bush plane. The flights are scheduled to make it in every day but low clouds and inclement weather can prevent this. Since the flights are already booked full or filled with cargo expect a bit of wait if you want to get out. Don't cut your return or incoming flight plans too tight here. Also there are no banks so bring plenty of ringgit. You can fly into the small landing strip from Miri or Marudi. You are best advised to set up your trip with one of the major outfitters in Miri. The best conditions for entry and travel are between March and October.

Getting Around

The following chart should not be used as a definitive trekking guide. Discuss the options with a Kuching or Miri-based outfitter and try not to bite off too much at one time. Keep in mind that if you get sick or hurt yourself it is a long way out of the highlands to a hospital. The times listed here are general and do not take into account any lollygagging or socializing along the trail. Guides will run about M$40 a day (don't forget they have to walk back home if you take a one way trip). Bring plenty of gifts, I recommend bringing a Polaroid, plenty of film and the traditionals: tea, shotgun shells, cigarettes or rolling tobacco, sugar, and other consumables.

Many connections such as hitching rides on local transport, hiring motorbikes and even the existence of supplies are highly variable so have a plan B.

Finally if you are going into or in and out of Indonesia via land routes make sure you fully discuss this with both Sarawak and Indonesian immigration so that you are aware of the vagaries of border crossings for travelers in this area.

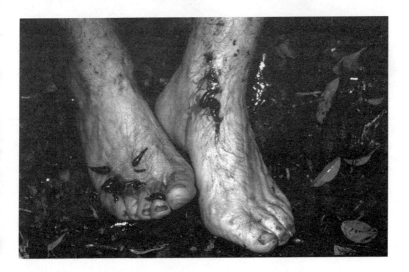

Ah, the joys of jungle trekking and feeding the local wildlife.

Trekking in the Kelabit Highlands

From	To	Time	Notes

AROUND BARIO

There are numerous opportunities for overnight treks into the surrounding areas. Items of interest would be understanding the local life-style, finding megaliths or tracking wildlife.

From	To	Time	Notes
Bario	Pa Tik	2 days	*A thriving Penan village*
Bario	Gunung Lawi	7 - 10 days	*The lower peak Gunung Lawi (2039m) is a stiff but non technical climb. The higher peak is a tough climb and should be planned out before attempting it. You will need to arrange a guide and equipment before you get to Bario. You will also need porters, and be prepared to hike to the twin peaked mountain first. The Kelabits used to believe that Lawi had evil spirits but porters are easily persuaded by cash.*
Bario	Gunung Murud	10 - 20 days	*The ascent of the more challenging peak of this twin mountain (2438m) would require some discussion with Kuching and Miri based outfitters before attempting on your own.*
Bario	Ulung Pallang	20 minutes	*Ulung Pallang is the site (the original longhouse has been replaced) where Tom Harrisson ran the Kelabit resistance during the war.*

NORTH: BARIO - BA KELALAN

This route lets you travel outward through the Apo Kayan, fly back to civilization via the airstrip at Ba Kelalan or try to hitch a ride to Lawas.

From	To	Time	Notes
Bario	Pa Umor	1.5 hours	*Take the path towards Indonesia (marked on trail at Pa Umor)*
Pa Umor	Kalimantan-Border	6 hours	*The trail goes across rice paddies and may be hard to follow. At the border the trail becomes a wide road.*
Kalimantan-Border	Lembudud		*The road heads to the east to the village of Lembudud where there is a longhouse for accommodations. Check in with the border police.*
Lembudud	Long Bawang	3 hours	*Follow the road or hire a motorbike to Long Bawang. Check in with the local police.*

From	To	Time	Notes
Long Bawang	Ba Kelalan	5 hours	If you want to head back into Sarawak, follow the trail through Long Api and Medang. When you cross the border you will need to reenter Sarawak and check in at the port. There is an airstrip in Ba Kelalan with morning flights to Lawas.

BARIO - LAWAS

This is a fairly easy and some say tedious trip along well traveled trails in the cool highlands.

From	To	Time	Notes
BARIO	Pa Lungun	4 hours	On the main northbound path watch for rock carving along the way. Stay at longhouse in Pa Lungun. You can hire guides and porters to make the two day walk to Gunung Murud from here. Plan about 10 days for an ascent try.
Pa Lungun	Pa Rupai	9 hours	Passes into Kalimantan. Stay in longhouse at village.
Pa Rupai	Long Medang	2 hours	Motor bikes can be hired here to take you to Long Nawang in Kalimantan. There is an airport in Long Nawang but flights out may be full.
Long Medang	Ba Kelalan	8 hours	There are daily morning flights to Lawas from the small airstrip.
Ba Kelalan	Buduk Aru	2 hours	There is a logging road that ends in Buduk Aru where you can (hopefully) find trucks going into Lawas.
Buduk Aru	Lawas	4 hours	In good weather it should take 4 - 5 hours to reach Lawas via 4 wheel drive vehicle.

Note: there is no guarantee of transport from Buduk Aru

SOUTH: BARIO - PA TIK

Those seeking more traditional longhouses and life-styles might want to try the more ambitious southerly treks. The total time requires a solid week or 9 days of trekking to complete. It is wisest to link up with any locals heading your way.

From	To	Time	Notes
Bario	Long Dano	8 hours	There is an idyllic 30 door longhouse at Long Dano where you may want to spend a day feeling the rhythms of life in this disappearing world.
Long Dano	Pa Dalih	2 hours	After 2 hours you will pass through Pa Dalih. There are 3 waterfalls near the border of Indonesia that are worth visiting (about a 7 hour hike)
Pa Dalih	Remadu	3 hours	If you skip Pa Dalih you can stay at the longhouse in Remadu.

From	To	Time	Notes
Remadu	Long Okan	8 hours	*This is the longest and most arduous part (about 32kms) of the journey through heavy jungle with a night in a simple shelter. If you want to cut it into two medium days, there is a jungle hut (Lepor Zinc) about 14 kms out of Remadu on sungai Dappur. From there it is only about 16 kms to Long Beruang.*
Long Okan	Long Beru-ang	4 hours	*Long Beruang is a Penan settlement where you have the opportunity to observe these unique people. Stay here before pushing on to Lio Matoh.*
Long Beru-ang	Long Banga	6 hours	*There is a longhouse here or stay at the kongsi (timber camp) 2 hours further in Lio Matoh.*
Long Banga	Lio Matoh	2 hours	*From Lio Matoh you can take a longboat down the Baram river to Marudi where you can catch a plane or the express boat to Miri.*

Getting Out

The Kelabit Highlands are ideal for one way treks. You can fly in from the north into Ba Kelalan and hike south to Bario. Or you can fly into Bario and hike out into Long Nawan and fly (or continue trekking through the Apo Kayan) into Kalimantan. The more adventurous can take a longboat into Lio Matoh and then hike north to Bario and beyond. The daily flight from Ba Kelalan is M$46; you can fly daily from Bario to Miri (M$70) or get off when it lands in Marudi (M$55). Twice weekly flights from Long Semado to Lawas are M$40.

INSIDER TIP

Before you get all excited about what the backpacker guides tell you about hiking Borneo, be forewarned. Jungle trekking can be tedious, frustrating and debilitating due to the dank forests, oppressive heat, long distances, constant wetness, slippery slopes, river crossings, hungry leeches and low caloric food. Expect to be bored, lose weight, get lonely and dream of alpine snowfields and ice cold beer. But c'est l'adventure.

Lambir Hills Park

12 kms (30 minutes) south of Miri

Popular with the locals, Lambir Hills (the highest is 465 meters) is a collection of sandstone hills, waterfalls, trails and picnic areas. There are chalets for overnighters. Gibbons and hornbills can be spotted at the park. Lambir's claim to fame is that its rich forests have among the most plant species of any place on earth. There are two waterfalls (Pantu and Tengkorong) that are about an hour hike.

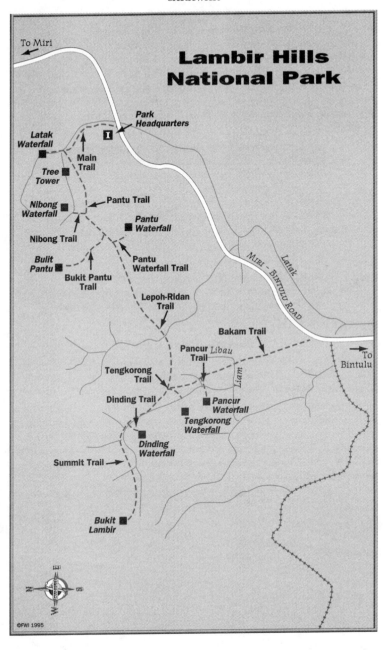

Lambir Hills National Park

Limbang

50 kms(2 hours) from Lawas by express boat

 If you like to do things the hard way you might want to visit Brunei or Gunung Mulu Park through the back door. It is a thin strip of land that must drive the Sultan of Brunei crazy because it has cut his country in half ever since his forebears gave a bunch of it to Brooke in 1890. In any case, this route called the Headhunters Trail provides a very different and unusual way into the park and you won't see anything twice. You can get here from Lawas, then take a boat or you can fly into Limbang from Kuching or you can come directly from Brunei.

Headhunter's Highway

In the late 19th century Kayan raiding parties, some containing up to 3000 warriors would travel down the Baram river in their 18 meter long canoes. At the Melinau gorge they would drag their canoes 3kms from the Melinau river to the Terikan river over a highway of logs. The raiding parties would then steal down along the Terikan to the Medalam and into Limbang where they would collect the heads of the Murut tribesmen and Chinese laborers.

You can follow this route today if you hike near Camp 5 near the Melinau gorge or just read about it in the description of our expedition to Mulu. Limbang was an ancient trading center and recent archeological digs have unearthed remnants of a Hindu influenced civilization.

Getting Around

Brooke sliced out the territorial sliver of Limbang between the Sultanate of Brunei in 1890. Limbang has little industry or population growth. The area was once important as the gateway to the riverine highway from the interior.

Limbang is rarely visited by tourists since the only attraction is the fort built by Charles Brooke in 1897. The fort is now an Islamic school. Limbang is also a good stopping off point if you are taking one of the two early morning express boats that make the 30 minute trip to Brunei or the 2 hour trip the opposite direction to Lawas. There is an airport 2 kms south of town with daily flights to Miri and Lawas. You can also catch a bus into Seria that will connect you to Brunei from Kuala Belait.

The Back Door to Mulu

From	to	time	Notes
Limbang	Kuala Medamit	.75 hour	*Take the minibus from Limbang to Kuala Medamit.*
Kuala Medamit	Mentakung	1 hour	*Take a longboat up the Limbang, along the Medalam to the 23 door Iban Longhouse at Mentakung.*
Mentakung	Kuala Terikan	4 hours	*Take a longboat to Kuala Terikan, the beginning of the trail to Gunung Mulu. It is a very scenic ride. The water can be very low and may require pushing the boat through numerous shallows. Park permits are checked at Mentawai.*
Kuala Terikan	Camp 5	3 hours	*The 11 km trail goes to Camp 5. Follow the red & white markings. From Camp 5 you can hike to the Pinnacles about 7 hours return. You may meet some people at Camp 5; ask if you can go back to Park HQ in their longboat.*
Camp 5	Kuala Berar	2.5 hours	*An easy walk to the Melinau river. There may or may not be a boat at Kuala Berar. Chances are if you wait a day, one will show up laden with tourists from the Park HQ.*
Kuala Berar	Park HQ	1 - 2 hour	*Take the longboat to Park HQ about 10kms via the Melianau river.*
Park HQ	Miri	full day	*From here you can fly out via the airport 2kms east of the Park HQ or arrange to go back down to Miri via longboat.*

Head Hunters

A Long Night In
A Longhouse

I am finally in Sarawak about to spend a night with the fabled headhunters of Borneo. I know enough about the pretense of visiting headhunters in Borneo to understand that the experience is about as authentic as a Hawaiian Luau on Waikiki Beach. My last authentic experience was in East Africa when I was invited to visit "authentic" Samburu tribespeople only to be crowded in a minuscule dark hut and have snotty babies and cheap trinkets shoved at me while the rest of the tribe blocked the door.

I am the American part of a multinational expedition through Sarawak and part of our cultural responsibility is to spend a night in this remote longhouse. We had heard horror stories of these tourist shows and how the drinking and dancing was more for the benefit of the inhabitants than the guests. Sort of an orgiastic prelude to a garage sale. The members of our expedition from Sarawak told me I could always just roll over and go to sleep if the gongs got too tedious. They lied.

There are over 1500 longhouses to choose from in Sarawak and all of their habitants will offer Dayak hospitality if their graciousness is primed with gifts or moldy ringgits (cash). We had chosen a remote longhouse where there were many elders and a mixture of Muslim, Christian and animist dwellers still carried on in relative shelter from karaoke bars, ghetto blasters and old ABBA tapes. It was also on the Skrang River that in 1849 Sir Charles Brooke massacred over 800 Ibans. Now it appears it is payback time. Before I regale you with our evening you must understand just what and who an Iban is.

The Skrang River is now the traditional home of the Iban people. This area was first settled by Ibans between the 16th and 18th centuries. Their proximity to the ocean earned them the name "Sea Dayaks" as opposed to the Land Dayaks, typically more sedate Bidayuh, Kayan or Kenyah, who lived further upriver. The Iban originally came from the Kapuas River basin in Kalimantan near the center of Borneo. They have a very distinct culture and look and probably are the most famous of the Dayaks.

The Ibans are truly fascinating people. Just as the Kenyahs are known for their rigid social structure, the Ibans are known for their classless, democratic society. Their appreciation and creation of artistic motifs and culture is second only to the Kenyah and Kayan. The Iban are probably most famous for their escalation of headhunting from a cultural necessity to a recreation. This may be partly due to Brooke's respect towards the indigenous people of Sarawak and his occasional use of their headhunting talents for political and military means. It would have to be said that the last real documentation of widespread headhunting was during the Japanese occupation of World War II, which was rekindled with the absolute support and encouragement of the British forces.

Today the Ibans, for the most part, have been converted to Christianity. Missionaries seem to have taken special pains to convert the "savages of Borneo" because of this propensity for lopping heads. It is important to understand that the Iban have a very strong set of beliefs and customs and that Christianity does not necessarily present a better option. In any case, the Iban are proud of their heritage, and unlike the Dutch who took special pains to confiscate heads, ban tattooing and stamp-out longhouses, the Iban enjoyed a gentle dominion under the White Rajahs and have preserved many of their customs and artwork to this day. In Sarawak, the further upriver (or *ulu*) you go, the less affected they are by western influences.

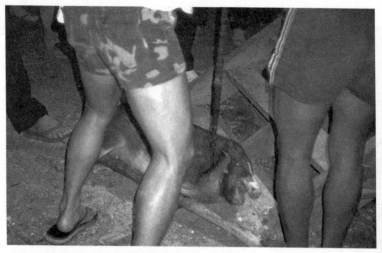

You may be asked to kill your dinner.

The most dramatic and visible symbol of Iban culture is the longhouse. The longhouse is the precursor of the townhome with fifteen to 20 houses joined together and built on stilts. The original longhouses were much higher off the ground with notched logs that were pulled up at night for security. The modern longhouses are rebuilt many times, each time getting slightly lower to the ground. Only the brave dare look under a longhouse.

There is one long common area in front of the homes and in front of each is proudly displayed a collection of blackened human skulls. Most of the skulls date back from World War II when the Japanese gave freely of their craniums. Nowadays the skulls serve the same purpose as jockeys on suburban lawns; a relic of days gone by. Strangely enough the role of the heads is to bring prosperity to the longhouse. In Sarawak the more heads, the more tourists, so maybe there is something to it.

Longhouses, besides being communal dwellings, also served as makeshift hotels back in the days when people travelled up and down the river. You can still find a dry and friendly place to stay if you travel along the rivers of Borneo upriver, but you must be prepared to endure the hospitality of your guests. I say "endure" because guests means party, and party in Borneo means all night and until your departure the next day. If you are lucky enough to visit a longhouse during a *gawai* festival in the beginning of June, be prepared to party for several days.

We arrived at the longhouse tired and dirty—although we were four hours late, our hosts told us the party was just beginning. The party commenced with the traditional killing of the pig. As we entered at one end of the longhouse we noticed a large pig had been tied up and we were invited to dispatch the evening's main course of dinner using a proffered spear.

Needless to say, the pig was about as happy with this custom as we were, but old traditions die hard. In this case, so did the pig. As he was shoved over to the side to contemplate his skewered state, we followed a group of dancing headmen preceded by musicians playing the traditional gong music. Not just a main street parade, this stuff was intense. The glazed look and rippling sinews of the elders told us tonight would be serious business. While the pig's eyes glazed over and the blood soaked into the warm ground, we entered the longhouse and began to make our rounds. Making the rounds in a longhouse is easier than you think. As we passed each front door of the twenty-odd homes that make up the longhouse, we were offered a drink of *tuak*; homemade moonshine that would probably do wonders as nail polish remover.

Drinking *tuak* isn't the hard part, it's trying not to drink the stuff by the time you get to the twentieth house. In this case, our hosts were so excited to be the recipients of such a grand delegation, they decided to take us around the longhouses again and again until the white sediment began to show at the bottom of the recycled whisky bottles.

They must have figured we liked the home brew because after countless musical parades around the longhouse, they broke into free form bartending as they chased us around, making us drink each bottle dry. So far so good. I was 20 minutes into experiencing a longhouse for the first time and I was drunk as a skunk.

After our bang-up reception we started to go deaf from the gong music and our heads were spinning from the *tuak*. Our hosts invited us to partake in another Iban tradition, bathing. The accumulation of dirt and sweat from our journey quickly disappeared in the Skrang River that flows nearby. We went skinny dipping by the light of the full moon, hoping that any waterborne predators would be repulsed by the amount and quality of dirt with which we were polluting the river. It was a magical feeling to be waist deep in the cool water, the moonlight making silvery wobbles off the black water and in the distance, the warm glow of candles and Coleman lanterns shining through the chinks in the wooden longhouse. The gong music faded in and out and the high-pitched chatter of native women painted an evocative picture. Then I got a shiver, not from the fish that kept bumping against my private parts, but from the fragment I remembered reading about Iban headhunting—how the night of the full moon was ideal for taking heads when the men bathed, their weapons left in the longhouse.

The women were watching us and giggling. We didn't feel embarrassed since we were eager to adopt the traditions of the noble savage. Later I was told that men and women never bathe nude but always wear some type of sarong or covering.

Back inside, cool and refreshed, the night began in earnest. The evening feast consisted of round after round of *tuak*, rice and a wide variety of well-cooked, chewy jungle animals. Our newly deceased pet pig had reappeared as chunks of greasy barbecued meat. To aid in our digestion there were speeches, not just one but many. As a matter of fact, one speech from every senior member of the longhouse. The speech was in the Iban dialect so it sounded like somebody listing electrical parts with great importance. Since the members of our expedition group were from Sweden, Turkey, Germany, France, Japan, the United States and Australia, we responded in kind with long-winded speeches in our own languages. Naturally, our guests did not understand one word but applauded wildly. We then gave gifts. I took Polaroids of the headman and presented them with a great flourish. I passed out baseball cards to the children and little trinkets to the women. Although I felt like I was negotiating a land deal, the genuine look of thanks was heartwarming. Later, one elder pulled me over and talked for 20 minutes about the picture I had just taken of him. His children and grandchildren sat silently, big-eyed, watching our conversation. Once again, it was enough to understand that he truly enjoyed our company. It was easy to forget that these people understood the meaning of ceremony, hospitality and friendship. My initial horror of having to spend an evening with the locals had become an educational and rewarding experience.

By midnight the food was cleared and we were ready for more dancing and drinking. The residents of the longhouse donned the ceremonial headdress of hornbill feathers, grasping a fierce, razor sharp knife, essentially a homemade machete with a deer antler handle and a decorative sheath. They danced in turn to entertain their guests. After displaying their prowess, they proceeded to drag up protesting members of the audience and challenge them to display their talents.

You better arrive hungry for a longhouse whoop up.

Heads once brought power and good luck to the Iban; now thay are curios from WW II and before.

There are not a lot of impressive dance steps that can be choreographed to a soundtrack that is a cross between banging hubcaps and a car crash. But try we did. Luckily the *tuak* removed any inhibitions we might have had and we played to our audience. The "funky chicken," the "mashed potato," whatever we chose they couldn't get enough of it. They laughed and laughed and laughed. They were genuinely amused by the clumsy self-conscious foreigners. It was a sweet and endearing experience.

The locals loved every minute of it and disregarded our inebriation or fatigue. As we got more exhausted they seemed to pick up speed. Screaming with laughter they would wake up and drag up victim after victim from the crowd. Every time the fuzzy headed victim staggered around they laughed harder. In between goofy foreign dances the Iban did imitations of us which inspired us to do imitations of them. By 4 a.m. we noticed a thinning in the foreign contingent. Realizing that us stalwart few were nearing exhaustion, our guests searched out the poor unfortunates who had sneaked off to the far reaches of the longhouse to sleep. Without missing a beat, they cracked open their mouths, poured in an invigorating slug of coconut wine, then led them on to the dance floor for more entertainment.

Close to dawn, I staggered to a dark corner of the longhouse to catch a few winks of sleep. Collapsing on the wood floor I felt hands under my head, my eyes flicked open in the blue dusk and I saw a woman putting a pillow under my head. Around her were the silhouettes of her family squatting, chatting softly. I drifted back to sleep, an hour later the strident roosters under the longhouse woke me. I now had a blanket on me. The family was still there chatting softly, squatting around me. They saw that I was awake and invited me to share their simple breakfast with them. As I got ready to leave I gave them whatever useful items were in my bag and wished them luck. The Iban did not take my head but my heart.

The Iban

The Ibans like most Dayaks of Borneo had no written language. It wasn't until almost a hundred years ago when Westerners promoted the concept of education that a written form of communication was developed.

The Iban pass down their history and culture through oral recitation of events. Like many indigenous tribes they use a singsong rhythm to help them remember the lengthy tales.

According to this oral history, the Ibans came from the Indonesian island of Java and from the north, in the area of what is now Cambodia. They settled in Sabah in the area of Merudu Bay.

Intense raids by the Sulu islanders from the Philippines forced them to the area now called Bintulu. The Sultan of Brunei forced them to move to Sambas in what is now Kalimantan.

The Ibans were industrious, gathered wealth and were working with the Majapahit government. When the government fell, the Iban fled to the upper Kapuas. Afraid that they would be under the control of another tribe, they decided to move to new ground. They had not learned how to build dugout canoes and their rafts broke apart in the fast water. In frustration they moved overland. Later migrations took them to the head of the Kapuas River. Further migrations took them up the Skrang river and the Padih River.

The Ibans are legendary hosts. An Iban will always house and feed a visitor without question.

They love to venture into the unknown. An unadventurous Iban male is referred to as a batu tungku, which is a resting stone in a fireplace. Men are actually expected to travel and test their ability to survive and overcome adversity. They used to cross over into Kalimantan to prey on the gentle inhabitants for sport until 1888 when a peace was arranged.

Ibans are very honest. They are known to always tell the truth. Theft is rare and any Iban caught lying or stealing will be reminded of it for the rest of his or her life.

Tuak

Tuak is a native drink made from glutinous rice, barley, tapioca, maize, wild palm or coconut. The potent drink is brewed just before festivals and celebrations. The yeast is dried and rice is soaked for ten hours in a running stream then cooked in bamboo cylinders over coals.

Tuak

The rice is drained and spread out over a mat, mixed with the yeast, and put into earthen jars. The large jars are made airtight and left to ferment for two weeks. The first brew is drained off into an assortment of bottles and corked. If the tuak is stored in a warm place, like above the fire, the brew will be higher in alcohol. The second batch is made by adding rain or river water to the original earthen jar and waiting another two weeks. The first brew is called ai suling, and the second, less potent brew, is called ai banchak.

The Iban are not heavy drinkers. Tuak is used during ceremonies to add a little gaiety to the celebrations.

Black Magic

Superstition has been, and still is, a major influence among Ibans. If the omen bird, (rufous piculet) flies from one longhouse to another, the inhabitants will abandon it until the evil omens are exorcised, usually by holding a gawai. Fighting cocks that carry ubat kebal, or protective amulets, are considered to be protected from razor cuts of opponents. Wild boar tusks and deer horns contain magic that can protect men from bullets and others can make a man invisible. There are charms called punti that, if buried under a jungle path, will cause lameness or pain when the intended victim walks over it. The quiet chant or puchau is used in emergencies or desperate situations. The puchau is used in emergency or to defeat severe illness, similar in use to the Roman Catholic Hail Mary.

Iban Customs

Hospitality is legendary with the Iban. An Iban will always house and feed a visitor without question.

They love to venture into the unknown. An unadventurous Iban male is referred to as a batu tungku, which is a resting stone in a fireplace. Men are actually expected to travel and test their ability to survive and overcome adversity. They used to cross over into Kalimantan to prey on the gentle inhabitants for sport until 1888 when a peace was arranged

Ibans are very honest. They are known to always tell the truth. Theft is rare and any Iban caught lying or stealing will be reminded of it for the rest of his or her life.

Just remember that you look as strange to them as they do to you.

Longhouses

Take a Motel Six, jack it up on telephone poles, cover it with bark and thatch and voila, a longhouse. No stay in Sarawak is complete unless you visit a longhouse. Longhouses are the indigenous housing of choice. Built on stilts for security and comfort, they are now becoming modernized and they look curiously like government housing instead of the massive fortresses they once were. Some used to run as much as half a kilometer long and sit seven meters off the ground. At night they would pull in the entry logs to keep out raiding parties. Today, most are between 10 and 20 doors long and are about 2–3 meters high. Color TVs, linoleum tin roofs and electric kettles are not unusual. There is still a common area with private apartments off the common veranda or *ruai*. Ancient longhouses made of *bilian* or ironwood are often rebuilt in new locations using old wood.

If you want to visit one of the 1500 or so longhouses in Sarawak, there are a few things you should know. First, it can be excessively tedious to have to drink homemade hooch and dance like a chicken until dawn, especially when accompanied by the dissonant banging of gongs. Second, choose your long-houses carefully so that you get the real thing, not a carbon copy. The best longhouses for short stays are actually at Iban settlements downriver where tour companies force the owners to keep their rustic ambience; for longer stays, you'll probably want to get to know the upriver longhouses of the

Kayan and Kenyah. They are the aristocrats of the Dayaks and do not have the boisterous nature of the Iban.

TIPS ON VISITING A LONGHOUSE

Make sure you have an invitation or are part of a tour. You can usually ask around and find a way to be invited if you are not part of a tour. Longhouses prefer to have tours visit since it is a big event for them. But single travelers will receive traditional hospitality if the headman is receptive.

The best time to visit is in June when the gawai or harvest festival is in full swing. Most longhouses will be partying up a storm whether they have visitors or not.

Bring gifts not only for the headman (tuai rumah), but also the other residents (there will be many). Cigarettes, alcohol, souvenirs of your country will do for the headman. Toys, photos or pens are good for the others.

Make a ceremony of giving the gifts as well as meeting the members of the longhouse. I bring a Polaroid and make a big deal of presenting each photo. You can also make a speech and present the photos in lieu of a gift. The Iban will also make speeches.

If you are with a large group and are asked to dispatch (kill) your dinner before entering (usually a pig) make a clean cut through the throat with the proffered spear. Chickens are beheaded.

Take your shoes off just as you enter. Observe most rules of conduct for Asian cultures. Ibans are animist or Christian.

You will be expected to take a sip from each of the proffered bottles. If you do not drink or have had too much, touch the rim of the glass with your fingers and then your lips with a thank you nod. Do not use your left hand.

You may be invited to take a wash in the river. Men and women always bathe wearing some type of light clothing such as a sarong or shorts.

If you see a white flag (a sign of mourning) or feel that your reception is rather chilly, offer a gift and beat a hasty retreat.

You may get hit up for souvenir sales such as weavings or parangs. People may also ask for payment for photographs when in costume.

The Ibans are hams and love to mimic guests. Don't take it personally; you can join in and mimic them. Be warned, if you are really popular they may make you repeat your performance until you keel over from exhaustion.

If you drink too much or act like a fool, don't worry—the Iban are party animals and have probably behaved much worse than you.

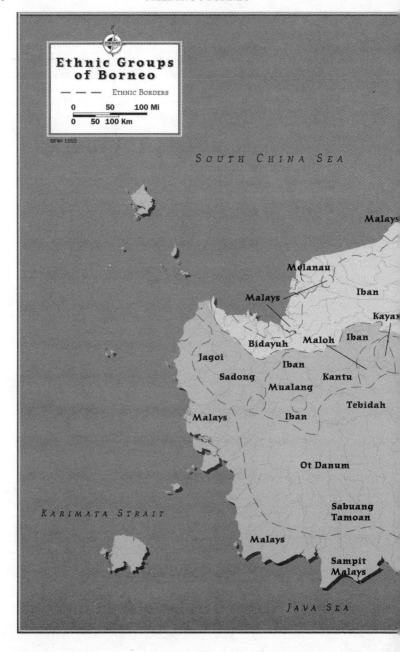

Kapit★

Four hours from Sibu

Kapit is the last major outpost before heading *ulu* or upriver, on the Rejang. The first of the two places to visit is the museum, which features an Iban longhouse and wood carvings. Fort Sylvia was used by Brooke to keep the Iban away from the Kayan and Kenyah upriver and vice versa. Kapit is a very colorful city because of its importance as a trading center and wilderness outpost. Here you will definitely get the feeling that you are on the back end of the world. Worth a visit. There are low cost accommodations in Kapit while you plan your trip upriver. The town feels like an Alaska frontier town. Plenty of hookers, pool halls, karaoke bars and cheap hotels. Sometimes you will run across Penan nomads who stop in to trade.

Fort Sylvia   ★

A wooden fort built in 1880 and then renamed after Vyner Brooke's wife in 1925, the fort was supposed to be an official presence to prevent the loco Ibans from picking on the upriver tribes. The gregarious and opportunistic Iban know that going upriver past this fort was forbidden.

Frail canoes are the best and only way to see the longhouses along the river.

Getting Around

The Shell and Petronas jetties seem to be the clearing house for finding out which longboat is heading to which longhouse or logging camp. If you want to do it the easy way there are plenty of guides in and around Kapit who will set up trips for about M$150-200 a day. If it isn't busy, negotiate amongst two or three to see what the best price is. **Tan Tech Chuan**, *11 Jalan Tan Sit Leong*, comes highly recommended ☎ *(084) 796352, FAX 796655.* The daily express boat to Belaga leaves Kapit at 9 a.m.

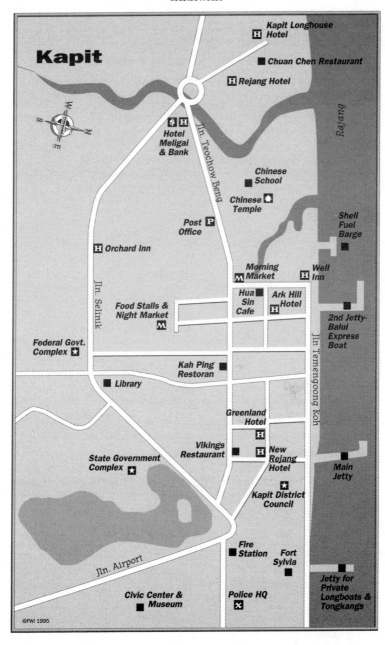

Kapit

Kapit Longhouse Hotel

Chuan Chen Restaurant

Rejang Hotel

Rajang

Hotel Meligai & Bank

Jln. Teechow Beng

Chinese School

Chinese Temple

Shell Fuel Barge

Post Office

Orchard Inn

Morning Market

Well Inn

Jln. Selirik

Food Stalls & Night Market

Hua Sin Cafe

Ark Hill Hotel

2nd Jetty- Balui Express Boat

Federal Govt. Complex

Kah Ping Restoran

Library

Greenland Hotel

Jln. Temengoong Koh

State Government Complex

Vikings Restaurant

New Rejang Hotel

Main Jetty

Kapit District Council

Fire Station

Fort Sylvia

Jln. Airport

Civic Center & Museum

Police HQ

Jetty for Private Longboats & Tongkangs

©FWI 1995

If you are not in a hurry there are trading boats run by Chinese traders who chug up and down the river when the water is high. Expect to pay around M$50 to get to Belaga. There is also MAS air service twice weekly to Sibu and Belaga.

Where to Stay in Kapit

Moderate

Hotel Meligai   **M$37–80**

Lot 3, 3 Jalan Airport, P.O. Box 139, ☎ *(084) 796611 FAX 76817*
If you are looking for luxury this is about all Kapit can muster. It has a nice view of the town, AC and phones.

Greenland Hotel   **M$45–55**

Lot 463-464, Jalan Teo Chow Beng, ☎ *(084) 796388, FAX 706708*
A newish and good compromise between luxury and roughing it. AC, bath, TV, hot water and carpeting. The rooms get cheaper the higher up you go.

Inexpensive

New Rejang Hotel   **M$40–48**

104 Jalan Teo Chow Beng, ☎ *(084) 796600, FAX 796341*
New, simple, cheap and clean with AC.Next to the Greenland Hotel and Main Jetty.

Well Inn   **M$35–38**

No. 40, Jalan Court ☎ *(084) 796009*
Some AC cheaper rooms with fan, video, and hot water

Ark Hill Inn   **$M38–50**

Lot 451, Shop Lot No. 10,Jalan Airport, ☎ *(084) 796168, FAX 796341*
AC, simple, clean rooms near the second jetty and fuel barge close to the Morning Market.

Budget

Rejang Hotel   **M$15–35**

28 Jalan Temenggong Jugah, New Bazaar, 300 meters from the dock, ☎ *(084) 796700, FAX 796341*
The most popular budget hotel and maybe the most fun. If you don't mind dragging your barang to the top floor you can pay as little as M$10 for the night.

Kapit Longhouse Hotel   **M$22–30**

on Jalan Temenggong Jugah
Historic hotel overlooking the river and down from the Rejang Hotel

Kuching retains a lot of its Chinese character.

Kuching★★

728km from Singapore, 811kms from KK

Kuching is the riverine capital of Sarawak with a population of 70,000. The oil center of Miri is the largest city. The Sarawak river bisects the city and most people prefer to travel back and forth by boat. The city was under White Rajah rule until 1941, when the Japanese invaded. It became part of the British crown colony of Sarawak in 1946 and a state of Malaysia in 1963.

Cat-town?

The story goes that when James Brooke first asked the name of this place a cat darted out from under a table. The locals thought he wanted the word for cat. According to the legend, the word for cat is Kuching. Just one more fable to add to Sarawak's legend. If this story was true then Kuching would be called Pussytown or something similar since the local Malay word for cat is "Pusa." The real source of the name is more likely "cochin" for harbor in Chinese. Kuching was a well established trading center and harbor for the Chinese 1200 years before Brooke showed up to rename it.

The major town and seaport of Kuching feels as exotic today as it must have felt when Brooke first saw it. There is a peculiar form of light here. As you sit on the banks of the Sarawak river watching the ferrymen oaring their boats you can feel the rhythm and sounds of this ancient place. The river winds through town. If you squint, you can see what it was like at the turn of the century. A casual stroll through town will take you past Indian temples covered with hundreds of brilliant figures, a dark rich Chinese temple, boisterous open air markets and crooked back streets. Everywhere there are splashes of

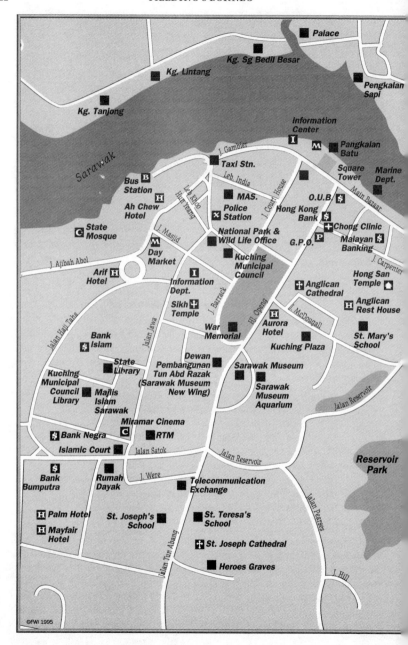

Palace

Kg. Sg Bedil Besar

Kg. Lintang

Pengkalan Sapi

Kg. Tanjong

Information Center

Sarawak

Pangkalan Batu

J. Gambier

Taxi Stn.

Leb. India

Square Tower

Marine Dept.

Bus Station

Ah Chew Hotel

Hun Yeang

Leb. Kilco

J. Court House

MAS.

Police Station

Main Bazaar

Hong Kong Bank

O.U.B.

State Mosque

National Park & Wild Life Office

Chong Clinic

G.P.O.

Malayan Banking

J. Masjid

J. Ajibah Abol

Day Market

Kuching Municipal Council

J. Carpenter

Arif Hotel

Information Dept.

Sikh Temple

J. Barrack

Anglican Cathedral

Hong San Temple

Anglican Rest House

Jalan Haji Taha

Bank Islam

Jalan Java

Hj. Cheng

J. McDougall

War Memorial

Aurora Hotel

St. Mary's School

Kuching Plaza

State Library

Dewan Pembangunan Tun Abd Razak (Sarawak Museum New Wing)

Sarawak Museum

Kuching Municipal Council Library

Majlis Islam Sarawak

Sarawak Museum Aquarium

Jalan Reservoir

Miramar Cinema

Bank Negra

RTM

Islamic Court

Jalan Satok

Jalan Reservoir

Reservoir Park

Bank Bumputra

Rumah Dayak

J. Were

Telecommunication Exchange

Jalan Pearses

Palm Hotel

Mayfair Hotel

St. Joseph's School

St. Teresa's School

Jalan Tun Abang

St. Joseph Cathedral

Heroes Graves

J. Hill

©FWI 1995

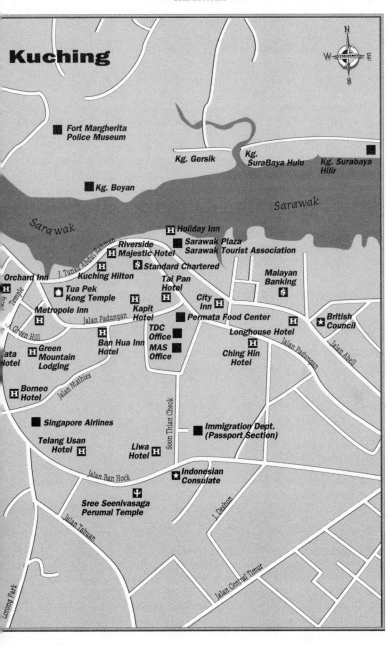

Kuching

Fort Margherita
Police Museum

Kg. Gersik

Kg.
SuraBaya Hulu

Kg. Surabaya
Hilir

Kg. Boyan

Sarawak

Sarawak

Holiday Inn

Riverside
Majestic Hotel

Sarawak Plaza
Sarawak Tourist Association

Standard Chartered

Malayan
Banking

Orchard Inn

Kuching Hilton

Tai Pan
Hotel

Tua Pek
Kong Temple

City
Inn

Metropole Inn

Kapit
Hotel

Permata Food Center

British
Council

Jalan Padungan

Longhouse Hotel

Ban Hua Inn
Hotel

TDC
Office

MAS
Office

Jalan Padungan

Jalan Abell

Green
Mountain
Lodging

Ching Hin
Hotel

ata
otel

Jalan Mathies

Borneo
Hotel

Singapore Airlines

Soon Thian Cheok

Immigration Dept.
(Passport Section)

Telang Usan
Hotel

Liwa
Hotel

Jalan Ban Hock

Indonesian
Consulate

Sree Seenivasaga
Perumal Temple

Jalan Tabuan

J. Dedon

Jalan Central Timur

Lorong Park

J. Tunku Abdul Rahman

Green Hill

Jalan Padungan

colors, smiles, loud noises and the myriad of unidentifiable smells that are only found in Asia.

There is a pleasant **Riverwalk** in Kuching, very modern looking and perfect for a nice after-dinner walk. At sundown in the middle of the Walk, there is a water fountain show where lighted water dances to the rhythm of classical music. A small park and numerous vendors line the walkway. The best thing about this Walk is that it's clean.

The **Sarawak Museum**, built in 1891 by Rajah Charles Brooke, houses wonderful tribal artifacts. **Istana** (palace) is now the residence of Sarawak's governor. **Fort Margherita** (named after Brooke's wife) is now a police museum but is still considered among the best colonial architecture left in Southeast Asia. **Masjid Besar** (Main Mosque) is famous for impressive contemporary architecture. Completed in 1968, the mosque incorporates the design of some of the first buildings constructed on the site, dating from 1852. There are many impressive Chinese temples, including **Tua Pek Kong** (1876); **Hian Tien Shian** (1877), dedicated to god of heaven; the **Temple of Kuan Yin** (Chinese god of mercy), which dates from 1908; and **Tien Hou** (goddess of seamen), built in 1927. Upriver are traditional villages accessible by small craft.

The graveyard of the old mosque

The Sarawak River

Cat Museum

Open Tuesday–Sunday 10 a.m.–6 p.m. Free admission
(in the DBKU building) Those who love cats should stop here (albeit briefly) for a trivial tour of things feline. It is a whimsical place full of photos, displays and other bric a brac designed to tie in to the city's namesake or *Kuching*.

Chinatown

Calling any place in Kuching "Chinatown" might be like calling any place in Beijing Chinatown. Kuching was built by the sweat of Chinese and is now the predominate ethnic group here. During the turn of the century and before WWII they created the unique look of old Kuching. On Jalan Satok there is a bustling market on late Saturday night and early Sunday morning until 1:00 p.m.

Downtown ★

Unlike Kota Kinabalu, Kuching was spared some of the wrath of Japanese and Allied bombers. There are still some heavy colonial buildings left around the waterfront. Visit the **Square Tower**, a mock fortress now converted to a dance hall, The **Post Office** was built by Vyner Brooke and across the street is the **Pavilion**.

Jong's Crocodile Farm

Open Daily 9 a.m.–5 p.m.
(18km south of Kuching, 25 minutes via #6 bus) The crocodiles of Sarawak used to be a major threat. At the turn of the century there was a bounty on man eating crocs who preyed on fishermen along the Sarawak river. Today the closest you will get to a croc will be at this breeding facility. There are no noble aspirations here though. Those evil saurians are destined to become handbags and suitcases when they out-live their touristic purposes. The crocs are fed at 9 a.m. and 3 p.m.

The Istana

(Across the Sarawak River) The Istana was built in 1870 by Charles Brooke to house him in the manner of a White Rajah. This former royal residence of the Rajahs sits amid beautiful gardens across the river from Kuching and now serves as the governor's home. It is closed to the public but it is lit up at night and adds to Kuching's romantic image.

Fort Margherita

Open Tuesday– Sunday 10 a.m.–6 p.m., Free admission.
(Take the ferry from Pangkalan Batu across the Sarawak River) This old fort is one of the few of twenty or so river fortifications built by the Brookes to pacify the rivers of Sarawak. The forts (and their cannons) acted as an effective deterrent against headhunting parties, uprisings and pirates who wanted to head upriver. The Fort commands the Sarawak river and was an important defense against seaborne attacks particularly from Bugis pirates who would attempt to raid the town or settlements upriver. It was burned down in 1857 when Chinese gold miners rioted, and then rebuilt in 1879 by Charles Brooke who named it after his wife. The building suf-fered damage in December of 1941 when the Japanese bombed Kuching. Since then it has been carefully restored and is now a police/military museum and land-scaped grounds. The museum has exhibits on the evils of piracy, drugs, counterfeit-

ing, Japanese occupiers, rebels and other such concerns that the governor was obliged to quell.

Sarawak Museum ★★★

Open daily except Fridays 9:00 a.m.–Noon and 1:00 p.m.–6:00 p.m. Free admission.
(Straddling Jalan Tun Haji Openg) Borneo was lucky when Rajah Charles Brooke was convinced by Sir Alfred Wallace Russel in 1855 to set up a museum to preserve the unique wonders of the region. Wallace is the lesser known creator of the evolutionary theory.

The museum opened in 1891 and has expanded past its original concept as a ragtag collection of curios and is now a world class exhibit of anthropological and natural wonders. Worth a trip in itself just to understand the art and culture of the peoples of Borneo. Originally housed in the 1891 building, it was expanded in 1983, as a new wing was added. This museum, in conjunction with the cultural center, is one of the best introductions to a country's indigenous peoples I've seen. I would definitely recommend that you spend some time here before heading ulu to understand the Iban and other indigenous cultures of Borneo.

The museum is split into two buildings. The old wing consists of natural history exhibits that will give some insight into the amazing range of natural life in the region. Upstairs is devoted to the peoples of Sarawak and can make your trip to the Sarawak Cultural Village more enlightening. Here you will see an authentic Iban longhouse along with artistry and crafts. The Penan, Kenyah, Kayan and Chinese are represented as well. Most of the artifacts such as gongs from Brunei, musical instruments and older craft are no longer found in the remote regions.

The new wing covers the history of Sarawak. Here you can understand the Chinese influence as well as the brassware: gongs, cannons, tea kettles and urns that have long been snapped up by collectors. There are also rotating exhibits in the main lobby.

Book lovers should check out the gift store if they are looking for a good selection of tomes on Borneo and its peoples.

Sarawak Cultural Village ★★★

Open 9:00 a.m.–5:30 p.m., Monday to Sunday. Admission charge.
(on the way to Damai Beach) When I first toured the almost finished site with one of the architects, I was blown away by the dedication to rebuilding the massive homes of Borneo's native and Malay peoples. What I didn't see was the cultural shows that are the main draw for tourists. About the only way you will be able to see just how the peoples of Borneo lived is in this well-executed recreation of various ethnic villages. Although this cultural Disneyland, complete with native dancing and gift shops may make veteran travelers run screaming, it is the only way most visitors will see how authentic longhouses are made, use real blow pipes, taste rice wine and see what goes into making the handicrafts. And you can do all this without having to stay up all night drinking! You can even take a class in one of many cultural handicrafts. The village is more that a low key version of the Las Vegas style Mormon owned pseudo-cultural villages of Hawaii. The Museum had a guiding hand in

ensuring that every building was authentic and that the local school children would be ensured of seeing a bit of the culture preserved. The Government, however, has added an "Aren't we happy savages in a happy multicultural pot " spin that some will find embarrassing. I recommend visiting it if only to gawk at the massive authentically-built longhouses. There are shows at 11:30 a.m. and 4:30 p.m.

Semonggoh Wildlife Rehabilitation Centre   ★

Open daily 8 a.m.–4:15 p.m.

(22km from Kuching, about 30 minutes by bus) If you are not going to Sepilok you should spend a half day taking a peek at a hodge podge of animals brought to the center for medical attention or rehabilitation. On any day you might see orang utans, sun bears, proboscis monkeys, birds or other native animals. You will see at least one orang utan. Say hello to Bullet a full grown orang utan who was shot by a hunter, recovered but won't habituate back into the wild. The Centre was opened in 1976 and a fairly low key affair. The animals are fed at 9 a.m. and 2:30p.m. Check with the National Parks & Wildlife people on Jalan Satok (☎ *248080*) about a km west of the center of town to see if it is worth the trip or just show up. Once you have seen the animals, there are trails where you can acquaint yourselves with some of Sarawak's plants via simple labels on each plant.

Timber Museum

Open Monday - Friday 8 a.m.–4 p.m. and Saturday 8 a.m.–12:30 p.m., Free admission (*Next to the stadium on Jalan Wisma Sumbar Alam*) In the mid '80s when the timber business was under a lot of criticism for its policy of clear cutting and exporting logs, one of their responses was to open a museum. Nothing truly edifying here but it may be the only chance you get to understand the logging process. Out in the logging camps there is little informative or educational. Better yet combine this trip with the Sarawak Cultural Center to get a feeling of irony.

A cure for AIDS?

There is much talk about just what is hidden in jungles. Recently the US National Cancer research signed an agreement to conduct research into the effects of the Bintangor tree on the AIDS virus. Two anti AIDs compounds, Costatolide and Calanolide have been discovered by American researchers. The compounds derived from this tree have now been approved for testing on animals. The Sarawak government has banned loggers from harvesting the two species of the Bintangor tree.

Where to Stay in Kuching

Luxury/Expensive

Like most large cities in Borneo, Kuching does not have much to offer the luxury traveler in town; most exotic spots are well out of town. Compared to mainland prices you don't get good value but compared to stateside prices any of these top rated hotels are a bargain. Use your credit card for the best exchange rate.

Kuching Hilton   **M$290–650**   ★★★★

Jalan Tunku Abdul Rahman, PO Box 2396. ☎ *(082) 248200, FAX 428984.*
322 rooms.

The most expensive hotel in Kuching delivers views of the Sarawak river and is walking distance to most of Kuching's attractions. The Hilton has the edge of the Holiday Inn for high rollers because it's nine years newer (built in 1988 and renovated in 91) and a tad glitzier.

Holiday Inn Kuching   **M$185–460**   ★★★

Jalan Tunku Abdul Rahman, Kuching. ☎ *(082) 423111, FAX 426169.*
320 rooms.

The Holiday Inn responded to the Hilton's makeover in '91 by doing it one better in '92. It still doesn't have the pizazz of the Hilton and the pricing shows it. This and the Hilton are the main business hotels in Kuching, travelers would be better served by the Damai Beach Holiday Inn.

Holiday Inn Damai Beach   **M$130–265**   ★★★

Damai Beach ☎ *(082) 411777*

This pricey resort hotel at the foot of Gunung Santubong and out of town is the favorite of most German and Australian package tourists. The modern 302 room resort is on 90 acres about 32 kms from Kuching and about 40 kms from the airport. Teluk Bandung beach can be muddy during monsoon season. This hotel tends to be more crowded because of the quantity of lounge lizards around the pool. The upside is that it is never hard to start a party in the private chalets. There is wheelchair access to some rooms and nonsmoking rooms are available. Those looking for a tropical resort complete with chalet type rooms and studios will enjoy themselves here. The hotel was first built in 1987 and was added to in 1993. A great place to do your laundry and burn off the mildew gathered in the jungle. To keep you occupied, the hotel offers tours, windsurfing, an 18 hole golf course designed by Trent Jones. The Sarawak Cultural center is close by but little else.

Riverside Majestic Hotel   **M$270–525**   ★★★★

Jalan Tunku Abdul Rahman. ☎ *(082) 247777, FAX 425858*

There is now a third alternative to the Hilton and Holiday in Kuching. The 1992 hotel is pure business with minibars, hairdryers, direct dial phones, coffee maker and other amenities. There are both wheelchair access rooms and nonsmoking rooms available, also sauna, tennis and squash for the active. Right downtown.

Moderate

Kuching is a bit more expensive than most budget travelers like. You may want to splurge and stay at the Holiday Inn out at Damai or cut a mean deal with one of the budget joints below.

Aurora Hotel   **M$95–140**   ★★★

Jalan Tanjong Batu, Bintulu. ☎ *(082) 240281, FAX 425400.*
Old musty 84 room hotel from 1955 but close to the museum and business area Fixed up in 1984 and is due for another renovation.

Liwah   **M$110–150**

Song Thian Cheok, ☎ *(082) 240222*

Mayfair Hotel   **M$90–140**
　　45 Palm, ☎ *(082) 421486*

Hotel Longhouse   **M$60–80**
　　Abell, ☎ *(082) 249333*

City Inn   **M$60–80**
　　275 Abell, ☎ *(082) 414866*

Fata Hotel   **M$60–80**
　　Tabuan, ☎ *(082) 248111*

Hotel Borneo   **M$50–80**
　　30 Tabuan, ☎ *(082) 244121*

Metropole   **M$40–80**
　　22 Green Hill Road, ☎ *(082) 412484*

Palm Hotel   **M$40–60**
　　29 Palm, ☎ *(082) 240231*

Cheap

Anglican Hostel   **M$20–30**
　　Behind St. Thomas' Anglican Church, ☎ *(082) 414027*
　　The hostel run by the Anglican church is the most popular crash site for backpackers. If the hostel is full or not to your liking check out The Kuching Hotel.

Selamat Hotel   **M$30–40**
　　6 Green Hill Road, ☎ *(082) 411249*

Kuching Hotel   **M$20–35**
　　6 Temple Street, ☎ *(082) 413985*

Getting Around

Kuching is a little out of the way compared to Kota Kinabalu. Sibu and Miri are the major air hubs. There are numerous tour and travel agencies in Kuching to help plan any flights or tours. Don't be afraid to shop for best tour prices and to work out your trip in detail using this and other guidebooks as the starting points.

Tour Companies

Borneo Adventure
　　No 55 Main Bazaar, ☎ *(082) 245175, FAX 422626*

Borneo Sightseeing,
　　Lot 173, Jalan Chan Chin Ann, ☎ *(082) 410688, FAX 415300*

East West Agencies
　　41 Jalan P. Ramlee, ☎ *(082) 241401, FAX 424529*

Ibanika Expeditions
　　Lot 4. 11, 4th floor Wisma Saberkas, ☎ *(082) 424021*

Insar Tour & Travel
　　524 Jalan Pisang, West, ☎ *(082) 416223, FAX 424206*

Inter-World
　　85 Jalan Rambutan, ☎ *(082) 252344, FAX 424515)*

Journey Travel Agencies
　　Lobby Floor, Hilton Hotel, Jalan Borneo, ☎ *(082) 240652, FAX 415775*

Life is a little slower in Sarawak compared to Sabah.

Longhouse Tours

First Floor, 253 Jalan Datok Wee Kheng Chiang, ☎ *(082) 422215, FAX 412728*

MBF Insight

Lot 260, First Floor Banguanan Lai Chin Hung, Jalan Chan Chin Ann,
☎ *(082) 241305, FAX 241557*

Pan Asia Travel

Second Floor, Unit 217-218, Sarawak Plaza, Jalan Tunku Abdul Rahman,
☎ *(082) 419754*

Samasa Tours & Travel

Lot 358, Lower Ground Floor, Jalan Rubber, ☎ *(082) 250603, FAX 481588*

Sarawak Travel Agencies,

70 Jalan Padungan, ☎ *(082) 243708, FAX 424587*

Vista Borneo

Level 3, Block G, Lot 13, Taman Sri Sarawak, Jalan Borneo,
☎ *(082) 417791, FAX 417781*

Wah Tung Travel

Teochow Association Building, Jalan Tambunan, ☎ *(082) 248888*

The express boats at Marudi

By Boat

Express boats are booked from the **Metropole Hotel Inn Hotel** *196 Jalan Padungan* at the office of **Ekspres Pertama** *196 Padungan Road,* ☎ *(082) 414735* or from **Concorde Marine** *Jalan Green Hill,* ☎ *(082) 412551* or **Ekspres Bahagia** *50 Padungang Road,* ☎ *(082) 421948.*

Imagine trying to navigate these unmarked logging roads without a guide!

By Road

Due to the lack of good roads around Sarawak air or river transport is highly recommended.

From Kuching

VIA AIR FROM KUCHING

The airport is 10km south of Kuching. Taxi is M$15 from downtown or take the #12A bus for M$3 into town. Miri is the central air hub for MAS.

Bintulu	5 dailiy	M$117	MAS
BSB (Brunei)	1 daily	M$192	MAS
Johor Baru	1 daily	M$169	MAS
Kota Kinabalu	3 daily	M$237	MAS
Kuala Lumpur	daily	M$186	MAS
Labuan	1 daily	M$199	MAS
Miri	5 daily	M$166	MAS
Pontianak (Kalimantan)	2 weekly	M$177	MAS
Sibu	1 daily	M$72	MAS
Singapore	2 daily	M$262	MAS, SIA
Long Semadoh	2 weekly	M$40	MAS

From Kuching

VIA BOAT

Express boats leave from Pedning, 6km east of city. Book one day in advance Taxi is M$8

Sibu	3 daily	M$35	4 hours

VIA LAND

Kota Kinabalu	daily	M$20	7:30am
BSB (Brunei)	daily	M$12	10:30 am

Miri is the gateway to Mulu National Park and the jungles to the south.

Miri

The Eastern end of Sarawak, near Brunei

Miri is a big expat center for Shell Oil employees. In fact Miri is larger than Kuching. Not surprising that Miri gave birth to Shell Oil. At the turn of the century, Shell was a puny trading company that traded lamp oil for fancy shells and pepper. When they hit oil on Canada Hill just behind Miri on August 10, 1910 things changed in a big way. Sarawak became an oil exporter and Shell later adopted a shell as its logo. Today the Miri Field supports 624 oil wells producing 80 million barrels of oil per year. Oil well number one was retired in 1972 having pumped out over 600,000 barrels of crude.

Today it is strange to emerge from the jungle to see a town populated with gaunt white skinned Dutchmen. For the visitor Miri is the origin of trips to Gunung Mulu National Park, Niah Caves, Lambir Hills as well as the Bareo or Kelabit Highlands. A few lucky tour operators have a lock on the Mulu trips because of their lodgings within the park. If you are planning to go to Mulu or beyond, I would strongly suggest booking the trip from Miri with one of these companies. They will be glad to customize your trip. It

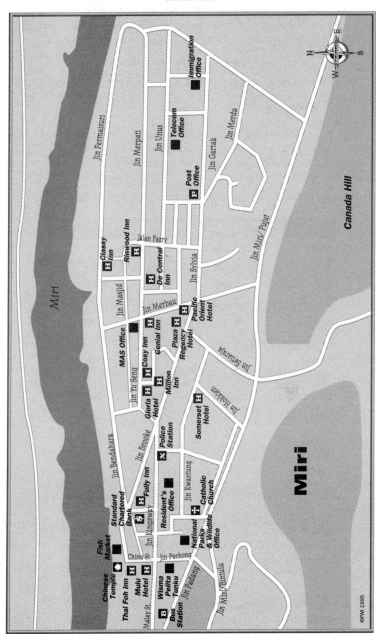

©PWI 1995

will not be cheap, but at least it will happen in the time allotted for the money allotted. Miri is the ideal place to get your permits for any trips to the National Parks or Jalan Raja. Pick up a map at the Land and Survey Office and book a tour. ☎ *(085) 36637*

Getting Around

Miri is a major terminus for travel in Sarawak. Most people will leave for Mulu, Niah and Brunei from this company town.

By Air

Miri is the central hub for air connections in Northern Borneo. If you are leaving from Miri there are frequent air connections to Kuching, KK, Marudi, Bario, Lawas, Long Lellang, Sibu and Bintulu. If you are traveling solo you are best advised to book a ticket on a Twin Otter to Bario and skip all the haggling, cost and effort of traveling by river.

All the flights listed are on MAS whose office is on Jalan Yu Seng ☎ *(85) 414144.*

By air from Miri			
Bario	1 daily	M$70	MAS
Bintulu	4 daily	M$69	MAS
Kota Kinabalu	7 daily	M$95	MAS
Kuala Lumpur	3 daily	M$425	MAS
Kuching	15 daily	M$164	MAS
Labuan	2 daily	M$57	MAS
Lawas	4 daily	M$59	MAS
Limbang	7 daily	M$45	MAS
Long Lellang	2 daily	M$66	MAS
Long Seridan	1 weekly	M$57	MAS
Marudi	2 daily	M$29	MAS
Mulu	3 daily	M$69	MAS
Pontianak	2 weekly	M$300	MAS
Sibu	8 daily	M$112	MAS
BY BUS			
Batu Niah	5 daily	M$3	2hours
Bintulu	frequent daily	M$18	4.5 hours
Brunei	2 daily	M$30	2.5 hours
Lambir Hills	frequent	M$3	1 hour
Marudi	frequent daily	M$3	.75 hour
Sibu	3 daily	M$35	8 hours

To the Kelabit Highlands

If you are heading for the Bareo Highlands a flight out of Miri can have you there in time for lunch.

To Niah Caves

There are several buses a day to Batu Niah (the closest stop to the park) that leave five times daily from the bus terminal on Jalan Raja. There are twice daily runs to Sibu that leave at 7:00 and 8:00 a.m.

To Brunei

You can also travel from Miri to Brunei via the six daily buses that leave Miri for the three hour trip to Kuala Belait in Brunei. It takes about a day to do the whole bus trip, the river crossing, customs and the trip to Bandar Seri Begawan. Best bet is the private minibus service for M$30.

Up the Baram River

This area is probably the last unexploited area available for travelers who want to understand something about traditional Dayak life-styles. There are no noble savages left but there is a definite lack of tourism along the Baram. You can book your own boat but the caveat is that once you are upstream things get a lot more expensive. Go to Marudi by bus or express boat then by boat to Long Miri and then a day by smaller longboat to Long Akah and then another day to Long Matioh.

Into Gunung Mulu

Pick a tour and don't be shy about haggling with the brace of tour companies that have organized tours into Mulu. Be realistic about how much time you should set aside to really see the vast park.

Tours and Expeditions

Most people come to Miri before they head up to Mulu. Having some experience here, I'll cut straight to the chase and recommend Alo Doda or Tropical Adventure. They pioneered trips into Mulu so start here in your quest for the ultimate Borneo experience. If you want to do something wild and crazy tell them, since they spend most of their time trying to reduce the hardship and suffering of their clients. There has been a rash of adventure tour companies all providing essentially the same services, so shop around and bargain hard. Star ratings denote expertise or skills in putting together unusual or more ambitious trips. Expeditions or trips to Gunung Mulu are not cheap but the tours are personalized and all inclusive. If you are traveling in a group or can put together a group to book your tour, your costs are much reduced. Boats into the park up to M$400, cave guide will run you M$20 per cave, porters cost M$35. If you want to go back and forth you will be bleeding ringitts to the guides and boatman as you are blood to the leeches. After all if you don't agree to their price what are your alternatives once you are in the park. Tours are about M$80–100 a night (cheaper the longer you stay) and they take care of all permits and food. If you are a solo traveler ask if they can hook you up with a group going in. This will defray costs for the group you are joining and you get to meet birdwatchers, corporate sales people, rich Chinese from Singapore or European oil execs. Use the fax numbers provided to cut your best deal. Keep in mind that the folks who run the tours all know each other so don't try to play them off against each other with bogus bids.

Alo Doda   ★★
    2 Jalan Setia Raja, ☎ *(085) 37408, FAX 415887*

Borneo Adventure
    Unit 9.02, 9th Floor, Wisman Pelita Tunku, Jalan Puchong, ☎ *(085) 414935*

Borneo Leisure
    Lot 227 Ground Floor, Jalan Majau Beautiful Jade Centre, ☎ *(085) 413011*

Borneo Overland
    37 Ground Floor, Bangunan Raghaven, Jalan Brooke, ☎ *(085) 302255, FAX 416424*

East West
    Lot 688, Mini Arcade, SEDC Complex, Jalan Melayu, ☎ *(085) 410717*

Hornbill Travel
    G26 Park Arcade, Jalan Raya, ☎ *(085) 417385, FAX 412751*

JLM Tours & Travel   ★★
    Lot 3002, Ground Floor, Morsjaya Commercial Centre, 2.5 Miles, Miri-Bintulu Road,
    ☎ *(085) 416051, FAX 414390*

KKM Travel & Tours
    Lot 236, Beautiful Jade Centre, ☎ *(085) 417899, FAX 414629*

Malang's Sister's Agency
    Lot 260 Beautiful Jade Centre, First Floor, ☎ *(085) 417770, FAX 417123*

Robert Ding   ★
    Lot 556, First Floor, Royal Snooker Centre, Jalan Permaisuri,
    ☎ *(085) 416051, FAX 414390*

Seridan Mulu
    Lot 140, Tinkkat 2, Jalan Bendahara, ☎ *(085) 416066*

Teland Usan
    Lot 166Tingkat Bawah, Bangunan Baram Trading, Jalan Permasuri,
    ☎ *(085) 387715, FAX 417588*

Travel & Tours
    288 Ground Floor, Bangunan Pei, Lot 1180B Lorong 2, ☎ *(085) 34250, FAX 514677*

Tropical Adventure   ★★
    288 First Floor, Beautiful Jade Centre, Jalan Majau, ☎ *(085) 414503, FAX 416452*

Vista Borneo
    Aras 3, Block G, Lot 13, Taman Sri Sarawak, Jalan Borneo,
    ☎ *(085) 417791, FAX 417781*

Car Rental

A&Z Motor
    Lot 108, Jalan Bendahara, ☎ *(085) 412692*

Mewah Bunga
    Jalan Permaisuri 81, ☎ *(085) 655639*

Where to Stay

With the oil and tourism business booming there is no shortage of high end for the oil patch consultants and middle range hotels here. Most people will fly in to stay a night and then head out to one of the parks the next day.

Luxury

Rhiga Royal Hotel Miri M$235–600 ★★★

Jalan Temenggong Datuk Oyong Lawai, ☎ *(085) 421121, FAX 421099*

The new top dog in town, or rather 3km out of town on Brighton Beach. This ultra luxury hotel has a choice of chalets or traditional rooms complete with 24 hour room service, even a concierge! Expect to lay out some mean green for the pleasure of a stay here. The Royal has 225 rooms all with bath, hair dryer, minibar, tea/coffee maker, direct dial phone and color TV with movies. Don't come for the beach, especially during monsoon season.

Dynasty Lutong M$160–180 ★★

Jalan Pujut, ☎ *(085) 421111*

Holiday Inn Miri M$150–170 ★★★

Jalan Temenggong Datuk Oyong Lawai, ☎ *(085) 418888, FAX 419999*

Shiny clean resort hotel just south of Miri, full to the brim with expats and tourists. You will have 168 rooms to choose from all with top of the line features. Although it is technically on the beach there is not much to recommend swimming in the muddy waters off Taman Salera Beach.

Somerset Hotel M$100–120

12 Jalan Cranking, ☎ *(085) 422777*

Rinwood Inn M$100–115

Lot 579 Jalan Yu Seng Utara, ☎ *(085) 415555 FAX 415009*

Park Hotel M$100–115

Jalan Kingsway, ☎ *(085)414555*

Your best choice after the Holiday Inn.

Hotel Plaza Regency M$80–110

47 Jalan Brooke, ☎ *(085) 414458*

Moderate

Most of the fair to middling dives are on Jalan Yu Seng Selatan and Jalan Yu SengUtara.

Gloria Hotel M$72–100

27 Jalan Brooke, ☎ *(085) 416699*

Million Inn M$63–69

6 Jalan Yu Seng Selatan, ☎ *(085) 415085*

Classy Inn M$60–65

Jalan Masjid, ☎ *(085) 412533*

De Central Inn M$60–65

14 Jalan Yu Seng Utara, ☎ *(085) 412518*

Genial Inn M$40–45

Jalan Yu Seng Selatan, ☎ *(085) 410966*

Brooke Inn M$40–45

Jalan Yu Seng Utara, ☎ *(085) 412881*

Fully Inn   **M$40–45**

    Jalan Yu Seng Utara, ☎ *(085) 412541*

Cosy Inn   **M$40–50**

    545 -547 Jalan Yu Seng Selatan, ☎ *(085) 415522, FAX 415155*

Mulu Inn   **M$37–52**

    Lot 2453 Jalan China, ☎ *(085) 417168, FAX 417172*

Budget

There is a certain standard of hotel that caters to the backpacker intent on extracting as much discomfort for the lowest price. These hotels are found off the marketplace near the waterfront off Jalan China.

Thai Foh Inn   **M$38–45**

    18 -19 Jalan China, ☎ *(085) 418395*

Fairland Inn   **M$25–40**

    Jalan Raja, ☎ *(085) 413981*
    AC with TV

South East Asia Lodging House   **M$7–38**

    Behind Cathay Cinema, ☎ *(085) 416921*
    None with private bath but you can choose AC at the high end or bunk it at the low end.

Tai Tung Lodging House   **M$8–45**

    26 Jalan China, ☎ *(085) 34072*
    Dormitory style beds or attached bathroom with AC.

Niah National Park★

100 kms(2 hours) from Miri, 130kms north of Bintulu

In the state of Sabah, the Niah National Park is a mysterious land which is inaccessible by road. The highlight here is the Niah Caves, one of the largest limestone caverns in the world. The park covers 7756 acres that includes Gunung Subis; at 1294 feet—it's one of the highest points in the state. Although you have to go to the museum in Sarawak to see the artifacts in 1959, Tom Harrisson, then curator of the museum, changed the way people viewed Asia's role in the evolution of man when he found evidence of human habitation as early as 37,000 years ago. Niah is also the only site of **cave paintings** in Borneo. Today, the 31 sq. km park is Sarawak's most popular tourist site. Man had been using the caves as a burial site leaving behind perfectly preserved skeletons, tools and handicrafts. Africa was once thought to be the cradle of man and now these and other finds in China and Malaysia have challenged that theory.

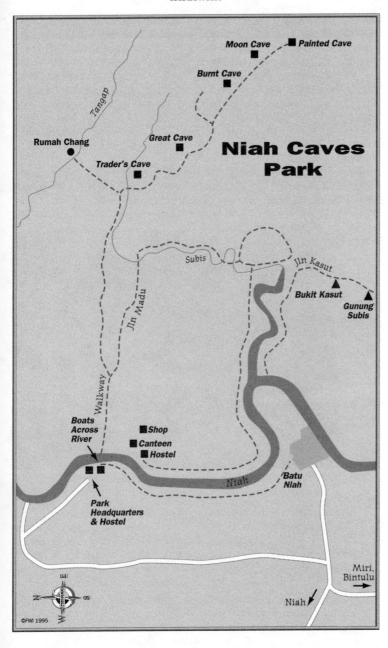

Birds' Nests

There are three types of nests built by the swiftlets. The highest and most treasured is the white nest built by the white nest swiftlet (Aerodramus fuciphagus). The swiftlets use the saliva to glue the nest to the rock and hold the nest together. There is the black nest built by the black nest swiftlet (Aerodramus maximus) which has a high proportion of saliva but more twigs and material. Down low is the mossy nest built by the mossy nest swiftlet (Aerodramus vanikorensis) and the white bellied swiflet (Collocalia esculaenta) that are inedible. The first harvest is between February and April just after the birds make their nests but before they lay eggs. They rebuild their nests and the collectors give them a rest until the second harvest between July to September after the eggs have hatched.

How do you eat a bird's nest? Well the sticks, twigs and other hard matter are removed and the hardened saliva of the swift is boiled to make Bird's Nest Soup. You can try it at the Marco Polo Hotel in Taiwan and the high end Chinese restaurants in Kuching.

Niah is the site of the oldest continuous habitation in Southeast Asia.

The Caves

(30 minutes from Park headquarters on foot) Make sure you take at least a couple of days to explore the caves. Don't forget to pack some food and water. Comfortable hiking shoes are a must if you want to explore the surrounding jungles and limestone massifs. Once there, you can branch out from the caves and explore one of many jungle trails in the surrounding area, climb a 400-meter tall limestone wall or visit Rumah Chang, an Iban longhouse located near the park boundary.

It is a thrilling hike to get to the caves from the Park HQ along a forested walkway.Plunged into the primeval sounds of the jungle you are buried in the cacophony of cicadas, monkeys and hornbills.

There is a turnoff to the left to the Iban longhouse where refreshments are sold. The first cave you come across is Trader's Cave where the birds' nests are collected.

Birds' nests

(in the Trader's caves and beyond) If you want to watch the triennial collection of birds' nests, plan on visiting in August to December or January to March. The nests hang from the roofs of the caves and collectors bring them down by climbing 60 meters up on rickety bamboo scaffolding. Then use long bamboo poles equipped with scrapers to flick them off the wall. The white nests are the preferred ones(built by the white bellied swiftlet), the black nests (built by the black nest swiftlets) contain feathers and require more cleaning.

Birds' nest soup is a delicacy in China and sells for up to U.S.$500 and more a kilo in Hong Kong. It takes about a 100 nests to make a kilo of bird's nest. The nests are not popular in Borneo (probably because the locals find nothing appetizing about eating nests that have tumbled into the cockroach-infested guano).

Bats & swiftlets

It is estimated that there are a half million bats in Niah. Eight species have been recorded. The bats live on insects and some eat nectar from fruiting plants. The swiftlets construct their nests in crevices in the roof of the Great Cave. It is their nests that are used in bird's nests soup.

The locals collect the rich bat and bird droppings and sell them as fertilizer to the surrounding plantations. The bats stream out of the cave at night and create an impressive black river as they head out to consume half their body weight in insects before returning. Since swiftlets are day fliers and bats are nocturnal, if you arrive at 6 p.m. you will be able to see the shift change as swiftlets return to the caves and bats stream out for the night.

Cave paintings

You will make your way along the slippery walkway through Great Cave, Burnt Cave, Moon Cave and end up in Painted Cave where ancient peoples buried their dead in wooden boat shaped coffins. These coffins date from around 1000 BC by use of the Chinese artifacts that were found among them. The wall paintings are hard to make out in the darkness so bring a flashlight. The crude paintings cover an area about 32 meters wide, depict people dancing and boats and are supposed to illustrate the journey from this life to the next.

Getting There

You can take one of the four daily buses ($M10) from Miri or take a cab ($M25).Cabs are $M30 from Bintulu. Take the 15 minute longboat from Park headquarters to visit the caves ($M.5). There is a 4 km plank walk to the mouth of the Great Cave. Continue through the cave to visit the Painted Cave, where you'll see the cave paintings. Make sure you stay long enough to experience the spectacle of the bats leaving the cave at sunset. Permits to visit the Painted Cave are available from the Museum in Sarawak or Niah Park headquarters.

The walk, in good weather conditions, takes roughly 45 minutes. To view the painted caves requires another 30 minutes of walking.

Where to Stay in Niah

A guide is recommended. There is a 36 bed hostel for $1 a night, 4 park chalets that sleep 6 - 8 people for $25 a night or you can stay in the cheap hotels in Batu Niah, 4 km away. If you want to stay in the park you must reserve space in Miri at the Park Office.☎ *(085) 248088.*

Santubong

32 km from Kuching

The mouth of the Sarawak River and the navigational aid of Gunung Santunbong made this area an important trading center during the Tang and Sung dynasties from 7th to 13th centuries A.D. Today there is a small picturesque fishing village, lush scenery complemented by odd shaped boulders and the 2500 meter high Gunung Santubong. The area is a good day trip from Kuching (take the frequent #2B bus from the Lebuh Jawa depot), have lunch at one of the simple restaurants or take a boat ride up the river.

Rock carvings

Chinese and Hindu rock carvings are found at **Sungai Jaong**, just 2 kms upriver from the village. The most interesting sculpture is Batu Gambir, a Kenyah warrior. Today, it's just a popular place for swimming and fishing. Government chalets may be booked through the District Office in Kuching or you can stay at the The Holiday Inn Damai Beach Resort (See "Where to Stay Kuching"). The other main attraction is the Sarawak Cultural Village.

Sematan

100kms west of Kuching

Those who want to poke around the most westerly limits of Sarawak will be surprised to find one of Sarawak's newest National Parks, Gunung Gading. Gading is an area set aside to protect the rafflesia, the large parasitic flower that grows to three feet across. If you don't charter a taxi, it can be too far for a day jaunt from Kuching so it may be worth a special trip if you are looking for rafflesia and won't be going to KK and the sites close to town.The town of Sematan is an idyllic getaway from the bustle of Kuching. The beach is fringed with coconut palms and the slow lazy life of a Sarawak fishing village. There is a turtle sanctuary on Palua Talang Talang. You will need permission to visit from the Park folks back in Kuching.

The way to Sematan by bus is via Bau (35kms) and then Lundu for a layover and then another hour onward to Sematan. You can take the daily STC buses to Bau (M$2, 40 mins) Lundu (M$6, about 2 hours) and from there take the bus to (M$5, 1 hour) to Sematan.

Gunung Gading National Park

(On the road 30 minutes from Sematan towards Lundu) The park is designed to protect the rafflesia and some would say to give tourists a reason to travel westward from Kuching. There are no facilities at the park but there are well marked trails from the park's headquarters that lead to a waterfall.

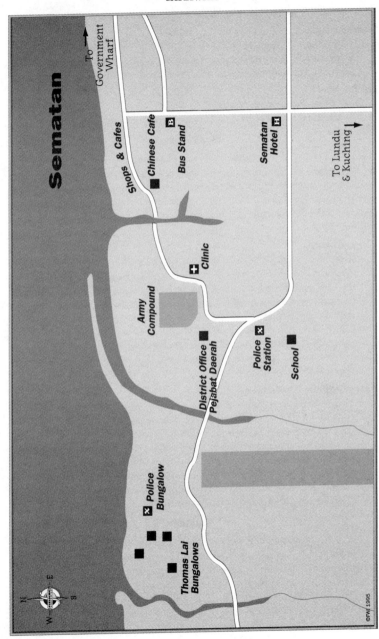

Where to Stay in Sematan

Sematan Bungalows   **M$25**

On the beach ☎ (082) 711133

Accommodations in Sematan are restricted to this picturesque cluster of chalets on the beach. You must phone in advance to arrange for the keeper to let you in.

Sematan Hotel   **M$25–40**

On the beach ☎ (088) 711162

Accommodations downtown but our preference are the oceanside bungalows.

Serian

65kms southeast of Kuching

Serian is not really worth a visit but it is the gateway to the longhouses that are along Sarawak's southern border with Kalimantan. These are longhouses of the Bidayuh, who were known as "land dayaks" for the their proclivity in building longhouses away from rivers and back in the hills and to differentiate them from the warlike, riverine "sea dayaks" or Iban.

Gunung Penrissen

If you stay in Kampung Abang there is a tough but worthwhile hike up Gunung Pernrissen at the headwaters of the Sarawak river. On the tortuous narrow climb to the 1300 meter summit you will pass through idyllic verdant jungle scenes of waterfalls and crystal clear streams. Towards the top is a Malaysian army post, a relic of the *Konfrontasi*. If you overnight here the view in the morning will be worth the misery. Make sure you hire a guide and a porter (if you are carrying camping or camera gear) since the last section of the climb is quite steep and requires using the built in rope ladders) Hire your guide in Kampung Abang or at any one of the longhouses in the area.

Across the border to Kalimantan

Border crossing is open 6 a.m.–5 p.m. Check with Indonesian embassy for details.
(Southeast from Gunung Penrissen) You can also take trails to Tebedu where you can then catch buses to Entikong on the Kalimantan side. You can also take the early morning buses from Serian to Tebedu. Don't just wander out of the bush and expect to enter Indonesia since even though Americans do not need a visa to enter the major air entry points, you will need special permission from the Indonesian embassy in Kuching to use this land crossing. From Entikong there are morning and early afternoon buses that travel to Pontianak.

Sibu

130kms (3 hours) from Kuching on the Rejang River

This is the second largest city in Sarawak 191 kms by air from Kuching. A Chinese timber trading town, Sibu is the springboard for Kapit and the river trips up the Rejang River, a colorful and photogenic area. You can also catch the buses to Miri and Bintulu at 6:30 a.m. and 12:30 p.m. at Jalan Khoo Peng Loong. There is an air connection via MAS to other major cities in Sarawak. The premier method are the burbling growling Express boats that slice up and down the Rejang.

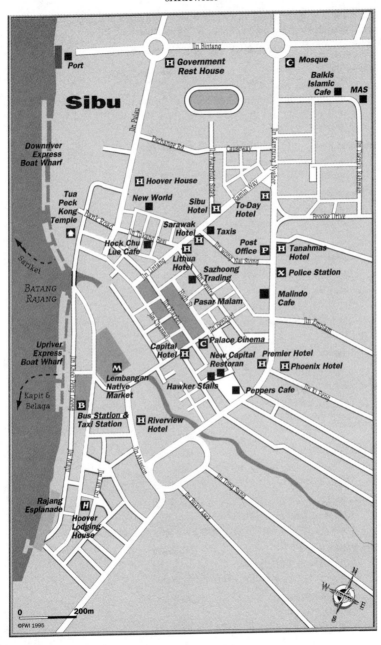

Sibu

Jln Bintang

Port

H Government Rest House

C Mosque

Balkis Islamic Cafe

MAS

Downriver Express Boat Wharf

Jln Pulau

Exchange Rd

Causeway

Jln Kampung Nyabor

Jln Maju Rahman

H Hoover House

New World

H Sibu Hotel

H To-Day Hotel

Ramin Way

Brooke Drive

Tua Peck Kong Temple

Bank Road

Sarawak Hotel

Taxis

H Hock Chu Lue Cafe

Jln Tukang Besi

H Lithua Hotel

Jln Wong Nai Siong

Post Office P

H Tanahmas Hotel

X Police Station

Sarikei

Jln Lintang

Sazhoong Trading

Pasar Malam

Malindo Cafe

BATANG RAJANG

Jln Central

Jln Channel

Jln Bengkel

Jln Emplam

Upriver Express Boat Wharf

Jln Chew Geok Lin

Capital Hotel H

C Palace Cinema

New Capital Restoran

H Premier Hotel

H Phoenix Hotel

Kapit & Belaga

M Lembangan Native Market

Hawker Stalls

Peppers Cafe

Jln Ki Peng

B Bus Station & Taxi Station

H Riverview Hotel

Jln Khoo Peng Loong

Jln Maju

Jln Mission

Jln Tong Sang

Jln Pedada

Rajang Esplanade

H Hoover Lodging House

Jln Lanang

0   200m

©FWI 1995

N W E S

Some Borneo trivia: Sibu is also home to Ting Ming Siong who according the Guinness Book of Records has been best man at 808 weddings since 1976.

Where to Stay in Sibu

Premier Hotel   M$150–270

Jalan Kampung Nyabor, ☎ *(084) 323222, FAX 323399*
Built in 1976 the Premier and the Tanahmas pickup most of the business from the business travelers. The old rooms are the cheap ones, the renovated ones are at the high end of the list.

Tanahmas Hotel   M$140–180

Jalan Kampung Nyabor, ☎ *(084) 333188*
The newest hotel in Sibu comparable to the Premier.

Li Hua Hotel   M$66–105

Jalan Longbridge Commercial Centre, ☎ *(084) 324000*
Business hotel with AC and good restaurant.

Moderate

Hotel Capitol   M$38–45

19 Jalan Wong Nai Siong, ☎ *(084) 336444*

River View Hotel   M$32–50

65 Mission Road, ☎ *(084) 325241*
The top rated budget bunk with TV, telephone, attached bathrooms, near the bus station.

New World Hotel   M$30—45

1 Jalan Wong Nai Siong, ☎ *(084) 310311*

Sarawak Hotel   M$30–36

34 Jalan Cross, ☎ *(084) 333455*
Newly renovated.

Budget

To-Day Hotel   M$15–30

40 Jalan Kampung Nyabor, ☎ *(084) 336499*
Older, but reliable.The more expensive rooms are the best bet.

Hoover House   M$15–25

Jalan Pulau (next to the church), ☎ *(084) 332973*
Clean rooms with western style bathrooms run by the Methodist church.

Sibu Hotel   M$15–30

Jalan Marshidi Sidek, ☎ *(084) 330784*
A little out of town, on the way to the stadium.

Hoover Lodging House   M$8–10

34 Jalan Tan Sri
Your last resort.

The Rejang River★★★

The major reason you will be in Sibu will be to travel to Kapit the last trading post before entering the dark interior. Kapit has no roads and the river is its lifeline. There is something hypnotic and romantic about lying on sacks of durians and palm oil in the hot equatorial sun. Below you are two thundering diesels that direct drive a massive prop that is propelling you in slow S's further and further upriver. Perhaps that's why Joseph Conrad was compelled to use the Rejang in his classic *Lord Jim*. Once you get to Kapit you need a permit from Pejabat Am office in the State Government Complex. From here you can charter a boat and explore the longhouses along the Rejang until you get to Belaga or really push up the Baleh to recreate Redmond O'Hanlon's hilarious book, *Into the Heart of Borneo*, now an adventure classic.

Despite the romantic allusions, you will not be the first traveler to go this way so you may be surprised at the less than friendly reception you get from some longhouses. See "Visiting Longhouses" for more info on protocol but the general tip here is bring gifts, chat up the *tuai rumah* or chief. The most visited longhouses are found close to Kapit and as you push upriver they become more laidback and a little happier to see you. See also Kapit and Sibu. Best time to travel on the Rejang is during the *gawai* or harvest festival during late May and early June when there is much celebrating and travel between the longhouses

Once you get past the limits of the express boats, these chariots await you.

Getting Around

Traveling up and down the Rejang is fairly easy albeit expensive for the independent traveler. Guides in Kapit, Kanowit and Song will hustle you when they see an orang puti in town so don't worry about how to find a guide. Naturally they all have access to a fine longboat that is probably made of their mother's clapboard house. The cost for guides should be about M$30 a day, for longer trips you should be able to negotiate this down to M$25. You will need a bowsman who should cost no more than M$20 per day. Longboats should go for M$20 a day (make sure you physically inspect the boat first) While you are inspecting the boat, check out the horsepower. You will be dunned about M$10 per horsepower plus fuel. This area will soon be under water if the Bakun dam begins so visit it now.

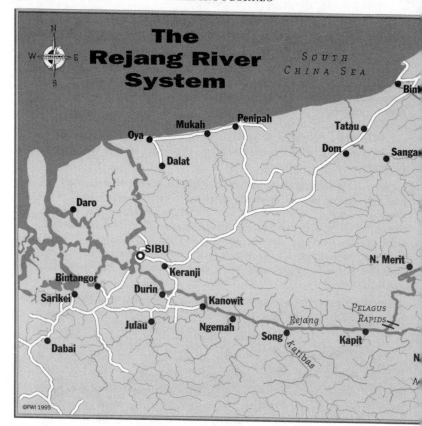

The Rejang River System

Along the Rejang		
Belaga	Take express to Long Murum	*Start of most upriver trips up the 20km long sungai Balui.*
Long Murum	3 hours north from Belaga via express boat on the Balui	*Kayan longhouse. About M$10 for a night's stay.*
Long Linau	2 hours further upstream from Long Murum	*A Kayan settlement at the mouth of the Linau river.*

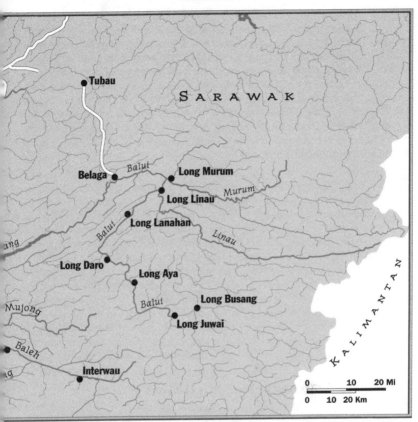

Along the Rejang		
Long Lanahan	**2 hours from Long Murum**	*Large Lahanan longhouse*
Long Daro	**1 day southeast along the Balui from Long Murum**	*Well known Kayan community with spectacular murals.*
Long Aya	**4 hours east of Long Daro on the Balui**	*Solitary Ukit longhouse. Ukits are a nomadic people who hunt and gather.*
Long Jawai	**Near the border with Kalimantan**	*Center for nomadic Penans and Ukit military operations against the Indonesians during Konfrontasi. This area is being heavily logged and can be reached by logging road.*
Long Busang	**2 days from Belaga**	*The last village on the Balui.*

Nuts & Bolts

To explore the sungai Balui you will need to start from Belaga. You can also reach many areas by using the logging roads that come in from Tubau. Belaga is an atmospheric town and may be worth just hanging around to see the **penanor,** the honey hunters that trek in from Kalimantan. March and September is the best time to catch the honey gatherers who trade their raw material for finished goods. It is also a good place to pick up stories and put together an itinerary while hanging with the locals. Those in a hurry might want to contact guides **Eddie John Balarik** through the Bee Lian Inn ☎ *(086) 461416* or **John Bampa** through the Belaga Hotel ☎ *(086) 461416* to set something up. You will also need to get a permit from the government office near the jetty. Permits are issued Monday–Friday 8 a.m. til noon and 2 p.m.–4:15 p.m.

It is very expensive to go *ulu*. Guides will run M$80–100 a day. Gasoline goes for about M$4 a liter (about three times the cost than in the cities downriver) and boatmen will charge a premium because of the scary waters that await you. Going upstream will require heavy horses that burn fuel at a rate equal to the U.S. deficit. You will need at least a 40hp engine that sucks up 20 liters to go just 10kms on slow water. If you are going the full 200 kms to the headwaters of the Balui that's M$1600 just for gas! A guide, your boatmen (you will need two) a longboat and gifts for the longhouses and a week's worth of supplies for the whole expedition will add another M$1500–M$2000 that doesn't include any overage of pocket money for any low water levels, screwups, gifts, souvenirs and any luxuries for yourself. Be happy if you get away with spending M$4000 on your little week long outing. Best bet is to get a flat bid before you charge off into the wilderness. Also you will need to be carrying all this money in cash. Also keep in mind that a week is the minimum you should put aside to explore this area. You may want to just hang around these sylvan longhouses and get to know the people you have paid so dearly to experience.

Similajau National Park

20kms northeast of Bintulu

The park is a long (32 km), thin (1.5 km) strip of beach and coastal estuarine. Visit to see the beaches (Pasir Mas), coral reefs (Batu Mandi), birds (185 species), turtles, dolphins, small mammals and the feared saltwater crocodiles. Sarawak was once the home of the world's largest crocs, but domesticated cattle (which crush the crocs' nests) and hunting (they used to eat people) has thinned their ranks to near extinction. The area's not very well known, but the park is a great place to spend a couple of days hiking, swimming and birding. There is a two hour walk north to Turtle Beach (cross the Likau in a longboat first) After one hour there is a trail that branches off to the Selansur Rapids about an hour and a half walk along the sungei Kabalak. An hour beyond Turtle beach is Golden Beach. Past this beach is a riverside trail that follows sungai Sebubong. You should reach a quiet pool after 15 minutes and then on back to the Park headquarters. If you don't want to walk back you can take the longboat from Golden Beach to the park headquarters.

Get a permit in Bintulu at the Bintulu Development Authority and stay at the chalet at Park headquarters. You can hire a speedboat from the Bintulu jetty for M$300 a day or take a taxi from town for M$40 If you would like to stay at the park, there are chalets, a hostel and a campsite. There is a small canteen at the Information center.

The information center open daily 8 a.m.–5 p.m.

Up the Skrang River

This area is home to the Iban, who settled in this area in the 16th century. Because of their proximity to the ocean and their alliance with seagoing Malays, the people were called Sea Dayaks. The Iban are warlike and the only group to make headhunting a sport rather than a tool of war. Headhunting had a very positive and spiritual significance to each longhouse. The heads are still kept in many longhouses though their protective magic has long worn off.

Conquered by James Brooke in 1849 on behalf of the Sultan of Brunei, the adventurer was given this area as a reward. Thus began Sarawak and the steady erosion of the Sultan of Brunei's land.

If you want to take a river trip complete with a longhouse stay, try to get past the long-houses near Lamanak and Pias (unless you want the standard tourist fare). You have to wonder if the Iban develop liver problems, with visitors showing up for a party and booze binge every day of the week! The concept of riverine hospitality has developed into a floor show of souvenir sales in some longhouses. Frequent visitors to Borneo will do anything to avoid another night in a longhouse. Once is enough for most. The area is 135 km from Kuching.

Brunei Darussalam

Worshippers at Bandar Seri Begawan's Saifudden Mosque

Epcot East

Walt Disney had a plan for thousands of acres of swamps he carefully bought up in Southern Florida. Unhappy with what had happened around his Disneyland project in Anaheim, he was determined to do it right. That meant control of the laws, the people, the land and the future. Epcot (Experimental Community of Tomorrow) was to be a city of the future. No crime, no pollution, no overcrowding. Just pure turn of the century Kansas with none of the evils of capitalism. There would be full employment, sunshine, fresh air and a bright future. Walt's plans were quickly ridiculed as Utopian, naive and possibly something out of political manifestos of the late 30s. Walt's dreams of a city nation ruled by a benevolent corporate dictator

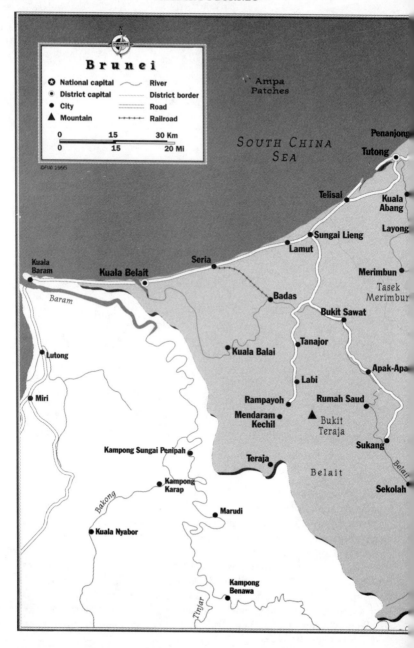

Brunei

- ✪ National capital
- ⦿ District capital
- ● City
- ▲ Mountain
- River
- District border
- Road
- Railroad

0   15   30 Km
0   15   20 Mi

©FWI 1995

Ampa Patches

SOUTH CHINA SEA

Penanjong
Tutong
Telisai
Kuala Abang
Layong
Sungai Lieng
Lamut
Merimbun
Tasek Merimbur
Seria
Kuala Baram
Kuala Belait
Badas
Bukit Sawat
Baram
Tanajor
Apak-Apa
Kuala Balai
Lutong
Labi
Miri
Rampayoh
Rumah Saud
Mendaram Kechil
▲ Bukit Teraja
Sukang
Kampong Sungai Penipah
Teraja
Belait
Sekolah
Belait
Kampong Karap
Bakong
Marudi
Kuala Nyabor
Kampong Benawa
Tingar

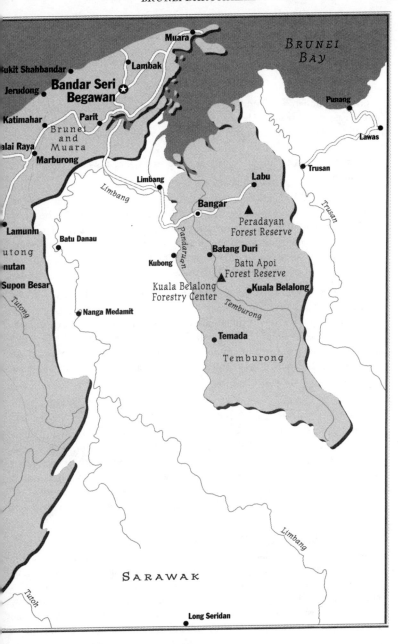

were quickly forgotten and Epcot, complete with artificial countries, became the largest cash cow of the Disney empire. Strangely, no one thought to compare his ideas to a little country tucked away on the north shore of Borneo.

An Abode of Peace

Today's Sultanate of Brunei or Negara Brunei Darussalam is out of place on the island of Borneo. There is little of the raw edge of Asia. It could be likened to a nice Midwestern city complete with theme park in the middle of Florida. Yes, Epcot East lives and it is called Brunei. The difference is that the theme park is the Sultan's palace and the attendance is somewhat limited to his family and invited guests.

The sultan and his nation are very wealthy, indeed. Per capita income is over $20,000, placing it among the world's wealthiest nations. To be sure, the $2 billion or so in exports earned annually from oil and gas is far more than the government can possibly spend, even though all food is imported and beef arrives from the country's own cattle ranch in Northern Australia. (The ranch is larger than Brunei Darussalam itself.)

The postage-stamp-size country of Brunei Darussalam became the world's 159th sovereign nation on January 1, 1984, ending nearly a century as a willing, loyal and wealthy protectorate of the British. About the area of Delaware (some 2228 square miles), little Brunei Darussalam is a 500-year-old sultanate carved from virgin rainforests in Northern Borneo like a succulent filet mignon sandwiched between the East Malaysian states of Sabah and Sarawak off the China Sea.

The first oil well in Brunei was sunk in Seri by Shell in 1929. It was a good thing since the major export of Brunei up until then was gambier, a dye extracted from the *bakau* mangrove tree used to tan leather. Since then Dutch Shell has been selling Brunei's oil almost exclusively to Japan. Everyone is happy with this simple and lucrative arrangement. The wealth of the Sultan of Brunei has not only allowed him to take care of his people, but has created some very impressive cultural and religious centers. Brunei has also preserved the culture and history of the people in its impressive museum and other public buildings.

Brunei has been independent from Britain since 1994 and its people have an extremely high standard of living. Most of the 305,522 people that come for tourism are from Malaysia (84 percent) and Singapore (5 percent). Although they don't need the extra money, Brunei does need to keep its 747's and hotels full. Tourism is growing rapidly and is expected to double every two years. Most "tourists" come to do business and are in transit from Sabah to Sarawak (and vice versa). Malays make up 64 percent of the population of

Brunei with Chinese being another 20 percent. Malays are favored over other races for political and high profile jobs.

For now Brunei and the Sultan still get most of their spending money from the oil reserves that lie offshore the tiny country. It is estimated that these reserves have another 25 years to go and then there will be plenty of natural gas for another 15 after that. Today Brunei supplies 5 percent of the world's oil and 9 percent of the world's natural gas, not bad for such a footnote sized country. With that kind of cashflow the Sultan has no problem spending a reputed $450 million on his main palace. When the oil reserves do run out, it will take a lot of gambier, coconuts or even computer chips to keep up with his life-style and the benefits the population is used to. Brunei is also highly dependent on Japan to buy most of its petroleum. The country does 67 percent of its export business with Japan, and the ASEAN countries make up the balance.

A Benevolent Monarch

The Sultan is the world's wealthiest man according to *Forbes* magazine but not according to the Sultan. The Sultan is the absolute ruler of the country (ever since he flushed democratic elections after the uprising in 1962 and after political parties were banned in 1988) and he is ably assisted by his hand picked cabinet ministers, two of which are his brothers. The country is still ruled under a state of emergency which is the simplest way for the Sultan to run things.

The 29th sultan is an absolute and benevolent monarch. He is said to have an easy sense-of-humor approach to life and his country. Educated at Sandhurst, the British military academy, he loves fast cars, polo and piloting his own helicopters. He shares the state's oil wealth with his subjects, in the form of electric, water, fuel, and basic staple subsidies. Medical care and schooling are free and the state picks up the tab for university study abroad. Pilgrimages to Mecca, medical care in Singapore and junkets to England are just some of the benefits for civil servants. There is no such thing as a personal income tax and interest rates are less than one percent!

He is a pleasant and just ruler but he has his quirks. His first wife was his cousin, Princess Saleha. He married his second wife, an airline stewardess, secretly. The Sultan also likes his toys. One would imagine in a land as tranquil and sedate as Brunei there is plenty of opportunity for recreation and travel. The Sultan owns over 350 cars, 200 polo ponies and likes fancy hotels. In fact, he owns the Dorchester in London and the Beverly Hills Hotel in Los Angeles. He lives with his two wives, four sons and six daughters in luxury in his 350 acre, $450 million palace. His second wife has her own palace.

The Sultan likes to spread his wealth around and has made donations to the Bosnian Muslims, the homeless in New York and an embarrassing $10 million donation to the Nicaraguan contras that was accidentally deposited in someone else's Swiss bank account. Locally the Bruneians do pretty well for themselves; there are 539 cars, 335 televisions and 276 phones per 1000 population.

The palace is Moorish-Islamic in design and flavor and features a private helipad, underground parking for 800 cars and his personal mosque, appropriately gold-domed. There are approximately 900 rooms in the family quarters for the sultan, his two wives and seven children, three brothers and their families. Landscaping is Japanese, the hardwoods are from the Philippines, the tiles from Italy and the furniture American-bought.

The sultan has invested wisely abroad and has some $20 billion in currency reserves—more than Britain or Switzerland. Hence, he can easily present $1 million to the United Nations Children's Fund on the occasion of his country's becoming the 159th member of that world body.

The Sultan has no problem flying in his personal 747 or enjoying the 1366 miles of roads in his Rolls Royces, but MTV and free speech will never really catch on. Much like Monaco, Brunei is a tiny and pleasant little anachronism tucked away in a backwater area. This happy land is ruled by the world's richest man who lives in the world's largest palace. The University of Brunei, in conjunction with the RGS, operates a rainforest study site that is open to scientists but not tourists or casual visitors. Brunei is included not so much for its position as a location for natural wonders, but as a historical journey that provides an interesting historical and cultural detour.

Just call me Sir

In case you wish to be more formal you should know that the current Sultan's full name is: His Majesty Seri Baginda Sultan and Yang Di-Pertuan, Sultan Hassanal Bolkiah Mu'issaddin Waddaulah Ibni Al-Marhum Sultan HaJi Omar Ali Saifuddin Sa'sdul Khairi Waddien, DKMB, DK, PSSUB, DPKG, DPKT, PSNB, PSLI, SPMB, PANB, GCMB, PANB, DMN, DK (Kelatan), DK (Johor), DK (Negri Sembilan), Collar of the Supreme Order of the Chrysanthemum, Grand Order of the Mugunghwa, DK (Pahang), BRI, Collar of the Nile, The Order of Al-Hussein Bin Ali, The Civil Order of Oman, DK (Selangor), DK (Perlis), PGAT, Sultan and Yan Di-Pertuan Negara Brunei Darussalam.

Facts, Fancies and Idle Rumors

A country this rich, this strange and this xenophobic is bound to create urban myths, bold lies and titillating tales. So since there is really nothing else to do at night in Brunei I thought I would give you this trivia test. Which of the following are true or false?

The Iban of Brunei combine their traditional customs with modern amenities.

True   False   The Brunei Gossip Test

☐   ☐   Bruneians have the second highest life expectancy at 71, second only to Singaporeans.

☐   ☐   Brunei owns a ranch near Willero in Australia that is larger than its own country just to make sure they have enough beef.

☐   ☐   They keep stray dogs under control with blowpipe-wielding dogcatchers.

☐   ☐   Brunei rents a battalion of Gurkhas from the British army to guard its oil fields for several million dollars a year.

☐   ☐   Civil servants get one free shopping trip in Singapore each year. One free trip to Mecca and trips for medical care.

☐   ☐   The largest crocodile captured in Brunei was 8.5 meters long and had eaten 12 Ibans near Kaula Belait.

☐   ☐   85 percent of Brunei is still forested, and no logs are exported.

☐   ☐   Upriver, Ibans are entitled to free TV sets for their longhouses There is one TV for each four people in Brunei.

☐   ☐   80 percent of all food is imported.

☐   ☐   The Sultan's house has over 200 toilets.

☐   ☐   The Sultan is actually quite average in wealth and all the oil money belongs to the state.

☐   ☐   The Sultan makes $100US a second.

☐   ☐   There are 90,000 cars in Brunei and the sultan owns 350 of them. Only the Sultan is allowed to ride in a Rolls Royce.

☐   ☐   Brunei has the world's largest stilt village, Kampung Ayer.

☐   ☐   Brunei's oil and gas reserves are predicted to run out in 2027.

☐   ☐   Gross Domestic Product is over $3.5 billion U.S. a year.

☐   ☐   Brunei is one of the world's smallest nations: 2226 square miles (5765 sq km).

True	False	The Brunei Gossip Test
☐	☐	There is no foreign debt.
☐	☐	The Sultan of Brunei is the richest man in the world earning approximately $5.5 million a day or $2 billion a year.
☐	☐	Islam is the official religion but locals can go to Labuan to party.
☐	☐	Brunei is actually divided into two separate parts with Sarawak in the middle.
☐	☐	The country consists of primary rainforest that has never been logged. The Temburong district is virtually pristine.
☐	☐	The Sultan has a younger brother Jeffri, who lives in the former Playboy Club in London.
☐	☐	Brunei forbids its citizens to sing, drink alcohol or dance in public. There are no discos or karaoke bars.
☐	☐	The royal family has their own country club, Jerudong Park, complete with a disco managed by DJs hired from Britain, and if they get tired of loading the CDs they import stars such as Elton John and MC Hammer to entertain them live.

OK, time's up. Well as you guessed by now all the above are true or as close to true as anyone has found out. Now this chapter has probably done more to whet your appetite to visit Brunei than all of the efforts of the sultanate over the last 2000 years.

History of Brunei

Although Brunei has been engaged in trade with China since the 6th and 7th centuries A.D., there has always been a certain wariness when it comes to foreigners. It seems that visiting Europeans and Asians have a bad habit of slicing off bits of the Sultan's country once they get friendly.

At the end of the 16th century, Brunei established trading with the Dutch East India Company. Brunei remained independent and was not absorbed into Indonesia. Although Brunei Darussalam means "Brunei, harbor of peace" it seems that they had a heck of a time with pirates and foreigners who were bound and determined to cut out the middleman when it came to trading in ivory, gutta percha and rattan. Brunei was wealthy because it controlled the trade between the gatherers and foragers of the deep interior and the traders from China, Arabia, Java and Asia. Between the 7th and 15th centuries Borneo (apparently named for the Arabic/Malay word *buah nyiur* or coconut) was a major stopping point for traders who traveled between China and Java as well as the Mollucan straits. The current Islamic sultanate was founded in about AD 1370 with Sultan Mohammad. Sultan Hassan, the ninth Sultan, created the current charter of today's government.

When Magellan's motley crew (without the recently demised leader) showed up on July 8, 1521, they were shocked to see such a splendid city complete with silk draped elephants and a royal palace. We only know because Pigafetta wrote it all down in his book *First Voyage Around the World.* He described a stilt town, with opulent wealth, a splendid palace and about 25,000 content happy people. Sounds familiar.

Things started to change in 1526 when the Portuguese muscled in and set up a trading post. The Spanish showed up in March of 1578 and had the impudence to demand tribute and to allow priests to begin converting the Bruneians to Catholicism. The Spaniards and the Bruneians fought off and on until 1645 when civil unrest and division drove the sultanate into poverty. Meanwhile the Sultan of Sulu in the Southern Philippines was expanding his control over the Eastern side of Borneo (now Sabah). Bugi Pirates (the original boogey men) from Sulawesi regularly made off with the cargo of trading ships. Finally in the closing part of the 1600s the Sultan gave the British the island of Labuan in return for protection from pirates. The trading post languished and the pirates ruled the oceans.

By the early 1800s Brunei was a ramshackle little town with a population of less than 10,000 people.

In 1839 James Brooke returned to the South China Sea. He had spent some time with Stanford Raffles, the founder of Singapore, and was impressed with how an Englishman with a bit of bluster and luck could set himself up as a potentate. Brooke was 36 years old when he first sailed into Kuching to deliver a letter thanking the local Sultan for rescuing some British sailors. At the time Kuching was the only positive ebb in Brunei's cash flow. Antimony had been discovered and the local *pangiran* Makota were busy abusing and rounding up the local Dayaks to dig it out as fast as they could. This did not sit well with the locals. Brooke saw an opportunity and returned a year later with 19 men, a few cannon and a small ship to offer his services to Rajah Mudah Hashim who was sent in 1837 by the Sultan of Brunei, Omar Ali Saifuddin, to quell the revolt caused by Makota. Hashim, who was not doing that well in his attempts to defeat the Dayaks, offered Brooke (who happened to have a very well armed schooner *The Royalist)* the Sultanate of the Sarawak River if he could quiet things down.

The White Rajah and the Three Thumbed Sultan

Brooke did so handily and was given the ill-defined region in September 1841. Hashim, having given Brooke his sultanate, then returned to Brunei where he and 11 other heirs to the throne were murdered by the evil and greedy Sultan. Brooke was not a fan of the three thumbed, cancerous, illiterate Sultan and decided to make his move. In June of 1846, Brooke invited British Admiral Cochrane to help him out and together they blasted Brunei down and burnt it to the ground. The Sultan fled into the jungle and Brooke wanted to be made Sultan of Brunei. Admiral Cochrane felt this might be politically gauche, so instead he allowed the nervous Sultan to rule if he pledged his allegiance to Queen Victoria. His slap on the wrist was having to give Labuan to the Crown on December 18, 1846. The Sultan also signed a treaty that protected him from further land grabs from Brooke in 1847. Although the Sultan had signed a treaty of Friendship and Commerce, the British did little to quell the pirates who regularly plundered trading ships and villages along the north coast of Borneo.

Brooke went after the pirates with a vengeance and in 1849 killed over 1500 and sank all but 11 of their 98 boats in one battle near Batang Maru. This impressed or scared the sultan so much that he gave Brooke most of the land between current Brunei and Sarawak.

Worried that the White Rajah would continue to push eastward. The Sultan signed a 10 year deal giving American consulate Charles Moses exclusive rights to develop the lands he controlled to the east in what is now Sabah.

The Lesser of Two Evils

Since the British were concerned about foreign encroachment into an area they assumed they owned, they viewed Charles Brooke, James Brooke's nephew, the lesser of the two evils. The British gave Brooke the Baram river basin and he neatly folded it into Sarawak as the Fourth Division. In 1890 Brooke annexed the valley of the Limbang river even after the Sultan had signed a protectorate agreement with Britain that would prevent the exact scenario from happening. At that point there was little to prevent Brooke from taking over Brunei proper. All it would take would be another revolt like the 1884 uprising in Limbang to force his hand. Since much of the jungle territory was ill-defined and amorphous it was acceptable to assume that he was simply expanding Sarawak into the Sultan's less defined regions. Brooke never got to make the final grab. In 1900 preliminary exploration work had determined that Brunei might have vast oil deposits. When oil was discovered in 1929 the British cozied up to the Sultan and made it clear that Brooke had better be content with what he had grabbed to date. Brunei was effectively a ward of the British empire having little say in its own government.

A miniature history of Brunei

900 AD	*First mention of Brunei by Chinese traders*
1521	*The first Europeans to visit are the remnants of Magellan's crew who documented the wealth and pomp of Brunei.*
1526	*Portuguese set up a trading post in Brunei.*
1888	*Brunei becomes a British Protectorate*
1899	*Oil exploration starts in Brunei.*
1906	*British sent advisors and administrators but Brunei does not become a colony of Britain.*
1928	*Oil discovered at Seria.*
1963	*Offshore oil deposits found.*
1967	*Sultan Omar abdicates in favor of his 21-year-old son, Prince Muda Hassanal Bolkiah, the 29th Sultan of Brunei.*
1973	*Arab oil embargo raises oil prices. Brunei goes from B277 million in revenue in 1970 to 9.7 billion in 1980.*
1984	*The independent nation of Brunei, Darussalam, was created and became the 159th member of the United Nations.*
1986	*The Sultan donates 10 million US dollars to the contras. It was deposited in the wrong bank account and finally returned in 1987.*
1987	*"By God's Will" an autobiography of the Sultan is written by the head of the PR firm hired to promote his new image of stern, political forward thinking center of Islamic stability. He also plays a lot less polo.*
1992	*The Sultan celebrates 25 years of power.*

The End of the Romantic Era

The anachronist structure of Northern Borneo came to a dramatic end in 1942. Sarawak, a private kingdom ruled by a familial line of potentates, British North Borneo, a business enterprise zone privately owned by businessmen and a feeble ward of the British colonial system, all became Japanese occupied territory. After the war Brunei was run by the British Military and then the Governor of Sarawak and then in 1959 Sultan Sir Ahmad Tajuddin was taken off the endangered list and given control of his country except for, of course, the military and defense which would be provided by Britain. When the surrounding regions of Singapore, Malaysia, Sabah and Sarawak wanted to create a great Malaysian state, partly to protect themselves from being made quick snack by China to the North and Indonesia to the south, Brunei opted out. They would rely on Britain's commitment to keep them free from the evils of communist expansionism.

However in 1962 the Sultan was rudely introduced to the evils of democracy when the party that was elected based their platform on removing the sultanate's power. Sultan Omar found new energy in exercising his sultanic powers and promptly forbade the Brunei Peoples' Party (PRB) from taking control. Naturally the party members organized a revolution and the British army quickly quelled the insurrection in less than a week. It pays to have friends in high places. This friendship allowed the Sultan to blow off the Malaysian federation, who would drain money out of Brunei's oil coffers to support their development plans. The angry Malaysians helped the PRB rabble rouse from nearby Limbang but when Prime Minister Razak died in 1976 they gave it up and Brunei was left alone.

When Indonesia made a grab for Sabah and Sarawak in 1963, Brunei allowed the British to operate from Brunei against the Indonesian rebels. But this fizzled out in 1966. Now that the old grudges had died down, Brunei was still under pressure to create a democratic government. In 1971 the ruling Sultan abdicated, putting his son, Hassanal Bokiah, in complete control, a new deal was signed with Britain allowing Brunei to rent-a ghurka for about $5 million a year.

On the morning of Jan 1, 1984 the sun rose on a fully independent Brunei. And Brunei has kept out of the limelight by diligently working to improve the quality of life in its small land and investing its wealth for the day that the wells finally go dry. (2027 in case you were calculating when to drop credit.)

The People of Brunei

Brunei is primarily a Muslim Malay country along the water with Iban tribes upriver. About 70 percent are Malay, with the balance being Ibans and Muruts. Despite the fact that business in the nongovernmental section is controlled by the Chinese, there are actually very few Chinese in Brunei, about 6000 according to a recent census and shrinking every day. Chinese were not automatically given citizenship on independence and must prove that they have lived continuously in Brunei for 25 years.

Brunei actively promotes the advancement and hiring of Malays in top business positions. The enforcement of Islamic tenants is increasing and there is little evidence of any relaxation as the Sultan adopts a sterner tone. The creation of the University of Brunei is designed to create a work force untainted by exposure to the evils of the outside world.

It is interesting to note that almost half of the 90,000 jobs in Brunei are held by foreigners (8000 are expats employed by Shell). All finished materials and most raw goods have to be imported.

Getting In

There is frequent service via most of the major Asian air carriers. Royal Brunei tends to be 50 percent more expensive than Malaysian Air Services. Brunei is not the best place to start your trip to Borneo since the prices are high, the ambience slightly cool and the infrastructure very poor. You are better off ending your trip in Brunei and starting your trip in Kota Kinabalu or Kuching.

To Brunei			
VIA AIR			
The airport is 11km outside BSB. If you are staying at one of the better hotels have them pick you up.			
Bangkok (Thailand)	3 weekly	B600	**Philippine Airlines**
Hong Kong	3 weekly	B690	**Royal Brunei**
Jakarta (Indonesia)	4 weekly	B680	**Royal Brunei**
Kota Kinabalu (Sabah)	6 weekly	M$83	**MAS**
Kuala Lumpur	6 weekly	M$441	**MAS**
Kuching (Sarawak)	3 weekly	M$420	**MAS**
Manila (Philippines)	Tues./Sat	B500	**Philippine Airlines**
Singapore	1 daily	S$377	**Singapore Airlines**
VIA BOAT			
Boats leave in the morning from Lawas and Limbang from Sabah. Boats leaving BSB depart from Jalan Roberts.			
Lawas	daily	M$25	leaves 11:30am
Limbang	frequent	M$10	
Palau Labuan	frequent	M$25	90 minutes away
VIA ROAD			
You cannot just drive or take the bus to Brunei. From Sabah you must leave from Lawas and take a taxi into the eastern district of Temburong, then via boat to BSB.			

U.S. citizens do not require visas for stays of up to 90 days, provided they are in possession of valid passports and onward or round-trip tickets—but always double check with your carrier for the latest in this regard. Entry is through Bandar Seri Begawan's international airport via Royal Brunei Airlines from Singapore, Hong Kong, Bangkok, Manila and neighboring East Malaysian states. Other Far East/Asian airlines also serve the area. A coastal highway links Brunei to the Malaysian state of Sarawak. Taxis to and from the capital cost about $12.50 to $19, depending on your destination, and airport buses start at about $1, but take the Sheraton Utama car service if you are staying at the only international hotel in the country. More information on Brunei can be obtained from:

Brunei Permanent Mission to the United Nations

866 United Nations Plaza
Room 248,
New York, NY 10017
☎ *(212) 838-1600*

Embassy of the State of Brunei Darussalam

Suite 300
2600 Virginia Ave., N.W.
Washington, D.C. 20037
☎ *(202) 342-0159*

Getting Around

Although Brunei is tiny it can be quite daunting. You can rent a car, take water taxis, land taxis or use the less than comprehensive bus service. Transit by taxis, buses and boats is excellent. There are some self-drive cars available, but traffic is British style (left-hand drive) and can be confusing. An International License is required and minimum age is 23. Hotels will arrange airport transportation with prior notice. Surprisingly, one of the best ways of getting around is with your thumb, especially if you're headed out of BSB. Not that the locals are trying to speed your departure out of town; it's just that they like to chat.

By Car

If you have come to see Brunei you should rent a car since the taxis will bleed you to death. You have to be between 23 and 60 and have an international driving license. The Bruneians drive on the left. Expect to pay between B$60 and B$180 a day depending on the kind of car.

Car Rental Agencies in BSB

Avis

21st Floor, Bangunan Hasbollah 4, ☎ *(02) 242284*
Avis also has offices in the Sheraton Hotel and Sheraton Utama.

Budget U-Drive

9 Bangunan Mengalait I, Jalan Gadong, ☎ *(02) 446343*

Ellis

3A Ist Floor, Bangunan Gadong Properties, ☎ *(02) 427238*

Roseraya

Ist Floor, Britannia House, Jalan Sungai Kianggeh, ☎ *(02) 241442*

Zisen Enterprise

7 Block C, Sufri Shopping Complex, Km 2 Jalang Tutong, ☎ *(02) 243848*

By Taxi

Taxis are expensive here. The airport run will cost you B$20. You can call a **taxi** on ☎ *(02) 26853* or *22214*. There are also water taxis which shuttle between the villages of Kampung Air. Short to medium trips shouldn't cost you more than B$2 and a charter should be about B$20.

By Bus

There is simply no way to get around the remote areas by bus. There are buses that leave when full from the bus station beneath the parking lot at Jalan Cantor.

Getting Out

Departure is via BSB International Airport, which can become congested during the annual period of pilgrimages to Mecca. There is a duty-free shop at the airport, but liquor is not sold, as this is a strict Muslim country. (Drinks are available to visitors in the restaurant here, however, except during Ramadan.) There is a departure tax of $B12 to all destinations, except Malaysia and Singapore, where the tax is $B5.

Airline Offices in BSB

British Airways

Jalan Kianggeh, ☎ (02) 243911

MAS

144 Jalan Pemancha, ☎ (02) 224141

Philippine Airlines

Suite B, 1st Floor, Wisma Hazzah Fatimah, Jalan Sultan, ☎ (02) 244075

Royal Brunei /Cathay Pacific

RBA Plaza, Jalan Sultan, ☎ (02) 242222

Singapore Airlines

49-50 Jalan Sultan, ☎ (02) 244901

Thai International

4th Floor, Complex Jalan Sultan, ☎ (02) 242991

Getting Sick

Statistics show that there is one doctor for every 1456 Bruneians but the wealthy will fly to Singapore or Europe for serious surgery. Health care is free for locals. Travelers can expect good medical treatment in this compact country. Brunei has eradicated malaria but outbreaks can occur. Water is potable in large hotels but you may wish to drink only bottled liquids or request boiled water.

Innoculations are not required for entry and local health officials claim the country is cholera free; however, Americans are advised to have a valid cholera certificate upon arrival. Brunei is relatively free of malaria but precautions should be taken.

Nuts & Bolts

Brunei has a hot sweaty coastal climate. There are no bars and whatever entertainment there is would put your grandmother to sleep. Any evening spots are buttoned down tight by 10 p.m. The locals head straight to Labuan (90 minutes by boat) where they can be subjected to intoxication, fornication and general good times. Brunei has wonderful jungles, excellent museums and an intriguing backwater ambience.

The only real mountainous area is in the southern part of the Temburong. The wet season is between November and February.

Business Hours

Business hours in Brunei are 7–8 a.m. to 4 p.m. Monday through Thursday, with a half day on Saturday. Friday is the official Muslim holiday and offices are closed on Sunday. Banks have slightly reduced hours, with lunchtime closing from noon to 2 p.m. Local markets are open from dawn and small shops stay open in the evening.

Currency

The exchange rate at press time (July 1995) is $B1.28 to U.S.$1.00.

The Brunei dollar ($B) consists of 100 cents. Brunei notes are in denominations of 1, 5, 10, 50, 100, 500 and 1000 dollars. Coins are in 5, 10, 20 and 50 cent pieces. The Singapore dollar is on a par and circulates freely; the Malaysian ringgit has a slightly lower rate. There is no limit on foreign or local currency imported or exported. The tourist will find travel expensive in Brunei. The standard of living is quite high and the people affluent by Southeast Asian standards. The average blue collar Bruneian makes about BS3.5 an hour and has significant benefits provided by the government. There is 6 percent unemployment in Brunei.

Drugs

The trafficking in and the illegal importation of controlled drugs are very serious offenses in Brunei. **The penalty for smuggling drugs is death**. Persons carrying amounts above specified minimum quantities (15 grams of heroin, etc.) are subject to the maximum penalty. There is no record of this penalty being carried out or any arrests of Americans for serious drug offenses in recent years.

Duty Free

Applies only to personal effects, including 200 cigarettes, 1/2 pound of tobacco and one quart of liquor (frowned upon). Customs officials are strict on imported items like small electrical appliances and cameras, so declare equipment at airport.

Electricity

Local current is 220-240 volts/50 cycles. The populace has all types of fancy, modern electronic entertainment equipment to keep them happy so the electrical power better be good. The PAL system is used by the local television network.

Embassy/Emergency

If you stop in at the embassy you get the local scuttlebutt but you may get a few tips on what is worth seeing.

American Embassy

3rd floor, Teck Guan Plaza, Jalan Sultan, Bandar Seri Begawan. ☎ *(02) 229-670*
Send mail to:

American Embassy

Box B, APO AP 96440
Bandar Seri Begawan

Police/Fire/Emergency ☎ *999*

Royal Brunei Police ☎ *22333*

Local Time

Local time in Brunei is Greenwich Mean Time plus 8 hours (13 hours in advance of Eastern Standard Time, 16 hours ahead of Pacific Standard Time). Brunei is in the same time zone as Manila, Singapore, Bangkok and Kuala Lumpur.

Official Languages

Languages in Brunei are Malay, with English widely utilized and understood in business circles. Do not expect to carry on long conversations upriver when Malay is the lingua franca.

Telephone, Telex and Fax

Services are good if you are in Brunei on business and stay within the confines of BSB. Radio and Television Brunei transmit locally produced programs and programs made elsewhere eight hours daily weekdays, 12 hours on Fridays and 15 hours on Sundays. News broadcasts are in Malay and English. Brunei does have its own color television station, and even longhouse dwellers in the jungle have their own TVs (and personal generators) provided by the government. There is a limited amount of reading matter on the country, but the weekly English-language *Bulletin* attempts to keep visitors informed about the outside world. Naturally the sultan owns or controls all the media.

BRUNEI

TO CALL ANY NUMBER IN THIS BOOK FROM THE USA:

DIAL 011 then 673 then the area code (no"0") and then the number

There are 4 area codes in Brunei: BSB, Muara district is 02, Belait is 03, Tutong is 04 and Temburong is 05 (Drop the "0"

To reach the operator when in Brunei dial 0124

International calls can be made from your hotel, cardphones, Central Telegraph office, the main Post Office and from the airport.

Public phones require phone cards. Cellular phone service is excellent and inexpensive.

Tipping

Tipping varies from person to person, place to place, in this prosperous nation. Tip according to services rendered and the circumstances. Hotels add a 10% service charge.

Tour Companies

Antara Travel & Tours
    102 Ground Floor, Bangunan Guru, Jalan Kianggeh, ☎ *(02) 448805, FAX 448817*

Mahasiswa Travel Service
    Bangunan Wisma Raya, 49- 50 Jalan Sultan, ☎ *(02) 243452, FAX 229457*

Travel Trade Agencies
    Bangunan Wisma Raya 49-50, Jalan Sultan, ☎ *(02) 224041*

Freme Travel
    Hong Kong Bank Building, Jalan Sultan Pemancha, ☎ *(02) 335025, FAX 223404*

Jasra Harrisons
    Jalan McArthur/Kianggeh, ☎ *(02) 243911, FAX 243904*

Ken Travel Teck
    Guan Plaza, Jalan Sultan, ☎ *(02) 223127, FAX 244066*

Borneo Leisure Travel
  Britannia House, Jalan Cator, ☎ *(02) 223407, FAX 240990*

Sunshine Borneo Tours
  Block A, 1st Floor, Abdjul Razak Complex, ☎ *(02) 441791, FAX 441790*

Telephone
The country code for Brunei is 673.

To dial Brunei from the United States punch in the international number (*011*). Then dial the country code (673) then the area code, don't forget to drop the 0 *(BSB area code is 02, Belait is 03, Tutong is 04 and Temburong is 05)*, then dial the six digit number. If you need help ask an international operator to help you.

Tourist Information

Economic Development Board
  Ministry of Finance, Jalan James Pearce 240243
  Open everyday except Sunday and Friday, 7:45 a.m.–12:15 p.m. then 1:30 p.m. til 4:30 p.m.
  As you can tell from the name, this department is not really set up for touristic advice. The hotels can do a better job of explaining the relative merits of BSB's and Brunei's attractions.

Weather/What to Wear

Brunei sits 298 miles north of the equator and is a coastal environment. The only real mountainous area is in the southern part of the Temburong district. The wet season is between November and February. Dress in comfortable clothes in this hot and humid climate. Unless you are invited to the palace, you will not need dressy or smart attire. Clean shirts and long pants are in. Shorts are not. Women should not wear shorts or anything too revealing in respect of Muslim tradition.

FESTIVALS AND HOLIDAYS

Primarily Muslim but Chinese, Hindu and Christian holidays are also observed.

January 1	*New Year's Day.*
January/February	*Chinese New Year celebrations.*
Variable	*Hari Raya Haji. Celebrated by Muslims to commemorate sacrifice of Prophet Abraham.*
Variable	*First day of Hijrah (Muslim New Year).*
Variable	*Maulud (tenth day of New Year).*
February 23	*National Day.*
May 31	*Anniversary of Royal Brunei Malay Regiment.*

FESTIVALS AND HOLIDAYS

July 15	*The sultan's birthday.*
Variable	*First day of Ramadan (fasting month).*
Variable	*Anniversary of Revelation of the Koran.*
Variable	*Hari Raya Aidilfiltri, a month's feast following the end of Ramadan.*
December 25	*Christmas holiday.*

Bandar Seri Begawan

Bandar Seri Begawan

This is a place you can call Bandar, or even BSB. It's the capital of Brunei and irrefutably the cleanest and most modern city on Borneo.

There is a surprising amount to do in such a relatively small area if you like museums. The town is nicely situated on an inlet of Brunei Bay and has a host of cultural stops and some eye-popping buildings.

You won't see a lot of the sights that are commonplace in other Asian cities, namely traffic congestion, garbage, roadside food stalls and beggars. Everything is very tidy in this capital of 80,000 residents.

BSB is split into three areas: the **Old Area**, built in the 1950s; the industrial area called **Gadong**; and the **Seri Complex**, found close to the Sultan's palace.

What to Do in Bandar Seri Begawan

As you would expect, in this closely run Muslim sultanate there is little infrastructure for pure tourism. However the largesse of the Sultan has created a number of very impressive museums and cultural centers. The hours are a little choppy here with closures for lunch and prayer but most attractions are free.

The Sultan's Residence (Istana Nural Iman)

4kms from BSB, best view is from the river at night when illuminated.

This is reputed to be the largest royal residence in the world. Having said that, I do not know who goes around measuring but the floor space is estimated to be 20 hectares! Inside this radiant space shuttle hangar are reputed to be 1780 rooms, 257 toilets, 44 staircases and all the trappings you would expect a monarch with his amount of money to have. All the juicy details are available in James Bartholomew's book: *The Richest Man in the World*. Imagine having to do vacation swaps with the Pentagon or the owners of the Sears Tower. The Vatican, Buckingham Palace and the White House wouldn't even match up for square footage.

We do know that the palace took two years and about $450 million or so to construct. Having eliminated the ability to make a profit by reselling the magnificent edifice, the architect made sure it would last. There are 38 kinds of marble, spectacular throne rooms with solid gold tiles(22kt) and a 4000 seat banquet hall, among other elegant touches.

Maybe when things get light the Sultan will take the lead of Queen Elizabeth and run tours through this amazing place. Having only seen it on TV, I would imagine that you could put in an Imax theater and a "Pirates of Borneo" ride and quadruple the tourist dollars coming into Brunei. I guess the sultan will worry about that when the oil dries up in about 20 years. If you can pass as a local you can tour the palace at the end of Ramadan, the Muslim fast. If you are a tourist you will have to content yourself with salacious magazine articles and speculation.

In any case, you are free to click off pictures and wonder what it would be like to be the world's richest man living in the world's biggest palace in one of the world's smallest most remote countries.

Taman Perangian Tasek

A small park from which the palace can be viewed. Inside is a tiny waterfall, picnic tables and a swimming area.

Istana Nurulizza

24kms from BSB, Not Open

Don't confuse this palace with the Sultan's. This is the home of the Sultan's second wife. It has a throne room to allow the Sultan to do a little regaling away from home. This lavish building was built in 1984 to commemorate Brunei's independence.

Brunei Museum   ★★

Mile 3, Jalan Kota Batu 5kms from BSB
Open weekends, Tuesday to Thursday from 9:30 a.m.–5 p.m., and Fridays 9 a.m.–11:30 a.m., 2:30 p.m.–5 p.m. Closed Mondays. Free

An attractive structure, it was opened by the Sultan and Queen Elizabeth II in 1972. It features views of Brunei River and houses a fine collection of bronzes, Chinese porcelains, Malay kris (inlaid swords), artifacts of Borneo life and antique Brunei brass, for which the sultanate was famous. There is also an art gallery featuring art from the Sultan's private collection. There is a Shell sponsored display on the oil business and a minor display of animals.

Chinese Temple & Market

Jalan Sungai Kianggeh and Jalan Elizabeth. Open to visitors

If you are not going to Kuching or Singapore this might be your best choice for Chinese temples. If you are staying in Brunei it will be your only chance since it is the only Chinese temple in the country. The temple is a riot of colors and is a great photo stop along with market across the way. The market is a great place to visit at night to sample the various taste treats.

Malay Technology Museum

1 km up from the Brunei Museum or walk down the path that connects the two museums.

Open weekends, Monday to Thursday except Tuesday from 9:30 a.m.–5 p.m., and Fridays 9 a.m.–11:30 a.m., 2:30 pm.– 5 p.m. Closed Tuesdays. Free

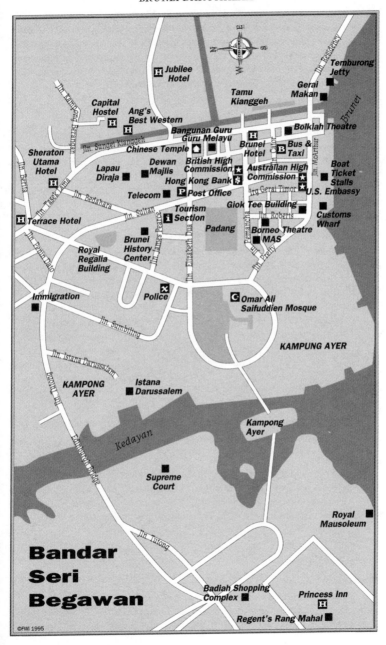

Bandar
Seri
Begawan

©FWI 1995

Jubilee Hotel

Capital Hostel

Ang's Best Western

Tamu Kianggeh

Gerai Makan

Temburong Jetty

Bangunan Guru Guru Melayu

Bolklah Theatre

Chinese Temple

Sheraton Utama Hotel

Brunei Hotel

Bus & Taxi

Boat Ticket Stalls

Lapau Diraja

Dewan Majlis

British High Commission

Australian High Commission

U.S. Embassy

Hong Kong Bank

Telecom

Post Office

Giok Tee Building

Customs Wharf

Terrace Hotel

Tourism Section

Padang

Borneo Theatre

MAS

Royal Regalia Building

Brunei History Center

Immigration

Police

Omar Ali Saifuddien Mosque

KAMPUNG AYER

KAMPONG AYER

Istana Darussalem

Kampong Ayer

Kedayan

Supreme Court

Royal Mausoleum

Badiah Shopping Complex

Princess Inn

Regent's Rang Mahal

Jln. Residency

Brunei

Jln. Kampong Peramuan

Jln. Sungei Kianggeh

Jln. McArthur

Jln. Berita

Jln. Pasar Lama

Jln. Bedahara

Jln. Sultan

Jln. Pemancha

Arg Gerai Timor

Jln. Roberts

Jln. Pretty

Jln. Pemancha

Jln. Elizabeth Dua

Jln. Penin Dua

Jln. Sumbiling

Jln. Istana Darussalam

Edinburgh Bridge

Jln. Tutong

This museum is a must see if you have included the museums in Sabah and Sarawak. There are a variety of intricate models showing how traditional Dayak and Malay houses are built. I shouldn't say models since many of them are full size similar to the cultural center in Sarawak. You can also get a better understanding of the traditional skills of the Malays: silversmithing, boat building. There is also a series of displays showing how the Penan and other indigenous tribes live.

Government & State Buildings   ★

Central BSB, All buildings closed to the public.

An architect would weep with envy at the sight of all the magnificent buildings commissioned to support the bureaucratic functions. You should visit these buildings just because so few people ever will. The Language and Literature Bureau Office with its mosaic mural, the **Royal Ceremonial Hall** (Lapau) and the **Parliament House** (Dewan Majis) are definitely worth having a look at.

Kampung Ayer   ★★

Near and around the Mosque.

This 400-year-old village is the world's largest habitation built over water—a city within the city and home to some 30,000 people. It is a series of 40 connecting villages where people live together in houses on stilts (each with its own TV antennae) and most commute into the more modern metropolis. Reached by small motor launches. A fascinating view of how people have lived for centuries. These folks do not give up luxuries—here most homes have AC, electricity, lighting and all the trappings of land based homes. They like the cooling breezes and social closeness. Poke around the antique shops and the last of Brunei's brass workers. Although there is continual pressure for the residents to move to more modern homes, they continually resist. If you wonder where the high rent district is, just ponder a while on where you would live in a city that has no sewage treatment, upstream or downstream? You also wonder how much fire insurance these folks have. There were major fires in 1981, 1990 and in 1993.

Omar Ali Saifuddin Mosque   ★★★

Open at all times for prayer. Non Muslims may visit between 8 a.m. -noon, 1 p.m.– 3:30 p.m., 4:30 p.m. –5:30 p.m., Saturday to Wednesday, open 4:30 p.m.–5:30 p.m. Fridays.

Focal point of Brunei. Named after the late sultan. Built with imported materials on reclaimed land beside the Brunei River. Exemplifies the fierce tradition of Muslim worship in an elegant atmosphere made possible only by petro dollars. Don't miss the lagoon in which floats a replica of a 16th century *mahligai* (stone boat).

If you would like a bird's eye view of the city take the elevator to the top of the 10 story minaret. The mosque was designed by British architects, built in 1958 at a cost of US$5 million.

Tomb of Sultan Bokiah

Jalan Kota Batu, towards the Brunei Museum 4 cams from BSB. Free

The fifth Sultan of Brunei,Bokiah lived during the golden age of Brunei from 1473 to 1521. A pretty place where they are busy unearthing the site of an ancient fort.

The Royal Regalia Museum

On Jalan Stoney, North of the Mosque in the city center.

Open 8:30 a.m.–5 p.m., Monday to Thursday, 9 a.m.–11:30 a.m., 2:30 p.m.–5 p.m. Friday and Weekends 8:30 a.m.–5 p.m. Free

Formerly the Sir Winston Churchill Memorial Museum, it was reopened in September of 1992 to commemorate the Sultan's 25th year of power. This celebration of the Silver Jubilee and tribute to the reigning monarch might be a bit much for political realists since the displays and constant extolling of the present Sultan's achievements might even make his mother blush.

The **Constitutional Gallery** looks like every school outing nightmare and the **Brunei History Centre** is probably more worthwhile for museum buffs.

Upriver

Upriver is found the lush jungle. It is possible to hire boats for excursions to the longhouse people, the Ibans from Sarawak. Dusun, Muruts, and settled Penan also live in villages upriver from BSB, but don't expect too much exotica. They also enjoy the material prosperity of Brunei.

An Islamic ruler and the benefit of petro dollars created the elegant atmosphere of the Saifudden Mosque.

Downriver

Downriver features some beautiful beaches along the South China Sea coastline. Good swimming while watching the offshore oil rigs. There are few organized tours available, so be creative.

Bandar Seri Begawan Environs

Muara
25km northeast of BSB

Although you'll occasionally find a lot of windsurfers at nearby **Serasa Beach**, the beach itself leaves a lot to be desired. A better bet is the locally popular but accessible **Muara Beach**.

Tutong
48km southwest of BSB

A rich agricultural region with an Agricultural Station. Tasek Merimbun is 27km inland from Tutong. The Sultan's beach home, Pantai Istana, is on Pantai Seri Kenangan.

Belait District

Sungei Liang Forest Reserve
500m up the Labi Road
A 14 hectare forest that has an information center, walking trails and picnic facilities.

Labi
25kms up Labi Road
An agrarian town with mountains of tropical fruits. Try the durian if you dare.

Longhouses
Go to the end of the improved road and follow the track.
There are a number of Iban longhouses on the way to Sarawak. (You sure you want to go this way?). None of these settlements provide any insight into traditional ways.

Seria
65kms southwest of Bandar

Seria is large by Brunei standards; about 25,000 people live in this oil town. It's the second largest "city" in Brunei. Like other Brunei towns, it was built on the familiar grid pattern. Seria is oil city and there is a large Ghurka army post (about 900 at any one time) to make sure nobody disturbs this lucrative enterprise. There's a golf course near here, but unless you're an oilman, forget it. If you are an oilman this is where Shell first hit oil in 1931. You can worship at the Billionth Barrel monument just out of town on the water if you are so inclined. Normal visitors should just keep going.

Kuala Belait
19kms from Seris

Twenty thousand people live in this small port city on the bank of the Belait estuary. There are shops and a central business district but not much else. Kuala Belait is the entry into Sarawak. Clean civilized and containing nothing you traveled this far to see. The only curiosity is the Buccaneer Steakhouse. Unusual for its dull Midwestern menu in the middle of rice and chicken country.

There are two clean hotels in town and you can change your money before heading into Sarawak. Buses leave about every two hours between 7:30 a.m. to 3:30 p.m. from the bus station. The bus fare includes the ferry and bus you need to get to Miri in Sarawak.

Where to Stay in Kuala Belait

Sea-View   **B$130–280**   ★

Lot 3678 Km 2.6 Jalan Maulana ☎ *(03) 332651, FAX 332654*
A very comfy hotel with 86 units built in 1973 but updated in 1982. The 28 apartments and supermarket/department store and car rental office make it popular with folks working the oil patch. Not all rooms are air-conditioned. 2kms out of town.

Sentosa Hotel   **B$130–155**

92-3 Jalan McKerron ☎ *(03) 334341, FAX 331120*
More expensive, six years older than the Seaview but at the same rates there is little to recommend it. The 37 rooms are air-conditioned and come with phone and TV. Its location by the bus station ensures that it's full of tired folks who didn't make the last bus.

Government Resthouse   **B$12**

On the beach, 500m from the bus station along Jalan McKerron ☎ *(03) 334288*
Not the usual place for folks to stay but a lot cheaper. If they have extra rooms they will give you one.

Temburong District

This is the 1288 sq km mountainous region of Brunei, accessible only by plane or longboat. The remote, thinly populated region is separated from the rest of Brunei by Sarawak's Limbang area, part of Brooke's 1884 grab.

If you continue up the Temburong River, you'll come upon Batang Duri. Also check out the following places of interest.

Bangar

48km Southeast of BSB by boat, 15 kms upriver from Brunei Bay
The district center is called Bangar; it's a sleepy little town with barely a thousand residents. Longhouses can be found here. Typical for Brunei, expensive cars and television antennas make this an incongruous setting.

Kuala Belalong Forestry Center   ★★

In the Batu Apoi Forest Reserve, on the Belalong River upstream from the Temburong River. Not open to the public without prior permisison from the University of Brunei.
This was the site of an important study of Borneo's rainforest conducted by The University of Brunei and The Royal Geographicial Society in London. The two year study completed in 1992 left a greater understanding of this pristine environment. There is a central Field Studies Center for schoolchildren and scientists. Around the center are walking trails and various ongoing studies. Visitors must get permission and make bookings through Biology Department of the Univeriity of Brunei

☎ *(02) 427001.* Once your visit is booked the center is reached by longboat from Batang Duri or with an escorted tour from BSB.

Peradayan Forest Reserve
(15kms from Bangar by boat)
If you don't have the time to visit Kuala Belalong but want to see the pristine forests, there is a park open to the pubic a short day trip from BSB just up the river from Bangar. Batu Patoi is a one hour walk from the Park entrance. The trail is steep in parts but the scenery is worth it. If you keep going you can then hike three hours along the marked trail to Bukit Peradayan. This trail comes back into the road about 12kms from Bangar right near the Labu 5km marker.

What do you mean rain forest, Daddy?

Rainforest is where annual rainfall exceeds 2000mm (or 80 inches) per year and where there is no dry season or wide climatic variations. Four million square miles of rainforest are found mainly along the equator. Tropical rainforests are found in South & Central America, Central Africa, India, Southeast Asia and various islands like Madagascar and Sri Lanka. But there are also temperate rainforests in places like British Columbia, Washington and New Zealand. In Borneo there is a Northeast Monsoon between December and March where the winds blow in a westerly and southerly direction in the north of Borneo, and then southerly and easterly below the equator in Kalimantan. The heavier Southwest Monsoon occurs between June and September when the wind direction reverses. In Sabah and Sarawak the Northeast monsoons are heralded by winds from the ocean and vice versa in Kalimantan. Continual rain, humidity and heat create the massive, slow-growing trees and lush canopy.

In equatorial Borneo the length of the day varies only one half of one hour with July having the longest day and December the shortest, and once again the reverse in southern cities of Kalimantan. The longest there may be a lack of rain would be one to two weeks in March, July or August with the heaviest rains in September through November. Temperature and humidity are affected more by altitude. The higher you go, the more it rains and the the cooler it gets. In lowland forests relative humidity is higher at night usually at the saturation level with clear days reducing the humidity. Winds are affected by thermal cooling and can reverse from night to day. The lack of strong winds, constant rainfall and temperatures create an ideal environment for plant growth. However due to the heavy rainfall the soils tend to leach their nutrients rapidly creating barren forest floors. The high level of leaf litter and detrius also support a large ephiphytic population. (Nonparasitic plants that exist on other plants.) The rainforests are called the lungs of the world for their ability to cleanse the air and return water into the atmosphere by evapotranspiration. Evapotranspiration caused by solar energy is about 1350mm in lowland Southeast Asian rainforests compared to average rainfalls of 2300mm. This means 650mm is lost to runoff or into the soil. The current triple canopy lowland dipterocarp forests are the most mature and stable of the forests. It takes 120 - 300 years to regrow them although there is no guarantee that the same species or mix would reoccur.

Where to Stay in Brunei

Sheraton Utama Hotel
B$235–495 ★★★★

Jalan Tasek, P.O Box 2203, ☎ *(02) 244272, FAX 221579.*
The Sheraton is the top hotel in BSB with rates that would make a New Yorker pause. Its 154 rooms are exactly as you would expect: CNN, well appointed, nice views, but look in the minibar and, ah yes, you are in Brunei. No liquor. Located opposite Parliament buildings, Churchill Memorial and Park. Transportation arranged from airport, just four miles away. There is a nice pool and rooms for non smokers. Try the Heritage continental restaurant if you are homesick for Western cooking.

Brunei Hotel
B$160–240 ★★

95 Jalan Pemancha, ☎ *(02) 242372, FAX 226196*
Older (1962) four story hotel with 73 simple rooms. Completely renovated in 1990. Restaurant/coffee shop with Western and Chinese dishes.

Jubilee Hotel
B$125–450

Jalan Kampong Kianggah, ☎ *(02) 228070, FAX 228080.*
Centrally located with supermarket and restaurant.

Riverview Hotel
B$110–230 ★★★

1 Jalan Gadang, ☎ *(02) 238238, FAX 236688.*
A spanking brand new hotel just to the north of town close to the airport.

Terrace Hotel
B$98–328

Jalan Tasek Lama, P.O Box 49, ☎ *(02) 2243554, FAX 227302*
An older hotel (1968) out of the city center but they will run you into town on their shuttle. A good budget alternative.

Ang's Best Western Hotel
B$75–100

Jalan Tasek Lama, ☎ *(02) 243553, FAX 23702.*
84 rooms. Simple but comfortable air-conditioned rooms. Friendly service. Restaurant serving Chinese and Western specialties. Bar, swimming pool, hairdresser/barber, meeting room.

Capital Hotel
B$70–138

7 Simpang 2, Jalan Kg Berangan (beyond the youth hostel), ☎ *(02) 223561, FAX 228789.*
Older 1968 hotel slightly out of town. Probably the lowest price place in BSB other than the government resthouse, all the usuals (AC, TV, refrigerator and safe).

Government Rest House
B$on application

Jalan Cator, ☎ *(02)223571.*
Not available for tourists unless you have received prior permission from the Municipal Chairman, Bandar Seri Begawan 2031 at least one week before arriving.

Sampling Local Fare in Brunei

Don't expect much entertainment in BSB, other than a friendly chat with other tourists at the Sheraton or the Royal Brunei Yacht Club—if you happen to know a member. And forget drinking. As this is a strict Muslim country, liquor is served only at designated places and strictly to tourists. The oilfield set have their own private clubs and entertainment, but these are hardly for the casual visitor.

There is plenty of good and interesting food in Brunei, including that succulent beef from Australia! Local dishes run the gamut from Malay curries and rice to Chinese noodles, excellent steaks and local seafood. There are also open-air stalls along the Brunei River opposite Kampong Ayer, which offer a tantalizing array of *satay* sticks, noodles and such.

Aside from the coffee shop, bar and Heritage continental restaurant at the Sheraton, visitors should inquire of the hotel concierge about good local places to try. There are several, like the **Chayo Phaya** in Klasse Department Store (Thai Muslim dishes) and the **Rasa Sayang** for reasonable Chinese (next to the Chinese Temple).

If you plan to spend a day at one of the lovely beaches, a short drive from BSB, be sure to take along your own food and drink. The Sheraton can pack a lunch and it also has a nice gourmet shop for snack items. (Be sure to include sunscreen and some insect repellent as well, for obvious reasons.)

There are also several private sporting clubs that serve meals, some of which welcome visitors by invitation. They are the **Brunei Tennis Club**, the **Royal Brunei Yacht Club** and the **Pantai Mentiri Golf Club**—all located in the environs of Bandar Seri Begawan. Brunei Shell Petroleum has two clubs in Seria—the **Panaga Club** and the **Shell Recreation Club**—that extend a welcome to visitors who have an introduction. Membership in the posh Jerudong Park Polo Club is by invitation only. Polo happens to be a passion of this sultan.

Shopping in Brunei

Locally made handicrafts include **brass cannons** and ornamental **kris** (the Malay knife)—and **rattan furniture** is also tempting if you can figure out how to get it home! Muslims are terrific gold dealers and **24-carat jewelry** is a good buy here, especially in gold bangles. Dealers are honest, as they sell it by weight according to the world market price.

Seri complex

The main shopping area is in BSB with its department stores, supermarkets and boutiques, which accept all major credit cards.

Brunei Arts and Handicrafts Training Centre

1 km north of BSB on Jalan Residency along the river
Open Monday–Thursday and Saturday 8 a.m.–12:15 p.m., 1:30 p.m.–2:30 p.m., Friday and Saturday 8 a.m.–noon, 2 p.m.–5 p.m.

An ideal place to see and buy handicrafts being made. You can browse through weaving, silver and bronze work, kris and kain songket (handwoven cloth) or just watch.

The Tamu Kianggeh Open-Air market

On the bank of the Kianggeh River, open daily from morning to late evening.
Another and cheaper source for arts and handicrafts.

Bahasa Malay Helper

Don't know your sungai from your bukit? Use this handy cheat sheet to figure out your ulu from your hilir.

Adat	custom or traditional law
Air	water
Air terjun	waterfall
bandar	port
batang	main branch of a river
batu	stone or hill
bukit	hill
genting	mountain pass
gua	cave
gunung	mountain
hilir	downriver or lower reaches
istana	palace
jalan	road
kali	river
kampung	village
kangkar	Chinese village
kota	fort
kuala	mouth of a river or where a tributary meets the river
labuan	port
laut	sea
masjid	mosque
negeri	state
orang	man
padang	open area
pantai	beach

pasar	market
pekan	market place
penghulu	chief or leader
pulau	island
selat	strait
sungai	river
tamu	market
tasik	lake
teluk	bay
ulu	upriver
ujung	cape

Into Indonesia

The Hard Way

Hard, face first and fast

It was now time to head into the unknown through the forbidden. I was getting bored and hungering for a little adrenaline. Although the army posts and remote jungle camps along the border were empty, there was still tension between Indonesia and Malaysia. The *Konfrontasi* between 1963 and 1966 had resulted in many armed clashes between the Indonesian Army and the British and Australian SAS. In 1963 Indonesia tried to destabilize Sabah and Sarawak and prevent them from joining the new federation of Malaysia. Indonesian President Sukarno also supported Chinese communist groups within Sarawak, Brunei and Singapore. Sabah and Sarawak turned to Britain, who sent in a large but mostly covert force of commandos and ghurkas to provide a strong deterrent to Indonesia's predatory goals.

Although the people who live here have little regard for political borders, I am curious as to why Indonesia continues to rigidly maintain its mountainous border with Malaysia. Rather than simply walk along the many migratory paths established by young men seeking work in the timber camps, I look for something spectacular and somewhat symbolic of this artificial line that separates the same peoples.

The end of our journey will be in "the Heart of Borneo," an area chosen as much for its total lack of definition on most maps, as for its very abused term in most books about the region. The central highlands of Borneo have yet to be completely mapped by satellite due to its continual cloud cover. Our maps simply show white areas with vague terms about undefined forest cover.

Borneo has many centers. The one I have selected is the center from which the great migration of the Kayan and Kenyah peoples began, the Apo Kayan. Nestled between Sarawak, Brunei and Kalimantan, the Apo Kayan is a remote area about 2000 feet in altitude, now thinly populated by remaining Kenyahs and the last of the original Kayan.

The Kenyah are the second oldest migratory tribe in Borneo. The Kenyah are known for their rigid social structures, complicated spiritual beliefs and their artistic skills. Their longhouses are decorated with the elegant symbols of life, fertility and death. They are also known for their headhunting, though their reputation for bloodthirstiness was eclipsed by the Iban. The Kenyah and Kayan are among the few aristocratic races of Borneo: ancient cultures with well developed cultures, beliefs and history.

As with most explorers, we are not content with doubling back and simply buying an airline ticket from Kota Kinabalu to Balikpapan, a detour of over a thousand miles. We, like old Hollywood stuntmen, want to go hard, face first and fast. I had been told that there is a wild river that cuts through the border between Sabah and Sarawak. If you carefully examine a detailed map you will see the one blue thread that defies the topography. There is one problem. Well, actually two. Although there are specific border crossings open to foreigners here, the border is still technically closed to all surface travel after 30 years. Earlier I had worked with a group of Malaysians who wanted to set up an expedition between the two countries and the answer had always been a simple "no."

"Beyond the limits of reliable information"

We survey the map carefully for a route. South of the Sabah border is a white featureless area with polite excuses like "RELIEF DATA INCOMPLETE," "GENERALLY FOREST COVERED" and "BEYOND THE LIMITS OF RELIABLE INFORMATION" replacing the usually accurate topographic data. There is a wrinkled landscape free from villages, roads, any other marks of civilization. There are a number of mountains that climb to 400 feet high in the area but none with names. A thin blue line captures our attention. There it is, the only river that cuts southward through the watershed from Sabah to Kalimantan—the Pensiangan River. Whether we can make it all the way through is a big question. We can find no one who has ever gone down this river. Even old SAS records from the war reveal information on short forays but never a complete penetration in the swamps below. We will be going blind. No boat, no equipment, no visa, no map worth a damn. We will simply talk our way down and out to one of the big cities on the coast. From there we will figure out how to get back into the remote highlands of the Apo Kayan. If we are arrested it will be very difficult to send us back. We all agree to give it a shot.

Our planning consists of bad maps, hearsay and a faith in luck.

There is another minor concern, we can find no one who has ever gone down the entire length of the river. Many people have never come back but no one has gone all the way down and back.

Since we will be running fast rivers and must be able to travel by any means, our expedition has to travel fast and light. The people picked to accompany me on this expedition number only two. Coskun Aral, a Turk from France; Jon Rees, a Brit from Malaysia and I (a Canadian from America) round out our multinational group. Indonesia will have its borders penetrated by six different nations at once. I can imagine the confusion if we are caught. C'est l'aventure!

First, we trim down to just our essential equipment. Just one pair of clothes with a spare shirt. No food, no tent, just the survival basics. Everything that is not necessary will be left behind. We will drive a four wheel drive Toyota along to Sapulut, as far as the roads will take us. Then, we will find a boat and boatmen crazy or hungry enough to take us south through the mountains and into the flat swamps of East Kalimantan. There will be a lot of "ifs" in this expedition. We get rough instructions on where we can find the river. We drive off into the mazelike logging roads of Sabah with a new sense of purpose. We will end up, after many stops and starts, tracing a little-used track that winds along the precipitous edge of a river gorge. Then the road will end and our adventure will begin.

Knowing that you are passing through terrain that you will only see once always makes journeys more interesting. As we jolt and bump our way along crude trails we gain in altitude beyond the flat, and the hazy landscape begins to fold and jut up like blue cardboard cutouts.

It is not wise to tailgate logging trucks.

We weave and dodge through a steady stream of logging trucks as we enter a boisterous logging town. Stopping for our last restaurant meal, we sit high on a wooden balcony and watch the long plumes of dust follow the trucks on their way down through the town and on to the sawmills. This is the wild west, dusty one road towns made out of hastily thrown together wooden buildings. Chinese shopkeepers making their fortunes on bad food, cheap women, flea infested beds and greed. The Yukon, Western Australia and Texas all have had towns like this at one time or another.

We stop one last time to view civilization from the top of the steep hill that runs into town. At the top of the ridge the drivers stop their groaning trucks to test the tire pressure by bouncing a rock off the tires. The drivers are dark, slight and eager to guide us upwards towards Sapulut as they begin their wild roller-coaster ride into mills in town and then home.

The blue cardboard cutouts of the distant mountains soon take on greener, more dramatic shapes. Hills loom above us as cleared forest gives way to secondary forest, and then to the cool green of primary jungle. We twist and turn, slipping on the muddy road, driving gingerly over long abandoned log bridges and swerving to avoid the washouts and potholes. The cool, wet air rolls down the hills and fills the dusk air with rich oxygen. Sensing that we have left the hot and ravaged jungle behind, we come to the end of the road. There is only the sound of the river and jungle. The Sungai Pensiangan runs wide and smooth here and in the small village we find a few boats and an odd assortment of battered motors stashed under a house. Surprised, but also pleased by the sudden appearance of three *orang putis,* the owner of the boats senses that he is about to negotiate a deal that is somewhat one sided. The lack of demand for boats has also reduced the number of boat owners to one. For a price, the owner can arrange two boats and three boatmen. (He obviously prefers to delegate this trip, preferring to live long enough to enjoy his money) He explains that the price will be steep because this trip should not be done and the river is dangerous. We get the idea that we would be better off buying his boats since he doesn't even address the problem of a return trip. Our final offer overcomes his concern for the boatmen's well being and a deal is struck. Here, it is called the Pensiangan and the name will change into the Sembakung River once we enter Indonesia. Once inside Indonesia we can follow the winding Sembakung to the ocean, or we can take a short trip by land over to the larger Sungai Sesaiap, then down to the Selatan, and finally to the oil port of Tarakan.

The hills of Sabah slowly rise into the mountains beyond.

The end of the road

Coskun and I spend the night in Kampung Salong while Jon finds someone in Sapulut to drive our truck back. The sound of babies crying, roosters crowing, people spitting and the constant laughter and chatter creates a relaxing rhythm. The villagers sit and stare at us with an impassive curiosity. It is very pleasant in the countryside. There is lush greenery everywhere and the pace of life is slow. The air is 10 degrees cooler and the sound the rapids create reminds us of tomorrow's venture.

We spend the evening in the local store/restaurant having beers and cigarettes (Marlboro, the people remind me). Coskun cooks for the owner. People come down from the hills just to sit and stare at the two curiosities. Children are taken away from their normal play and stare for minutes. When we explain that we are going to Kalimantan by boat their brows knit for a moment. "Kalimantan?" they ask puzzled. "This is the hard way."

We spend the night in a community building. Every movement sways the building on its delicate stilts. The sounds of talking and laughing softly into the early hours is only occasionally broken by an old woman spitting out the window.

In Borneo, man's best friend is his rooster.

The next morning is cool and fresh. The roosters of our village awake long before dawn and a crowing competition begins with their counterparts across the river. We go down to the local store for breakfast. They have a modest collection of goods neatly stacked in small pyramids. A small mayfly larva crawls up from the grass and across the floor. A puppy sniffs and knocks it along with its nose, never quite able to pick it up. An adult dog walks over, sniffs it and decides that it is not edible. Reading a well-thumbed copy of the *Borneo Mail*, we find there has been a second pirate attack just off the island where we photographed the Sea Bajau a few days ago. People make their way to the river to defecate, wash and brush their teeth. Our boatmen arrive and they sit patiently waiting for us to finish our breakfast and coffee. I ask how long the trip will take. One boatman shrugs his shoulders. His partner says someone told him two days, depending on the river. I add, "Or if we get arrested." He smiles, but does not reply.

The entire population of the tiny *kampung* comes to help us load the boats. I hand out whatever goods I can as tokens of our brief, but pleasant stay. They stand shyly holding our gifts in both hands like ceremonial symbols. As they leave, one small boy says, "Good-bye, Mr. Robert. Sweet traveling."

Into the unknown

On June 25, we leave Salong at 8:00 a.m. to begin our trip downriver. Seeing the size of his passengers and speed of the river, our boatman stops to change to a more powerful outboard down the river. About a dozen people have walked in from the villages and are waiting here for boats that will take them upriver to Sabah. It is a wilderness bus stop, of sorts. There is no scheduled boat, just the hopes that there will be room on a passing boat. No one is going in our direction.

Our boatman returns with a 25 horsepower motor. He ties down the motor and then adds a length of strong rope. He says there is a very strong river ahead. He hopes it is enough. This gave us an inkling of what lay ahead. I have a strange feeling but I cannot understand why.

Traveling down the river we enjoy the stark beauty of the area. The shores of the river are naked rock. There are no signs of human habitation after the "bus stop." Soon we come across a remote army outpost on a hill overlooking the river. This is Sabah immigration. We climb up to find an official. We have to wake him. He sleepily puts his hat on and wonders what we want. He says we are the first white people he has ever seen cross the border here. Far from being suspicious, he finds it an opportune moment to practice his passport stamping. He spends an inordinate amount of time looking at each of our passports, reading the stamps from the different countries and giggling as he compares our current appearance to our passport photos. He reads the name of each country on the cover of the passport carefully. After spending another considerable amount of time searching to find the proper stamps and ink pad, we officiate our crossing with handshakes and gifts. I don't think I can recall when someone has been so happy to see us leave.

Since we are going through a military zone, we must check with the military police next door. Same routine, same comments, all except why. This time there is less levity but still genuine interest in making sure the proper documentation is filled out. We can't help but notice that as the officer fills out all the paperwork: name, age, country of origin in a careful, meticulous hand, there are no other names in the large ledger. We sit politely as each person fills out enough personal information to apply for a mortgage. Baking under his tin roof there is a wide-carriage, Remington typewriter used for filling out military paperwork and his beret is hung neatly above his well-maintained jungle boots. A faded map on the wall clearly delineates the territory to be patrolled. Since we are on the edge of his area and leaving, I assume that we are of no interest to him. Once again after all the paperwork is filled out we shake hands and he wishes us well.

Back on the river we enter the unknown. This area was once hotly contested at one time. Now there is nothing. We have a ways to go before we even leave no man's land and see our first Indonesian outpost. The river is deserted. I now know why I have felt so strange since we left the village this morning. Having canoed and run rivers since I was ten, I am used to rivers becoming tamer and wider as you travel downriver. Here we were travelling miles downriver and the banks were climbing higher and higher, the water was becoming darker, deeper and more powerful. The more we travelled downriver, the faster the river ran. Looking down the river, it gave the impression that we were climbing. But, one look at the black water scouring and sucking the sheer rock sides told me otherwise.

Oh boy, just like Raging Waters!

Screaming white water

We are in Indonesia and are officially criminals. The first people we see are nomadic Penan hunting along the rocky banks of the river. As soon as they see us they dart into the bushes, pausing briefly before disappearing into the jungle. Maybe they mistake us for military with our khaki shirts and sunglasses. It is obvious we should not be here. Another group of hunters do a double-take when they see three white people in two boats coming from the wrong direction. We wave and pass them rapidly since the current is quite fast. They do not move a muscle until we are well out of sight.

We come across a Dayak family on the river a few kilometers further. Their boats are simple, unpainted wood but with an elegant arching bow. They too are quite surprised to see white people traveling on the river. A Brahminy kite carrying a silver fish flaps along the river and into the jungle. The fast water is filled with small and urgent rapids. Not dangerous, just shuddering reminders of the water's speed and power. The rapids grow in size, length and volume as we start to drop in altitude. Although we have absolute confidence in our boatmen, we have no confidence in our boats. There are two ways of appreciating boats. One is to assume that native engineering and supple natural material have created an elegant and simple solution to shooting these deadly rapids. The other theory is that we are large 200 lb. men with too much equipment sitting in three pieces of crude, hand shaved wood planks. This continually becomes the more accepted theory. Our canoe is simply one, 1/2 board forming the bottom and two, 10 foot by one foot boards forming the sides. The boards are created from split logs, hand shaved, nailed, roped, tied and glued together to form a temporarily buoyant device. I say temporary because the concept of being waterproof creates unnecessary engineering. This problem is taken care of by the steersman incessantly bailing with a tin plate.

The only catch is when the steersman is occupied with navigating three to eight foot bow waves he tends to forget about his tin plate. That's where we come in. When the tin plate floats around the bottom of the canoe, one of us grabs it and tries to put more water outside of the boat than is inside. Any physics teacher or boatman will tell you that the real reason for the passengers bailing is to distract them from the hopelessness of defeating the Titanic-sized waves and screaming whitewater hell around them.

Going down one set of rapids our boatman decides to have some fun. Dropping into the thundering white water, our steersman guns the engine and shoots the boat directly towards the rocks on our left, the other bowmen jump up in fright, stare open-mouthed at the stern and point in the opposite direction. The look of fear on their faces is unmistakable. The steersman laughs as the boat just scrapes through a passage they had not seen. The bowmen return sheepishly to their vigil while the steersman keeps laughing.

The fun part just before we stopped taking pictures and started bailing.

Something Dark and Evil Awaits

By now you can appreciate that the Sembakung River is a series of ever-deeper, ever-faster moving waters interspersed by severe drops through rocks and ledges. The calm areas are filled with deep violent currents and whirlpools upwelling from unseen obstructions. We are careful to stay away from endless vortexes that would trap us and enslave our leaflike canoe.

The tempo and different moods of the river seem to take on a definable rhythm—almost symphonic in structure. There is a prelude building up to an almost choral sounding din. Then with little warning, there is the *prestissimo* of the white water and echoing canyons followed by the sombre *adagio* between rapids like the slow parts of a symphony introduced by a *ritardando*. The rapids are *fortissimo* complete with the crashing of boat against wave. After each rapid there is calm and silence, a *largo* of calmness and deepness. Visually each new crescendo is accompanied by dead silence of the black waters and a fine sparkling white line up ahead as we are propelled *accelerando* in the white *allegro assai*. As the noise and the bright white light from the rapids builds, small flecks of water fly up from the rapids below, then like a crash of cymbals, we are tossed like a javelin into the maelstrom. Soon the rapids become too serious to wax poetic. We are in big trouble.

From this point there is no turning back.

Each set of rapids is larger than the previous. Unable to get a firm hold on our vessel, the rapids throw us forward and smack us down, sometimes pulling back to see if we will tumble off the front. Angry at the inability to have us, the river surges up from below and with a sharp kick sends us into the chute—hoping to smack us against rocks and into the cold water. But the boat threads its way along the hard back of the water and up and over the raging storm. Finally, bored and spent, our craft is ejected into the eddying pools below; bent, bedraggled and bruised.

There are a couple of rapids that even I would not choose to be poetic about. These rapids are like black ice or tornadoes. They are not dangerous —they are treacherous. Like most good river travelers, or even like most river runners who are still alive, we rightly assume that all will be lost in these rapids and plan accordingly.

Our boatman pulls to one side, walks along the bank of the river to survey the rapids, then the men converse quietly among themselves as they plan how best to maneuver the boiling water. During the most severe drops and rapids, our boatman has us portage the equipment to the base of the run while he grimly fights his way past waves that tower over his head.

Deep into Indonesia now, we are going through steep canyons with lush overhanging greenery. I can't help but think that this would be a perfect place for an ambush. Sedimentary rocks point straight up in the river, making sawtooth ridges like the spine of a dragon. The dark water bends and curls around sensuous boulders the size and color of elephants sculpted like Henry Moore's. There is something dark and evil ahead.

Has anybody seen Elvis?

At the bend in the river we stop below a simple wooden house. It is our first contact with inhabitants. A row of faces peers down at us from the slit-like window. An older man in a green Indonesian army T-shirt waddles down to chat with us amicably and asks us to write our names in a tattered old notebook. We don't quite know whether we are going through customs or just making friends. I very carefully print, "Elvis Presley, Memphis, Tennessee." Jon and Coskun write in their equally silly *nom de guerres* in a hasty scribble. I can imagine what the Indonesian APB on us will sound like : "The government is on the lookout for Elvis Presley, Topogigo and Captain Biggles in the jungles of Borneo."

Amused with ourselves we forget the ominous warnings of the river behind us. As we turn the corner, all hell breaks loose. The river changes from its normal rhythm of smooth black swells with occasional rapids, to an ocean of nonstop, angry, churning white caps with ridge-back waves. The boulders are larger, the water faster and the sides of the canyon steeper. We can plainly see the river dropping at an alarming angle. We are not going downriver, we are falling downhill. There is no going back.

Hurtling through the rock canyon we pick up speed. Decisions have to be made at lightning speed and there can be no mistakes. Once we are in the rapid's grip, all we can do is trust the skills of the boatman. He does not trust us with paddles since we are only two inches from flooding the tiny canoe. If two of us paddle at the wrong time, we will sink like a rock. As usual we get to bail. Cautiously, with short jerky motions of the throttle, the steersman maneuvers into position then, twisting the throttle, we descend into the maelstrom. The power of the thundering water can be felt as it squeezes, bends, twists and bucks every board in the frail craft. The rapids grab us, slam us through and then spit us out like a watermelon seed. Each time we are shot into the churning water below we manage to exit the rapids in one piece. At one point our boat was four feet in the air before it slammed down, shuddering with the force. We are too exhilarated to be scared.Our bailing takes on red line frenzy as a continuous stream of water exits out the boat but never really lowers the water inside.

Somehow we survive. Since we do not know the name of this rapid or even where we are, we decide to name this rapid Cereberus after the two headed dog that guarded the gates to hell.

During calm spots I use my Swiss army knife to clean the contacts on the 15 horsepower Suzuki motor, which is starting to sputter and stall at increasingly critical moments.

We are in virgin jungle now, gliding by large black rocks polished by the fast water. The deep clear water eddies and swirls as currents are being pushed up from far below. Creepers hang down the sides. Our vision is only forward as each rapid pulls us further into Kalimantan. Two big hornbills fly overhead in the direction we are heading. A good omen.

In the deltas of Kalimantan

Hot and slow

After descending down from the mountains, the thrill of the river gives way to monotony. The river, content that we have earned the right to pass but eager to keep us, begins to relax, widens and begins to take long meandering turns. Where previously our view was blocked by the steep canyons on either side, we can now see hills that rise up in the background. The calmness and richness of the river also begins to bring out a menagerie of wildlife. Fish eagles, hornbills and butterflies appear to inspect us and then continue on with their business. The drone of the motor and the cool breeze carrying the smell of mangoes and durian lulls us to sleep. A loud splash from the edge of the river tells us there are monitor lizards here. The look in our boatman's eyes tells us that means dinner in his book.

There is evidence of violent erosion and constant flooding of the river. The river leaves its evidence here in the calmer waters. The sides of the river are made of alternating one-foot-thick bands of dark and light silt which creates an unnatural man-made appearance similar to the cathedral in Orvieto. In some areas there are 20 foot deposits of silt that are sliced through by small waterfalls that cut down to the rock.

We pass Penan hunters and fishermen with their blowpipes, spears and fishing poles. This means that we are now getting closer to habitation. They still stare at us, never taking their eyes off us. We are in the outermost reaches of their world. To see someone come from further upstream is truly a novelty. We wave and they pause for a few seconds before politely waving back.

The mood is languorous. The coolness of the mountains gives way to the close heat of the lowlands. Our clothes begin to dry in the sun and our skin begins to turn reddish brown. Baking in our little wooden casserole dish, we doze off to the vibration of the outboard motors.

Our first sign of civilization is an incongruous brightly-painted white and blue church with an oversized cross. A polite distance away sits a dull, official-looking building with an equally oversized red and white flag: Indonesia. These two painted buildings surrounded by casual squalor tell us that this must be an official border town of sorts.

It is now time to face the music since we have no intention of being picked off as we cruise down the river. We decide to take the issue of our arrival face to face.

Our first contact with Indonesians

Strangers in a strange land

As the entire population peers at us from the village, we walk up to register officially at Labang, the Indonesian border station. We have no idea what our reception will be like—a quick gift and an entry stamp or a few weeks in jail. Luckily, we never find out because no one is there. It appears the man has gone off hunting. We are sure that the men upstream wearing army green T-shirts who had us write down our names have radioed our presence by now. We know there will be a confrontation with a lot of questions and suspicions once we are discovered. We have a pow-wow and agree that if there is a problem here, it would be too easy to send us back since our method of travel is obvious and available. If we press on further downstream, we would be closer to Tarakan, a diplomatic solution and we would be closer to our final destination, the Apo Kayan.

More importantly, the thundering river is still fresh in our minds. We could imagine going down, but going up would be a whole different proposition.

Pressing on, we officially discard our quasi-lost status and officially begin our tour of Indonesia. There is a marked difference between the stolid people and cultures of Sabah and the more exotic, sensual appeal of Kalimantan. The construction of the boats, houses and people of Indonesia are more delicate with a pronounced artistic flair. We make good time on the calm river. We pull into Mensalong just as the sun is setting. As we pull up to the shore it is time for the locals' ablutions along the river. The Indonesians' twice daily trip to the riverbank is twofold as we find out. It seems that one half of the people are bathing and brushing their teeth in the brown water, the other half is defecating off the crudely constructed jetties. We would get used to this sight as we traveled through Indonesia, but the fact that every second person was ingesting what every other person was passing was a still a little unsettling.

Our descent from the pristine jungles into the squalor and filth of our first major town is an unpleasant welcome to Indonesia. We step gingerly through the water to unload our boat. In the dusk we try to get our bearings. It seems we have arrived at the closest thing to an inhabited junkyard. The village is one long street strewn with trash, stray dogs and abandoned vehicles. The only two buildings of note, or at least with light, are Chinese-owned stores. There is a handful of goods in each store and the bare light-bulb hanging in the center of the room draws us in like moths.

We inquire at one of the stores about rooms for the evening. By coincidence the ever-smiling Chinese shopkeeper does have rooms upstairs; he just needs a few minutes. On command the family drags up mattresses, furniture and sheets, and the empty upstairs becomes a deluxe hotel. We take note of our newly furnished surroundings: bare flyspecked bulbs, grubby wallpaper dangling from the ceilings and walls, the luxury of worn out linoleum and even a pile of mewling newborn kittens in the halls. Tired, wet and hungry, it is definitely five star.

A souvenir or a bad dream

After a generous and spicy dinner we decide to take a walk through the village at night. This is a ramshackle neighborhood with no electricity. Only the two Chinese stores have tiny generators to run their televisions. That means the Chinese get to watch the call to prayer on TV while the mosque down the road calls the people to prayer in real time. The other houses have no doors, no screens, no windows. The people squat on the floor by the dim orange light of oil lamps. Their simple unpainted walls are decorated with posters of politicians, rock stars and cigarette ads.

Visiting the other store with its equally meager supplies, we chat with the family, asking how to get to the next village. When we buy a pack of Winstons, we hand out cigarettes to everyone. All the people take a cigarette except one dour-faced person who enters the store and stares intently at us. He is introduced to us by the nervous shopkeeper as the Chief of Police.

A most urgent request

The police chief politely refuses our offer of a cigarette and adopts an I-don't-believe-my-fucking-eyes look. We say our good-byes and exit backwards like scalded cats. We figure it won't be long before word gets around. Our boatmen have disappeared probably to the local whorehouse, so we cannot warn them.

It does take a little longer than we guessed, about three hours. After all this is Indonesia. That night at about midnight we receive a knock on our door with, "a most urgent request to report to immigration please." We tell our polite envoy that we are not going anywhere and that we will see him in the morning. To stop his protestations, we ask him where he thinks we will go in the next few hours. Lacking a quick answer, the policeman wanders back into the darkness muttering about crazy "orang putis."

The next morning police and immigration officials are sitting on the front porch of the store waiting for us to get up. We are amazed at their politeness. They even let us have breakfast before they arrest us. We take a pickup truck taxi and go to the immigration headquarters. For such a one horse town there is quite a large military/police complex. We find our three boatmen sitting glumly in the simple waiting area. They have been there a while longer than we have, probably all night. They manage a half-hearted smile as we go in to talk with the crisp military officer in charge. He suggests that this is a most perplexing problem. He explains to us that we are not supposed to be here and most definitely, we are not supposed to get here from Sabah. He asks why we didn't come from Tarakan. We reply, "because we are going to Tarakan." The officer is very polite but obviously does not quite know what to do. Not understanding why he is perplexed we think that maybe this is an overture for a financial settlement.

I ask politely if there is a charge for processing a visa from this area. The officer looks at me with an, "are you crazy" look, and says, "No, this is much too serious." To prove his point he brings out a voluminous sheaf of papers about an inch thick that explains in great detail why no one shall travel down the Pensiangan/Sembakung River, cross at the border post, or be admitted into the country by any landborne or waterborne means. After lengthy examination we find that this is not a minor law but one that goes into great detail. We can only wonder what the punishment is.

He takes our passports and confers with another official. This official has neither the politeness nor concern the officer has. He takes one look at us over the officer's shoulder and waves his hand in the direction of Sabah. "Get rid of them" is written all over his face. His biggest concern is the amount of paperwork required just to describe our transgression. Our officer returns saying he has a problem. This is his last day on the post and the person he was just talking with is the new commander. The new commander wants us sent back; no ifs, ands, or buts. He would be lenient but he is not officially in charge.

"He thinks you are crazy to come down that river." Unfortunately, he does not take charge until tomorrow, which is where my problem begins. To send you back I must first admit that you were here. That means I not only have to fill out a lot of paperwork, but I must explain how you managed to get this far. This would cause problems for me and the other men who are stationed upriver."

"If I let you continue, I cannot stamp your passport, since if you are arrested again they will want to know why I did not capture you, so they will know that you came through here." "As you can see, quite a perplexing problem."

Surprised at his candor and his integrity we offer an equitable solution. We had previously taken the time to get a valid visa for Indonesia, but it showed Tarakan as our port of entry. I suggest that we continue to Tarakan and simply get our passports stamped there. If anyone asks how we arrived we would say "by boat" and not go into specifics. Strangely enough, we truly sympathize with the outgoing officer. More important, we want to get this thing solved before his replacement has any more helpful hints.

We definitely downplay the standard approach of "we're important." I avoid explaining that Coskun is a famous war photographer for SIPA press, or that I am writing a book about Borneo, or even that Jon Rees is a well known tourist guide and outfitter. We choose to dwell on the fact that we have been misled by travel guides in Sabah in telling us that the border is open. A statement that is true but somewhat dubious considering our zeal in picking this place to cross the border.

In light of our innocent intentions, and lack of incriminating evidence, he strikes a bargain with us. If we proceed directly to Tarakan and not tell anyone how we arrived in Indonesia he will forget this incident ever happened. We ask him about our boatmen. He waves his hand and says they should know better. There will be a fine and they will be sent back. We don't ask how but expect that they have a long walk ahead of them. There is some comfort in the fact that they can sell their boats and motors for a premium here and we paid them handsomely.

The look of relief on our faces is apparent. Sweet clove or *Kretik* cigarettes are passed around to celebrate this solution and as a precaution, the officer will send one of his men along to make sure we get on the boat to Malinau, where the scheduled riverboat will take us down the delta to Tarakan. He arranges our departure with an aide and we breathe a silent sigh of relief.

We congratulate ourselves on doing quite well as we stumble out into the bright sunlight. Instead of one escort, there are three.They are all well armed with automatic rifles and it seems that the third gentleman is a blue uniformed police officer. We have not yet begun our escape. The police chief would like to talk to us.

Old enemies, new friends

We all dutifully pile into the pickup truck, rifles and all, and march up to the police compound. The chief has gone out and will be back. With the broadest smiles we can muster, we explain our unusual predicament and our novel solution to the young officer holding the fort. He looks at us skeptically, and only after our immigration escorts second our story does he relax. Since our escort is impatient to send us on our way, he asks the policeman to fill out the necessary paperwork. It seems that since we are in his police district without valid visas or authorization, he must fill out a police report. Procedure. The young policeman who originally assumed we were being escorted to jail erroneously assumes our well armed friends are to actually protect us.

He dutifully gathers up the long forms in triplicate and carefully inserts well used carbons between each sheet. After asking us each person's name, he slowly hunts and pecks each letter onto the form. Hoping to speed things up, we offer to fill out the forms for him. We entertain the young policeman by taking Polaroids and handing out stickers. Thinking we are capital fellows, he reciprocates by insisting on typing each of our forms one letter at a time.

About halfway through the last form and just as we think we might be getting out of this mess, in walks the dour-faced chief of police we met in the store last night. The young policeman quickly hides the Polaroids and stickers we had given him. Things do not look good. The chief takes one look at our happy expressions, the paperwork, the guilty smile of his officer filling out the forms and says, "What the hell are you doing?" The officer explains. The chief looks at us and at the forms and shakes his head: "No way." Our hearts sink.

While the police chief confers with our escorts and immigration, we are given a chance to inspect the jails from the inside. They are actually cleaner and cooler than where we had spent the night. It was the three rusty hooks about eight feet off the ground in a stained anteroom that has us wondering. It looked like this might be home for awhile.

Later we are rousted and sent back to immigration, as the police chief would have none of this. "You must go back. Put everything back in the boat," he says, with the same wave of his hand as our nemesis used back at immigration. We begin the negotiation process anew. We explain how we can't possibly go back and magnify the size and ferocity of the rapids. This time we find out that the police chief is not only a Murut but is not impressed because he knows there are dozens of trails that connect the two countries. In fact, he is a veteran of the *Konfrontasi*. He reasons very democratically and correctly that if the boatmen have to return back to Malaysia, then why not take us with them. Luckily the immigration official, like many senior Indonesian officials, is obviously from Jakarta and, coming from a major urban center, views the jungle as an enemy. He completely sympathizes with the odious concept of being sent back into the jungle without food, water or supplies. The police chief, on the other hand, sees no reason why we need to travel all the way to the big city when it is much easier to return to Sabah from whence we came.

Jon chats with the police chief and learns that he is from Long Pasia, the site of the worst fighting between the British and the Indonesians. Jon's British accent and our military-looking clothes probably do not bring back a lot of good memories for this man. As they chat, they learn that they have common friends in the area. Although the border splits Indonesia from Malaysia, tribal relationships run stronger than government rules. This area is predominately Murut and it is not uncommon for people to have family on both sides of the border. At immigration, the chief of police discusses the matter with the chief of immigration; actually, with both chiefs of immigration because even though he doesn't take charge until tomorrow, the new head still seems intent on sending us back up the river.

It is becoming obvious that there is no easy solution. Sending us back is no guarantee that we wouldn't just turn around and come back. This is a real possibility because not only did we not have supplies and food for the lengthy return, the police chief is the only one who knows what we are really up to. He knows that Jon runs river rafting expeditions and he has seen people like Coskun and I before. The kind of crazy people that do these things just for the fun of it.

The law they are enforcing is a tough one to enforce because even though the conflict in the '60s is still fresh in some people's minds, there is no real reason other than political to seal the border. As far as these people know, we are the first outsiders to come down the river since the war. They are convinced that the officials in Tarakan wouldn't believe we came this way and we insist they would just deny it.

At last a consensus is reached. They would escort us to the next river and we would be somebody else's problem after that.

They would "escort us" and put us on a navigable river system far enough away and out of their jurisdiction that they would not be suspect even if we were apprehended again. They select two soldiers, one burly and young, the other one elderly and thin. We all cram into the back of a pickup truck and take the long, hot ride towards civilization. Along the way we bump and tumble sitting face to face with our armed captors. We exchange polite smiles. They stare at every item we are carrying. To ease the tension we take a few Polaroids of the soldiers. Because it is so bumpy, the best we could get are blurry representations, but they seem to be pleased with them.

When we finally arrive at the river, the soldiers bang on the door of a small cabin. The soldiers apprise a young man of the situation and tell him to take us to Malinau, the most remote terminus of the riverboat that will take us down the delta to Tarakan. We are told there is a fee for the pickup truck, approximately equivalent to its purchase price and that the soldiers have negotiated a special rate for our river trip. We are discussing cab fare with two armed men in the remote terminus. We consider our options, pay the soldiers and the driver. We refuse to pay the exorbitant rate for the boat fare and tell them we will negotiate the rate for the boat if and when we arrive in Malinau. The soldiers content with their wad of rupiah wish the boatman luck and clatter off down the road. I notice the soldiers and the boatman wear the same type of Ray Ban aviators.

Lost in the land of chain smoking monkeys

The trip to Malinau is tedious and uneventful.Upon arrival our boatman informs us that the fee has doubled from the previously agreed upon usurious fee. Our boatman, sensing that our arrival by armed military escort does not exactly make us VIP's, has decided to take advantage of our situation. Luckily, since the boatman has neither a machine gun or the smarts to agree on a price before we leave, I just smile and offer him the money we had originally agreed upon. He screams and harangues us drawing a crowd of curious onlookers. I counter by being very Asian and cool. We just continue to smile and unload the boat. He makes a great show of being insulted, threatens us with arrest and marches off to the police station. By now we really don't care, at least we will save the cost of a hotel room for tonight.

I knew that smoking stunts your growth.

An older man, watching this age-old charade from the pier, smiles and says, "He will make trouble for you." Jon goes off to find a room for the night; I sit with the gear in the shade. I buy some peanuts and cookies from a vendor and share them with the old man. The children refuse our gifts and step back in fear. We sit in the shade and chat in broken English and Indonesian about life in general as children stare in amazement at us.

Soon the boatman comes back in a high state of agitation.

This continued charade obviously means the local *penghulu* or police chief is not in. He harangues the crowd in Indonesian but after realizing that the crowd isn't going to stone us for cheating him out of his fare, he stomps off. We make use of the time and find a simple pension across the street. The boatman meekly returns a third time once the crowd has disappeared and takes the money. He disappears (along with some of our possessions, we found out later) having never once taken off his Ray Bans.

When we are asked for our passports by the hotel owner we play musical chairs. Since we have no entry stamp and the police chief would be equally agitated at our presence we decide to play a shell game. Whenever he would ask one person for their passport, the person that isn't there has them. In this fashion we manage to put the manager off until the police station closes that night.

While all the confusion is going on, a delicately-framed man overhears Coskun and I speaking in French. He identifies himself as Ari, the son of the former Indonesian ambassador to Paris. He invites us to have coffee and to allow him to show us around his town. He apologizes for the boatman's behavior but says no harm was done. The people like us and were impressed by our handling of the situation. After our previous welcome, Ari's offer is a surprise. But we are getting used to surprises.

We go with him to his small cafe to sit in the shade. A baby macaque monkey jumps up and grabs the cigarette out of Coskun's mouth and begins to puff rapidly. They are trained to pick coconuts and amuse the people in their spare time. An older macaque monkey down the road elicits howls of laughter from the locals when he runs down the tree, sticks his bright red rump in the air and points to it. The poor monkey repeats this obscene gesture over and over again like a comedian on speed, all the while grimacing and shrieking to feign laughter.

Ari's monkey is small and has the stale urine smell of winos. His trick is to crawl up your shoulder, grab the lit cigarette from your mouth and tear off the filter. He then puffs madly like a locomotive until the butt burns his fingers. He sniffs the burning piece of tobacco, flicking it from hand to hand until it is burned out. He, like the older monkey down the road, never tires of this trick. He also has the nervous tick of a confirmed nicotine addict.

That afternoon, Ari takes us on a tour of the village of Malinau. He takes us to see furniture being made from jungle rattan and a man who dives for ancient Chinese jars and porcelain in the muck of the riverbed. He also collects ancient dragon jars from the Dayaks in the interior. The dragon jars are the most valuable possession a Dayak has. Only aristocrats could afford to own one. The oldest dragon jars start at 800,000 rupiah; a lot of money for any country.

We see the crumbling symbols of colonialism. There is an iron steam roller that has been parked since sometime around the turn of the century and has been sitting rust-free and immobile ever since. It's made of German steel and its massive structure seems to be impervious to rust. It will probably be there 500 years from now. In a more contemporary vein, we come across a 12 cylinder aircraft engine of World War II vintage from either a Japanese or American aircraft. Now it is used as an anchor for a jetty.

Jesus and the dragon dog

We walk a ways out of town to visit with the local missionary. He had spent most of his life in Laos and Vietnam. He is assisted by a group of doe-eyed Timorese boys who sit reverently on the steps and hang on every word he says. The missionary is an accomplished linguist and switches easily between

English, Indonesian and French as he tells us of his travels through the Apo Kayan in the '70s and fills us in on the region and its people.

The missionary takes us proudly through his church which is a curious blend of Kenyah and Roman Catholic imagery. The last days of Christ are interpreted in Kenyah motifs and imagery to create a truly hallucinogenic version of the age-old story. His pulpit is a shield and the altar is a synthesis of the *asu* or dragon dog and the Holy Trinity; an interesting touch. Coskun, who is starting to miss European cuisine, asks him if he has any pasta or tomatoes to make spaghetti. The missionary takes a long time to realize that Coskun thinks that because he is Italian, he still eats Italian food. He explains that he has been living on rice in the jungle since he was a young man. As he gestures around him, he explains that this is home. We ask him if he wants to come with us to visit the more remote regions of the Apo Kayan. He says that sadly that is a young man's interest and he has plenty to do where he is.

He mentions that MAF (Mission Aviation Fellowship) might be able to fly us directly into the Apo Kayan to a place called Long Bawan. From there we could take a canoe or walk south to Long Nawan. We walk to the simple grass strip to check on flights. All that exists is a rusting scale, an ancient cargo price guide and dozens of bashed and dented oil drums full of fuel. The locals say that a plane comes through once a week, but we would have to go to the coast to get more information.

On the way back we enjoy the setting sun and quiet village. Our calm tour is interrupted when we are accosted by a silver-haired man who insists that we are not supposed to be here. He becomes quite demonstrative and begins to yell that we must immediately report to the police. In order to avoid a mob scene we walk by the police station. Luckily no one is in. Ari tells us not to worry since he knows the police chief and would take care of the details. That night we are questioned by two surly looking military-types in plain clothes. Ari again tells us not to worry and that the police chief is now aware of our presence. If we are arrested at this place, it would be a very tall job to deport us back up the river we had come down. We are not too worried since we are only a day by riverboat from Tarakan. We find out later that Ari's assurance hinged on the promise to the police chief that we would be on the riverboat the next morning.

That would explain why bright and early the next morning there is a military escort standing patiently by the riverboat. They watch us drink coffee and even help us load our gear onto the boat. Unsmiling, they watch us disappear around the bend and towards Tarakan.

Rolling on the river

I must say that in all my travels I have never met so many people who were so happy to see us leave. Thankfully our boat trip down the delta to Tarakan is uneventful and restful. Rather than subject ourselves to the stifling heat and repetitive Indonesian music that blasts from the speakers below, we ride on top. The bowman on this run is quite a character. A deaf mute he speaks in grunts and barks. Throwing his head back (like Errol Flynn) he howls (not like Errol Flynn) when he plays a practical joke on someone. He has a wicked sense of humor. When we tell him we are riding on top, he arranges a comfortable throne among the luggage and produce, then turns to us as we settle in and makes deep sniffing sounds with his head in the air. He then walks to the front of the boat, pretends to be urinating and measures the angle and drift of the imaginary spray. He gives us a sly thumbs up sign and howls with mirth. There are no toilets on the boat. Etiquette dictates that number one is done off the bow, number two; off the stern. Women perform all functions on the stern while the captain dutifully stares forward. Unless of course he is grunting and motioning for us to come back and a have a look. We decline.

The riverboat is a simple structure. The boats are designed thin and long to ride the ocean waves that come up on the estuarine area of Eastern Indonesia. There is a large diesel engine that drones into your subconscious. The rich smell of spice, mangoes and durians baking on the hot asphalt roof mixes with the acrid smell of the slow moving, well polluted river. As we get closer to the ocean the boat rocks and creates a cooling bow spray as it rises and splashes into the gentle swells of the water. After weeks of being careful not to drink too much from the rivers, I realize that I am inhaling gallons of vaporized sewage from the bow spray. And, I am at the most polluted point, downstream from thousands of habitations. Oh well, just one more thing learned too late.

Our adventure has been one part Conrad and one part Monty Python.

The river snakes slowly to the ocean, creating patterns identical to the Chinese dragons found on Brunei gongs or the tendrils motifs of the Kayan or the scorpion tatoos of the Iban. Mangroves and nipah palms line the sides in monotonous green walls. The riverboat is the bus of the delta and our eight hour trip is broken by meal stops at small villages, where we eat meals of curry and rice. This is definitely a once in a lifetime trip—meaning that once in a lifetime is enough. I think I have seen enough mangrove swamp to last a lifetime.

Mata hari, or the eye of the day in Indonesian, stares down on us without mercy. As the equatorial sun climbs in the sky, the heat on deck is massive. Baked by the sun's rays amplified by their harsh reflections off the water, we soon turn from a crimson shade of red to ocher, then to black. It can only be described as a furious tan. I am burned by the sun right through my pants, my shirt, even my wool socks. The stiff breeze and constant spray make the heat somewhat bearable but we keep sticking to the melting tar on the roof. As the muddy-brown river mingles with the clear green ocean, the spray from the bow instantly crystallizes on our skin and hair encrusting us with brine.

The long, lazy trip to Tarakan.

In the low deltas of mangrove and mud flats there is not much scenery. We see the occasional *menares* tree standing like a lone white marker to jungle that has been long dead. Villagers ride out in small canoes to flag our boat down. The boatman slows down as they load their *barang* on board and then continues the monotonous trip. The scenery is much like the Amazon as we glide along under the endless panorama of puffy white clouds.

We come across fishing boats with the faded white and red flag of Indonesia. Coming around a corner we see the rusty oil town of Tarakan.

"Next time, take the plane"

Our plan is simple. Meet the ferry from Tarakan, mingle with the crowd and get our passport stamped. There was one problem. Customs for the ferry is done on Nunakan, a small island, miles north of Tarakan just south of Tawau. Scratch Plan A.

No problem, switch to Plan B. Off to immigration headquarters. Closed. Scratch Plan B. Next, check the seaport. No customs here. We are told to go to the head office. Plan C gone. Try the house next to the immigration office, there is always someone there we are told. No immigration here. Knock on the door next to the office. Nobody home. Plan D dead. Try the airport. Sorry, all planes have landed today. Plan E shot. As we start to leave, the man points to a distinguished officer leaving the terminal building and says he might be able to help. We accost the important looking official with a locked briefcase leaving the building. His epaulets clearly say "Immigrasi." When we begin to ask our questions he replies politely in perfect English, "Immigration is closed. Come back tomorrow."

The officer, who is also carrying what looks like the results of a recent shopping trip, is more concerned with helping an attractive woman into a minibus. The woman is the one who has been doing all the shopping. So much shopping, it seems that it requires the personal attention of Customs and Immigration.

Just before the side door is slammed in our face, we wave our passports under his nose. His trained eye sees the visa but no entry stamp. He understands the problem instantly and then says, "Follow me. I will stamp them at my house."

We arrive at his simple but comfortable home. He unlocks his briefcase, lays out his stamp, a pad, smooths out the required entry visas and motions that he is now ready to begin the job of checking and stamping our visas.

"How did you get here?" he asks.

"By boat." We all chime in.

"What was the name of the boat?" He prepares to fill out the name in our entrance visa.

"We don't know...uh, it didn't have a name...it was a small boat."

Expecting a different answer he realizes that this is not routine. He looks up.

"You took a small boat? How small?"

"Just big enough for five people."

"That is a prahau (canoe), not a boat."

"Yes, a prahau."

"You took a prahau all the way from Tawau to Tarakan, on the open ocean?"

"In a way."

"In a way?"

"Well, we took more than one boat."

"What was the boatman's name?"

"We didn't ask."

"Where is the boatman?"

"He went back."

The officer thinks he is either truly in the company of madmen or people who don't wish to tell him how they arrived. He recaps the situation politely just in case we don't realize how stupid our story sounds:

"You came 200 miles on the open ocean in a canoe and you expect me to believe you?"

"Well, how else could we have got here?" I ask.

This is a tough one. This takes a while for the official to ponder. Being an official of Indonesian customs and being experienced with many illegal forms of entry, he either can't be bothered listing the various creative ways of illegally entering Indonesia or he truly can't think of how we got here. To save time, since it will be his dinner time soon, he decides to explore who we are rather than how we got here.

He looks at the forms we have just filled out. He looks at me. My passport takes a good deal of his time as he carefully looks at every country I have visited in the last four years. He compares the dog-eared passport to the information in my visa form.

"You are a "manager." He speaks the words carefully and with an unmistakable note of cynicism. "What do you "manage?" The word "manage" definitely had spaces on either end of it, as if he were picking up a dirty sock.

I point to a poster on the wall to make sure there is no confusion. I tell him that I do design and create advertisements.

He smiles politely to show that, "Yes, I do understand."

He then looks at Coskun and his passport. Coskun's Turkish passport is overflowing with stamps for popular vacation spots like Afghanistan, Lebanon, China, Croatia, Cambodia, Chad. He has introduced himself as an artist to our host.

"And you are an "artist?"

Coskun was the only one in our group who routinely obscures his occupation since, "war correspondent" does not open a lot of doors in the Third World.

"Of sorts."

"Of sorts?"

"I am interested in primitive cultures and I take pictures for reference."

The officer nods his head. Good answer. "You are a Muslim?" Coskun touches his chest and nods enthusiastically. The official smiles politely, not because he cares, but more because this is the first straight answer he has received.

To Jon he says, "And you are a "businessman?" Again, those same distinct spaces at the beginning and end of he word. Jon simply nods to avoid further questions. We just smile stupidly.

"So a manager, a businessman and an artist take a canoe across the ocean and end up in Indonesia without a good explanation of how they got here?" He seemed to take extra care to add extra spaces around the word, "artist."

This is obviously a rhetorical question so we simply smile and do our best to look pleasant.

Coskun, figuring that the official is teetering on the edge of indecision, suddenly goes for an Academy Award and begins bemoaning our long days on the boat and swears that we will never travel by boat again. He curses the boatman and his stupidity in trusting him.

The officer's head tilts back a few degrees as he watches this amazing piece of acting.

Now he truly knows he is in the presence of the insane and decides that it would take too much effort on his part to really figure out how we got here. It is obvious he doesn't believe a word of what we are saying but he can't think of a better reason why three tattered, grubby, leech bitten, beet-red "orang putis" are in Tarakan without an entry permit. We are obviously too stupid to be smugglers, too western to be pirates and too polite to be criminals. There haven't been any reports of mercenaries, missionaries or madmen, so he doesn't have any reason to detain us. And, we are in Tarakan with a visa to enter Tarakan. It's just that he can't figure out how we got here. We, on the other hand, have not technically lied yet and if we are frog-marched off to jail we could credibly backtrack. We had come from Tawau (we had just driven inland a few hundred miles), we did come by boat and we were somewhat practitioners of the professions we claimed.

The official fingers his visa stamp cautiously. He is still deciding our case. Coskun is still going on in mangled English using his best Turkish/French accent: "Next time I will take the plane. Never by boat, never again will I trust a boatman." His eyes roll up to the heavens to implore Allah to forgive him.

Now there is one very tangible piece of evidence that lends credence to the fact that we have spent some time on the open water. The three of us are sunburned to a painful reddish ocher. In fact, Coskun's hair and eyelashes are bleached white by the intense sun of the past few days.

Finally, swayed by either hunger pains or pity, or a rendezvous with the attractive lady he was escorting from the airport, the officer looks at his watch and begins to stamp our passports. As each passport is signed, there is an audible sigh of relief from each of us.

Later, when we meet the same official in the Tarakan airport on our way out of Indonesia, he reminds us, "Next time, take the plane."

Konfrontasi

Konfrontasi was an outgrowth of "Maphilindo" Sukarno's image of an empire that included the Philippines, Malaysia and all the territory of Papua New Guinea and Borneo.

It began with Indonesia trained and supported communist agitators who were sent to destabilize Singapore, Brunei, Sabah and Sarawak. The first armed attack on Sarawak came on April 12, 1963, when a platoon of Indonesian soldiers attacked the police station in Tebadu. One policeman was killed. In Sabah the upper reaches of the Pensiangan river and the Saliler was used to supply Indonesian troops at Lipaha, Nantakor, Lumbis and Labang. Each base had around 100 soldiers at any one time. Sabah and Sarawak fought back with SAS commandos from Britain, Australia and New Zealand, Ghurkas stationed in Burma and Malaya and local Muruts. In Sarawak the Commonwealth forces of regular British troops and SAS commandos and Ghurkas were supported by Iban scouts. In all, three divisions kept the Indonesians from invading Kuching or Kota Kinabalu. The British policy was to contain harassment and interdiction within 3000 yards of the border. This was later increased to 10,000 yards. In July of 1965 Operation Claret took the war deeper inside Indonsian territory. In August of 1965 Sukarno became very ill and on October 1 a group of army officers tortured and killed 6 generals in a failed attempt to overthrow Suharto's regime. They failed when loyal troops crushed the coup.

The largest single loss of lives occurred when Ghurkas operated a clandestine operation in which 27 Indonesians were killed in a single operation in September of 1965. The "confrontation" between the new Federation of Malaysia and Indonesia under Suharto resulted in 150 Commonwealth and Malaysian deaths and 206 wounded. On the other side 590 Indonesians died and 222 were wounded. 771 Indonesians were captured and later released unharmed by British forces. Many soldiers were felled by leptospirosis, malaria and amoebic dysentery. Injuries were also caused by the effect of the damp environment on unstable explosives. Konfrontasi briefly reintroduced headhunting to Borneo. The conflct ended on August 11, 1963 with the signing of the Bangkok accord.

Indonesia

Kalimantan is geographically linked with Malaysia and Brunei yet delivers a totally different experience when compared to Borneo's northern regions.

Indonesia is one of the truly exotic travel destinations left on this planet. Like India and China it is a vast country that cannot be summed up in one or two paragraphs. There are as many commonalities as there are disparities between the chauffeured executive in Jakarta's high rises and the stone age tribes that have recently been discovered in the Irian Jaya. They all possess complex social structures, languages, religions and cultures and they all are Indonesians. So it is with Kalimantan. There is little, if any reason to unite a Bugi pirate from the waters off Sulawesi with a Kayan nobleman from the misty highlands of the Apo Kayan under a common flag but Indonesia has done it.

Kalimantan

★ CAPITAL CITIES   — - BORDER
▲ ATTRACTIONS   ═══ ROAD
■ NATIONAL PARKS   ● CITY

0   30   60 Mi
0   30   60 Km

©FWI 1996

SOUTH
CHINA SEA

Bintulu
Tatau
Dom
Sibu
Sarikei
Kanowit
Hutan Sambas
Reserve
Bako
National Park
Dabai
KUCHING
Pamangkat   Sambas
Bandar Sri Aman
Semonggoh
Orang Utan
Sanctuary
Telagus
Danau
Reserve
Putussibau
Singkawang
Pinang   Ngabang
Nanga
Tepuai
Mandor
Reserve   Pusatdamai   Sintang
PONTIANAK   Kapuas   Sanggau
Nanga Mahat   Nanga Pinoh
Teluk Bahang
Sukadana
Bukit Raya-Bukit
Baka Reserve
Kepulauan Karimata
Marine Reserve
Nanga Tayap   Tumbang Samba
Memala
Ketapang
KARIMATA
STRAIT
Sukaraja
Kendawangan   Pangkalambun
Sampit
Tanjungpandan
Manggar
Maura Kendawangan
Reserve
Tanjung Puting
Orang Utan Reserve

JAVA SEA

Miri

Gunung Mulu
National Park

Rumah
Lagan

Long Lama

Pa Dali

Lio Matoh

SARAWAK

Kayan
Sungai Mentarang
Reserve

Ulu
Sembakung
Reserve

Muara
Sobuku
Reserve

Tarakan

SULAWESI
SEA

Tanjung Selor

Gunung
Berau Reserve

Tanjung Redeb

Muara
Blemlelakidau

Sankulirang
Reserve

Muarabu

Biatanbepinang

Lasan

Kongbeng
Caves

Sangkulirang

Pulai

Batu Kelau

Muara Wahau

Muara
Kaman Reserve

Sengata

Betapau

Genting Tanah

Kutai
National
Park

Tajung Balai

Kersik Luwai
Orchid Forest
Reserve

Mahakam

SAMARINDA

Muara Badak

Tenggarong

Seipinang

Samboja

Muara Merunga

Balikpapan

Muara
Koman

songan

PALANGKARAYA

Tanjung

MAKASSAR
STRAIT

Amuntai

Tabudarat

Rantau

Kandangan

BANJARMASIN

Kuin
Floating
Market

Martapura

Kotabaru

Pelaihari
Martapura Reserve

Pelaihari

History of Indonesia

The island of Borneo is the largest of the 17,508 islands (6000 inhabited but only 992 full time) that form the archipelago of Indonesia. The largest states in order are Kalimantan (Indonesian Borneo), Sumatra, Irian Jaya (West Irian), Sulawesi and Java. Although Kalimantan is the largest in land areas, nearly two-thirds of the population lives on Java, one of the most densely populated areas in the world. Kalimantan contains 30 percent of Indonesia's land mass and only five percent of its population. By contrast the next largest island, Sumatra, contains 25 percent of Indonesia's land area and 20 percent of its population.

Indonesia has had a fairly aggressive history of laying claim to as much land as it can with its ocean area being three times larger than its land area. Indonesia shares land borders with Malaysia and Papua New Guinea and sea borders with Australia, India, Singapore, Vietnam, the Philippines, and the US-administered Trust Territory of the Pacific Islands. Both PNG and Malaysia had uneasy feelings about its borders and Indonesia was behind a lot of unrest in both areas in the early '60s. That mistrust still exists to this day.

Although most of Indonesia is part of the "ring of fire," a highly active volcanic chain, the island of Borneo is not volcanic. The last volcanic activity was over 50,000 years ago and the gradual process of deforestation and erosion is sending much of the thin topsoil back into the ocean.

Indonesia is by no means a poor country and exports oil, gas, coal, timber and other minerals to Japan, the U.S., the EC, Singapore, and Hong Kong. The country is rapidly investing in factories and agriculture programs that produce textiles, shoes, electronics, processed food products, tea and coffee, rubber, timber and forest products.

In A.D. 300, the islands now forming Indonesia were the site of small kingdoms established under the influence and culture of India. After the Buddhist kingdom of Srivijaya in Sumatra declined in the 14th century, the Hindu kingdom of Majapahit in Java succeeded in gaining control over most of what is now Indonesia as well as much of the area now forming Malaysia. By the end of the 16th century, Islam was established as the dominant religion in most of Indonesia. The remote areas of the Philippines, Borneo, Sumatra and Malaysia were large sultanates with fuzzy to unknown knowledge of where their control stopped and their neighbors started.

Early Traders

The Chinese were the first people to discover the riches of Borneo. Blocked from trade with India, the Chinese looked south for new trade partners.

The depths of the Mahakam river continue to turn up treasures that date back as far as the 5th century B.C. Local divers mucking about in the sediment of other estuaries and rivers regularly turn up Chinese pottery, weapons, brass cannons and other treasures. The Chinese were active on the south and west where they dug for diamonds and other precious stones.

What's in a name?

Indonesia maintains that Kalimantan means "river of diamonds." Understandable if you have a vested interest in attracting investment and settlers. However others say that it comes from the less glamorous lamata or the starch from the Sago palm. The correct name for the entire island is both Borneo and Kalimantan. Borneo being the British word to describe the northern view while Kalimantan has always been the Dutch and Indonesian way to describe their southerly view of the island. The Arab traders called the vast island Kalimantan after a type of mango, meaning that Kalimantan is the Island of Mangos. Local Malays say that the current name for the island comes from Buah niyor, Malay for coconut. Visitors since Pigafetta (1521) have called the island Brunei or Borneo after the sultanate of Brunei. Brunei Darussalam means Abode of Peace, just like Dar es Salaam in Tanzania means Harbor of Peace. Sabah, the area of the former British North Borneo Company, comes from the Arabic Zire bad or land below the wind. Sarawak means serawak or antimony in Malay. Malaysia is easy. It means land of the Malays.

Kalimantan has always been a rich source of natural products. In ancient days Chinese would trade pottery and brass implements for honey, bezoar stones, bird's nests, rattan and gutta percha. The British took control of the north while the Dutch grabbed the south. Spices, mostly pepper, were the major riches of the islands. When oil was discovered, Royal Dutch Shell became wealthy from the pure and cheaply derived oil. It would be a mistake to assume that the Indonesian part of Borneo is similar to the Malaysian and Bruneian parts.

Kalimantan is the largest of the islands (there are more than 17,000 if every tiny island is included) that make up the archipelago of Indonesia. Unlike genteel Malaysia or content Brunei, Indonesia is a seething powerhouse of 190 million people, the largest Muslim nation in the world. On these equatorial isles are found 300 ethnic groups who speak over 500 languages and dialects. For all its diversity there is little strife. There is an ongoing tension in East Timor, Aceh in Northern Sumatra, and sporadic tribal warfare in Irian Jaya but Indonesia can be considered a safe travel destination with relatively good services and infrastructure.

To the adventurous traveler, Indonesia ranks along with India and the Middle East as one of the most exotic and mind expanding regions. Traveling through Indonesia's 1,919,317 sq kms, you can't help but wonder how these people have existed peacefully, let alone are united under one flag. The distance from one of Indonesia's islands to the other is the same as traveling from Ireland to Azerbaijan.

Their oxymoron slogan is "Unity in Diversity" and has little to do with the real reason for Indonesia's strength. The real reason lies in the martial looking national symbol, The Garuda or eagle. Warfare has united Indonesia and the threat of quick and brutal retaliation keeps it together. Any independence movement is quickly crushed as in Timor or Aceh for the good of the country as a whole. Although many ancient sultans, kings and warriors combined large sections of what is now Indonesia into pocket sized kingdoms, it took the greed and military power of the Dutch to unite these diverse but warlike peoples.

The Dutch first arrived in 1610 in Malacca on the Malaysian Peninsula. In 1811 the Dutch East India Company began their ruthless and completely mercenary annexation of the outlying islands with control of Java.

The Dutch came for cloves and then nutmeg and the profits were one of the major reasons for the wealth of the Netherlands. The Portuguese were expelled in 1660 and the English were ousted six years later. Their goal was to obtain an absolute monopoly on the spice trade and control over important shipping routes to Asia. Diamonds from Borneo actually began the diamond cutting business in Amsterdam.

Using an army of 1000 Europeans and 2000 mercenaries, mostly Bugis and Ambons, the Dutch managed to knock off one tiny sultanate after another because of the division and ongoing conflicts in the region.

This tiny trading company had united all of Java and most of Sumatra by the end of the 1700s and had made inroads into Kalimantan when in 1800 the Dutch East India company was declared bankrupt and the territories given to the Dutch government to control. Their trade monopoly was broken in 1811 when Napoleon occupied Holland in 1811 and the British invaded several major trading ports in Java and the surrounding area. In 1824 the Netherlands traded some of their holdings in India and the Malay peninsula for British settlements in the Dutch East Indies. Meanwhile the Indonesians still battled against the colonial oppressors. One five year rebellion that ended in 1830 claimed the lives of 8000 Europeans, 7000 Indonesians and 200,000 people on Java died from starvation and disease.

Throughout this, Borneo kept its independence and relative peace until the Dutch overcame the sultan of Banjarmasin in the late 1800s.

Colonial Aspirations

The Dutch gradually gained control of most of the islands, occupying them until Indonesia gained independence in 1949. (The first Europeans to arrive in Indonesia were actually the Portuguese, who controlled the eastern half of the island of Timor until it was occupied by Indonesia in 1975.) As the Dutch exploited the rich islands, Indonesia became one of the world's richest colonial possessions, supplying tea, rubber, rice, sugar and petroleum up until the beginning of World War II.

The Dutch controlled Kalimantan until 1942 when the Japanese captured the vital oil industries—so much oil that Kalimantan, Brunei and Sabah provided 45 percent of the Japanese military's fuel.

Japanese Occupation

Japanese forces occupying the islands in 1942 stimulated resentment against the Dutch in order to control the area. When Japan surrendered in 1945, Indonesian nationalists proclaimed the independence of the country from Dutch control. The Netherlands failed to defeat the Indonesian nationalists and a war of independence started.

Independence

Four long and arduous years followed as Indonesians fought a revolution to regain their land from the foreigners who had occupied it for so long. It took world opinion and some discussion in the United Nations before the Dutch bowed and returned the sovereign rights of The Netherlands East Indies back to the new Republic of Indonesia. Queen Juliana finally signed the official document on December 27, 1949.

Achmed Sukarno became the new nation's first president, a post he held until deposed in 1965. He was a brilliant and charismatic man, whom his fellow countrymen called "Bung" (brother) Karno. Some said his manner was so mesmerizing that he could persuade and cajole just about anyone. However, in his later years of power he seemed to "run amok" and misuse the trust bestowed upon him by the people. He married a Japanese call girl, who called herself Dewi (goddess), and lavished jewels and furs upon her while most of the country lived in poverty. He elected himself president "for life" and put forward a "guided democracy," against all that was written in the Constitution. He erected costly monuments to his glory and entered into an unnecessary confrontation with neighboring Malaysia. He withdrew membership of the Republic from the United Nations and espoused "Nasakom," an acronym for nationalism, religion and Communism.

The Foiled Communist Takeover

An attempted Communist coup in September 1965 failed but instigated more than a year of intense bloodshed, as Indonesians turned on each other in an attempt to rid the country of inside and outside Communist influences. Almost half a million lives were estimated lost—sometimes whole villages— before the Sukarno regime was deposed. The "father of the country" died a broken man, under house arrest. He was succeeded by Major General Suharto, who was installed as president of the Republic in 1968. He was conveniently reelected in 1973, 1978, 1988 and 1993.

Today Indonesia continues to modify its stance on socialism as it develops stronger trade ties with America and Europe. Indonesians have lost little of the fiery spirit of independence and continue to build their economy through exploiting natural resources, social programs and investment in their own country.

The Future

Indonesia still has an aura of political incorrectness as it aligns itself with the new Southeast Asian tigers of Singapore, Thailand and Malaysia. The country is taking full advantage of its free access to millions of hectares of precious hardwoods, coal and oil needed to fuel development, social programs and education. Like the Malaysian states of Sabah and Sarawak, timber has been ripped from Kalimantan's hinterland in ever increasing amounts.Oil, minerals and timber from East Kalimantan provide a quarter of Indonesia's exports so there is little chance that ecotourism will have a major impact on slowing down the deforestation.

It is not just the ground and natural resources that have been invaded. The minds and bodies of the tribes of Kalimantan have undergone dramatic change. Beginning in the '30s Dutch and American missionaries have attacked the Kalimantan region from the inside out using float planes to fly into the interior and proselytize the locals until even the most remote jungle village looks like a small town in Minnesota. Much of the local culture and artistry have been submerged as being subversive and then artificially resuscitated by government programs designed to attract tourism. Needless to say there is little "authentic" about most of the remote regions and peoples. If you do get a chance to get way upriver you will meet the last remnants of the once flourishing Dayak people. Most upriver people have converted to Christianity and have adopted the dress, manner and attitude of newly converted Western Indians. They wear T-shirts (usually castoffs and donations from American and European missionary groups), sing hymns on Sunday and live in small Western style houses—a far cry from their days in spectacularly decorated longhouses and animistic practices. Many villages used to the new wave of eco-tourists demand money for photographs and have learned to adapt to their new role in society.

Indonesia's attempts to put on a new face of openness were dashed in November 1991, when security forces in Dili, East Timor, fired on a crowd protesting Indonesia's incorporation of former Portuguese territory in 1976, killing about 50 people while being caught on camera. East Timor is still a tense area with little chance that it will achieve independence.

Although Indonesia tries to be a good neighbor through its membership in the Association of Southeast Asian Nations (ASEAN), (founded in 1967 with Thailand, Malaysia, the Philippines, and Singapore) they got into a shouting match in late 1991 over the islands of Ligitan and Sipadan islands. Since then they have agreed to negotiate an equitable settlement.

Best Bets In Kalimantan:

•*Apo Kayan*

•*River trips along the Mahakam, Kapuas, Berito rivers*

•*Diving*

•*Jungle Trekking*

•*Dayaks*

•*Collecting the art of the Kenyah*

•*Visiting Birute Galdikas and her orang utan rehabilitation center.*

River of the Precious Stones

Kalimantan is the Javanese word for "river of the precious stones." Today Kalimantan is the vast southern region of the island of Borneo. The border between Malaysia and Indonesia follows the central mountain ranges, becomes high plateaus and then descends into low lying swamps. The 549,000 sq km area has much of its future ahead of it and for now is a frontier where prices are high and tourist facilities are few. On the positive side there are some dramatic plateaus and mountains to explore along the Muller and Schwaner range. The highest point is Gunung Murut at 2438 meters high near the Sabah/Sarawak border. Most of Kalimantan is under 150 meters in altitude. That means hot, humid heat. Around 80 percent of Kalimantan is forest covered. The typical terrain looks like rumpled Astroturf broken by snaking brown rivers. The entire island is undergoing a continual erosion into the ocean. The erosion is aggravated by logging which removes the thin layer of leaf litter and by dramatic forest fires which have burned away more than 20 percent of East Kalimantan's forest.

But despite the monotonous appearance of Kalamantan there is much to be discovered. The rare Sumatran rhino still hides in Banamuda in East Kalimantan. There are fresh water dolphins in the Mahakam river; the proboscis monkey and the orang utan (sharing 95 percent of humans' DNA) still live in the vast forests and swamps. Wild elephants wander over the border from Sabah, while the sun bear and the clouded leopard exist mostly unseen in the dark forests.

Hassles with police

The former paranoia about Malaysian expansionism and the militaristic attitude of the Indonesian government means the government is also represented well in the remote areas. Although the Konfrontasi is over, there is still a fairly tight control over the borders and border regions between Sarawak, Sabah and Kalimantan. If you go deep into the interior you will be expected to "humma humma" (a term I use for long gratuitous conversations that result in little except a healthy distrust of people's other intentions) with whoever is running the local government. You will rarely be asked for a direct bribe or payment but you will pay through the nose for anything you need that is in the control of the local government. Remember that negotiation for supplies that come from one source do not necessarily lead to tough bargaining on your side. If you need gas and are going upriver the military or police are about your only bet.

There is much said about corruption and use of authority by these local politicians, policemen and soldiers. My experience, as you will read, is both positive and negative with the scales tipping toward the negative in the remote regions. It seems that tourists are an important part of their financial diet, so make sure you travel with someone who knows their way around if you know what I mean. Purchase of artwork, gasoline, supplies and other necessities tend to lead back around to the village government. Rental of canoes, guides and other materials will also lead you to them. This is not a negative it is just a part of life in this poor but entrepreneurial region.

Since Kalimantan has been the focus of government directed industrial development you will find much of the forest along rivers and populated areas has long since disappeared. The very accessibility of the forest has created an easy resource.

The financial, political and cultural center is centered on the island of Java and the chaotic city of Jakarta. The people of Kalimantan view the Indonesians in the army, police and government agencies the same way they viewed the Dutch and missionaries. They stick to their own cultural world and go about the same daily business that has been occupying their lives for decades. To the experienced traveler Kalimantan does feel like it is in the grips of an occupying army. There are political slogans everywhere, officers tend to be Javanese, not from local towns, and the local dialect is used when people are among friends. Bahasa Indonesian is used when conducting business or talking with strangers. The people of Kalimantan live under a sterner set of social conditions than their neighbors to the north. Many of the people are displaced from crowded areas of Java and Sumatra. These people are forced to move from their homelands and given plots of land in areas outside of major urban centers. Although it is easy to criticize this policy, there have been no other solutions to the increasing population on the tiny island of Java. The elite group of businessmen, politicians and high ranking military essentially run Indonesia and profit enormously by controlling many of its major industries.

The regime of Suharto is considered to be corrupt, his wife is vigorously involved in politics and business and even his daughter Siti controls the construction of all the toll roads around Jakarta. His other children have benefited the opening of television to the private sector. It is estimated that up to 30 percent of Indonesia's $1.9 billion in foreign aid disappears through leakage through project delays or misappropriation. The army (Suharto was the former army chief of staff) will continue to have a strong hand in running the country and the two opposition parties; the Christian dominated Democratic Party (PDI) and the Muslim dominated United Development Party are tolerated but given no real power. The upside of Mrs. Suharto's involvement has been the increasing equality of women.

Also there is a noticeable lack of Chinese in many areas. There is a fear and distrust of them. The Chinese play a major role in Indonesia's economy and have been distrusted ever since Chinese were shown to be major supporters of the October 1965 PKI communist uprising. Indonesia has not been a fertile ground for many Chinese. In 1963 in Bandung, 1974 in Jakarta and 1980 in Semarang there were major riots against Chinese businesses. Although Kalimantan has a large percentage of Chinese, they are not in evidence as much as they are in Sarawak.

Relations with Papua New Guinea with whom Indonesia shares an artificially created border were improved by the visit of Papua New Guinea Premier Paias Wingti to Indonesia in February 1993, but there are still groups that do not accept Indonesia's control of their country. There are many negative things that can be said about Indonesia. It is the least developed country in the ASEAN group with a high debt service ratio. There is some concern that Suharto who has held absolute power since 1971 will die (he was born in 1921) leaving the country fractured and in disarray. The army has chosen Vice President Try Sutrisno as his successor and accordingly his picture is being widely distributed to be put up next to General Suharto's. Suharto is not so happy with this decision and is said to prefer a member of his family to succeed him and protect his rather extensive holdings.

On the good side is the robust growth at a sustained average of over four percent a year in per capita GNP and the country's wealth of natural resources. The people have endured imposed hardship. Dayak, Javanese, Chinese, Dutch, or from other origin continue to live in harmony, retain their own unique culture and still look enthusiastically into the future. It is not unusual to see an Indonesian listen to disco records, speak at least three languages, pray at a mosque, wear Western clothes, drive a Japanese car and practice ancient ceremonies handed down from grandparents. It is this ability to accept complexity and their sense of good will that makes the Indonesian people unique.

The Indonesian Calendar

There are many local celebrations on Kalamantan. Keep in mind that the Muslim calendar is linked to the lunar calendar and holidays occur on different times on our solar based calendar.

FESTIVALS AND HOLIDAYS

January 1	New Year's Day Tahun Baru	*A religious holiday for some with church services and visiting of friends and neighbors*
Jan/Feb.	Al Miraj	*When Mohammed returned with the five prayers from the archangel*
February	Imlek	*Chinese New Year*
March/April	Good Friday	*Christian Holiday*
April 21	Kartini Day	*The birthday of the founder of women's emancipation; Raden Auneg Kartini*
May	Waisak Day	*The birth and death of Buddha on Java*
June	Idhul Adha	*A holiday to commemorate the willingness of Abraham to sacrifice his son*
June/July	Muharram	*Muslim New Year*
August 17	Independence Day	*The biggest national holiday*
August/Sept.	Garebag Maulad	*Birthday of the prophet Mohammed*
October 1	Hari Pancasilia	*The five basic principals of Pancasilia*
December 25	Christmas Day	*Christians celebrate the birth of Christ*

The Food of Indonesia

As with religions, peoples, races and customs it is difficult to describe the foods of Indonesia without lengthy background as to their origins.

Overall the food of Indonesia is unusual to Western palates. Rice is the basic filler, chicken is the meat of choice and creative spicy sauces and coconut add the tropical flavor.

The most famous dish is not one dish but a staggering offering of up to 16 dishes served with dramatic flair. The *rijstaffel* or rice table is a groaning board of Dutch and Indonesian delicacies usually served in hotels or fine restaurants.

Sate is the Asian version of kabobs. They are ordered by the fistful and are eaten with a sweet creamy peanut sauce usually as an appetizer. Choose from chicken shrimp or beef marinated and then cooked over hot charcoal.

Rendang is a hot dry curry of beef seasoned with coriander and tumeric.

Nasi means rice and there is a bewildering variety of both sweet and spicy dishes built around rice.

Nasi campur is a simple dish with a selection of bean curd and chicken. *Nasi goreng* is fried rice usually with bits of meat, shrimp and vegetables. *Nasi gudeg* is a sweet dish that uses jackfruit, chicken cooked in coconut milk. *Nasi kining* is a beef and rice dish cooked in coconut milk similar to *nasi liwet. Nasi uduk* is a spicier version.

Opor ayam is chicken cooked in a rich coconut sauce.

Sayur lodeh is the vegetable version.

Nuts & Bolts

Indonesia is on the metric system. The language is Bahasa Indonesian but many people in the tourism and hotel business speak English. When you lump the whole country together into a big melting pot most Indonesians are Javanese (45%) followed by Sundanese (14%), Madurese (8%), Malays (8%) and others at 25% covers a wide range.

Indonesia's growth is fueled by, what else, fuel. Timber and oil are the big exports. Seventy percent of Indonesia is covered with forest and there are almost 6 billion barrels of oil still to come out of the land and seas. Indonesia is also rich in natural gas, timber, gold, coal, bauxite, tin and nickel. The economy has grown by 7% a year for 25 years. Oil output from existing wells is falling forcing exploration further into the wilderness of Irian Jaya and Borneo.

Tourism is not a big money earner but is growing at 24% a year. Most of the 3.1 million visitors head straight for Bali, followed by Java and Sumatra. Japanese tourists make up the bulk of visitors followed by Brits and Americans. Germans, Dutch and Australians are also fans of Indonesia.

The people of Indonesia can be considered poor by any standard. The ownership of cars is only seven per 1000 people which is higher than Malaysia's two per 1000. Television sets are owned by only 55 out of 1000 people compared to 144 for Malaysia.

Facts

Area: 752,410 sq. miles

Official Language: Bahasa Indonesian

Population: 192,810,000

National religion: Islam

Currency: Rupiah

Indonesia has the world's second largest rainforest area after Brazil.

The world's longest archipelago almost 5000 kms wide.

There are 17,508 islands, 6000 inhabited but only 992 full time.

The five largest islands in order are Sumatra, Java, Kalimantan, Sulawesi and Irian Jaya.

Most of Indonesia's domain is water.

Indonesia's largest trading partner is Japan, who also provides 75 percent of its bilateral aid.

Eighty-eight percent of Indonesians are Muslims, 7.4 percent are Christians.

Kalimantan is divided into four conveniently named provinces:

South Kalimantan - Kalimantan Kalsel - Kalsel

Central Kalimantan - Kalimantan Tinggi - Kalteng

East Kalimantan - Kalimantan Timur - Kaltim

West Kalimantan - Kalimantan Barat - Kalbar

Getting In
Visas

Valid passport and onward or return ticket required. A visa is not required for tourist stays up to two months (non-extendable). Your passport must be valid for six months beyond the end of the two month visa. For longer stays and additional information consult:

Embassy of the Republic of Indonesia

2020 Massachussetts Avenue., N.W.
Washington, D.C. 20036
☎ *(202) 775-5200*

or the nearest Consulate:

The Indonesian Consulate

645 South Mariposa
Los Angeles, CA
☎ *(213) 383-5126*

or contact consular offices in San Francisco ☎ *(415) 474-9571*, Chicago ☎ *(312) 938-0101*, New York ☎ *(212) 879-0600* or Texas ☎ *(713) 626-3291*.

If you are in-country and you need to extend your visa most people will simply fly out and back in again. Now remember the U.S. Consulates will only provide visas through approved entry ports. That means major airports. You should not try to enter the country through a back door or remote areas without a visa specifically for the border post you will pass. This creates serious hassles and sets you up to pay a whopping bribe to get your exit visa. You are almost better off losing your passport. (Read "Into Indonesia, The Hard Way"). You must have an onward ticket or they will make you buy one at the airport. If you are going to get creative about your port of entry, get your entry visa at the neighboring country first not from the U.S.

In Kalimantan the official port of entry for Westerners is Pontianak and Balikpapan although you can enter through Tarakan by ferry or cross country from Kuching. Entikong became an international entry point in January 1994. The same rules apply at Entikong as other major airports and seaports. It is always advisable to check this and do not change your intended port of entry. Red tape in Indonesia would make an Indian postal clerk cry. If you try to squeeze every day out of that two month pass remember that a two month visa is good for one day less than the stamped entry date. (Enter on the 10th means you must leave on or before the 9th). Here are some local Indonesian embassies or consulates to check on entry or visa questions:

Embassy in Brunei

Simpang 528, Sungai Hanching Baru, J/n Muara ☎ *(02) 330180*

Embassy in Singapore

Wisma Indonesia, 435 Orchard Road, Singapore ☎ *(73) 774422*

Embassy in Kuala Lumpur

Jalan Pekeliling 233, KL ☎ *(03) 421011*

Consulate in Kota Kinabalu

Jalan Sagunting 1, KK, Sabah ☎ *(088) 54100*

Documents

It helps to have an International Drivers License, photocopies of your passport photo page, letters of recommendations, medical records, prescriptions for eyeglasses or medicines, your scuba diving card, phone numbers and addresses to send postcards to, photos of friends, family, your house, a student ID card (it has very limited value here).

Inoculations

Unless you're coming from an endemic area, inoculations are not required, but tropical diseases such as malaria are still a threat in the jungles of Kalimantan, so before venturing into unknown regions, please check with your doctor or the **Center for Disease Control** in Atlanta: ☎ *(404) 639-3311*.

Customs

There is no one right way to avoid offending everyone in Indonesia just as you would have a hard time pleasing everyone in your home town. There is some measure of comfort in knowing that Indonesians can be rude, criminal, obnoxious and annoying too.

Since the biggest single common denominator is the Muslim religion it is important to understand the basic likes and dislikes of Muslims. The Islam of Indonesia is not the hard flat Islam of the Middle East but a lush rich combination of ancient traditions and even a dash of Buddhism. Even the converted Kenyah of the Apo Kayan manage to attend church every Sunday, sing hymns and still believe in the spirits of the forest. The common denominator is *adat* or a rigid belief in the need for customs and tradition.

Islam

Islam is a simple but powerful religion. It binds together a billion people around the world. Their actual practice and interpretation of the Koran varies from casual to fundamental but they all believe in the five pillars of Islam: Faith, Prayer, Concern for the Needy, Self Purification and the Haj, or pilgrimage to Mecca.

Prayers are performed five times a day; at dawn, noon, midafternoon, sunset and nightfall. A Muslim can pray anywhere although it is preferred they pray at a mosque. In Indonesia it is quite common to see people praying in front of their TV sets while prayers are being led on the channel. Muslims pray towards the direction of Mecca which is why you will notice the green arrows showing the direction on the roof in hotel rooms. Muslims used to pray to Jerusalem but Mohammed changed it to Mecca.

The Zakat (purification or growth in arabic) states that all wealth belongs to God and that mortals have temporary possession. The idea of sharing one's wealth with the less fortunate is similar to tithing where Muslims donate two and a half percent of their income to the needy.

The Haj is the pilgrimage to Mecca, the place of worship God commanded Abraham to build 4000 years ago. God then commanded Abraham to summon all people to visit this holy site. This is only necessary for those who can afford the trip. There is a huge business in haj trips complete with charters, hotels, souvenirs and special white clothes that equalize all pilgrims. The Haj requires travel to Mecca where the pilgrim circles the Ka'ba or meteorite type rock, seven times and travels seven times between the mountains of Safa and Marwa. Upon their return they may wear the white cap of the haj and have the title haji after their name. About 2 million people travel on pilgrimages to Mecca in Saudi Arabia each year.

The haj is based on Mohammad's hejira (Migration in arabic) in which he traveled from Mecca to Medina in AD 622. The haj takes place during the 12th month of the Islamic calendar which is lunar not solar like ours. The end of the Haji is marked by the Eid al Adha festival celebrated with prayers and exchanges of gifts. It is also the end of Ramadan the main event of the Muslim calendar.

Ramadan is when healthy Muslims must abstain from food, drink and sexual relations during the day to understand the plight of the needy. If a Muslim cannot fast they may make up the time in increments during the year.

When dealing with Muslims, cleanliness and protocol are very important. Do not offer or eat with the left hand and do not offer alcohol or pork. If the person begins his prayers, do not stand and stare. When dealing with Christians restrain yourself from yelling out "Christ" or "Jesus, Holy Mother of Mary" when you trip or hurt yourself.

Wakee, Wakee

You're sleeping peacefully after a late flight into Kalimantan. Your cheap and picturesque hotel is across the street from a large mosque. At dawn you are jolted awake by what seems to be a nightmare. A man is yelling at the top of his voice into a megaphone that is connected to an amplifier which is connected to loudspeakers all turned past MAX. This is not a dream. Welcome to Islam. Your first call to prayer on your first day in country is always the most exotic. After you get used to this foreign sound it actually becomes quite comforting. But what they are saying here for your edification is the muezzin's call to prayer:

"God is most Great, God is most great

God is most Great, God is most great

I testify that there is no god except God

I testify that there is no god except God

I testify that Mohammed is the messenger of God

I testify that Mohammed is the messenger of God

Come to prayer, Come to prayer

Come to success in this life and the Here after, Come to success

God is most great, God is most great

There is no god except God."

A typical Malay mosque

Muslims in Indonesia pray in *mesjids* or mosques. Most mosques in Indonesia are modest affairs usually with a metal dome and a simple wooden interior. The mihrab is the niche that directs the congregation towards the direction of Mecca. The *muezzin* used to be the fellow that climbed up to the *menara* or minarets to call the faithful to prayer. Today his call to prayer is tape recorded and played back at a most unholy volume. The most holy time for praying is Friday afternoons when many businesses and government offices are closed. The devout pray five times a day and make use of any private corner. In many large airports or public places there are prayer rooms. Although many Americans have an image of Islam as a symbol of anti-American sentiment, there is little if any political connection between Islam in Indonesia and anti-Western sentiment. The Indonesian's view of Jews is similar to our views of Muslims—exaggerated and mostly diffused upon actual contact. It would not be wise however to wear your religion on your sleeve since Indonesians will assume that you are a Protestant Christian and will rarely ask what your religion is.

As for peculiar Indonesian taboos it is hard to define where they came from but I will rattle off some.

First off, all Indonesians are very sensitive to forms of address. Given that you are going to mangle the language anyway, you will be excused in many cases but if you are the guest of a headman or town leader keep the following in mind: an older man should be addressed as *bapak* or *pak*. The word means "father" in Bahasa Indonesian and it is akin to our using "sir" instead of "dude" or "hey buddy" when meeting your girlfriend's parents and shows your gratitude and respect. His wife or any older woman should be addressed as *ibu* or *bu*. If you are in the presence of real officialdom or in danger of being thrown in the pokey by a midlevel military official always use *tuan* to raise yourself in his estimation. Women can be called *nyonya* if married and *nona* if single.

Correct clothing is not an issue but incorrect manner of dress can lead to some uncomfortable moments. Both men and women should not wear speedos, tight shorts, tank tops, thong bikinis or revealing clothes except in resorts. Wear long pants, clean clothes, long sleeve shirts and try to avoid loud colors or logos. Don't tousle kids' hair. Asians feel the head is the center of a person's soul. The left hand is used for washing your private parts in the river after you perform your scatological duties so don't be eager to pat people on the back, offer cigarettes or pass food with the left hand. Sorry Lefties. If you really want to look slick with that girl's parents, get in the habit of bowing slightly when introduced and using both hands to pass food or objects. The next worse thing than your left hand is the soles of your feet so do not cross your legs or sit with your legs straight out. The person to whom your feet are pointed may view it as a form of mooning. Sitting James Dean style with your feet crossed on the table is akin to giving someone the finger. Sit with your legs tucked under you or to one side. Don't point with your finger, you can use your thumb. Take your shoes off when entering homes, mosques or any area that has shoes scattered around.

Displays of affection or emotion are considered very Western and very embarrassing. Screaming, gesticulating or throwing a tantrum portrays you as a fool and your intended victim will be embarrassed for you or pity you. Do not kiss or hug in public for the same reasons. Always stay calm and avoid the American habit of yelling louder when you think your point is not being understood clearly. The only place I have seen yelling get anything done is at the high end hotels that cater to Westerners. Indonesians do not associate something going wrong with their actions. So if a plane is late, your room is booked or even if a cabdriver is ripping you off, yelling produces few results except drawing a crowd of curious onlookers.

Timeliness or the lack of it is something that will drive you to drink in Indonesia. Rubber time (a Malaysian term) is a phrase to describe the infuriating habit of promising to meet someone or do something and having it never happen. Lateness would be a definite improvement. At least you could set your meetings an hour earlier. Keep in mind that rubber time applies more to the Malays than the Chinese or Dayaks.

The bottom line is to be cool, observe what your hosts do and laugh when you do something really stupid.

Language

The *lingua franca* of all of Indonesia is Bahasa Indonesia which is essentially the same trading language called Malay. Just as Arab traders created Swahili to converse with trading partners in the Indian ocean and Africa, Malay is used as the trading language along the coasts of Southeast Asia. In the 1920s the Indonesian nationalist movement adopted Malay as a symbol of modernity and progress and it is now taught in all schools. All signage, printed materials and written and spoken media communications are in Bahasa Indonesia. In Kalimantan, Dayaks, Javanese, Chinese and other ethnic groups still use their native tongues to converse among themselves.

Bahasa Indonesia Cheat Sheet

Remember there is no "the", "a" or other articles. Think of a caveman when you speak, "me hungry," "car broken" etc. The plural can be expressed by doubling the noun or adding the word many (banyak). Verbs are not conjugated and sudah (already) is used to show your past actions and akan (will) to show your intentions. When in doubt point, or just smile, put your thumb up and say "bagus" or good.

Good morning	*Selamat pagi*
Good day (11 a.m. til 3 p.m.)	*Selamat siang*
Good afternoon (3 p.m. til 7 p.m.)	*Selamat siang*
Good evening	*Selamat sore*
Welcome	*Selamat datang*
See you later	*Selamat tinggal*
My name is...	*Nama saya...*
What is your name?	*Siapa nama saudara*
I, you (sing./plural) he /she/it), we, they	*Saya, saudara, dia/ia, kita/kami, mereka*
Have a good trip	*Selamat jalan*

Bahasa Indonesia Cheat Sheet

Thank you	*Terima kasih*
Please	*Tolong*
Excuse me	*Permisi*
Stop	*Berhenti*
Let's go!	*Jalan jalan!*
Great! (Good)	*Bagus! (baik)*
Eat (restaurant)	*Makan (rumah makam)*
One more... (or just point)	*Satu lagi...*
I would like to pay now	*Saya mau bayar sekarang*
How much money (kms)?	*Berapa harga (kilometers)*
How much is a room?	*Kamar berapa harga*
Does this room come with...	*Ada kamar yang ada...*
...AC/hot water/bathroom?	*Aircon (AC)/air panas/kamar mandi?*
Can I see the room?	*Saya mau lihat kamar dulu?*
Bathroom (toilet)	*Kamar mandi (kamar kecil waysay)*
Toilet paper	*Kertas waysay*
Yes (OK)	*Ya (baik)*
No (lack of)	*Tidak (bukan)*
Too expensive	*Mahal*
Discount	*Potongan harga*
I want to go to...	*Mau pergi ke...*
Where is...?	*Di mana ada...?*
Tomorrow	*Besok*
Here	*Di sini*
Bus	*Bis*
Ship	*Kepal*
Station	*Stasiun*
Left/right/straight ahead	*kiri/kanan/terus saja*
North, south, east, west	*utara, selatan, timur, barat*
Tourist office	*Kantor parawisata*
Telephone (number) (card)	*Telepon (nomor) (kartu)*
Police (hospital)	*Polisi (rumah sakit)*

Days of the Week	
Monday	*Hari Senin*
Tuesday	*Hari Selasa*
Wednesday	*Hari Rabu*
Thursday	*Hari Kamis*
Friday	*Hari Jumat*
Saturday	*Hari Sabtu*
Sunday	*Hari Minggu*
today	*hari ini*
yesterday	*hari kemarin*
tomorrow	*hari besok*

The Currency

The currency of Indonesia is the rupiah and each rupiah is about RP1855 to US$1.
The average farm laborer makes about RP100,000 per month and professionals in the larger cities make about RP 1.5 million.

Counting your rupiah			
1	*satu*	**100** *se ratus*	
2	*dua*	**1000** *se ribu*	
3	*tiga*	**10,000** *se puluh se ribu*	
4	*empat*	**100,000** *se ratus ribu*	
5	*lima*	**1,000,000** *se juta*	
6	*enam*	**10,000,000** *se puluh se juta*	
7	*tujuh*	**100,000,000** *se ratus se juta*	
8	*delapan*		
9	*sembilan*		
10	*se puluh*		
11 - 19	*add "belas" to the end eleven is "se belas"*		
20 - 29	*add "dua" then "puluh " to the front then the number: 21 "=dua puluh satu"*		
30 - 39	*add "tiga" then "puluh" to the front then the number:31 ="tiga puluh satu"*		

Electricity

Electricity is 220 volts/50 cycles in the main cities. Business hotels usually have 110v/ 60 cycle razor outlets. In small cities electricity is provided via unreliable or wildly fluctuating and sporadic sources. Always carry a flashlight since streets are not lit and houses have very rudimentary lighting. Electricity usually consists of a single bare bulb hanging from the center of the ceiling. Those with electrical devices needing recharging should consider carrying a socket to outlet adapter since there are few outlets.

Water

Water is not safe to drink for Westerners except in upscale hotels or bought in bottles. Under no circumstances should you drink from rivers or streams since Indonesians use the waterways for defecating and urinating. Most sewage is dumped directly into the rivers and oceans including discharge from industrial plants.

Bottled water purchased in any store is safe and natural water sources should be boiled and then purified using tablets to prevent ingestion of bacteria, worms or other unpleasant life forms.

Health Services

Overall there is an average of one doctor for every 7372 people in Indonesia. In the remote areas of Kalimantan there are no doctors or any medical services. There are clinics in most small towns and health care is improving. Hospitals are found in large cities only with about half of them privately run.

What to Wear/Weather

Since all of Borneo straddles the equator you can expect hot humid weather broken up by wet spells. The wettest time is between October and March and the dry season is July to September. It rains frequently throughout the year but the rains can be very heavy and disrupt travel in the monsoon seasons.

Clothing should be light cotton, khaki in color to hide dust and not too tight. Indonesians do not wear shorts and in small Islamic towns women should dress very conservatively. Try to avoid wearing T-shirts which have logos or political statements printed on them.

Photography Tips

Other than Jakarta, Balikpapan, Banjarmasin, Tarakan and Pontianak you are out of luck if you run out of film. Try to buy film in Singapore, KL, Hawaii or another large city on your way in and don't be afraid to buy more than you need. If you do come across film in your travels it will have been baked, aged and definitely be off color. If you have a choice, old funky slow ASA print film holds up much better than slide film. Black and white is even more stable. If possible have your print film developed in the large cities at one of the many one hour photo places. If the prints look like hell you can always have them reprinted correctly stateside. If you are not picky about slide film you can wait till you get to Singapore or KL but most pros wait till they get back to their favorite lab. Keep your film cool especially after it has been exposed. Kodachrome must be processed outside the country or when you get home. If you are fussy and don't mind losing a couple of frames, have your slide film "clip tested" by a professional lab. Then you can adjust the rest of the roll or batch accordingly. This can only control ASA or speed variances. Fujicolor print film is widely available. Batteries are sold in camera and one hour photo stores. When it comes to video tape, age is not really an issue but price will be.

As for the ambience of Kalimantan, there isn't much scenery worth photographing in the middle of the day. There is a perpetual haze on the the lower deltas that can make midday photos extremely unphotogenic. Conversely this yellow haze early in the morning or late in the afternoon can infuse a golden glow. Since there can be an awful lot of sky in island scenic shots, concentrate on closeups, people and don't be afraid to set up the kind of picture you want. What you will end up bringing home with you will be hundreds of shots of people, exotic handicrafts, fascinating architecture and remote lands.

Most Indonesians are flattered that you are taking their picture and will drag out family members, pets, neighbors to get into the picture. In fact Indonesians are proud people and will be quite amenable to direction. Many will ask for a copy of the photo and it is wise to decline rather than lie and tell them you will send it. You can offer a business card with a request to write you in exchange for the photo. I always carry a Polaroid SX-70 and take at least one group shot per mob. If I see a mother with a new child I will make sure I take a portrait just for them. In Indonesia very few people have photographs of themselves and a few seconds of your time can create a treasured family heirloom.

The most common phrase of "Hey Mister gimme one shot" does get a bit old as you are constantly followed around by bouncing children. One solution is to wait until you have a large enough gaggle and then take one group shot. You can have a little fun and pose them in the most convoluted groupings.

As a photographer you will be invited to come in to many houses. Don't forget to take your shoes off and be respectful of their generosity. Typically they will want you to photograph a wedding, a gift, a new infant. Once again try to reciprocate with a business card, small gift or a Polaroid photo.

If you are videotaping let them have a look at themselves and they'll go crazy since most rural people have never seen themselves on tape.

There is a practical use for this gift giving, business cards and Polaroids. If you find yourself in trouble with the local law or in need of a favor, these same people will come to your assistance immediately. If you have no need of their friendship the next traveler will be more than surprised at their warmth. Also, if for some reason you leave something behind as photographers are wont to do, they can at least tell the local police.

As for the damage and duress the tropics will do to your cameras, there is plenty of first-hand experience covered in the "Malaysia" chapter. There is no special paranoia in Indonesia about taking pictures of military but you will be admonished to go away if you point a camera at a soldier on duty or a military base. Airport police are a little jumpy if you are not taking standard type photos and the military in remote regions may grill you on your reasons for being there.

Other subjects you should avoid are devout Muslim women usually wearing veils and traditional dress, inside mosques during prayer, or people bathing.

Tipping

Thankfully tipping is an alien concept in Indonesia. The swankier hotels and big city restaurants will nick you for a 10% service charge but the only time you will be expected to part with your change will be when people carry your bags. In some rural areas they may ask extraordinary fees for carrying your bags from the airstrip into town. This is work for hire, though, so chalk it up to free market prices not settling down to the appropriate level. Simply give the person what you think it is worth and keep smiling as he heaps all sorts of abuse on you.

Shopping

You will come across a wide variety of fascinating objects when you browse the markets and souvenir shops of Kalimantan. If you are looking for the real McCoy don't waste your time in the boonies, head straight for the large antique shops in Balikpapan and Samarinda. Why? Well where would *you* get the most money for a real antique? The locals are not stupid—when they need money they head downriver. There is also a thriving business between local crafstmen and traders who act as middlemen. It is very rare to find any object of value in the hinterlands of Borneo.

Jewels, diamonds, black opals and *ikat* (native weaving) can be bought in smaller centers but unless you know what you are buying you will pay too much.

How do you get good stuff cheap? Simple. All it takes is a lot of time and an engaging manner. If you have a plane to catch in an hour and want to get souvenirs you will get stung. If you just want to get something cheap, then you will get what you pay for.

The way to bargain in Indonesia is very simple. Introduce yourself and explain that you want to purchase the finest items. As you are shown various items write down the price and the item. After you have seen what the seller has to offer thank him and tell him you are now going to shop around. Tell him in a pleasant manner that these are prices for tourists, that you really are only interested in a good deal for a number of items. He will ask you to make an offer. At this point whatever price you set will end up being one end of the midpoint you will actually pay. Most people will offer half of the asking price and the final price will be around 25 percent to 30 percent off. I always buy at 50 percent or less simply because I buy good items and am prepared to walk away.

He will tell you that your price is far too low but he would sell it to you for slightly less than his price. At this point whip out pictures of your children and ask him about his children, share a cigarette, tell a few jokes and generally win him over. Be prepared to leave and come back the next day with a slightly higher offer. Consider shopping in Indonesia like playing badminton—you must volley and the person who makes the other blink gets the best of him.

So congeniality, patience and an unrelenting fixation on your price are important. Now some secret weapons:

Asians believe that the first sale will set the tone for the rest of the day so start your sharklike circling at the start of the business day.

Help him sell to other customers as they walk in the shop. If you can convince a tourist to buy that horrid spear and shield, the shopkeeper will warm up to you instantly.

Don't just think about money. You may own something that is worth a lot to the shop-keeper—lighters, cameras, clothing, watches and other Western items that are hard to get in Indonesia can be traded for handicrafts.

Shop from a Muslim shopkeeper towards the end of Ramadan when they need money to throw parties.

Bring the shopkeeper a small gift such as a Zippo lighter or other item—he will be truly blown away and provide a good price.

Go for the gimmes. As your deal is consummated tell him that your wife or children would love to have a necklace, small carving. He will usually throw it in free.

Shop with a local guide. If the owner knows your friend he will make sure he keeps his good reputation for having the best price.

Finally, keep the list of items and the owner's business card. When you realize how little you paid for that artifact, you may ask him to sell you the rest of his shop once you have struck a deal.

Some tips to make sure you get royally screwed: Argue loudly and insult the owner as a bandit. Make fun of the goods as crap, mock the origin or wave money around and say take it or leave it. Sounds stupid but I have watched folks do this. Suddenly, they realize their bus leaves in five minutes, and buy a cheap trinket for five to 10 times its value.

Telephones and Faxes

All major hotels provide direct dial service. Smaller towns have spotty phone service and limited lines. Perumtel and Wartel telephone offices are your best bet for international telephone calls outiside the major cities. Wartel offices also send faxes to the U.S. for about RP8000 per page. Remember that the east half of Kalimantan is 16 hours ahead of Los Angeles time so that when it is 8 a.m. in Malaysia it is 4 p.m. the previous day in Los Angeles. West Kalimantan is 17 hours ahead.

INDONESIA

TO CALL ANY NUMBER IN THIS BOOK FROM THE USA:

DIAL 011 then the country code, city code (no "0") and the number

Long distance calls to the US cost about RP5000 per minute. There is a 25% discount for calls placed between midnight and 6 a.m.

For local directory information dial 108

For help placing a local call dial 100

For help placing an international call dial 101

For long distance operator assistance dial 106

South Kalimantan

Kalsel is dominated by Banjarese Muslims and home to the most important ancient sultanate in Borneo after Brunei. Banjarmasin means "salty garden" an apt description of the coastal areas of Kalsel and the Venice of the Orient: the city of Banjarmasin. Kalsel is the most densely populated region of Kalimantan—a predominantly Malay/Muslim area with timber being the major source of revenue. About half of the region is still unlogged particularly in the most remote region, the "Range of 100 Mountains" or Pengunungan Meratus. Kalsel is a major rice producer reclaiming vast areas of mangrove areas to use as rice paddies. The rice areas are planted during the dry season and then the deep water paddies are flooded to a depth of two to three meters when the rains come. The rice is harvested from boats. The water world of Kalsel has also created the swimming water buffalo who think nothing of swimming through the flooded paddies from one raised area to another in efforts to graze.

Getting In

VIA AIR

Jakarta	2 weekly	RP190,000	Sempati
Balikpapan	3 weekly	RP78,000	Sempati
Pangkalan	1 daily	RP114,900	DAS

VIA BUS

Martapura	frequent	RP15,000
Banajarbaru	frequent	RP15,000
Tanjung	frequent	RP7500

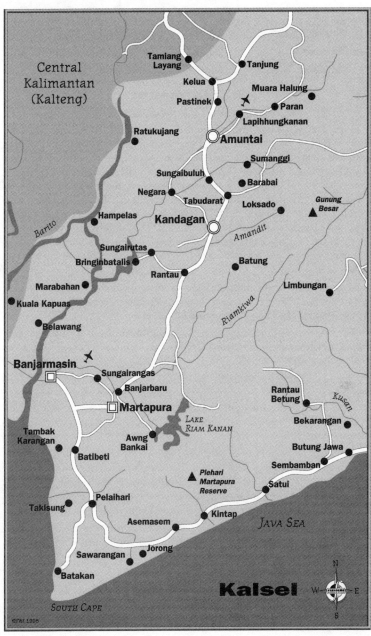

Central
Kalimantan
(Kalteng)

Tamiang
Layang

Tanjung

Kelua

Muara Halung

Pastinek

Paran

Lapihhungkanan

Amuntai

Ratukujang

Sumanggi

Sungaibuluh

Barabai

Negara

Tabudarat

Loksado

Gunung
Besar

Hampelas

Kandagan

Amandit

Sungairutas

Bringinbatalis

Batung

Rantau

Barito

Marabahan

Limbungan

Kuala Kapuas

Riamkiwa

Belawang

Banjarmasin

Sungairangas

Banjarbaru

Rantau
Betung

Kusan

Martapura

Bekarangan

Lake
Riam Kanan

Tambak
Karangan

Butung Jawa

Awng
Bankai

Sembamban

Batibeti

Plehari
Martapura
Reserve

Satui

Pelaihari

Takisung

Kintap

Java Sea

Asemasem

Jorong

Sawarangan

Kalsel

Batakan

N
W · FIELDING · E
S

South Cape

©FWI 1998

VIA BOAT

Surabay	2 weekly	RP87,500	PELNI
Semarang	2 weekly	RP103,500	PELNI
Pangkalanbum	3 weekly	RP24,000	Ferry

Banjarmasin

22 miles from the ocean

Founded in 1526, Banjarmasin is home to an ancient kingdom that succumbed to the Dutch in 1860. Starting with the Hindu ruler Pangeran Samudera (Prince from the Sea) Banjarmasin was ruled by an unbroken succession of 22 sultans. The city has always had close links with Java and Hinduism and ruled the surrounding sultanates to the West and East coastal areas of Kalimantan. Legend says that the city was actually founded in the 12th century by Ampu-jatmika from the Cormandel coast of India. The Dutch arrived in 1603 to trade with the sultan. In 1607 a Dutch ship was attacked and the following reprisal by the Dutch chased the sultan to Martapura. The Dutch had a pepper trade monopoly by 1635 until the English broke their monopoly 20 years later. The Dutch gave up their grip on Banjarmasin but returned in 1733 to build a fort at Tabiano and send settlers.

Banjarmasin was also the center of a viscious uprising against the Dutch in 1860-1864 led by Pangeran Antasari who was born in nearby Martapura. He rallied the Bugis, Dayaks and Banjarese and is now an Indonesian national hero.

The town is a former pirate hangout turned devout Islamic center. Because of the sawmills, diamonds and sea trade, the residents enjoy a level of prosperity envied by other cities along Kalimantan's coast.

Little known outside of Indonesia, Banjarmasin is popular with Indonesian tourists who come from Java and Bali to visit the dramatic architecture and floating market (*paser terapung*). It is a good starting point for trips to the diamond fields and jungle trekking through the Pengunungan Meratus as well as visiting the Hill Dayaks around Loksado along the Amandit River.

Banjarmasin is famous for its architecture. The traditional houses are called *bubungan* (ridge of the roof) or *tinggi* (high) houses. The large *bubungan tinggi* are carved from belian or ironwood and have ornate carved motifs that incorporate hornbills, flowers, Arabic calligraphy and geometric designs. The best place to see traditional bubungan tinggi is in the town of Marabahan about 50kms north on Banjarmasin on the Barito river.

The city is also built where the dirty red Barito and Martapura rivers meet. Most of the inhabitants live in houses built over the water on piles. Transportation is by boat via a series of canals. The people live above and, sometimes it seems, in the sediment-filled water as they brush their teeth, wash, defecate, spit and bathe.

When to Go

March is the best time to catch a traditional Banjar wedding, visitors are welcome. Independence day is when the canoe (*prahu dayung*) races are held on the river.

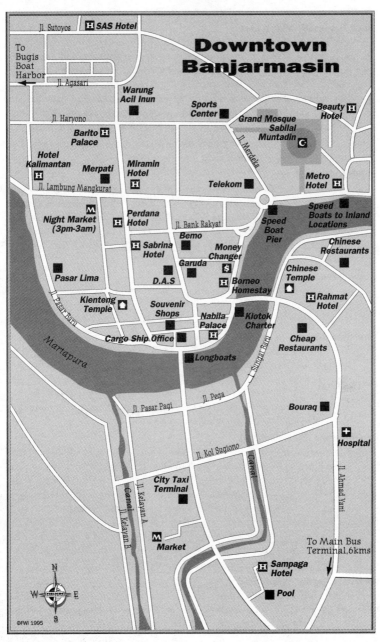

Downtown Banjarmasin

Jl. Sutoyos

H SAS Hotel

To Bugis Boat Harbor

Jl. Agasari

Jl. Haryono

Warung Acil Inun

Sports Center

Grand Mosque Sabilal Muntadin G

Beauty H Hotel

Barito H Palace

Jl. Merdeka

Hotel Kalimantan H

Merpati

Miramin Hotel H

Telekom

Metro Hotel H

Jl. Lambung Mangkurat

Night Market (3pm-3am) M

Perdana Hotel H

Jl. Bank Rakyat

Speed Boats to Inland Locations

Bemo

Speed Boat Pier

Chinese Restaurants

Sabrina Hotel H

Money Changer $

Pasar Lima

Garuda

D.A.S

Borneo Homestay H

Chinese Temple

Rahmat Hotel H

Pasar Baru

Kienteng Temple

Souvenir Shops

Nabila Palace H

Klotok Charter

Cargo Ship Office

Martapura

Longboats

Cheap Restaurants

Jl. Sungai Baru

Jl. Pasar Pagi

Jl. Pega

Bouraq

Jl. Kol Sugiono

Canal

Hospital

Jl. Ahmad Yani

City Taxi Terminal

Jl. Kelayan A

Jl. Kelayan B

Market M

To Main Bus Terminal, 6kms

Sampaga Hotel H

Pool

N
W — FIELDING — E
S

©FWI 1995

What to Do

Pasar Terapung/Floating Market   ★★★

Get up at about 5:00 a.m. and head out to the western edge of town on the Barito River, preferably by *klotok* or floating taxi. Get here at first light (6:00 a.m.) or you will miss most of the action. Everyone will have gone home by 9 in the morning since they will have been here since 4:00 a.m. Bring your camera, your wide angle lens and a lot of film since the joint will be jumping as Banjarese go about the business of stocking their larders, fixing things, getting medical checkups, filling up their outboards with gas, eating and generally catching up on the day's gossip.

A great place for breakfast or a quick snack from one of the floating tea shops (Banjarmasin's version of the push cart).

Sabila Muhtadin Mosque

The central focal point of Banjarmasin is this 45 meter high (built in 1980) copper domed mosque that houses over 15,000 worshippers. All of Banjarmasin's population (98 percent) are Muslims and it is said that there are more mosques and *surau* (small mosques) per person here than anywhere else in Indonesia. It is estimated by the locals that there is one mosque for every 40 people here. Visitors will be requested to pay a small fee to see the unusual interior.

Grave of Pangeran Samudera

On your back from the floating market you might want to stop in at Kuin village to visit the grave of the Hindu ruler who founded the city in 1526. When Pangeran Samudera converted to Islam in 1540 he changed his name to Pangeran Suriansyah.

Bugi Shipyards   ★

There is a booming shipbuilding industry in Banjarmasin just upstream from the floating market where the Barito and Andai rivers meet. Here the Bugis build their dramatic seagoing ships in the traditional manner. These *perahu layar* (sailing ships) carry a crew of 30 men and carry goods and people to nearby islands of Java and Sulawesi. The sawmills in town provide the lumber the Bugis need to make these ancient looking ships. Other sawmills create plywood.

Monkey Island (Pulau Kembang)

Downriver (thank goodness) is Flower island, better known as Monkey Island. Here gangs of macaques entertain and insult tourists. The long tailed macaques congregate like bored teenagers near the old Chinese temple. The fact that they are spoiled rotten by visiting Chinese on Sundays doesn't help their greedy and petulant dispositions. The Chinese give the monkeys grotesque amounts of bananas and nuts in the hope they are doing good. The monkeys of course simply digest and defecate the offerings. If you have been sinning in the whorehouses of Banjarmasin you can buy bags of peanuts on the island. Make the monkeys work for it though because they will simply steal the whole bag if they get a chance.

Proboscis Monkeys/Palau Kaget

A better way to spend your time (a lot of tours to the floating market include Monkey Island to kill time) is to visit Pulau Kaget 12 kms downstream where you'll see the rare proboscis monkey. It is called *kara belanda* or "the monkey that looks like a Dutchman" because of its large nose, pot belly, spindly legs and awkward demeanor. The curious creatures can be seen early in the morning or at dusk. *Nasalis larvatus* is found only on Borneo and if you're not going to Sabah to visit the Kinabatangan River area this may be your only chance. The whole trip takes about five hours and 50,000 rupiah from local tour operators or half that if you rent your own klotok. You should plan on leaving about 2–3 a.m. (depending on the direction of the tides).

Where to Stay

Banjarmasin is devoutly Muslim, tightly controlled and not really used to Western tourists. Many cheap hotels may turn you away even if they have rooms. Accommodations run from overpriced business hotels to the usual fleabags all in the center of town. Cheap accomodation can be found by cruising Jalan Ahmad Yani along the Martaupra river.

Barito Palace   **RP120,000–600,000**   ★★★★

Jalan Haryono MT 16-20; ☎ *(0511) 67300, FAX 2240*
The most luxury you're going to get here along with the Kalimantan. All the goodies including satellite television.

Hotel Kalimantan   **RP127,000–1,76,000**   ★★★

Jalan Lambung Mangkurat; ☎ *(0511) 66818, FAX 67345*
Recently built with A/C, small rooms, centrally located, restaurant, pool. A world class hotel complete with the obligatory karaoke bar. Expect to be up at dawn thanks to the mosque next door.

Hotel Maramin   **RP78,000**   ★★

Jalan Lambung Mangkurat 32; ☎ *(0511) 68944, FAX 3350*
Eclipsed by the Kalimantan and Barito Palace, the Maramin is still a luxurious hotel and its lower prices make it popular with business travelers. It is noisy on the top floors (unless you love thumping from the sixth floor nightlclub that is thankfully closed on Monday, live groups every night 10 p.m. till midnight) bar, A/C, convention center, restaurant, in room videos.

Nabilla Palace   **RP98,000–147,000**   ★★

Km 3.5 Jalan Jend. A Yani 126; ☎ *(0511) 62707*
On the road to the airport, tennis courts, A/C, restaurant.

Sampaga   **RP37,000–50,000**   ★

Jalan May. Jend. Sutoyo S 128; ☎ *(0511) 62480*
A cab trip from the center of town could save you a few rupiah (add in the cab fare though). In the northern part of town, A/C restaurant, clean rooms.

Hotel Metro   **RP16,000–24,000**

Jalan May Jend. Sutoyo S 26 (near the Grand mosque); ☎ *(0511) 62427*
Not all rooms with A/C. Rooms with fan and private mandi start at 24,000 rupiah.

Perdana Hotel   **RP28,400–44,000**

Jalan Brig. Jend. Katamso 3; ☎ *(0511) 63276*
Clean airy rooms, restaurant. Rooms with private mandis are RP20,000–23,000, rooms with two beds from 25,500 and A/C RP37,600–44,000 rupiah.

Hotel Sabrina   RP18,000–35,000

Jalan Bank Takyat 21; ☎ *(0511) 54442*
Middle of the road accommodations with a good price range depending on your budget. A/C, restaurant 15,000–118,000 rupiah for rooms with fan, 20,000–25,000 for fan and shower, 27,000–30,000 for A/C and TV.

SAS   RP22,500–34,650

Jalan Kacapiring 2; ☎ *(0511) 53054*
A traditional Banjari house. Not all rooms with A/C, restaurant.

Rakmat   RP9900–13,750

Jalan Jend. A Yani 9; ☎ *(0511) 54429*
No A/C, ask for a room with fan.

Hotel Beauty   RP6500–7500

Jalan Haryono M.T. 176; ☎ *(0511) 54493*
Cheap, some with A/C, bathrooms outside rooms, ungainly but serviceable.

Borneo Homestay   RP7500–11,000

Jalan Pos; ☎ *(0511) 66545, FAX (0511) 66418*
A favorite of backpackers. Owners Johan and Lina Yasin also run low budget tours.

Wisma Batung Batulis   RP45,100–60,200

near the Mesjid Raya
A government resthouse with 18 rooms. Usually booked but when space is available they have oversized rooms with A/C.

Losmen Noormas   RP2500

Jalan Baru 120; ☎ *(0511) 52014*
Cheap, grubby but what do you expect for RP 2500 a night.

Losmen Abang Amat   RP4000

Jalan Penatu 17; ☎ *no phone*
Popular with Indonesians because of its central location.

Getting In

Most people fly into Syamsudin Noor Airport from Jakarta or Balikpapan via Bouraq or Sempati. The best way in from the airport to Banjarmasin is to buy a ticket for a taxi inside the terminal for RP9000. You can walk the 2-1/4 kms from the terminal to the Banjarmasin-Martapura highway and then catch a bemo for about RP500. That's if the bemo driver cuts you a fair deal.

Getting Around

If you want to go anywhere except up the Barito or to Palau Kembang you will need permission from the police. You will need copies of your photo and info page of your passport (make sure you have one copy for every place you plan on staying). Sometimes you can get by with a copy of the hotel registration form from the hotel in Banjarmasin. Make sure it has the police stamp on it.

Take a what?	
bemo	An archaic and tiny pickup truck with a bench seat on each side.

Take a what?	
bajaj	A three wheel taxi usually found in Jakarta.
ojeks	A motorized becak about half the fare charged by bajaj.
becaks	A man-powered tricycle cab or rickshaw. Always cut your deal before.
taxi kuning	Yellow minicab. Standard cabs, agree on rate first.
klotok	Motorized canoe, the cheapest form of river transport.
taxi sungai	River ferry that carries goods and has bunks on the upper level.
taxi air	Riverboat. Slow, overcrowded riverboats, wet, leave when full.
speedboats	Chartered, cost ten times taxi air, wet, fast and expensive, same price for one or many.

The six travel agencies in Banjarmasin that can help foreigners (that means you) can make sure you have the right permission, boat times, costs, etc before you go. Most remote areas require that you have a guide.

Touring Banjarmasin by Boat

The best way to see Banjarmasin is to hire a motorized canoe or klotok for about 5000 rupiah an hour. As with any transportation deal in Indonesia, make sure you agree to the total cost before you get in. Figure on two hours to see the highlights of the city. You can pick them up by the wharf near Jalan Lambung Mangkurat and Jalaln Pasar Baru. Don't be shy about pulling over a floating vendor or tea vendor and negotiating breakfast or a purchase.

Upriver

Via double decker boats

Passenger boats leave from the Bajaraya pier, on the western end of Jalan Sutoyo. The boats go to Palangkaraya (24hrs, 5100 rupiah) Muara Teweh (48hrs, 12,000 rupiah), and Puruk Cahu 60hrs, 13,000 rupiah) except in the dry season where you must transfer to canoe at Pedang and recast your schedule (longer) and your budget (downward). The cost past Pedang via less luxurious motorboat to Muara Teweh (3hrs, 10,000 rupiah), Puruk Cahu (60 hours, 13,000 rupiah) may make you change your mind.

The doubledecker boats that travel past Palangkaraya have beds (1000 rupiah a night), warung, toilets and prayer rooms. Make sure you reserve a bed a day before the ship leaves. Schedules are posted on the outside of each boat. The normal departure time is 11 a.m. with ticket offices open 8 a.m.–2 p.m. To get to the Bajaray pier take a bemo for 250 rupiah or bajaj for 2500 rupiah from Pasar Malabar.

Via Motorboat

Daily speedboats that travel from Janjarmasin to Palangkaraya leave from the dock at the end of Jalan Pos. They cost about 21,000 rupiah. The boats usually leave once they are close to sinking. You can buy your tickets at the dock.

To the Tanjung Puting National Park and orang utan Sanctuary: The 18 hour trip to Tajung Puting National Park via Pangkalanbun is via the Karakatau which makes the journey every two weeks.

Via Road

The Terminal Taksi Anta Kota at Km 6 is the main terminus for all land based travel. The variety of transportation is as bewildering as it is cheap. Taxi kotas around town run 250 rupiah.

Bajaj and becak drivers will automatically demand whatever the market will bear from orang putis (white men).

Minibus (Japanese built mini van) the low budget, long distance hauler, usually leaves when full. *To Balikpapan:* Overnight minibus (12 hours, 12,000 rupiah) leave between 4 -5 p.m. Buses are A/C and non A/C. *To Samarinda:* Overnight buses leaves between 4– 5 p.m.

Taxi: leave from Terminal Taksi Anta Kota at Km 6. to destinations around Kalsel. Negotiate fare with driver first.

To Java
Via Schooner

Bugi Schooners leave for Surabaya and other points from the port of Trisakti. It will cost you about 250 rupiah to take a bemo from the Jalan Samudera taxi kota station to the harbormaster office to get your ticket. The harbormaster in Trisakti (Jalan Barito Hilir, ☎ 4775) can tell you what is happening or walk across the street to buy a ticket from any one of the ticket agents. Fare is between 15,000–20,000 rupiah one way.

Via PELNI Ferries

Jalan Martadinata
☎ (0511) 3171, 3077

You can take a 1000–1500 passenger ferry Kelimutu to Surabaya (18 hours, 25,000 rupiah for Class V) and Semarang (19 hours, 26,000 rupiah for Class V) via a modern passenger ship complete with A/C, bar, restaurant and cafeteria. You can choose from first class cabins with televisions and bathrooms, all the way down to fifth class which entitles you to wander the decks and hang out in a large air conditioned room.

By Air

The Syamsudin Noor airport is 27 kms east of town along the road to Banjarbaru about halfway to Martapura.

Taxis to the airport run about about 9000 rupiah and can be picked up outside large hotels or the Garuda office. There are regularly scheduled flights to Jakarta and Ballikpapan. The Missionary Aviation Fellowship (MAF) can charter light planes (usually Cessna 185's) to smaller fields but they are usually busy and don't like to fly certain types (probably you) into the remote areas. Banjarmasin is served by Garuda, Merpati, Bouraq, Kalsel, Asahi and DAS to most major Indonesian cities.

Banjarmasin Nuts & Bolts

Population 2,600,000.

Area: 3, 700,000 hectares, 37,600 sq miles.

Area code: 0511 long distance calls can be made from the office on Jalan Pos.

Best time to Visit: Dry season between June and September

Language: Banjarese, Bahasa Indonesian, Tribal

Banjarmasin: A center for diamonds, rattan and lumber and the central jumping off point for treks into Central and East Kalimantan.

Banks in Banjarmasin can be found along Jalan Lamung Mangkurat.

Maps can be purchased at the Toko Cenderawasih Mas on Jalan Hasanuddin 37 near the Garuda office.

Post Office: Jalan Lambung Mangkurat and Jalan Samudra

Airline Offices in Banjarmasin

Garuda, *Jalan Hasanuddin 11A,* ☎ *(0511) 4203*

Merpati, *Jalan Let. Jen Haryono,* ☎ *(0511) 4433*

Bouraq, *Jalan Lambung Mangkurat 50,* ☎ *(0511) 2445*

DAS, *Jalan Hasanuddin 6,* ☎ *(0511) 2902*

Local Tour Operators in Banjarmasin:

Adi Angkasa

Jalan Hasanuddin 27; ☎ *(0511) 3131, FAX 66200*
Run by Pak Mariso who also happen to be the only folks that will take credit cards.

Arjuna

Ground Floor; Arjuna Plaza; Jalan Lambung Mangkurat 62; ☎ *(0511) 65235, FAX 4944*

Borneo Homestay

Jalan Pos 123; ☎ *(0511) 665545, FAX 66418*
Owners Johan and Lina Yasin also run a homestay and will undercut their competition on various trekking and boat tours. Most travelers and even guidebook writers recommend Johan for his prices and demeanor.

Pujo Santoso

Jalan Nagasari 80; ☎ *(0511) 3023*
For more information contact the tourist office for brochures and tour operators.

Kalsel Tourist Office

Dinas Pariwisata Kalimantan Selatan; Jalan Panjaitan 23 ☎ *(0511) 2983*
This is an excellent source for information on trekking the surrounding region. This office also is the South Kalimantan Tourist Guide Association which can hook you up with adventure tour operators. Guides run between 20,000–30,000 rupiah a day for local trips and double that for remote tours. Note: They are planning to relocate the tourist office to the BNI Bank building in Arjuna Plaza.

Excursions from Banjarmasin

Cempaka Diamond Fields

43 kms from Banjarmasin, take the green minibuses from the Bemo terminal in Martapura, about RP5000 roundtrip.

Just 10 kms from Mardapura are the 150 year old diamond fields. Cempaka is just one of six major diamond fields in the area. The fields are worked by hand with workers washing and panning each basketload of earth carried from the shallow shafts below.

Although laborious, some fairly impressive diamonds (and other precious gems) have made the work worthwhile. In 1965 a 167.5 carat diamond was unearthed, in 1990 a Liz Taylor size, 48 carat bauble was unearthed. The ground has many more years of productivity in it yet. You have to walk from the road to visit the mine. Don't let the primitiveness fool you; there are also Australian owned mines that do it more professionally in the interior.

Loksado

3hrs from Banjarmasin by road

This area is populated by Banjaris who did not want to convert to Islam in the mid 1500s when the sultan converted. There are about 20 villages populated by the descendants of these refugees over a 2500 sq km area. The area has become a popular trekking spot for Westerners with Padang Batung being the first stop to check in with the police. If you have checked in with police in Banajarmasin they will give you a permit to tour the area. It is said that the permit is just a courtesy but it doesn't hurt just in case you wander off in your trekking bliss.

Most villages have simple rooms or balai that run between 1000 up to 5500 rupiah a night. Muara Hatib is the most touristed since it has road access.

Martapura

40kms, 45 mins from Banjarmasin about RP750 via colt

A center for precious gemstones for a century and a half, Martapura is usually a day trip from Banjarmasin. The heady prospect of discovering stones has created a strange "karma" in this village of dreamers. Diamonds are worshipped as having spirits like virgin princesses who can be easily offended by a variety of uncouth behavior. The miners do not smoke, whistle or even allow sour tasting food in an effort not to scare away the delicate female diamond spirits. The stores and polishing factories are closed Fridays but Friday is the best day to visit the local vegetable market next to the regular market (Pasar Niaga).

Let's make a deal, politely

If you want to take home a few baubles remember to haggle like hell (but don't offend the diamond spirits), don't waste your time on Friday (the stores and factories are closed) and focus your chiseling skills on the owner of Kayu Tangi on Jalan Sukaramail 4/J where they will guarantee the quality of the stones. Remember that even if you cut a mean deal you will have to have your stone fine tuned (the stones are not well cut or polished) and mounted in whatever jewelry you choose.

Getting Around

Buses leave for Kandangan throughout the day from the terminal in Banjarmasin (3 hours, 3000 rupiah), then charter an ojek (30 minutes, 2500 rupiah) or local bus (20 minutes, 1000 rupiah). Make sure you stop in Padang Batung to register, then on to Mawangi. From there most people hike in and then raft down from Loksado to Kandangan on a bamboo raft for about 45,000 rupiah.

Negara

3.5 hours from Banjarmasin by road

A swampy homeland for Banjars. What makes the area interesting is how the Banjars have adapted to swamp dwelling. Not only are their homes built on stilts but they raise water buffalo on raised platforms. They also catch serpent fish using baby ducklings as bait.

Where to Stay

There is a tiny losmen with shared mandi for 4000 rupiah.

Getting Around

Take the river taxi from Banjarmasin river taxi pier (6500 rupiah, 24 hours), or the bus to Kandangan and then to Negara (3.5 hours, 5000 rupiah).

Jungle Trekking

The best places to explore are the Meratus Dayak near Loksado on the Amandat river and the Mt Besar (1892m) in the Pegunungan Muratus area about 190 km from Bansarmajin. The area to the Southeast offers treks around Lake Riamkanan. You will need a guide to get the most out of any of these areas so the best advice is to shop your needs with the local tour operators. Most tour operators will want to have a party of at least two people.

Banjarbaru

30 minutes from Banjarmasin by minibus

Other than the museum there is little reason to visit this town.

Lampung Mangkurat State Museum

In Banjarbaru near Martapura, open Tuesday–Sunday 8:30 a.m.–2:00 p.m. closes 11 a.m. Friday and 1:00 p.m. Sunday.

Kalsel's official museum features a lot of weapons from wars with the Dutch, artifacts found in Hindu temples around Kalimantan and a *tambangan* or traditional Banjar river boat. There are dance performances on Sunday around 9 a.m. It can be skipped if you are in a hurry.

Long Houses/Balai

There are over 30 longhouses in the Loksado area. Request material from the Kalsel tourism office that provides an overview of the various treks along with times and distances.

Getting In

From Banjarmasin take a minibus (1200 rupiah) or a taxi (30,000 rupiah) or speedboat (10,000 rupiah) from the Dermaga Pier near the Grand Mosque.

East Kalimantan

East Kalimantan is the most remote and rugged part of Kalimantan. It is also the wealthiest, most visited and second largest province in Indonesia after Irian Jaya. Comparable to Alaska to the U.S. or Siberia to Russia, the government of Indonesia is in a rush to pull out as much timber, coal and oil as they can to fill the government coffers back home.

Stone poles with Sanskrit inscriptions have been found on the East Coast that date back to the 5th century. Javanese fleeing the Majapahits founded the kingdom of Kertannegara. The Chinese who traded up and down the coast of Borneo called this region *Kutai* or "great land" to describe its vastness and richness. Not being very creative the Chinese also named the major inland trade route the *Mahakam* or "Great River." The Mahakam River was also the gateway for the Hindus who arrived in AD 400. Later Kutai became an Islamic sulatanate (until 1960) following the lead of Banjarmasin in late 1565.The Hindu kingdom of Martapura, based along the Mahakam river, warred with Kutai until a marriage united the two regions. A second conflict 200 years later resulted with Kutai losing and being added to the Martapura domain.

During the 18th century, Kutai's capital was moved inland to protect it from the many pirate attacks from the neighboring Bugi of Sulawesi. In 1781 Tenggarong became the capital.

Joseph Conrad used his experiences from his multiple visits to Berau and Tanjung Redeb in *Lord Jim*, *Almayer's Folly* and *Outcast of the Islands*. Kutai or modern day Kaltim cannot shake off its image of vastness and great expanse. Few people will travel over the entire region. Many people will visit this region with little understanding of the vast forests beneath their airplane. Others will spend weeks exploring remote jungles or traveling the rivers of the Apo Kayan. Most will fly into Balikpapan, take a tour and then leave.

Today the major centers of Kaltim are Balikpapan, a major oil producing and refining center and Samarinda, a major logging center. Tarakan to the north is another oil producing area but slowly running out of oil.

Balikpapan

Sitting high above the noisy street in air-conditioned comfort at the Benakutai hotel I watched as the offshore rigs flamed off excess gas. Below the ocean was tropical blue and the sky full of spectacular white clouds. This is Borneo?

Balikpapan may look more like Galveston, Texas or some other modern oil port. There is little here to remind you that you have come half way around the world. The government owned Pertamina oil company is the major reason for Balikpapan being here. Out on the street are air-conditioned shopping centers that rival anything in Los Angeles or Singapore, hotels and restaurants that cater to expense account visitors and bars full of men with cowboy boots and aluminum briefcases. The upside to this wealth is the quality of native crafts shops, antique stores and tourism infrastructure. The downside is that Balkipapan can drain your wallet faster than a losing streak at the Flamingo.

The World's Biggest Fire

Starting with the great conflagration in 1982 and 1983 the great forests of East Kalimantan have been burning almost continually. Most point to logging as the main culprit, others point out the large seams of coal that can burn underground for years. In any case over 20% of the rainforest was destroyed in the '83 fire. The fire sent clouds of haze as far as Singapore.

Where to Stay

There is a 21 percent surcharge on all room rates in Balikpapan.

Hotel Benakutai   **RP242,000–682,000**   ★★★★★

Jalan Jenderal Achmad Yani; ☎ *(0542) 31896, FAX 31823*

The primo hotel in Balikpapan since 1980 with 176 well kept rooms with views of the offshore oil rigs. The first and only stop for the oil patch, businessmen and tour groups. The hotel is used to mud splattered trekkers showing up with two weeks of mildewed laundry. The bar beyond the lobby is a popular expat hangout.

Dusit Inn Balikpapan   **RP150,000–400,000**

Jalan Jend. Surdirman, ☎ *(0542) 20155, FAX 20150*

A beach resort about 4 kms from the airport. 208 rooms built in 1994. Swimming pool, tennis, fitness center and two restaurants.

Blue Sky Hotel   **RP78,000–126,000**

Jalan Let. Jend. Suprapto 1; ☎ *(0542) 22268*

A friendly place to stay if the Benakutai is full. Billiards, A/C, massage, satellite television complete with in house videos.

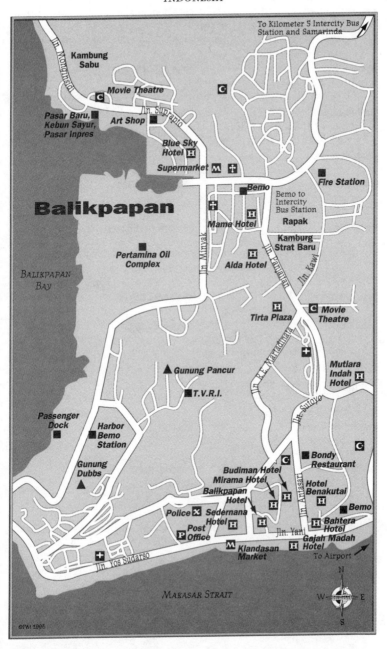

Balikpapan

To Kilometer 5 Intercity Bus Station and Samarinda

Kambung Sabu

Movie Theatre

Jln. Monginsidi

Pasar Baru, Kebun Sayur, Pasar inpres

Art Shop

Jln. Suprapto

Blue Sky Hotel

Supermarket

Bemo

Fire Station

Bemo to Intercity Bus Station

Rapak

Mama Hotel

Kamburg Strat Baru

Pertamina Oil Complex

Jln. Minyak

Aida Hotel

Jln. Panjaitan

Jln. Kawi

BALIKPAPAN BAY

Tirta Plaza

Movie Theatre

Jln. R.E. Martadinata

Mutiara Indah Hotel

Gunung Pancur

T.V.R.I.

Jln. Sutoyo

Passenger Dock

Harbor Bemo Station

Bondy Restaurant

Gunung Dubbs

Budiman Hotel

Mirama Hotel

Balikpapan Hotel

Jln. Antasari

Hotel Benakutai

Police

Sedernana Hotel

Bemo

Post Office

Bahtera Hotel

Jln. Yani

Gajah Madah Hotel

Klandasan Market

To Airport

Jln. Yos Sudarso

MAKASAR STRAIT

N
W — E
S

©IWI 1995

Hotel Balikpapan   RP66,500–78,650   ★★

Jalan Erry Suparjan 2;☎ (0542) 21490
Another businessman's special complete with "health club" disco, restaurant A/C
etc.

Mirama   RP50,000–105,000

Jalan A.P. Pranoto 16; ☎ (0542) 33906
Big clean hotel with plenty of rooms when the Blue Sky and Benakutai are full.

Hotel Budiman   RP45,000

Jalan Jend A. Yani; ☎ (0542) 36030
Low budget, passable with A/C.

Gajah Mada   RP22,500–50,000

Jalan Jen. Sudirman 14; ☎ (0542) 34634

Bahtera Hotel   RP42,400–60,500

Jalan Jend. Sudirman 2; ☎ (0542) 22603, FAX 31889
Businessman's hotel, A/C, restaurant.

Wisma Patra   RP 40,000–100,000

Jalan Prabumilih; ☎ (0542) 33011
For oil folks. Away from downtown but overlooking the Pertamina oil refinery. You
can ask for one of the detached bungalows if the view doesn't turn you on. Tennis
court.

Hotel Senderhana   RP14,000–44,000

Kelandasan Ulu ☎ (0542) 22564

Hotel Aida   RP12,000–30,000

Jalan Jend. A Yani 1/12; ☎ (0542) 21006
A popular backpacker hangout.

Surya   RP5000

Jalan Karang Bugis; ☎ (0542) 21580
A hotel that charges by the half hour can't be all that bad. At least plenty of vacan-
cies open up each night.

Penginapan Murni   RP4000

Jalan S. Parman1
Simple accommodation.

Penginapan Royal   RP4000–6000

Near Pasar Baru, near Jalan Pengeran Antasari corner
Simple and clean with shared mandi, some with A/C and breakfast.

Best Time to Visit

June to November are the driest and coolest months. March, April and May are the
wettest and hottest ones. It makes little difference since it is always hot and humid.

Tour Companies

Kaltim Adventure Tour

Blok C-1/1 Komplex Balikpapan; Permai Jalan Jend. Sudirman;
☎ *(0542) 31158, FAX 33408*

Musi

Jalan Dondang (Antasari) 5A ; ☎ (0542) 24272, FAX 24984

Natrabu

Jalan Ned A. Yani 58; ☎ *(0542) 22443*

Tomaco

Hotel Benakutai; Jalan Jend. A. Yani; ☎ *(0542) 22747*

Tourist Information Office; Seppingang Airport, ☎ *(0542) 21605.*

Getting In

Sepinggang Airport is a short 10km from downtown Balikpapan. The airport has a money changer, souvenir shop, restaurant and a telephone that you can use to make international calls usings credit cards.

Taxis into town are 7500 rupiah, taxis to Samarinda run 55,000 rupiah.

Flights on Asahi, Bouraq Garuda, Merpati and Sempati, connect to most major cities in Kalimantan and Indonesia.

Getting Around

Via Land

Buses to Samarinda (2hrs) leave every 30 minutes from 5:30 a.m. to 8 p.m. from Km 3.5 on Samarinda road. You can also get to Samarinda via taxi from the Batu Ampar terminal (RP6000 per person). Getting around town is usually done via yellow Toyota minibuses. (RP250 anywhere in town) Ojeks are RP500.

Via Boat

The PELNI ferries Tidar Kernicni and Kambuna travel every two weeks to Jakarta, Surabaya, Tarakan, Toli Toli and Ujung Padang. Buy your tickets at Jalan Pelabuhan near Jalan Yos Sudarso ☎ *(0542) 22187* and catch the ferry at the dock west of the city center off Jalan Yos Sudarso.

Getting Out

There are five flights a day to Jakarta from Balikpapan and PELNI sailings every two weeks.

Nuts & Bolts

If you want English language magazines, books or newspapers, the shop in the Benakutai hotel is your best bet. The post office is on Jalan Ahmad Yani and there is one at the airport. Post office hours are from 8 a.m. till 6 p.m. (5 p.m. on weekends and holidays) with the airport being open in the morning hours only.

Bank Negara Indonesia on Jalan Pengeran Antassi is your best bet (and rate) for cashing travelers checks.Banks are open 8 a.m. to noon, 1:30 pm to 3 p.m. Monday through Friday and then Saturday 8 a.m. to 11 a.m. The major hotels and airport money change will also oblige.

The immigration office is on the corner of Jalan Ahmad Yani and Jalan Sudirman.

Author's Tip

Make sure you cash plenty of traveler's checks or get advances on your credit cards if you plan to go inland. They may take heads but they don't take American Express. Gasoline, boatmen, food and supplies will be exorbitantly expensive and everyone expects to get paid in big fat rolls of rupiah.

Samarinda

120km north of Balikpapan,
60 kms upstream from the mouth of the Mahakam river

Most travelers will blow through Samarinda on their way up the Mahakam river or to catch a plane to the Apo Kayan. It is primarily a trading town (founded in 1730). Most of the trees that used to exist upriver have passed through Samirinda on their way to Japan and Europe. The town has grown rich from the timber industry. Sights worth seeing are the Bugis schooners tied up on the left bank near the east side of town and Kampung Sulili, a small town built on stilts downriver. After that there is not much. It is advisable to hook up with one of the recommended tour companies in Balikpapan or Jakarta. There are plenty of eager tour guides in Samarinda who will dun you 30,000 rupiah or more per day. You will probably end up paying much more for hidden extras like gas and permits than if you went with a tour group. The tour companies also own houseboats designed for tourists that take much of the misery out of the river trip.

Getting In

Most people fly in from Balikpapan, Banjarmasin, Tarakan, and other major cities outside of Kalimantan. The airport is on the northeast side of town.

Getting Around

Samarinda is a central point for most tourism in East Kalimantan.

Where to Stay in Samarinda

Hotel Mesra   **RP68,000–187,000**   ★★★

Jalan Pahlawan 1; ☎ *(0541) 32772, FAX 21017*
56 Rooms. The best hotel in Samarinda but out of town. Swimming pool, tennis court, coffee shop, restaurant and all A/C.

Kota Tepian   **RP40,000–90,000**   ★★

Jalan Pahlawan 4; ☎ *(0541) 32513*
Clean, expensive, A/C restaurant 30,000–105,000 rupiah.

Hotel Sewarga Indah   **RP29,000–55,000**

Jalan Jend. Sudirman 11; ☎ *(0541) 22066, FAX 23662*
69 rooms. Clean, economical, and centrally located. Price includes breakfast, and tax/service fee. A/C restaurant. Service is not up to the price.

Aida   **RP17,000–32,000**

Jalan K.H. Mas Tenunggung; ☎ *(0541) 42572*

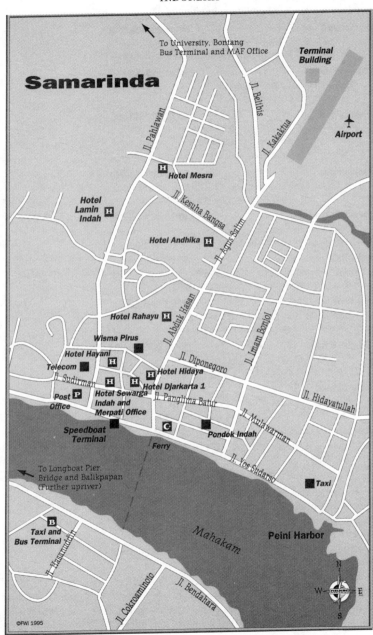

Samarinda

To University, Bontang
Bus Terminal and MAF Office

Terminal Building

Jl. Pahlawan

Jl. Belibis

Jl. Kakaktua

✈ **Airport**

H **Hotel Mesra**

Jl. Kesuha Bangsa

Hotel Lamin Indah H

Jl. Agus Salim

Hotel Andhika H

Jl. Abduk Hasan

Jl. Imam Bonjol

Hotel Rahayu H

Wisma Pirus

Hotel Hayani H

Jl. Diponegoro

Telecom

H **Hotel Hidaya**

Jl. Sudirman

H H **Hotel Djarkarta 1**

Post Office P

Hotel Sewarga Indah and Merpati Office

Jl. Panglima Batur

Jl. Hidayatullah

Jl. Mulawarman

Speedboat Terminal

C

Ferry

Pondok Indah

Jl. Yos Sudarso

■ **Taxi**

To Longboat Pier,
Bridge and Balikpapan
(Further upriver)

B

Taxi and Bus Terminal

Jl. Hasanuddin

Mahakam

Peini Harbor

Jl. Cokroaminoto

Jl. Bendahara

N
W — E
S

©FWI 1995

A/C colorful location next to market, a popular budget stop.

Hotel Hayani   RP10,550–66,750

Jaland Pirus and Jalan Nenderal; ☎ *(0541) 42653*
Across the street from the Wisma Pirus with restaurant.

Hidayah I Hotel   RP18,150–33,275

Jalan K.H. Mas Tenunggung; ☎ *(0541) 31210*
Near the morning market.

Andhika Hotel   RP14,520–22,990

Jalan H. Agus Salim 37; ☎ *(0541) 42358*
50 rooms. Cheap with restaurant, about a ten minute walk from town center.
Mosque across the street for early risers.

Wisma Pirus   RP10,000–70,000

Jalan Pirus and Jalan Nenderal; ☎ *(0541) 21873*
A wide selection of rooms with friendly staff.

Hotel Djarkarta 1   RP10,000–25,000

Jalan Jend. Sudirman 57
Cheap, good in a pinch, A/C .

Hotel Rahmat Abadi   RP9000–12,800

Jaland Serindit 215; ☎ *(0541) 23462*
Near the airport, rooms include breakfast.

Hotel Rahayu   RP7200–19,200

Jalan K. H. Abul Hasan 17; ☎ *(0541) 22622*
20 rooms. Cheap and cheerful with shared bathrooms.

Hidayah II Hotel   RP11,000–20,000

Jalan K.H. Khalid 25; ☎ *(0541) 41712*
Some rooms with A/C.

Hotel Sukarni   RP7500–20,000

Jalan Panglima Batur 154; ☎ *(0541) 21134*
A popular brothel, for people who have no intention of sleeping.

Penginapan Maharani   RP5500–11,000

Jalan H. Agus Salim 35; ☎ *21057*
Cheapest.

Nuts & Bolts

You can change your U.S. dollars (last chance if you are going upriver) at the Bank Negaro Indonesia on the corner of Jalan Sebatik and Jalan Panglima Batur. If you have traveler's checks or currency other than American you must go to the Bank Dagang Negaro on Nalan Mulawarman. Hours for both banks are 8 a.m.–12:30, 1:30 p.m. to 4:30 p.m. Monday to Thursday, Friday from 1:30 p.m. to 4:30 p.m. and Saturday from 8 a.m. to 11:30 a.m.

The tourist office is off Jalan Kesuma Bangsa at Jalan Al Suryani. ☎ *(0541) 21669.* Many people stop in at the Hotel Rahayu, and ask for Jailaina, a local guide. The post office is on the corner of Jalan Gaja Mada and Jalan Awanglong. The morning market is just north of the Mesra Hotel and is best between 6 a.m. and 8 a.m. The tourist trade going up the river means this is a good spot for shopping. Items are expensive so bargain, bargain, bargain.

Airline offices in Samarinda

Garuda
   Jalan Jendirman Sudirman 57; ☎ *(0541) 22624*

Merpati
   Jalan Iman Bonjol; ☎ *(0541) 23928*

Bouraq
   Jalan Mulawarman 24; ☎ *(0541) 21105*

Sempati
   Masnum Anindya; ☎ *(0541) 22624*

Asahi
   Jalan Imam Bonjol 4; ☎ *(0541) 23928*

MAF
   Jalan H. Agus Salim 13B; ☎ *(0541) 22644, FAX 320080*

MAF
   Post office Box 82; Samarinda
   The airport is close if not almost in town.

Tarakan is a sleepy backwater oil town.

Tarakan

35 minutes by air from Tawau in Sabah

Tarakan is a fading oil port tucked away in the northeastern part of Kalimantan. The only reason to visit is to take the plane to or from Tawau in Sabah. Tarakan was the site of a major battle in May of 1945. The Island's airfield was needed to launch further attacks into Borneo, but the airfield was so badly damaged it was unusable. Over 200 Australian soldiers died in the six week battle. You can still see the Japanese defenses and rusting gunboats around the city. Today Tarakan is a tough dirty city spread out along a single street. There are cheap hotels along Jalan Jenderal Sudirman and expensive hotels along Jalan Yos Sudarso.

Where to Stay in Tarakan

Hotel Tarakan Plaza   **RP77,000–99,000**   ★

Jalan Yos Sudarso ☎ *(0541) 21870.*
This is where everyone stays including all the pilots.

Wisata Hotel   **RP10,500–20,000**

Jalan Sudirman ☎ *(0541) 21245.*

Barito Hotel   **RP16,500–33,000**

Jalan Jenderal Sudirman 133, ☎ *(0541) 21212.*

Getting Around

Merpati

Jalan Yos Sudarso 8, ☎ *(0541) 21875*

Bouraq

Jalan Yos Sudarso 9B, ☎ *(0541) 21248*

Asahi

Jalan Yos Sudarso ☎ *(0541) 21871*

From Tarakan

VIA AIR

The airport is a RP3500 taxi ride. Drivers may jack you up on arrival so agree to a fare including any baggage you have.

Balikpapan	daily	RP138,000	Bouraq
Tawau (Sabah)	3 weekly	RP122,000	Bouraq

VIA FERRY

The ferry makes its twice weekly run between major Indonesian ports. Check with the PELNI office at the port at the end of Jalan Yos Sudarso.

Balikpapan		RP66,500	PELNI
Ujung Padang		RP122,500	PELNI
Surabaya		RP154,800	PELNI
Jakarta		RP375,500	PELNI

VIA LONGBOAT

The boats leave at dawn from the pier just over the bridge. Boats to Nunakan and then to Sabah leave from Pelabuhan Tarakan

Tanjung Selor	daily	RP5000	Longboat
Nunakan	daily	RP15,000	Longboat
Pulau Bunju	daily	RP7000	Longboat
Tawau	charter	RP40,000	Speedboat
Nunakan - Tawau	charter	RP25,000	Speedboat

Nunakan

A minor stop on the way to Tawau. This timber town exists to change money and to house and feed Indonesian immigration officials.

Excursions

The Mahakam River ★★★

In 1991 when Bill Dalton first wrote his *Indonesia Handbook* for Moon Publications he figured that only 1000 people made the trip up the muddy Mahakam. Today this river is the most popular tourist attraction in Kalimantan. Over 15,000 tourists take boat trips up the lazy 920km long Mahakam River to visit the tribes and get a lifetime full of "authentic" tribal goods and dances. Strangely enough because of the exodus from the Apo Kayan there are more Kenyah and Kayan peoples along the river than up in their ancestral homelands. The lower Mahakam River is from Samarinda to Muara Muntai. This takes in the Tenggarong and the three lakes. This is the most touristed section. The middle Mahakam begins at Kuara Muntai to Long Bagun. Here you run out of public transit so you must negotiate a boatman and canoe to take you further. Tour operators will set this trip up for you. You will travel from Long Gelat and as far up into the Muller range as you'd care to go, or your wallet and nerve will take you.

Those expecting ancient history or loin clothed savages will be sorely disappointed. The modern world has arrived. There is no jungle, no towering mountains, no authentic longhouses. The atmosphere is similar to any new settlement where people are busy making a living. If the intrepid traveler pokes around the smaller tribtutaries or spends time exploring the side roads, he will be pleasantly surprised. Your choice of chariot are the riverboats that ply the waters on regular schedules. You could charter a longboat with a high powered engine, or a less powerful *ketingting* or *ces,* cheaper but slower.

The lower and middle stretches of the river could be described as tedious. Romantic types bring along *Heart of Darkness* to experience a Conradian transformation. You can cut to the chase by simply flying on Asahi airlines to Data Dawai airstrip in Long Lunuk and start from there.

It takes at least a week to get a decent ways up the river. The further upriver you go, the better the sights. A 5–9 day tour will cost you about US$800 per person for a group of 4–6. You can get as far as Long Iram. Fourteen days will get you as far as Long Bagun 523 kms upriver. If you want to walk for two days the mighty Boh River awaits or the Benahan.

Up the Mahakam	
Sungai Kanjung	Boats leave early morning
Kota Bangung	9 hours
Tanjung Isuy	14 hours
Muara Muntai	12 hours
Melak	24 hours
Long Iram	30 hours
Long Bagun	40 hours

Tenggarong ★★

40km upriver from Samarinda

If you are interested in the most interesting spot in Kalimantan for culture and you are not the adventurous type, this is your best bet. Every September 23 they hold the big five day Erau festival. You have the opportunity to see a wide variety of Dayak tribes perform their dances, sports, and Indonesia's biggest water fight after launch of a great floating Dragon.

Erau Festival ★★★

September 23–28

Formerly celebrated the coronation of the Sultan of Kutai. The original wing-ding was 40 days long. This may explain why the Dutch had no problem conquering this part of Borneo. This is a photographer's fantasy with colored costumes including the Hudoq dance (seen on most of the tourist posters back in Balikpapan and Samarinda). This dance looks very similar to Haida costumes and dances held in the Pacific Northwest of Canada and Alaska. The dance and grotesque masks are designed to scare away pestilence, bad weather and other evil things that could interfere with a good rice crop.

There are also sporting events that involve everything from top spinning to boat races to mock combat. The gory part is when they recreate a *mamat*. This is the ceremony that was held to welcome back warriors returning with heads. In this case orang utan skulls are used and a water buffalo is sacrificed to celebrate. For those who like their ceremonies more cerebral there is also a *belian* healing ceremony where devils and evil spirits are cast out by the *shaman*.

Naturally the event is crowded with tourists brandishing Nikons, but it is worth scheduling a trip around.

Muluawarman Museum

Open 10:00 a.m.–2:00 p.m. every day except Monday.

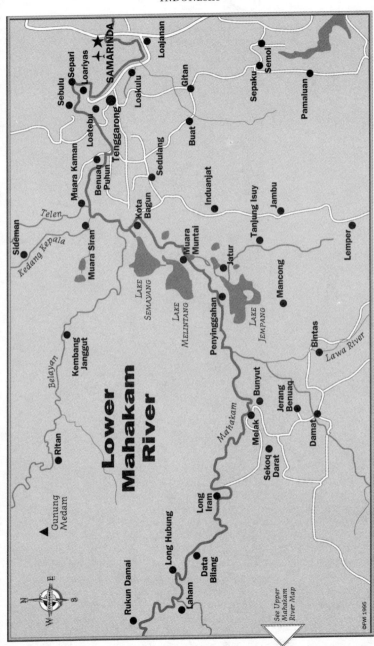

Lower Mahakam River

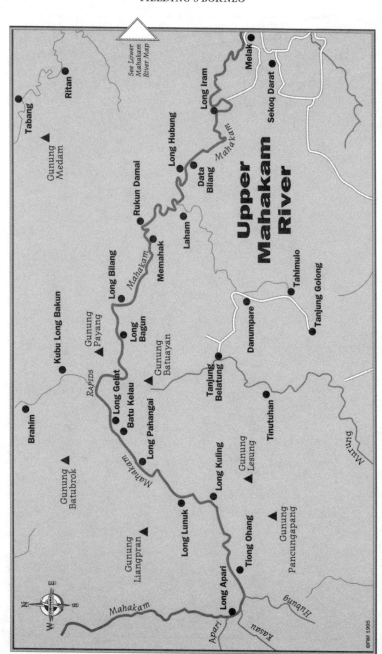

See Lower Mahakam River Map

Upper Mahakam River

©FWI 1995

A stilted poorly done replica of the former Sultan's palace that was destroyed by fire in 1936.The Dutch architect who designed the replica didn't quite get the knack of recreating the opulence the Sultan was accustomed to. Around the turn of the century, coal and oil had made the Sultan a very wealthy man—a situation very similar to the Sultanate of Brunei today. The Sultan had a well stocked harem, an ice machine, and three cars. His "house" was furnished with the finest that Europe and China offered. Today the museum has an excellent introduction into the history and culture of the region. There is also an orchid garden in the back and cultural shows in the main hall on Sundays.

Muara Kaman

6 hours upriver from Tenggarong, 2 hours downstream from Kota Bagun

This ancient Hindu Mulawarman site is the start of the **Sungai Telen** tributary and the kampungs of Muara Bengkal, Batu Ampar, Long Noran and Muara Wahau (where there can be a connection between Marapan via a 2.5 ride to Marapan) and from there a 12 hour riverboat trip to Tanjng Redap and then 10 hours to Tarakan. A little further up the river is the sungai Kedang Kepala for trips to Senyiur and beyond. A half hour walk downstream from Muara Kaman will take you to Muara Kenyak a Kenyah village.

Just before Kota Bangun is the sungai Belayan with Long Bleh, Ritan and Tabang. There is a footpath between Tabang and Muara Merak. It is 11 hours upriver on the sungai Kedang Kepala to Muara Ancalong. There is a cave that holds statues of Hindu gods. Gua Kombeng is east of Muara Wahau via an 8 hour trek or a half hour upstream walk beyond the Slabing lumber camp. There are MAF airstrips in Long Sefar, Miau Baru and Merah.

Sungai Kedang Kepala

Regular longboat services travel north to **Muara Wahau**. (3 days and 2 nights, RP16,500) and 16 hours to **Muara Ancalong** (a Kenyah village). From this point it might be possible with time and money to travel to Tarakan via Sungai Kelai.Just past Batu Ampar the river narrows. The last village on the river is Ben Hes a settlement of some 70 Modang families.

Sungai Mahak

There is a tiny airstrip at Makar Baruthat that is occasionally serviced by MAF flights.

Sungai Belayan

A 2–3 day trip to the Kenyah village of **Tabang** is on this tributary of the Mahakam if you charter a *ketingting* for about RP100,000. There is also a foot trail to Tabang from Muara Merak. MAF has irregular flights in and out of Tabang.From Tabang there is a two day trek to skirt the rapids and then a three day canoe trip up Sungai Tabang and a two day trek to the Penan settelement of **Long Suleh**.

Sungai Kayan

Tanjung Selor is the entrance to the Kayan river. There is regular riverboat service to Mara I and Mara II. A set of rapids prevent river travel into the Apo Kayan. There is a twice weekly flight for RP41,800 to Long Ampung in the Apo Kayan.

Kota Bangun

This backwater Muslim town is 8 hours upriver from Tenggarong, the start of the flat lake country on the north bank of the Mahakam. You can reach Kota Bangun via a rough 84km road from Tenggarong .

Muara Muntai

10 hours from Tenggarong, 3 hours from Kota Bagun
A stilt village raised above the flood level of the Mahakam. From here it is possible to hire a guide to hike into the Bario river basin and then take a boat downriver to Banjarmasin.

The Lakes

Lake Jempang, Lake Melintang, and Lake Semayang are the only fresh water lakes in Borneo. The lakes of the Mahakam are famous for their freshwater dolphins and proboscis monkeys .

Tanjung Isay

2.5 hours from Muara Muntai.
A major stop for tourists due to its dance performances. You should report to the police station if traveling solo, on the Mancong River. There is a longhouse at Mancong about 10kms, 3 hrs by foot or 2.5 hours by canoe from Tanjung Isay. You can get a ride on a motorbike for about RP15,000.

Melak

12 hours from Kota Bagun, 29 hours from Samarinda, 51 kms by road from Long Iram.
A Muslim town where there are also good longhouses.There is also an **Orchid Reserve** named Kersik Luway 16kms to the south where black orchids are in bloom in April, at the end of the rainy season. There are 112 species of orchids on display at the Reserve. At this point there are many villages who practice the Kaharingan religion.If you want to get off the river and do a bit of mild trekking, the area of Barong Tongkok awaits. Melak is the gateway to the Barong Tongkok area to the southwest.

Barong Tongkok

18kms south of Melak by road
This area consists of flatland and rolling hills with lush landscaping and welcoming people. Barong Tongkok is an ideal starting point to visit the many animist and traditional longhouses in the region. From Barong Tongkok try to visit the longhouses of **Engkuni** (12kms south) **Geleo Baru** (13km northeast) **Papas** (17km southeast) **Eheng** (15 km southwest) and **Mengimai** (6 kms south). You can hire a motorcycle or 4 wheel drive to take you to the various villages.

When you're ready to continue upstream hike out the 30kms north to Tering Lama to get back on the riverboat or hike the extra 7kms, 1.5 hours to Long Iram. You must cross the Mahakam at Tering Sebarang to Tering Lama for about $1000 rupiah. There is a good road network that leads to the Barito basin and to the surrounding villages. To find out what is happening at the various longhouses around Barong Tongkok spend a few minutes at the *camat's* office. You can stay at the simple losmen or at the longhouse.

Tering

12kms downstream from Long River
A collection of three villages (Old Tering, New Tering and Tering Sebarang). There was a Roman Catholic mission here in the early 20s and there is a well decorated meeting house in Tering Lama and some ancient carved posts. Gold mining is the latest topic here but it is handled by an Australian company.

Long Iram

114kms, 21 hours from Long Bagun, 583kms, 33 hours from Samarinda
This may be where your river trip ends if the river is low or if the boat can't make headway up the river. At this point most tourists figure they have seen all there is to see and head back. Little do they know that the scenery begins to become spectacular and the people are friendly. From Long Iram your best bet to get upriver is to get aboard an eight passenger ces with its powerful outboard motor.

Datah Bilang

5 kims downstream from Long Bagun
Now things get interesting. Visit the the two town halls above the river. Here you'll find the look and feel of the more remote Apo Kayan without having to travel all the way there. There is also a giant canoe painted in the traditional Kenyah designs. There are traditional dances every Sunday night. There are many traditional Kenyah who retain the tattoos and traditions. Long Hubung a few kms upstream will put on an ad hoc *hudoq* dance if you have the cash. The sheer limestone cliffs (many with large caves) and lush vegetation let you know that you are heading into the heart of Borneo.

Rukun Damai

4 hours upstream from Data Bilang
A Kenyah village with two longhouses. There is a dilapidated longhouse in the Bajau town of Matalibag.

Long Bagun

523kms upriver from Samarinda, 140kms, 8 hours by longbot from Long Iram
The end of the line for the riverboats and the beginning of adventure into the interior. This is the land of the Benauq, the Kenyah and the Tunjung. It will cost about RP32,000 per person to travel to Long Apari. Travel beyond Long Bagun will require chartering a longboat complete with boatman and bowsman. In between here and the next settlement (Long Pahangi) is a one day boat trip over a set of rapids. There is little to see in Long Bagun except a logging company. This is the town to plan your trip to the Apo Kayan if you want to do it the hard way. From here you can take the two day longboat up the Boh and then the Benahan to Muara Benahan. Expect to pay about RP600,000 for the one way trip. The Boh has a set of very dangerous rapids requiring you to to take the Sungai Benahan to Muara Tanit and then walk two days to Mahak Baru. Plan B is to take the Sungai Uga from the Boh and then to Long Metalung. From here trails lead to Long Ampung and Long Nawan.

This is the beginning of authentic longhouses and dayak villages. There are some excellent wood carvers in Long Bagun Hilir (downstream) There is an airstrip in Data Dawai with a Thursday and Sunday Asahai flight to Samarinda for RP42,000.

Beyond Long Bagun

From this point on you are adventuring in the purest sense of the word. Although many people and some books will tell you how to get from point A to point B, there is a lot of misery in between those two points. The first Westerner to make this trip was Dr. A. W. Nieuwenhuis in 1897. He recorded the natural habits and lifestyle of the Kenyah in his photographs and notes at the time. He did much to convince the Kenyah and Kayan of the Apo Kayan that Dutch rule would be beneficial. The fact that the Iban had decimated and terrorized the region in 1885 did much to convince the Kenyah that they needed help. The Iban had sent a huge raiding party and had traveled into the region of the Upper Mahakam and Apo Kayan and burned every Kayan and Aoheng village. The region came under Dutch administration in 1907 and saw its first missionary school in 1927 in Batu Ura.

Today the region is losing more and more young men to the timber camps of Sarawak. In Sarawak men make more money in a month (about $1700 per month) than their parents ever made in their lives, if any. Their culture has been subverted into dances performed for tourists and their religion is either Catholic or Protestant. There is an acute shortage of simple items like salt, sugar, tobacco or medicine and any items they need cost about twice what the downriver communities pay since simple items like outboard motors or gas have to be either carried in or flown in. If you attempt the trip upstream remember that there is a reason why travelers are not seen here. The rapids between Long Bagun and Tiong Ohang are fierce and you can spend a lot of time in the same spot fighting the fast current. Most people fly to Data Dawai, the airstrip within walking distance from Long Lunuk. From there you can travel downsteam to Long Pahangai or upstream to Tiong Ohang.

Tiong Ohang

This is the land of the Penihang. Sungai Huvung is one day upriver from Tiong Ohang. At Sungai Huvung you can walk to a tribtutary of the Kapuas river. There are two interesting longhouses here. There is also a small store. This is the kecamantan center for the region. You should check in with the local camat. There are also guides who will take you across the Muller Range into the Kapuas Basin.

Long Pahangai

There are quite a few rapids between Long Bagun and Long Pahangi so expect to spend two days. The Catholic Mission has created some impressive Apo Kayan motifs.You can take side trips up the Sungai Pahangai to visit the jungle and revel in the solitude.

Long Apari

The uppermost village of the Mahakam. It takes 5–6 hours from Long Lamuk. The four day trip to Malaysia can cost as much as RP 500,000 It is about three days to the headwaters of the Mahakam from here.You can also arrange treks to the Kapuas basin here. Three days of trekking will take you to Long Metalung in the Apo Kayan.

Getting Around

Your best bet is to set up a tour in Balikpapan or Samarinda. Those who push further up the river should take their time and explore the little visited tributaries. The riverboat is the only way to get up the Mahakam. The boats provide sleeping areas on deck and will stop for meal breaks along the river. The better boats will have food on board and mattresses and lockers. The fare up the river may fluctuate depending on whether the river is running high or low. To get to the dock at Sungai Kunjung take a taxi kota from downtown (RP500). Keep in mind that once you leave the scheduled riverboat service behind, you are at the whim of whatever boatman you hire.

To prepare for the trip you should bring something to read, sunglasses, binoculars, plenty of bottled water, snacks and some type of supplement to the bland food served on board. Bottom line for this region is to take the plane. There are many flights into the remote airstrips of the region. Also consider flying in and taking longboats downstream where travel is faster and cheaper.

Where to Stay Along the Mahakam

Most visitors sleep aboard the riverboats. If you want to get off there are rest houses at all major stops. Most budget hotels charge RP5000 for a night's rest. There are many longhouses beyond Long Bagun and most people are welcoming of visitors. Once you get *ulu*, longhouses are your only choice.

Up the Berau

Tanjung Redeb

59 kms from the mouth of the Berau river, 55kms, 9 hours north to Tarakan

The Berau is a little traveled river starting at the small town of Tanjung Redeb. Once the capital of the tiny kingdom of Berau (founded in the 14th century) the Indonesian government abolished it in 1960. Tanjung Redeb is the starting point for trips into primeval rainforest in the upper Bahau area. There is another palace in Sambaliung .

There are museums that have a minor collecton of artefacts at Istana Sambaliung. You can travel to Tarakan from Tanjung Redeb for about RP12,000. You can also travel up the Kelai and Sagan rivers. Only 8 boats a month call at this remote port.

The Krayan

Tucked into the corner of Sabah and Sarawak is the most remote region of Kalimantan and possibly the least interesting. Missionaries have been hard at work since 1927 converting the mostly Murut peoples from their traditional animist ways to the more industrial modern beliefs. The best way in is to fly into Long Bawan. You can fly into Long Bawan via the twice weekly Merpati flights. MAF flies in from Malinau but check with them to ensure you can get back out. Fares from Tarakan to Long Bawan are RP250,000 and from Long Bawan to Melinau about RP150,000.

There are also smaller missionary airstrips in Binuang, Harapan Karya, Long Rungan, Pa'Upan, Kampung Baru, Lembudud and Long Umung.

From Long Bawan you can trek west into Ba Kelalan in Sarawak or from Sabah into Long Pesiat. Much of the land has been cleared and is not that lush. It's an easy four hour trek to Lembudud. From there it is six hours to Ba Kelalan or Bario in the Kelabit Highlands. From there, there are frequent flights to Lawas or Miri. Make sure you have your visa in order before you leave.

If you just want to wander around and not attempt a border crossing you could easily spend a week visiting the longhouses in Kurid.

If you want to walk out to Malinau and take the riverboat to Tarakan it is a good 60kms or 8 days southeast of Kurid.

Kutai National Park   ★

120 kms north of Samarinda

This 200,000 hectare park contains over 239 species of birds and a large population of proboscis monkeys and orang utans especially around Teluk Kaba. Inside this vast area is a whole lot of virgin forest. To get to the park you will need to get to the refinery town of Bontang. Most folks pick up a local tour in Balikpapan and don't have to worry about where to stay and where to eat. An all expense paid 3 -4 day tour of the park costs about RP500,000 for a group of 4 -6 people. Transportation for regular folks consists of a bus from Samarinda (3 hrs, RP3000) or a passenger boat (RP10,000) from Samarinda. You can charter a plane (45 minutes) from Balikpapan.

Once in Bontong there are speedboats for hire that will take you to the park within 30 minutes. If you show up by your lonesome you will pay an arm and a leg for the brief trip. If you are going solo make sure you pick up a permit (free) and a guide (RP10,000) per day) from the PHPA Office in Bontang.

In Town

Equator Hotel

PT Pupuk Kaltim (Persro Komplex); Loktuan, Bontang; ☎ *(0542) 3845286*
There is not much to say about this hotel except that you are smack on the equator. A/C bungalows, TV, RP30,000.

Tour Companies

There are three ground operators in Balikpapan who can take you up the Mahakam, to the Apo Kayan or to places beyond. The best bet is to shop all three with the exact tour you have in mind. If they are not busy you get a deal. Worst case is you will get to take advantage of their 15 percent walk-in rate for published tours. Remember that the dry season is between June and October. Travelers upriver may want to go when the waters are higher.

Tomaco

Hotel Benakutai, Jalan Jend. A. Yani. ☎ *(0542) 22747*
The biggest and most efficient of the tour operators operating out of Balikpapan. They can get you just about anywhere and seem to be able to cut some mean deals doing it. They are also a full fledged travel agency so they can handle your connecting flights while you are out in the bush.

Kaltim Adventure Tours

Blok C-1/1 Komplex Balkipapan, Permai, Jalan Jend. Sudirman, ☎ *(0542) 31158, FAX 33408.*
Specialists in the Mahakam with five full time guides and cooks. They also run two houseboats based out of Samarinda.

Musi Holidays

Jalan Dondang(Antasari) 5A, ☎ *(0542) 24272, FAX 24984.*

The Apo-Kayan

Descent Into The Dark Heart

T he smell of leaking fuel was not a good omen. I checked that the pilot and crew were ok and threw open the rear exit door. My first thought was to throw our exposed film as far away as possible from the plane in case of an explosion. The impact had sprayed all our camera equipment towards the front of the plane and slammed it hard against the bulkhead. No one was hurt. Hard to believe. As we threw our gear out the back door, the pilot and co-pilot sat dazed in the front.

I had never been in a plane crash before. I am sure most of those who are never live long enough to talk about it. We had just broken through a mighty wall of clouds and had about ten minutes to find the landing area—if there was one.

Seeing the longhouses with the clearing by the river was enough for us. There was just enough fuel to fly us into the center of Borneo and then for the pilot to return to Balikpapan. The choice of this clearing as a landing sight was a foregone conclusion. We had been flying for the right amount of time and we didn't have a choice. My early years of aerobatic flying with my father in his Citabria and dozens of close calls with bush pilots in the Yukon, had removed my fear of flying. But, like they say, it's not the flying that kills you, it's what stops you from flying that kills you. I had faith in our pilot who told me of his experience flying relief missions in war torn Africa. Since we had the luxury of two pilots I felt that if this strip was doable then that was fine with me. I got my first butterflies when he set up for a full power, full flaps, combat landing. I climbed to the back of the plane and tightened my seat belt when I saw that the landing strip was actually made up of a cliff, a river bank and a tiny clearing. We hit hard. So hard that I thought we did a "touch and go." I remember the equipment floating in the air in slow motion and then, as if we had hit warp speed, accelerating towards the front of the plane and smashing against the bulkhead. The sound of the bamboo hitting the plane echoed like a hundred baseball bats pounding on a drum. Roaring props smashed and shattered the wood into splinters as we careened into the forest. Waiting for the final sight of the front of the plane turning inward towards me I was relieved to discover that we were actually stopped. The pilots screamed at each other to kill the battery, shut down the engine. They madly flipped switches and then sank into a long silence.

After our gear was out, we had time to review where we were. The plane was at a grotesque angle, resting a few feet from a large ancient Kenyah burial tower. We had been saved by the thick bamboo along the side of the narrow grass strip. The four inch thick bamboo groves had beaten the leading edge of the wing and more importantly had bent to absorb the impact and slow us down. The soft earth had gripped the landing gear, destroying the front gear and trapping the rear. We were lucky; very lucky. We were told later that the spirit of the elder chief entombed in the large platform had saved us. All I could remember were stories that a Sabahan doctor had told me of having to cut the fingertips off all of the various dismembered limbs of crash victims and putting them in plastic bags so they could be identified back at the lab.

Boom Bang Crash... Welcome to the Apo Kayan.

An old man appeared. He had a permanent toothless grin, a deformed or mutilated left hand and a weathered old parang. He began to cut a length of bamboo into two foot lengths. Calmly and methodically, without really noticing our presence, he stood under one of the engines, held up his bamboo container and began to collect the leaking fuel. Only then did he nod to us as if we were waiting for a bus. The fact that he could be blown into a pile of wet jelly if the gas hit the exhaust pipes did not seem to faze him.

Gradually, more people from the village appeared. Never having seen a plane of this size, particularly in this bizarre position, they peered under, over and inside. The villagers took their cue from the old man and began to cut short lengths of the thick bamboo.

Soon the ladies were placing pots and bamboo leaves under the fuel tanks while we ran around hoping that nobody would light up a cigarette while waiting for his container to fill.

We helped the pilot remove the batteries and the crew's belongings.

The pilot was apologetic. He continued to apologize for crashing. I tried to explain that any landing you walk away from is a good landing. He didn't see the humor in this old saying since he had just cracked up a very expensive piece of oil company property in a very remote place.

In our conversation with the villagers we found out we were in Long Nawan not Long Ampung. The runway in Long Ampung is supposed to be 1000 meters long. We paced off the distance of the clearing and it was about the length of a football field. Well, to be more accurate, it was a football field.

The villagers did not question the fact that we had just crash landed a 20 passenger cargo plane on this tiny spot. We persuaded our audience into dragging the plane to a level area where the damage could be better assessed.

For some strange reason the tone of the crowd became more serious. It seemed the local police official had arrived. Acting stern and concerned, as all Indonesian police chiefs seem to do, our spectacular descent in his small village took on an ominous tone. Why were we here? Who gave us permission? Who was responsible for the damage? The pilot and navigator sidled up to us and in soft voices told us to walk slowly towards town, act stupid and not answer any questions. The official was more concerned that we did not ask his permission to crash. The reasoning being that if we would have had permission, we would not have crashed. This is not an argument we were going to win with logic so we concerned ourselves with finding shade and a place to figure out our next move.

The group of young men who came with the police chief offered to help carry our gear to the village. The pilot nodded that it would be prudent to provide employment if only to get them away from the scene of the negotiations.

We diplomatically left and it seemed that the senior chief had left for town with bundles of local artifacts for sale. The junior official was quickly argued out of his perception that our misfortune was financial opportunity for him. Since he couldn't send us back or keep us there his minor attempts at creating a fuss soon fizzled out. And, since we seemed to have ingratiated ourselves with the locals by helping them collect fuel, taking pictures and distributing gifts, they also told the official to "lighten-up." This was the second time in Indonesia that our appearance on the scene had been swayed to the positive not only by our refusal to be intimidated but by the locals' help in smoothing things over.

As we walked towards the village we paced off the grassy area leading up from the edge of the river to the cliff-face. We had crash landed on a patch of dirt less than 400 yards long. Our pilots spent the evening calculating the various ways in which the plane could be extracted. They would not be back home for awhile.

Backcountry Kalimantan

Initial discussions with the boatman started at one million rupiah for two boats, for two days. The standard negotiating ploy is to negotiate the price of the boats from usurious to only outrageous. The boatman mentioned that there was a small problem with gas. There wasn't any. Our price for renting two boats was 500,000 rupiah but the cost of the fuel was 250,000 rupiah.

We naively discussed a variety of options; like draining kerosene from the crashed plane and using that. The boatman didn't know if the low octane gas used in the turbo-prop would burn in his engine. The engineer said they would need the fuel from the plane to give to the helicopter pilot when he brought in the spare parts. Since we would be no help and had no desire to fly out with the pilots, we left them to their fate. We found out later that huge Bell 204s were used to bring in spare parts and pieces as well as the chief oil company pilot from Jakarta. Then the plane was rebuilt, repaired, stripped of seats, excess fuel and flown out on a newly expanded runway.

Further Into the Interior

The police had some fuel and after a bit of back and forth, mostly forth, we secured enough to take us into the interior and, hopefully, back.

The boatmen couldn't remember the last time someone went to Data Dian. Maybe in the early seventies; 1972. Everyone goes upriver. Sometimes people come here from Data Dian but why would anyone go there from here.

The boat was constructed of a carefully scooped out keep with two long flexible boats that overlapped end to end. There were no cushions or seats of any kind. One boat was new and freshly painted. Its position in the water showed it was well designed. The other boat was without paint, caulking or design. It rode a full foot in the air and wobbled like a drunk on a skateboard. Just turning your head left to right made the gunnel veer towards the waterline. Unlike the sleek outboard engines of the coastal areas, we were now using a converted pump motor. Clamped to the stern of the boat, it delivered power directly through an outboard drive shaft that doubled as a steering device; similar to an oversized hand mixer. The primitive nature of the engine was such that the rpm was kept at a constant rate, there being no, or little, control of the throttle. After two days of this chugging, our hearing had a dead spot.

The flexible nature of the boat was apparent when we descended into the rapids. The sides undulated and squeezed against us as we passed through the churning water. The water was a little lower than usual and as our boats slithered over the rocks, we could feel them hitting our butts.

Downriver to Data Dian

Once again it seemed we were going the wrong way. We should have been going upriver to find remote tribes, not down. Once again the concept of remoteness was determined more by the river than by the lay of the land. Just beyond Data Dian there is a great series of impassable rapids forcing the Kayan to cross over to another river by going up and then down. The village of Data Dian is essentially the last stop before pure wilderness leaving it in a timeless backwater. Cruising down the lazy river we were lulled to sleep by the chug-chug of the primitive engine. I was awakened by the sound of someone shaking out hundreds of rubber car mats. That is about as close as I can get in finding a comparison for the sound. As the sky darkened with these black, glistening gargoyles, we saw we had disrupted a colony of giant flying foxes. I use the world "giant" accurately when comparing these bats to typical bats. The first sight of Flying Foxes is always startling and somewhat similar to seeing small dogs fly. Thousands of these half-pteradactyl, half canine, animals leapt from the canopy and began to circle overhead. It took well over half an hour for them to begin their large, lazy, circular holding pattern. After the first wave were in synch they gathered in a more purposeful direction and flew along the river to find a more peaceful place to nap. As we slowly cruised down the river we pushed the circling hordes ahead of us. We watched for over an hour as they blocked the sun creating an awe inspiring sight.

Flying foxes circle overhead.

The curious thing about these animals is the soft gentle look of their heads and torsos combined with the demonic hooked hands and transparent leather wings. One could assume that these gentle animals had committed some heinous evolutionary crime and were condemned to being out of evolutionary sync with the rest of the world.

A Kenyah bridge

Flying Foxes can have wing spans of up to five feet across and are the largest of the bat species. They live on fruit and pose no harm to humans—although, they have been known to send people collecting fruit toppling out of trees due to the shock of waking these creatures.

We arrived at Data Dian as the sun kissed and hid behind the high jungle canopy. We were finally with the people we had come to see. This is the last Kayan village left. The young men have left to work in Sarawak, only a handful remain. We see mostly young children, women and old men. A young man brings out his grandson to be photographed. The children smile shyly. Women pound rice in the longhouses as they have done for hundreds of years. The deep booming sound resonates along the river and across the hills. In small groups the people return from the *ladang*, or rice fields. These are old women, young women and children. Very few young men. Watching from the veranda the people look up at us shyly, not breaking step. They are hungry and the pounding of the rice means there is still dinner to prepare.

There are two great longhouses left. Fifty years ago these longhouses would stretch for a quarter of a mile. Now only five families live in one long house, eight in the other. A clouded leopard skin, a squirrel, a headless python, a freshly killed deer, chicken coops, baskets and hats fill the room. An old woman squats holding a pot of water in her hand. She starts a fire in one of the metal suitcases, fanning it with her hand. Other women winnow the rice.

Rice is the staple diet of the Kayan.

Longhouses are rebuilt every 5–15 years from giant hardwoods. Some floor panels are four feet wide, polished smooth by years of shuffling bare feet. Every piece of wood is rough hewn. Each longhouse has a giant drum centered in the eaves in case of an emergency. There is also a large gong that is hit in case of emergencies. There are a few signs of civilization here. The water is supplied by a long plastic hose that stretches across the river.

Data Dian

The influences of the missionaries and the government, who have a small airstrip just outside of town, are obvious. There is one satellite dish in the village but no TV or electricity. Gas for generators must be flown in. There is a sports field across from the new school for the children. There is one church and a small airfield just outside the town which is serviced by MAF; the Missionary Aviation Fellowship. Missionaries frown on longhouses. The government views them as archaic. They are trying to get people to build and live in separate dwellings.

Across from the schoolteacher's house is the new school. It will be a large modern looking building when it is done. The trouble is they are waiting for the roof to be delivered. The teacher points to a tiny pile of corrugated roofing. He explains it has to be flown in.

We understand why MAS has little space for passengers. It seems they have been busy flying heavy tin roofing in for the past few months. Since the missionaries use a tiny Cessna 185, it will be a long time before the rest of the materials will be brought in. I almost ask the teacher to look around at the jungle that hems in the village or even the longhouse 30 yards away. Their roof is made of iron-hard bilian wood woven with rattan. It insulates, keeps the people dry and can be repaired with simple hand tools. The practice of making these simple people dependent on materials and technology that must be flown in is questionable. It is not my place to question or discuss this practice, but it saddens and confuses me.

Two generations at Data Dian

As it gets dark the last stragglers come in from the rice fields. Old women, more young men and small boys arrive carrying kettles, parangs, blowguns and other paraphernalia in their wicker backpacks. The women trail behind, burdened with rice, cooking utensils and children while the men carry only a blowpipe with a spear attached to one end. It is not chauvinsism. The men keep their hands free to hunt if they spy game coming across the trail.

They are dirty and tired. But at night, the primitive village is alive with music. Across the road there is choir practice and in each house a large radio is on playing melodic, Indonesian pop songs, torch songs, even an Indonesian version of Alvin and the Chipmunks.

That night we slept in the house of the schoolteacher. It seemed one of us was missing a Swiss Army knife. Coskun remembered it being in our room moments earlier. We did not see who had taken it but we knew that the native people do not lie, steal or conceal the truth. We couldn't accuse our boatmen and we felt that maybe we had tempted someone by leaving it out. Jon broke the matter to the head boatman. He told the story as if it had not happened yet. He communicated that if someone were to leave something out and if someone was to pick it up out of curiosity and forget to give it back, it might create the appearance of being taken. The boatman listened attentively and then pondered the proposed problem. We judiciously extinguished the candle in our room and waited outside for a polite interval. When we returned, Coskun's knife was sitting exactly where he left it.

With no hard feelings we shared our freeze-dried food with the teacher's family and the boatmen.

The boatmen slept in the hallway, lit by a tiny kerosene lantern. Each one snoring, making his unique sound. The dull light from the lamp flickered across the features of the men as they snored and mumbled, recreating a scene from *Snow White and the Seven Dwarfs.*

In the morning the villagers headed off into the fields again, happy and chattering. We asked a couple of tattooed women to pose for us. Like all commuters they were shy, in a hurry and wanted to get going.

Back in the village we felt like we were playing hookey from work, as the rhythmic thumping of grain began. Dogs sprawl deathlike in the sun while others snap at flies that feed on the many open sores. Puppies hide under the longhouses to avoid the angry hens with their chicks.

Children rocked a heavy log back and forth over two carefully carved logs as an old blind woman pushed sugarcane under the heavy log. She poured water from an old blackened kettle to drain the crushed sugar through the grooves in the logs and juice gathered below in a pot. The juice would be boiled down later to make a concentrated syrup. In some cases, the concentrate is sealed in bamboo holders to make a light alcoholic beverage called *ja-kan*. The Kayan very rarely drink. At the other end of the log, the children in charge of rolling the log back and forth sneaked their own fixings into a small plastic bag.

There is little for the next generation in the remote regions of the Apo Kayan.

The women sat on the verandas waving long bamboo poles with animal skins tied to one end to scare the chickens away from the rice drying on the grass mats. More enterprising and less labor intensive families put fishing nets over the rice and attended to other business. Old women wandered through the field looking for greens and very old women wove mats, winnowed rice and mended clothing.

In midafternoon we headed off upstream, satisfied and sad that we had found what we had come to find.

Now, with the finality of death, we had come to the end of our trip. We had penetrated the heart of this island in a long spiral route. Now it was time to return, but not quickly. As we departed, we built in technology. First, by small canoe, large canoe, chartered turboprop, large turboprop, 737 and finally, by a 747-400.

Kenyah mask worn during rice harvest festivals.

There were adventures ahead, but they would not be sequential or part of our story. We had pushed hard and overcome many obstacles to reach this remote point. Going back was like coasting downhill. The timing was good. I was excited to be heading back: the plants would have grown, people would have changed, there would be news to catch up on, mail to plow through, stories to tell. My beard was like a clock.

Going upstream gives you more time for reflection. Returning is like watching a movie backwards. You know what to expect and it looks a little different when you see it.

The clouds created liquid shapes all day long; billowing, flattening and dancing against the deep blue sky. Ginger grew in sprays along the side of the river. Bright red flowers spiked the centers. Trees grew gently down to the bank and hung on tenaciously with gnarled desperate roots as if holding on for dear life. The twisted shapes of the vines mimiced the rolling coils of the water. We used one as a swing. Swifts darted in and out of the V-shaped canyon created by the trees and monitor lizards wriggled into the water.

I finally used my Therma-Rest with the Pelican case as a back rest. Once in a while a fragrance of incense, fruits or flowers wafted across the water. My suntan was now a sunburn.

As we pulled into Long Nawan the light greeted us. Black thunderclouds ripped by pure white lightning threatened in the distance. A hard, strong shaft of sunlight illuminated the small town. I dropped my gear and ran up to the hill above the town to take pictures. Patiently the sun held on and, as if to reward me for my effort, gave me a perfectly positioned rainbow.

Then the light vanished and rain fell in big fat drops.

We were sitting in the resthouse when the cook ran in asking us to come quickly. It seemed that three kittens had cornered an eight-inch black scorpion under the table and it was holding the kittens at bay. The kittens flicked nervously at the scorpion and he scurried and angled to make sure he would not be cornered. The scorpion was given a few moments of fun and then put into the fire to crackle and pop. The cook was genuinely concerned when we asked her later at dinner if the scorpion was ready yet.

Long Nawang

Long Nawang is a government administration center. There are a large number of people of noble birth in Long Nawang. This is considered to be the birthplace of the first people of Borneo. Long Nawang is also a tourist's nightmare. People rubbing their fingers together asking for money. People who find people for a fee so you can take their picture. One guide wanted 75,000 rupiah for a day of guiding. The fee should be 10,000. An old man, on seeing my camera, stuck his head out as if he were sunbathing and then, proud of his professional modeling, demanded money, even though I didn't take his picture. The fact that I hadn't bothered to take his picture didn't phase him in the least.

Old couples stop us, demand money and then pose. They repeat a word over and over. When I ask Jon what "sobik" means, he says, "you mean Sobek, the tour company." We realize that someone has done a number on these remote villages, teaching people to demand money for photos. Not just pocket change, but professional modeling fees. One young lady wanted 10,000 rupiah to have her earring photographed. Other people, upon seeing a camera, will double their efforts at whatever primitive pastime they are engaged in and then demand money. Boatbuilding, winnowing, weaving, babysitting, evening napping are all now paying spectator sports in Long Nawang.

Long Ampung

It's 2-1/2 hours by boat to Long Ampung; a sleepy town, chickens walk slowly, dogs are scattered throughout the village. The neat government precision of Long Nawang contrasts with the randomly scattered layout of Long Ampung. A haphazard collection of ramshackle, run down, unpainted houses and longhouses, sprawling on both sides of the river connected by a rickety, pieced-together suspension bridge, using old pieces of wire, rattan, sticks, wood and string.

Here, people seem to be marking time. The word, "hillbillies," comes to mind. People say, *selamat soreng*, for "good afternoon" or just, *soreng*. It sounds like they are saying, "sorry." Missionaries dump all the abandoned T-shirts of the world here—Ninja turtles, Batman, etc. The roads are as wide in Long Nawang, but here, there is a thin meandering path scuffed into the middle. People don't change direction much.

Upon our arrival at Pempung's, he saw we had no rice. Our protestations that we had freeze-dried food fell on deaf ears. He hobbled to his rice barn and got a large basket of rice and picked some tapioca leaves and pakus, or fern shoots.

The Penghulu's longhouse

Pak (uncle) or *Bapu* (uncle), Pempung Anya (he is called "Pemgpung" and visitors call him, "Ping Pong") was born in 1912. He built houses for the Dutch in the 50s. He used to walk for five months to the coast and back with the other villagers for salt, cotton and household articles. Each man would carry a hundred pounds.

Having worked up a sweat, he gave the ingredients to his son's wife and invited us to "makan," or eat. Even though we were cooking beef bourguignon, fettuccine alfredo and various other freeze-dried specialties, he insisted that we drop our pretense of having enough and eat his food. We gave him a sample of our food. He politely held it in his hand and then disappeared into the back of the longhouse, probably to throw the disgusting tasting stuff to the chickens. Meanwhile, we busied ourselves stuffing rice into the empty foil packets to give to the dogs later. When he returned he looked at how much we had eaten and ordered more. This time we had to grimly stuff down as much as we could under his watchful eye. He was proud of his daughter because she made pure white rice, not a husk or dark grain to be found.

The wall of the headman's house is decorated with the traditional art of the Apo Kayan. When Pak is quizzed on the origins of this art he bluntly responds by saying that someone came by and painted it. All he knows is that the traditional bit is the jar in the middle and the tiger. The Tiger is a Hindu symbol. Tigers are found on the Malayan Peninsula. When he first painted his longhouse, Pak asked the Dutch to show him a tiger skin so that he could copy it. The tendrils are modified with modern images and symbols.

We asked him if the villagers could dance and show us their costumes after church. There are three churches; Protestant, Catholic and Gospel, all within spitting distance of each other. A few of the villagers showed up complete with their street clothes under their ill-fitting Kenyah costumes and crudely painted war shields. It looked like a fifth grader's version of a night in a longhouse. Disappointed, we realized that this event would be about the lowest on the cultural scale we had experienced to date. We wisely declined their offer to put on a "cultural show" for us.

We asked to take pictures of them individually in the setting sun. They said, "No, we must do the usual dance we do for tourists." We declined. Pempung was embarrassed. It was hard for him to tell us that now the Kenyah of his village only dance for tourists' money. They do not dance for heads or for harvest, just money. They are embarrassed to be photographed in these outfits.

Pempung spent hours chatting with us even though we could barely understand what he was saying. He would talk in his soft sing-song manner, ocassionally putting his hand on our arm for emphasis or stopping to scare a rooster off the veranda. He told us stories of hunting bears. He told us to wait until the sun bear rears up because the spear will not penetrate its thick hump. He told us how he kills a pig; sending dogs to frighten it, then shoving his spear through its shoulder into its heart. He told us of using the blowgun to kill the elusive deer. He acted out the parts we didn't understand and even pantomimed the blowgun part. He went out, got his old blowgun and showed us how to use it.

Pak's friend came from next door and brought with him the two parts of the poison used to rub on the bamboo darts. He explained the two kinds of poison used and how to mix the two parts of the poison. He even told us to be careful not to prick our fingers once we had put the poison on the darts. He told us how the Kenyah used to get their pockets picked when they went into town. Then they began putting sharpened bamboo splinters with poison in their top pockets in a piece of paper. The practice of bilking country bumpkins ended quickly. Suddenly, he thought we must know how to make darts and dashed out of the longhouse.

Pempung came back breathless with a length of seasoned bamboo he had hacked from the jungle and began to carve. As he carved, the years fell away. He began to hum a song to himself. Rapidly the three-inch round bamboo became chopstick-sized sticks. He sharpened each one into rounded, pointed darts.

When we brought the video camera out, a big smile came across his weathered face. Slowly, he began stamping his feet in a gentle urgent rhythm. Then he began chanting, bending his neck and back in the birdlike position of the Kenyah war dance. He was enchanted. He promised to tell us many stories that night.

Two cultures collide.

He invited his friend over to help him sing the old songs. We went into the back of the longhouse so the rest of the village could not hear. He told us they don't like him to do this since the whole village likes to charge for shows. He began to sing the sing-song, talking songs that are the oral history of the Kenyah. The songs were long and took a long time to finish but there was an insistent rhythm and a need for these stories to be told.

He then asked if he could dance for us. Since there were no instruments, each man took turns singing the musical accompaniment while the other danced. Pempung pretended to play a sambe, an ancient Kenyah guitar. Looking like a 14-year-old doing his version of Jimi Hendrix, he imitated the sound of the sambe while he strummed and fretted all the notes on his imaginary guitar while his friend danced.

Between songs we would play back the music for the entertainers to hear. They would yip and stamp their feet and sing in harmony with the music. "This is magic!" they insisted. They enjoyed it to the fullest. It was a sight to see the old man, his elongated ears flapping below the high-tech stereo headphones, dancing and clapping his hands like a teenager as he relived the tales of his youth.

Late into the morning they finally turned to us and said, "That is all we have to sing." Then, after talking to each other, they said they had one more song. It was a traditional song that they modified for us. They told of our trip in the airplane that crashed, our boat trip and how tomorrow we would have to carry all our luggage to the airport and fly away. It was a fitting gift for us. We thanked them and gave them gifts. The old man gave Coskun, who collects weapons from the wars he covers, his blowgun. We all went to sleep. In the morning his daughter had made us rice wrapped in bamboo for the ride home to civilization.

The next morning we gave away what we didn't need to the men who we thought would carry our gear to the airport. Instead, they dumped our gear for the women to carry. After the women had staggered to the airport, they showed up later to collect payment. We mentioned the gifts. They shrugged their shoulders. We said, "screw it." We now recognized the same group that had offered to carry our gear in when we first arrived.

At the airport there was quite a bit of commotion. The runway is being lengthened by carrying large round stones from the nearby river. A group of young men break the rocks into gravel and then the gravel is dumped in neat piles in preparation for the extension of the runway. A very labor intensive way to lengthen the runway. Obviously, a government sponsored job. I sat by the river and talked with two men from Samarinda who were cleaning the morning's catch of Ikan (fish). They had come here for jobs. The runway project is supposed to provide jobs for the locals but the locals just want to get out. The government of Indonesia is trying to stem the exodus of people from this region. The Apo Kayan had been the home of most of the indigenous people of Borneo. Once, they were forced deeper into the heart of the country by pirates, colonists, adventurers and marauding headhunters. Now, they are streaming downriver into the cities and timber camps looking for well paying jobs. Meanwhile the unemployed of the big coastal cities are attracted by easy government jobs in the interior.

The airport has a terminal that is further from the runway than those at LAX or JFK. Inside the tiny building there are wornout aircraft tires, broken tools, a broken generator and a worn, old radio run by two car batteries. The radio beacon does not work and the runway only offers about 4–5 hours of visibility per day before the clouds come in and the rains begin.

The villagers know that there will be a plane here today and they have turned out as if a politician were visiting. The drone gets louder. The man from the "terminal" chases the people off the runway with an official-looking stick. The workers scattered as if they were being strafed.

Much later our plane finally landed in a cloud of dust as they reversed props on the usable center portion of the strip. They were late for our rendezvous. They went to the wrong runway, but fortunately did not land. With them they brought cartons of salt and gifts of candy for the children. In exchange, a man gave them four bottles of local honey. There is a desperate lack of salt, sugar and coffee in the Apo Kayan.

Traditional grave decorations of the Kenyah

Kenyah and Kayan women wear heavy earrings to extend their earlobes.

The man who cleared the runway of workers with a stick also takes care of the landing and ground handling fees. He also mans the radio that doesn't work. We assumed this was a joke, but not so. The same man made sure we filled out our names and passport numbers in his grade school, three-hole punch notebook. The pilot thought the program to widen the runway was a farce, but he was keeping his mouth shut. This was Indonesia, opinions were only for politicians.

There were some candies for the children, who looked upon this airplane the way farmers in the twenties looked at barnstormers. They peered inside at the cavernous plane and at the amazing hydraulic cargo ramps that opened in the back. We sat in the plane and enjoyed the simple cartons of juice and candies. Small luxuries after rice and tapioca. We were sad to leave because we knew this place must change. In ten years the old men and women will be dead. The new generation with their Superman T-shirts and Nike football shoes will never carry on the traditions of their forefathers.

We may be among the last to experience the true Apo Kayan. It is not there in substance but in songs sung late at night, in the mischievous twinkle of an eye or in the war whoop of young men eager to be tested.

As we gained altitude, the solid green canopy gave way to scars and then to wholesale destruction. Logging roads like yellow varicose veins ripped into soft green hills, leaving dirty brown patches. It was here, in Kalimantan, that one of the world's largest disasters occurred without the world even raising an eyebrow. The forest below burned for a year destroying an area the size of Holland, filling the sky with choking smoke as far north as Singapore. To-day, the loss is not as dramatic but it is relentless. We flew for miles and miles over wasteland. As we neared the coast, smoke stacks and mile-high dirty black smoke billowed upwards. Out to sea, offshore rigs sent huge flames from bright silver candles high into the sky. There was industry here, there was sweat and toil but I longed to turn back to sit at the edge of a crystal clear stream and hear the villagers laugh, to hear the elders tell stories, to dance the war dances, to dream the future. But not this future. I felt that there was death below. Death for a culture, an ecosystem and for a people. But the only hope is that with each tree that crashes to the ground, they die like thunder, awaking the rest of the world to their plight.

The Apo Kayan★★★

The Apo Kayan *(apau Kayan)* is the highlands of the Kayan river and its tributaries. It means "space above the great rapids of the Kayan." The area also includes the Boh river and its tributaries. Surrounded by mist covered mountains, cut off by impassable rapids, uncharted due to the continual cloud cover and difficult to fly into due to its violent weather patterns and dearth of landing strips, the Apo Kayan is truly the dark heart of Borneo.

There is no logging here, no development or even roads since the lack of direct river transport or logging roads make it very difficult to enter and leave. All goods that aren't flown in must be carried by canoe from the coast, portaged and then carried by canoe again. The Kenyah and Kayan are cut off from the rest of the world. Most people of the Apo Kayan walk into Sarawak and their tribal language is spoken. Today the Kenyah of the Apo Kayan take their name from the longhouses along the Iwan river. Others say the Kenyah came from the Belaga river in Sarawak. The once dominating but gentler Kayan warred with the Kenyah until the Kenyah dominated the region.

The capital of the Apo Kayan region is Long Nawan. "Long" means confluence of a stream and a tributary. It is 575 meters above sea level, cool in the evenings and tends to be hot, but less humid, during the day. At the turn of the century the Apo Kayan boasted one of the most sophisticated and well run social structures in Borneo. The area is famous for its lavishly decorated longhouses of the aristocracy. Although most people have been converted to Christianity, the government encourages the Kayan to maintain the appearance of their ancient culture.

The first Dutchman appeared in the Apo Kayan in 1901 having walked and canoed from the Mahakam. In 1907 the Dutch set up an outpost at Long Nawan to offer some resistance to Brooke's marauding Iban troops and stem his continual ingestion of other people's territory. In 1911 there was a permanent military outpost in Long Nawan. The Dutch and Indonesian soldiers' jobs were to curtail raids by Kenyah on Iban on the British side.

The border between Sarawak and Dutch Indonesia began as a vague line drawn in London on September 28, 1915. A Dutch photographer named Nieuwenhuis explored the Apo Kayan in May of 1900. The photographs he brought show a proud people living in massive longhouses. They had a unique style of artwork, a rigid societal structure and well developed animist religion. The photographs are surprisingly reminiscent of the coast Indians of British Columbia.

SARAWAK

Malisambo

Long Poh

Long Lemiliu

Nahakramo

Long Sungan

Data Dian

Iwan

Kayan

Long Irun

Pura

Long Marong

Long Metun

Sai Anai

Pegian

Long Betoah

Long Payau

Long Nawang

Nawang Baru

Long Temunyat

Dumu

Long Sungai Barang

Long Ampung

Boh

Long Uro

Lidung Payau

Long Lebusan

The Apo Kayan

Mahak Baru

Dumu Marak

Metulang

Mahak

Uga

N

W E

S

FIELDING

Benahan

Muara Tamit

0   5   10 Mi

0   5   10 Km

To Long Bagun

Boh

Muara Benahan

©FWI 1995

Kenyah tendril decoration

These dramatic photographs along with the detailed descriptions of head hunting and pagan rituals were enough to set any missionary's heart a-flutter. The next seminal visit was by American missionary George Fiske in 1940. Fiske was part of the Christian Missionary Alliance, who had been saving souls in Tarakan since 1929. He managed to land a floatplane on a smooth and wide stretch near the Kayan village of Data Dian. Soon animist ways were discarded and churches started springing up. Some villagers like those at Nawang Baru moved across the river to get away from these new spirits that were destroying thier old beliefs.

The war brought more stress as Japanese troops, Dutch and Javanese soldiers brought more of the outside world than they cared to know about. During the Konfrontasi, Long Nawan and the Apo Kayan became a garrison for about 100 Indonesian troops. In 1972 a small airstrip was put in at Data Dian to supply building materials and to shuttle people to and from the large cities.

This is the ancestral home of the Kayan and the Kenyah. The population of about 5000 *ulu* or upriver people were originally from Sarawak driven into the upper reaches by continual raids by the Iban. The Dutch had an administration center here from 1907 through 1911. The end of headhunting and warfare between the Iban and the Kenyah came about in 1924 when the Sarawak government negotiated a truce. The population has shrunk to a tenth the size it was 100 years ago as young men head for the timber jobs in Sarawak and Kalimantan.

The area survives on hill rice grown by slash and burn techniques. The rice fields, or ladang, have consumed a large amount of jungle along the rivers in the Apo Kayan. Jungle is cleared and burned and ash is spread over the ground. Holes are made and rice is thrown in without being covered. As the rice germinates, so do the weeds. Weeding takes up an inordinate amount of time and labor as does keeping out birds, animals and insects. The poor nature of the soil only allows one harvest every five to ten years. The people also grow cassava, tapioca, sweet potato, maize, sugarcane, pisang and even pineapple.

Most travelers go upriver from Long Ampung to reach the interior of Borneo. In fact, downriver is more remote because of the impassable waterfalls that block passage downstream. An expedition in the early '70s portaged around for the sake of publicity, but for all practical purposes the waterfalls of the lower Kayan create a barrier to trade and development.

The Apo Kayan is divided into Kayan Hulu (upriver) and Kayan Hilir (downriver) with about 5000 people living upriver and less than 400 people living downriver. About 10 percent of the upriver men work in Sarawak. Seventy five per cent of the people are Protestant, the rest being Catholic. Long Nawan is the center of the region and many trekkers start their journey at any one of the area's seven crude landing strips. The local economy is subsistance farming with rice being the major crop. Every year the locals still manage to pull out about 10 tons of damar resin, six tons of fragrant *gaharu* wood and a puny three kilos of gold. Tourism should be a big source of cash but most people come in self sufficient and the most the locals can make is the 6000 rupiah per person the headman gets for room and board. Native dancing runs about $50US and is usually part of larger tours. Most people survive on the money their husbands bring back from jobs in Sarawak.

Depending on the levels of the rivers your longboat trip could be tedious or life threatening.

Getting In

Most people come here on a tour using Merpati or Asahi (2.5 hours, 100,000 rupiahs) from Samarinda. From Samarinda to Long Ampung it's about one and half hours and 350 kms. The 21 passenger planes are usually booked well in advance but there are frequent cancellations.

Make sure you read "Getting Out" to find out how many people can leave the Apo Kayan. Missionary Aviation Fellowship doesn't run by any particular schedule but they can fly you in and out depending on how full their planes are. They fly in everything from tin roofing to gasoline so your best bet is to book a regular ticket.

Journey of Death Part I

As remote as the Apo Kayan seems, it didn't help a group of Dutch, American and British refugees many of whom fled to Long Nawan starting in February of 1941. A group of fifty women and their children trekked overland from Kapit in Sarawak to the Dutch military outpost in hopes of escaping the Japanese who had invaded Sarawak on Christmas Day a month earlier. Here there was a small group of Dutch soliders, American missionaries, Javanese troops and local Kenyah.

The Japanese troops got wind of this safe haven and sent in troops. When the Dutch commander was told that the Japanese troops were only two days away he didn't believe them. The Japanese executed all 109 men, women and children.

Getting Around

Alright here we go jungle trekking. Just what is jungle trekking you ask? Well jungle trekking is what the locals have to do to get around. If there is no river, or the river is impassible it means walking. The average elevation of the Apo Kayan is about 2600 feet above sea level so it is cooler than the lowlands and much chillier at night. The villages of the Apo Kayan are connected by wide walking paths, especially the ones along the Kayan river—many of which are not sheltered from the sun. It takes about a week to ten days to walk between Long Nawang and Long Sungai Barang, the last village on the Kayan river. Most people walk one way and then hire a canoe for the return journey. If you want to go past Long Sungai Barang you can hike for two and a half days over the mountains to the headwaters of the Mahak and then by a short day by canoe to Mahak Baru.

For hikers, July and August are the driest months of the year; it also means lower water levels and slower going for canoes

Considered the holy grail of jungle trekkers many people have little idea what awaits them in the cool high plains of Kalimantan. Most tours are at least 9–10 days with plenty of walking, canoeing and partying. Be forewarned, many visitors are shocked at the clean civilized villages they see. Many sport old T-shirts and baseball caps. The missionaries and government are hard at work in these remote fields making sure the last vestiges of Kenyah and Kayan culture are stamped out. Villagers now prefer single houses to the longhouse and only the elders sport tattoos and tribal regalia. Most villages have radios, soccer fields, even badminton courts.Sunday is spent dressing up in Western finery and singing hymns translated to the tribal dialect. The rivers are peaceful and wide, and if you squint, the scenery is almost reminiscent of the English countryside painted by Constable. Tours to the Apo Kayan cost about $900 US per person for a group of 4–6 and include airfare from Balikpapan or Samarinda. It is said that the tribes along the Mahakam are more authentic and have escaped much of the outside pressures.

Long Nawang

The government administrative center complete with bridge, school, more churches than an Iowa farm center and neat little rows of houses with badminton courts. There are plenty of interesting things to see but most folks head across the river to Nawang Baru to admire the carvings and paintings in the main longhouse.

Nawang Baru ★★

30 minutes across the river from Long Nawang

If you cross the suspension bridge from Long Nawang and follow the trail along the river for about 20 minutes (turn left after the bridge) you will discover an idylic Apo Kayan village. Here you will see the massive wood carvings and painted walls of the Kenyah. Although not entirely authentic, the people and atmosphere are laid back. There are also gravesites along the way. The inhabitants of this village did not want to adopt the western ways and religion of Long Nawang.

Long Ampung

5 hours on foot from Long Nawang

You can walk or take a longboat to Long Ampung. There is not much here other than some interesting rice barns and a dilapidated longhouse. There are some interesting old times left in this village.

Long Uro

2.5 hours on foot from Long Ampung

One of the original aristocratic villages a short walk from Long Ampung. If you are walking onward to Sungai Barang ("river of things" in English) take the left trail as you leave Lidung Payau.

Long Sungai Barang

The usual terminus of most jungle treks is rewarded with an impressive longhouse well decorated with the tendril-like Kenyah artwork. It is possible to hike to Long Lebusan (1.5 days) and Mahak Baru about a half day further.

For more in depth information on trekking, along with usable maps, pick up Bill Dalton's *Indonesia Handbook* from Moon publishing or get the latest on tours by contacting one of the tour companies in Samarinda or Balikpapan.

Costs for staying in longhouses are only about $5–10US dollars, porters go for about $10US a day (don't forget the return trip) and canoes go for about $100US a day with boatmen. If you rent a motorized canoe (called *ces* or *ketinting*) prepare to cough up about double that.

The landing strips that can accommodate small planes are: Mahak Baru, Lebusan, Long Sungai Barang, Long Nawang, Long Ampung, Data Dian and Long Sule.

Getting Out

Naturally you can just wander around and leave the way you came. Not so fast, there is a catch. Since the airstrips are at higher altitudes and are quite short, *outbound* flights can only carry 10 passengers (aren't you glad you read the whole chapter?). Tour organizers and medical cases have first dibs on the outbound seats so don't be surprised if you get stuck for a couple of weeks. You may also be delayed by low rivers or conked out outboards so keep this in mind if you are connecting to international flights.

You can fly out of any airstrip you have a reservation for.

Into Sarawak

The chances of you being allowed to stroll from Indonesia to Sarawak are slim at best. The cost can also be prohibitive since you may be turned back if you go through customs. If you sneak in, you will have to figure out how to get your passport stamped with the Sarawak entry visa. The closest town to Sarawak is Long Nawang.

You can take a four hour canoe trip on the Pengian river northwest to Long Betao, a tiny Kenyah village. From here it is a full day by canoe to the border. Few boatmen will make this trip because of the hazardous conditions before you get to the Rejang river. Be prepared to pay for the trip back, for your guide and boatmen.

To the Mahakam

If you have all the time and the money in the world you could fly in and then make your way back down the Mahakam river. First you have to get around the mighty rapids of the Boh river (near where the Benehan and the Uho river meet). This means a rugged lonely day and a half hike west from Mahak Baru to Muara Tanit before you can hire another boat to continue on down the Boh to Long Bagun.

Journey of Death Part II

The guardian of the Apo Kayan are the impassable rapids of the Kayan river as it heads east to the town of Tanjung Selor. The Brem-Brem rapids or Giram Ambung, loosely translated as "the rapids of spray," have been an ancient barrier to travel and commerce. In the 1930s a group of eight Kayans were handpicked to run the 20 mile long series of rapids. They all drowned.

A Trekking Primer

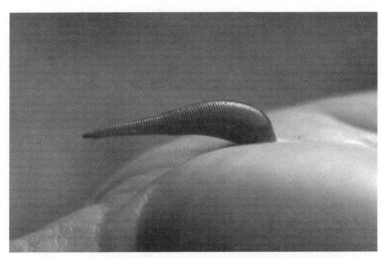

The leech, your constant companion in your jungle trekking adventures.

Be forewarned—trekking is a Dutch word and had nothing to do with pleasurable hiking. Trekking is miserable, makes you complain a lot, but is free. It is no surprise then that you see Dutch travelers trekking through Kalimantan complaining, not having a good time but glad that it's free. Not everyone has a good time walking through empty jungles with only the prospect of a rice dinner and a chilly evening on a grass mat ahead of them.

My own opinion slides both ways on the scale. Sometimes I am enraptured by the primitiveness of it all, other times I am just plain fed up with the endless prospect of a day in the gloom of the deep forest. As you may have gathered, I much prefer the open vistas and deadly excitement of river travel.

There is a complete packing list at the end of this book for your trip to Borneo. However if you decide to get seriously remote here is a brief list of things to think about. Then you should make some modifications. Here's what you should be doing if you want to do some trekking:

Get light:

Strip down to the essentials: Only one set of clothes, snap the handle off your toothbrush, strip down your first aid kit, toss your Metallica tapes and Walkman, forget your deodorant, camera, shaver, tent and whatever else you don't absolutely need. If you hire a guide, he will carry some of your junk. Every ounce will gobble up calories. Hey how come Jenny Craig and Richard Simmons don't recommend jungle treks for lardos?

Get serious:

You will need a spare pair of shoes, antibiotics for infections, a compass, waterproof matches and lighter, flashlight, extra batteries, foot powder, toilet paper, a light sleeping bag, a poncho or rain cover, ground sheet. If you get lost out here, you can die. Hire a guide, always introduce yourself to the headman and tell him where you are going and think on your feet. You don't want to trip and break your leg.

Get friendly:

You will need friends to survive. Bring plenty of gifts and think of what is light and in demand. Salt, tobacco, cigarettes, and a flask of booze (I carry Armangac). Gifts are the currency out here and don't forget that currency is also the currency out here if you need to pay your guide or rent a canoe. Bring plenty of rupiah and ringgits if you are going to sneak into Sarawak.

Get wet:

Everything you bring will be soaked 24 hours a day—either from downpours or from sweat. If you travel by canoe don't be surprised to find your barang floating in water, stepped on and dumped ignobly about two feet short of the river bank at the end of the day.

Get positive:

Don't let anyone tell you that jungle trekking is fun. Just like banging your head on a wall, it feels so good when you stop. You will spend a few moments panting with exhaustion, staring at your muddy, blood-stained, bruised body wondering whatever possessed you to leave home. Worse is the effect of low caloric meals (Yumm, love that bland rice) continual twilight from the forest and the nonstop assault by insects, leeches, thorns and tree roots.

A final tip

You probably noticed that there isn't a single toilet once you leave the smaller villages. It's OK to do your thing in the river or along the trail. It is ecologically better if you dig a six inch hole, do your do and then cover all including paper well. This way plants will grow and flowers will flower. I doubt you will be able to convince your boatman that the river may be convenient but ecologically tacky. It doesn't do the locals downstream one bit of good to make their morning tea out of his leavings.

Customs and Beliefs of the Kenyah

Alarm Drums

The large drums are found in the center of every major longhouse, typically in front of the chief's room. They are used primarily to sound the alarm in case of fire or attack. They are also played during ceremonies. The drums are tuned with wooden wedges used to keep rattan stringers in place.

Baby Carriers

Parents are very careful to protect not only the physical body, but the second soul or *berawa*, of small children against evil spirits. Every baby must have a baby carrier. To strengthen the carrier's effect against evil spirits, coins, bear tusks, beads, shells and other valuable items are added. The beaded decoration is also an indication of the family's status. A full human figure is a symbol of very high birth as well as tiger or dragon symbols. Only people of high birth can wear or use the dragon symbol. People of lower birth can only use portions of mythical figures.

A woman would never sell her own baby's carrier because some of the baby's soul is still in the cradle.

If twins were born, the first one was killed. It was believed that it would take away the vitality of the other. The babies of unmarried mothers were killed for it was thought they would bring misfortune to the tribe.

Baptism

The Kenyah baptismal rite consists of three parts. The first occurs three to ten days after birth. The child is given a name. The name gives the child spiritual vigor. This event is attended by family members only.

The second part is the rebaptism when the child is given a new name. It usually occurs after the rice harvest and is celebrated with a great feast by the village. A pig is sacrificed and its blood, or water of life, is given to the father.

The third part is the *lemewa*, the purifying and strengthening rite. The child and parents are marked with the blood and soot from burning bamboo that is extinguished in the pig's blood. The objects used in the *lemewa* are given to the parents to be wrapped and stored in the rafters of the longhouse. If these objects are lost it can bring bad luck to the child.

Blackened Teeth

Teeth are blackened by making a paste of tannin-rich leaves and earth-rich iron. The paste is held over the teeth at night with a piece of banana leaf.

The blacker the teeth, the more beautiful the woman. Black teeth are considered good by the spirits. They assume that the owner has had the teeth pulled and has given them up as offerings to them.

The blowpipe or sumpit

Blowpipes

Blowpipes or *sumpit* were usually made by the nomadic Punan from bilian or ironwood. They were patiently drilled with a metal chisel. There is a slight curve to the hole. If you look through the bore of a well made *sumpit,* you will see a half moon. Rotated 180 degrees, it becomes a full moon. This curve is to compensate for the bend when held. The dart is a piece of bamboo that is carried in a bamboo quiver with a sliding top. The poison is mixed and added just before shooting. Hunters usually carry some flint steel and tinder in the quiver to make fires. Most *sumpit* have a spear attached to the end for hunting pigs, sun bear and self defense.

Burial Houses
(Liang)

On the way into many villages you will see ornately carved burial houses. These are miniature versions or *liangs* of burial houses of the noble people. These miniature houses are believed to contain the souls of the dead. Many are decorated with personal belongings in case the departed needs them. The *liangs* are supposed to be three feet off the ground and supported by highly decorated and painted posts.

Dancing the Kanyet

The Kenyah enjoy dancing the *kanyet*, a rhythmic, almost hypnotic dance that is accompanied by the *sambe*, the two stringed guitar.

The epitome of Borneo haute couture: plucked eyebrows, blackened teeth and extended earlobes.

Earrings

The Kenyah and Kayans carefully extend earlobes using heavy brass earrings. It takes many years to extend the earlobes using a plug at first and then the earrings. In some cases an earlobe will tear. This is considered a great blemish and most women hide the torn ear while proudly displaying the good ear.

Headhunting

Headhunting is not unique to Borneo but it is probably the most infamous tradition of the island. No one knows why headhunting started but it is well established among most Dayak tribes throughout the island. Headhunting has been practiced by many cultures even in Yugoslavia, by the Montenegrins as late as 1913. The Jivaro tribe of Ecuador is famous for shrunken heads and the natives of Papua New Guinea combine head taking with cannibalism. In Borneo, headhunting was a necessary part of manhood and contributed greatly to the overall well-being of the tribe.

Headhunting was considered a currency of sorts. The more heads one collected, the better off his village and his longhouse would be. Heads brought good luck, prosperity and fertility. Collecting heads also reduced the number of enemies and was a good judge of a man's worthiness.

To kill an enemy was looked upon as doing a favor for the dead. The spirit of headhunting was both religious and tribal. Religious beliefs taught the Dayak that when a loved one died he would be lonely. By bringing back heads, the deceased would have a companion to accompany him to heaven.

If the recently deceased were alone he might try to take one of his relatives with him. Mourning was a way to not attract attention lest the spirit of the dead takes you with him. Headhunting gave you, *"bali akang,"* or the spirits of courage. To take heads is to prosper and to be blessed by your ancestors.

To not take heads would result in sickness, death, hunger and other disasters for your longhouse. This fear has come true. Since the first banning of head-hunting in 1841 by James Brooke in Sarawak, the fortunes of the Dayak have dwindled.

Head Swords
(Mandau)

Once carefully crafted head swords, mandaus are the indispensible jungle tool. Today many are made from car springs or chainsaw blades. Head swords can be bought as souvenirs now and are still used for clearing the *ladang* (rice fields) or for construction of wood buildings. Most mandaus are made in small villages using hand run blowers and small fires.

The Human Spirit

The Kenyah believe that humans are a combination of *beruwa* (soul) and *luhan* (body). At death, the spirit is freed from the body and goes up to join its ancestral spirits. It then becomes the *bali matei*, or spirit of death. The people are very afraid of the ancestral spirits. Earthly life is the highest attainable form and once dead, the spirits become angry and envious of those still alive. During all ceremonies, offerings are made to the spirits of the dead. The spirits of the dead continually tempt the spirits to leave the body so that the person will die. This is why people who do not have their soul and body firmly joined together, such as children, need greater protection from the *bali matei*.

When a person of nobility dies, they bang the alarm drum to scare the spirits away, making as much noise as possible.

An innocent spider, a human skull or an evil spirit. You decide.

The body is immediately washed and dressed in its best finery. A dead person receives certain objects that will be buried with him. The dead man is always equipped with a spear, an oar, a *kediri*, a shield, a sitting mat, a basket in which there is an empty quiver, tobacco, a flint tinder, a plate and spoon, a rainhood, a sword with *poe* and a *laaf* with some salt. The family can supply other equipment as well. In older days, many heads would be taken to be sent along with an important chief, sending outlying villagers scurrying into the forest for protection.

The body cannot be taken through the door of the dwelling because the door is strictly for the living. Planks are taken from the front wall of the dwelling and the body and personal possessions are displayed for up to eight days in the front gallery. A funeral meal is held because no one is allowed to go to the grave site hungry. This would make the *beruwa* angry because it must suffer hunger on the way to heaven.

The old graves were resplendent with Chinese jars, brass gongs, hats, swords and other expensive items. Today, the possessions are more modest and possibly, more useful. Just outside Long Nawang, there is a modest little grave decorated with an old, faded umbrella.

There are records of stone graves and markers throughout the Apo Kayan, around Long Uru and other older villages, but nothing is known of the people who created them or their meaning.

The Lepo Tau

Although the Lepo Tau are the most famous headhunters of Kalimantan they were preyed upon by the Iban of Sarawak. Unlike the Kenyah who took heads for good harvest and omens, the Iban took heads for sport.

The Lepo Tau were the protectors of the rice farmers and did little work other than practice their fighting skills. Famous for being bad or lazy rice farmers, the Lepo Tau of Long Nawang charged a fee for protection against the Iban of Sarawak. When Nieuwenhuis and the Dutch offered protection to the Lepo Tau against the Iban headhunting raids, they eagerly accepted.

The Lepo Tau was the the warrior tribe from the three villages of Long Uru, Long Nawang and Long Temonyet. They are the *paran bio*, the aristocrats of this fertile region.

Napo Sang Festival

Napo sang, is a ceremony performed after the rice harvest. The leaf of the sang plant emits an unpleasant smell and is believed to have a magical power. *Sang* leaves are hung on long rows of sticks. Later, chicken heads are added after being sacrificed.

Sharp stakes are cut with the ends shaved into curls of wood to catch the blood of sacrificed chickens and piglets. Blood has a very strong magical power, both repelling and purifying. The stakes are put up only when help from the spirits is needed. Today, you will see these decorations, sans sacrifices, at weddings and when politicians visit.

Penis Pins

A *palang*, or penis pin is another unusual Dayak custom. A small rod of bamboo, wood or bone, is inserted sideways at right angles below the glans of the penis and is supposed to provide additional sexual pleasure to the female. Today, it is more a macho symbol of the ability to withstand pain than anything else.

Historically it is not much different from the female's need to be tattooed, stretch earlobes or blacken teeth. Today it is against the law because of its understandably painful side effects from infection and amateur infliction. It is not known exactly who the first volunteer was for this operation. There is a theory that the Dayaks were emulating the unusual-shaped penis of the rhinoceros.

Palangs are not just a painful figment of the imagination. Many Dayak males still have this modification done after puberty and usually before marriage. Anything from outboard motor sheer pins to pig bristles can be used.

The method of insertion is as simple as it must be painful. The man and the "administrator" (I am told the operation can be self administered!) go down to the river in the early morning and the recipient endeavors to use the cold water to shrink the organ as much as possible. This has a slight anesthetic effect as well. The penis is held by a simple jig and then a sharpened bamboo spike is quickly pushed through the stretched organ. The length of the insert can be lengthened as the woman bears more children.

There is a milder version today. When some Dayak men are circumcised, they will have the doctor create small flaps from the foreskin. It is often described as "my little elephant."

Plucked Eyebrows

It is a sign of good grooming when both men and women have their body hair plucked, including eyebrows and eyelashes.

Rice Barns

Rice barns are used to store rice away from the main longhouse. This is a precaution due to fire, insects and other animals. The rice barns are also the storage place for valuables or *tajaus*, the large ceramic jars. Each rice barn has its own ladder. The rice barns of aristocrats are decorated with the familiar dragon and hornbill motifs and spirals. The house is supported on curved supports, much like the bottom of a canoe, to keep rats out.

Rice Masks

Rice masks are found in Long Ampung longhouses. A dance is held when the rice stands in the field after weeding. It is performed to keep harmful influences away from the fields. These are rice eating animals and evil spirits that hinder the rice spirits. The Kenyah believe rice has a spiritual essence.

The Season of Fear

After the forest was cleared in the *ladang* and the rice was put in few Kenyah slept well. The season of fear was the time between planting and harvest when men would caulk their war canoes, sharpen their head swords and wait for the omens to signal the beginning of their raids. All tribes raided each other for heads in a test of strength and to gather slaves to harvest the rice. Fresh heads brought power, good luck and prestige to a village. Slaves made the difficult work of harvesting the rice crop easier and many of the women carried off gave sons to their new husbands.

Sunhats

Apo Kayan sunhats used to feature intricate beadwork with smaller cotton fabric trim. Now the decorative area is mostly given to clothwork. The hats are made of dried leaves from the forest. A woven crown fits snugly above the head and creates an umbrellalike shade. The hats can reach large sizes to shade both mothers and babies at the same time.

Tattooing

Tattoos or *metik* are now out of vogue among the Kenyah and banned by the government as being unsanitary. *Paran* or upper class women once endured weeks of agony as complex tattoos were applied over their legs and arms. The women of Kenyah carry complex tattoos that are symbols of high birth and aristocracy. The greater the tattooed area, the more desirable the woman. The amount of tattooing would also communicate to men how much pain the women could endure.

Tattoos were administered with the consent of the village chief by a specialist. The tattooist had a collection of soft wooden blocks in many traditional designs. Once the tattoos were chosen the block was coated with soot and pressed on the area to be tattooed. The tattoos were given with a heavy three-pronged stick that penetrated about three mms when hit by an iron or heavy wooden rod. An assistant held the skin taut and the mixture of soot and water was rhythmically pounded in by the tattooist. Every tattoo had a symbolism ranging from the throat tattoo that allowed the soul to escape when decapitated to the small rings tattooed on men's knuckles that showed how many heads had been taken.

The magic created by tattooing women affected men unpleasantly and was only allowed every six years. When the process was completed a celebration was held to counteract the bad influences.

Tattoos and the Journey of Death

When a woman dies her soul goes on its way to heaven. On the difficult journey the soul must cross a ravine using a log bridge. The bridge is guarded by a watchman who must give permission for the soul to cross. The log is in constant rotation, so the soul cannot pass until the log is at rest. The watchman stops the log rolling if it appears the woman has been a good wife to her husband, a good mother to her children and, if she has tattoos, they must be complete. Unfinished tattoos are unacceptable or else the *beruwa* (second soul) of the woman cannot enter heaven.

If everything is in order, the watchman stops the bridge so that the woman may pass over it. Once across, the soul comes to a dark part of the journey. The tattoos radiate light so that the women may continue. The darker the color, the more light they will emit. Everything in heaven is the opposite of earth. Light is dark, black is white, yes is no. The greatest misfortune Dayaks can experience is to be reunited with the souls of their ancestors in heaven.

Totem Poles

Villages in the Apo Kayan were once all protected with the *belawing*. Topped by a fearful warrior, these large totem poles were designed to frighten away evil spirits and protect the villages. Sacrifices at the base were given during the *mamat*, or headhunting feast. During the *mamat* warriors were possessed by the spirits and would dance wildly. Women and girls were not allowed for they displeased the spirits. The structures were also covered with *sang* leaves.

After a freshly cut head had been offered at the base of the *belawing*, a *keramen* was erected to shelter the souls inside and outside the house. After the ceremonial meal, during the mamat, leaves were hung on the *keramen*. The design can be seen in the grave markers of modern Apo Kayan graves. A *keramen* is a large spear-shaped spike coming from a *tajau* (jar), usually with a hornbill on top.

KENYAN WORDS

asu	dragon-dog motif
bali statues	crude carvings of spirits with erect phalluses who roar and scare away sickness-bearing spirits.
bali akang	spirit of courage, bravery
bali matei	spirit of the dead
bali uma	house spirit
hampatong	carved ritual post
lamin	apartment, room
liang	grave, mausoleum
panyin	commoner
long	confluence of rivers
panyin ja'at	bad commoner
panyin tiga	good commoner
paran	aristocrat
paran bio	big aristocrat
paran lep, uma	ordinary aristocrat
paran iot	low aristocrat
pasanggrahan	rest house
pejaka	ceremonial homecoming of headhunters
poe	small knife that comes with mandau
pui	elder term of respect
suhan	status, grade
uma	longhouse
ula	slave
uyat	carved (protective) human image

KAYAN WORDS

bali uma	house guardian spirits
bali akang	spirits of bravery
mamat	headhunting rites
bali	spirit
adat	customs
mandau	head sword; now a glorified machete
perahu	canoe
ba	baby carrier
udo	human face motif

West Kalimantan

West Kalimantan or Kalbar is the last remote area in Kalimantan. Largely devoid of indigenous people inland, lacking any major natural wonders and patrolled like an inner city high school, it is and will be the last region in Borneo to be made available to outsiders. The major business here is timber with rubber plantations springing up soon after the flat land is denuded.

In the 14th century there were Malay sultanates that controlled trade in and out of the major rivers. The two major ones were Sukanda (south of Pontianak) and Sambas (north of Pontianak). These entrepreneurial folks would trade with the Dayaks that came down from the interior with natural goods. In 1770 the Arab trader and adventurer, Abdul Rahman founded Pontianak at the confluence of the Landak and Kapuas rivers and decided to consolidate these fly speck sultanates. The sultans immediately complained to the Dutch who then acted as referees for the next 150 years.

Diamonds were a profitable but dwindling resource for the sultanates but in 1780 gold was discovered in the Sambas area. The Sultan of Sambas imported thousands of Hakka Chinese to dig it out. During the 18th century the gold fields in western Borneo produced up to one seventh of the world's supply of gold. The Chinese didn't need an MBA to figure out that they could make more money if they dug it out and sold it themselves, so they set up *kongsi* based on family ties.

More Chinese were invited to come to the gold fields as the 1700s came to a close, and of course, the sultan of Sambas was there to sell them what they needed and to extract his piece of the action. By 1820 there were 40,000 Chinese working and running the gold fields of Mandor and Montrado with the gold being sold back to closely connected Chinese back in China. The Java rebellion (1825-30) was occupying the time and energy of the Dutch colonial rulers so they didn't catch on until the gold fields were mined out.

The *kongis* battled amongst themselves and the Dutch for control of other areas. The Dutch army finally got around to quieting Borneo's wild west. The Chinese *kongsi* were broken up and the workers that were unable to pay for fare back home settled in the cities of Singkawang, Pontianak and Sambas.

West Borneo became a backwater region so quiet that the Dutch colonial presence consisted of only two representatives, one in Sambas and the other in Pontianak.

Quiet Kalbar received a rude shock when the Japanese occupation forces arrived in October of 1943. They rounded up the cream of Kalbar's business, religious and ethnic leaders and simply shot them. It is estimated that 21,037 people were killed by the Japanese. Mass graves exhumed after the war revealed that over 1000 in Mandoor had been killed in one day.

In 1945 a guerilla group called Majang Desa fought back resurrecting the old tradition of headhunting.

Things again quieted down after the war until Chinese communist groups, no doubt with backing from the Chinese government, began a war of insurrection in the late 60s. The entire border area was declared an operations area and the border was closed in 1975. The Indonesian army was successful in pushing the insurgents into Sarawak and after a cooling off period the border was reopened in 1991.

Getting In

Kalbar, a little visited area, (English is not a common language) is centered around the Kapuas river basin, providing the only real link between Sarawak and Kalimantan. The border post at Entikong is the only real land gateway between the two regions. At one time the Dutch were terrified that James Brooke, the Rajah of Sarawak would try to add this region to his ever expanding fiefdom. They beefed up Pontianak and the surrounding areas. Paranoia creeped in again in 1968 when warfare between Indonesia and Chinese insurgents turned the area into an occupied area. The rebels were pushed back over the border into Sarawak but the border was locked down to make sure they didn't return. The border between the two countries was closed in 1975 but in April of 1990 the border reopened. You can now travel by land from Kuching in Sarawak to Pontianak by bus.

Getting Around

Today travel in the region can be daunting for a variety of reasons. The large military presence and resulting bureacracy, the lack of tourist facilities, empty region, few people that speak English , the presence of legal and illegal loggers inland and the general high cost of travel make most adventurers pick the Apo Kayan, Berau or Mahakam region. If you do want to explore this region it is strongly advised that you link up with a local tour operator who can guide you through not only the wilderness but the paperwork jungle as well.

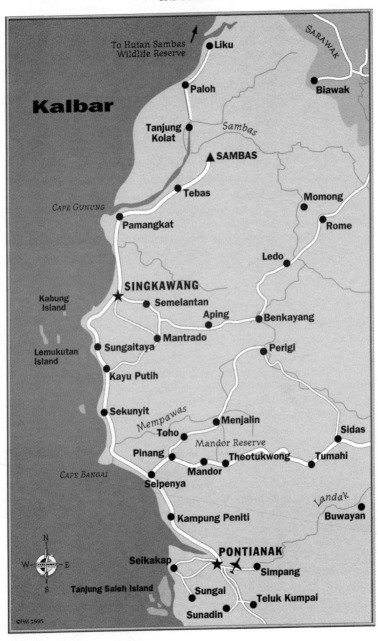

SARAWAK

To Hutan Sambas
Wildlife Reserve

Liku

Paloh

Biawak

Kalbar

Tanjung
Kolat

Sambas

▲ **SAMBAS**

Tebas

Momong

Rome

Cape Gunung

Pamangkat

Ledo

SINGKAWANG

Semelantan

Aping

Benkayang

Kabung
Island

Mantrado

Sungaitaya

Perigi

Lemukutan
Island

Kayu Putih

Sekunyit

Mempawas

Menjalin

Toho

Sidas

Mandor Reserve

Pinang

Theotukwong

Tumahi

Mandor

Cape Bangai

Seipenya

Landak

Kampung Peniti

Buwayan

N
W— ⊕ —E
S

PONTIANAK

Selkakap

Simpang

Tanjung Saleh Island

Sungai

Teluk Kumpai

Sunadin

©FWI 1995

To travel up the Kapuas river (or anywhere past the capital city of Pontianak) you must check in with the police and fill out the proper paperwork. Military intelligence and the camat will then be notified. They may ask you to fill out more paperwork or check in with them. They will radio ahead to the next town to ensure that you check in like a good boy. You may be asked to fill out paperwork as you go upriver (with little or no guidance in English). If you are traveling alone they will assume that you are up to no good since no tourists in their right mind would visit the logging destroyed and remote regions in the interior.

By water

The 1243 km long Kapuas is the focal point, major artery and the entire reason for being in Kalbar. Ocean-going ships can sail as far as Putussibau.

Getting Out

There is little that the Indonesians can do to stop the locals from traveling to and from Sarawak. Traditionally they have trekked along their *jalan tikus* (mouse trails) for centuries. Foreigners were absolutely forbidden and Malaysians were barred from entering until 1991. Malaysians can now visit relatives in Pontianak by taking the 400 km bus ride from Kuching. Surprisingly, most of the lineups are on the Kalimantan side as Indonesians use Entikong as a duty free exit port.

The People of Kalbar

Like the rest of Kalimantan, the 3.9 million people of Kalbar live along the coast and rivers—split evenly between Malay (40 percent) and Dayaks (40 percent).

Kalbar has the highest concentration of Chinese (450,000 or 11 percent of the total population) left over from the great gold rush of 1790–1820. Pontianak has a Chinese population of 35 percent Chinese and Singkawang is 70 percent Chinese. Today immigrants come from matriarchal peoples of Minangkabau, from southern Sumatra and from the crowded island of Java.

Entikong

9 hours from Pontianak by road

All Indonesians must pay a tax of RP250,000 when they leave the country. This anti-tourist tax not only keeps most Indonesian families stuck at home but discourages even the idea of normal folks making the haj to Mecca or even visiting relatives back in Singapore, Malaysia, India, Hong Kong or China. For some strange reason Entikong is the only exit port that does not require this stiff tax. There is enough incentive for large families to fly to Pontianak, take the bus to Kuching and then depart to their next destination.

Pontianak

Pontianak is the largest city in Kalimantan, and timber is the major business here with 9.5 million hectares of virgin timber coming out as fast as the loggers can pull it out. Approximately 3 million hectares are supposed to be protected from logging. In the meantime, Kalbar is the least explored of the provinces of Kalimantan. Most travelers will hear the story that a *pontianak* is a blood drinking ghost of a woman who has died while giving birth.

You can cruise through Pontianak in about one day. Even though Pontianak is Borneo's largest city, there is little to recommend a special visit unless you are into rubber or plywood. Pontianak is primarily a Chinese town with 60 percent of its inhabitants being Hakka Chinese descendants from gold rush days. The city is a collection of quarters that were once separate villages. The center of the city is the area around the sultan's palace (*kraton*). If you walk around this bustling town of 450,000 people you can take in most of the sights in a full day. There is a large central, indoor market (Kapuas Indah) and an early morning fishmarket (Pasar Ikan) downriver and a collection of interesting temples and the architecturally interesting remnants of the sultanate era. The Museum is definitely worth a visit but take along a guide to help you figure out what you are looking at.

What to See in Pontianak

Abdul Rachman Mosque (Mesjid Abdurrakhman)

Take an air taxi across the sungai Landak from the harbor. Next to the Kadriyah palace.
A 250 year old Malay style mosque built by trader, adventurer and pirate Syarif Abdul Rahman who founded Pontianak in 1770. He became respectable by making himself the first Sultan in 1771 and proceeded to build this great mosque to add to his new respectability. The area is a great place to take pictures as the sun goes down and the people are on the river. Across the river is the picturesque harbor.

Equator Monument (Tugu Khatulistiwa)

The *tugu Khatulistiwa* is the Indonesian word for equator. If you are a collector of snapshots of various signs that signify this position then take a minibus heading northeast out of town. When the monument was built in 1928 it was simple *belian* obelisk with an arrow. In 1930 a circle was added and in 1938 another circle was added to make it either an astrolab or a gyroscope. Lovers of trivia will be glad to know that on March 23, and September 23 the sun is positioned directly overhead. In 1991 they covered the original wooden monument inside a concrete building and erected a 20 foot high column on top of that. If you can't be bothered taking the bus out through the grubby industrial area to visit this "monument" you can buy it in miniature from the town shops or you can get a free signed certificate from Pontianak's City Hall across from the Kartika Hotel. In any case, when the shadow disappears during the March and September equinox it is a good excuse for the locals to party in Pontianak which tells you how much there is to do here.

Harapan Kita

Take the bridge across sungai Landak, turn right.
Technically not a tourist attraction but worth a look-see if you are all karaoked out. A curiosity to rival Hamburg's Reeperbahn, a one stop shopping waterfront brothel. Mockingly called kampung Brunei or Harapan Kita (our hope), this village

of over 250 prostitutes is Pontianak's way of making sure you know where your husband is. Instead of allowing prostitution throughout the city, the girls are only allowed to ply their trade in this ramshackle village of lust.

Kadriyah Palace (istana Kadriyah)

Open daily 9 a.m.–5:30 p.m., RP500 donation requested.

The sultan's palace is built entirely out of ironwood (*belian*) by Sultan Abdul Rahman and commands the confluence of the Kapuas and Landak rivers. Abdul Rahman died in 1808. The palace has since been home to eight sultans. The sixth Sultan and his son were killed by the Japanese during the occupation. The eighth sultan died in 1978. Syarif Yusof Alkadri, the indirect descendant of the Sultan's family, now looks after the palace. Yusof is more than happy to show you around or to pose for pictures.

National Museum (Musium Negeri)

Jalan Ahmad Yani, south of the city center near the University
Open Monday - Sunday, 9 a.m.–4 p.m., Friday, 9 a.m.–11 a.m.

Probably the second best museum in Borneo (The Sarawak museum is the best). The Pontianak museum has a very comprehensive collection and display of native art, musical instruments, clothing, weapons, tools and crafts. There are models of longhouses, tattoo blocks, basketry. There is also a good selection of ceramic jars (*tempayan*) dating back to the 16th century. If you intend to spend a lot of time upriver, unfortunately this is where you will see traditional artistry and materials. It is worth spending some time here although the museum information is in Indonesian. Just off Jalan Jend. At Yani, there is a full size replica of a longhouse built in 1985.

Pinisi Harbor

Jalan S. Muhammmad south along the the Kapuas Kecil

Here is where the East Javanese and Bugi schooners dock. You can also find the houseboats (*bandung*) that take advantage of the Kapuas' deep depths. They stock up with goods in Pontianak and then slowly travel up and down the Kapuas stopping at each village, becoming floating Wal-Marts.

Where to Stay in Pontianak

There is nothing close to five star or even four star in this working man's paradise. We can be accused of being overly enthusiastic in awarding stars. Accordingly accommodations are overpriced and unappealing.

Luxury

Hotel Mahkota Kapuas   **RP55,000–385,000**   ★★★

Jalan Sidas 8; ☎ *(0561) 36022, FAX 36200*
105 rooms. New hotel A/C , small rooms, swimming pool, billiards room, restaurant, tennis courts and bar. Best bet for clean rooms.

Kartika Hotel   **RP52,000–98,000**   ★

Jalan Rahardi Usman; ☎ *(0561) 34401, FAX 38457*
45 rooms. Central location (right across from city hall) filled with businessmen. You can reserve rooms that face the river. This is our best pick if location overides luxury or service. All rooms with A/C.

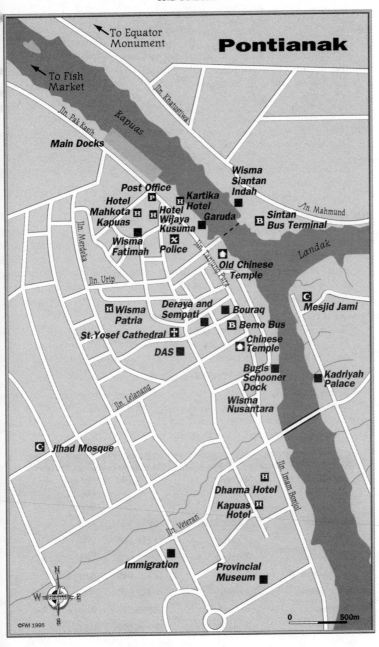

Pontianak

To Equator Monument

To Fish Market

Kapuas

Jln. Khatustiwa

Jln. Pak Kasih

Main Docks

Jln. Merdeka

Post Office

Hotel Mahkota Kapuas

Hotel Wijaya Kusuma

Kartika Hotel

Garuda

Wisma Siantan Indah

Jln. Mahmund

Sintan Bus Terminal

Landak

Wisma Fatimah

Police

Jln. Tanjung Pura

Old Chinese Temple

Jln. Urip

Mesjid Jami

Wisma Patria

Deraya and Sempati

Bouraq

Bemo Bus

St. Yosef Cathedral

Chinese Temple

DAS

Bugis Schooner Dock

Kadriyah Palace

Wisma Nusantara

Jln. Lelanang

Jihad Mosque

Jln. Imam Bonjol

Dharma Hotel

Kapuas Hotel

Jln. Veteran

Immigration

Provincial Museum

N W E S

FIELDING WORLDWIDE

©FWI 1995

0 500m

Moderate

Kapuas   **RP42,000–62,000**   ★★

Jalan Iman Bonjol; ☎ *(0561) 36122*

67 rooms. Towards the airport. Not a palace but a sprawling low rise complete with
shopping center and 100 meter swimming pool. Overall ambience is musty and
dank but pool and large apartments are a change. If you are homesick you can ask
for an apartment complete with carport for 58,000 rupiah. Cottages are about
10,000 rupiah cheaper. Most rooms with a/c, restaurant.

Hotel Dharma   **RP22,000–40,000**   ★

Jalan Imam Bonjol 10; ☎ *(0561) 34759*

90 rooms. Fading large hotel displaced by the Mahkota. The fact that the top floor
has been turned into a whorehouse may give it an edge over the other business
hotels.

Budget

Hotel Wijaya Kusuma   **RP20,000–32,500**

Jalan Musi 51 -53; ☎ *(0561) 32547*

68 rooms. A/C in some rooms, fans in others. A good location on the river, and
across from the indoor market. Caters to Chinese businesmen so don't be shocked
to find that you're staying in a den of iniquity (mostly gambling and prostitution).
Rooms go up in price depending on whether they come with shared or attached
bathroom (*mandi*). Rooms facing the street are noisy.

Wisman Patria   **RP18,000–20,000**

Jalan Hos Cokroaminoto 497; ☎ *(0561) 36063*

37 rooms. Hos Cokroaminoto does not mean house of cockroaches but it could.
Budget accommodations, friendly staff (they have to be to keep guests).

Getting In

Most people will fly into Supadio Airport (about 20km out of town). Taxis into town
(RP10,000, 10 minutes) are plentiful. Buy your ticket at the counter in the airport. All
major Indonesian airlines fly into Pontianak from Balikpapan, Jakarta, Ketapang, Medan,
Pankalanbun and Puta Siban. You can fly directly to Singapore or Kuching.

By air from Pontianak			
Jakarta	3 daily	RP179,700	Merpati, Bouraq, Sempati
Ketapang	1 daily	RP75,000	DAS
Kuching	2 weekly	RP165,000	MAS
Nangapinoh	1 daily	RP128,000	DAS
Pangkalanbun	1 daily	RP103,000	Deraya
Putussibau	1 weekly	RP149,000	DAS
Sintang	3 weekly	RP65,000	Deraya
Singapore	3 weekly	RP205,000	Garuda

Getting Around

Your best bet is to cover the coastal area by bus and the interior by boat. Long distance buses leave the Batu Layang terminal at km 8 on the Sambas road. Buy your tickets at the bus station. You can charter a taxi for about RP65,000 an hour.

Buses From Pontianak		
Kuching (via Entikong*)	**RP30,000**	**6–8 hours**
Mandor	**RP2000**	**1.5 hours**
Sintang	**RP15,000**	**10 hours**
Singkawang	**RP 4000**	**3–4 hours**
Sambas	**RP2000**	**3.5–4.5 hours**

You must walk across the border to catch buses at Serian and then onward to Kuching.

Getting Out

Daily buses leave Pontianak for the 9 hour trip to Kuching at 6 a.m. You can buy your tickets from **Insan Worldwide Tours and Travel (ITT)**, *Jalan Tanjungpura 149*, directly here from Kuching. The border at Entikong is open 6 a.m.–4 p.m. (west Indonesian time) and 5 a.m.–5 p.m. Malaysian time. You must change buses at the border and pickup a Malaysian bus on the other side.

By Boat

The *Tanjung Priok* sails for Jakarta on the first and third Monday of every month and the *Belawan* sails once a month for Sumatra. Buy your tickets at the **Pelni** office at *Jalan Pelabuhan 2*, ☎ *(0561) 34133*. The PELNI ferry *Lawit* travels to Jakarta every 10 days (RP91,000, 2 days, 2 nights). You can also see if there any cargo ships in the harbor.

Pontianak Nuts & Bolts

Area:
146,807 sq km, 56,682 sq miles

Population:
450,000

Best Time to visit:
December to April is the wet season and May, June is the dry season.

Post Office
Jalan Rahadi Suman 1

Hospital
Dr. Sudarso Hospital, Jalan Adisucipto , Sei Jawi Hospital Centre, Jalan Merdeka Barat

Airline Offices

Bouraq
Jalan Haji Juanda 169, ☎ *(0561) 2371*

Garuda/Merpati
Jalan Rohadi Usman 8A, ☎ *(0561) 2106*

DAS

> Jalan Gajah Mada 67, ☎ (0561) 583

Deraya/Sempati

> Jalan Sisingamangaraja 145, ☎ (0561) 4840

PELNI Ferry

Pelni Ferry

> Pelni office at Jalan Pelabuhan 2; ☎ (0561) 34133

Tour Companies

Ateng

> Jalan Gajah Mada 201; ☎ (0561) 32683, FAX 36620

Insan Worldwide (ITT)

> Jalan Tanjungpura 149; ☎ (0561) 64257, 62841, 66349

Jambore Express

> Jalan Pahlawan 226; ☎ (0561) 36703

Kalbar Tourist Office

> Jalan Achmad Sood 25, ☎ (0561) 36712 and at airport.

Excursions from Pontianak

Singkawang

Take the minibus from Pontianak (3.5 hours, 5,000 rupiah)

A predominantly Hakka Chinese settlement and trading center for the gold fields in nearby Mantrado. Today it is a busy backwater town that keeps pretty much to itself. Primarily a farming area and a city more likely to be found in Sarawak than Kalimantan.

Where to stay in Singakawang

There are five cheap hotels to choose from in-town. My advice would be to look into the resort and day trips that leave from this area.

Hotel Mahkota   **RP70,000–175,000**   ★★

> Jalan Diponegorar 1; ☎ 31244
> Your best bet in Singkawang (the name of a locally grown turnip). All A/C, a swimming pool, and disco. Any other hotel is cheaper and passable except the Hotel Kal-Bar Jalan Kepole ☎ 21404 which is a brothel and gambling center that shuns foreigners.

Hotel Palapa   **RP26,000–52,000**

> Jalan Ismael Tahir 152; ☎ 31449
> Not to be confused with the beach hotel of the same name. Out of town but clean and cheap.

Hotel Diponegoro   **RP9200–21,500**

> Jalan Diponegoro 32; ☎ 21430
> Best bet for a cheap crash. Rooms are as small as they are clean and cheap.

Hotel Bandung   **RP5000–8000**

> Jl. Pasar Tengah

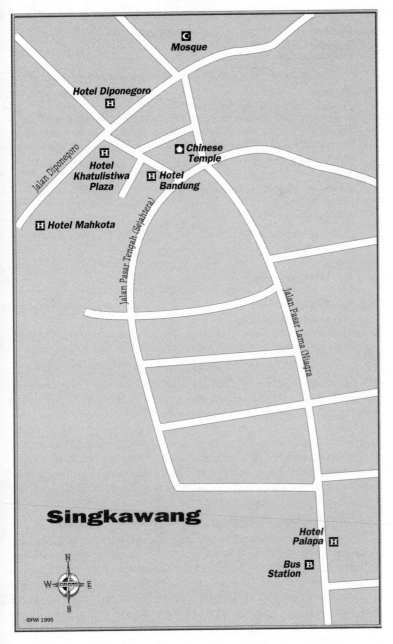

Mosque

Hotel Diponegoro

Jalan Diponegoro

Hotel
Khatulistiwa
Plaza

Chinese
Temple

Hotel
Bandung

Jalan Pasar Tengah (Sejahtera)

Hotel Mahkota

Jalan Pasar Lama (Niaga)

Singkawang

Hotel
Palapa

Bus
Station

N
W E
S

©FWI 1995

Inexpensive, basic and an eight minute walk from the bus station.

Hotel Khatulistiwa   **RP5000–8000**
Jl. Selamat Karman 17; ☎ *20510*
Small and also near the bus station.

Excursions from Singkawang

Pulau Randayan
2 hours by boat from Singkawang by boatd
A 12 hectare island that offers good snorkeling along its coral reefs. You can stay at one of the simple but new lodges on the island. Check in with Mr. Sukartadj the owner of the Palapa hotel in Singkawang who will set you up for the boat ride and overnight accommodations.

Palua Temajo
60km south of Singkawang by boat.
Just off the coast from Kampung Sungai Kunyit village. Palua Temajo is another good dive site or a good day excursion.

All inclusive one day diving trips will cost you RP25,000 from Pontianak through Ateng Tours and Travel.

Pottery village
7kms south of Singakawang
You can buy replicas of Chinese vases in this little cottage industry town.

Pasir Panjang Beach
15 kms south of Singakawang
A pleasant weekend retreat for the locals. There is a beachfront hotel called Hotel Palapa (15,000 rupiah) or camping where you can rent watersports equipment.

Sambas★

A stilt village built over the Sambas river. Formerly the center of a small 400-year-old sultanate and then a major gold and diamond mining center. You can visit the remains of a diamond mine. Visit the Sultan's palace (built in 1812) and the mosque built in 1893. There is a type of cloth produced here called *kain sambas.* The cloth is hand stitched using gold thread. The Hutan forest preserve will be an important park designed to protect the watershed and will be linked with an area in Sarawak. Although the region is appealing for adventurers, there is heavy police and military presence and explicit permission is required to enter.

Mount Palung Wildlife Reserve

This 90,000 hectare area is a scientific research center and offers nine campsites within the park. If you want to go in you must be self sufficient and arrange for permission from the **PHPA Conservation Office** in Pontianank *on Jalan Abdurrahman Saleh 33.* Mr Tan Yong Senh of Ateng Tour and Travel seems to have a lock on tours going into the park. Once inside the park you can expect sightings of proboscis monkeys and orang utans as well as the range of lowland dipterocarp flora and fauna.

The Kapuas River

The 1243 km long Kapuas was explored in 1822 by Dutchman Major George Muller. In 1826 he lost his head (literally) while attempting to cross the self named Muller Range. The Sultan of Kutai had second thoughts about letting the Dutch explore the dark interior of his country for him. Unrelated author Kal Muller retraced and completed Major Muller's journey backwards from the Mahakam to the Kapuas in his part travel guide, part travelogue; *Borneo, Journey into the Tropical Rainforest.*

The area north of the Kapuas was the site of many skirmishes between British SAS soliders and the Indonesian army during the Konfrontasi (1963–65) as well as the Chinese Communist insurgency in the late '60s. Tension has subsided but suspicion of strangers lingers like the morning mist on the far off Muller range. You will need to be diligent about checking in with the local officials. You won't see much along this deep muddy river but you will get to know the people and the rhythm of the place.

There is still some gold panning going on both in the rivers and by digging up large chunks of real estate. The trip on a *bandung* is cheap (about 50,000 rupiah) but the 4–5 days you would normally spend reading trashy novels could be put to better use exploring the headwaters.

Your best bet is to go directly to Sintang via bus, or if the road is completed by the time you get there, continue all the way to Putussibau.

Pah Auman

120km from Pontianak on the way to the border crossing at Entikong. Take an eastbound bus from the Batu Layang bus station (RP3,500)
There is a 30 door traditional longhouse 12 kms from Pah Auman . The Kamung Saham longhouse is your best bet if you want to see or experience an authentic Kedayan longhouse in this region. Ask permission from the headman who will graciously accept your gift and most likely let you stay.

Sintang

245 km east of Pontianak by bus (RP9,000 , 8 hrs)
Sintang was a Chinese trading town whose residents got rich trading hard goods for jungle items brought downriver by the Dayaks. You can take the two hour walk to the top of 900m Dark Mountain (Gunung Kelam) or you could head up the Melawi or Pinoh to visit with the Ot Danum tribes that live at the headwaters. You take sungai Melawi to Nangapinoh where there is rudimentary accommodation and travel by canoe to the villages of Kotabaru and Nangasokan. There is an airport in Nanga-

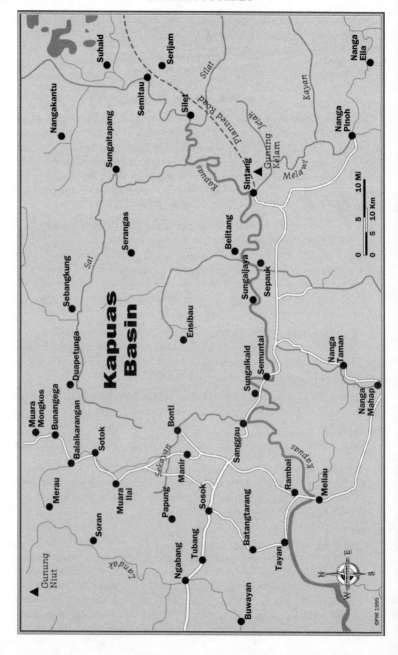

pinoh with direct flights to Pontianak. The trip is recommended for its wild river sections and rarely visited Dayak tribes.

Semitau

Midway between Sintang and Putussibau

Students of Dayak artistry may want to visit with the Maloh Dayaks to see what they can do with silver and gold. There are three "black" lakes in the area (Luar, Sentarum and Sumpa) that are settled by Ibans from Sarawak. The water in the shallow lakes is stained by the natural tannins from the soil and leaf litter.

Putussibau

1000kms upriver from Pontianak

The last stop before heading into the Muller Range above the Kapuas. The descriptive name *putussibau* or *putus* Sibau means "cut off at Sibau" in reference to river traffic having to halt at the Sibau river. On the other side of the Range the mighty Mahakam begins its long journey to Samarinda. There are few Dayak longhouses in the area. Two worth visiting are the Malapi I and the Semangkok. Once in town you are well advised to stop in at the mayor's *(bupati)* office and explain your intentions.

Many longhouses along the Kapuas are a blend of the traditional and practical.

Beyond Putussibau:
Across Kalimantan

Many will find the remoteness of the upper Kapuas appealing. Even fewer will embark on a major trek over the watershed of the Muller range and then

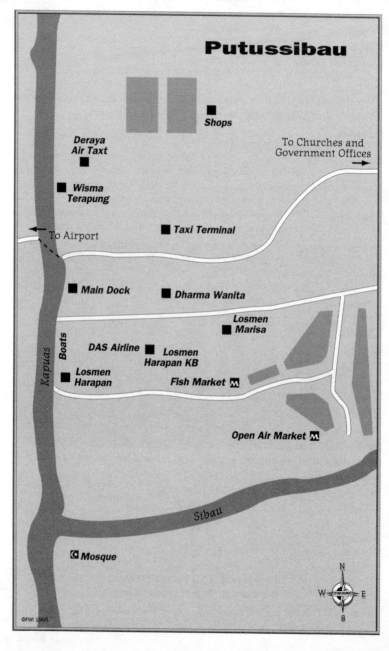

Putussibau

Shops

Deraya
Air Taxt

Wisma
Terapung

To Churches and
Government Offices →

To Airport ←

Taxi Terminal

Main Dock

Dharma Wanita

Losmen
Marisa

Kapuas

Boats

DAS Airline

Losmen
Harapan KB

Losmen
Harapan

Fish Market

Open Air Market

Sibau

Mosque

©FWI 1995

N
W   E
S

down the Mahakam. If you want to go further upriver you must cut a pretty mean deal with the local boatmen. It can run you RP100,000 *an hour* to go exploring beyond Putussibau. If you are determined to go all the way to Long Apari, the headwaters of the Mahakam, you will need to contact a guide in Putussibau or one of the travel companies in Pontianak.

House boats (*bandungs*) take about four days and three nights to get to Putussibau. The fare includes minimal food, so come prepared with supplements. The scenery is as tedious as the pace of the *bandung*. Travel up the river is better accomplished by taking the bus to Sintang (about 700kms by river !) and then a shorter, 36 hour trip by boat to Putussibau. The chart following gives a fairly ambitious trek from Pontianak to Samarinda, past the regular scheduled riverboat service to Putussibau at which point you will need to purchase supplies, arrange a guide and a boat to Nangabungan. The bupati in Putussibau will assist in this endeavor. Provision yourself and your guides for the 7–10 day journey (don't forget to estimate the food required for your porters and guides' six day return trip from Log Apari). Basic food supplies are available in Putussibau. Take your time cutting your best deal for a motorized canoe (this will run about RP500,000) to make the one day trip upriver to Nangabungan. From here you switch to smaller canoes. (Each canoe should cost about RP100,000) for a day long trip to Tanjung Lokan. You are now in the boonies and if you made it this far without a guide you will definitely need one now to pick your way along the overgrown mountain trails. The walk is six days of steep terrain and jungle. There is a logging road and camp about a day west of Long Apari. At this point your guides will make the long trip back. From the logging camp you hike your way (4 hours) to the river. There you should be able to hire a canoe for about RP40,000. It is a 2–3 hour boat ride downstream to Long Apari depending on the water level. From Long Apari you can continue downstream to Long Lunuk the terminus of regularly scheduled riverboat service to Samarinda.

Pontianak to Samarinda			
Samarinda - Sintang	RP15,000	2 days	Riverboat
Sintang - Putussibau	RP15,000	2 days	Riverboat
Putussibau - Nangabangan	RP500,000	1 day	Hired boat
Nangabungan - Tanjung Lokan	RP75,000	1 day	Hired boat
Tanjun Lokan - Long Apari	RP150,000	1 day	6 day trek with guides
Long Apari - Long Lunuk	RP30,000	1 day	4 hr trek/3 hour boat
Long Lunuk - Samarinda	RP15,500	3 days	Riverboats

You are now back in civilization at which point you can take the 3 day / 2 night riverboat down the Mahakam river to Samarinda or fly to Samarinda from Long Lunuk (RP50,000) to Samarinda.

You will have spent about two weeks in the more remote parts of Borneo.

Young orang utans are rehabilitated into the wilds at Tanjung Puting.

Central Kalimantan

This is the largest, least visited and least populated province in Kalimantan. Set up as a separate homeland for the indigenous peoples of Borneo in the 1950s, it is now a remote mountainous area to the north with vast swamplands to the south with a population of 1.4 million people. The major attraction here is **Tanjung Puting** where Dr. Birute Galdikas runs an orang utan rehabilitation center. There is also a major month long festival every so often when the Dayaks celebrate **Teweh,** when those who have passed away but have been in temporary graves can be buried. The capital city of Palangkaraya was only built in the '50s and is known only for its **museum**.

Getting in

From		Cost	Via
BY AIR			
Jakarta	daily	RP109,900	Garuda
Balikpapan	daily	RP58,700	Garuda
Pangkalanbun	daily	RP42,100	DAS
Pangkalpinang	daily	RP23,800	Merpati
Sampit	daily	RP29,800	Merpati
Surabaya	daily	RP85,200	Merpati
Banjarmasin	twice daily	RP96,300	Bouraq

Most independent travelers get to Palangkaraya via riverboat from Banjarmasin. It is a long 12 hour trip. You can fly here from Jakarta(RP109,900) aboard the one daily flight this area supports. Garuda also flies in from Balikpapan (RP58,700).

Getting Around

Bouraq, *Jalan A. Yani 6*, ☎ *(0514) 21622*, **Merpati**, *Jalan A. Yani and Garuda, Jalan Sudirman 45, 21121* have offices in Palangkaraya. To get to Tanjung Puting take a klotok to Kumai (RP50, 5 hours) and then from Kumai to the Sekunyer River. You will need to have a permit from the PHPA office in Kumai to visit Tanjung Puting. The major rivers are the Arot, the Barito, the Kahayan and the Sampit.

Nuts & Bolts

You'll be somewhat pleased to know that the Indonesian tourism folks don't even include this 154,000 sq km region in their tourism brochures.

Palangkaraya

13 hours by riverboat from Banjarmasin

The provincial capital is too recent to offer any historic or culturally rewarding experiences for the traveler. The entire town was built in 1957 as a mini Brasilia to be the province's capital. The Russians got into the act and helped out by building a well engineered road to Kasungan to the north. When the Indonesians turfed out the Russians in 1965 they had completed one 31km road (the Indonesians built 3kms of it). What exists is a less than inspiring city with a beautiful road to nowhere. Until drag racing or road hockey gets big here the road will probably remain unused and still in perfect shape. If you are going upriver this is the only spot to book flights, change money or cash travelers checks. After you take in about 20 minutes of the flat uninspiring landscape, the bureaucratic architecture and general malaise, you will be ready to head for the mountains up north or to Tanjung Puting to the southeast.

Museum Balanga

A pretty setting for Dayak handicrafts, Chinese ceramics, a small zoo and large gardens.

Where to Stay in Palangkaraya

You have one semi-luxury hotel and some cheap losmens along the Sungai Kahayan.

Dandang Tingang   RP39,000–127,000

Jalan Yos Sudarso 11, ☎ *(0514) 21805*
A ways out of town but the only luxury digs.

Hotel Adidas   RP38,000–43,000

Jalan A. Yani 90, ☎ *(0514) 21770*
AC rooms, not much else to recommend it.

Hotel Virgo   RP15,000–30,000

Jalan A. Yani 7B, ☎ *(0514) 21265*
You get fans at the low end and AC at the high end.

Losmen Putir Sinta   RP8500–11,000

Jalan Nias 2, ☎ *(0514) 21132*
Bottom of the heap, but you get a fan and mandi.

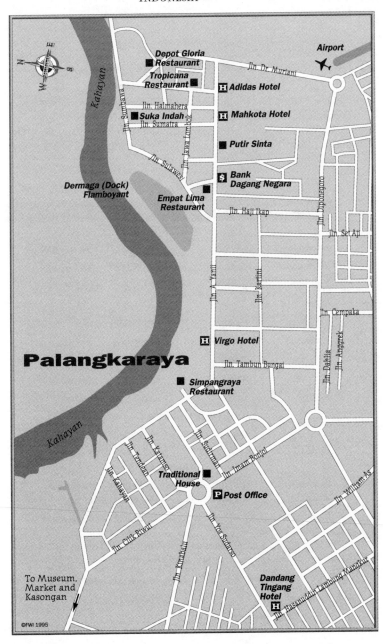

Depot Gloria
Restaurant

Tropicana
Restaurant

Airport

Jln. Dr. Muriani

Kahayan

Jln. Sumbawa

H Adidas Hotel

Jln. Halmahera

Suka Indah
Jln. Sumatra

H Mahkota Hotel

Jln. Jawa Lombok

Putir Sinta

Jln. Sulawesi

Jln. Diponegoro

Bank
Dagang Negara

Jln. Set Aji

Dermaga (Dock)
Flamboyant

Empat Lima
Restaurant

Jln. Haji Ikap

Jln. Cempaka

Jln. A. Yani

Jln. Kartini

Jln. Dahlia

Jln. Anggrek

H Virgo Hotel

Palangkaraya

Jln. Tambun Bungai

Simpangraya
Restaurant

Kahayan

Jln. Kanarias

Jln. Sudirman

Jln. Imam Bonjol

Jln. Tandun

Jln. Kahayan

Traditional
House

P Post Office

Jln. William As

Jln. Cilik Riwut

Jln. Karhaili

Jln. Yos Sudarso

To Museum,
Market and
Kasongan

Dandang
Tingang
Hotel

H

Jln. Hasanuddin Landung Mangatur

©FWI 1995

Losmen Mahkota   RP7000–35,200

Jalan Nias 5, ☎ *(0514) 21672*
Choose between this and the Putir Sinta across the street.

Pangkalanbun

2 hours by air from Banjarmasin

This is a stopping off point for trips to Tanjung Puting National Park. The nondescript city is on the banks of the Sungai Arot and is essentially a harbor town. There are good boat connections here to other ports along the Kalimantan coast. There are also banks, stores and other services before you head into the park.

Getting Around

From		Cost	Via
BY AIR			
Palangkaraya	daily	RP100,000	Bouraq, DAS
Banjarmasin	daily	RP100,000	Bouraq, DAS
Surabaya	3 weekly	RP162,800	Bouraq
Sampit	2 weekly	RP89,600	DAS
Semarang	daily	RP143,000	Deraya, Merpati
Pontianak	3 weekly	RP100,000	Deraya
Ketapang	2 weekly	RP84,000	Merpati
Bandung	daily	RP198,000	Merpati
Jakarta	daily	RP206,000	Merpati
VIA FERRY			
Semarang Banjarmasin	2 monthly	RP27,000	PELNI (Krakatoa)
VIA BOAT			
Pontianak Semarang	3 days, 2 nights	RP32,000 -46,000 w/bed	Cargo boat
Banjarmasin	1 -2 days	RP25,000	Charter boat

The DAS and the Merpati offices are near Wisma Anddika east of the downtown area back from the river. The passenger pier is really the center of most of the town's business.

Where to Stay in Pangkalanbun

Blue Kecubang   RP40,000–71,000

Jalan Domba, ☎ *(0514) 21211*
A good (and only) choice if you want TV, AC, a restaurant and telephone service.

Wisma Andika   **RP15,000–42,500**

Jalan Hasanuddin, ☎ *(0514) 21218*
Clean rooms, AC and with a tasty restaurant.

Wisma Sampurga   **RP10,000–15,000**

Jalan Domba
AC and mandi.

Budget

Nothing special here just low buck losmens for travelers heading into the park. Jalan
P. Antasari, the street that runs along the river, has three budget accommodations to
choose from (Bahagia, Mawar, and Abadi in order of preference) expect to pay RP6000–
8000. If you go back one street along to Jalan Kasumayuda, the second street parallel to
the river you will find Losmen Rahayu and Antrek. Here you can get by parting with
RP5000–7500.

Tanjung Puting National Park★★

4 hours by boat from Kumai

This 305,000 hectare reserve was established in 1937. The land is comprised primarily of tea colored swamp, swamp forest, heath forest and lowland ditperocarp forest to the north. Although the main attraction is Camp
Leakey where there is one of the world's three orang utan rehabilitation centers you can explore the network of trails in the parks. Here you will find
proboscis monkeys, crocodiles, sun bears, wild pigs, monitor lizards, crab
eating macaques, gibbons, deer and otters. Bird watchers will discover her-
ons, storks, flycatchers and hornbills. The hiking can be a little wet. Unlike
the Florida everglades where walkways let people forget what a swamp is really about, here you will learn to hate swamps close up. Many of the trails require walking through deep water and constantly tripping over mangrove
roots. Many nasties abound: crocodiles, leeches, malarial mosquitos are in
great numbers. The actual study area is 3500 hectares.

Camp Leakey

When loggers cut down trees, many times female orang utans are killed, but their
offspring survive. There had been a flourishing trade in baby orang utans who were
sold as performers or pets. There was also a dark trade in decorative or ceremonial
orang utan skulls to replace the once plentiful human skulls. I have seen examples
of these skulls for private sale in the antique shops of Balikpapan. Now, if loggers or
police come across an orphaned orang utan, it is taken to this center to be fed and
hopefully reintroduced into the wild. The total number of orang utans in Kalimantan is estimated to number between 10,000 and 15,000. There are about 100 orang
utans in the park—half of which are introduced and the other half native.

There are feedings at the camp at 3:00 p.m., 4:00 p.m. and 5:00 p.m. On most days
you will be able to see about two dozen young orangs come to eat. If you want to
do a little one a favor you can offer it fruit or nuts and it will be glad to take it off
your hands. Please note that orang utans can catch human colds or other diseases
and that any visitor who is sick is not allowed in the park.

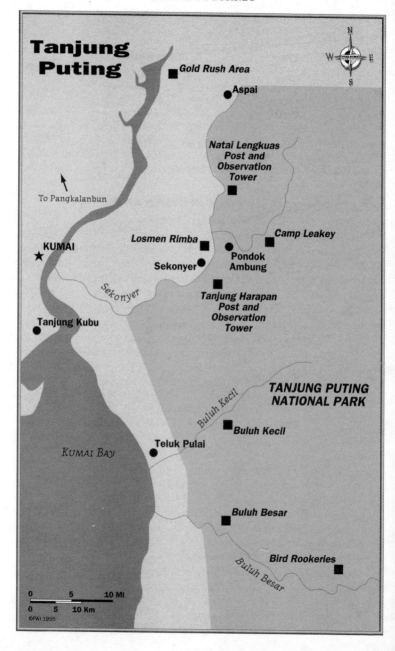

Tanjung Puting

Gold Rush Area

Aspai

Natai Lengkuas Post and Observation Tower

To Pangkalanbun

Camp Leakey

Losmen Rimba

KUMAI

Sekonyer

Pondok Ambung

Sekonyer

Tanjung Harapan Post and Observation Tower

Tanjung Kubu

Buluh Kecil

TANJUNG PUTING NATIONAL PARK

Buluh Kecil

Teluk Pulai

KUMAI BAY

Buluh Besar

Bird Rookeries

Buluh Besar

0   5   10 Mi
0   5   10 Km
©FWI 1995

The Ape Ladies

In case you didn't know, Birute Galdikas is one of the "ape ladies" sent out by Dr. Leakey to study and help preserve the three major species of apes. American Dian Fossey went to the Mountains of the Moon in Rwanda and Uganda to study the silver back gorilla, British researcher Jane Goodall went to Gombe on the shores of Lake Tanganyka in Tanzania to learn about the chimpanzee and Canadian Birute Galdikas came here as a young UCLA graduate of 25 to understand the orang utan. All three have managed to create a much higher level of awareness, particularly Dian Fossey, who was murdered and then became the subject of the movie Gorillas in the Mist *starring Sigourney Weaver.*

Although Galdikas keeps up a hectic schedule outside of Indonesia promoting her books and raising funds, she can usually be found here taking care of and studying her red headed charges.

Tanjung Harapan

(2 hours by boat south of Camp Leakey) This is the overflow center built in the 80s to handle the increasing flow of tourists that visit the park. There is also a third rehabilitation camp two hours north of Camp Leakey at Natai Lengkuas. At Tanjung Harapan you can rent dugout canoes (RP75,000–14,000 per day) to explore the park.

Getting In

Starting from Pangkalanbun you must check in with the Kantor Polisi for a park permit from the Conservation or PHPA office. You will need to bring your passport with you. You should have a copy of the photo page to get your permit. They may offer you a guide for RP7500 per day but there is little use for a guide since your boatman will take you to all the usual places. If you plan to get ambitious you may want the services of a guide to act as an interpreter, cook and porter. When you get to Kumai you drop off the copy of your passport and police letter/permit that you received in Pangkalanbun and then go to register at the PHPA office. The registration will cost you RP2000 and you must give them a copy of your police letter from Pangkalanbun and a copy of the photo page in your passport. Then the PHPH folks will give you three letters, one of which you keep and the the others are for the the Park Ranger at whatever point you visit and the third for the Orang utan Research and Conservation Project at Camp Leakey.

Most visitors stay in Pangkalanbun to get their permit and then take the 25 km minibus (RP7,500) southeast to Kumai. Colts do the same route in about 30 minutes and cost RP800. From Kumai you must hire a klotok to make the 4 hour trip to the park and for your sleeping quarters. Reccommended klotoks are the *Garuda 1* (6 passengers, RP60,000 per day) and *Garuda II* (10 passengers, RP70,000per day). They can be chartered at Jalan H. M. Idris; Kumai Hulu is the most popular choice. There are a variety of klotoks for hire in Kumai that range in price from RP 45,000–70,000 per day. You can organize the complete tour from Banjarmasin.

Longboats can be hired from Kumai to Tanjung Harapan (2 hours) or Natai Lengkuas (6 hours).

Where to Stay in
Tanjung Puting National Park

Most visitors stay either on the klotoks or at the Rimba Hotel in Kumai. There is no accommodation in the park other than wilderness camping.

Rimba Hotel   **RP90,000**

Sekonyer village near Tanjung Harapan
The only game in town. The price includes meals and an attached mandi.

Muara Teweh

56 hours by boat from Banjarmasin

If you want to skip Palangkaraya and head straight upriver, it is a *loooong* (56 hours, RP13,000) longboat ride from Banjarmasin to Muara Teweh. You can sleep and eat on board. You can fly via DAS for RP62,900 or take a klotok for about RP60,000. Faster and smaller speedboats will soak you almost RP350,000. Once in Muara Teweh you can hire guides to northeast to the Mahakam down to Samarinda or overland to Long Iram in East Kalimantan. An interesting side trip would be to Gunung Pancungapung on the border between Central and East Kalimantan where concrete markers note the exact geographical center of Borneo.

Where to Stay in Muara Teweh

There are a handful of cheap losmen that will run about RP6000–12,500 per night. The Barito, the Permai and Gunung Sintuk are first choices.

Fly the Bumpy Skies

Having had the dubious experience of crashing into the green jungle of Borneo it might be a good thing for me to warn you on the dangers of flying in this rugged land. Weather can be extremely violent with thunderstorms, updrafts and wind shear. It is quite common for helicopters and planes to go down and not be found for months. Survival experts give most people about 7 days to survive once their plane is down.

Recently rescuers had to resort to a psychic to find a downed Sikorsky S-5BT that went down with 18 people on board in July 26 of 1994 in the Kutai district in East Kalimantan. During the initial search they found another helicopter in the Bulungan district that had gone down a year earlier.

Pack List

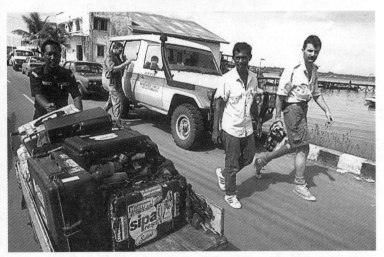

Loaded down with cameras, computers, video gear and digital recording equipment, the author blithely ignores his sage advice to travel light.

Heading off on any trip produces a frenzy of shopping, packing, repacking, more shopping, and then in desperation, the cruel act of cutting what you have just packed in half. If you plan on taking an expedition the process is worse. How much food will you eat? What is available locally? What about batteries, film, medicine, spare straps? The list goes on.

Explorers in the 19th century would hire dozens of porters who would be responsible for cooking, hunting, setting camp and collecting samples. The major implements brought by the explorers were weapons, ammunition, survey and navigation equipment, gifts, clothing (including dress uniforms) and in some cases, even a Victrola to liven up the long nights.

Just remember all that "gotta have it" stuff as well as your own sorry carcass might have to all fit in one longboat.

Today most travelers can provision themselves just fine from any of the department stores in Kota Kinabalu, Singapore or Jakarta. Adventure gear such as tents, hiking boots, sleeping bags, backpacks, miniature stoves, high tech flashlights and other modern survival gear should be purchased stateside.

Film, cameras, video equipment, recording equipment can all be purchased in Singapore, KK or KL much cheaper than the States but you will not have the chance to test your equipment before heading out to the bush.

Medicines and prescriptions are readily available (sometimes without prescriptions) from pharmacists in the larger towns in Borneo.

Here are the various modes of travel and what you should think about before leaving:

Business:

Everything your heart desires is available in major cities and five star hotels. Travel light. Laundry and cleaning services are available in all major hotels. Tailors are cheap and plentiful. Bring power adaptors for computers and access codes for phone cards. Overnight delivery is common in large cities and faxes are widespread. Interpreters can be hired, and entertaining is considered a major part of any business transaction. Remember that Muslims do not drink or eat pork. Chinese will feed you till you burst and asking a favor of anyone may result in a much larger favor being asked of you later.

Tours and Cruises:

Film and video supplies are available in major tourist towns. It will be slightly old but not out of date. One hour processing labs are readily available as well as low end cameras and accessories. Shopping malls are ideal for souvenirs but bargain hard if you buy at a market stall. Don't be afraid to walk away and then bargain some more. Do not buy butterflies, animal skins or other forbidden items or they may be confiscated by U.S. Customs upon your return.

Make sure your boots and your temperament can handle mud. A too familiar point of view after a miserable section of winching in the mountains of Sabah.

Backpacking:

Outdoor clothing is available but limited to smaller sizes. Western food and groceries are available in all towns. Basic supplies like coffee, tea, matches are found in most villages but expensive. Maps and books are only available in major towns. Shoes are limited to small sizes. Simple utensils and supplies are readily available in markets and shops. Flip flops, a sarong, an umbrella and straw hats are available in all markets.

Making our way through the Maliau. When your smiling outdoor shoe salesman tells you how waterproof those new hiking boots will be, show him this picture.

Hiking/Soft Adventure:

Simple and low quality camping supplies are available in major shopping centers in the main cities—including fuel for stoves, sleeping bags, tents, chairs and diving equipment. Local guides can be hired from most villages. High-tech freeze dried food is not available but noodles (*mee*) and dried foods are common staples in all stores. Boots are hard to find and most guides wear soccer shoes with cleats in the jungle. Make sure everything you bring can be carried in one-man loads since porters are readily available. Bring plenty of gifts for stays in longhouses. Carry a first aid kit, guidebooks and phrasebook.

Is this the shrunken skull of an expedition member who told his boatmen he ran out of money or just the crunchy bits of a gibbon? You decide.

Hard core adventurers:

Bring lots of money. Carry it in cash and be prepared to spend it faster than a cab driver at a racetrack. Bring all off-roading, scuba, caving, climbing and rafting equipment from the States. Local clubs, dive sites and outfitters can supply worn but usable equipment. All gear must be waterproof and have straps or backpack straps for carrying. Do not pack any one bag to weigh more than 50 lbs. Do not travel with more than three people—a boat carries two passengers max. Trucks carry three passengers. Helicopters carry three passengers. Porters are small and tough but don't kill them. Plan on carrying plenty of gifts in addition to your supplies. Shotgun shells, tobacco and salt are still in demand in remote regions. Hair clips, small makeup kits and combs are ideal for women or children. Bring photographs of your family, house, dog etc. Have them laminated. Order the aviation maps of Borneo and bring a GPS. Walkie talkies and high powered radios are forbidden without special permits but can be disguised as AM/FM radios. Contact scientific, military, political and special interest organizations in advance. Their contacts and advice can be very helpful.

Prior arrangement with local clubs can provide most heavy expedition equipment. Outfitters may agree to purchase some specialty items based on the length of rental. Food and cooking supplies consist of local fare and a lot of noodles. There are off-road clubs, caving clubs and dive clubs in Kota Kinabalu and Kuching. Try to arrange resupply points with smaller airlines. Bring first aid and survival equipment, manuals, Swiss army knife, compass and binoculars.

Travel and exploration of remote regions will require permission from local police, logging camp concessionaires, and in many cases, participation of local guides or cooperation with local government agencies.

Helicopters can be chartered from Kuching, Kota Kinabalu, Miri, Balikpapan, Samarinda and Pontianak. Private planes, oil company planes, mission owned planes can be chartered by going directly to the airport or major hotels where the pilots stay to discuss the rates with the chief pilot. Tour operators can get you better prices on small planes than if you negotiate directly.

Boats and vehicles can be chartered through tour companies or by negotiating directly with boat owners.

Guides are best acquired through tour groups or by referral from other travelers.

Pack List

I am always surprised at the number of generic pack lists that have little to do with jungle travel. Redmond O'Hanlon follows the SAS advice on clothing; one wet, one dry. In other words keeping the wet set on during the day and sleeping in your clean and drys. The problem is that after your first torrential downpour your drys will start to funk and be wetter and fouler than your wets. My solution is to sleep naked or with light boxers, wash my clothing in the morning, drying it in the sun before the rains and then packing it away before the 2:30 p.m. rains. If you spend enough time in the jungle you will end up going native and wearing shorts, a T-shirt and football shoes. Locals wear a sarong and flip flops after bathing and when doing laundry. The bottom line is expect everything you bring to turn to junk. All those magical, breathable, wicking synthetics that do so well on the ski slopes will bake you alive and breed bacteria faster than a mad scientist. Stick to light cotton. Stay away from any groovy new boots that will be stinking mildewed sponges. Buy simple leather boots with Vibram soles. Look for a minimum of foam padding or gizmos. Remember they will be soaking wet the first day you hit the bush and probably will end up in the trash when you get home. I wear either Converse high tops or my self designed, hand made, leather-only boots made by Viberg in Victoria, British Columbia. Durable and simple is the watchword when it comes to protecting the most important part of your body – your feet.

If you really must take a 747-load of camera gear, books, clothing and camping gear along, consider leaving some of it in a hotel and just taking what you need on treks. If you want to be well prepared, a few faxes back and forth with your local outfitter will pare down your list. Seasoned adventurers will bring their gear and food in packs already broken up into 20–50 lbs per porter.

Keep in mind the physical limitations of small canoes, Cessna 185s, local buses, etc. The following pack list is based on my experience. Let me know if you discover a few secrets of your own and I will pass them along in the next edition.

Heavy Duty Pack List

Use clear Tupperware containers to separate and sort small materials. Use garbage bags to wrap clothing and use rafting sacks and waterproof Pelican or Sea King cases for delicate equipment. Carry it all in dive bags or loose packs with shoulder straps. Write in your own items of necessity following our list.

PERSONAL

- [ ] **Passport**
- [ ] **Visa (if needed)**
- [ ] **Permission for remote regions, caves, Indonesia - Malaysia border**
- [ ] **Airline Tickets**
- [ ] **International Drivers license**
- [ ] **Vaccination Certificate, Eyeglass prescription, medication prescriptions**
- [ ] **Money, credit cards, travelers checks**
- [ ] **Itinerary, address list, phone numbers, letters of introduction**
- [ ] **Waterproof holder, photocopies of above**

TOILETRIES

- [ ] **Toothbrush**
- [ ] **Toothpaste**
- [ ] **Floss**
- [ ] **Hairbrush/comb**
- [ ] **20 Cotton Swabs**
- [ ] **Small Swiss army knife with scissors, tweezers**
- [ ] **Plastic shavers**
- [ ] **Eye drops**
- [ ] **Squeeze soap (biodegradable, use for laundry too)**
- [ ] **Condoms, birth control, feminine hygiene items**

FIRST AID

☐ **Clear Plastic Box or Tupperware, containing:**

☐ **Pepto Bismol (minor runs)**

☐ **Stop Trot (dehydration)**

☐ **Ciprio (infection), available by prescription only**

☐ **Anacin (pain relief)**

☐ **Antifungal creme (crotch/foot rot)**

☐ **Bullfrog sunscreen (SB #18) (sun, dryness)**

☐ **Hydrogen peroxide (cuts)**

☐ **First aid cream**

☐ **Gauze/compress**

☐ **Various bandages, sewing needles**

☐ **2 bottles DEET insect repellent**

☐ **Malarial pills (bring extra pills)**

☐ **Prescription medicines**

☐

☐

☐

☐

☐

☐

☐

☐

☐

☐

☐

CLOTHING

- ☐ Spare glasses/contact lenses
- ☐ Polarized sunglasses (with straps to prevent loss)
- ☐ Watch (with glow in the dark dial)
- ☐ 4 Shirts (2 long, 2 short)
- ☐ 1 Pair boots (Must dry out quickly). Avoid foam packed linings and synthetic uppers. Order one size larger with wool socks on due to heat and shrinkage.
- ☐ Spare laces
- ☐ 1 pair flip flops (for showers and nighttime)
- ☐ 1 pair running or street shoes
- ☐ 3 pairs pants (short/long pant combinations are ideal)
- ☐ 1 money belt
- ☐ 1 Goretex tropical weight raincoat or olive green military style poncho
- ☐ 5 pair wool socks (pure wool, avoid synthetics)
- ☐ 4 pair thin wool or wicking socks (use as liners)
- ☐ Bush hat (cotton with wide brim)
- ☐ Spare hat with brim
- ☐ 2 pairs boxer style underwear (doubles as bathing suit)
- ☐ 1 small towel
- ☐ 1 belt
- ☐ 1 tie or buy the traditional mens batik shirt on arrival
- ☐ Small packets laundry soap
- ☐ Utility or safari vest with mesh back and inside pockets
- ☐
- ☐
- ☐
- ☐
- ☐

CAMPING EQUIPMENT

- [ ] 1 two-man mesh tent with rain flap or 9 by 9 tarp
- [ ] 1 sleeping bag with crush bag (use a synthetic filling with cotton liner)
- [ ] Therma Rest sleeping pad
- [ ] 1 Mini Maglite flashlight (must use AA batteries)
- [ ] 2 spare bulbs for Mini Mag flashlight
- [ ] 1 REI waterproof head flashlight/spare bulbs (AA batteries)
- [ ] Stainless steel/copper bottom cooking pots with lid, handle and carrying bag
- [ ] Knife/fork/spoon
- [ ] Steel cup
- [ ] 2 canteens with straps or waist belt
- [ ] 3M synthetic pot scrubber (cut into small strips)
- [ ] Clear Tupperware bowl w/lid for spare food
- [ ] Freeze dried breakfasts (try them first!)
- [ ] Power Bar Energy snacks
- [ ] Freeze dried dinners (make sure you bring a variety)
- [ ] Guidebooks, stripped down in plastic zip-loc bags
- [ ] Maps and phrase books in plastic zip-loc bags
- [ ] MSR multi fuel stove with MSR bottle
- [ ] Silva compass with mirror and measuring marks
- [ ] Katadyne water filter with spare filter
- [ ] Water purification tablets
- [ ]
- [ ]
- [ ]
- [ ]
- [ ]

PHOTOGRAPHY LIST

- ☐ Tamrac camera bag with dustproof zipper seal (for carry-on)
- ☐ 2 cameras bodies, one with winder (manual, non autofocus if possible)
- ☐ Extreme wide angle lens (19 - 24mm)
- ☐ Medium wide angle lens (35 - 28mm)
- ☐ Standard or macro lens (50- 65mm)
- ☐ Short telephoto or macro lens (90- 100mm)
- ☐ Long telephoto lens (135 -250mm) lens
- ☐ Extreme long lens (300 - 600mm) lens
- ☐ Tele-extender, extension tubes or close up lenses
- ☐ Auto strobe with small soft box
- ☐ Tiny weatherproof automatic camera with flash
- ☐ Slow film (ASA 50 - 100)
- ☐ Fast film (ASA 200)
- ☐ Ultra fast color or black and white (ASA 1000 or faster)
- ☐ Mini tripod
- ☐ Palm sized tape recorder
- ☐ 6 mini cassettes
- ☐ 1 notebook and spare pens & pencils
- ☐ Spare camera batteries
- ☐ Sony shortwave radio
- ☐ Compressed air can, soft brush, small towel to wipe hands
- ☐ AA batteries
- ☐
- ☐
- ☐
- ☐

LUGGAGE

- ☐ Two waterproof Pelican or Tundra cases inserted in luggage or back packs with straps. Extra material is packed in dive bags with straps.
- ☐ One Pelican case contains tent, mattress, sleeping bag, pots in backpack
- ☐ One Pelican with all else in backpack
- ☐ One carry-on camera bag with waist strap
- ☐ One cardboard box of food, film, gifts
- ☐ Small backpack
- ☐ Fanny pack
- ☐ Straps or locks for luggage
- ☐

LUXURIES/GIFTS

- ☐ 20 packs of gum or sugar-free mints for dusty roads
- ☐ Baby wipes (for chafed rear end and quick washes)
- ☐ Swiss Army knife with tools
- ☐ Compact binoculars
- ☐ Gift items: pens, pins, patches, stickers, etc. (200 count)
- ☐ Malay/Indonesian phrasebook
- ☐ 10 extra Zip-loc freezer bags
- ☐ 2 marker pens (Sharpies: black and red)
- ☐ 2 highlighters (for maps)
- ☐ 5 pens (extra ones for gifts, order by dozen with name imprinted)
- ☐ Shotgun shells, 12-gauge
- ☐ Tobacco
- ☐ Assorted hair clips for girls
- ☐ Photographs
- ☐

The Parks of Borneo

The Parks of Sabah

Sabah's aggressive tourism development policy has favored creation of parks and lodges to attract ecotourists. There is still much back and forth between the pressure for development and long term management of resources. Long term management is still the loser. In relative terms, Sabah is well ahead of Sarawak and Indonesia in creating and maintaining wilderness areas.

The government has recently gazetted the flood plain of the Kinabatangan river and the coral reefs of Semporna, including Pulau Sipadan. The future of the Maliau Basin is still in the balance but will be included in Danum Valley as a conservation area.

Crocker Range National Park
(139,919 ha)

Hill montane forest.

Danum Valley Conservation Area
(42,755 ha)

A scientific research center with facilities for tourists. There is a jungle lodge specifically for eco-tourists.Visitors can stay in the Borneo Rainforest Lodge and explore well marked trails in the area. There are more ambitious hikes leading to the Research Center.

Gomantang Forest Reserve
(3600 ha)

Limestone caves with colonies of over one million swiftlets and two million bats.

Kulamba Wildlife Reserve
(20,682 ha)

Coastal swamp forest with tembadau and large colonies of flying fox bats.

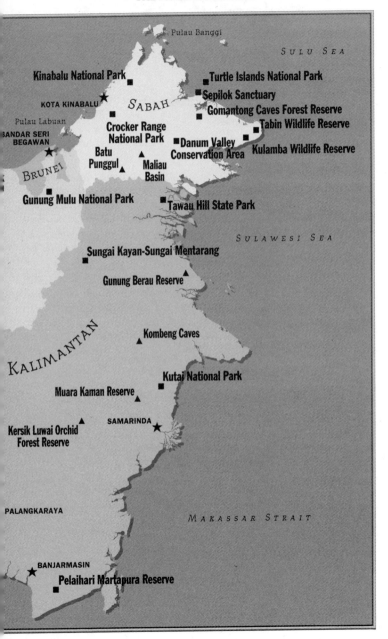

Pulau Banggi

SULU SEA

Kinabalu National Park ■

■ Turtle Islands National Park

★ ■ Sepilok Sanctuary

KOTA KINABALU *SABAH*

Pulau Labuan

■ Gomantong Caves Forest Reserve

■ ■ Tabin Wildlife Reserve

BANDAR SERI BEGAWAN

★ Crocker Range National Park

■ Danum Valley Conservation Area ■ Kulamba Wildlife Reserve

Batu Punggul ▲

BRUNEI ▲ Maliau Basin

■ Gunung Mulu National Park

■ Tawau Hill State Park

SULAWESI SEA

■ Sungai Kayan-Sungai Mentarang

▲ Gunung Berau Reserve

KALIMANTAN

▲ Kombeng Caves

■ Kutai National Park

Muara Kaman Reserve ▲

▲ SAMARINDA ★

Kersik Luwai Orchid Forest Reserve

PALANGKARAYA

MAKASSAR STRAIT

★ BANJARMASIN

■ Pelaihari Martapura Reserve

The Parks of Borneo

Mount Kinabalu
(75,000 ha)

The highest point in Southeast Asia. There is a well known trail up to the peak with simple accommodations just below the summit. The best area to experience montane forest habitat with nepenthes, rhododendrons and other species found at high altitudes. There are a wide variety of accommodations and facilities for visitors. Guides can be hired at the park.

Sepilok
(4530 ha)

Lowland dipterocarp forest that features a rehabilitation center for young orang utans. The center is open daily and is an excellent place to photograph and observe the orang utan. There are no accommodations and most of what is interesting can be hiked in a day.

Tabin Wildlife Reserve
(120,521 ha)

The only protected area set aside exclusively for the preservation of the Asian rhino. Logged forest around an unlogged central area. Visitors need special permission from the Sabah Wildlife Department to visit this center.

Turtle Islands Park
(1700 ha)

Marine park on islands of Selingan, Gulisan and Kecil where green and hawksbill turtles come ashore to lay eggs.

The Parks of Brunei

Eighty percent of Brunei is covered by virgin forest, and with little demand or pressure to develop this land, it is a safe bet that Brunei will be the site of some very good parks in the future. The only obstacle is the Sultan's policy of not wanting tourism or travelers. The only major project that may lead to the development of a national park is the Brunei Rainforest Project being developed in conjunction with the University of Brunei and the Royal Geographical Society. Currently, schoolchildren, invited scientists and VIPs are allowed on site.

The Parks of Borneo

The Parks of Sarawak

Sarawak is well advanced in its campaign to maximize its timber harvest. With the creation of Mulu as a park and a biopreserve, the value of national parks as generators of income has been established. It has also led to some questionable resettlement policies with the nomadic Penan and has highlighted the inability of the government to prevent illegal logging in its own parks.

Bako National Park
(2728 ha)

Close to Kuching Bako, this park is of interest to the botanist. There are several species of monkey and small bat caves.

Gunung Mulu National Park
(52,900 ha)

A biosphere with some massive cave systems and limestone spires. Good area to visit lowland and montane habitats. Few large mammals but much to be explored. Of 4000 species of butterfly specimens captured in the late 80s, 75 percent turned out to be unknown to science.

Lambir Hills National Park
(7000 ha)

Mixed dipterocarp and heath forests. A haven for plant, wildlife and bird enthusiasts.

Lanjak Entimau Wildlife Sanctuary
(168,000 ha)

One of the larger protected areas for orang utans in Malaysia

Niah National Park
(3100 ha)

Niah is home to one of the largest and most accessible bat caves in Borneo with an estimated 300,000 bats. The caves are the site of Niah man; one of the earliest records of homo-sapiens remains.

Samunsam Wildlife Sanctuary
(6000 ha)

An area of nipah, mangrove and lowland forest. An excellent place for observing proboscis monkeys.

Similajau National Park
(7000 ha)

A coastal park with sandy beaches, turtles and rocky headlands; 24 species of mammals, 185 bird species, famous for saltwater crocodiles.

The Parks of Borneo

The Parks of Kalimantan

Kalimantan has been chosen as a repopulation site for the overcrowded island of Java. It is also rich in timber, coal and diamonds. When the stated priorities are moving settlers in and developing industry, parks are of little concern. Kalimantan was also the site of one of the 20th century's biggest forest fires. The peak of the fire's destruction was in March and April of 1983 and resulted in the destruction of more than 13,000 square miles of woodland. Yes, the rainforest can burn. There was a reoccurrence in 1994 when fire spread through the great forests. Although Indonesia understands the importance of national parks for attracting tourism and preserving species, there is little infrastructure to allow the visitor access to these unique regions. Most parks are vast areas still awaiting basic improvements and management programs.

Bukit Raya
(170,000 ha)

Central Kalimantan includes the highest mountain peak (2278m) in Southern Borneo.

Gunung Bentung and Karimun
(600,000 ha)

In West Kalimantan adjacent to Sarawak's Lanjak-Entimau Wildlife Sanctuary.

Gunung Palung
(30,000 ha)

In West Kalimantan.

Kutai
(200,000 ha)

A vast unimproved area in East Kalimantan.

Pelaihari Martapura
(30,000 ha)

In South Kalimantan. Part of the Meratus Range.

Sungai Kayan - Sungai Mentarang
(1,600,000 ha)

The largest park in Borneo in the interior of East Kalimantan.

Tanjung Puting
(300,000 ha)

Probably the best known and most visited of Kalimantan's parks in Central Kalimantan. Coastal swamp and dryland forest with large populations of orang utans and proboscis monkeys. Birute Galdikas has provided considerable publicity for the area with her work with rehabilitation of orang utans.

The Animals and Plants of Borneo

The flora and fauna of Borneo boast some fairly impressive extremes. Although scientists have not cataloged all of the species found on the island, the best guess is that there are 222 mammals (93 are bats, 61 are rodents and 26 are carnivores), over 9000 species of flowering plants, 570 species of bird, 250 species of fresh water fish and over 1000 species of butterflies. Keep in mind that in Borneo about 2700 new species of flowering plants are discovered each year! It is interesting to note that although about 99 percent of the 4020 estimated mammal species have been discovered on this planet, only one percent of the 2 1/2 million bacteria species have been named.

Forest Types of Borneo

Beech
Sandy soil with predominance of Casuarina trees, a commonly found tropical pine.

Mangrove
Low lying saline areas flooded by the ocean. Nipah palms, Nibung, Api-Api and Pedada are found along esturaries and low regions.

Peatswamp
Found further inland from the mangroves. Soil is peat built up from leaf litter. Meranti trees, Tamin, and Terentang are found here along with trees that can reach 80 meters in height. These forests are easy to reach and therefore easy to log.

Riparian
Found along the river banks of Borneo these forests line the river systems and have many blossoming trees. Ensure and Gapis trees create graceful covers over the river and the Aping palm creates a lush tropical environment.

Lowland Dipterocarp
The classic triple canopy forest found at low elevations (Dipterocarp describes the two winged seed). These are the most common forests in Sabah and Sarawak and are home to the giant, slow-growing hardwoods. There are as many different species in one acre of Borneo's lowland forest as there are in the entire country of England. Many of these species are rare and found in specific areas.

Hill Dipterocarp
Poor soils, large trees found on sloping regions.

Montane
As you climb in altitude past 700 meters in elevation the trees shrink in size and the moisture increases. Gone are the lofty canopies and the daylight is often softened by mist and fog. Shorea trees, oak and laurel trees grow wooly coats of moss while on the ground nepenthes or pitcher plants are found. Ferns abound and animal life disappears. Trees begin to lift their roots out of the ground like women hiking their skirts to stay dry and the forest can be eerily silent.

Belukar
Native name for secondary forest that occurs after logging.

Ladang
Areas cleared for shifting cultivation that are left to regenerate.

Lalang
Overgrown areas once cultivated but overgrown with elephant grass

Life is tough for the animals in the jungle. In Bornean forests most plants are high in fibre and tannins and most leafy material is high above the ground. Soils in many regions of Borneo are very poor in minerals, and salt water springs and mud volcanoes are patchy in distribution. The major rivers act as natural barriers to separate the animals. Not exactly the best place for wildlife to exist.

Most of the ecological changes in Borneo have taken place in the last 27 years due to logging. Swidden agriculture or slash and burn crops do not dramatically affect the animals or forests. Three threats to animals and their forest are logging, hunting and forest clearing.

The dipterocarp forest supports the largest number of animals.

The most threatened animals are the Asian rhinoceros *(Dicerorhinus sumatrensis)*, the *tembadau* or wild ox *(Bos javanicus)* and the Dugong *(Dugong dugon).*

The shy, hairy, and rapidly disappearing, Sumatran rhino

According to very rough estimates there may be only about 30–50 rhino left in eastern Sabah and possibly in all of the interior of Borneo. The horn and other parts of the body fetch high prices for medicine in Chinese shops throughout Asia. The *tembadau* is more numerous but is continually hunted for its meat. The Asian elephant *(Elephas maximus)* population is estimated to be at between 500–2000 with 1000 being a good estimate. The elephants or Borneo are found only in Sabah and threatened by loss of habitat. They are found in logged areas as well as virgin forest. In fact, the best place to see elephants is in the logged areas of Danum Valley. There is a spot in a logged area near kilometer 20 where droppings can regularly be found.

There are many books on the wildlife of Borneo in the better bookshops of Kuching, Balikpapan, BSB and Kota Kinabalu. The results of a recent study in Brunei are featured in a new 389 page color book called *Belalong, a Tropical Rainforest.* The Insight *Guide to Southeast Asia Wildlife* is also a good introduction to the region.

Leopard cat

MAMMALS

(Mammaliia)

There are 222 recorded species of wild land mammals in Borneo with bats (93) being the largest group followed by rodents (61) and then carnivores (26). The largest is the Asian elephant and the most interesting is probably the orang utan.

ASIAN ELEPHANT
(Elephas maximus)

Gajah

Of the two species of elephants, African and Asian, the Asian elephant is the smallest of the two. The elephant is the largest land mammal in Borneo. The elephants of Borneo are slightly smaller than those of the mainland. The distribution of elephants is restricted to Sabah and they are found in flat, fertile areas that are also ideal for human population.

Elephant areas can be identified by their large, bowling-ball-size droppings and large footprints. Elephants are active from about two hours before dusk until two hours after dawn. They need water and lots of monocotyledonous plants including soft grasses and the growing parts of palms and banana stems. The elephant is fond of feeding on agricultural crops, particularly oil palms. Groups contain between three and forty individuals. Elephants are also found in dipterocarp forests and sometimes enter swamps and nipah groves to feed. They can swim across rivers or travel though gardens and plantations mainly at night or during rainy weather.

Elephants are found in Sabah between Sungat river in northeastern Sabah and Sembakun river in northern East Kalimantan. They have been exterminated from the Tawau Semporna areas and the Sandakan Peninsula during the last two decades. Elephants are quite common between the Labuk river, the upper Kuamut river and Tanjung Darvel. Prior to 1983, elephants rarely crossed the Labuk river, but loss of habitat has forced them northward. It was assumed that the wild elephants in Borneo were descendants of imported logging elephants that were let loose during the Japanese occupation in WWII. However Magellan's chronicler Pigafetta described the highly decorated elephants of the Sultan of Brunei when he visited in the 1500s. Others believe that either the Sultan of Sulu or Sultan of Brunei introduced elephants from the mainland several hundred years ago.

Elephants in Borneo are found only in Sabah and they prefer overgrown recently logged areas where there are young shoots and plants—they can easily find the 300 lbs (136 kg) of food an adult elephant needs every day. They can also communicate via low frequency calls that are too low for humans to hear, but can be heard by other elephants up to 12 miles (19 km) away.

The Asian elephant found in Borneo is smaller that its African or mainland Asian relatives at 18 ft (5.5 m) tall and 9000 lbs (4080 kg). It is estimated that there are about

50,000 Asian elephants in all of the world and about 1000 in Borneo.

ASIAN TWO HORNED RHINOCEROUS
(Dicerorhinus sumatrensis)

Badak berendam

The rhinoceros is probably the most reclusive animal in Borneo. Their three-toed tracks and mud wallows with distinct horn marks are the last remaining proof that this species still exists. In five years of looking for this gentle animal I frequently came across rhino tracks but never once caught sight of the elusive animal. The Borneo rhino is the smallest and most primitive of the five rhinoceros species on earth. The species found in Borneo most closely resembles the forms of rhino found in Europe 30 million years ago. Unlike the African species, the Asian rhino is hairy and quite small, about 8 ft (2.5 m) long and 1990 lbs (900 kg). When disturbed it runs away emitting a series of short, hoarse barks. The rhino and its tracks can be confused with the bearded pig or Tapir.

Rhinos are active in the late afternoon to mid-morning and rest during the hot hours of the day in a mud wallow, shaded spot or ridge top. Their diet consists of mature leaves and twigs from a wide range of woody plants including saplings, lianas and small trees. They can be found near natural mineral sources and salt licks. All records of recent rhino encounters in Sabah have been within 9 miles (14 kms) of these sources.

Fossilized remains found in the Niah Caves show that the rhino was once physically larger and more prevalent than today. Rhinos are hunted for income received from the sales of the horn and other parts to Chinese medicinal stores across Asia. Although rhino were once hunted by hunting parties with spears, they are now trapped in large camouflaged pits dug near wallows and streams. The hunters then visit the pits once every few months since the only item they are interested in is the horn. There are no Javan or one horned rhinoceros on Borneo. There are only about 50 left in Unjong Kulong Park on the island of Java. The last Javan rhino in Malaysia was shot in Perak in 1932.

BORNEAN GIBBON
(Hylobates muelleri)

Ungka

The distinctive hooting of the gibbon is a familiar sound of the rainforest. Gibbons usually live in families of four to five animals consisting of male, female and their offspring. They can be heard crashing through the trees when disturbed using their long arms to swing from branch to branch. The members of the ape family live in groups of four to five and can be heard calling out to other groups in the early morning. A similar gibbon, The Agile Gibbon *(Hylobates agilis)* or *ungka tangan hitam* is found between the Kapuas River and the Barito in Kalimantan.

ORANG UTAN
(Pongo pygmaeus)

Orang utan or *kogiu*

The *orang utan* is Malay for "man of the forest" but its Dayak names are *kogiu* in Sabah and *maias* in Sarawak. The orang utan is the largest of the primate species. Found only in Borneo and Northern Sumatra, the only other great apes are found in Central Africa. The long armed, arboreal ape is identified by its reddish brown coat. The adult male Sumatran orang utan does not have the large cheek pads of the Bornean orang utan male.

Adult males weigh up to 220 lbs (100 kg) and stand about three feet tall (one meter). They can live up to 30 years and may have three to five offspring in their lifetime. Orangs reach adulthood and sexual maturity at about seven years of age. Most females give birth to their first child at age eight. The gestation period is nine months, the same as hu-

mans. The young stay with their mothers for up to five years.

Sabah has the largest number of orang utans in the world. Secretive and solitary in the wild, the World Wildlife Fund Malaysia estimates their numbers between a minimum of 2000 and up to a maximum of 20,000. Male apes live alone and females usually live with one to two children until they are chased away at around age four. Each ape needs about 1200 acres (500 hectares) in the wild due to the sparsity of fruit trees. Because of this they do not live in groups and travel 1300 ft (400 m) a day due to their large size.

Logging of habitat and poaching of babies to sell as pets are the most serious threats to the orang utans' survival. Orphaned orangs are brought to Sepilok Sanctuary near Sandakan, Semenggoh Wildlife Rehabilitation Centre in Sarawak or Camp Leakey, Natai Lengkuas and Tanjung Harapan in Tanjung Puting National Park in Central Kalimantan for rehabilitation into the wild. Their arm span can reach seven feet (two meters). Considered to be four times stronger than humans, the orang utan is not aggressive and will avoid human contact in the wild. In captivity they enjoy the company of humans and interact well. They communicate by long burbling calls, squeaks, whines or loud roars.

The orang utan is found primarily in swamp forests and in the vicinity of rivers in primary dipterocarp forests. They build a new nest daily out of twigs and small branches to rest or sleep.

Their diet includes fruits, bark, insects, honey, leaves, durians, figs, rambutans and other jungle fruit.

LANGURS or LEAF MONKEYS
(Presbytis hosei)

Cenaka **or** *kelasi*

There are three species of leaf monkey; most are found only in Northern Borneo usually in fairly high densities in dipterocarp forests. They are also found in plantations or raiding gardens around kampungs. They live in groups of 6–15 and can be identified by their peaked hairdo and long tail. There are also other langurs found on Borneo including the more common reddish colored maroon langur (*kelasi*), silvered langur, white fronted and banded (*cenaka*)—found in Sarawak these are usually called leaf monkeys.

PROBOSCIS MONKEY
(Nasalis larvatus)

Bekaleh **or** *Orang Belanda*

With a nose up to six inches long, it is hard to figure out why nature blessed this otherwise attractive animal with such a huge honker. Only found on the male of the species, he uses it to attract the opposite sex. The females have quite a pert nose and are half the size of the male. The large nose (or proboscis) is used to deepen and amplify the calls the male makes.

The 45 lbs (20 kg) male and 22 lbs (10 kg) females are herbivorous and feed almost exclusively on the young shoots and leaves of the Sonneraita mangrove. They are most visible feeding at dawn or dusk in the mangroves bordering water. They are very vocal and make a variety of grunts, squeaks and loud roars.

The proboscis monkey loves the water and is typically found in coastal mangrove and riverine environments like Banjarmasin in Kalsel or Kinabatangan in Sabah. The locals call them "Dutchmen" or *orang belanda* because of their large nose, white skin and awkward walking motion in the water.

The proboscis monkey is found only in Borneo and is best seen along the tributaries of the Kinabatangan in Sabah, Bako National Park in Sarawak and Tanjung Puting in Kalimantan. It is estimated there are 3000 left in Northern Borneo. There has been no census in Kalimantan.

PIG TAILED MACAQUE (Macaca nemestrina)

Beruk

This monkey gets its name from its curly tail. Macaques live in large groups of between 16–18 animals. They have a social structure that allows them to forage in packs. Their favorite foods are fruits, tubers, leaves and many crops.The average size of the full grown macaque is 18 lbs (40 kg) and up to two feet high.

When the macaques raid human crops they usually scope the area first and then silently pick out the best fruit or vegetables while a sentry will stand guard at the edge of the field.

Because of their intelligence people will keep macaques as pets, teaching them to smoke cigarettes or make rude gestures. They are also trained to pick coconuts. There is a long tailed or crab eating macaque (*Macaca fascicularis*) or *kera* that can be differentiated by its longer tail, smaller size and more pronounced sideburns.

PANGOLIN
(Manis javanica)

Tenggiling

The Malayan pangolin is a smaller version of the six foot long (two meters) African pangolin *(manis gigantiea)*. The toothless pangolin eats ants, is nocturnal and walks on its knuckles to prevent its digging claws from wearing down. Its strong claws are used to break up ant nests. It then uses its sticky tongue to mop up the rest. The brown colored pangolin has been known to open its scales to let in ants, close-up his scales and then take a bath and eat the ants later as they float away. The pangolin has a prehensile tail. Although there are no natural enemies of the heavily armored pangolin, the powder made from the ground-up scales of the pangolin is considered an aphrodisiac by the Chinese and is collected for this purpose.

When surprised the pangolin will curl into a tightly armored ball.

WILD OX or GAUR
(Bos javanicus)

Tembadau or Seladang

The wild cow can be differentiated from its domestic cousin *(bubalis bubalis)* by its white stockings and buttocks. It has been hunted to near extinction because of its sedate nature and good meat.

Mainly nocturnal, it feeds primarily on grasses with some herbaceous and low woody vegetation. The large bovine can also be spotted near natural mineral sources or salt including the sea. Wild examples are found only in Eastern Sabah and are often seen in groups of 8–10 individuals—usually one adult male with females and young. Prior to the 1940s, Tembadau were common along the banks of most major rivers in Eastern Sabah. The widespread use of guns led to rapid extermination.

SUN BEAR
(Helarctos malaynus)

Beruang Madu

The sun bear is the smallest of the bear species found in the world, about five feet long (1.5 meters) and about 22 lbs (50 kg). It can be spotted at any time of day on the ground and in tall trees. It builds nests of small branches in trees similar to those of the orang utan, but nearer the trunk and less well woven. Diet includes entire bee nests, termites, small animals, fruits and the heart of coconut palms. The sun bear is found in extensive areas of forests and occasionally enters gardens in remote areas. It is called the honey bear by locals because of its love of bees' nests.

Signs of the sun bear's presence are claw marks on tree trunks or the remains of bee or termite nests ripped open in standing or fallen trees. You may hear the loud roar or hoarse grunts which are similar to the sound of an adult male orang utan or the rhinoceros. Like all bears, the sun bear has an excellent sense of smell but poor eyesight and hearing. For this reason the animal will stand up on two legs to sniff. The sun bear and the elephant are two of the few mammals that can be dangerous to man due to the unpredictability of their nature. The sun bear attacks by running quickly on four legs, then rearing up and crashing against the victim with a loud roar. Hunters use this habit to spear the bear just as it rears up.

SLOW LORIS
(Nycticebus coucang)

Kongkang

This cuddly, bug-eyed animal is actually a tiny primate. Brown to reddish brown in color, this nocturnal animal can swivel its head 198 degrees and has excellent night vision. If you shine a bright flashlight into the canopy at night their eyes will reflect back like two red taillights. The solitary loris lives on insects and fruit that they meticulously pick out of smaller sized trees. Some locals keep them as pets when they are found in plantations or gardens. The loris is easy to identify due to its curious slow motion movements and its "space alien" fingers and hands.

LESSER MOUSEDEER
(Tragulus javanicus)

Napoh, Pelanduk or *Kancil*

The mousedeer, along with the greater mousedeer (*Tragulus napu*), are the smallest hoofed animals on earth. These animals are found in the lowland dipterocarp forests and stand only about 6–12 inches (15–30 cm) off the ground. They subsist on fungus, fallen fruit and tender shoots. The mousedeer is not a deer and is considered to be a crafty, intelligent animal.

The greater mousedeer is found at higher elevations.

TARSIER
(Tarsius bancanus)

Tangkasi

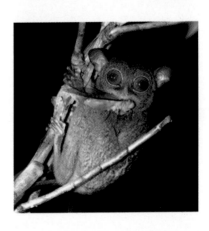

The tarsier is a rather quick, nocturnal animal but is sometimes confused with the slow loris as it romps around the lowland canopy. One way to tell the difference from a distance is that the tarsier's eyes will not reflect back when you shine a flashlight at them. They frequently make high pitched calls during the night. The tarsier is the smallest species of monkey.

BEARDED PIG
(Sus barbatus)

Babi hutan

Easily the ugliest denizen of the forest floor. The bearded pig takes part in mass migrations as the trees begin to fruit. There are great pathways or "jalan babi" created by these annual but irregular migrations. The pig has always been a staple food of the native peoples of Borneo who hunt them with spears and traps. A note of caution, if you come across a pig wallow, usually a wet area where the mud has been turned over and mashed—watch out for ticks. The animals are diligent in ridding themselves of these tiny bloodsuckers who immediately scramble up the legs of any other warm blooded victim, ideally you.

The bearded pig is also known to build large nests from saplings and vegetation. You can come across them in cleared areas where the pig has chewed off all the young trees in a 50 ft (15 m) area. The final nest is about one meter high. Here they give birth to their young, usually 3–11 at one time.

LARGE FLYING FOX
(Pteropus vampyrus)

Of the 93 species of bats found on Borneo (11 percent of the world's total) none are as dramatic as the flying fox. Bats are harmless to humans and exist on either insects and/or fruit. They are also important in the process of pollinating fruits like durians and bananas. They also disperse seeds in their droppings.

The flying fox is the largest bat in the world weighing between 22–40 oz. (645–1100 g). The bats are found in large colonies in the open branches of trees, often in mangrove or nipah palms. At dusk they circle the trees gathering in large groups, then fly long distances to feed on flowering or fruiting trees. They also eat orchard fruits such as rambutan and mangoes helping to pollinate the flowers of many forest trees.

SAMBAR DEER
(Cervus unicolor)

Rusa

The sambar deer is a nocturnal animal that can usually be seen in the early morning and late afternoons. Their diet includes grasses, herbs, shrubs, young leaves and fallen fruits. Sambar deer visit salt licks or mineral sources. A solitary animal that is heavily hunted, it is common in secondary forests on gently sloping terrain. They will also enter gardens and plantations to feed.

RED MUNTJAC
(Muntiacus muntjac)

Kijang

Active during the day, the common barking deer eats a diet of herbs, young leaves, grasses, fallen fruits and seeds. It gets its name from its barklike call. Often seen in pairs of male and female, it can be found in the low hill ranges and coastal regions. There is also a Bornean yellow muntjac deer.

CLOUDED LEOPARD
(Neofelis nebulosa)

Harimau

The clouded leopard is the largest cat found in Borneo. Nocturnal and arboreal, the leopard is sometimes active during the day as it hunts for pigs, deer, monkeys, orang utans and smaller mammals. They are found in tall and secondary forests. There are no tigers on Borneo even though they are featured in the artwork of the Kenyah.

BEARCAT
(Arctictis binturong)

Binturong

This bearlike animal is actually a member of the civet family and uses its tail to navigate through trees in its nightly search for fruit. It is two meters in length, covered with black fur and found in low branches.

MALAY CIVET
(Vierra tangalunga)
Tangalung **or** *Musang*

Members of the civet family are common in Borneo. They can usually be found at night in trees by using a powerful spotlight or the headlights of a car. Civets are strictly nocturnal animals whose wanderings can be discovered by their brightly colored droppings (usually pure fruit). Civets are found around settlements and will also visit campsites to forage for scraps. Although gentle animals, they do fight with rats or other animals and can liven up the jungle night with their terrifying screams and cries. Their diet also consists of invertebrates and small vertebrates taken from the forest floor. The Malay civet has distinctive banding around its tail that makes it easy to identify.

There are eight diverse species of this commonly seen animal.

FRESH WATER DOLPHIN
(Orcaella brevirostris)
Pesut Mahakam

The Mahakam and its upper lakes are famous for fresh water dolphins. These animals are sometimes confused with dugongs, an even rarer mammal found in the rivers of Borneo. The dolphins are seen in small groups of three to six animals and they are bluish grey. The fresh water dolphin is also found in the large rivers of Thailand, Vietnam and Myanmar.

OTHER MAMMALS

Other small mammals include the half meter long white moonrat or *tikus ambing bulan*, a white nocturnal rat that leaves a strong odor. There are 11 species of squirrel or *tupai* found only on Borneo including the 31 inch (800 mm) long **giant squirrel** or *kerawak* (*Ratufa affinis*) and the **red giant flying squirrel** (*Petaruists petaurista*) or *tupai terbang*. There are many rats or *tikus* that include (you guessed it) the **giant mountain rat** (*Sundamys infraluteus*). There are three types of **porcupine**—many times you can find the long 12 inch (30 cm) banded spines along trails. In Borneo you can spot **martens**/*mengkira*, **weasel**/*pulasan*, **badgers**/*teludu*, **mongooses**/*bambun* and **otters**/*berang-berang*.

The **cat** family includes five species including the marbled cat and leopard cat, smaller felines that are sometimes confused with the larger clouded leopard.

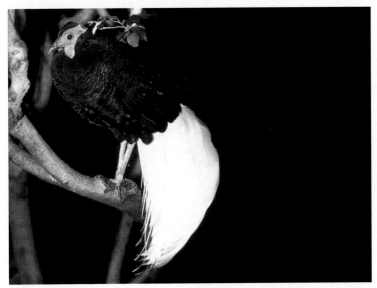

Bulwer's Pheasant

BIRDS

There are over 600 species of birds in Borneo, about half of them migrants from as far away as Europe and China. The most spectacular are the hornbills, owls and eagles that live in the canopy. Borneo is also home to the world's smallest bird of prey the white fronted falconet (*Microhierax latifrons*). Borneo is a popular spot for birdwatchers. *The Birds of Borneo* by B.E. Smythies is the bible of birding. Those who find the tome too much to carry can also take along a condensed version published by the The Sabah Society. The *Pocket Guide to the Birds of Borneo* helps in identifying birds but provides no written background.

ARGUS PHEASANT
(Argusiansus grayi)

Kuau Besar

This rare bird is a member of the partridge family. This name comes from the mythological Greek monster with 100 eyes, an all seeing monster who guarded Io, the mortal maiden loved by Zeus.The argus pheasant can be identified by its rows of eyelike patterns on its feathers. The male argus puts on an elaborate mating dance, strutting his feathers to attract a female. The Dayaks use the tail feathers of the argus for their native ceremonial costumes.

EDIBLE NEST SWIFTLETS
(Collocalia)

The caves at Gomantang and Niah are the major harvesting grounds for the swiftlets' nests, an ancient Chinese delicacy. Bird's nest soup is made from the saliva the swiftlet uses to construct its nest. Contrary to myth, the soup is not made from boiling the whole nest. The raw material is separated from the nest material and then added with other ingredients to create an enervating, glutanous and mildly aphrodisiacal meal.

RHINOCEROS HORNBILL
(Buceros rhinoceros)

Enggang Gading **or** *Kanyolang*

If you are traveling down a river and hear a flock of geese honking, you are probably listening to the hornbills flapping and making their famous "ha-honk" sound. The rhinoceros hornbill is the largest and most colorful hornbill. Its red and yellow casque contrasts dramatically with its black and white feathers. In Borneo the hornbill is considered to have magical power. Voyages, battles and rice planting were planned based on the direction and time of the hornbills travel. The Dayaks bestow the tail feathers as proof of bravery. The Iban call the bird the *kenyalang* and create large ornate carvings to protect their longhouses. The birds have an unusual method of protecting their young. The female is sealed in a hollow tree for three months by both partners sealing the entrance with bird droppings, mud and grass. The male then feeds the female through a small orifice. When the chick has hatched the female chips her way out. There are nine types of hornbill found in Borneo.

The crocodiles of Sarawak are among the largest in the world.

REPTILES

Although Sarawak was famous for its giant crocodiles, there are few if any left in the major rivers. Turtles, the largest reptiles are much friendlier. The leatherback turtles grow to six feet and can be seen around Sipadan and the other offshore islands when they come up to lay their eggs. Frogs and toads make up the largest mass of reptiles. Lizards range from house geckos to flying lizards who can travel 20–50 ft (6–15 m) between trees by using the skin along the side of their body to give them lift, to chameleons who run like a two legged sprinter when surprised. The water monitor is the largest lizard.

CROCODILE
(Crocodilus porosus)

The crocodiles of Borneo were once feared. Now they are all but gone. They reach a length of up to 33 ft (10 m) and are found in the rivers and lakes of Borneo. It is a rare sight to see a crocodile today. The smaller relative is the Malayan gharial (*Tomistoma schelegeli*) an eight foot freshwater reptile that concentrates on fish for its diet.

FROGS
(Anura)

There are over 50 species of frogs found on Borneo. They can be found clinging to leaves, near waterfalls, or in mangrove areas. Some are poisonous, like the rock frog *(Rana hosei)*, unusual like the Bornean horned frog *(Megophyrys nasuta)* or large, like the giant river toad (*Bufo juxtasper*) which grows up to 8.5 inches (215 mm) in length. The tinkling sound heard at night is courtesy of the tree frogs *(Rhacophoridae)*. The Wallaces flying frog *(Rhacophorus nigropalmatus)* can fly from tree to tree using its webbed fingers and toes. Also watch for what looks like foam on tree branches above ponds. These are nests of frog eggs that when ready drop down from the nest to the water below.

GREEN TURTLE
(Chelonia mydas)

There are seven species of sea turtle. The green turtle can be found in all tropical waters and the Mediterranean. They attain a length of five feet (1.5 m) and weigh up to 400 lbs (180 kg). The leatherback is the largest species of sea turtle and can reach six feet in length. The breeding season is between October to February and turtles can be seen mating on the surface of the water. Female turtles return to the same beach they were born on and lay about 100 eggs at night. The eggs hatch in two to three months during the night and the odds of a hatchling surviving to adulthood is only two out of 100. The green turtles' favorite food is sea grass that is found in shallow warm waters. Turtles need to surface to breathe but can stay submerged for up to five hours. The sex of sea turtles is determined by the incubation temperature of the eggs; 82°F (28°C) will produce all male offspring and 90°F (32°C) will produce all females.

MONITOR LIZARD
(Varanas salvator)

There are seven lizard families in Borneo. The rarest is also the largest—2.5 m (8 ft) long monitor lizards can be found along Borneo's riverbanks. They usually announce themselves with a splash as they drop from an overhanging tree branch and swim away. The lizards are very fast on land and usually scamper up trees if cornered on land.

SNAKES
(Serpentes)

There are over 20 species of snakes in Borneo ranging from the large carnivorous python to tiny tree snakes to water snakes. The most dangerous is the king cobra when it becomes highly protective of its nest.

Another poisonous snake family in Borneo is the krait *(Bungarus fasciatus)* with their distinctive black and yellow stripes. Kraits do not attack humans but can strike if stepped on. Coral snakes *(Maticoreae)* are the other major poisonous snake species found in the water. They do not strike out like other snakes since their fangs are located too far back in their mouths.

RETICULATED PYTHON
(Python reticulatus)

Borneo is home to the world's largest pythons, measuring as long as 30 ft (9 m) and weighing as much as 300 lbs (135 kg). Pythons kill their prey by coiling around their victims and suffocating them to death. Pythons found in the swampy areas of lowland Borneo are usually very docile and have not been known to attack man.

KING COBRA
(Ophiophagus hannah)

The king cobra can attain an average length of 13 feet (4 m) with record specimens reaching 18 ft (5.5 m).

When attacked a large cobra can raise itself up to a man's eye level or higher. This snake is also highly venomous with half inch long fangs allowing it to deliver enough venom to kill a grown elephant if it bites a sensitive region like the trunk. The favorite foods of the king cobra are frogs and small mammals but it is known to attack humans and other snakes particularly during the period when the females protect the young in their nests. Nesting season is in April. Cobras mate with their lifelong partners by intertwining and lying together for hours.

In Borneo, king cobras are usually found around water and will use the river to escape when threatened. The large snake is a good climber and can also chase victims into trees. King cobras can be found in all regions of Borneo.

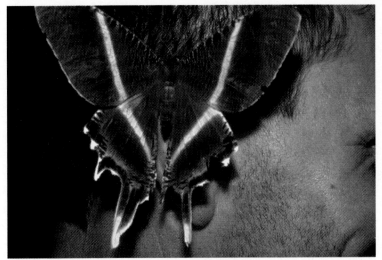

Bright lights will attract some interesting friends.

INSECTS

Insects are really the king of Borneo's jungle. On close inspection it seems that every square inch is populated with some industrious species that has been doing the same thing for the last few million years.

ANTS/TERMITES
(Formicidae)

There are over 100 species of ants ranging in size from over an inch like the giant 1.2 inches (3 cm) long elephant ant (*Campono-tus gigas*) to the tiny but painful fire ant (*Tetraponera rufunigra*) who will swarm and bite until washed or flicked off.

HONEY BEES
(Meliponinae)

There are 29 species of bees identified on Borneo although over 100 may exist. Some are stingless like the *Trigona collian* that lives in subterranean nests. Some are aggressive like the giant honeybees (*Apis dorsata*) who make their open combed nests in the towering mengaris (*Koompassia excelsa*) trees.

BUTTERFLIES & MOTHS
(Lepidoptera)

There are 950 recorded species of butterflies and an estimated 3750 moth species in Borneo. The most famous butterfly is the Rajah Brookes' birdwing *(Troides brookiana)* named by naturalist Alfred Wallace for his friend and supporter James Brooke. The most dramatic moth is the swallowtailed moth *(Nyctalemon patroclus)*. Moths are attracted by any light source at night; headlights or Coleman lanterns, even settling on flashlights. Butterflies are attracted to the salt in seepage along roads and rivers and are attracted to perspiration.

SPIDERS
(Arachnida)

Spiders and their close cousins, mites and ticks (*Acari*) are found in all parts of Borneo. Many of the spider species are of the jumping variety. Ticks are carried by wild pigs and are found in wallows. Ticks can be carriers of disease so trekkers should inspect all parts of their bodies on a daily basis.

RHINOCEROS BEETLE
(Chalcosoma)

Borneo depends on its 1600 plus species of beetles to be caretakers of the forests. They pollinate plants, remove dead animals, and even process the decayed organic matter. It is not unusual to come across one of these massive three horned atlas or rhinoceros beetles moving slowly across the forest floor. This docile but fierce looking beetle grows to a length of 2.1 inches (5.5 cm) and can actually fly when disturbed.

LANTERN BUGS
(Fulgoridae)

Although not related to the proboscis monkey this tiny insect has an ungainly nose that lights up the jungle night.

CICADAS
(Cicadidae)

Cicadas live most of their lives underground but they make up for lost time once above ground. The loudest noises in the forests of Borneo are cicada symphonies brought on by temperature changes. Cicada calls begin usually at noon when the temperature is at its highest. Variations in temperature and/or humidity can throw off the timing of what the libation-ready colonials used to call the "cocktail bug" or "6 o'clock bug" that begins its loud screech at dusk until it is replaced by the frogs who begin after dusk. After the frogs calm down, the grasshoppers are the main noise makers. Cicadas make their whine or screech with a rapid series of clicks or vibrations created by a stiff shell vibrating against a hollow air sac. Grasshoppers, katydids, butterflies, moths, crickets and other insects also join in the jungle chorus.

WALKING STICKS
(Phasmida)

Borneo is home to 300 of the 2900 identified stick insect species in the world. These varied insects are nocturnal and feed on soft plant tissue. The world's largest insect, the walking stick, can be found hanging around the forests of Borneo. Perfectly camouflaged among the grass and trees, these 2–20 inch (5–50 cm) insects do not bite. When startled some stick insects secret an acidic, strong smelling fluid.

MANTISES
(Mantodea)

These predatory insects with swivel heads come in an amazing variety of camouflages. Some like the orchid mantis *(Hymenopus mantis)* look exactly like a white orchid. Others look like dead leaves, green leaves or twigs. The sex life of a male mantis is not enviable. When the male and female begin mating the female will calmly begin eating the head and thorax of her partner. The mantis is the only species to whom a good meal and great sex are one and the same.

MILLIPEDES/CENTIPEDES
(Diploda/Chilopoda)

Millipedes are the harmless multilegged denizens of the forest floor that look like 100 men carrying a canoe. Centipedes are the nastier relatives with only only one pair of legs per segment. Centipedes feed off of other insects and smaller vertabrates. The three most common millipedes are the large pill millipede *(Oniscomorpha)* who will roll up into a thumb sized ball when disturbed, the long red centipede and the large brown millipede *(Thyropygus)*. These harmless critters live off leaf litter.

SEGMENTED WORMS
(Annelida)

The most memorable of Borneo's creatures might be the leech family. Annelids also include earthworms of which there is one five to six foot giant variety on Mt. Kinabalu.

Land leeches come in several odius types —the common leech, the tiger leech (identified by its painful bite and cowardly yellow stripe), and the large ground leech, which is just as greedy as its smaller brethren. All leeches are tiny when first attached and then swell up when engorged with blood. Leeches are found on the ground and attached to moist low vegetation. When walking through the woods try to be in the middle of the group and avoid being the first or last in line.

COMMON GROUND LEECH
(Haemadipsa zeylanica)

Unlike most wildlife in Borneo, this is one creature that will eagerly come to you. In fact, they will want to ride along with you. Leeches are found on trees, on the ground and particularly around mud wallows.

They will actually "sniff out" humans. They raise up on their posterior and inch as quickly as they can to attach to their host. They suck blood through the skin using an anticoagulant called hirudin to stimulate blood flow. Leeches can be burned off with salt, cigarettes or tobacco juice or, you can just smash them or yank them off. In any case, there are plenty more where the one you just pulled off came from. The white marks they leave take a while to heal. You can take heart in the fact that leeches were applied by ancient doctors to invigorate clients by blood letting. The open sores the leech's bite creates can become infected if not taken care of.

The Rafflesia, the world's largest flowering plant.

PLANTS

If you could pick a place to study plants there are few places more diverse than Borneo. Although the original forest areas are under attack by logging, there are still large areas untouched and unexplored by man. Rare and wild orchids are a major attraction of the forests. The vast diversity of tree, flowering and fruiting species have yet to be fully classified. Borneo has more fern species than any other region. Bamboos, palms, mengaris, heaths, shrubs mosses, herbs, flowers and dipterocarps make for one of the most diverse plant regions on earth.

MANGROVE PLANTS

SCREWPINE
(Pandanacae)

The 15 foot (4.5 m) high pandanus palm is found in the low mangrove areas of Borneo and is used to weave roofs. The wide regular leaves are strong and fibrous and are arranged in spirals around the stem.

MANGROVE
(Rizophora mucronata)

The mangrove swamps are full of this drab tree with arching or buttress roots. The seeds develop in long spear type shapes that drop down to embed themselves in the soft mud below.

DILLENIA
(Dilleniaceae)

Ten species of dillenia are found in Malaysia and Borneo. Red sepals cover the large flowerbuds and fruits. The flowers are fragrant and the oval leaves are up to 11 inches (28 cm) long. The trees can grow to 115 ft (35 m) tall.

FOREST PLANTS

DURIAN
(Durio)

The durian is the most famous and odius of Bornean fruits. Soft, creamy and with a pungent smell, the durian is an acquired taste. The smell of ripe durian was designed by nature to let animals know where the fruit is ripening. The spiny outer shells act as perfect protective cases for the soft inside. The Malaysians have been busy trying to breed the nasty aftertaste out of the fruit but so far have been unsuccessful. There are many types of durian, some of them completely inedible so be selective when trying the noxious fruit in the wild. Of the 27 known species of durian, 19 are found on Borneo. The white durian (*Durio putih*) is the favored edible type.

FIGS
(Moracae)

Figs in Borneo are fast growing fruiting trees that are pollinated by the *Blastophaga* or fig wasp.

The wasp larvae develop inside the flowers and then seek out the opposite sex in other flowers. The females then emerge to lay eggs in other figs carrying pollen along the way. Figs are an important source of food for apes, monkeys, hornbills, pigs, squirrels, deer and bats. Some of the most impressive figs are the strangler figs which climb up the host tree, encircling the host with roots, and then finally replacing the tree and dropping further roots to spread its domain.

MENGARIS
(Koompassiae)

Shorea or red meranti is a common hardwood tree identified by its three winged fruit. They are easy to identify by their lofty North American looking form and white bark. They are the tallest trees in the forest. There are often large combs of the giant honey bee *(Apis dorsata)*. Dayaks will not fell the trees to ensure a supply of honey (many of the individual trees are owned by locals) and loggers pass them by because of their tendency to shatter when they hit the ground. A cubic foot of mengaris wood weighs about 50 lbs (23 kg). The mengaris trees drop their leaves between February and May.

DIPTEROCARPS
(Dipterocarpacea)

Dipterocarps are any tree that produces a two winged seed (*Di-ptero-carp* in Greek). Some plants like the meranti have more than two wings on their seeds. The purpose of the winged seeds is to spread the incidence of the tree beyond the shaded area. Other trees are the bright barked tristania or pelawan trees that shed their bark like a eucalyptus.

RAFFLESIA
(Rafflesiaceae)

The world's largest and foulest smelling flower is named for Stanford Raffles of Raffle's hotel fame. They are only found in Southeast Asia and very unpredictable as to when they bloom.

The plant is a parasite and exists usually as a network of fine roots inside the absorptive stems of the ground trailing *Cissus liana*. The hard flowerbud bursts through the bark of the host plant to create a reddish brown, caldron-shaped flower. The flower is pollinated by flies and has the smell and look of putrefied meat. Size is 3 feet (1 m), weight around 18 lbs (8 kg).

PITCHER PLANT
(Nepenthes kinabaluensis)

Periuk kera

The pitcher plant or, "*nepenthes,*" is an epiphytic plant found in the lowlands and mountains of Borneo. The Malays call them *periuk capa* or monkey cups. Mt. Kinabalu is the only home on this planet to the largest nepenthes (up to 18 inches (45 cm) long) *Nepenthes raja*. Borneo contains 40 percent of the world's 70-odd species. They thrive on poor soils and get subsistence from insects that slip into the pitcher and then drown. An enzyme in the nectar dissolves the insects. Peek inside, but be careful: 68 species are known to live in the pitchers! The most interesting is the drummer ant who will vibrate the top lid of his pitcher plant home when alarmed.

RHODODENDRONS
(Rhododendron brookeanum)

Rhododendrons come in many shapes and sizes on Borneo. They can be identified by red bell shaped flowers. There are 26 different species of rhododendrons found on Mt. Kinabalu alone, six of them unique.

A Gallery of Orchids

Renanthera bella

Dendrobium anosmum

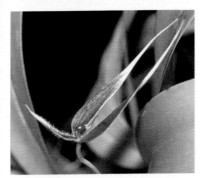

Bulbophyllum blumei

Bulbophyllum beccarii

Flickingeria comatum

Dendrobium anosmum

EPIPHYTES

Orchids are among the epiphytes family. Epiphytes are plants that live on other plants but do not destroy them like parasitic plants. The middle and lower canopy of the forests are full of various plants that trap the rainfall and live off nutrients that they catch with the runoff. If you venture up to the upper canopy you will finally see the lushness that escapes most visitors on the dank ground. Among the more spectacular squatters in the forest are the bird's nest fern *(Asplenium nidus)* and the many orchids *(Orchidaceae)*, pitcher plants *(Nepenthes)* and ferns *(Pteridophytes)*.

CLIMBERS

The jungle is full of vines, climbers and rattans. These plants use other plants to support their long arduous climb to the sunlight in the canopy above. Along their way some create beautiful sculptures and designs. Some climbers cover open areas with large leaves.

Rattan is a thin thorny vine that has been collected for thousands of years by the Penan and sold in coils. The major use of rattan was for woven furniture. Rattan only grows in primary forest and seeing long natural coils of thorny rattan usual means the area is uninhabited. There are versions of lianas that can be cut and contain water. Doing this however kills the entire upper length of the plant, and despite what jungle survival schools tell you, is not a good way to get water in the jungle.

FLOWERING PLANTS

There is no shortage of color in Borneo. Gingers, bananas, begonias, figs, even fungi can look like flowers or glow pale green in the night.

Jackfruit is a domesticated jungle fruit.

DOMESTICATED PLANTS

There are many native and introduced fruiting plants in Borneo. Mangos, durians, breadfruits, ginger, starfruit, Malay apple, water lemon, passionfruit and cocoa are just some.

BANANA
(Musaceae)

The banana is a native of Malaysia and a common backyard adornment. There are only two genera (*Ensete and Musa*) in the banana family and they range in height from three feet (one meter) to over 65 ft (20 m). Bananas found in the wilds of Borneo are inedible to humans. They are pollinated by bats and bees. The banana plant can only flower and fruit once in its lifetime and then must be cut back to produce more shoots. The banana is actually a giant herb with no true stem above ground. The stem is underground. Domestic bananas are seedless and sterile and are propagated using cuttings. Borneo's smaller bananas (*pisang*) are eaten as fruit and used in cooking. The larger types are cooked and eaten as a starch product.

The banana began its journey around the world 4000 years ago and was carried by trav-

elers to India, Africa and the Philippines. Europeans brought the banana to Haiti in the 1600s and the fruit is now a staple of all tropical diets. The name Banana Republic came from the political influence wielded by the United Fruit Company who in the early 20th century were owners of vast tracts of land in Latin America.

It is a testament to modern transportation that bananas can be found in all supermarkets from Alaska to Florida yet bananas are not grown commercially in North America. Today Brazil is the largest exporter of bananas.

BETEL NUT
(Piper betle)

Betel vine is the source of the leaves that are chewed with areca nut, slaked lime, gambier and tobacco leaves. There is no betel nut. They are actually the round seeds of the Arieca palm (*Areca catecu*), a hard seed that contains arecoline. The tobacco in the betel nut not only stains the teeth but is said to also polish the teeth and contains a strong astringent.

COCOA
(Therbroma cocoa)

These medium sized bushes (about five feet (1.5 m) tall) are transplanted from the Andes of South America. The pods are ripe when they rattle or turn yellow. The seeds are bitter but the soft white pull is tart and refreshing and can be eaten to quench thirst.

KAPOK
(Ceiba pentandra)

The kapok tree was a native of South and Central America. The light fluffy flowers are used for fiber, insulation and in the old days to create flotation in life preservers.

PEPPER
(Piper negrum)

Once pepper was the most valuable of Asian spices. A native of India, pepper is still a major crop in Sarawak. Pepper is a climbing bush and bears a strand of peppercorns. The pepper is ripe when the seeds turn yellow. The peppercorns are then dried until black. White pepper is also derived from black pepper after the husks are soaked off. The hotness in pepper is due to the chavicine resin.

Salak
(Sallaca edulis)

This fruit looks suspiciously like it is the offspring of a snake. The fruit is popular in east Kalimantan and tastes like an apple. The fruit is harvested from a vicious spined thorny shrub.

Bahasa Malay

The kids will get a kick out of the stupid orang puti *who can't understand a simple language like Malay.*

Bahasa Malay is not a language you can pick up in one day but it is easy. Although some words and phrases may be easy to remember, you'll realize that it's nothing like any language in the West, and you'll thank God, or Allah, or whatever deity rules this part of the land, that many people in both Malaysia and Singapore speak English. However, here are a few words and phrases that may prove helpful.

ENGLISH	BAHASA MALAY
Good morning	*Selamat pagi*
Good afternoon	*Selamat tengahari*
Good evening	*Selamat ptang*
Good night	*Selamat malam*
Goodbye	*Selamat jalan*
Thank you	*Terima kasih*
How are you?	*Apa khabar?*
My name is...	*Nama saya...*
May I know your name?	*Boleh saya tahu nama awak?*
I come from...	*Saya datang dari...*
Could you help me?	*Bolehkah awak tolong saya?*
How much is it?	*Berapakah harganya?*
Please give me a receipt	*Tolong beri saya resit*
I have no small change	*Saya tidak ada duit kecil*
Good	*Bagus*
Big	*Besar*
Small	*Kecil*
Left	*Kiri*
Right	*Kanan*
Open	*Buka*
Close	*Tutup*
Soup	*Sup*
Vegetables	*Sayur*
Fish	*Ikan*
Beef	*Daging lembu*
Chicken	*Ayam*
Mutton	*Kambing*
Crab	*Ketam*
Egg	*Telur*
Bread	*Roti*
Water	*Batu*
Coffee	*Kopi*

ENGLISH	BAHASA MALAY
Tea	*Teh*
Sugar	*Gula*
One	*Satu*
Two	*Dua*
Three	*Tiga*
Four	*Empat*
Five	*Lima*
Six	*Enam*
Seven	*Tujuh*
Eight	*Lapan*
Nine	*Sembilan*
Ten	*Sepuluh*
Sunday	*Ahad*
Monday	*Isnin*
Tuesday	*Selasa*
Wednesday	*Rabu*
Thursday	*Khamis*
Friday	*Jumaat*
Saturday	*Sabtu*
Now	*Sekarang*
Later	*Nanti*
Soon	*Tidak lama lagi*
Today	*Hari ini*
Tomorrow	*Esok*
Yesterday	*Semalam*

The Travel Journal

The travel experience is made richer by capturing the small seemingly insignificant events and impressions.

A Proof of Passing

We all have them—dog-eared postcards never sent, stacks of weather-beaten, spiral notebooks, small plastic binders with rusted spines, even tattered airline ticket holders covered with addresses and notes. We all need to record our passing in some manner. Many of us find it hard to sort out items of interest in our day to day existence. Routine dulls perception. Travel forces thousands of fresh experiences upon us—so many, that we need to really reflect on them back in our humdrum existence. By capturing as many of these new experiences and our immediate interpretation of them, we reconstruct or reinterpret the frantic days of travel. It seems that one day of travel can de-

liver as many indelible memories as a few years of normal existence. Your
travel journal will help you get the most out of your journey. Writing your
experiences down will help others understand your enthusiasm and possibly
help you truly understand who you are.

The Travel Journal:
A Guide for the Serious Traveler

A travel journal is more than a notebook. It is the foundation for a great
book, a reference manual, a record of history, an undeniable proof of a
stranger's passing and recollections.

Every good travel book starts with a good journal. In the age of electronic
and visual information a handwritten notebook may seem archaic. Until we
can capture smells, emotions and personal interpretations, the journal will be
the guardian of true vision.

The Physical Journal

Choosing a travel journal depends on a lot of factors—how long you will
be gone, what type of clothes you wear, the conditions under which you will
be traveling. I have carried a variety of journals: small plastic binders with
looseleaf pages that fit perfectly in the top pocket of my jean jacket, but split
open when too full like a ripe pomegranate. Large, fat spiral binders that I
tucked into my camera bags, turned into soggy mush in the jungle. I have
used a small recorder while traveling in vehicles at high speeds through Africa and Borneo, careful to transcribe everything upon my return. Whatever is
comfortable for you will be your journal. Consider the following when making your choice.

Format:

Whatever is comfortable. Think about durability. Keep it cheap so it will not be cov-
eted by the locals. Keep it conservative so that writing in it does not invite suspicion
and most important, keep it at hand.

Weight:

Better two or three small books. Use your writing style to determine how many
pages you will need for each day. Don't forget all the pages you will tear out when
other people ask you for an address or directions.

Pens:

Bring lots of pens. The kind you get from gas stations can be bought with your
name and address. They make great gifts. Always bring a mechanical pencil as a last
resort. Use indelible ink. Don't use a fountain pen unless you are a true classicist and
bring an entire writing kit. Don't be afraid to try your hand at drawing.

Binding:

    Make sure the book will hold together. Looseleaf lets you add or delete pages and looseleaf lets you reorganize.

Cover:

    Should be unobtrusive and stand up to a lot of abrasion.

Paper:

    Unruled paper lets you draw, format or even write sideways.

Writing Your Journal

It would be too simplistic to just say write down anything you want. There is a definite discipline to travel journal writing. It is not enough to have pages full of "had a great meal, saw a lot of interesting things, nice hotel too." It is important to establish a purpose and a format to help you get the most from your experiences.

Consistency in Reflection

Once you have selected your journal of choice, think of when and what you will write. This consistency will give you perspective. The most typical time of writing is in restaurants, in your hotel and while in transit. In order for you to get the most from your travels, write what you hope to see, achieve, buy, experience. You may be pleasantly surprised by the time your trip finishes.

Set Yourself a Goal

Promise to fill out four pages a day, for example. Even when you did nothing but sit in one place, write down what you hope to see, why you are traveling, descriptions of fellow passengers; describe your boots. These all become interesting side notes later.

Everything is Important

Your linear recollections of your trip are just one half of the journal. The thousands of little things that do not fit in neatly with your travels become the spice that adds variety to your account. Colors, sounds, the music heard on the radio, names of train stations.

Make lists. Write down headlines of newspapers, prices of food, people's names. Single words that capture small truths.

I write on the right hand side leaving the left side open for phone numbers, addresses, comments and other small margin notes. You can develop small habits like always writing a description of where you are when you make the day's entry.

Write down quotes, draw maps, floor plans, architectural details. Include everyday items: tape in bus tickets, wine labels, clippings, whatever strikes your fancy. The more observant you are, the more perceptive you will become.

Refer to others. Do not forget to include the observations of others, whether they be long-dead explorers or your companion. It is always interesting to compare impressions.

Borneo in Books

Travelers to Borneo seem to find a way to capture the exotic, romantic island.

It would seem that Borneo is not the favorite haunt of the armchair traveler. The Amazon, Kenya and even the Poles dominate the book shelves in the adventure section. Borneo is the passion of the British, the Dutch and the Germans. Few movies other than *Farewell to the King* have been made in or on Borneo in recent years and yet the island has all the cinematic elements that make for high adventure: headhunters, dramatic artwork, giant caves, towering limestone cliffs, sparkling oceans, not to mention pirates, White Rajahs, gold rushes, diamond mines, uncharted territory. Maybe the lack of bestselling books or blockbuster films is because of the intense scientific scrutiny Borneo gets. Maybe it's because it is just so difficult to travel, film or photograph here. Maybe it's because nobody knows just exactly where the world's third largest island sits. For now let's just keep Borneo our little secret.

If you are not a fan of the oft pedantic travel guides and just want to get into the mood, get the following books before you go. I should mention that Oxford in Asia has a serious Borneo Jones and has reprinted just about every old book on Borneo they could find. Start with their excellent compilation work on Borneo entitled what else but *Best of Borneo* and then expand into the book that covers the area you are going to visit.

The most popular book on Borneo has to be Redmond O'Hanlon's 1984 farcical quest for the rhino. He has a thing for birds and a way with words. I don't know what attracts smart, irreverent people to Borneo but multitalented men like Tom Harrisson is another one. Despite his sense of humor he has played a major role in the military, cultural and natural development of Borneo. Curator of the Sarawak Museum, proclaimer of Niah Man and jungle commando, he is another chip off the Rajah Brooke's block. His book *World Within* is worth taking along for his in-depth descriptions of the Kelabit.

Shooting the Boh by Tracy Johnston is a good book recounting her introduction to Borneo. She tells it like it is and it's a good read for anyone who has not been on expeditions before.

There are a few large coffee table books you might find in the airport or hotel gift shop when you get to Borneo. My advice is buy them because you will have a hard time getting them once back at home. If you want the best selection, head to the book section at the nearest department store.

NONFICTION BOOKS ON BORNEO

The First Voyage Round the World by Magellan
Antonio Pigafetta (Hakluyt Society, London published 1874)
By far the first western description of Borneo. Written in 1521 by the expedition's chronicler. Magellan set off around the world from Seville, Spain on August 10, 1519 and returned home on September 8, 1522. Magellan died during the three year voyage on March 27, 1521 only four months before the fleet reached Brunei in early July. The account tells of the fleet being welcomed to the Sultanate of Brunei while riding silk-decorated elephants and carrying gifts in porcelain vases. Their visit with Rajah Sirapada is brief and they even are unlucky enough to be attacked by Filipino pirates. The work was first published in French in 1525 and only excerpts have survived.

A Voyage To and From the Island of Borneo
Captain Daniel Beeckman (T. Warner and J. Batley, London 1718)

In 1713 Captain Beeckman set sail from England to acquire pepper from the Sultanate of Banjarmasin. The only catch was the Sultan had tossed out the English after a brief war some years before. After much haggling he was successful and returned to England two years later. He then wrote this travel guide to help other ship captains interested in opening up trade in the region.

Borneo and the Indian Archipelago ★
Frank S. Marryat (Longman, Brown, Green and Longmans, London 1848)
Probably the first talented artist to visit Sarawak, Marryat was a midshipman aboard a British survey ship. He arrived in 1843 and proceeded to create a wealth of illustrations on Dayak life-styles and scenes. He also wrote his recollections, which were then published in the *Illustrated London News* and in book form.

Sarawak, Its Inhabitants and Productions
Hugh Low (Richard Bentley, London 1848)
Hugh Low was the British major domo in Labuan, the British trading port northeast of Brunei. This book is not by any means the most readable or easy to find.

Adventures Among the Dayaks of Borneo
Frederick Boyle (Hurst and Blackett Publishers, London 1865)
Boyle was an Englishman who toured Sarawak in 1863 with his brother. Although this very Western account of his travels is over 130 years old many readers will experience deja vu as he describes his longhouse nights.

Life in the Forests of the Far East
Spenser St. John (Smith, Elder and Co., London 1862)
St. John was Sir James Brooke's personal secretary, and British Consul General to the native states of Borneo in 1856. He is probably best known for his ascent of Mt. Kinabalu in April of 1858. His record of 13 years in Borneo makes for an interesting read without a lot of scientific detours.

Ten Years in Sarawak.
Charles Brooke (Oxford in Asia Reprints, 1866)
The nephew of Sir James Brooke ruled Sarawak from 1869 until his death in 1917. Between 1852 -1863 he kept a detailed diary of his governmental work in the service of his famous uncle. The 746 page book is the best single insight into the most adventurous period in Borneo.

The Malay Archipelago, The Land of the Orang Utan, and The Bird of Paradise
Alfred Russel Wallace (Macmillian and Co. London, 1869)
Alfred Wallace traveled over 14,000 miles on over 65 journeys to the equatorial region of Borneo and Indonesia. Sir James Brooke was a major sponsor as were the Dutch and British governments. Traveling in small expeditions he collected over 125,000 specimens in Asia that took over seven years just to sort and catalog. Wallace is credited with creating the groundwork for the theory of evolution and the Wallace line is his lasting legacy.

The Head Hunters of Borneo
Carl Bock (Oxford in Asia Reprint, 1881)
A Norwegian travels up the Mahakam in 1879 on a surveying mission for the Dutch. His travels up the Mahakam and along the Barito make for good reading.

Although nobody was optioning books for screenplays back then, it appeared the Bock was doing his best to attract interest in his search for men with tails, bloodthirsty headhunters and high adventure. His rip roaring yarns pepper this supposedly scientific tome and make an interesting counterpoint to Lumholz's work.

Two Years in the Jungle: The Experiences of a Hunter and Naturalist in India, Ceylon, The Malay Peninsula and Borneo

William T. Hornaday, (Paul, Trench & Co. London 1885)

The Exploration of Mount Kinabalu, North Borneo

John Whitehead, (Gurney and Jackson, London, 1893)

The Home-Life of Borneo Head Hunters Its Festival and Folklore

William H. Furness (Lippincott, Philadelphia, 1902)

Wanderings in the Great Forests of Borneo

Odoardo Beccari (Archibald Constable and Co. 1904)

Beccari spent two and a half years in Borneo in pursuit of specimens. He managed to off over 40 orang utans as he shot them out of the trees, many too mutilated to use. He traveled up the Rejang and the Baleh and also into Brunei. He eventually had to leave due to ill health. Even though the period of his trip was in 1861 and 1864 the book was not published until 1902 and then translated from Italian to English in 1904.

The Pagan Tribes of Borneo

Charles Hose (Macmillan, London 1912)

A Naturalist in Borneo

Robert W. Shelford (T. Fisher Unwin, London, 1916)

Through Central Borneo   ★ ★

by Carl Lumholz (Oxford in Asia Reprint, 1920)

Dr. Lumholz (calmer and more perspicacious than his countryman Bock) does a sequel to Carl Bock's epic trip and gathers more information than any one explorer could use in a lifetime. Like many others before and after him, the author was caught in the spell of the native peoples of Borneo. He had a healthy dislike for the Malays and was indifferent to the Chinese. He traveled up the Kinabatangan, along the coast and down the Mahakam making copious notes along the way. He has a descriptive touch and records many native legends along the way. The book was published in 1920 and Lumholtz died two years later with even more notes and collections still to be committed to paper.

Among the Dayak Headhunters

William O. Krohn (Oxford in Asia Reprint, 1927)

An American's turn to journey up the Mahakam. First published in 1927, the book is his account of his journey through headhunter country. Much of the same ethnographic information is found in Lumholz's book without the emotional connection or intellect. The 327 page volume is a good addition to Borneo libraries for its in-depth descriptions of Dayak life-styles and cultures.

The Field-Book of a Jungle Wallah. Shore, River and Forest Life in Sarawak.

Charles Hose (H.F. And G. Witherby, London, 1929)

His 23 year stint as a civil servant under Sir Charles Brooke was put to good use in Hose's case. He spent a great deal of that time studying the flora and fauna of the region, collecting both natural specimens and cultural objects for the Museum at Cambridge. In his later years he lectured extensively and wrote other books on Borneo.

Borneo Jungle

Edited by Tom Harrisson (Oxford in Asia Reprint,1938)

This is a 254 page account of the Oxford University Expedition of 1932 wherein five young men in their early 20s decide to explore Borneo. This scientific tome is recommended for Harrisson's breezy style and the good combination of tale telling and scientific background. Now in print from Oxford Press.

A Journey Among the Peoples of Central Borneo in Word and Pictures

H.F. Tillema (Oxford University Press Reprints, 1938)

One of my favorite books on Borneo. Hendrik Freerk Tillema was a Dutch pharmacist who traveled to the Apo Kayan at the age of 62. He worked out of Long Nawang and took hundreds of photographs and made films of the Kenyah.

This large format 248 page book contains 336 black and white photographs. Tillema died in November 1952.

Borneo People

Malcolm MacDonald (Jonathan Cape and Random Century, 1956)

MacDonald probably chalked up more longhouse visits than any other traveler in his position starting as Governor General of Malaya and British Borneo in 1946 and ending as Commissioner General in 1955. His book describes his relationship and changes within the Iban of the Kapit-Belah region.

World Within. A Borneo Story ★★★★★

Tom Harrisson (Oxford in Asia Reprint, 1956)

If there is one man who typifies Borneo it is Harrisson. Just as T.E. Lawrence symbolized Arabia, Harrisson was a true romantic role model for many British schoolboys. Adventurer, archeologist, author, soldier, hero, ethnologist, naturalist and explorer, Harrisson would be hard to invent if he was not a real person.

A cocky graduate of Oxford, he first came to Borneo in his early twenties on a sponsored scientific expedition (See Borneo Jungle). He then was sent into the Kelabit highlands as a major to organize resistance against the Japanese towards the end of WWII. He then was curator of the Sarawak Museum from 1947 to 1966 and is credited with the discovery of Niah Man. *World Within* is the story of his adventures in the Bario in 1944 and is the best book on the traditions and culture of the industrious Kelabit.

Longhouse and Jungle: An Expedition into Sarawak

Guy Arnold (Chatto and Windus, London, 1959)

Ulu, The World's End

Jorgen Bisch (George Allen and Unwin, London, 1961)

A Season in Sarawak

Mora Dickson (Dennis Dobson, London, 1962)

Orang-Utan

Barbara Harrisson (Collins, London, 1962)

Panjamon

Jean Yyves Domalain (Rupert Hart-Davis, 1972)

My Life with the Headhunters

Wynn Sargent (Arthur Baker Ltd, 1974)
The title should be a dead giveaway.

A Stroll Through Borneo ★

James Barclay (Hodder and Stoughton London, 1980)
I don't get it. Why do all these Westerners want to walk around Borneo? Not as well done or as interesting as Eric Hansen's later book but a pretty impressive feat (no pun intended) let alone a book. This book is hard to find outside of Malaysia.

Expedition to Borneo

David MacDonald (J.M. Dent, London, 1982)

Into the Heart of Borneo

Redmond O'Hanlon (Salamander/Penguin, 1984)
By far the funniest book on Borneo. O'Hanlon drags Oxford poet and former SE Asian correspondent, James Fenton up the Rejang and Baleh Rivers in Sarawak in search of the mythical rhino. He obviously never achieves his goal but his misadventures along the way make for great reading. O'Hanlon is overly educated, degreed in both philosophy and literary vices. He also is a bit of a twitcher and makes numerous references to ornithological trivia as he quotes directly out of *Birds of Borneo* by Betram Smythie.

A Stranger in the Forest, On Foot Across Borneo ★★★

Eric Hansen (Houghton Mifflen, 1988)
A solo trip through Sarawak, and ending up in the Apo Kayan where the author is mistaken for a *bali saleng*, a wandering ghost who collects blood. His 1982 trip is full of insights and adventures along his 1500 mile journey.

Wild People ★★

Andro Linklater (The Atlantic Monthly Press, 1990)
Linklater was hired by Time-Life to add a book on the Iban to their series *The World's Wild Places*. The idea was that a writer and a photographer would live with the Iban and document their lives. The longhouse chosen was Rumah Langga along the upper tributaries of the Rejang. When the team arrived they realized that the Iban were quite happy living in the present and did not really make good stone age subjects for series. The project was canceled and thankfully this book is what was salvaged. Linklater writes in an engaging style and casts a trained reporter's eye on the disappearing life-style of the Iban. The 208 page book is also a candid and sympathetic introduction to the culture and myths of the Sea Dayak.

Shooting the Boh ★★★

Tracy Johnston (Vintage Departures, 1991)
Happily married, premenopausal Johnston decides to have an adventure in the Apo Kayan. She signs on to do a recce trip with Sobek down the thundering Boh river. She is teamed up with an odd assortment of fellow adventurers who turn out to be

nothing of the sort. The trip is a disaster due to poor planning, bad chemistry and a total lack of romantic allusions on the part of the participants. What Johnston does capture is the brutal lack of grace and pleasure that awaits the overly romantic and a great book on the ups and downs of adventure travel. A funny and sensitive book.

The Best of Borneo Travel

Compiled and introduced by Victor T. King, Oxford in AsiaReprint, 1992)

This 1992 collection of stories covers a wide gamut. From Antonio Pigafetta's description of his visit to Brunei in 1521 to contemporary nonfiction from Redmond O'Hanlon and Eric Hansen, the 315 page book contains 19 stories and excerpts. It is the ideal book to read by flashlight in the jungle. The paper is a bit too smooth for toilet paper or cigarette paper but makes our list for the only book to pack along with this guidebook.

ILLUSTRATED BOOKS ON BORNEO

There are many scientific books on Southeast Asia and the Indonesian archipelago, Malaysia and even Brunei. You'll have to pick and choose since there are many species and subspecies unique to Borneo. There are major works on butterflies, coral reefs, forests, birds, reptiles and what have you. I have listed just the major books unique to Borneo. Keep in mind that most of these books focus on Northern Borneo. When you are at the nature center you may want to pick up the massive two part guide to *Orchids of Borneo*.

Borneo

J. MacKinnon (Time-Life 1975)

Although long in the tooth you can usually pick this well written book up at a garage sale.Originally part of a *Wild Places* series, this is still one of the first and better books on Borneo.

The Birds of Borneo

B.E. Smythies (Sabah Society/Malayan Nature Society 1981)

A massive work on the native and migratory birds of Borneo. A definite acquisition for any Borneophile along with portable companion, the Pocket Guide. You will have to bone up on the descriptions or read them later since the Pocket Guide consists of visuals only.

Pocket Guide to the Birds of Borneo

(Sabah Society/WWF 1984)

A tiny condensed version of the larger classic by Smythies.

Field Guide to the Mammals of Borneo

J. Payne, C. M. Francis and K. Phillips (Sabah Society/WWF 1985)

A must have hardback that covers all the major mammal species. For some strange reason they include whales, dolphins and other sea mammals that have never been sighted, but omit the rare freshwater dolphin found in the Mahakam. Keep in mind that most of the mammals you will sight will be bats, squirrels, rats, civets and the odd tarsier.

Wild Malaysia

J. Payne & Gerald Cubitt (New Holland, 1985)

Another good photo book with shots of rare animals by South African nature photographer Cubitt.

Sipadan ★★

by Michael Patrick Wong(Odyssey Publishing 1992)

Big, beautiful and expensive but a great souvenir of a dive trip to Sipadan. Order direct from the publisher. Born in Sarawak and now a dentist in London, Wong spent a long time putting together this coffee table book. You won't find it many places other than the airport bookstores in KK so buy it if you see it.

Beyond the Java Sea. Art of Indonesia's Outer Islands ★★★

Paul Michael Taylor, Lorraine V. Aragon (Harry N.Abrams, Inc, 1991)

An excellent book on Indonesian art including Kalimantan. Although only 25 pages of the book's 318 pages are on Dayak art it is well illustrated and allows the reader to understand the art of Borneo in context with other Indonesian art forms.

Hornbill and Dragon. Arts & Culture of Borneo ★★★★★

Bernard Sellato (Sun Tree Publishing 1992)

The best single book on the art of Borneo is not widely available. It features the work of 15 photographers and provides a good background on the island and its cultural influences.

The Nature of Borneo ★★

Steve Yates, Terry Dominico (Facts on File, 1992)

A 208 page photo book for the nontechnical. Despite the fact that they managed to put a few of the pictures upside down (a frog, a tree with pronounced roots no less) the book makes a good souvenir.

WORKS OF FICTION RELATED TO BORNEO

Joseph Conrad loved the seamy, dark side of men on the verge of insanity. If you came to Borneo for dark, take Conrad on the plane and for those interminable river trips into the interior. One personal note, I found the African structure of *Heart of Darkness* backwards in Borneo. The interior is where men are sane, the land is calm, it is only as you travel downriver to the coast (read Miri) that the insanity becomes more and more evident. On a more trivial note, the Flashman series by George MacDonald Fraser has an interesting chapter on James Brooke and the evil Makota in *Flashman's Lady*. Although the lovable scoundrel survives his adventures, they truly pale next to some factual adventures. For those who like a dash of fantasy and artistry with their Borneo education, I recommend works by the following authors.

Joseph Conrad

Conrad only spent a few weeks in Borneo, all of them downriver from Tanjung Redeb in Berau. Yet this short layover yielded four novels. *An Outcast of the Islands, Lord Jim (1902), The Rescue* and *Almayer's Folly*. (Although *Heart of Darkness(1902)* is set in Africa, it is a great novel to read on river trips in Borneo). Conrad set some of his short stories in Borneo as well, *Freya of the Seven Isles and Karain* being among them. I recommend *Great Short Works of Joseph Conrad* (Perennial Classic). *Almayer's Folly*, written in 1889, is based on the village of

Berau in Borneo where fans can search for the grave of a Mr. Ohimeyer, the Dutchman that inspired the fictional title character.

Somerset Maugham

W. Somerset Maugham was a curious student of the Far East: an educated witty man, secret agent, gossiper and the Dalton Trumbo of his time. Once again a perfect visitor for Malaya, Borneo and Singapore in its colonial heyday. Like Conrad, the line between fact and fiction was thin but always accurate. In *Borneo Tales* he tells of his near drowning in the tidal bore in 1929 Sri Amanin in "Yellow Streak." His depiction of bored, gossiping civil servants in *The Outstation* is an excellent picture of colonial times.

PERIODICALS ON CURRENT EVENTS IN ASIA

Asia Week

Asia Week is the *Time* magazine (or the *Economist* if your prefer) of the East. The straightforward news stories give you insight into the relative importance of issues plus are a great balance to the typical Western image of Asia as a newly born economy. In other words they typically feel sorry for overworked, overtaxed Americans living in a crumbling economy.

Far Eastern Economic Review

A weekly "*Economist* cum *Business Week*" out of Hong Kong. Tight reporting with good background.

MOVIES FILMED IN BORNEO

For those who like to watch rather than read, there is not much to recommend. Many films such as *Bat 21* and *Farewell to the King* and a few adventure flicks have been filmed in Malaysia. Few can capture the same feeling of being there. The main reason these two movies were filmed in Malaysia is because of the government's largess in flying over entire film crews to promote the region as a film location. I guess somebody should have told the governments of Sabah and Sarawak that Hollywood exists because of the lack of rain and the fact the stars can be back in bed by 9:00 p.m.

Bat 21 ★★★

(1988, 105 minutes, R, Directed by Peter Markle)
Bat 21 is the only Hollywood film shot in Sabah. Normally the film folks head for the Philippines (*Apocalypse Now*) or Mexico (*Rambo 2*) when they want steaming jungles. In this case there is little difference as Gene Hackman runs around in the jungle and Danny Glover flies above it. Hackman is a desk-bound officer who gets shot down while checking out troop movements while Glover is a FAC (Forward Air Control) pilot who doggedly stays with him. This real life Vietnam era story is worth watching for the plot and the Sabah jungle scenes.

Farewell to the King ★★

(1989, 117 minutes, PG. Written and directed by John Milius)
This is probably the only movie made in recent times that captures some of the appeal of Borneo. Screenwriter/Director John Milius spent four months in and around Sarawak filming this Asian *Heart of Darkness*. Since Milius also wrote *Apocalypse Now* (based on Conrad's *Heart of Darkness*) for Coppola you get the feeling

that the two movies are somehow connected. Nick Nolte plays Learoyd (Get it? Le Roi, or "the king" in French) and Eton-educated Nigel Havers plays an unnamed paratrooper/botanist who is obviously about as close as one can get to Oxford-educated Tom Harrisson, a paratrooper/anthropologist without having to pay royalties.

The movie is based on Pierre Schoendoerffer's novel of the same name and is set on a nameless island. The story is about a shipwrecked American sailor who is taken in by the natives. Three years later he ends up being the head cheese instead of a smoked head and lives an idyllic life surrounded by native babes and loyal subjects. We are never told how he went from AWOL sailor to king but since Milius is known for action flicks it doesn't take long for Nolte to change from Gandhi to Rambo.

Overall the movie turns out to be a machine gun flick with some interesting interpretations of Iban longhouses and native customs. The jungle scenes are quite scenic if you don't mind the fact that the rivers are usually floating with Japanese corpses.

TRAVEL GUIDES ON BORNEO

Travel guides to Borneo are generally either timeless or out of date. If they are a litany of prices, addresses and recommendations you can rest assured that the world changes very quickly here. Here is a list of major travel guides to the region. Since this is the only travel guide to Borneo proper, you will need to double up on some of these guides to create some type of continuity to your trip if you plan to travel between Indonesia and the other countries. When buying a travel guide peek at the copyright date in the front and subtract about 6–12 months. There is a gaggle of expats whose work seems to pop up on books on Malaysia: American writer/photographer Kal Muller, Canadian photographer Ian Lloyd and writer Wendy Moore.

Fielding's Guide to Borneo

Robert Young Pelton (Fielding Worldwide, 1995)
Wait, I'm having deja vu. Aren't I reading this book? This and the following two guides are our contribution to the glut of travel guides on Southeast Asia. The difference is we try to focus on the unusual and the adventurous.

Fielding's Guide to Malaysia & Singapore

O.Sam Mitani.(Fielding Worldwide, 1994)
I dragged Sam from his day job as an editor at *Road & Track* to cover the Trans - Pen, a nine day expedition from hell through Peninsular Malaysia. If that wasn't enough, he was hooked enough to return to write an entire book on the place. His book is a good intro into the main sights of Malaysia and Singapore. I wrote the Borneo section while Sam continually tries to one up me with the cushy mainland part.

Fielding's Southeast Asia

Robert Young Pelton, Wink Dulles, (Fielding Worldwide 1995)
An adventurous guide to Southeast Asia including the latest on the more remote, ever changing regions like Myanmar and Cambodia. Updated with passion by our Southeast Asian Bureau Chief Wink Dulles. He is also the author of Fielding's *Viet-*

nam. Wink's excellent book on Vietnam was banned by the Vietnamese government. The government hates his book so much they even grab them away from people visiting their tourist hungry country. Wink lives in Los Angeles and Bangkok.

Insight Guides to S.E. Asia Wildlife

(Apa, Insight Guides)
A 430 page color book that includes some of the best photography of the region's plant and animal life. Nature photographer Alain Compost is a major contributor to this book along with well written and knowledgable sections written by scientists.

Indonesia, Malaysia and Singapore Handbook ★★★

(Trade & Travel Passport Books. 1995)
This annually updated guide is a 1152 page miniencyclopedia and telephone book in one. The compact hardbound guides have excellent information and maps and are surprisingly free from most travel writer opinions. The sidebar information was well researched and worth the price alone (just under $30). Although the cover doesn't mention it, the book has room for Brunei as well. There is exhaustive information on history and culture as well as probably more numbers and addresses than you can possibly use in one trip. The section on responsible tourism is humorous to say the least (It should simply read: Send money, stay home.) and there is a little too much boilerplate creeping in to the front of these books. However you do get 128 teensy weeny type pages on Sabah and Sarawak, 34 on Kalimantan and 33 on Brunei. My advice is to lighten the book by using the politically correct sections for rolling smokes and toilet duty and keep the meaty stuff for your travels.

Malaysia, Singapore & Brunei ★

Hugh Finlay, Peter Turner (Lonely Planet, 1994)
The newest 540 page guide is long on details and short on adventure. But then again aren't most travel guides bought by cautious people? The focus here is on budget accommodation and how to get around. Good solid information with plenty of maps (even to hamlets like Beaufort and Tenom that don't really need them). Minor chunks on history and culture far fall short of *Trade & Travel's* intellectual coverage but the guide offers more price guidelines and hotel recommendations. For $16.95 you get 115 pages on Sabah and Sarawak and 23 pages on Brunei. Maybe you can find another traveler and trade the mainland and Singapore sections for a Kalimantan chapter.

Malaysia, Singapore & Brunei

Charles de Ledesma, Mark Lewis, Pauline Savage (The Rough Guide, 1994)
This relative newcomer to travel guides on Asia hits the ground running with a comprehensive 615 pages of in-depth information on hotels, restaurants and transportation. Very complete coverage of Borneo with precise maps. Better than Lonely Planet for its coverage of remote regions but lacking in specificity on room rates and treks. It packs a chunky 140 pages on Borneo regions along with good maps for remote regions. The downside? They make the remote regions sound as civilized as Kansas and deal very little with the realities and vagaries of bush travel.

Borneo, Journey into the Tropical Rainforest ★★★★★
The Passport Guide East Malaysia and Brunei ★★★★★
Wendy Hutton, Kal Muller (Passport/Periplus, 1992, 1994)
The best illustrated books and guidebooks on Malaysia and Indonesia are published out of Singapore. Actually two separate books that could be glued together into one extraordinarily knowledgeable and entertaining guide to Borneo. The newer Malaysia/Brunei book is edited by Wendy Hutton with help from 17 other regional experts including Kal Muller who is author of the older Kalimantan guide. A bargain at $17.95 and worth it just for the photos and maps.Kal Muller is an American with a doctorate in French literature and is a well traveled photographer and writer. His work seems to pop up in numerous guides to Indonesia and Borneo.

Indonesia ★★
Storey, Spitzer, Nebesky, Lyon, Wheeler (Lonely Planet, 1992)
This 938 page book is slowly gaining in page size on Bill Dalton's Moon Handbook. Focused almost entirely on go here, do that, go there, stay here, it doesn't leave much room for having a good time. The work is industrial at best but the information is useful to the budget traveler. Considering the target market, there is not much adventure packed in here. Their 61 pages on Kalimantan are perfunctory but not as usable as Moon's guide or the annual Passport Books.

Indonesia ★★★★★
Bill Dalton (Moon, 1995)
Bill Dalton began Moon publications with this book just as Tony Wheeler's *Across Asia on the Cheap* started Lonely Planet in the'70s. Unlike the globe trotting and prolific Wheeler, Bill has stayed focused and expert on Indonesia. Every trekker in the remote regions relies on this book to figure out how to get around and back out. No book can match Bill's for thoroughness or coverage on remote areas. His only fault is that he seems to write about places even locals have no interest in going to. The best book to take if you are planning on trekking through Kalimantan.

There are also Fodor's, Frommer and other mainstream and imported Asian and European photo guides to Borneo. None of these provide in-depth, on the ground coverage and stick mainly to the tourist ruts. There is little the adventurous traveler can get out of these books which are written more for Ma & Pa Kettle go to (fill in the blanks). They do cover the large hotels and major attractions. They rarely dabble in the great green beyond.

A final warning on guidebooks. If you buy an armload of guidebooks and research the various treks and boat trips described in these books you will find that many do not jibe. This may be due to the writer's interpretation of directions or because of a specific source's propensity for an alternate route. Also keep in mind that every region in Borneo is changing very rapidly due to logging and aggressive tourism development programs.

So do not use any guidebook to estimate exact times and costs. In all cases the laws of supply and demand are in effect. Borneo is not a cheap destination if you plan to go *ulu* and none of these guidebooks will identify which trips they have taken and which have been written from secondary sources.

Hey, if it was easy it wouldn't be an adventure would it?

INDEX

Favorite People, Places & Experiences

ADDRESS:	NOTES:

Name

Address

Telephone

Name

Address

Telephone

Name

Address

Telephone

Name

Address

Telephone

Name

Address

Telephone

Name

Address

Telephone

Favorite People, Places & Experiences

ADDRESS:	NOTES:

Name

Address

Telephone

Name

Address

Telephone

Name

Address

Telephone

Name

Address

Telephone

Name

Address

Telephone

Name

Address

Telephone

Favorite People, Places & Experiences

ADDRESS:	NOTES:

Name

Address

Telephone

Name

Address

Telephone

Name

Address

Telephone

Name

Address

Telephone

Name

Address

Telephone

Name

Address

Telephone

Favorite People, Places & Experiences

ADDRESS:	NOTES:

Name

Address

Telephone

Name

Address

Telephone

Name

Address

Telephone

Name

Address

Telephone

Name

Address

Telephone

Name

Address

Telephone

Favorite People, Places & Experiences

ADDRESS:	NOTES:

Name

Address

Telephone

Name

Address

Telephone

Name

Address

Telephone

Name

Address

Telephone

Name

Address

Telephone

Name

Address

Telephone

Favorite People, Places & Experiences

ADDRESS:	NOTES:

Name

Address

Telephone

Name

Address

Telephone

Name

Address

Telephone

Name

Address

Telephone

Name

Address

Telephone

Name

Address

Telephone